PLAINS INDIANS, A.D. 500–1500

PLAINS INDIANS, A.D. 500–1500

THE ARCHAEOLOGICAL PAST OF HISTORIC GROUPS

EDITED BY KARL H. SCHLESIER

UNIVERSITY OF OKLAHOMA PRESS : NORMAN AND LONDON

Other books by Karl H. Schlesier

(coauthor) *The Rights of the Indians of the Americas* (Amsterdam, 1980)

The Wolves of Heaven: Cheyenne Shamanism, Ceremonies, and Prehistoric Origins (Norman, 1987)

This book is published with the generous assistance of the Wallace C. Thompson Endowment Fund, University of Oklahoma Foundation.

Book design by Bill Cason

Library of Congress Cataloging-in-Publication Data

Plains Indians, A.D. 500–1500 : the archaeological past of historic groups / edited by Karl H. Schlesier.
    p. cm.
   Includes bibliographical references and index.
   ISBN 0-8061-2593-4 (alk. paper)
   1. Indians of North America – Great Plains – Antiquities. 2. Great Plains – Antiquities. I. Schlesier, Karl H.
   E78.G73P528 1994 c.2
   978 – dc20   93-46120
                                            CIP

1 2 3 4 5 6 7 8 9 10

For all the old peoples of the Great Plains and their descendants, and for those, more recently, who worked to reconstruct the past, both Indians and anthropologists. And for Bob Alex and Al Schroeder, who were our friends.

CONTENTS

List of Illustrations   ix
List of Tables   xiii
Preface   xv
Introduction   xvii
  1. Cultures of the Northwestern Plains: From the Boreal Forest
       Edge to Milk River   *J. Roderick Vickers*   3
  2. Late Prehistoric Cultures on the Montana Plains
       Sally T. Greiser   34
  3. Cultures of the Mountains and Plains: From the Selkirk
       Mountains to the Bitterroot Range
       Philip Duke and Michael Clayton Wilson   56
  4. Archaeological Complexes of the Northeastern Plains and
       Prairie-Woodland Border   *Michael L. Gregg*   71
  5. Neighbors to the North: Peoples of the Boreal Forest
       David Meyer and Scott Hamilton   96
  6. Cultures of the Upper Mississippi River Valley and Adjacent
       Prairies in Iowa and Minnesota   *Guy Gibbon*   128
  7. Cultures of the Middle Missouri
       R. Peter Winham and Edward J. Lueck   149
  8. Cultures of the Heartland: Beyond the Black Hills
       L. Adrien Hannus   176
  9. The Central Lowland Plains: An Overview   *Patricia O'Brien*   199
 10. The Central High Plains: A Cultural Historical Summary
       Jeffrey L. Eighmy   224
 11. Cultural Continuity and Discontinuity in the Southern Prairies
       and Cross Timbers   *Susan C. Vehik*   239
 12. Holocene Adaptations in the Southern High Plains
       Timothy G. Baugh   264
 13. Development in the Southwest and Relations with the
       Plains   *Albert H. Schroeder*   290
 14. Commentary: A History of Ethnic Groups in the Great Plains,
       A.D. 150–1550   *Karl H. Schlesier*   308
The Contributors   382
Bibliography   387
Index   477

ILLUSTRATIONS

MAPS

I.1.	Vegetation map of the central North American grasslands, indicating area covered by this volume	xviii–xix
1.1.	The Northwestern Plains: the study area	4
1.2.	Mortlach/One Gun Phase material and various Indian groups, ca. A.D. 1730	27
2.1.	Archaeological complexes on the Montana Plains, ca. A.D. 500	36
2.2.	Archaeological complexes on the Montana Plains, ca. A.D. 850	44
2.3.	Archaeological complexes on the Montana Plains, ca. A.D. 1250	47
2.4.	Archaeological complexes on the Montana Plains, ca. A.D. 1600	52
3.1.	Selkirk Mountains to Bitterroot Range: northern principal locations	57
3.2.	Selkirk Mountains to Bitterroot Range: southern principal locations	58
4.1.	Archaeological complexes in the Northeastern Plains, A.D. 500 to 600	75
4.2.	Archaeological complexes in the Northeastern Plains, A.D. 800 to 900	80
4.3.	Archaeological complexes in the Northeastern Plains, A.D. 1100 to 1200	84
4.4.	Archaeological complexes in the Northeastern Plains, A.D. 1400 to 1500	90
5.1.	The boreal forest: the study area	97
5.2.	Vegetation zones	98
5.3.	Rivers, lakes, and archaeological sites	101
5.4.	Laurel distribution, ca. A.D. 500.	102
5.5.	Laurel distribution, ca. A.D. 750.	107
5.6.	Populations making Laurel and Blackduck pottery, ca. A.D. 1000	113
5.7.	Selkirk, Blackduck, Duck Bay, and Sandy Lake cultural materials, ca. A.D. 1250	118
5.8.	Selkirk, Duck Bay, and Sandy Lake cultural materials, ca. A.D. 1500	124

6.1.   Major vegetation regions in Iowa and Minnesota before Euro-
       American settlement   129
6.2.   Archaeological complexes in Iowa and Minnesota, ca. A.D.
       650 to 800   131
6.3.   Archaeological complexes in Iowa and Minnesota, ca. A.D.
       1100 to 1200   134
6.4.   Archaeological complexes in Iowa and Minnesota, ca. A.D.
       1500   140
6.5.   Native American linguistic/tribal groups in the Upper Valley,
       ca. A.D. 1650   141
7.1.   The Middle Missouri region   150
7.2.   (a) Truman Mounds, Cross Ranch, and unassigned Woodland
       sites; (b) Valley phase   156–57
7.3.   Great Oasis, Initial Middle Missouri, and the Flaming Arrow
       site   158
7.4.   Extended Middle Missouri   165
7.5.   Initial Coalescent and Terminal Middle Missouri   170
8.1.   Northwestern Plains, with prominent drainages   177
8.2.   Pelican Lake sites   183
8.3.   Besant sites   187
8.4.   Avonlea sites   189
9.1.   The major physiographic regions of the Central Plains   200
9.2.   Hopewellian complexes or phases on the Central Lowland
       Plains, ca. A.D. 1 to 500   202
9.3.   Plains or Late Woodland complexes or phases on the Central
       Lowland Plains, ca. A.D. 500 to 900/1000   208
9.4.   Central Plains Tradition phases on the Central Lowland
       Plains, ca. A.D. 900/1000 to 1500   212
9.5.   Historic Indian tribes on the Central Lowland Plains, ca. A.D.
       1500 to 1700   219
10.1. Late Woodland components in the central High Plains   230
10.2. Upper Republican and Intermountain secondary utilization
       of the central High Plains   236
11.1. Southern prairies and Cross Timbers, A.D. 500   240
11.2. Southern prairies and Cross Timbers to A.D. 1450/1500   244
11.3. Southern prairies and Cross Timbers to A.D. 1750   247
11.4. Southern prairies and Cross Timbers, Early Historic A.D. 1541 250
11.5. Southern prairies and Cross Timbers, Early Historic A.D. 1601 252
11.6. Southern prairies and Cross Timbers, Early Historic A.D. 1720 253
12.1. Plains Woodland manifestations on the southern High Plains   268
12.2. Early Plains Village manifestations on the southern High
       Plains   274
12.3. Middle Plains Village cultures on the southern High Plains   284
13.1. Culture districts, ca. A.D. 500   292
13.2. Culture districts, ca. A.D. 1000   295
13.3. Culture districts, ca. A.D. 1500, and locales of historic period
       tribes   302
14.1. Archaeological cultures to ethnic groups, A.D. 150   364–65

14.2. Archaeological cultures to ethnic groups, A.D. 500   366–67
14.3. Archaeological cultures to ethnic groups, A.D. 850   368–69
14.4. Archaeological cultures to ethnic groups, A.D. 1200   370–71
14.5. Archaeological cultures to ethnic groups, A.D. 1550   372–73

FIGURES

1.1.   Carbon-14 dates per century for Besant, Avonlea, and Old
       Women's/Mortlach/One Gun phases   8
1.2.   The Great Late Prehistoric Guessing Game: cultural
       relationship proposals   10
1.3.   Projectile point types   12
1.4.   Ceramic vessel forms of the Avonlea, Old Women's, and One
       Gun phases   16
1.5.   Shield-bearing warrior motifs sometimes considered to
       represent Shoshone   29
2.1.   Generalized projectile point sequence for the Late Prehistoric
       period   45
2.2.   Cultural sequence for the Late Prehistoric/Protohistoric
       period   53
4.1.   Climatic episodes and cultural chronology, A.D. 500 to 1500   73
4.2.   Plains Woodland ceramic vessel of the A.D. 500–600 period   77
4.3.   Plains Woodland ceramic vessel of the A.D. 800–900 period   82
4.4.   Plains Village ceramic vessel of the A.D. 1100–1200 period   87
4.5.   Plains Village ceramic vessel of the A.D. 1400–1500 period   92
5.1.   Laurel vessel   104
5.2.   Avonlea vessel   109
5.3.   Blackduck vessel   114
5.4.   Selkirk vessel   119
5.5.   Duck Bay vessel   121
14.1. Kutenais, Kiowa-Tanoans, Algonquians, 400 B.C. to A.D. 1550 311
14.2. Sarcees and Southern Athapaskans, A.D. 50 to 1550   325
14.3. Western Siouans, A.D. 100 to 1550   340
14.4. Plains or Northern Caddoans, 50 B.C. to A.D. 1550   349

TABLES

3.1	Regional Cultural Chronologies	65
7.1	Woodland Sites in the Middle Missouri Region	153
7.2	Great Oasis Sites in the Middle Missouri Region	159
7.3	Initial Middle Missouri Sites in the Middle Missouri Region	160–61
7.4	Extended Middle Missouri Sites in the Middle Missouri Region	166–68
7.5	Initial Coalescent Sites in the Middle Missouri Region	172
7.6	Terminal Middle Missouri Sites in the Middle Missouri Region	173
11.1	Southern Prairies and Cross Timbers, A.D. 500	241
11.2	Southern Prairies and Cross Timbers to A.D. 1450/1500	243
11.3	Southern Prairies and Cross Timbers to A.D. 1750	246
11.4	Available Historic Population Data and Estimates, A.D. 1540–1850	257–58
11.5	Possible Plains Epidemic Events	259
13.1	Southwestern Neighbors, A.D. 500	291
13.2	Southwestern Neighbors, A.D. 1000	294
13.3	Southwestern Neighbors, A.D. 1500	301

PREFACE

THIS volume deals with a thousand-year period of cultural dynamics in the Great Plains and some important adjacent regions prior to the passage of the first killing smallpox epidemic and the arrival of Europeans during the early sixteenth century. It attempts to extend ethnohistory back in time beyond its present limits and to identify cultures ancestral to historic groups. This is an important although difficult task, and it has not been tried before.

The presentation is perhaps unusual in that the organizer and editor is an ethnographer/ethnohistorian when all other contributors are archaeologists/prehistorians. If there is a dividing line, it may not be as sharp as feared because each writer also considered the ethnography and ethnohistory of the region concerned.

No attempt was made to paper over differences. On the contrary, it was deemed essential that incongruities in theory and interpretation be made visible and be left to stand. The common bond was the attempt to read a thousand years of Indian cultural dynamics. Where regional essays reveal disagreement among archaeologists in regard to the interpretation of archaeological entities overlapping more or less artificial regional boundaries, it is due to the difficulty of explaining traditions and securing origins and ethnic identities.

I do not see disagreements as a problem and take solace from a recent statement by Ian Hodder (1988:x): "Archaeology no longer has to be 'new' and unidirectional, presenting a unified front. It has the maturity to allow diversity, controversy and uncertainty. From catastrophe theory to sociobiology, it is all being applied to the archaeological past. But through this onslaught a more seasoned genre emerges, recapturing the old and redefining the new to form a distinctive archaeological enquiry."

Answers are suggested here but some will be controversial. I want to thank an international group of scholars who joined the initial symposium held at the Forty-sixth Plains Anthropological Conference, Wichita, Kansas, November 2–4, 1988, because of the need for such a volume. At the University of Oklahoma Press I want to thank John N. Drayton and Barbara Siegemund-Broka for their unflinching efforts to make this complex book a success. Until its publication no work of this scope and intention existed. I believe that Indian peoples of today, linear descendants of populations discussed here, whose genuine interest in the past has too often been ignored, will follow the stations of our search with impassioned concern and critical anticipation.

KARL H. SCHLESIER

Corrales, New Mexico

INTRODUCTION

THIS book deals with the cultures of the Great Plains and some neighboring regions in the period A.D. 500–1500. These neighboring regions are included because their populations contributed significantly to cultural developments in the Great Plains.

The end of the period here covered is marked by the arrival of European-derived diseases during the sixteenth century. The greatest slayer of Indian people, smallpox, made its first appearance in the New World in 1516, having crossed the Atlantic Ocean on a Spanish ship. It was transmitted in 1519 by men of Panfilo de Narvaez's fleet to the Mexican coast where Fernando Cortez's army prepared the attack on the Aztec empire. Because American populations had long been isolated from direct contact with the Old World, they were highly susceptible to virulent bacteria and viruses that had evolved there. While members of Cortez's invading army were immune to the disease, the contagion swirled around them through central Mexico, killing native people there and beyond by the millions. During a four-year period it spread north and south through many of the most densely populated regions of the Americas. Henry Dobyns (1983), one of the major researchers of Native American depopulation, has estimated that this first smallpox epidemic killed about 75 percent of the inhabitants wherever it reached.

Although the epidemic passed through Central America into South America, Dobyns's interpretation of a genuine pandemic has been challenged in regard to North America. Some critics (for instance, Henige 1986) find fault with his documentation; others (for instance, Snow and Lanphear 1988) have argued that smallpox did not enter northeastern North America until the early seventeenth century, although they admit to the presence of earlier episodes of European diseases in the region. They agree, however, on the terrifying results of a first smallpox appearance. Dobyns's proposed casualty rate is not exaggerated. Snow and Lanphear (1988:28) are confident that the overall mortality from the 1616–19 and 1633–39 epidemics in New England stood at no less than eighty-six percent of the Indian populations.

This is not the place to enter the continuing debate about Dobyns's interpretation. It should be remembered, however, that the first smallpox appearance in North America, in contrast to events in Mexico, was beyond European observation. But the invading army of Hernando de Soto, which meandered through southeastern North America from May 1539 to September 1543, found irrefutable evidence that epidemics had emptied whole regions before its arrival. Said de la Vega: "The Castilians found no people in Talomeco because the previous pestilence had been more rigorous and devastating in this town than in any other of the whole province, and the few Indians who had escaped had not yet reclaimed their homes" (de la Vega 1962:315).

And a Knight of Elvas wrote of the arrival of the Spanish in Cufitachiqui: "About the place, from half a league to a league off, were large vacant towns, grown up in grass, that appeared as if no people had lived in them for a long time. The Indians said that, two years before, there had been a pest in the land, and the inhabitants had moved away to other towns . . . This country, according to what the Indians stated, had been very populous" (Elvas 1904:66–67). If the 1520–24 smallpox epidemic was not a pandemic, it may very well have reached at least into some densely populated areas of North America. Whether it passed into the Great Plains is yet unknown.

The Americas had achieved their highest population levels in the early sixteenth century. The continent had not been touched before by devastating diseases such as the variants of plague, smallpox, measles, influenza, diphtheria, scarlet fever, typhus, malaria, and cholera that had affected Eurasian populations for a long time. All of these came to the Americas with the Europeans and had terrible results. Considering

---

Shortgrass plains

Mixed grass prairie

Bluestem prairie

Aspen parkland (trembling aspen, willow)

Cross Timbers (blackjack oak, post oak and little bluestem)

Maple-basswood forest and oak savanna, with spruce-fir forest in the northern parts of Minnesota, Wisconsin, Michigan

Oak-hickory forest and bluestem prairie

Boreal forest (white spruce, black spruce, balsam fir, jack pine, white birch, trembling aspen)

Shrub and mesquite savanna

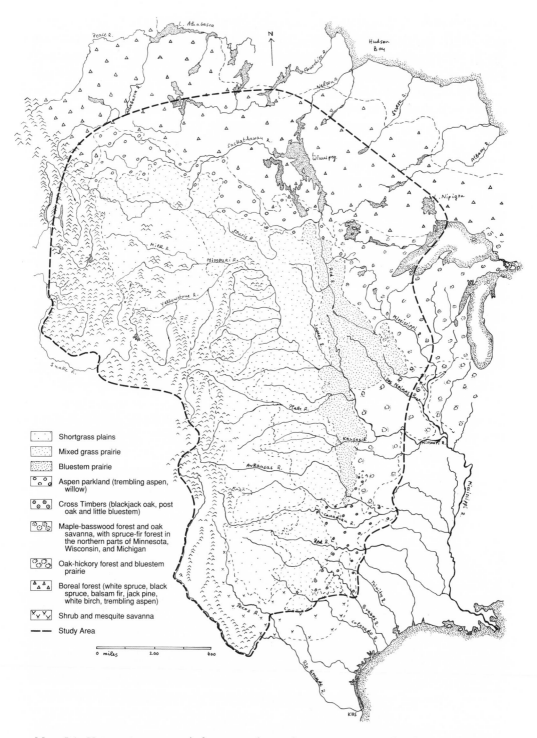

Map I.1. Vegetation map of the central North American grasslands and adjacent areas, indicating the study area covered by this volume. Boundaries were simplified from Kuechler (1964) for the United States and Rowe (1972) for Canada.

the long and undisturbed growth rate, Dobyns (1983:42) has estimated that at its peak the population of North America north of civilized Mesoamerica may have numbered approximately eighteen million. He assumed an average density of about 2.35 persons per square kilometer for horticultural populations in the great Mississippi River valley and on its major tributaries, and 1.4 persons per square kilometer overall for North America outside the arctic region.

It may be interesting to apply an estimate to the area covered by this book. The total area (map I.1) comprises approximately 3,607,500 square kilometers. If a more conservative estimate of 0.8 person per square kilometer were used, the population of the area would have stood at well over two million. Although we will never know the exact number, this estimate appears to be reasonable.

If the population of the area had been that large in 1520, European observers may never have had an opportunity to see the cultures in their original state, nor to witness the associated density and complexity. When Cabeza de Vaca crossed the southern edge of the Texas plains in 1535, and Francisco Vasquez de Coronado reached into the Kansas plains above the great bend of the Arkansas River in 1541, an epidemic may already have passed before them. In addition, at least parts of the Southern Plains seem to have suffered a measles epidemic in 1531–33, and an epidemic of an unidentified disease in 1535 (Dobyns 1983:17, 23). Coronado's visit seems to have been followed by the appearance of bubonic plague in the Southwest, 1545–48 (Dobyns 1983:20). If this indeed occurred, it is unlikely that its extent was confined to this region alone. Later episodes of epidemic diseases in North America (Dobyns [1983:15–23] lists no fewer than ninety-three for the period 1520–1918) lie outside the scope of this book.

Vaca and Coronado at least had still seen large, independent populations. Europeans eventually following in their footsteps found only scattered groups and much of the wide country devoid of people. Unaware that they had come in the wake of the ravages of epidemics which had stripped the land, they made reports that fixed indelibly in the European perception the notion of the Great Plains as a vast and empty hunting ground. It was easy for European colonials here and elsewhere to raise flags and take possession in the names of distant kings when the original masters of the land had perished. Until very recently, even in anthropology, the role of European diseases in conquest of the continent was played down. For instance, the *Northeast* volume of the *Handbook of North American Indians*, published by the Smithsonian Institution in 1978 and covering one of the areas of North America originally most heavily populated, mentions epidemics only seven times, and in passing. Only the reevaluation triggered by a research thrust on epidemiology and population dynamics is beginning to address the historical facts.

It would be fortunate if this volume could show the rise and cultural sophistication of populations in our area from A.D. 500 through 1500. This is a difficult task, and many questions will remain unanswered. It is especially difficult because the bands or little tribes profiled in the ethnographic fieldwork of the late nineteenth and early twentieth centuries were only shadows of the powerful societies that had occupied the area in 1500. The term tribe, as applied to groups with ethnic boundaries, may be acceptable for Indian systems from the early nineteenth century onward but is wholly inadequate for the period preceding the arrival of the epidemics and even the following two centuries, despite continuing dramatic population losses. It remains to be seen whether the term can be used even for the period around A.D. 500. If developments in other areas of the Americas are compared, and if these were synchronous, events in the area covered here may already have led to systems larger than tribes by A.D. 500. Vast parts of the Great Plains were indeed a marvelous hunting ground. A cultural sink, to use a term once frivolously and wrongfully applied to southern Texas, they were not.

For much of the period, we have to think in terms of large conglomerates of loosely associated, far-flung populations, connected by a common language or dialects of a common language, often including participants of different language stocks, bound together by overarching national symbols which gave them the power and security of a common tradition and history. We have to think of large confederacies much like those observed by early European travelers in eastern North America. In the eastern half of the Great Plains remnants of such confederacies existed to the end of the eighteenth century, from the Kitsais and Wichitas through the Iowas, Omahas, Pawnees, Skiris, and Arikaras to the Mandans, Hidatsas, and the Dakotas. Even the equestrian groups of the nineteenth century, such as the Blackfeet, Crows, Arapahos, Atsinas, Cheyennes, Kiowas, and Kiowa Apaches, had centuries earlier consisted of numerous divisions organized much like their horticultural neighbors and trading partners. Cultures of the Great Plains after 1782, when they had been reduced to between 5 and 10 percent of their pre–European contact population levels, had become poverty cultures when compared with the richness of the past. That they stubbornly preserved important aspects of earlier cultural life and exhibited impressive adaptations to detrimental, ever-changing conditions is nothing short of a miracle. These they carried into reservation time, and some are with us even today.

Another erroneous assumption, widely held, is that the fragmented groups (tribes) of the late historic period had no historical depth as definite, bounded systems, that they had become groups with ethnic identities late, virtually under European observation. This assumption once allowed the unquestioned dispossession of Indian groups; it has no time perspective. It ignores the fact that many of the groups had been in the area for a millennium or much more before they saw the first European. Even those groups who migrated into the area shortly before or after the initial European presence, running away from disasters elsewhere and taking land emptied by epidemics, had been participants in large-scale alliances earlier in their history. Their immigration did not dissolve ethnic boundaries. A good example are the Dhegiha groups (Omaha, Ponca, Kansa, Osage) who came into the area as refugees in the early seventeenth century.

Humans need ethnic space for survival as much as they need belief systems, techniques for food production, shelter, and well thought-out social organizations. Ethnicity is already present, I believe, in the Upper Paleolithic of Eurasia and, according to some French prehistorians, even in the Middle Paleolithic. It would be wise to search in our area and in our time frame for the evidence. In an apparently very controversial book I have recently interpreted the Cheyenne Massaum as an earth-giving ceremony which forged groups of the eastern subphase of Besant into the ethnic entity Cheyenne (Tsistsistas), sometime between 500 and 300 B.C. The time level seems to have disturbed many, but evidence or convincing arguments to contradict it have yet to be presented by those who prefer to disagree.

We stand to learn nothing more than we already know if we close ourselves to radically new theories based on fresh lines of inquiry. We should test them rather than wish them away. I agree that ethnicity is an elusive quantity and that the identification of ethnic groups in the archaeological record is imbued with problems. But whether we want this or not, we are essentially discussing the prehistory of ethnic groups in a volume such as this because the archaeological entities we are exploring represent depositions of features and artifacts as well as manifestations of mental concepts ancestral to those of historic Indian populations. We are in the unique situation that Indian groups on reservations today are linear descendants of the people whose archaeological record we are tracing.

Given the incompleteness of the archaeological record and the impact of change, how can we with any certainty identify historic ethnic groups with ancestral prehistoric groups? The following remarks are general but are area-specific and may not be applicable elsewhere.

First, ethnicity. Ethnicity requires boundaries in mental and physical space; it cannot exist without them. Mental space means identification with a specific system of values and behavior modes and, beyond language, with a specific world perception expressed symbolically in religious practices, myths, ritual, oral tradition, objects imbued with sacred power, sacred places, and so on. Physical space means biological identification with a specific population. Boundaries in physical space exclude "others" from "us"; members generally call themselves "people," or "the people," to define separateness. In historic time, such terms, in many different languages, often became "tribal names." Physical space also refers to the area or territory within which ethnicity exists.

It may be obvious that physical space is subordinated to mental space. Essentially members of a people, or a culture, represent a closed congregation of those who participate in an ongoing tradition. Tradition is largely based on religion. It was created and is maintained by chief performers: visionaries, "culture heroes," shamans, "medicine people," bundle keepers, and the like. Their interpretation of origins, of the perceived and institutionalized covenant of their people with spiritual forces and the obligations to these, explained in myth and ceremonies, draw and maintain ethnic boundaries.

Today these boundaries have been obscured among Indian groups because of the aggressive intrusion of alien influences. Still, as an example, a Cheyenne is but a person registered on a Bureau of Indian Affairs tribal roll; that person may be a Christian and assimilated into the dominant society. A Tsistavostan is a Cheyenne who accepts the ancient covenant of Tsistsistas as expressed in *Nimahenan*, the sacred arrows, the foremost sacred objects of this old ethnic group, and in the two surviving major ceremonies, the *Maxhoetonstov* (Ceremony of the Sacred Arrows) and the *Oxheheom* (New Life Lodge, "Sun Dance").

That the physical is subordinated to the mental, or spiritual, is also evidenced by the fact that outsiders, biological aliens, were quite often adopted. In this process the outsiders rejected their earlier ethnic identities and acquired the new, eventually becoming practitioners in its spiritual dimensions. Indian cultures were the original melting pots of the continent, constantly enriched biologically and culturally from without.

Now, the manifestations of ethnicity. It is obvious that ethnicity is expressed in all aspects of culture. It is expressed visually in all facets of material culture, from artifacts of the profane to artifacts of the sacred. There is no clear dividing line between the two. No artifact belongs exclusively to one or the other category. One could say that each artifact assumes a number of levels of association. What to us may appear to be an everyday, mundane little chert artifact on a laboratory table originally may have functioned on a number of different levels of meaning. An arrow point, for instance, may have been the tip of a "lucky" arrow prayed over for success by a ceremonial person, may have been found as an "antique" at a special place and reused, may have been made by a special person, received as a gift, or used for ritual cutting or killing, and eventually may have become part of a necklace or hair ornament, or been added to a bundle as a special object.

Because material culture is ethnically specific, it symbolizes the identity of an ethnic group to both insiders and outsiders. Nearly all its manifestations are imprinted with information that gives signals to those who can read it. This is clear in the case of highly pronounced features such as pictographs and petroglyphs, village sites, pounds, burial mounds or burial sites, and shrines. But it extends to countless items of everyday and special use, from hair ornaments to dog harnesses, children's toys to garment bags, ritual objects to footwear. Often the clue is in the detail, in the specifics of manufacture, style, or decoration. For a contemporary person, a single arrow found embedded in a tree trunk without association would clearly spell its ethnic identification. The clue might not be in the projectile point itself, which could belong to a "horizon style" (a term copied from Peruvian archaeology) category, but in the shaft and fletching: type, size, decoration, subtle ways of binding. These signals are mute to us today.

Ethnicity also is manifest in "territorial markers," territorially based sacred sites acting as land claims. Historic and prehistoric Indian populations have used sacred places (e.g., springs, mountains, perceived spirit lodges underground, caves, and prominent cliffs or trees) explained in myth and ceremonial lore. In many cultures these places were or are visited regularly by delegations of ceremonial people or became the locale where events were conducted. Human-made features (e.g., burial mounds or sites, shrines, and medicine wheels) served the same purpose and were considered inviolate. Here we must distinguish between core territories and wider areas of utilization. Syms's (1977:5–8) co-influence sphere model is certainly applicable; it separates core or home areas from regions of secondary and tertiary utilization. Ethnic groups overlapped in the latter two regions freely and often without friction. Evidence suggests that core territories were defended against hostile intruders but open to invited guests. Core territories were bounded by sacred places and marked with sacred sites.

Some prominent natural sacred places might be shared with neighboring ethnic groups, but human-made sacred sites were not. Archaeologists who believe that some burial mounds were shared by a succession of ethnic groups are wrong. The places of the dead are ethnically specific and were avoided by outsiders. For instance, in historic time a Kiowa would never be interred in a Cheyenne burial ground, nor vice versa. This holds for all ethnic groups and certainly extends into prehistoric time. The spirit of an outsider would be helpless and lose identity in an alien sacred site. Even when some burial mounds in the northeastern Plains were used continuously over many centuries, perhaps for a millennium, the dead should belong to one ethnic tradition regardless of the associated artifact inventory and how it may have changed over time. A conceivable exception might be that an ancient burial mound was taken for a natural rise by a group new in the region, and used by mistake.

The territories of ethnic groups often changed over time. In new territories, new ethnic markers were established. Often the sacred places of earlier—even evicted—groups were adopted because they were natural landmarks and powerful, impressive locations. In a sense, immigrating groups brought their sacred places with them. For instance, when the Suhtais lived in eastern South Dakota their sacred mountain was located in the Timber Mountains of southwestern Minnesota. When they moved to the Black Hills region around 1670, they adopted Bear Butte as their foremost sacred place and transferred to it the origin story of the New Life Lodge ceremony that had belonged to the Minnesota mountain. Bear Butte was not a territorial marker but an important spiritual place for a number of ethnic groups in historic and prehistoric time.

Many of the old ethnic markers are unknown to us today. Some are not, but they puzzle us. But what do we do with the early ethnographic information that, for instance, besides Bear Butte, Devil's Tower in northeast Wyoming was an important Kiowa sacred place, and that the Kiowas traced their early presence in the Great Plains to the mountains of the "extreme north" (speaking from Oklahoma; Mooney 1898:247), to "their first remembered home, the 'Kiowa Mountains' near the Gallatin Valley in Montana" (Scott 1911:368)? If we test Kiowa oral tradition and search for their ancestors in the archaeological complexes of southwestern Montana, we should be able to find them. We also might be able to document their later shift eastward to the Devil's Tower and Bear Butte areas of the Black Hills, where they were located well before the beginning of the historic period. Because the mountains around the Gallatin basin were "their first remembered home," not their earliest home, we might trace them from the archaeological remains in southwestern Montana back in time to A.D. 500 or beyond, regardless of where the search might take us.

One further line of inquiry might yield additional information. The Kiowas shared an important ceremonial aspect with the Kutenais, a major ceremony featuring sacred dolls (Schlesier 1990). I believe that both ethnic groups were in direct contact in the northwestern Plains before the arrival of groups ancestral to the Blackfeet, and perhaps later. A third ethnic group, whose archaeological remains overlap with those of the two in regions of secondary and tertiary utilization, was ancestral to the Kiowa Apaches. Mooney (1898:247) learned this from old Kiowa Apache informants: "They have not migrated from the southwest into the Plains country, but have come with the Kiowa from the extreme north, where they lay the scene of their oldest traditions, including their great medicine story. Their association with the Kiowa antedates the first removal of the latter from the mountains, as both tribes say that they have no memory of a time when they were not together."

This should be taken as a hypothesis worth testing. Bear Butte, or more specifically, Bear Butte Lake, was also a Kiowa Apache holy place in the Black Hills region. McAllister's (1937:162) informants told him in 1933: "Long ago the land of the dead was visited by a Kiowa-Apache who brought back and gave to the people one of their worship bundles. This place is generally located under the ground, sometimes specifically located under the waters of 'Medicine Lake,' a mythical body of water said to be located in the Black Hills region of Dakota."

For the Kiowas and the Kiowa Apaches, both Bear Butte and the lake near it were important. The oral traditions of both ethnic groups confirm a long, close association in the northern Plains.

I return to the question of how ethnic groups in our area can be identified in the archaeological record. Archaeologists conduct minute, often excruciating, investigations of features and fragments of material culture. But tipi rings, sherds, bones or stones do not speak, and the intricacies of style, easily read by a contemporary, escape our comprehension. We have gone as far as we can go. Material culture, of course, also changes over time, and we may be thrown off by perceived similarities and sequences that are insignificant for the larger picture. We may have arrow points to compare, but without the shafts, we may lack the key information. In short, we are operating with great handicaps. But some among us are forever asking for more of the same material, trying to beat the odds with ever changing models and new theoretical tricks. I do not deny the need to look carefully at the remains of material culture, and I do not belittle efforts to squeeze knowledge from them, but this small sample alone will never tell us what we want to know. Fortunately, we are not dealing with the Upper Paleolithic of the Loire Basin or that of the middle Danube River plain, where our colleagues have no source other than what they take from the ground.

Some aspects of culture change less than others. Those that change least I have mentioned as categories of mental space in ethnicity: specific world perceptions expressed symbolically in religious practices, ritual, myths, objects imbued with sacred power, specific systems of values, and behavior modes. Sometimes a ritual may have been lost (especially under the impact of traumatic population decline) and new ones developed or were adopted from outside influences. But even a new ceremonial feature was reinterpreted on the basis of a continuing tradition (e.g., the so-called Sun Dance, Schlesier 1990). If we concentrate on objects of material culture alone, we will miss the most important clues. There is a tendency to do this because it does not bring results; sometimes to say nothing is considered prudent scientific behavior.

To work out a true prehistory of the Great Plains, we must read for details in everything from material culture to perceptions of the sacred and its manifestations, including myths and oral traditions, but not in one or two cultures alone. We must emphasize these manifestations more because they are the best embodiment of ethnic continuity. We are fortunate that we possess considerable information regarding Indian mental space in early (late nineteenth- and early twentieth-century) ethnographic field reports. Because the clues are in the details, we must read these reports for details and make deep-level comparisons. To this most have only paid lip service. The direct historic approach, as developed by Strong (1935), Wedel (1940), and Steward (1942), is still a valuable method to use for reconstruction, provided we include in it a detailed and comparative reading of the sum of the ethnographies.

What I argue for herein I have applied in chapter 14. Readers will decide where I have failed and where I may have succeeded. Rational and frank discourse is now of the essence.

PLAINS INDIANS, A.D. 500–1500

CHAPTER 1

CULTURES OF THE NORTHWESTERN PLAINS: FROM THE BOREAL FOREST EDGE TO MILK RIVER

J. Roderick Vickers

THE study area for this chapter includes the plains and parklands of Alberta and Saskatchewan, and a small portion of Montana and North Dakota north of the Milk/Missouri rivers (map 1.1). Unlike the rest of the Great Plains, the main streams of the region—the Saskatchewan and Red rivers—drain ultimately into Hudson Bay and the Arctic Ocean. This area forms the most northerly grasslands of the Plains. Beyond are the aspen parklands, the Rocky Mountains on the west, and the continent-spanning boreal forests of the north. These Northwestern Plains are the land of the Blackfeet, the Blood, the Piegan, the Sarcee, the Assiniboine, and the Plains Cree.

Arcing around the northern section of the study area is the aspen parkland (map 1.1). This is a transition zone between the boreal forest to the north and the grasslands to the south. The aspen parkland zone is characterized by groves of aspen trees (*Populus tremuloides*) dotted among the rough fescue (*Festuca scabrella*) grasses; the groves form at least 15 percent of the ground cover (Strong and Leggat 1981). Similar woodlands extend along the river valleys in the grasslands of the region (Morgan 1979). The woodland zones were especially important for the Indians of the region; their winter camps were situated in these sheltered locales where firewood could be gathered (Ewers 1958).

Various classifications of the grassland community have been formulated (see Morgan 1979, 1980), but a simplified version of the scheme proposed by W. L. Strong and K. R. Leggat (1981) will suffice for our purposes. Ignoring details, I will describe only the mixed grass and shortgrass ecoregions. The mixed grass ecoregion curves around the southern edge of the aspen parkland and is replaced by the shortgrass zone farther to the south. Both zones are dominated by a grama–spear grass (*Bouteloua gracilis, Stipa comata*) association with wheat grass

I would like to thank Alwynne B. Beaudoin and Brian M. Ronaghan for reviewing a draft of this chapter; their comments were most helpful. I am pleased to acknowledge Wendy Johnson for her fine drafting of the figures. I am grateful to Yves Beaudoin for help with the computer production of this chapter. It is with pleasure that I thank all for their aid. Of course, any errors or omissions are solely my responsibility.

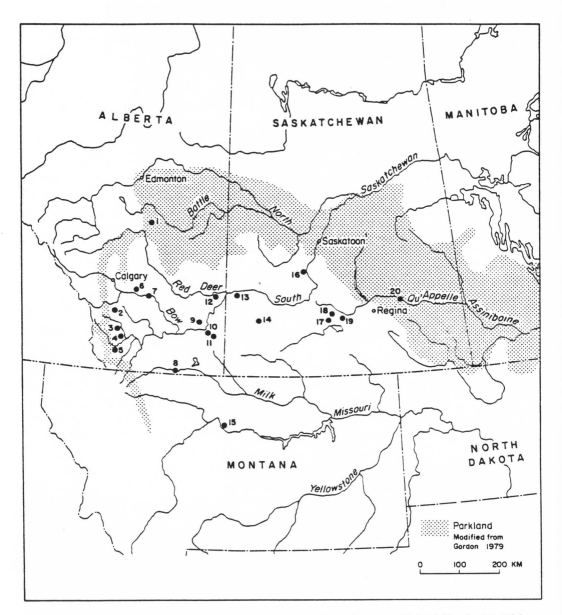

Map 1.1. *The study area, showing sites mentioned in the text: (1) Muhlbach; (2) Old Women's; (3) Morkin; (4) Head-Smashed-In; (5) Kenney; (6) Hartell Creek; (7) Cluny; (8) Writing-On-Stone; (9) Ramillies, EcOs-41; (10) Ross Glen; (11) Larsen; (12) Empress; (13) Estuary; (14) Gull Lake; (15) Lost Terrace; (16) Sjovold; (17) Mortlach; (18) Walter Felt; (19) Garratt; (20) Lebret.*

(*Agropyron* spp.) in moister locales; soils are brown chernozems. The areas differ in that the moister mixed grass zone yields about 25 percent greater biomass (475 kg/ha) than the shortgrass zone (see Strong and Leggat 1981:12). It is these grassland zones that formed the summer pasture for the great herds of bison (Morgan 1980). From campsites situated along the river valley margins, the Indians could exploit the summer bison herds.

A brief sketch of the regional weather may help the reader visualize the year (Potter 1965; Longley 1972; Strong and Leggat 1981). By the end of April, snow is gone from the region, although spring snow storms are not uncommon and frost may occur until mid-June. Temperatures rise quickly throughout this period. Precipitation is low in March, but rises through the following two months to a June peak in the grasslands. Summer, June–July–August, is short; July is the warmest month and the month of greatest precipitation in the parklands. Fall includes September–October–November, but one should note that the ground is usually snow covered by mid-November. Little precipitation occurs in the fall. Winter, December–January–February, is cold and snowy. By the beginning of December, lakes are frozen and snow covers the ground. Most of the area sees about thirty to fifty inches of snow. Blizzards are somewhat infrequent.

ADAPTATION

Within this land of sweeping plains and wooded valleys, bounded by mountains to the west and shaded by aspen groves in the north, lived the Blackfeet tribes (the Blackfeet proper, the Blood, the Piegan, and their Athapaskan-speaking allies, the Sarcee), the Plains Cree, and the Assiniboine. Until the coming of the Northwest Mounted Police in 1874, European settlements — primarily fur trading company forts — were located along the North Saskatchewan River and north into the woodlands where furbearers were plentiful. In this section I will briefly discuss the historic adaptation of the Blackfeet, and develop inferences about the Late Prehistoric pedestrian adaptation. As well as the season-al round described by Ewers (1955, 1958) for the historic Blackfeet, models of the pedestrian round have been developed by R. G. Morgan (1979) for the northern plains and J. H. Brumley (1983) for southeastern Alberta. This will serve as a general model in which to consider cultural-historical developments.

For the historic Blackfeet, March was often a time of hardship since the bison were drifting away to the open plains but the people might not be able to follow immediately (Ewers 1955:126). However, except for this interval when alternate prey species were hunted, the bands were soon separately pursuing the bison on the open plains. For pedes-trian days, Morgan (1979) suggested that in early spring, the river valley winter camps were abandoned and people moved to adjacent uplands to avoid runoff moisture. For bands wintering in the parklands, dried provisions were needed for the march to the summer bison pasture in the plains.

Among the historic Blackfeet, J. C. Ewers (1955) noted that the tribal summer communal hunt and Sun Dance were the centerpieces of the season. By early July the bands had assembled and were chasing bison on the level plains. The pantribal sodalities (warrior societies) were active at their duties of policing the hunt. The Sun Dance was timed to the ripening of the Saskatoon berries, generally in early July, depending on weather. The ceremonial encampment lasted eight to ten days, after which the bands again dispersed. In prehistoric times the summer communal hunt may have been more difficult (Morgan 1979; Frison 1978:250). As well, Morgan (1979) has noted that surface water (sloughs) would disappear by midsummer, and the bands, lacking horse transportation, would be forced to camp nearer secure water supplies along the river systems. Morgan suggested that as well as bison, dried provisions and alternate game species were drawn upon for sustenance.

Following the Sun Dance encampment, Ewers (1955) stated that the Historic Period Blackfeet bands separated and concentrated on hunting cows. Berries were collected, and each band tried to put up as much dry meat as possible. Morgan (1979) has modeled prehistoric pedestrian band occupations along the river valley rims until late fall. At that time, the complete lack of surface water drew the bison to the river valleys and intensive communal hunting occurred. By the end of October the bands would establish their winter camps.

According to Ewers (1955), river valleys with shelter, fuel, water, and pasture for the horses were selected for winter camp locales. The bands wintered separately, but camps were established several miles apart along a reach of the river. Unless fuel or grass became exhausted, the winter camp was occupied throughout the season. Bands with large horse herds were obliged to shift camp more often, but such moves were usually only a day's march apart. Morgan (1979) has followed G. Arthur (1975) in noting that large encampments of several hundred lodges might occur in association with pounds in the winter season. Such camps must have been occupied by several bands.

This then, must serve to approximate the human-land relationships for the last two thousand years. No matter the coming and going of archaeological phases or historic tribes, all must have structured their adaptation to the seasonal availability of resources. Deviation from the seasonal round outlined here would seem to be impossible for a hunting people on the Northwestern Plains. Climatic change may have advanced or retarded the schedule of resource exploitation slightly, but the basic adaptation must have been constant.

CHRONOLOGY AND SYSTEMICS

In Alberta the classificatory scheme used to organize Plains prehistory is derived from W. Mulloy's (1958) original formulation, subsequently modified by B. O. K. Reeves (1969, 1970) and W. J. Byrne (1973). The Alberta scheme is based on presumed changes in weapon technology: Late Middle Prehistoric Period cultures are said to have relied on the atlatl while Late Prehistoric Period cultures used the bow (Reeves 1970:18). The Protohistoric Period covers the time when European manufactures were being added to the material culture, and horses were appearing from the south, but before frequent European observation occurred (see Vickers 1986).

The Saskatchewan classification also relies on a technological definition, and I. Dyck (1983) defines the Late Plains Indian Period by the appearance of arrow points and ceramics. Dyck (1983:110) rather arbitrarily selects two thousand years ago for the initiation of the Late Plains Indian Period, while noting that defining "the beginning of the period is something of a guessing game." He thus avoids the curious Alberta situation where both Middle and Late Prehistoric Period cultures, as defined by weapon technology, are contemporary.

It is not my intention to dwell upon the details of period classification in this essay; T. A. Foor (1985) has provided a convenient summary for the interested reader, while Reeves (1985) has offered an amusingly vitriolic attack upon those who diverge from the path of righteousness as defined by Mulloy (1958). Suffice it to say that the last two thousand years of native dominance of the Northwestern Plains were years of accelerated change. The atlatl and dart were replaced by the bow and arrow, and ceramics were added to the material culture inventory at the beginning of this interval. At the very end of this time, pedestrian hunters swiftly, and briefly, became horse nomads.

For this chapter, the time of interest includes a number of phases or complexes which have long been recognized. These include the last gasps of the Besant phase, most of the Avonlea phase, all of the Old Women's phase, the Mortlach phase, and the One Gun phase (figure 1.1). While I will continue to use the term "phase" in this essay, the reader should note that its use in the Northern Plains is not identical to the G. R. Willey and P. Phillips (1958:22) definition. Reeves (1970:21) removed the geographic limits from the definition, in effect blurring the distinction between phase and horizon (see Syms 1977:64–72 for a useful discussion). The phases are defined primarily upon the presence of "diagnostic" projectile points, with occasional modification based on ceramic data; the phases range from formal constructs to ad hoc arrangements of convenience.

Any discussion of this period of Northwestern Plains prehistory must necessarily be complex. A number of contrasting relationships

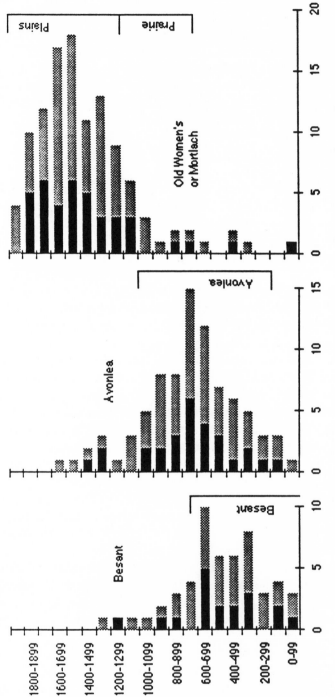

Fig. 1.1. Number of carbon-14 dates (uncorrected) per century for Besant, Avonlea, and Old Women's/Mortlach/One Gun (undifferentiated) phases, Alberta data only. Note that each date has been graphed three times; midpoint (black) and with standard deviation added and subtracted (grey). Vertical brackets indicate accepted ranges for phases. Data compiled by John H. Brumley (pers. comm. 1988).

have been proposed, and are discussed below. I recognize that this situation is confusing, and have provided a chart to enable the reader to navigate through the various schemata (figure 1.2). While I would like to recommend a single interpretation, I am forced to conclude that they all lack a firm scientific foundation. This is not to say that the observations and opinions expressed below are incorrect; many are based on intimate familiarity with at least portions of the data base. Nevertheless, the material should be considered as inductively derived models which have never been adequately tested.

Besant

The Besant phase, classified within the Late Plains Indian Period by Dyck (1983:110), is considered by Reeves (1970:18) to be the last expression of the Late Middle Prehistoric Period. The presence of atlatl points—Besant side-notched—accounts for the latter classification. However, some Besant phase components also contain an arrow point—Samantha side-notched—and occasional ceramics; thus Dyck's classification is also supported. Problems of terminology aside, it is apparent that the Besant phase represents a culture in technological transition. Atlatl technology was being replaced by the bow, and ceramics were being added to the material culture inventory.

The Besant point type was first named by B. N. Wettlaufer (1955) at the Mortlach site, and detailed typological description was undertaken by T. F. Kehoe (1974). He proposed a number of morphological varieties, but his study was inhibited by small sample sizes and the variety terminology is seldom used. Besant side-notched points are lanceolate specimens with notches which are about twice as wide as they are deep (Dyck 1983:115). The notch is often placed low on the point and may even remove the basal edge, giving a corner-notched morphology (Kehoe 1974, Reeves 1970:42). Points are about 30–78 millimeters long, 19–23 millimeters wide, and have an internotch width of about 14–16 millimeters (Dyck 1983:115). Workmanship ranges from crude to well controlled. Bases are often ground.

Based on the data from the Walter Felt site, Kehoe (1974) also defined several varieties of Samantha point. In general, the term is used for points morphologically similar to Besant but with smaller mensual attributes (Reeves 1970:52). At the Felt site, Besant points occurred in Layer 13 only, while Samantha points were primarily distributed in the overlying layers (Layers 12 and 10). Kehoe suggested that Besant points spanned the early part of the phase, from about the time of Christ until A.D. 400. Subsequently "they were transformed into the transitional Samantha point, to about A.D. 700, when they became the Prairie Side-notched point" (Kehoe 1974:109). The similarity of Samantha to some of the later Prairie side-notched specimens has also

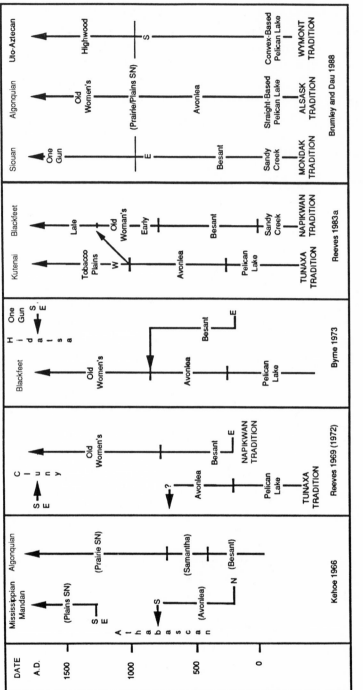

Fig. 1.2. The Great Late Prehistoric Guessing Game: cultural relationship proposals. Projectile point names are in parentheses; other names are phase names. The general direction of phase entry/exit from the region is indicated.

been noted by a number of other archaeologists (e.g., Reeves 1970:53; Duke 1988:268).

Reeves (1970) described other artifact types from Besant assemblages, but other tools generally are not recognized as being phase-diagnostic. Local lithics are often used extensively, although some sites show very high frequencies of Knife River flint from North Dakota. Avon chert from Montana may also occur in abundance. Wyoming-derived obsidian is very rare. Although this phase was once considered to be aceramic (Byrne 1973), recent research suggests that ceramics occur in small frequency in western Besant assemblages (Quigg 1986; Dyck 1983). These are described by Dyck (1983) as simple shoulderless vessels with cordmarked or plain surface finish.

A possible post-in-ground dwelling was noted at the Mortlach site in Saskatchewan; Dyck (1983:113) has compared this to a more complete example from South Dakota. Such elongate structures are more similar to mat- or bark-covered houses of the woodlands than to the familiar Plains tipi. However, it seems likely that the common dwelling was the tipi, represented archaeologically by stone circles. T. J. Brasser (1982:309) has argued that the true tipi with smoke-hole ears is a recent innovation (postdating A.D. 900). Nevertheless, attributes such as the shape of Besant phase stone-circle floor plans conforms to historic tipis. At the Ross Glenn site in southern Alberta, central post molds in the stone circles are thought to represent tie-down stakes, another attribute of the tipi (Quigg 1986:132). Indeed, several of the stone circles showed rock clusters which appear to indicate tipi pole locations. These may have resulted from rolling the rocks off the cover and clustering them around the poles when the lodge cover was raised for ventilation. All these observations suggest that the Besant dwellings were, indeed, true tipis.

A number of archaeologists (see Brumley and Dau 1988:36) have noted that Besant tipi rings are sometimes large. At the Ross Glenn site, for example, Besant tipi rings averaged 6.8 meters in inside diameter (N = 5, Quigg 1986:192); the average inside diameter of a large sample of Alberta tipi rings is 4.6 meters (N = 651 rings, Brumley and Dau 1988:263). What, if any, social significance should be attributed to this observation is unclear. Obviously, Kehoe's (1960) reasonable hypothesis that tipis increased in size after horse traction became available is not supported, but I am hardly the first to note this.

Besant origins are obscure, but recent speculation suggests that the phase may have developed from the Early Middle Prehistoric II Oxbow phase (Reeves 1983a:14); Oxbow, Sandy Creek, Besant, and the later Old Women's phase are linked into the *Napikwan* tradition by Reeves. The Sandy Creek complex (Dyck 1983:108), which contains a Besant-like projectile point form, is seen as technologically intermediate between Oxbow and Besant. Sandy Creek components occur in the

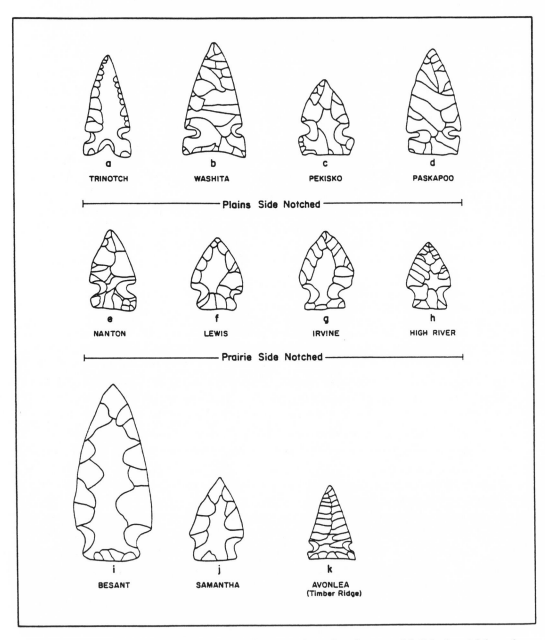

Fig. 1.3. Projectile point types. Type definitions based on base width/blade width and base height/notch height ratios, as well as overall morphology (see Vickers 1986 for review). Provenience: (a) Kobold (Frison 1970: fig. 13j); (b–h) Old Women's (Forbis 1962: figs. 12a, 12d, 12l, 12p, 13c, 13g, 13j, respectively); (i) 24HL101 (Reeves 1983: fig. 11, no. 14); (j) Leavitt (Reeves 1983: fig. 17, no. 8); (k) Head-Smashed-In (Reeves 1983: Fig. 15, no. 18).

plains of both Alberta (Head-Smashed-In) and Saskatchewan (Sjovold, Mortlach, Walter Felt sites) and appear to bridge the time between late Oxbow and Besant. However, relatively few Sandy Creek sites are yet known, and the details of transformation to Besant are unclear. Perhaps all that is yet reasonable to say is that Besant seems to be a culture indigenous to the Northwestern Plains and is visible by about 200 B.C.

By about the time of Christ, Besant was widespread over the Northwestern Plains. Besant components occur in Wyoming and the Dakotas, as well as the Canadian plains. The western edge of the distribution is more or less coincident with the mountain front; a few specimens are found in Pelican Lake sites in the mountains. The northern limits include the parklands, but few specimens occur within the boreal forest (Reeves 1983a:8); Besant sites are primarily the remains of plains-adapted hunters. Indeed, G. C. Frison (1978:223) suggests that Besant represents the climax of bison hunting cultures in the arid Wyoming area, while Dyck (1983:113) considers Besant the single best represented phase in Saskatchewan. A careful consideration of Alberta data, however, indicates that Besant components are no more frequent than earlier (McKean, Pelican Lake) or later (Old Women's) ones. Besant components are about three times more common than those assigned to the coeval Avonlea phase (Vickers 1986:14).

Besant sites include the full gamut of typical Plains sites; examples include bison jumps such as Old Women's (Forbis 1962), pounds such as Mulbach (Gruhn 1971), river valley winter campsites such as Kenney (Reeves 1983b), and warm season tipi ring sites such as Ross Glenn (Quigg 1986), to name but a few. Other examples are briefly described in Dyck (1983) and Vickers (1986). Burial mounds occur along the Missouri River (R. W. Neuman 1975) and must be mentioned here since they have played a role in our culture history formulations. The mounds contain multiple bundle burials and bison bone; along with bone uprights, Besant/Samantha points, and a great emphasis on Knife River flint, these traits form the Sonota subphase of Besant (Reeves 1983a: 10–13; cf. Syms 1977:88–90). Some sites as far west as the parklands of central Alberta contain similar high frequencies of Knife River flint (Gruhn 1971) and surely must represent actual movements of people from the quarry area in North Dakota.

As noted earlier, Besant is partially coeval with the bow-using Avonlea phase on the Northern Plains. When Reeves (1970:91) first considered this period, he suggested that Besant phase initiation was earliest in the Middle Missouri area. He was thus challenged with the task of explaining how Besant could expand from the Middle Missouri area in the face of Avonlea's superior weapons technology. Reeves (1970:212–16) argued that Besant was an active participant in the Hopewellian Interaction Sphere and traded grizzly bear teeth, Knife River flint, obsidian, and the products of the hunt eastward. Among other things, Besant peoples learned how to be "buried in style," hence the burial mounds. Reeves further speculated that the warrior societies (pantribal sodalities) controlled the trade surplus from the communal hunt and remained active for a greater portion of the year. This superior organization enabled Besant society to expand against the less organized Avonlea peoples. The motive for the expansion was a desire to control another trade commodity: the obsidian quarries in Wyoming.

The evidence necessary to support the model remains ambiguous; Knife River flint, a frequent constituent of Besant (Sonota subphase) sites near the quarries in North Dakota, is rare in Hopewell sites (F. Clark 1982). Obsidian is also rare in both Hopewell and Besant sites. Thus, there is little evidence of a particularly strong Besant-Hopewell trade interaction. The burial mounds are obviously derived from Woodland cultures, but the concept was reworked: the Sonota mounds appear to be unranked group repositories of the dead, rather than evidence of a ranked society as postulated by Reeves (see Neuman 1975; review in Syms 1977:88–90; Vickers 1986:86). Reeves's (1970) and Kehoe's (1974) observations that there was strong communication eastward into the woodlands, and between the Middle Missouri subarea and the western Plains, is certainly correct. What, if any, impact this had upon the social organization of the western bison hunters of the Besant phase remains uncertain. Away from the Middle Missouri region, the only evidence for possible social differences in comparison to other archaeological phases is the large tipi ring diameter data noted earlier.

In any case, with better dating control, it is now clear that Besant was resident in the Northwestern Plains before Avonlea appeared (Reeves 1983a; R. E. Morlan 1988); both were present before A.D. 500. However, the problem of Besant and Avonlea interaction still remains to be discussed. Before pursuing this topic, it will be necessary to describe briefly the entity known as Avonlea. For now, suffice it to say that Besant phase materials persist in the region until about A.D. 750 or 850 (Reeves 1983a:8, Morlan 1988). The ultimate fate of the Besant phase is inextricably intertwined with Avonlea, and both with the appearance of the Old Women's phase; these problems must be left for later in this essay.

Avonlea

The Avonlea phase is the first of the Late Prehistoric Period cultures in Reeves's (1970) classification; Dyck (1983) placed the phase within his Late Plains Indian Period. Avonlea phase sites contain only arrow points, and the phase is considered to be the first to employ exclusively bow technology on the northern plains. It is hypothesized that this technology diffused from Asia, perhaps through the mountain interior of British Columbia (Reeves 1970). Unlike western Besant assemblages, Avonlea sites seem more commonly to contain ceramics; these are thought to derive ultimately from the eastern woodlands (Byrne 1973).

Avonlea points are triangular and exceedingly thin; small, shallow side notches are situated very close to the concave base (Dyck 1983: 122). Average length of the point type is about twenty-one millimeters, width averages about thirteen millimeters and internotch width averages about ten millimeters. Flaking generally is very well controlled. The thinness and careful flaking have consistently impressed archaeologists working with this material. Triangular (unnotched) points are also present in this and later phases; they will be considered here to be preforms, perhaps especially manufactured for trade as recently argued by R. J. Dawe (1987).

The Avonlea point type was named by Saskatchewan archaeologists (T. F. Kehoe and B. McCorquodale 1961), and Kehoe (1966) again was responsible for systematic description of the type and its varieties. However, examination of a recent compendium of Avonlea research papers (L. B. Davis 1988) indicates that few archaeologists now use the complete type/variety terminology. Nonetheless, the variety names "Timber Ridge Side Notched" and "Head-Smashed-In Corner Notched" (Reeves 1970:49–52), are still occasionally encountered in the literature.

Other lithic tools are not recognized as being phase diagnostic. The use of local lithics, or rather the lack of exotic lithics, is commonly considered characteristic of Avonlea assemblages. However, Morgan (1979:212) noted that a high frequency of Knife River flint was used for Avonlea artifacts at the Garratt site in southern Saskatchewan, and Kehoe (1966:829) stated that more than 10 percent of the points at the Gull Lake site were of that material. S. T. Greiser (1988:127) has reported that about thirty percent of flakes at the Lost Terrace site in Montana were exotic to the area. Until it is statistically demonstrated, the general proposition that Avonlea lacks exotic lithics should be considered questionable. It would obviously be unwise to assume that Avonlea was isolated from extant trade networks.

Avonlea ceramics are relatively common and include a number of forms (Byrne 1973). Vessels are primarily simple "coconut" or conoidal forms, and a large range of sizes are known. Surface finish includes a fabric/net-impressed variety, and a parallel grooved type (A. M. Johnson 1988); the latter vessels appear to be larger than the former (Dyck 1983). Smoothed variants of each also exist. Decoration is very simple, usually being confined to a row (or rows) of punctates below the rim.

Avonlea sites include bison jumps such as Head-Smashed-In (Reeves 1978, J. Brink et al. 1985, 1986) and Gull Lake (Kehoe 1973), pounds such as Ramillies (Brumley 1976) and Estuary (G. F. Adams 1977), winter

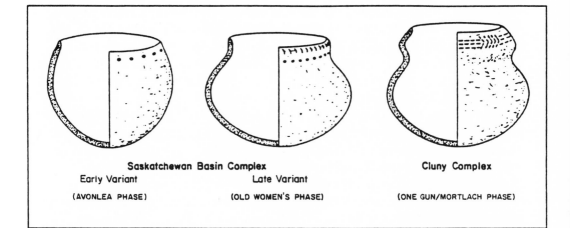

Fig. 1.4. Ceramic vessel forms of the Avonlea, Old Women's, and One Gun phases. (Redrawn from Byrne 1973.)

campsites such as Irvine (L. A. Milne 1988), Morkin (Byrne 1973), and Garratt (Morgan 1979), and tipi ring sites such as Empress (Hudecek 1988). In addition, an Avonlea fishing station—presumably a weir trap employed during the spring spawning run—is known from the Qu'Appelle valley in the Saskatchewan plains (Smith and Walker 1988). In general, the site types appear not to differ from those of the Besant phase. However, the total number of sites is very different. For example, in Alberta some 142 Besant components had been recorded by 1986, but only fifty Avonlea components were known (Vickers 1986:14). Dyck (1983:123) notes a similar situation in Saskatchewan.

Despite the smaller total number of known sites, the distribution of Avonlea phase sites is at least as extensive as that of the Besant phase. The distributions are not, however, totally coincident. While sites of both phases occur in the plains of Alberta and Saskatchewan, Avonlea sites are also known from the Kootenay and Flathead rivers on the west side of the continental divide (Roll 1988), and from the forest margins of northeast Saskatchewan (Meyer, Klimko, and Finnigan 1988). Unlike Besant, Avonlea materials appear to be very rare or absent in eastern Montana, the Dakotas, and southwestern Manitoba (Joyes 1988, Fraley 1988, Brumley and Dau 1988).

Avonlea appears on the Northwestern Plains about A.D. 150–250, or slightly earlier; earliest dates are from the plains of Alberta and western Saskatchewan (Morlan 1988). As one moves outward from this area, initial Avonlea dates become progressively younger. In the northeast periphery, Avonlea sites postdate A.D. 1000. Few sites dating before A.D. 600 occur on the Missouri drainage in Montana, and none are known before A.D. 800 in the Kootenay basin.

Avonlea origins are even less clear than is the case with Besant. Kehoe (1966:839) postulated that the appearance of the Avonlea point marked the migration of Athapaskans from the boreal forest to the plains. He based this premise on the lexico-statistical inference that the southern Athapaskans (Navajo, Apache) split from the northern Athapaskans about A.D. 650, a date which also marked the termination of the Avonlea components at the Gull Lake site. He further suggested that large-scale communal hunting of bison appeared with Avonlea, and represented an extension of caribou-driving common to circum-boreal regions. The latter observation turned out to be erroneous, and bison drives substantially predate the Avonlea phase.

No technological ancestor for Avonlea has been discovered in the boreal forest (Reeves 1983a; J. W. Ives pers. comm. 1988). Moreover, the northernmost Avonlea sites located in the forest margins of Saskatchewan, and the westernmost ones across the continental divide, are also among the most recent Avonlea sites (Morlan 1988). If the Athapaskan hypothesis were correct, the oldest Avonlea dates should occur in the north and west. Thus, while one still sees this hypothesis in the literature (e.g., Wilcox 1988), present data are inadequate to support it.

Reeves (1969, 1970) considered Avonlea to be a sequent phase in the *Tunaxa* cultural tradition which also included the McKean and Pelican Lake phases of the Middle Prehistoric Period. On the basis of early Avonlea dates at Head-Smashed-In Buffalo Jump, and the occurrence of Head-Smashed-In corner-notched points, which are morphologically similar to Pelican Lake points but technologically similar to Avonlea, Reeves postulated that the transition occurred in the eastern slopes or Rocky Mountains. However, R. E. Morlan (1988:298) has observed that a series of conflicting citations regarding provenience and cultural associations exists in Reeves's Head-Smashed-In data, which surely must cast doubt upon their reliability. It would be unwise to assume that Avonlea is, in fact, particularly early in the Alberta foothills. As well, no transitional components have been discovered despite rather intensive archaeological investigation of the area, and Reeves (1983a: 18) has become less certain of this hypothesis.

Brumley and Dau (1988:44) have disputed Reeves's unilineal Pelican Lake-to-Avonlea transition, since a different pattern of lithic source utilization occurs in foothills sites of each phase. If the transition had occurred, there should be continuity in lithic quarry use between the phases. Instead, they suggested that the foothill variants of Pelican Lake (termed convex-based Pelican Lake [see Dyck 1983:105] or Keaster II [see Greiser this volume]) lead to other stemmed and corner-notched arrow points, such as are common in Wyoming (see Frison 1988:170). In a core area centered on the Alberta-Saskatchewan-Montana boundary, Avonlea appears to derive from straight-based Pelican Lake variants. Avonlea was said to expand then to the south and west, displacing convex-based Pelican Lake from lands north of the Missouri. Much of eastern Montana, and North Dakota, continued to be held by Besant.

In the end archaeologists must plead ignorance in understanding the appearance of Avonlea on the Northern Plains. It seems we can state that Avonlea is a culture of the western Saskatchewan River basin and that it expanded southward into central Montana, westward over the Rocky Mountains, and northeastward into the forest margins. We are unable to derive the phase from any external area — recent dates suggest it is not an intrusion from the mountains to the west; the somewhat poorly known point technology in the boreal forest does not appear to be antecedent; the northeast manifestations are late; and a derivation from Mississippian cultures to the southeast (Morgan 1979: 220) would seem to be precluded by Sonota distributions (Joyes 1988:233; Syms 1977:80). If these limited data are then interpreted to indicate an *in situ* development from earlier cultures, then the hypotheses of Reeves (1970) and Brumley and B. J. Dau (1988) will need to be pursued. It seems unreasonable to derive Avonlea from Besant; Reeves's arguments that the phases are more or less contemporaneous and the products of different cultural traditions is generally accepted. The alternative is therefore to derive Avonlea from the antecedent Pelican Lake phase, or some subphase thereof. This suggests that late Pelican Lake, early Avonlea, and Besant occupation and interaction within the Saskatchewan basin may be more complex than is commonly modeled.

Besant and Avonlea points occasionally, but rarely, co-occur in apparently unmixed assemblages (Reeves 1970). Some major Besant sites (e.g., Old Women's Buffalo Jump — Forbis 1962) do not seem to have been used by Avonlea peoples, while some Avonlea sites (e.g., Estuary — Adams 1977) show no Besant presence. Conversely, Avonlea and Besant occupations at a number of sites (e.g., Morkin — Byrne 1973, Hartell Creek — E. M. Murray et al. 1976) may represent simultaneous occupation or may simply reflect patterned site selection processes with subsequent mixing of components. In any case, one need not model a Besant-Avonlea interaction predicated upon continuous warfare and population displacement. Certainly in the early historic period literature, it is not uncommon to find reference to multiple ethnic units within one camp (see Brink 1986). The Cree-Assiniboine and Blackfeet-Sarcee associations are particularly well known, and even involve members of different language families (Algonquian-Siouan and Algonquian-Athapaskan, respectively). Still, the impression remains that Besant and Avonlea distributions are primarily disjunct.

As noted previously, Avonlea sites are relatively rare; there are about a third as many Avonlea as Besant or Old Women's phase sites. There is no reason to believe that Avonlea peoples were any less well adapted to life on the northern plains than were those bearing Besant or Old Women's material culture. Presumably the site frequency phenomenon reflects a smaller Avonlea population. One is therefore faced with more or less the same genre of problem that Reeves perceived for Besant: How does Avonlea expand in the face of large, resident Besant populations?

Brumley and Dau (1988:46) have suggested that Avonlea social groups may have remained aggregated for longer periods of the year and this, combined with superior weapons technology, may have enabled them to compete successfully despite a smaller overall population. The vast majority of upland sites, removed from river valleys in the region, constitute small (three or fewer tipi rings) habitation sites; these are thought to represent dispersed groups stalking bison in the spring and early summer while surface water supplies (sloughs) were available. In contrast, a number of Avonlea communal kills (Ramillies and EcOs-41 in Alberta, Three Buttes and Timber Ridge in Montana) occur in the upland region, suggesting large Avonlea population aggregates in the same areas, and presumably at the same time of year, as other groups were dispersed into small encampments.

Brumley and Dau (1988) further argue that the fine craftsmanship evinced in Avonlea projectile points indicates that strong social control was exercised in point production. Assuming that Avonlea competitive success was partly grounded in their innovative weapon system, there may well have been magico-religious sanctions associated with the production standards and use of the bow and arrow. That is, there may have been an attempt to prevent the spread of their weapon technology, at least in detail, to others. Before dismissing this idea — after all, if one observes a bow in action, the principle should be obvious — one should consider the complexity entailed in the production of sinew-backed bows or of arrows with good flight characteristics. It might, indeed, be possible to limit or slow the spread of such production technology, especially if production was a craft specialty (see Dawe 1987). Brumley and Dau (1988:48) speculated that the "degeneration" of flaking quality in late Avonlea and post-Avonlea points may reflect the breakdown of such social sanctions concomitant with the perfection of the weapon system by other groups.

Besant seems to disappear from the western Alberta/Saskatchewan plains by about A.D. 850 at the latest. Avonlea persists until roughly A.D. 1150 in the region. At first blush, it would seem reasonable to suggest that Avonlea displaced Besant, and that the latter need no longer be considered in this chapter. However, things are not so simple! A series of side-notched points, collectively called "Side Notched Arrow" (Byrne 1973), but more properly classified minimally as Prairie or Plains side-notched, and usually assigned to the Old Women's phase in the region, appear in the archaeological record. These styles are earliest in the eastern (Saskatchewan) area, where they appear after A.D. 550, and a little later in Alberta, where they postdate A.D. 700 (Morlan 1988). It is apparent that the earliest variety of these points — Prairie side-notched — begin just as the Besant/Samantha points are fading from the scene. This, as well as morphological similarity among the Besant-Samantha-Prairie group, may suggest cultural continuity. We will explore this issue in the next section, and consider the termination of Avonlea, and its relationships to subsequent cultural manifestations.

Old Women's

The Old Women's phase was a term coined by Reeves (1969) to subsume post-Avonlea, Late Prehistoric Period material culture remains. However, Reeves did not actually provide a phase definition until over ten years later. Citing a manuscript report not generally available (Reeves 1980:88 in Reeves 1983a:19), he supplied the following description:

Old Woman's [sic] Phase is characterized by ceramics, emphasizes local Plains or Montana lithics to large measure, and has a technology characterized by the extensive use of split pebble techniques to produce blanks for end scrapers, points, pieces esquilles, and burin-like spalls. There is also extensive use made of petrified wood. Projectile point styles are micro-stylistically descrete [sic], particularly those representative of the close of Prehistoric times (Washita).

The taxonomy of late projectile points on the Canadian plains was developed by R. S. MacNeish (1954), R. G. Forbis (1962), and Kehoe (1966). The points can be ordered into two major groups: Prairie side-notched and Plains side-notched (Kehoe 1974). From work at Old Women's Buffalo Jump (Forbis 1962) and at the Gull Lake site (Kehoe 1973), it is apparent that the Prairie side-notched series appear earliest. Dyck (1983:129) estimated the group dates A.D. 750–1250 in Saskatchewan, which is more or less concordant with Kehoe's (1973) and D. Meyer's (1988) estimations, although Forbis (1962) demonstrated that the styles last in diminished frequency until the Protohistoric Period. Plains side-notched points appear about A.D. 1200/1300 and last until the introduction of metal points in the Protohistoric Period.

   The Prairie side-notched group is characterized by mediocre bifacial flaking and irregular body outline. Notches are generally wider than they are deep and often asymmetrically placed on the point, and the base is generally narrower than the blade (Kehoe 1974:830). Varieties within this group include Irvine, High River, Nanton, and Lewis (Forbis 1962). The similarity of some of these forms with the earlier Samantha point has already been mentioned. Kehoe (1974) explicitly linked them in an evolutionary sequence, while Reeves (1970:53) actually reclassified some of the Old Women's Buffalo Jump points as Samantha.

The Plains side-notched group of points is characterized by symmetrical body outlines, sharper angles at points of juncture, symmetrical notch positioning, notches placed higher on the point, and bases that are usually wider than the blade. Common varieties within this group include Paskapoo, Pekisko, and Washita (Kehoe 1974, Forbis 1962). Rare to the region are Buffalo Gap Single Spurred from extreme southern Saskatchewan and north-central Montana, and several forms which contain basal notches in addition to side notches — sometimes called "tri-notched" in Alberta — which appear to be more common in Montana than on the Canadian plains. Dyck (1983:132), as well as Kehoe, noted general esthetic and formal similarity between Plains side-notched and Avonlea. Reeves (1983a:20) presumably refers to this observation when he notes a strong technological link between Avonlea and "late" Old Women's material.

Ceramics from the Old Women's phase have been described by Byrne (1973). He classified these under the rubric Saskatchewan Basin Complex: Late Variant. The terminology reflects Byrne's belief that attributes of the vessels are derived from the east across the Canadian plains, and are unrelated in any specific way to the ceramics of the Middle Missouri area. Vessels have an elongated globular form, shoulders are common and often pronounced, necks are shallow and short, rims either flare or are vertical, and lips are usually flat. Most vessel exteriors were textured by the application of a cord-wrapped paddle or through fabric/net impressing. About one-third of the vessels were then smoothed, almost obliterating the textured surface. Another one-third of the vessels show truncation of the surface finish; that is, the surface was scraped or polished after hardening but the textured surface was not completely obliterated. The vessels bear little decoration; punctation is the most common technique although incision and impression also occur. Motifs are simple and include oblique impressions on the lip or at the lip edge. Decoration below the lip consists of a few rows of elements, usually oriented horizontally (Byrne 1973:331–35).

The origin of the Old Women's phase is obscure. Reeves (1970) initially proposed that Besant ultimately dominated the Alberta/Saskatchewan plains and Avonlea was displaced southward; Besant then gave rise to the Old Women's phase. More recent radiocarbon dates, however, indicate that Avonlea outlasted Besant in this region (Morlan 1988). Still, there is a slight overlap between late Besant dates and initial Old Women's phase dates (see Brumley and Rushworth 1983, Vickers 1983, Morlan 1988). As well, Avonlea persists until A.D. 1150, and thus overlaps the first four hundred years of Old Women's emergence. This would seem to suggest that two cultural traditions, represented by Old Women's and Avonlea, continued to persist side by side in the region, as Besant and Avonlea had done previously. The most parsimonious explanation is to consider Old Women's as the bow and arrow continuation of Besant (Vickers 1986:100). This is consistent with Kehoe's and Reeves's reconstruction, and with the observed similarity between Samantha and Prairie side-notched points.

Byrne (1973) reexamined the derivation of the Old Women's phase from the perspective of ceramic analysis. He suggested that there were similarities in both pottery and projectile points between Avonlea and the Old Women's phase, and that the latter derived from Avonlea, or from a merger of Besant and Avonlea (1973:469). He disputed the similarity in shape between "Side Notched Arrow" points and Besant/Samantha, on the basis of a Penrose Population Distance test, the details of which unfortunately remain unreported. Byrne's more telling argument was based on ceramics; specifically his statement that "the pottery evident throughout the Late Prehistoric Period in southern Alberta belongs to a single ceramic tradition, the Saskatchewan Basin complex" (1973:469). Thus, Byrne saw continuity between ceramics associated with Avonlea and with "Side Notched Arrow" points, and objected to deriving the Old Women's phase from the aceramic (as it seemed at the time) Besant phase. However, he was unwilling to dismiss Besant completely: "After apparently coexisting in the same region for some 500 years it would seem probable that the Napikwan and Tunaxa traditions would be able to integrate rather quickly; in contrast, the sudden emergence of conflicts sufficiently strong to result in the elimination of one or the other of the traditions would seem to be a somewhat dubious thesis" (Byrne 1973:470).

Duke (1988) also favored the amalgamation interpretation, suggesting that the earlier Prairie side-notched points (especially Irvine and Nanton) are derived from Besant phase Samantha types, while the pottery is derived from Avonlea. He suggested that increasing climatic aridity led to reduced bison and human populations, people adopted an exogamous marriage system, and Avonlea and Besant hunters shared information as well as mates; this led to cultural amalgamation visible as the Old Women's phase.

The argument for an Avonlea, or a merged Avonlea and Besant, origin for Old Women's as put forward by Byrne and Duke is no more compelling than any other. The projectile point similarity study by Byrne remains unreported. Besant appears to not be aceramic; there is some evidence for at least the limited presence of ceramics in Northwestern Plains Besant assemblages (Dyck 1983:115), as well as in the Sonota subphase of Besant in the Middle Missouri subarea (Syms 1977:88, Neuman 1975). Further, Morgan (1979:390) suggested that at least one of Byrne's persistent modes (cord-impressed surface finish) varies in conjunction with the percentage frequency of Side Notched Arrow points throughout the Morkin site levels. That is, instead of indicating cultural continuity, the mode reflects the degree of mixing between levels. She concluded: "There is no evidence to suggest that the Avonlea and side-notched ceramics [*sic*] represent a single cultural development" (Morgan 1979:391).

Past discussion of the Old Women's phase with neither definition nor analysis is unfortunate; it is possible that more than one cultural manifestation has been subsumed by the term. Despite the morphological variation among the projectile points which was clearly demonstrated in the initial work of Forbis (1962) and Kehoe (1966), subsequent researchers have tended to assume that only one cultural entity — Old Women's — was represented. Indeed, many archaeologists so inadequately record morphological variation that one cannot always discern Plains from Prairie side-notched in the literature (Dyck 1983: 129). It seems entirely possible that excessive "lumping" has obscured the cultural variety in the post-Avonlea record. This may account for some of the conflicting origin theories discussed above. Indeed, there may be no need for complex environmental/cultural amalgamation or cultural replacement theories at all.

Brumley and Dau (1988:51) have recently confined the use of the term "Old Women's" to components containing pottery of Byrne's (1973) Saskatchewan Basin Complex: Late Variant in association with Prairie and/or Plains side-notched points. This emphasis upon the presence of Byrne's (1973) Late Variant of Saskatchewan Basin Complex pottery as the phase diagnostic, rather than projectile point morphology, is most reasonable. They then suggest that the Old Women's phase develops from Avonlea in southern Alberta and adjacent Saskatchewan, the two being sequent phases in the Alsask tradition. Again a multilineal evolution is suggested, with other Besant and Avonlea "subphases" leading to other Prairie/Plains point-using cultures; the latter, of course, lack Saskatchewan Basin Complex ceramics. The scheme presented by Brumley and Dau (1988) is no better supported than the others but does acknowledge the complexity in the Late Prehistoric record. Given the confused state of current reconstructions, even that is a step forward.

Meyer (1988) has adopted the ceramic-limited definition for Saskatchewan Old Women's phase sites containing similar side-notched points and Saskatchewan Basin Complex: Late Variant pottery. Initial components of the phase, dating generally from A.D. 800 to 1300, are characterized by Prairie side-notched points. After A.D. 1300, Plains side-notched occur with increasing frequency although Prairie side-notched points persist throughout the sequence. Continuity is based on ceramics, as Meyer (1988:57) has noted: "The ceramics do not appear to have changed much throughout the history of the Old Women's Phase, although some decorative attributes from neighbouring ceramic assemblages were adopted."

Sites dating to the initial period of the Old Women's phase are distributed over a large area of the Northern Plains. This distribution includes all the Alberta and Saskatchewan plains and parklands, but the forests north of the parklands were not penetrated (Meyer 1988). The material certainly extends into the Milk River drainage in northern Montana. Brumley and Dau (1988:55) suggested that an aceramic cultural unit, which they name the Saddle Butte complex, also occupied that region; that is, they suggest a cultural boundary or tension zone in the region.

The later part of the Old Women's phase, after A.D. 1300, is one with a more circumscribed distribution. It appears that the Old Women's phase was expelled from the plains of Saskatchewan by the Mortlach phase, although Meyer (1988:60) suggested that the area west of Saskatoon continued to be occupied. At the same time, Selkirk phase groups — the presumed ancestral culture of the historic Cree — pushed south and west along the parklands almost to the Alberta border. From the Missouri River area of Montana, the Highwood complex — defined by Buffalo Gap Single Spurred and Emigrant Basal Notched varieties of the Plains side-notched point series (Kehoe 1966) — appears to push northward (Brumley and Dau 1988:57). The precise timing of these events is uncertain, although it appears that the time of greatest stress upon the Old Women's phase was in the Protohistoric Period, about A.D. 1730–50. However, I must defer consideration of Protohistoric events until the Mortlach and One Gun phases have been considered more closely.

Mortlach and One Gun Phases

The Mortlach phase has been characterized as one containing Plains side-notched points and ceramics which show attributes derived from the Middle Missouri area (Joyes 1973; Meyer 1988:62; Syms 1977:125). In Saskatchewan, Plains side-notched points appear about A.D. 1300 and persist until contact in A.D. 1750. Kehoe (1973:78) suggested that these points derived from the Mississippian cultural tradition via the Middle Missouri village populations. Dyck (1983:132) also suggested a source area in the Middle Missouri. Meyer (1988) noted that the Mortlach phase ceramics, although related to Middle Missouri materials, also show attributes derived from Selkirk ceramics in the forest/parklands, and traits derived from the Saskatchewan Basin Complex: Late Variant of the Old Women's phase. For the period postdating A.D. 1300, he suggested that the Old Women's phase had been displaced from the Saskatchewan plains by the Mortlach phase, except for the area west of Saskatoon between the two branches of the Saskatchewan River.

In Alberta, Byrne (1973) defined the One Gun phase to subsume Protohistoric materials similar to those which have been designated the Mortlach phase in Saskatchewan. Artifacts which show strong affinities to the Middle Missouri region include Cluny complex pottery, pitted handstones, grinding slabs, and scapula knives. The pottery surface finish is commonly check or simple stamped, subsequently smoothed to the point of obliteration. Minor quantities of brushing or fabric impression also occur. Vessels tend to be squat and globular in form, shoulders are rounded and unthickened, and necks are either short and sharply curved or long and shallow. Although direct or vertical rims occur, the rims are usually collared or braced, giving an S-shaped profile. Lips tend to be flat, insloping, and unthickened. Many vessels show a considerable amount of decoration. Linear dentate stamping is the most common technique, but cord-wrapped object impressions and fine line incision also occur in some frequency. Motifs are complex and include oblique impressions across the lip surface, but seldom at the lip edge (lip-rim juncture). Numerous closely spaced horizontal elements are present on the rim, collar, and/or neck. As well, triangular and chevron motifs occur (Byrne 1973:335–38).

The Cluny site, located on the Bow River downstream from Calgary, is the type site for the One Gun phase (Forbis 1977; Byrne 1973). The site consists of a semicircular ditch which terminates at a terrace edge; a channel of the Bow River likely flowed along this side of the site. The ditch is about 250 meters long, 2.5 meters wide, and 1 meter deep, and is bridged by at least three causeways. A palisade, constructed of poplar posts set in a shallow footer trench, is present about 4 to 8 meters inside and parallel to the ditch. Eleven large pits are located between the ditch and the palisade. These pits may be the remains of earthlodges, although their location in regard to the fortifications is unusual; excavation failed to yield much structural information. Except as noted previously, most tools recovered are not distinguishable from those of the Old Women's phase. Two fragments of brass and some horse bones were recovered. The site is thought to have been occupied briefly in the period A.D. 1730–50.

The Cluny site certainly represents an actual migration of people participating in the Middle Missouri Plains Village tradition. Byrne (1973:471) documented the migration hypothesis evidence. The Cluny site and Cluny complex pottery are clearly anomalous vis-à-vis the indigenous Old Women's phase. The One Gun phase material is all contemporary. The material is obviously related to the Middle Missouri area and intermediate (Mortlach phase) sites in Saskatchewan. The Hidatsa/Crow fission offers an historic analogue to such migration. Epidemics and intertribal conflict on the Middle Missouri provide reasonable motives for such movement. As well, Byrne (1973:476) suggested that the cultural material from the upper level at the Morkin site — Cluny complex ceramics, scapula knives, and nut stones — and a bell-shaped cache pit, may indicate another site unit intrusion. Most other One Gun phase material occurs as isolated specimens within Old Women's phase campsites, or in cairns. Many of these finds are poorly documented.

It seems reasonable to suggest that a progression of dates from A.D. 1300 to A.D. 1730 should document the Mortlach/One Gun spread from east to west. However, the data are not yet adequate to demonstrate this. Thus, while the Mortlach/One Gun replacement of the Old Women's phase attained its maximum extent in the Protohistoric Period, it is unclear how much earlier this may have occurred.

Byrne (1973:699) noted that, unlike the ubiquitous Old Women's phase distribution, One Gun phase materials are confined to the South Saskatchewan River drainage. The North Saskatchewan River and its tributaries (the Battle River and Sounding Creek) in Alberta appear bereft of Cluny complex pottery. This area is just west of the region of Saskatchewan where Meyer (1988) noted that no Mortlach phase material occurs. It thus appears that the Mortlach/One Gun phase intrusion did not penetrate the parklands and adjacent plains in western Saskatchewan and Alberta. The latter area continued to be occupied by the Old Women's phase.

FROM ARCHAEOLOGY TO ETHNOGRAPHY

Perhaps about A.D. 1730, the Piegans sent messengers to the forest Cree to aid them in war against the Snake, according to a story told to fur trader David Thompson in the winter of 1787–88 (Tyrrell 1916:328). The Cree, in contact with English traders on Hudson Bay, responded, outfitting themselves with their weapons:

There were a few guns amongst us, but very little ammunition, and they were left to hunt for the families; Our weapons was a Lance, mostly pointed with iron, some few of stone, A Bow and a quiver of Arrows; the Bows were of Larch, the length came to the chin; the quiver had about fifty arrows, of which ten had iron points, the others were headed with stone. He carried his knife on his breast and his axe in his belt. Such was my fathers weapons. (Tyrrell 1916:329)

So begins one of the most famous passages in Canadian plains historic literature – the Saukamappee story. Saukamappee (Young Man) was an aged Cree Indian living among the Piegan when he told his tale to David Thompson. His tale recounts the only pedestrian battles known for the Northwestern Plains; it provides a direct insight into prehistoric warfare. It further covers the first occasion that the Blackfeet tribes encountered the horse. And it leads to two unresolved controversies: What was the tribal territory of the Blackfeet at contact, and who were the Snake?

Speculation linking archaeological cultural materials with the historic tribes of the region is as old as archaeology. It is safe to say that the

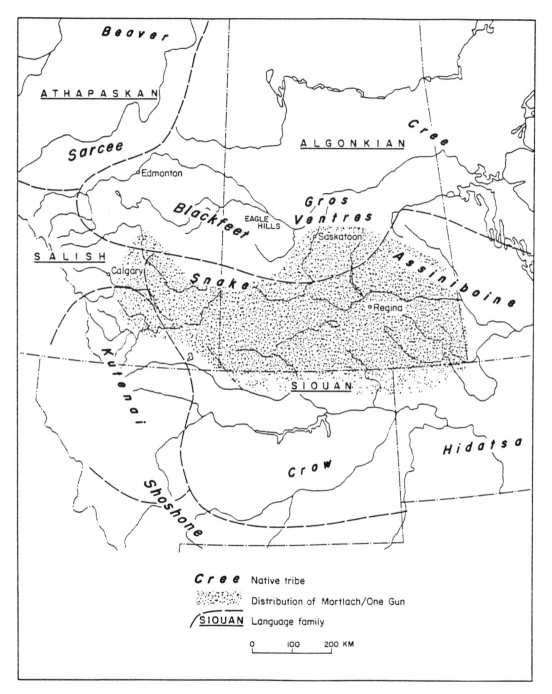

Map 1.2. *The distribution of Mortlach/One Gun phase material and postulated location of various Indian groups about* A.D. *1730.*

link between the Selkirk phase in the boreal forest of Saskatchewan and Manitoba and the Cree is generally accepted (see Meyer and Hamilton this volume; Syms 1977:141). It is also true that most archaeologists working in the region believe the Old Women's phase material represents the prehistoric Blackfeet, although with less secure justification (Brumley 1985:211–27, see Forbis 1963). Other ethnic units—the Atsina/Gros Ventre, Hidatsa/Crow, Assiniboine, Kutenai, Sarcee, and Shoshone—are even more difficult to identify archaeologically. The best summaries of this complex topic are presented by J. M. Brink (1986), Byrne (1973), and D. Russell (1982), while divergent opinions are presented by J. D. Keyser (1977), E. J. McCullough (1982), and Brumley and Dau (1988). M. P. R. Magne (1987) has compiled a series of maps showing tribal locations every fifty years from A.D. 1700 to 1850. These are particularly interesting in that they represent a compendium of contributions by Alberta and Saskatchewan archaeologists, and may be taken as current conventional wisdom.

Assuming that the Old Women's phase, at least in its latest prehistoric manifestation, represents the ancestral Blackfeet tribes, it is likely that the Blackfeet were confined primarily to the North Saskatchewan River basin west of the forks at the beginning of the Protohistoric Period. This is, indeed, exactly where the Saukamappee story would place them. The first Cree expedition was feasted on the north side of the North Saskatchewan near the Eagle Hills in western Saskatchewan. The Cree and Blackfeet, upon learning the location of the Snakes in the plains to the south, crossed the river in canoes or on rafts; they made sure to secure their vessels in case of retreat, so the battle must have occurred immediately south of the river. About 350 Algonquian-speaking Cree and Blackfeet warriors were assembled; the Snake were even more numerous.

After some singing and dancing, they sat down on the ground, and placed their large shields before them, which covered them: We did the same, but our shields were not so many, and some of our shields had to shelter two men. Theirs were all placed touching each other; their bows were not so long as ours, but of better wood, and the back covered with the sinews of the Bisons which made them very elastic, and their arrows went a long way and wizzed about us as balls do from guns. They were all headed with a sharp, smooth, black stone [flint] which broke when it struck anything. (Tyrrell 1916:329)

The battle proceeded until nightfall, when both sides, suffering no deaths, retired from the field.

Some years later, the Snake acquired horses and the Blackfeet (Piegan) again sent for Cree aid. This time the Cree brought a few flintlock muskets and created great slaughter among the Snake line; the latter were not mounted in the encounter. In subsequent years the Blackfeet contested the land and advanced southwestward to the Red Deer River area. Then smallpox swept the Plains, and the Snake disappeared from Alberta. The Blackfeet tribes continued to expand southwestward until the treaties ended native political autonomy.

A number of inferences can be drawn from the Saukamappee story. The first has been mentioned: the Blackfeet tribal location on the North Saskatchewan River conforms to the area where no Mortlach/ One Gun phase material is known to occur. If continued research confirms this impression, then the proposition that the Old Women's phase cultural material represents prehistoric Blackfeet will be enhanced.

Secondly, the story bears on the question of the identification of the Snake. The latter are traditionally taken to be the Shoshone (see Brink 1986, Magne 1988); only Forbis (1963:11) and especially Byrne (1973: 520) have suggested an alternate scenario. The Saukamappee story clearly demonstrates that the Snake were located south of the Battle River, and more important, that they were primarily a pedestrian culture. That is, the Snake were already in control of southern Alberta while a pedestrian, stone-using people — they were the latest Late Prehistoric or earliest Protohistoric residents of the South Saskatchewan drainage. This distribution conforms temporally and spatially with the distribution of Mortlach/One Gun phase material. The conclusion seems inescapable: the Snake are the ethnographic expression of Mortlach/One Gun. The material culture represented by Mortlach/One Gun is undoubtedly derived from Siouan cultures of the Middle Missouri area. Thus, the Snake of the Saukamappee story should be (generic) Sioux. Presumably, like the Crow, the Snake derived from the Hidatsa; whether they are identical to one or the other, or represent another, unknown offshoot is unclear.

VARIABLE SCALES

Fig. 1.5. Examples of shield-bearing warrior motifs sometimes considered to represent Shoshone. (From Keyser 1977: figs. 9, 14.)

Of course these need not be the only Snake in the grasslands. Keyser (1977) has argued that the shield-bearing warrior motif, common among the many petroglyphs at Writing-On-Stone on the Milk River in southern Alberta, represents Shoshone. Brumley and Dau (1988:58) suggest that the Highwood complex, which is characterized by Buffalo Gap Single Spurred and Emigrant Basal Notched (tri-notched) points, also represents Late Prehistoric or Protohistoric Uto-Aztecan speakers; that is, Shoshone. To this, one should add intermontane pottery as a Shoshone-associated trait.

As Byrne (1973:521) notes, few tri-notch points and almost no intermontane pottery occurs in site collections north of the Milk River in Alberta. The portable material culture evidence for Shoshone, or any other Montana group, is mostly absent from the archaeological record in this area. Both P. Barry (1991) and Magne and Klassen (1991) dispute the Shoshone/shield warrior correlation. Thus, contrary to the usual interpretation, I would argue that any Shoshone presence in the region was minor and short-lived.

Material culture correlates for the other historic tribes of the region — the Atsina/Gros Ventre at the forks of the Saskatchewan, and the Assiniboine of the Saskatchewan plains — are even more difficult to suggest. D. Meyer and S. Hamilton (this volume) suggest that the Assiniboine may be defined by the distribution of Sandy Lake ware of the Northeastern Plains and adjacent forests. Such a correlation appears to answer both the historic Assiniboine distribution data and their close connection with the Cree, as represented by the Selkirk phase. As for the Gros Ventres of the prairies, perhaps they and the Blackfeet are subsumed within a general Algonquian correlation with the Old Women's phase. In any case, I have attempted enough bridging of the Protohistoric/Historic gap and will pursue the topic no further.

DISCUSSION

A variety of interpretations of the last several thousand years of Indian occupation of the plains and parklands in Alberta, Saskatchewan, and Montana north of the Milk River have been explored in this essay. It is an attempt to represent fairly the differing views of cultural definitions and relationships in the Late Prehistoric and Protohistoric periods. Yet I confess to being most skeptical of this exercise. As indicated early in the chapter, these reconstructions lack scientific credibility; it is necessary to comment further on this notion.

Projectile points have formed the basis for definition of prehistoric cultural units in the region (see especially Reher and Frison 1980:94– 100). Despite attempts to incorporate variation in other tool classes, in lithic technology, in feature forms, and so forth (Reeves 1970), it is the projectile point that is, in the end, diagnostic. While ceramics have been used to define cultural units in the forest and parkland areas of Saskatchewan (Meyer and Hamilton this volume), and to some extent in the Brumley and Dau (1988) work on the Alberta plains, most assemblages can be classified only by their associated projectile points.

Interpretation of the meaning of point varieties from the Late Prehistoric Period has been a contentious issue since Forbis (1962) dug at the Old Women's Buffalo Jump. That site was identified in Blackfeet mythology as the place where men and women began cohabitation, and would seem to have been ideal for use of the direct historical approach (Forbis 1963). That is, the latest prehistoric occupation could be assigned to the Blackfeet on the basis of Blackfeet myth, and the artifacts should thus be diagnostic of that tribe.

However, as Forbis pursued the question, things became less simple (Forbis 1962, 1963). He encountered other legends and historical accounts which suggested that the Blackfeet were recent immigrants to the area (see Brink 1986). As well, since the term "Blackfeet" refers to people speaking that language, did the term become meaningless when applied to the past due to the process of language change? Indeed, how does an archaeologist determine the point at which linguistic and culture change make the application of Historic tribal and linguistic nomens to material culture traits inappropriate? In the end, Forbis (1962:71) concluded that the variation reflected "horizon styles" in use among various peoples; that is, the projectile point styles were seen to be widespread chronological indicators not relatable to specific ethnic groups.

In Saskatchewan, Kehoe (1966, 1974) had little hesitation in ascribing projectile point variation to linguistic or ethnic units. He assigned the Avonlea point to Athapaskan speakers migrating southward, Prairie side-notched was seen to be the product of Algonquian speakers, and Plains side-notched indicated Siouan speakers. However, Forbis's (1962) work at Old Women's Buffalo Jump had demonstrated that there was no simple replacement of types; rather, these changed in frequency and formed classic seriation curves (see Vickers 1986:99). These data were hardly compatible with Kehoe's ethnic model and its emphasis on migration and replacement. Nevertheless, without ever addressing Forbis's concerns, almost all other archaeologists have assumed that there is some equation between projectile point style and ethnic units.

When he wrote his thesis in 1970, Reeves specifically denied any relationship between his phases and linguistic units: "These linguistic speculative ideas and suggestions are antiquarian in nature and add nothing to Plains anthropological archaeology" (1970:217). It is thus ironic that, in the introduction to the published version of his thesis, he could discern not only linguistic units, but even detailed sociopolitical divisions: "The Old Woman's [sic] Phase in this model, while representing the prehistoric Blackfoot/Gros Ventre, can be regionally and

temporally segregated into variants which represent the various 'tribal' constituents—North Piegan, Blood, Atsina and Gros Ventre, for
example" (Reeves 1980:89–90 in Reeves 1983a:20). While it is most
unlikely that this can actually be done, most archaeologists would like
to believe that there is some sort of ethnic relationship between our
phases and historical tribal or linguistic groups. Even when specifically denied, as by Reeves in 1970 or more recently by Duke (1988),
society soon comes creeping through. Thus Reeves's Besant phase
archaeological unit develops burial customs and a hankering for trade
items, and Duke's Avonlea and Besant archaeological units begin
swapping wives. It is time to get our ethnic units out of the closet—let
us explicitly formulate our social models so that we can criticize and
test them. Until we do this, we cannot hope to approach a scientific
prehistory.

Another problem that inhibits a scientific prehistory concerns not
our models, but our data. Syms (1977) had a number of criticisms of
Reeves's Besant phase, noting among other things that this represented
a horizon based on projectile points having shallow corner notches.
Reeves (1983a:10–13) was incensed and argued against Syms's interpretation. He continually justified his position by arguing that his
analysis "was based on a 'hands-on' examination of all collections;
Syms' was not" (Reeves 1983a:12). Curiously, most of us consider this a
valid point—data description in the archaeological literature of the
Northern Plains is so inconsistent that an impression arrived at by
handling the collections may have more validity than one based on
examining reports. A similar situation can be seen in the new Brumley
and Dau (1988) model—the vast majority of data they cite are from sites
and collections which they have handled personally. We, like R. H.
Thompson (1956), must therefore evaluate the validity of an archaeological model by our impression of the quality—or at least the "hands-
on" experience—of the archaeologist offering the model. L. R. Binford
(1968) clearly noted that this is not the way to establish a scientific
archaeology.

Lastly, we should consider the methodologies that have been used to
construct the phases themselves. Reeves (1970) took a very structured
systems approach to constructing and comparing the Pelican Lake,
Besant, and Avonlea phases. His rigor of methodology has been attained
by no one else, and his conclusions still form much of the foundation
for the region's prehistory. However, one must also note that Reeves
provides virtually no quantitative data, either to examine morphological variation in his key artifact classes, or to compare trait frequencies.
Reher's (1988:283) comment on the Avonlea symposium seems especially relevant in this regard: "Where are the detailed studies, by site
and by region, that refine our knowledge of the 'Avonlea point'? Such
will continue, I suspect, to be our main evidence for cultural dynamics,

ethnic identity and other considerations, but where are the detailed stylistic and functional studies that are needed to answer these kinds of questions?"

Unfortunately, such studies are not being undertaken. Despite the fact that microstylistic variation was demonstrated in projectile point style early in Northwestern Plains archaeology, and that methods of quantitative comparison of archaeological assemblages are well known in the discipline, our phases remain impressionistic, qualitative constructs. Indeed, the qualitative examination by Reeves, being at least systematic, stands as one of the few lights in the darkness of regional reconstruction of prehistory. That this remains the case, especially with the increasingly ad hoc adjustments necessary to accommodate new data, surely argues against our having a scientific understanding of prehistory.

Archaeology in the Northern Plains is plagued by a lack of reporting consistency and, while site-specific studies have advanced greatly, integrative models have been inhibited by noncomparable data bases. It seems likely that microstylistic studies of specific artifact classes such as projectile points and ceramics, quantitative studies of artifact classes and lithic raw materials, and a general systems approach such as that pioneered by Reeves (1970), could lead to a prehistory in which we could place more confidence. While the necessary methodologies are clear to most archaeologists, implementation of such a study among collections containing thousands of items, scattered in several states and provinces in two countries, remains a task beyond our ability.

This discussion is intended to make the reader skeptical about the prehistoric relationships offered in this and other chapters. Archaeologists have put forward a variety of models of cultural relationships in the Late Prehistoric Period. However, none of the current models can be demonstrated to be other than guesses and, as Forbis (1977:16) observed: "So long as a guess is still a guess, it adds nothing to historical or archaeological understanding."

CHAPTER 2

LATE PREHISTORIC CULTURES ON THE MONTANA PLAINS

Sally T. Greiser

FOR the Late Prehistoric Period in the Northwestern Plains, a site occupation is ascribed to a particular cultural unit primarily on the basis of projectile point type. (The nature of the cultural unit or nomen varies with the investigator. It may be a phase of a cultural tradition or a "technocomplex.") A site may produce reliable radiocarbon dates, a well-defined hearth, ceramics, or a particular type of drill, yet, without the telltale or hallmark projectile point, we hesitate to ascribe cultural affiliation. The result, of course, is a skewed picture of prehistoric lifeways because of the necessity for at least one diagnostic projectile point to be present to render a site classifiable. Therefore, sites in which tasks not exclusively related to hunting were carried out are seldom part of our data base. Also excluded are sites from which projectile points have been removed by the occupants, subsequent peoples, or natural processes. We are clearly working with less than a full deck.

To add to our dilemma of inadequate data, we don't understand how projectile points, as we categorize them, relate to human groups. Although implicit in much of our writing, we have no proof that projectile point types can be equated on some level with linguistically defined social groups. Arrow decoration and fletching styles may have been more diagnostic of social groups than the points, yet the perishable arrows rarely survive for our inspection.

To address ethnicity with this partial deck is a nearly overwhelming challenge. Fortunately, the number of sites with ceramics is increasing and researchers are getting closer to defining typical ceramics for each cultural complex. Rock art, including petroforms, is becoming an important clue to ethnic identification. Burial practices should provide additional important information. For the present, I will proceed on the basis of the limited data currently available to speculate about the possible identity of prehistoric peoples on the Northwestern Plains.

Acknowledgments: I would like to thank Karl Schlesier for inviting me to participate in the symposium that led to the creation of this volume. Several colleagues reviewed various drafts of this chapter prior to publication and their comments and insights have been incorporated wherever possible. These reviewers include Philip Duke, David Wilcox, Gregory Campbell, and Leslie B. Davis. I'm grateful for their assistance.

ENVIRONMENT AND PALEOCLIMATE

The portion of the Northwestern Plains defined here as the study area is drained from southwest to northeast by the Missouri and Yellowstone rivers and from east to west by the Milk. Both the Milk and the Yellowstone eventually drain into the Missouri. These well entrenched drainage systems crosscut rolling sedimentary plains interspersed with outlier mountain ranges in the western portion and badlands in the east. From a narrow strip south of the Missouri River and extending northward, the land was glaciated. The Rockies bound the area to the west and southwest.

Climate is continental, with great seasonal extremes. Low precipitation and short growing season essentially precluded native peoples from developing reliance on horticulture. However, these same conditions facilitated bison proliferation. The combination of reliable water in the many rivers and tributaries, and the diversity of available resources contributed by outlier ranges, made this part of the Northwestern Plains especially conducive to a hunting and gathering lifeway, successfully focused on bison.

Through time, conditions have not been constant in the region. Plains archaeologists have generally assumed that the long drought episodes have had adverse impacts on bison populations. Data would seem to confirm this for the Atlantic climatic episode (ca. 6500–2730 B.C.), and perhaps also for the Scandic episode (ca. A.D. 280–870). Conversely, cool and moist periods apparently were the most conducive to bison proliferation, such as the "Little Ice Age," referred to here as the Neo-Boreal climatic episode (ca. A.D. 1550–1850). Although these trends appear to be real, we do not yet understand the complex ramifications of climatic change and stress on bison populations. For example, Clark and Wilson (1981) note dental anomalies in bison at a site that dates to the Sub-Atlantic episode, presumably marked by cool, cloudy, wet summers. A similar situation has been documented for bison at the Henry Smith site, dating to the Neo-Atlantic (Wilson 1988). These anomalies are interpreted as a sign of significant stress on the bison population. Clearly, we have much to learn, not only about past climates, but about how past climates affected resident game populations and the hunters who depended upon them.

THE SCENE: A.D. 500 ± 250

Reeves (1970) proposes that around A.D. 100–200, resident populations of the Pelican Lake phase of what he calls the *Tunaxa* cultural tradition were partially displaced by an intrusive population of Northeastern Plains origins, the Besant phase of the *Napikwan* cultural tradition (ca.

A.D. 100–700). For evidence of the continuation of the *Tunaxa* tradition
he cites the Avonlea phase, most commonly recognized by the hallmark artifact, the Avonlea arrow point. I agree that the two noted
horizons, Besant and Avonlea, are present in the study area at A.D. 500,
but I disagree with the conclusion that Avonlea represents a continuation of the tradition to which the Pelican Lake phase belonged. Rather, I
believe that both Besant and Avonlea intruded on the resident population, as will be discussed below.

Besant

Most researchers concur that Besant originated in the Eastern or
Northern Woodlands. The means by which we recognize the displacement of indigenous populations by Besant phase peoples is the presence
of side-notched dart points that replace corner-notched points and an
accompanying suite of definitive characteristics that distinguish Besant from Pelican Lake.

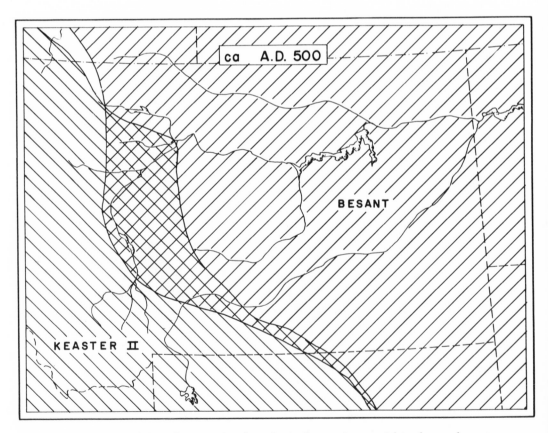

Map 2.1. *Proposed distribution of archaeological complexes within the study area, ca.*
A.D. *500.*

In addition to Besant dart points, Reeves (1970, 1983) suggests that the Besant phase includes Samantha arrow points, as defined by Kehoe and Kehoe (1968). At this time, well-defined occupations bearing Samantha points are few. (See Vickers this volume for discussion.)

Clusters of Besant sites occur along most of the major drainages in the Northwestern Plains as far north as the Missouri and Milk rivers. From the Milk, sites extend north into the Saskatchewan headwaters. While Besant sites are not common along the upper Yellowstone, they do occur in great frequency downriver and further south, along the Middle Missouri, the Belle Fourche, and in the Powder River basin.

Within the study area, although dozens of Besant sites are known, few have been professionally investigated, and these are generally limited to bison kill or processing sites. This lack of professional research precludes generalizing about certain aspects of Besant lifeways.

A few background observations are in order. Woodland pottery, high frequency of Knife River flint, and platform burial mounds clearly tie Besant phase peoples to the Middle Missouri trench. The distribution of Besant sites suggests that these were plains/riverine-adapted peoples who appear to have spread southward and westward along major drainages, perhaps in waves akin to the Eskimo/Aleut migrations eastward across the arctic (Dumond 1965).

With an expanded and refined data base, subgroups will undoubtedly be defined for Besant. Sites in the eastern portion of the territory contain significantly higher percentages of Knife River flint and ceramics than most sites to the west. Burial mounds are most common along the Middle Missouri trench. Other burial mounds, apparently associated with Besant occupations, have been reported from the plains of Montana (Johnson 1977) and Wyoming (Susan Hughes pers. comm. 1989). Sites in the Wyoming plains display highly developed communal bison hunting in addition to ceremonialism (Frison 1978). Sites in the study area and further north in the plains of Alberta indicate a focal bison economy.

Although Knife River flint is much less common than in the sites to the east, a preference for similar material is well documented along the upper Missouri (Greiser 1986; Shumate 1950). Furthermore, commonly used lithic materials are those available on the plains along river courses rather than those of the mountains to the south and west of the study area. Davis and Zeier (1978) noted that obsidian use at the Antonsen bison kill site appeared to be a matter of trial and error, based on the high frequency of hinge fractures and other flintknapping faults. Only two Besant sites are known in this southwestern portion of the study area which apparently was on the western fringe of their range.

To summarize, peoples of the Besant horizon were widespread throughout the Northwestern Plains by ca. A.D. 200. The earlier resident population recognized by Pelican Lake dart points was clearly impacted by the arrival of Besant groups and by the subsequent intrusion of Avonlea (ca. A.D. 400–900) (map 2.1).

"Keaster II"

Evidence from at least three locations in Montana, and confirmed by evidence from southern Alberta (Brumley and Dau 1988:44), strongly suggests that the resident population was not entirely displaced or subsumed. Rather, the tradition was carried on by people who made corner-notched arrow points virtually identical to their Pelican Lake precursors except for their reduced size. Terminology becomes a problem at this point because of the ethnic implications of Reeves's classification. *Tunaxa* is a Kutenai word, reflecting Reeves's belief that these people ultimately became known as Kutenai, just as *Napikwan* is a Blackfeet word, again reflecting an inferred ancestry. (For lack of a better suggestion, the name "Keaster II" is applied in keeping with Reeves's [1970] Pelican Lake subphase for the area.) These locations include several sites at the southern end of Canyon Ferry Reservoir on the Missouri River near Helena (Davis and Helmick 1982; Greiser 1984, 1986), the Hastings site west of Great Falls (Davis 1988), and the Birch Creek site in the area of White Sulphur Springs (Davis 1988). Stratigraphic evidence from the Hastings site clearly shows a corner-notched arrow point horizon below an Avonlea component.

The extent of the Keaster II complex or phase is unknown. Frison (1978) notes corner-notched arrow points in the mountains of northwestern and north-central Wyoming around A.D. 300–500. Cultural Level 3 at Mummy Cave produced a large assemblage of these points dated at A.D. 734 (McCracken et al. 1978). Now that we know what to expect, I predict that the number of occupations bearing these points will be increasingly recognized in the future. We have not recognized this point type previously because our taxonomy didn't accommodate the phenomenon. Due to the lack of information, a temporal range is not currently available. I would preliminarily suggest that this phase slightly predates but is roughly contemporaneous with Avonlea.

Assemblages from several sites at Canyon Ferry Reservoir show that lithic material selection was nearly identical between the makers of corner-notched dart points and arrow points (see Greiser 1986), demonstrating continued domination of the best lithic sources in the southwestern periphery of the study area including Obsidian Cliff in northwestern Wyoming and Madison chert sources in central and south-central Montana.

These data suggest that this tradition continued seemingly uninterrupted in some parts of the study area, especially along the eastern front of the Rockies along the upper Missouri River. However, much remains to be learned regarding cultural dynamics during this time. A case in point is the abandonment of the Schmitt Mine site (Davis 1982a), after fifteen centuries of intensive use by Pelican Lake phase people. Mine abandonment, by A.D. 200–300, roughly coincides with the transition from dart to arrow within this tradition. If indigenous groups continued to occupy the area and to control the lithic sources, why did they abandon this important mine? We might speculate that the resource was virtually depleted, or that extensive tunneling had made the quarry unsafe, or that arrow points required so much less material than dart points that these people simplified their lithic procurement activities and no longer worked the mine.

An unrelated, but equally plausible, explanation for mine abandonment might be that the arrival of a competitive group made people too vulnerable working this mine in its open location overlooking the Missouri basin. To investigate this line of inquiry we might seek evidence of warfare.

Avonlea

That Avonlea arrow points (Kehoe and McCorquodale 1961) mark the transition from dart to arrow in the Northwestern Plains is a commonly held belief. As noted, the Hastings site presents the first clear indication that corner-notched arrow points preceded Avonlea, at least in the southwestern portion of the study area. This is not to say that the bow and arrow originated in this region, but rather that indigenous people made the transition from dart to bow and arrow locally before the arrival, through whatever means, of Avonlea projectile points (see also Dyck 1983:107).

Researchers disagree on how and from where Avonlea arrow points made their way onto the Northwestern Plains. Kehoe (1966) asserts that Avonlea material culture is evidence of the Southern Athapaskan migration, using lexico-statistical data and a theory of transplanted circumboreal caribou hunters for support. Wilcox (1988) updates this theory with data accumulated during the last two decades.

Dumond (1969) has attempted to trace earlier Athapaskan movements and, with other authors (e.g., Sanger 1967), has noted a relationship between side-notched points (in this case, dart points) and microblade tools. In passing, he identified Avonlea points as perhaps representative of a later Athapaskan migration. However, he qualifies his theory because of an absence of microblade technology. Interestingly, microblades and prepared microblade cores have since been recovered from a number of Avonlea sites (Greiser 1988; Reeves 1983).

Husted (1969) disagrees with the attribution of Athapaskan affiliation, claiming that distributional data indicate Siouan peoples as the most likely bearers of Avonlea points. A third suggestion for ethnic connections comes from Syms (1977), who advocates upper Mississippi Valley origins for Avonlea. Morgan (1979), on the basis of ceramic characteristics, suggests an actual population movement from the upper Mississippi.

Reeves (1970, 1983:167) suggests that Avonlea point varieties origi- nated in the upper Saskatchewan basin and diffused across the Missouri basin to the Powder River–Black Hills area by A.D. 400–500. He con- tends that the stimulus for this technological change probably came from interaction of peoples in the parkland–Rocky Mountain Trench area of Alberta and British Columbia, suggesting that bow-and-arrow technology was introduced from the west, in interior British Columbia. The absence of sites documenting such a transition caused Reeves (1983) to question his earlier theory of Avonlea origins. As he states, "Although origins remain enigmatic, based on research of the last decade, it is quite clear that Avonlea did not originate in the northern forests" (1983:18). Although he is not specific with regard to what makes this "quite clear," it is perhaps because, if he accepts the possibility that these are Athapaskan peoples, they certainly could not become the modern Kutenai (cf. Reeves 1970, 1983).

In addition to the presence of Avonlea arrow points, Reeves (1970) defines Avonlea on the basis of a number of characteristics. He ac- knowledges the difficulty in defining a complex on the basis of skewed data, in this case an extreme reliance on bison kill site data. Several sites of more diverse type, studied within the last decade, have since expanded our knowledge of Avonlea. As mentioned, the presence of a microblade tradition as part of Avonlea stone tool technology has been documented, as have bipolar pebble technology and various ceramic types.

Although points typed as Avonlea have been reported as far south as Colorado, few of these match the defined type and they should be regarded with caution. As part of a cultural tradition, Avonlea-like points from other defined complexes such as Beehive (Fredlund 1981, 1988; Frison 1988) may represent subphases.

In 1970, Johnson (1970:48) suggested that the zone of concentration for Avonlea points is in the Plains area bounded by the Missouri, Saskatchewan, and Qu'Appelle rivers. The tributaries extending south of the Missouri should be added to this area of concentration, although Avonlea is glaringly absent along the Yellowstone outside of the head- waters area (Greiser 1984). The Beehive complex is tightly clustered in north-central Wyoming and adjacent parts of Montana.

The vast majority of Avonlea sites in the region are bison kill sites or habitation sites associated with bison processing. At the Lost Terrace site (Davis 1976; Davis and Fisher 1988), pronghorn killing and process- ing were the focal activities. In the study area, Avonlea sites are concentrated along the Missouri and Milk rivers in north-central

Montana with dates clustering between A.D. 750 and 1000. Of the recorded sites within these bounds, no burials have been found with associated Avonlea projectile points. The absence of ritualized burials would support the contention of an Athapaskan identity because of their universal fear of spirits, as evidenced by such practices as *chindi* hogans (Haskell 1987).

Distributional data indicate that the Avonlea range did not extend into the southwestern portion of the study area until very late (ca. A.D. 1000 or later). The indigenous Pelican Lake phase (Keaster II) apparently continued in this foothill and mountain fringe of the Plains until this time. It is interesting that the Pilgrim stone circle site (Davis et al. 1982), which produced a limited Avonlea component, has the earliest date by several centuries for Avonlea in the study area. If we accept this date as accurate, taken in conjunction with the early date from Head-Smashed-In (Reeves 1978, 1983), this evidence may be indicative of an early Avonlea orientation along the Rocky Mountain front with a subsequent shift out onto the plains. However, given the plethora of later dates it is more likely that this date is simply too early.

The gap of three hundred years or more between the earliest Avonlea dates, such as Head-Smashed-In at about A.D. 100–300, and the concentration of dated sites along the Missouri and Milk rivers of north-central Montana between A.D. 750 and 1000 is intriguing. Perhaps the early dates are representative of seasonal forays into bison country from the west, much like forays of the Kutenai and other Plateau groups several centuries later. Perhaps the successful adaptation of Besant phase peoples on the plains throughout much of the study area during these centuries prevented Avonlea encroachment eastward. Why, then, were Avonlea hunters so successful as plains bison hunters by A.D. 750?

Let us imagine for a moment that Besant society was more complex than that of Avonlea. Because Besant peoples had enjoyed the comforts of a thriving bison population which aggregated in predictable enough fashion to allow large communal hunts, they had developed a hierarchy, of sorts, to maintain and organize large numbers of people (see Bamforth 1987 and Fawcett 1987). (Reeves [1970] suggests that Besant phase peoples were sophisticated due to participation in the Hopewellian Interaction Sphere. However, the data do not seem to support this contention.) Such complexity gave them a strong advantage over Avonlea peoples who, prior to venturing onto the plains, had followed a more generalist subsistence strategy. In the montane and boreal forest, hunters generally stalk prey singly or in small groups. Only the salmon run provided a large enough food base to allow large groups to congregate, but these groups were nowhere near as large as the Plains rendezvous.

The technological breakthrough made possible by the bow and arrow that had improved hunting so significantly in the forest did not seem to make that much difference in communal bison hunts. Once the animals were impounded or driven off a cliff, they could be dispatched with a dart as effectively as an arrow, more or less.

It was not until the effects of a climatic shift toward drier and hotter conditions had seriously reduced bison numbers that the bow and arrow had gained a clear advantage over the dart. When the bison population and herd size were reduced, small group hunting with bows and arrows was more effective than trying to organize large, communal kills. This is not to say that communal kills ceased during this time, but evidence is strong for drastically reduced communal hunting within a more restricted area concentrated along the Missouri and Milk rivers. In eastern Wyoming, complex, highly organized and highly ritualized communal hunts by Besant hunters, evidenced at such sites as Ruby (Frison 1978), came to an abrupt halt by about A.D. 400. Based on currently available data, large-scale communal bison hunting in eastern Wyoming did not resurge until the sixteenth century (Greiser 1983). In Montana, as well, except for a few sites in the northern portion of the study area, communal kills are rare between A.D. 400 and 750. At Head-Smashed-In a similar pattern is apparent, with a gap in dates between ca. A.D. 305 ± 130 and 760 ± 90 (Reeves 1978:162). These centuries roughly coincide with the Scandic climatic episode (Bryson and Wendland 1967).

Based on the foregoing speculations, I suggest that Avonlea peoples ventured into the Northwestern Plains to hunt during the early centuries A.D., but were kept at bay by the dominant Besant phase peoples throughout much of the region. However, by about A.D. 700, climatic stress and concomitant changes in resident big game populations allowed Avonlea peoples an advantage due to their bows and arrows. At this time, they became the dominant group throughout much of the area, displacing Besant peoples, some to the north and northeast. Besant peoples, to be competitive, adopted bow-and-arrow technology (which they may previously have sneered at and otherwise maligned), and continued to make forays into the Milk and Missouri basins to obtain bison through communal kills, as contrasted with the smaller scale hunting to which they had resorted in the northland. Thus, within four hundred years, their roles had essentially reversed, with Avonlea peoples gaining dominance in the Missouri basin and relegating Besant peoples to outlier areas from which they made forays into this apparently prime and contested territory.

THE SCENE: A.D. 1000 ± 250

Besant and Avonlea Whereabouts

In the study area by A.D. 850, Besant is no longer recognizable. Samantha points are not common and other derivatives of Besant have not been well documented. Whether this absence is due to investigator unfamiliarity with point types or an actual dearth is unclear. Local varieties of Prairie side-notched points may represent the subregional descendants of Besant, but, until more is known, this remains speculative.

Avonlea is well established in the study area. South of the Yellowstone the Beehive complex occurs in the Tongue River area and Keaster II continues in the mountains to the southwest (map 2.2). As noted previously, Avonlea appears to "phase out" of the study area around A.D. 1000–1100. Depending on whether investigators believe Avonlea to represent Athapaskan speakers on their way south or people who stayed in the Northwestern Plains, opinions vary substantially regarding the descendants of Avonlea.

The question at this juncture is: What phases or complexes are recognized during the centuries following the "disappearance" of Besant and Avonlea projectile points? Several attempts have been made to define a projectile point chronology for the last millennium of prehistory on the Northwestern Plains (Forbis 1962; Kehoe 1966, 1973; MacNeish 1954; Mulloy 1958), based on seriation of a variety of side-notched arrow points (fig. 2.1). The samples are from stratified bison kill sites. Lacking well-defined, single-component sites, and having little or no understanding of bison kill organization during this time, we are left with a shallow understanding of what such point differences mean. Two general categories have been defined, each of which subsumes a number of point types.

In Kehoe's (1966) small point chronology, an outgrowth of MacNeish's work, these point types include "Prairie side-notched" points dating from ca. A.D. 700 to A.D. 1200–1400 and "Plains side-notched" points dating from ca. A.D. 1200 into the historic period. Projectile points of the Plains side-notched type occur throughout the continent at this time, for example, Desert side-notched in the Great Basin. Accordingly, they are not considered to be particularly useful indicators of ethnic identity unless much finer resolution is achievable.

Researchers disagree about the origins of peoples who used the various Prairie side-notched points. Kehoe (1973:78) believes that Prairie side-notched points represent a resurgence of indigenous Woodland peoples (possibly Algonquians), using a reduced and modified point designed specifically for bison pounds. The poorer quality of these points in comparison to Avonlea is explained as a reflection of the "fairly haphazard manufacturing techniques and ill-defined style from the Eastern Woodlands." Similarly, Reeves (1983) suggests that the earlier side-notched forms (e.g., Nanton and Irvine or Samantha) derive from Besant. In contrast, Byrne (1973) believes it more likely that the side-notched points were an outgrowth of Avonlea rather than Besant or Samantha.

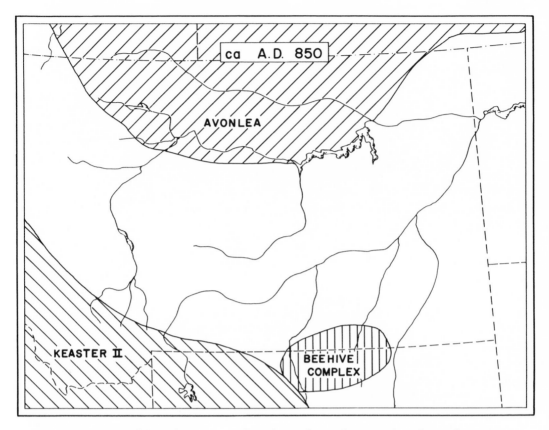

Map 2.2. Proposed distribution of archaeological complexes within the study area, ca.
A.D. 850.

With regard to the later Plains side-notched points, Kehoe (1973:200)
believes that, around A.D. 1200, another group entered the area from the
east who brought with them Mississippian influences. Reeves (1983:20),
following Forbis, refers to this entire sequence as the Old Woman's
phase, which he believes represents the prehistoric Blackfeet/Gros
Ventre, and that regional and temporal variants can be segregated
which represent the various "tribal" constituents (e.g., North Piegan,
Blood, and Gros Ventre). As has been pointed out by Vickers (1986:101),
until ceramic complexes are better defined for the region during these
centuries, it will be difficult to go beyond speculation with regard to
ethnic relationships.

Kehoe's reconstruction of changes in point types indicates a somewhat linear progression from Avonlea through Prairie side-notched to
Plains side-notched, recognizing some time-transgressive patterns (see
Kehoe 1966:833, fig. 1). Perhaps an explanation of time transgression is
overly simplistic in that it might conjure up an image of unidirectional
movement. The variations in onset and distribution of these point

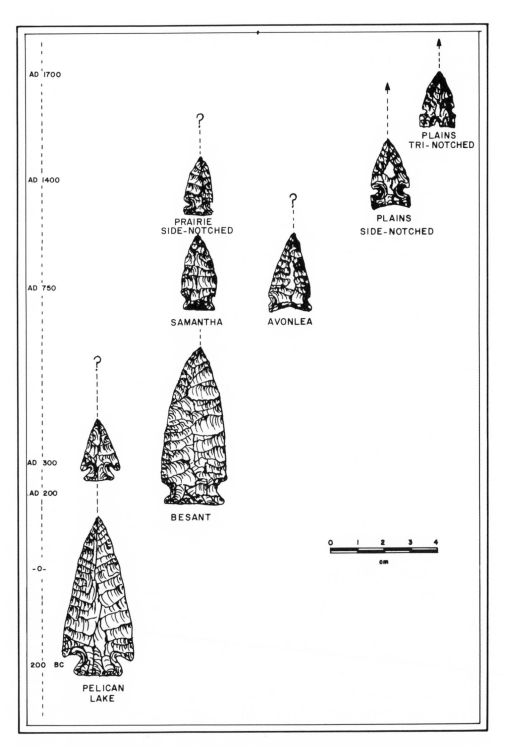

Fig. 2.1. *Generalized projectile point sequence for the Late Prehistoric Period in the Northwestern Plains.*

varieties might just as well reflect fluctuating territorial boundaries or fluid ranges of the local inhabitants. Substantially more research is needed to clarify these issues, especially for the centuries between A.D. 1000 and 1500.

Vickers (1986:99) provides a useful graphic summary of Forbis's (1962) relative chronology of Old Women's phase point type varieties, illustrating the possible connection between Besant and subsequent Irvine and Nanton types. He notes that Reeves (1983) reclassified two of the Irvine types from the Old Women's Jump as Samantha, thereby documenting his belief that these points are evidence of Besant progenitors. Reeves (1980:89–90) weaves a complex picture of Avonlea and Besant developments. With regard to Avonlea (as ancestral prehistoric Kutenai), he sees a strong technological link "to a 'late' Old Woman's (North Piegan?) variant . . . antecedents to which lie in 'early' Old Woman's (Blackfoot) and Besant traditions within the northwestern Plains region."

We know relatively little about life in the study area during the A.D. 1000–1500 period. Of the few investigated sites, again most are bison kills in north-central Montana (map 2.3). Bison kill sites radiocarbon dated to the Late Prehistoric Period peak between about A.D. 750 and 1100 (see Davis 1982b). In conjunction with other evidence, this might be indicative of relatively low bison populations earlier and later. Certain environmental indicators support this contention. Interestingly, along the Milk River, a few multicomponent bison kill sites with Avonlea points are roughly contemporaneous with multicomponent bison kills conducted by people using Prairie side-notched points. From this we might infer that at least two ethnic groups were using the same basins for bison hunting and other subsistence activities, and that resident populations during these centuries were subjected to pronounced stress and change. This co-occurrence of two point types in close proximity may reflect changing territorial boundaries as different groups competed for bison, especially during the late centuries of the first millennium A.D. when climatic conditions perhaps did not favor bison proliferation.

As must be obvious from the foregoing presentation, we know very little about the prehistory of this area during the centuries in question. Furthermore, what we do know is predominantly restricted to bison killing along the Missouri and Milk rivers in north-central Montana. Very little is known about the entire Yellowstone basin or the Missouri headwaters during these centuries. Given this substantive gap in the record, it is especially difficult to trace ethnic relationships. However, given the purpose of this volume, I will suggest that varieties of Prairie side-notched points represent local descendants of people who made Besant points (who may have been Algonquian speakers), and that at least some of the Avonlea people (who may have been Athapaskan speakers), left the study area during this time.

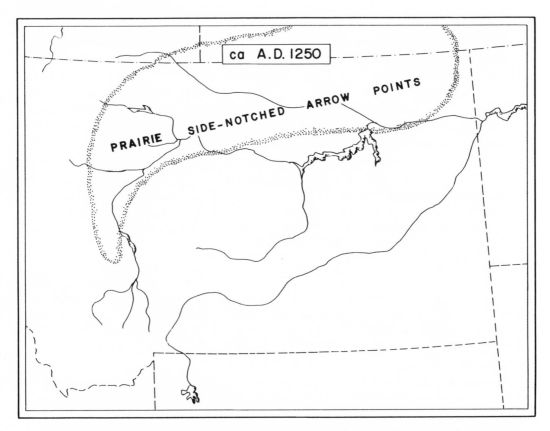

Map 2.3. Proposed distribution of archaeological complexes within the study area, ca. A.D. 1250.

THE SCENE: A.D. 1500 ± 250

The three centuries preceding Lewis and Clark's historic journey up the Missouri were marked by the heyday of communal bison hunting on the Plains. Furthermore, and as a reflection of this boom in bison populations, human populations on the Northwestern Plains were in flux: apparently everyone wanted a piece of the action.

Let us consider what we know from the historic record regarding ethnic groups identified as occupants of the Northwestern Plains and compare that information with data from terminal prehistoric archaeological sites. A preliminary study of early tribal migrations in the region by Gordon Hewes (1948) remains one of the best summaries of the data and is a provocative document in terms of relevant research questions. Accordingly, his work will be drawn upon liberally in the following discussion.

For the Blackfeet in the northern portion of the study area, there is near consensus today that they have long been inhabitants of the

Northern Plains. Historic records place them (or perhaps the Gros Ventre) west of the South Saskatchewan River by 1690 (Kelsey in Lewis 1942), with subsequent expansion to the west and southwest, reaching the Milk River by the early eighteenth century. Hewes (1948:53) suggests that their position reported by Kelsey in the late seventeenth century may have been the result of a temporary displacement (to the northeast) by the expansion of Shoshoneans. Hewes's (1948:53–54) consideration of the Blackfeet question is worthy of citation:

The solution of the early location of the Blackfeet would shed great light on the later prehistory of the N Plains. If the ancestors of the Blackfeet did in fact occupy the NW Plains as far back as 1400 or before, one might see them as a surviving northern portion of an old western Algonkian stratum in the Plains, pottery-using and quasi-agricultural, which might have been responsible for all or part of the early Woodland manifestations W of the Missouri, prior to the arrival of Siouan and Caddoan peoples in the centuries after 1400. If, like the proto-Cheyenne and proto-Arapaho, the early Blackfeet dwelt in Minnesota or the Red R. Valley between 1200–1300, the identification of the carriers of the early Plains Woodland culture becomes more of a mystery. Of the language families known to have occupied the Plains in historic times, only the Athapaskans seem a reasonable alternative.

Archaeological evidence of the transition from Late Prehistoric Old Women's phase to historic Blackfeet is problematic. Brumley (1985) has suggested that the death lodge type of medicine wheel (see Dempsey 1956) may document prehistoric Blackfeet distribution. Other areas of future research should include refined ceramic classification, Blackfeet projectile point definition, and lithic material selection patterns.

As of this writing, the most parsimonious explanation for the ethnic identity of groups responsible for the pre–A.D. 1500 archaeological remains in the area north of the Missouri River, and especially along the Milk River, is that they were one of the ethnic units that comprise the Blackfeet, most probably the Piegan and perhaps the Gros Ventre, as well. In terms of projectile points (our inadequate but key link to the past), this translates to Besant dart points followed by Irvine, Nanton, and perhaps other currently undefined varieties of Prairie side-notched arrow points, followed by Plains side-notched points of known historic Blackfeet affiliation.

Whether or not the Kutenai were Plains inhabitants prior to the protohistoric period remains a topic of controversy. Their own mythology claims an early Plains-adapted lifeway (Turney-High 1941). Hewes (1948:55) cautions that these reminiscences may represent a "temporary eastward shift of a tribe really long stationed in the Rockies." For justification, he notes that "many of the Plains elements in recent Kutenai culture seem post-horse." Furthermore, Shoshone expansion from the south could have resulted in Kutenai displacement.

The possible distant linguistic link between Kutenai and Algonquian (Voegelin 1941) fits Reeves's model of some ancient link between Avonlea (as proto-Kutenai) and Besant (as proto-Blackfeet). Additional support comes from information supplied Turney-High (1941) by a Kutenai informant who claimed that the Piegan were, at one time, the Kutenai.

From Kehoe's point of view, such a relationship between Kutenai and Piegan would have to be denied or explained away due to the premise that Avonlea represents an intrusion of Athapaskan speakers from the north whereas the Algonquian-speaking Blackfeet came from the east, bearing a distinctive toolkit: therefore neither would have become Kutenai. Perhaps the similarities noted by Voegelin resulted from centuries of interaction and, in some cases, amalgamation (see Duke 1981), as opposed to origins from a common language family. Whatever the case with the linguistic questions may be, the answers are buried so deeply in time that we can only speculate about their implications.

We know very little about a Salishan presence on the Plains prior to the historic period. The two major ethnographers to investigate these groups disagree about the subject. Teit (1930) proposed the theory of a former "Plains Salish" people who became the Flathead, pressured west of the divide by populations to the east. Turney-High (1937, 1941) disagreed, concluding that the Flathead were always an intermontane group. Archaeological evidence from which to address this issue is not available because of our inability to identify groups at this time.

A similar situation exists for the Pend d'Oreille, who may have been in the Milk River area prior to Blackfeet domination (see Graspointer 1980:38 for discussion). Until archaeological remains can be attributed to these particular ethnic groups, this void will continue.

Archaeological evidence supports Shimkin's (1941) proposed date of A.D. 1450–1500 for Shoshonean expansion northeastward from the Great Basin. Indicators regarded as diagnostic for prehistoric Shoshone in the Northwestern Plains include: distinctive flat-bottomed pottery known as Intermountain Ware (Frison 1971; Mulloy 1958; Wedel 1954); carved steatite bowls, also with flat bottoms (Frison 1982), and perhaps carved, tubular steatite pipes (Davis and Zeier 1978); tri-notched obsidian arrow points (Gruhn 1961; Malouf 1968); and distinctive semilunate knives (Frison 1978). Researchers have suggested the possibility that shield-bearing warriors found on rock art panels are of Shoshonean origins (Keyser 1975; Loendorf 1973).

Dates around A.D. 1450–1600 are available for a number of sites that contain Intermountain Ware in mountainous eastern Idaho and western Wyoming and adjacent plains of north-central Wyoming and south-central Montana (see Wright 1978). Tri-notched arrow points appear to occur somewhat later in the record, perhaps around A.D. 1650 (Davis and Zeier 1978).

Pre-horse, shield-bearing warrior rock art scenes recorded in the Bitterroot valley of southwest Montana (Keyser 1975) and as far northeast as southern Alberta (Keyser 1977), have been cited as evidence for pre-horse Shoshonean expansion well into the Plains (Bamforth 1987). (The Shoshone obtained horses from their Comanche relations ca. A.D. 1690–1700). Before we consider this rock art as proof of Shoshonean expansion, it is important that we briefly review some data that seem to refute, or at least alter, these suppositions. Loendorf (1988) has recovered what appears to be good evidence of an A.D. 1100 date for a shield-bearing warrior pictograph in south-central Montana. This predates all other indications of a Shoshonean presence by some four hundred years. A second area of doubt about the Shoshonean derivation of this motif is its fairly widespread occurrence in both the Gobernador and Rio Grande areas of New Mexico (Schaafsma 1980). Given the date of A.D. 1100 and the spread of this motif to the Southwest, we might speculate that this motif is more likely of Athapaskan origin. If so, this makes Avonlea an even stronger candidate for the archaeological manifestation of the Southern Athapaskan migration.

Temporal and spatial data indicate that the Shoshone occupied the southern reaches of the study area as early as A.D. 1500 and may have spread north to the southern Alberta plains by 1700 (see Vickers this volume for discussion). Evidence of a break in the archaeological record in several mountain sequences around 1500, in which one cultural tradition seems to disappear and a new one is introduced (see Butler 1981a and Wright 1978), is interpreted as evidence of Shoshone arrival.

One area of difficulty in identifying Shoshone sites that lack ceramics is that obsidian tri-notched points (as well as tri-notched points of other materials) are also associated with sites attributed to Crow occupations (Frison 1967, 1978). Davis and Zeier (1978) studied the distribution and frequency of obsidian tri-notched points as part of their investigations of the Antonsen site, a multicomponent bison kill site with the terminal Late Prehistoric component attributed to the Shoshone (ca. A.D. 1650–1800). They note the restricted distribution of tri-notched points to "the Plains/Foothills interface and intermontane valleys within the Northwestern Plains region" (1978:232). Tri-notched points rarely occur farther north than Great Falls (see Shumate 1950), and those that do may represent forays by Shoshone into Blackfeet territory.

Frison suggests that tri-notching had functional utility and that the Crow may have acquired this trait through contacts with the intermountain region (Frison 1967). The mixing of Intermountain Ware and "Mandan tradition" pottery at a number of sites may further document such interaction. During the early historic period, we know that the Crow had an established trade relationship with the Shoshone (Ewers 1958) and this may simply be an early expression of such practice.

Historic Crow territory extended from the Yellowstone River valley in Montana south principally along the Bighorn, Powder and Tongue rivers, that is, just adjacent to the study area (see Hannus this volume).

The Kiowa and Kiowa Apache may have been the resident groups displaced by the Shoshone. Kiowa traditions place both groups at one time close to the Shoshone and west of the Crow in the vicinity of the Missouri and Yellowstone headwaters (Mooney 1898). Occupations such as Cultural Layer 2 at Mummy Cave (ca. A.D. 1114 — McCracken et al. 1968), may be good candidates for researching ancestral Kiowa.

A somewhat different early homeland area for the Kiowa Apache is referred to by Gunnerson and Gunnerson (1971). They quote a nine-teenth-century source in which a Kiowa Apache informant claimed that "many years before" they had lived in a "broken and desolate country" between the headwaters of the Missouri and the Platte. Turning to the archaeological record, we have reviewed good evidence for an influx of Shoshonean speakers into the Yellowstone headwaters area by about A.D. 1500–1600. At roughly the same time, Siouan speakers were moving into the Tongue River valley and surrounding area. Prior to an apparent hiatus of a century or more, people of the Beehive complex, with its Avonlea-like points, were resident in the "broken and desolate country" described above. Considering the hypothesis that Avonlea and Avonlea-like projectile points and associated material culture represent Athapaskan speakers, it is possible that the Beehive complex (Fredlund 1981, 1988) represents a precursor to the Kiowa Apache branch of the Athapaskans.

Kiowa Apache is believed to have diverged from other Apachean dialects sometime around the twelfth century A.D. (Hoijer 1956, 1971), which roughly coincides with the end of the Beehive complex in north-central Wyoming and environs and the end of Avonlea as a recognizable technocomplex in the region. Perhaps the ancestral Kiowa Apache became more isolated from other Athapaskan speakers in the North-western Plains at that time as they shifted first to the west into the mountains with the Kiowa, later to move into the Black Hills, as suggested by Wilcox (1988), and eventually to the Southern Plains. The occurrence of shield-bearing warrior petroglyphs in the Black Hills (Keyser and Sundstrom 1984) may lend credence to this line of inquiry.

Returning to the archaeology of these terminal prehistoric cultures, we again see a record dominated by bison hunting. Literally hundreds of bison jumps and corrals are known for the period A.D. 1500 to 1850, although few have been professionally investigated. Fewer habitation sites have been studied that can be attributed to this period. As discussed, some terminal prehistoric archaeological sites can reasonably and tentatively be attributed to particular ethnic groups, for example, certain Shoshone and Crow sites. However, a larger number of sites cannot be assigned, some because of inadequate data and others because of complexities with shifting populations and recognition in the record (map 2.4).

SUMMARY AND CONCLUSIONS

As we attempt to link history to archaeology, we are confronted with significant changes that transpired among native peoples as a result of the horse and myriad changes resulting from the arrival and spread of Euro-Americans. Linking pre-horse with post-horse archaeology is difficult. In working with the data, it is substantially easier to work forward, rather than back, through time (fig. 2.2).

Working from the ethnographic and ethnohistoric data base, combined with historical archaeology, we can only trace the Shoshone and some Siouan group with any degree of assurance, and then only back to the fifteenth or sixteenth century. The Blackfeet and perhaps the Gros Ventre, who presumably have a much longer tenure in the region, are only tentatively traced back through time.

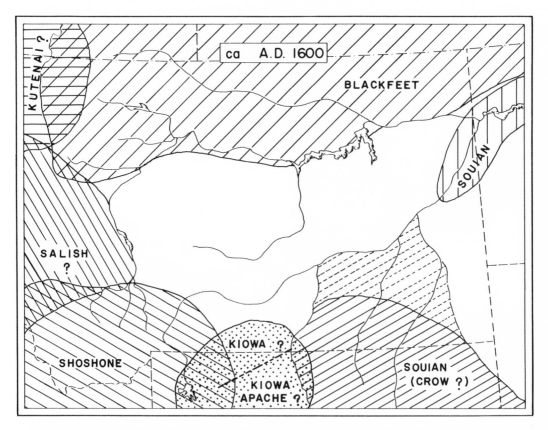

Map 2.4. Proposed distribution of archaeological complexes within the study area, ca. A.D. 1600.

AGE | CULTURAL SEQUENCE AND RELATED PROJECTILE POINT TYPES

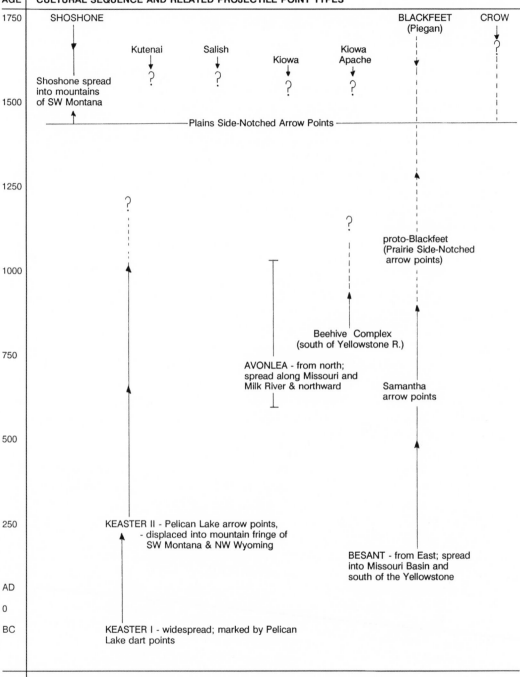

Fig. 2.2. Cultural sequence for the Late Prehistoric/Protohistoric Period in the study area.

For other groups known or thought to have been in the area, including the Kutenai, Flathead, Pend d'Oreille, Kiowa, and Kiowa Apache, we lack solid archaeological evidence of their identity and residency. Finally, archaeological verification of the Southern Athapaskan migration remains elusive although several lines of research await investigation.

Tackling the ethnicity problem from the perspective of archaeology and working our way up to history, we appear to do substantially better, at least in terms of being able to follow complexes through several centuries. Of course our limited data may provide us with the perfect opportunity to oversimplify. To review, at A.D. 500, two cultural traditions were present in the study area: one indigenous group referred to here as Keaster II and intruders from the north or east known as Besant. Keaster II withdrew or were pressured into the adjacent mountains. These people may be antecedents to the Salishan peoples of western Montana, to the Kiowa, or they may have moved on and left no further clues to their identity. At this time there is no way to link these remains to an identifiable ethnic group. Besant, on weak footing, is believed to be antecedent to the Blackfeet/Gros Ventre and perhaps the Kutenai as well.

By A.D. 750–850, Avonlea peoples from the north, who may have been Athapaskans, spread throughout the northern portion of the study area. Groups probably related to them, (perhaps ancestral Kiowa Apache), represented by the Beehive complex, spread southward into north-central Wyoming. Eventually, the Beehive complex people may have moved eastward into the Black Hills area. Avonlea hunters abandoned their bison-hunting lifeway, at least for a while, probably due to reduced bison populations. Their point type may have changed as a reflection of a subsistence focus shift away from bison. Perhaps they slowly shifted southward, eventually to become what we refer to as Southern Athapaskans. Similar point types of the Blue Dome complex appear west of the divide around A.D. 1000 (see Duke and Williams this volume for discussion).

The period around A.D. 1200–1450 is poorly known archaeologically. By about 1450, Siouan speakers were present along the Yellowstone and to the south into Wyoming. This early migration may have been up the Belle Fourche River. Later groups of Crow and other Siouan speakers came along the Missouri and Yellowstone (Johnson and Kallevig 1988) and the Saskatchewan (Byrne 1973).

Such "waves" of Woodland peoples from the east may have been an ongoing phenomenon throughout prehistory. Even what we call Besant is probably representative of numerous bands of people, probably connected linguistically, but not necessarily so, who shifted westward from the Middle Missouri or from further to the north. There is no reason to expect that the Crow (or the earlier Besant peoples) migrated in one mass movement. Examples from North America and from around the world suggest that the wave model is more appropriate.

By about 1550, Shoshone were moving into the mountains of south-western and south-central Montana. Whether or not their spread onto the Plains was pre- or post-horse continues to be problematic. The best evidence is that they occupied the mountains and periphery in south-central Montana, including the Missouri and Yellowstone headwaters areas, during the last centuries of prehistory.

Early relationships among these groups are unclear. The steady increase in obsidian at sites throughout the region may suggest an active trade network. Presumably, the Shoshone, given their distribution and power, controlled the obsidian trade. In historic times, they traded with Crow, Kutenai, and Salishan groups (Ewers 1958; Laroque 1910), and this pattern may have been established during prehistoric times. In later years, warring groups institutionalized formalities to allow trade relations to continue. This practice, too, may have its roots in prehistory.

That warfare existed during pre-horse days is documented through rock art of the region. We know that, as competition increased for the bison, intergroup warfare was common, but we have yet to document the extent.

Although more threads are left dangling than have been neatly tied up, the data await research directed toward solving questions of ethnic identity of Late Prehistoric cultures in the Northwestern Plains. Too little work has been done in the area of ceramics. In my opinion, such efforts will eventually paint the clearest possible picture of ethnic relationships. Rock art is another avenue for ethnic identity refinement, as is the study of burial customs. Detailed, systematic study of large assemblages of lithic tools from well-defined sites is a fourth research direction worthy of more attention.

CHAPTER 3

CULTURES OF THE MOUNTAINS AND PLAINS: FROM THE SELKIRK MOUNTAINS TO THE BITTERROOT RANGE

Philip Duke and Michael Clayton Wilson

THIS chapter examines the types and extent of cultural contact between Plains and Plateau peoples during the past fifteen hundred years of prehistory, concentrating on an area delimited by the Selkirk Range in Canada and the Bitterroot Range in the United States of America (maps 3.1 and 3.2). We argue that the fluidity between cultures of the Great Plains and Interior Plateau should be seen as representing more than simply the transfer of traits, but rather is also reflective of similar adaptive strategies, which were only intensified by European contact and the acquisition of the horse. We also examine the degree to which the historic groups of the study area can be recognized in the prehistoric archaeological record.

Unlike other chapters in the volume, this one is concerned with an area that extends outside the Plains. We discuss, therefore, not only their culture histories, but also the nature of cultural relationships between Plateau and Plains peoples. Our arguments are selective rather than comprehensive, expository rather than descriptive.

THE NATURAL ENVIRONMENT AND HUMAN ADAPTATIONS

Physiographic changes in the vicinity of the Forty-ninth Parallel are of great importance to our arguments. North of the international boundary an orderly mountain front and, behind it, a nearly linear continental divide seem wall-like and forbidding to plains travelers. To the south, the divide becomes sinuous. It is not surprising, therefore, to find that cultural groups in Montana and Wyoming moved back and forth from mountains to plains with great facility, whereas their neighbors to the north in what is now Canada were limited to a few narrow conduits.

The Bitterroot and Beaverhead mountains constituted an important barrier between the upper Missouri drainage in Montana and the Salmon and Clearwater rivers of Idaho. Western groups came into the area in the historic period to capture horses in winter drives, the country south of the Kootenay River headwaters being rich in horses

(Coues 1897:708). In addition, eastern groups would travel westward in quest of anadromous fish (primarily salmon). Thus, most of the groups considered here had ties that extended far to the west as well as eastward onto the plains.

The highly varied and "patchy" ecology of mountains and valleys provided a varied fare of resources. The fundamental food resource over much of the Interior Plateau was a group of anadromous fish, the salmon, especially the sockeye (*Onchorynchus nerka*). Salmon could at times provide a food surplus, as could bison herds on the plains to the east. Bison were occasionally available in mountain valleys, especially

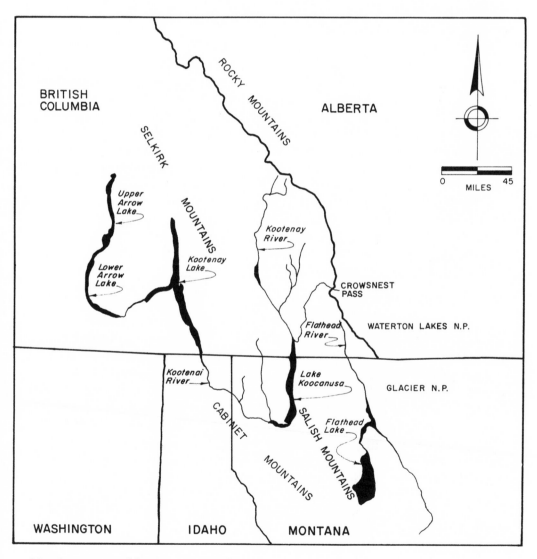

Map 3.1. Principal locations in study area.

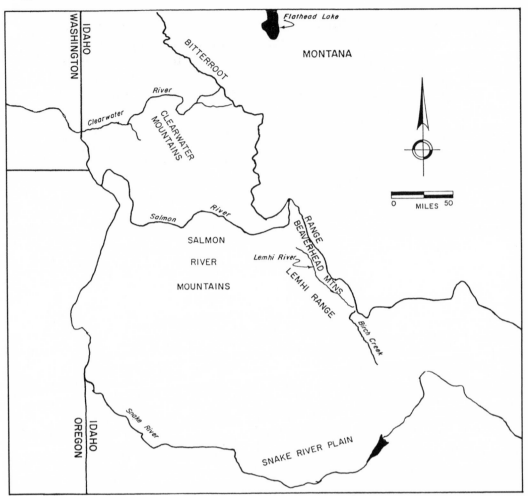

Map 3.2. Principal locations in study area.

in western Montana, but, generally, they were neither dependable nor
numerous. Through much of the area, other ungulates such as mule
deer, white-tailed deer, wapiti, moose, mountain goat, and mountain
sheep were available. In more open valleys to the south there were
pronghorn antelope, and a small resident population of woodland
caribou was occasionally harvested.

Vegetable foodstuffs were vitally important to human groups, especially in bison-deficient valleys. They included berries of many kinds
as well as roots, such as camas (*Cammassia quamash*), bitterroot
(*Lewisia rediviva*), biscuit-root (*Lomatium* sp.), and wild turnip
(*Psoralea esculenta*). Some of these required sophisticated processing
techniques to render them edible. Camas gathering took on territorial
implications, individual families tending to return to the same patches,
with their already prepared earth ovens (Turney-High 1933; Hart 1976:

16–17). Importantly, almost all resources were susceptible to annual variation in yield; root yields were relatively secure but berries had distinctly good and bad years, as did salmon runs. Game was susceptible to winter kills, drought, and hunting pressures.

Given the seasonal availability of specific plant and animal resources and the presence of passes through the Rocky Mountains, it was of great adaptive significance that transmontane mobility emerged, and this pattern formed the structural basis for social and political patterns of typical groups (Walker 1967; Wilson 1980:10). Certain resources would be harvested directly, but others could be acquired only through trade. The intensity of quarrying for lithics in this region likely reflects this, because Montana lithic materials (particularly Mississippian cherts) are widespread in Northwestern Plains sites. One possibility is that food, in the form of dried meat, was moved westward into an area that appears to have had a low carrying capacity for ungulates.

Flexibility in resource procurement helped to overcome the vagaries of annual yield in any one system (Walker 1967:9). In addition, mobility (including both sociostructural adaptations and the appropriate technology for transport) allowed groups to compensate for variable food quality by moving to better resource areas. Although the "bison realm" and the "salmon realm" did not, in nature, overlap, it was possible to make these two dietary realms overlap artificially, thereby raising carrying capacity for human populations.

Therefore, we argue that mobility, including transmontane movement, was a fundamental survival strategy on the Plateau both in historic and prehistoric times, and that it was possible for people to move seasonally from localities within the bison realm of the Plains to sites within the salmon realm of the Columbia drainage. Of course, not all such movements were tied closely to subsistence activities such as hunting or trade. Other movements occurred for raiding by war parties, to allow groups to combine temporarily for defense (Malouf 1967), and simply to satisfy curiosity.

It is important to note that this pattern of mobility by Plateau groups was evidently established in terms of salmon exploitation long before it was extended to hunting of bison. Groups were drawn to downriver fisheries because of the relative unreliability and poor condition of upper tributary salmon; having harvested the salmon they were rapidly drawn again upriver because the relatively wet climate of the lower Columbia was less favorable than inland sites for drying fish (Walker 1967:13). The pattern of historic period seasonal bison hunting can, therefore, be seen as the logical extension of a Plateau trait rather than the simple diffusion of a Plains trait (Walker 1967:1). An interesting possibility is that the arrival of the horse simultaneously precipitated the extinction of the plateau bison herds (because of greater efficiency in hunting) and allowed rapid movement onto the plains to provide an alternative bison source (Blake 1981:12). Adoption of the horse, while it did allow the infusion of Plains traits, was, therefore, entirely consistent with Plateau adaptive strategies favoring mobility and the storage of surplus food.

As a result of the patchy distribution of resources, there lay in the midst of the present study area a large tract of land on the west slope that was "neither fish nor bison," and in which groups relied upon smaller ungulates (especially deer and mountain sheep) and an array of other animal and plant species. Storage of plant foodstuffs was pivotal in the survival of such groups, as was long-distance trade, but even more lucrative was the mobile life style that led them seasonally either east or west. This area, extending from Montana into British Columbia, has been named the Barrier Falls subarea of the Northern Plateau (Roll 1988), and we shall examine this concept in more detail below.

The development of exchange systems, as noted above, countered local unavailability of resources. Bison products such as hides and dried meat were traded even further westward to groups that did not participate in either Plains or Plateau hunts. The specialized roles of some groups as brokers between neighboring resource-rich groups was undoubtedly established well before the historic period, however much it may have intensified at that time. Certainly, the increased mobility afforded by the horse allowed greater infusion of coastal goods to the Plains and vice versa (Griswold 1970:22), but *Dentalium* shells were arriving in the Northern Plains hundreds of years earlier (Wood 1972a: 161) and in central Washington by seven thousand years ago (Fryxell and Daugherty 1962:25).

Although some authors have preferred to view Plains influences on Plateau peoples as largely of historic period origin, associated with the coming of the horse (e.g., Ray 1939:145–47; Spencer 1965:216), we feel that the positive adaptive value of external trade for people in this bison- and salmon-deficient area fostered the arrival of at least a few Plains traits at a much earlier time. For example, projectile points from Middle Prehistoric components at the Lehman and Nesikep Creek sites on the Fraser River between Lytton and Lillooet, British Columbia, suggest "ideas in point manufacture emanating from east of the Rockies . . . without any other apparent borrowing of Plains' traits" (Sanger 1969:198). Moreover, many of the trade items documented in the historic period were perishable and would be invisible archaeologically.

HISTORIC TRIBES

In the historic period, the study area was largely occupied by the Shuswap, Kutenai, Flathead, Coeur d'Alene, Pend d'Oreille (Kalispel), and Nez Perce. To the northwest were the Lakes, who traded with Shuswap and Kutenai. Immediately to the west were the Spokan, Sanpoil, and Wallawalla. To the south of the study area, across the Bitterroot-Beaverhead divide, lay the northeastern tip of the Great Basin culture area, occupied by Numic speakers, specifically the Northern Shoshone, and a closely allied group of Northern Paiute speakers, the Bannock.

Although the distinction has seldom been explicitly noted, these groups can be divided into an eastern assemblage, many of whom were displaced westward from the Plains proper or from the intermontane grasslands where bison were obtainable, and a western assemblage, who either remained more or less in their traditional territories despite the disruptive effects of the contact period, or were forced into similar environments. The importance of this is that the eastern groups brought with them bison-hunting traditions and were able to develop new, long-distance, transmontane journeys to perpetuate this adaptive strategy. At the same time, they built new links with the salmon realm; western groups already had long-established mobile systems relating to anadromous fish and were able to adapt these, with little social or structural change, for use in hunting bison.

By the historic period the Shuswap were largely outside the study area, remaining only in its northern extreme in the Rocky Mountain Trench from north of the Kootenay/Columbia divide (which is at Canal Flats, British Columbia) northward and westward (Wilson 1980: 10–11). South of the Shuswap and along the western periphery of the study area were found the Lake Indians.

The Kutenai are divided into the Upper Kutenai, situated along the upper reaches of the Kootenay River and uppermost Columbia River in British Columbia, and the Lower Kutenai, situated along the lower reaches of the river in northwestern Montana and the adjacent Idaho panhandle. Early in the historic period some Kutenai were apparently located in the Fort Macleod area in southwestern Alberta (Teit 1930:311; Turney-High 1941). The Upper Kutenai were primarily buffalo hunters, though lake and river fish remained an important part of their diet. The Lower Kutenai relied more heavily on fish, fowl, deer, carnivores, rodents, and wild plants (Turney-High 1941; Thoms 1984:10).

Of particular interest is the Upper Kutenai subsistence pattern, in which people traveled eastward across the mountains up to three times each year, in June, September, and January, to hunt bison on the southern Alberta plains. Peter Fidler in the winter of 1792 encountered thirteen Kutenais camping on the Oldman River (MacGregor 1966:74–77). Based on Fidler's description, the Kutenais returned home by way of Crowsnest Pass. A similar group was encountered as late as 1877 near Lundbreck Falls, at the east end of Crowsnest Pass (Dempsey 1973:131). In prehistoric times a similar round likely existed, but may

well have lasted longer than a single year and involved intergroup
cooperation (Blake 1981:11).

The arrival of the horse, which brought drastic changes to the Upper
Kutenai, affected the Lower Kutenai much less. The Lower Kutenai,
while less mobile than the Upper Kutenai, also came together seasonally, undertaking journeys to major fishing stations as far west as
Arrow Lakes to obtain salmon, which in dried form was the staple
winter food. They seldom traveled east to the plains, though individuals occasionally went along with the Upper Kutenai on such hunts
(Blake 1981:11).

The attractiveness of the plains for bison and other items was not
lost on other groups. The Flathead evidently left their Salishan relatives at an early date and settled parts of western Montana in or before
the historic period (Turney-High 1937:11–21). On average, two bison
hunting expeditions were made eastward each year, one in winter
(January–April) and the other in summer (mid-July–September), some
reaching into Blackfeet territory during the horse period. Most trips
were made to the Three Forks area, their old homeland and a fairly good
bison range.

The Lower Pend d'Oreille based their subsistence on the fishing and
harvesting of local game and plants, and in historic times expanded
their range westward into the Kettle Falls area of Washington (Malouf
1982:24). The Upper Pend d'Oreille, on the other hand, were seasonal
bison hunters, especially after acquisition of the horse. A more or less
permanent Plains group of Pend d'Oreille lived along the upper Sun
River valley west of Great Falls, Montana and were bison hunters
linked in exchange systems with Pend d'Oreille to the west (Taylor
1973:117; Malouf 1967:3, 1982:17).

The Coeur d'Alene occupied territory north of the Nez Perce and
west of the Pend d'Oreille on the western fringe of the study area. James
A. Teit (1930) referred to general similarities between some of their
items of material culture and those of the Blackfeet, and to the
acquisition of Plains traits after introduction of the horse. Having
acquired horses, groups of Coeur d'Alene began to hunt regularly on the
plains with the Flathead and other tribes.

The Nez Perce formerly lived south of the Coeur d'Alene in central
Idaho, southeastern Washington, and northeastern Oregon (Swanton
1953:401). Teit (1930:97) noted a Coeur d'Alene belief that the Nez Perce
began to hunt bison on the plains only after the Coeur d'Alene had
begun to do so, despite the proximity of herds east of the Bitterroot
Range to Nez Perce territory.

The move to bison hunting was, as with other groups, less of a "Plains
influence" than a logical development of Plateau strategies. Although
the pattern of mobility and lengthy travel formerly related more to
anadromous fish, the transformation to bison was easy and required no

fundamental structural changes. Because of their strong participation in both salmon-fishing and bison-hunting systems, the Nez Perce became brokers *par excellence* and served as intermediaries in far-reaching trade systems. Although their acknowledged territory covered some seventy thousand square kilometers, they customarily exploited an area of at least six hundred thousand square kilometers, extending in all directions from their core territory (Walker 1967:1). Their forays onto the Plains reached at least as far as Crow territory and apparently even further; one group reached St. Louis in the 1830s (Walker 1967:1, 24). They played the largest role in bringing Plains traits to the Plateau (Walker 1967:16).

The Northern Shoshone and Bannock occupied the extreme southern part of the study area on an intermittent basis, living largely west of the Bitterroot-Beaverhead divide and south of the Salmon River during the historic period (Hultkrantz 1957; Murphy and Murphy 1986). They did travel seasonally into the area, though the bulk of their seasonal travels were into that part of the Plains south of the study area. The Shoshone were seen by Julian H. Steward (1938) as the only horse-mounted bison hunters of this area, but he concluded that their adaptation was recent. Although Teit (1930:305) saw this as a recent development, Ake Hultkrantz (1957) felt that these movements dated back to a time before the arrival of the horse. Certainly these groups, like others to the north, redoubled their efforts in plains hunting when bison were depleted in the west, but this event need not mark the start of their plains incursions.

Northern Shoshone and Bannock culture and social organization suggest a somewhat "intermediate status" between the Great Basin and Plains (Murphy and Murphy 1986:287). Such a proposition is fraught with many difficulties. At a material culture level, it might be obvious, while, in terms of basic adaptive strategy, it might not. Many Northern Shoshone and Bannock were closely similar to Plains groups in hunting bison on horseback, using the technique of bison jumping at the Challis site (Butler 1971), and living in tipis. Horses, acquired in the late seventeenth century, allowed them to move permanently onto the Northern Plains where the Plains Shoshone were, for a time, a force with which to be reckoned. However, once the Blackfeet acquired the horse and gun, the Plains Shoshone were pushed back into their original homeland.

As we have argued above, much of the study area constitutes the area of overlap or interaction between the bison realm and the salmon realm. Anthropologists have never clearly formalized a concept parallel to that of the ecotone in ecology, so it is necessary to assign the study area to either the Plateau or Plains category. Most of the tribes are assigned to the Plateau culture area, though arguably it was a zone of great interchange and transition between Plains and Plateau cultures.

Thus, a model can be adopted of Plateau groups onto whom Plains traits and, to some extent, a Plains life-style were grafted.

However, Verne F. Ray (1939:145–46) argued that the Plains element was misleading, being "in large part recent and superficial." His discussion is avowedly a reaction to Herbert J. Spinden's (1908:270) suggestion that "the culture of the [Plateau] area, as shown by one of its representative tribes, was purely a transitional culture." Spinden erred, as pointed out by Ray (1939:3), in taking the Nez Perce to be typical of Plateau peoples and in basing too much upon too little field work. We also suggest that in emphasizing individual cultural traits rather than the underlying adaptive pattern, Spinden saw the trees at the expense of the forest.

The adaptive characteristics that we have outlined above served at all times to modulate the patterns of acceptance of cultural traits from other areas. Ray's arguments about the limited time depth of most Plains traits (many of which were associated with perishable elements not preservable in the archaeological record), while important, were therefore irrelevant as a defense of the area's analytical unity. Ray was deeply involved in the listing of traits and gave less coverage than one might wish to the underlying adaptive pattern, though his suggestion of the "subjective guise" of Plateau culture undoubtedly signals his keen awareness of this pattern. Ray also made an operational decision to treat Plateau groups as essentially fixed in territories, whereas the traits could move back and forth. This facilitated the building of trait distribution maps but violated what we believe is one of the fundamental adaptive strategies of the region: mobility (see, for example, Walker 1967).

PREHISTORIC CULTURAL DYNAMICS

The permeability of the Plains-Plateau boundary, demonstrated in the historic period, is also seen in the prehistoric period. Plains traits did enter the Plateau and mountains, and, to some extent, vice versa. For example, tipi rings have been found as far west as Monida Pass (Ranere, Ranere, and Lortz 1969), the Flathead Lake area (White 1959), and Deer Lodge Pass on the Montana continental divide (Sharrock and Keyser 1975). Conversely, Yellowstone obsidian has been found as far east as Saskatchewan in a putative long-range exchange network (Burley, Meyer, and Walker 1981), and there was an increase in obsidian in the Late Prehistoric period on the Northwestern Plains (Davis 1972).

Much archaeological work in the northern part of the study area has focused not only on the distinctiveness of Plains and Plateau cultures, but also the degree to which the east slope formed an *independent* culture area. In the mountains, Besant points are rare: in the Crowsnest Pass, they have been recovered in quantity only at one site (Driver

1978), and a low frequency of Besant points is also reported in Pass Creek valley in Waterton Lakes National Park (Reeves 1972). During the period A.D. 500–1500, there seems to be evidence that there was an increasing cultural boundary between the eastern slope and the Plains (table 3.1), manifested most clearly in the definition of the geographically discrete Tobacco Plains and Old Women's phases (A.D. 900–1850), which are different from each other in their subsistence economies and, to some extent, artifact styles (Loveseth 1980). In the Arrow Lakes of southern British Columbia, Christopher J. Turnbull (1977) defined the Slocan phase (A.D. 650–1750). Points included the Avonlea type, used in a wide-spectrum subsistence economy.

The largest and most fully digested body of data in northwestern Montana and adjacent British Columbia comes from the Libby Dam and Reservoir (Lake Koocanusa) area and related water regulation projects on the Kootenai (Kootenay in Canada) River. A scheme devised by Wayne Choquette and C. Holstine (1980), and later updated by Choquette (1984), used a variety of cultural characteristics to develop a case for in-place continuity of prehistoric manifestations with historic Kutenai over at least the past few hundred years. Between the time of Christ and A.D. 1000 there is an undefined transitional period marked by a drop in the use of Kootenai argillite. The Akiyinek complex (ca. A.D. 1000–1450) has been identified in the Big Bend area of the Kootenai River; points of this complex are "strongly reminiscent of the Avonlea type of the Plains" (Choquette 1984:314). Material includes red and dendritic cherts from southeast of the project area. The latest complex

Table 3.1
Regional Cultural Chronologies

Rocky Mountain Trench	
Avonlea Phase	A.D. 200–900
Tobacco Plains Phase	A.D. 900–1850
Kookanusa Lake Area, Montana	
Undefined transitional period	50 B.C.–A.D. 950
Akiyinek Complex	A.D. 950–1400
Weis Rockshelter, Idaho	
Rock Canyon Phase	100 B.C.–A.D. 1670
Camas Prairie Phase	A.D. 1670–
Birch Creek Valley, Idaho	
Blue Dome Phase	A.D. 500–1750
Lemhi Phase	A.D. 1805–1840
Snake River Plain	
Dietrich Phase	A.D. 1300–1650

is the Akahonek, characterized by small side-notched points, initially similar to Avonlea points, and Top-of-the-world chert.

Tom E. Roll (1988) has designated the area west of the continental divide but beyond the upstream limit of slamon runs on west-slope drainages as the Barrier Falls subarea of the northern Plateau, which encompasses the drainages of the Kootenay and Flathead rivers. Certainly the absence of salmon strongly distinguishes this area from the rest of the northern Plateau, and the documentation of the historic period movements from this area onto the plains is suggestive of a Plains-like, rather than Plateau-like, adaptive pattern. Reeves (1974) in his earlier argument for consideration of the eastern slope in Alberta as a separate culture area appears to have made the same observation as Roll (1988) but lacked a clear definition of the boundaries of the proposed area.

However, Roll's (1988) use of the continental divide as a boundary has the effect of excluding virtually all of Reeves's key sites (for example, those in the Crowsnest Pass and Waterton Lakes National Park areas) from consideration, despite Reeves's contention that they are clearly separable from those of the open plains. It is, therefore, arguable that the boundary of Roll's Barrier Falls subarea could belong further to the east, however convenient the use of drainage boundaries may appear.

The Barrier Falls subarea of the Northern Plateau was largely the homeland of the Kutenai in the historic period. The consensus of scholars is toward a Plains origin for at least part of the group (Schaeffer 1940; Turney-High 1941). Ray (1939) is one of the few to disagree, preferring a strictly Plateau origin for the Kutenai, with an overlay of Plains traits. Ethnohistorical evidence suggests that the Kutenai, known as the Tunaxa, may once have been the indigenous occupants of the southern Albertan plains, living in the vicinity of present-day Fort MacLeod, Alberta. At some undetermined time in the past, about half of this group moved westward onto the Plateau and became the Kutenai. The remainder of the Plains *Tunaxa* later joined the other Kutenai to the west after they had been hit by an epidemic (Turney-High 1941:11). A Plains origin is perhaps suggested by a Kutenai legend of having once used buffalo cliff drives (Boas 1918:205).

Turney-High (1941:16) suggested the Tobacco Plains as the Kutenai center, and from this both upper and lower groups radiated. Whether westward movement was forced on them by the incoming Blackfeet is still unclear, although by the time Peter Fidler crossed southern Alberta and entered the Canadian Rockies in the winter of 1792–93, the plains of southwest Alberta were occupied by the Blackfeet. An earlier split of the Kutenai is also alluded to by Dee Taylor (1973:118); division of a Plains and Plateau Kutenai may have considerable time depth.

Models provided by Taylor (1973) and Reeves (1974) serve as points of departure for discussion of the archaeological evidence. In relating prehistoric cultural manifestations to historically documented groups in the area, three possibilities have been addressed: (1) *in situ* cultural evolution with forcing mechanisms for change being environmental change and culture contact; (2) movement of Kutenai peoples from their core area to the plains at a late time, with retrenchment in the Rockies during the Historic period; and (3) the arrival of Kutenai from the plains during Late Prehistoric times, with displacement of indigenous groups.

Reeves (1974) opted for the third hypothesis, regarding the Kutenai as the principal residents of the eastern slopes of Alberta in latest prehistoric times. Their westward displacement by the Blackfeet (particularly the Piegan) in the eighteenth and nineteenth centuries resulted in displacement of the Shuswap northward into the upper Thompson–Fraser River area of British Columbia and the Athabasca valley of Alberta, which itself had previously been utilized by Athapaskans (possibly Sarcee, Beaver, or Sekani). Reeves (1974) observed that displacement may well have begun many centuries earlier, because fishing stations in Waterton Lakes National Park were evidently abandoned around A.D. 200 to 400.

The choice by Reeves (1969:69) of the terms *Tunaxa* and Napikwan for his two major Northern Plains traditions also alludes to the presence of Kutenai in southern Alberta. Byrne (1973) accepted Reeves's classification and presented a scenario for linking Avonlea with Kutenai, who were in this view driven off the Plains into their historic homeland by the incoming Besant, which represented the prehistoric Blackfeet. Karl Schlesier (1987) places Kutenai affiliation even further back; to the preceding Pelican Lake phase. Reeves (1983:20) later developed his early model, suggesting that the Avonlea phase in the mountains was technologically ancestral to the Tobacco Plains phase, a phase that he took to be ancestral to the historic Kutenai. The Old Women's phase of the adjacent plains was broken into temporal and spatial variants which represent tribal groups such as the North Piegan, Blood, Atsina, and Gros Ventre.

Willingness to link prehistoric manifestations to historic social groups was taken even further in Choquette's (1984) identification of historic bands in prehistory. Kutenai band names were applied directly to the latest prehistoric assemblages where location, geographical orientation, and other factors warranted. Others have noted that studies in the area are only in a "first approximation" stage, and have further made it clear that the large villages of the Historic period have no prehistoric counterpart, suggesting important culture change at contact (Thoms and Schalk 1984:377).

According to Taylor (1973), persistent use of small corner-notched points west of the mountains in Late Prehistoric times could reflect ethnic distinction from Plains groups. If the Kutenai were, for example, a Plains group pushed westward at a very late time, these points might be associated with another group, likely of Salish affiliation (possibly the Shuswap). Certainly in the Historic period, the Kutenai were ultimately nearly excluded from the Plains by the Blackfeet, who possessed both horses and guns. As Taylor (1973) notes, it is also worth considering that the separation of Kutenai groups may itself have significant time depth. Rather than talking of the Kutenai *as a whole*, it is probably realistic to consider that the historic division noted above is of long standing, with one group being seasonal buffalo hunters and the other more closely tied to the homeland along the Kootenai River. Westward movement of both groups could have occurred, but at different times, with different archaeological consequences. As one possibility, westward movement of the upper or Northern Kutenai might have been linked with the appearance of small side-notched projectile points (including Avonlea) west of the divide.

The southern part of the study area covers the Idaho panhandle. The Salmon River–Snake River region is especially important for understanding this southern section, since it is essentially an extension of the plains and provides a corridor between the plains and the intermontane regions to the west. Excavations at the Weis rockshelter, located close to the Salmon River, provided an initial chronology (table 3.1) for the central part of the Idaho panhandle (Butler 1968). A continuous occupation from 5400 B.C. to the historic period was documented, with changes manifested mostly in projectile point forms. Two late period phases were identified. The Rock Canyon phase (100 B.C.–A.D. 1670) was identified by new projectile point styles, the gathering of plants and freshwater mussels, and the hunting of deer, elk, and mountain sheep. The succeeding Camas Prairie phase is interpreted as late prehistoric Nez Perce, with similarities between the phase and historic Nez Perce seen in house forms and specific artifact types. Historic documentation suggests also that the locality of the rockshelter was the home territory of a specific Nez Perce band (Butler 1968).

Recent syntheses by Robert Butler (1981b, 1986) provide further information on the later prehistory of the Salmon River–Snake River region. Here, two cultural traditions are represented. The earlier of the two, Fremont (belonging to a Formative stage), is represented only sparsely by pithouses and specific pottery and does not extend much beyond the Snake River. Butler (1986) has suggested that sometime after A.D. 300 peoples from the Northwestern Plains may have moved across the continental divide into the area north of the Snake River Plain and introduced Plains elements into Northern Fremont. These may have been ancestors of the Southern Athapaskans.

The second tradition represents prehistoric Shoshone, and Swanson's excavations at Birch Creek valley (Swanson 1972) provide a base for investigating this tradition (table 3.1). The Blue Dome phase, on the basis of geomorphological cross-dating, was dated to 950 B.C.–A.D. 1250 and later amended by Butler (1981b:252) to A.D. 500–1750. The phase is characterized by a variety of points, mostly corner-notched, although side-notched, stemmed, and triangular forms are also present. The Blue Dome points bear a superficial resemblance in shape and size to Avonlea points of the Northern Plains but lack the finely controlled flaking characteristic of true Avonlea points.

The historic Lemhi phase (A.D. 1250–1850) is the first clear evidence of the Shoshone in eastern Idaho (Butler 1986:133). These dates were later refined to A.D. 1805–1840 (Butler 1986:133). Butler (1986) has suggested, however, that Shoshone may have been present in the area earlier, with the main occupation of southern Idaho later on in the eighteenth century after they had been displaced from the Plains by the Blackfeet. The Lemhi phase projectile points are mostly triangular, "squat" lanceolate, and side-notched, although some corner-notched forms are also present.

Idaho archaeologists have paid great attention to the prehistoric identification of historic groups. In the case of the Shoshone, opinion has polarized between a relatively recent immigration and a long-term occupancy. On the basis of her occupations at Wilson Butte Cave in south-central Idaho, Ruth Gruhn (1961) posited a relatively recent Shoshone presence evidenced in Wilson Butte VI (post-A.D. 1300) by Wilson Butte Plain Ware and Desert Side-Notched points, and supported by independent linguistic evidence.

However, Butler (1981b, 1986) has argued that Gruhn's identification of these late period Dietrich phase materials (A.D. 1300–1650) at the west end of the eastern Snake River Plain as prehistoric Shoshone is fallacious, preferring to see the phase as part of the Great Salt Lake Fremont. The phase preceding the Dietrich phase in the western end of the plain may be represented by the Blue Dome phase initially defined by Swanson (1972) at Birch Creek valley.

In contrast, Swanson (1972), on the basis of excavations at sites in Birch Creek valley, has argued for long-term Shoshone occupation. Arguing that similar adaptations and cultural continuity might reflect similar ethnic identity, he has suggested that the Northern Shoshone might in fact be represented archaeologically by the Bitterroot culture (5000–1000 B.C.). Butler (1981b:252) opposes this view, suggesting that the cultural hiatus between the Blue Dome and Lemhi phases argues against continuous occupation by Shoshone from the prehistoric period. The possible emigration of the Shoshone into the Northern Plains prior to their eviction by the Blackfeet, and the archaeological evidence for this movement, has been dealt with by J. Roderick Vickers (this volume).

The later prehistory of the Snake River–Salmon River region and surrounding areas is further complicated by the possible infiltration of

Athapaskans on their southward movement (Butler 1981b). C. Melvin Aikens (1967) argued that proto-Fremont originated on the Northwestern Plains and were probably Athapaskans. They moved southwest into Utah about A.D. 500, where they encountered a Desert Archaic culture who already had perhaps adopted some Anasazi traits. Consequently, Fremont culture became a blend of Anasazi and Plains traits. By A.D. 1600 Fremont people were pushed back into the central Plains by the Shoshonean expansion. Richard J. Perry (1980) proposed that in the early part of the Late Prehistoric period, Athapaskan populations occupied the area from the Canadian Rocky Mountains as far south possibly as northern Colorado. Their abandonment of this area sometime by the fifteenth century allowed (or was caused by?) Shoshone moving into the region from the Great Salt Lake area. A revealing chart in Butler (1981b:247) alludes to an Athapaskan identification, represented by Avonlea, or Avonlea-like, assemblages of the Blue Dome phase. However, it is not certain that Avonlea points are indeed Athapaskan (cf. Reeves 1983).

A line of argument similar to Swanson's was used by Butler (1968) in his discussion of the origins of the Nez Perce. His original hypothesis was that the Old Cordilleran culture was perhaps ancestral to groups like the Nez Perce (Butler 1968:100). Excavations to test this hypothesis were conducted at the Weis rockshelter, located in historic Nez Perce territory. Cultural continuity was traced from 5400 B.C. to the Historic period, with the most obvious changes being manifested in projectile point style.

CONCLUDING SUMMARY

In this chapter, we have attempted to demonstrate the great amount of cultural contact between the Plains and Plateau regions during the period in question. We suggest that it is necessary for archaeologists to gain a greater understanding of how archaeological assemblages in the area are representative of "peoples," however that term be defined (cf. Duke 1991). Clearly, such a problem will not be resolved until we move away from a primary reliance upon ethnographic models to a more independent approximation of prehistoric social organization. This will help us understand better not only the nature of prehistoric social organization, but also, by extension, prehistoric subsistence and settlement strategies, and the nature of contacts between prehistoric peoples. We also suggest that archaeologists should be wary of assuming that ethnographically defined culture-area boundaries have any analytical relevance to the prehistoric archaeological record.

CHAPTER 4

ARCHAEOLOGICAL COMPLEXES OF THE NORTHEASTERN PLAINS AND PRAIRIE-WOODLAND BORDER, A.D. 500–1500

Michael L. Gregg

SEVERAL important cultural adaptations evolved within the Northeastern Plains and adjacent prairie-woodland ecotone area before they were taken up by groups situated further to the west in the Plains. Among the foremost of the evolutionary developments in the study area were the beginnings of Plains Woodland lifeways by 400 B.C. and Plains Village lifeways around A.D. 1000. References to this region as peripheral to either the western Plains or the eastern Woodlands are inappropriate (e.g., Lehmer 1971:29; Wedel 1961:23).

This chapter is organized by time periods and research topics. The time periods are: (1) A.D. 500 to 600, (2) A.D. 800 to 900, (3) A.D. 1100 to 1200, and (4) A.D. 1400 to 1500. The research topics are paleoenvironment, cultural chronology, artifact styles, regional interaction, technologies, settlement, and subsistence. Combinations of time periods and research topics provide a framework for touching upon the most important aspects of what is known regarding the area's prehistory between A.D. 500 and 1500. This approach is complicated by the continuity of some archaeological cultures and changes in others through time. It is also complicated by differences in contemporaneous archaeological cultures across the study area. People who lived in different parts of this geographically expansive archaeological subarea adapted differently to diverse ecological settings. The primary objective of the chapter is to summarize major prehistoric cultural developments. There is no intention to explore fully the systemic organization or material cultural variation of any archaeological or ethnographic cultures that are mentioned. A concluding section presents evidence and speculations regarding ethnic groups and population densities in the study area around A.D. 1500.

Paul R. Picha provided important input at several stages in the preparation of this chapter. Michael G. Michlovic offered valuable critical comments on a draft. Linda Olson drew the pottery illustrations based on sketches by the author. Special thanks to Karl Schlesier and E. Leigh Syms for the opportunity to have a part in the compilation of this volume.

THE CHRONOLOGICAL FRAMEWORK

Figure 4.1 presents the cultural chronology used in this chapter. This chronology involves only cultural traditions and archaeological complexes, not variants, phases, aggregates, and so forth. More detailed chronologies involving additional archaeological unit terms have been developed for some parts of the subarea (e.g., Benn 1986; MacNeish 1958; Syms 1977).

Cultural traditions are lifeways or general adaptive strategies defined in terms of variation in reliance upon hunting, gathering, and gardening for food production, and the use of ceramic containers for cooking and food processing (Gregg 1985). The Plains Archaic tradition was based on hunting and gathering but did not involve gardening or the use of pottery. The Plains Woodland tradition was primarily based upon hunting and gathering, but sometimes involved gardening and the production and use of ceramic vessels. In the Plains Village adaptive strategy, food production was often balanced between hunting, gathering, and gardening, and ceramic vessels were commonly produced and used in everyday life. People were probably living different lifeways in different parts of the study area at most times during the thousand-year-long era of concern (fig. 4.1). This was the case historically when groups such as the Awaxawi Hidatsa, Ioway, and Cheyenne had Plains Village adaptations while others such as the Middle Dakota, Assiniboine, and Plains Ojibwa had Plains Woodland adaptations. Further, based on ethnographic analogy, different groups within one society or of one ethnic affiliation may have employed different adaptive strategies. There was a time, for example, when some Cheyenne lived as Plains Villagers while others lived as equestrian nomads (cf. Wood 1971b:67).

Archaeological complexes are groups of distinctive material remains that have been found at multiple sites in a given area. A complex in this sense is similar to a composite as defined by Syms (1977:71) and employed by Meyer and Russell (1987:4), among others. The material remains that typify a particular cultural complex include technologically and stylistically similar artifacts such as ceramic wares, points of particular types, and unique grave offerings. The distinctive material remains of a complex sometimes also include settlement traits such as certain kinds of residential lodges and mortuary features. Archaeological units that are named in the primary literature as phases, patterns, variants, and aggregates are identified here as complexes.

A.D. 500–600

Changes in cultural complexity and human population density appear to have been correlated with times of xeric and mesic climatic regimes in the late prehistory of the entire Northern Plains. There was a peak of

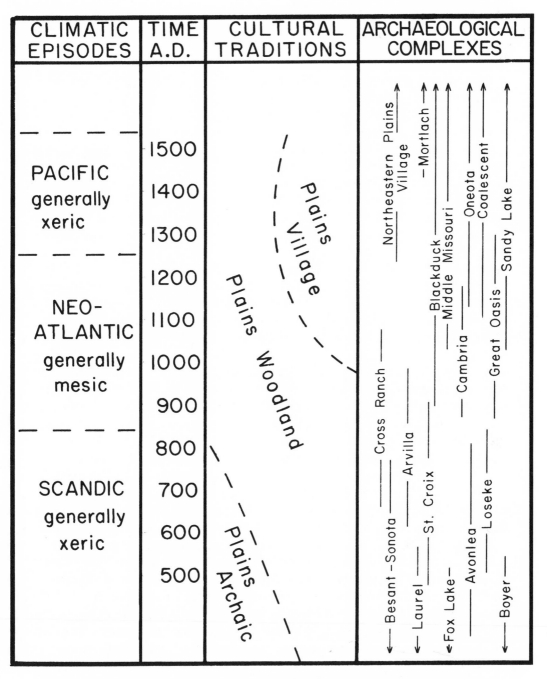

Fig. 4.1. Climatic episodes and cultural chronology postulated for the Northeastern Plains and prairie-woodland ecotone study area, A.D. 500 to 1500.

cultural developments about two thousand years ago when the mesic conditions of the late Sub-Atlantic climatic episode prevailed. By A.D. 500 or 600, during the more arid Scandic episode, there seem to have been fewer occupation sites in the Northeastern Plains. With less rainfall, the overall biomass and human carrying capacity of the subarea would have been lessened, but there was no occupational hiatus. For example, one of three episodes of use thus far identified at the Jamestown Mounds mortuary site (32SN22) along the upper James River is dated A.D. 380 to 670 (Snortland-Coles 1985:4.25).

A.D. 500 was a time of transition for Northeastern Plains Woodland cultures. In addition to adaptations of hunting and gathering lifeways to reduced biomass, the bow and arrow supplanted the atlatl, and significant advances were made in ceramic technology. Archaeological complexes named for distinctive ceramic styles and other diagnostic remains of that time include Boyer, Arthur, Lake Benton, and Fox Lake in the south (Benn 1981b, 1982b, 1983, 1986, 1990; Bonney 1970), Sonota in the central and northern regions (Gregg 1987a; Neuman 1975; Syms 1977), Besant and Avonlea in the west (Reeves 1983a; Schneider and Kinney 1978), Laurel (Stoltman 1973) in the prairie-woodland ecotone to the northeast, and St. Croix in the east (Gibbon and Caine 1980:61– 62; map 4.1). These complexes are often referred to as late or terminal Middle Woodland cultures. If all of these complexes were contemporary and represent ethnic and social diversity, then the maintenance of group territories was likely a continual problem. Mounds may have served as territorial markers in addition to cemeteries (Lofstrom 1987:11), a practice which may have originated in Archaic times (cf. Charles and Buikstra 1983:130). Prominent topographic features such as the Missouri escarpment, the edges of the Prairie Coteau, and the high beach ridges of the former Glacial Lake Agassiz may also have served as markers.

Sonota and Besant were the predominant complexes in the central, northern, and western areas, although the peak population and cultural complexity of these groups occurred several centuries earlier. Sonota and Besant can actually be viewed as variations of the same complex. They were originally described together by Reeves in 1970 (see Reeves 1983a), and they are considered collectively here as Besant-Sonota. Some consider Besant a Woodland complex related to Sonota (Johnson 1977). Much of the debate over Besant and Sonota and the differences between them relates to terminology and whether these entities are considered as archaeological complexes or regional phases or some sort of expansive cultural traditions.

Artifact styles are deliberately perpetuated, repetitive, patterned characteristics of material culture. Some artifact styles endured to the extent that they are presently recognized as diagnostic of certain archaeological complexes. Styles of patterned artifacts were some- times coincident with social groups and at other times had geograph-

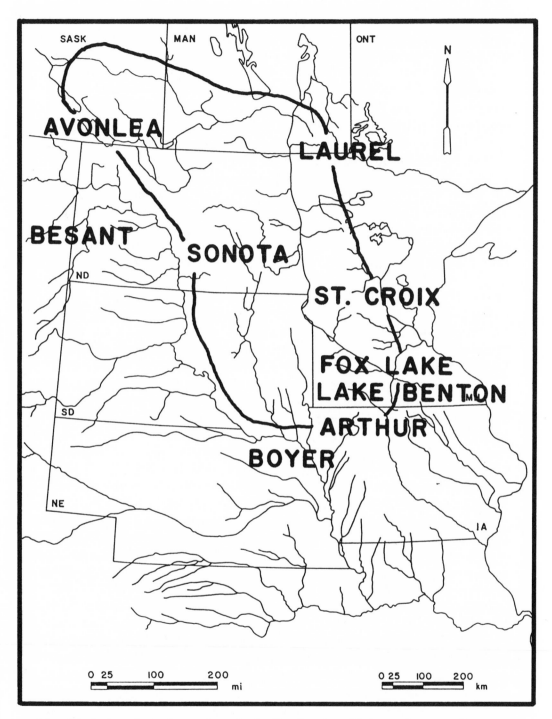

SASK   MAN   ONT

N

AVONLEA

LAUREL

BESANT

SONOTA

ND

ST. CROIX

FOX LAKE
LAKE BENTON

SD

ARTHUR

BOYER

NE

IA

0 25   100   200
                    mi

0 25   100   200
                    km

Map 4.1. *Archaeological complexes in the Northeastern Plains and surrounding areas on an* A.D. *500 to 600 Middle Plains Woodland time level.*

ically broad distributions that transcended territorial and ethnic boundaries (cf. Croes 1989:124). Besant and Sonota share the same stylistically diagnostic artifacts in the form of conoidal pots (fig. 4.2), Besant side-notched dart points, and Samantha side-notched points (Reeves 1983a: 140). Around two thousand years ago, Samantha points were small-sized atlatl dart points, perhaps used to tip special-purpose lightweight, high speed, low impact darts (cf. Gregg 1987a:278–80). They continued in use as atlatl dart points until A.D. 500 or so when it seems they were adapted for use as arrow points (Reeves 1983a:63).

Middle Woodland cultures are known for extensive exchange networks. The principal routes of long-distance interaction were probably the waterways. The Red River–Bois de Sioux River–Lake Traverse–Big Stone Lake–Minnesota River waterway links Lake Winnipeg and Hudson Bay with the Mississippi River and the Gulf of Mexico. This route was undoubtedly important prehistorically as it was historically (cf. Brown 1989). An east-west segment across southern Minnesota is a direct link between the western portions of the Eastern Woodlands and the Northeastern Plains. A north-south segment involving the Red River of the North links the study area with the boreal forest. Parts of the Northeastern Plains were also connected directly to the Middle Missouri subarea by permanent tributaries of the Missouri such as the Big Sioux and James rivers.

Occurrences of artifacts made from nonlocal materials or made in accord with nonlocal styles evince varying degrees of interaction with distant peoples in all directions. Besant-Sonota interaction materials included obsidian from the Rockies, Knife River flint (KRF) from North Dakota (Loendorf, Ahler, and Davidson 1984), copper from the upper Great Lakes region, *Anculosa* sp. shells from the Illinois and Ohio rivers, and *Busycon* sp. and *Marginella* sp. shells from the Gulf and Atlantic coasts (Gregg and Picha 1989). People with Laurel material culture were also involved in these exchange relations (Clark 1984). As a result of such interaction, populations in the study area were exposed to numerous important innovations such as plant domestication that were developed elsewhere. Most of the exchanges of exotic goods, however, seem to have been curtailed by A.D. 500.

The approximate time of transition from the exclusive use of the atlatl to the use of the bow and arrow seems to have been A.D. 500. Occasionally, claims are advanced that the bow and arrow was introduced across the Plains much earlier — such as during the first or second millennium B.C. — but none of those claims is unequivocally substantiated. With the shift in projectile weapons technology, there were changes in projectile point production technologies and styles. Flint-knapping reduction procedures shifted from the production of large thin patterned bifaces by percussion flaking to the production of small thin patterned bifaces by pressure flaking (Ahler and VanNest 1985).

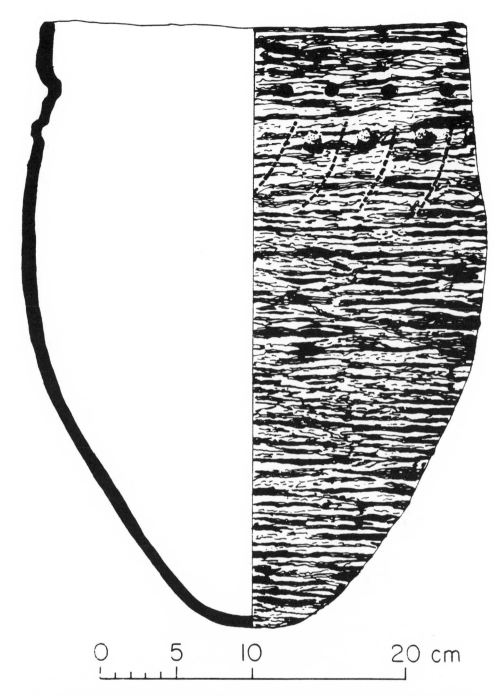

0   5   10   20 cm

Fig. 4.2. Illustration of a generic Plains Woodland ceramic vessel of the A.D. 500 to 600 period. Vessel shapes are characteristically conoidal and rim profiles straight. The vessel form in this illustration is adapted from Neuman (1975: pl. 25). Exterior surface treatments are usually cordmarked, horizontally, obliquely, or vertically. Rim interiors are also sometimes cordmarked. Cordmarkings on these and later pots are in some cases impressions from fabrics that were used to line molds; in other cases they are impressions from malleating with a cord-wrapped paddle. Rim exteriors are sometimes decorated with punctates, nodes, or bosses, and roulette or dentate stamps. Lips decorations include plain tool impressions and cord-wrapped tool impressions.

The kinds of archaeological sites representing all of the prehistoric occupations being considered in this chapter may be viewed as varieties of residential bases, field camps, stations, locations, caches, and mortuary sites (cf. Binford 1980). Although this classification was developed for hunter-gatherers, it also has utility for describing the settlements of Woodland groups as well as village horticulturists. Residential bases are domestic sites that were occupied by nuclear families, stem families, bands, or multiband groups (cf. Hanson 1983). Field camps were temporary operating centers for task groups. Stations were places such as hunting lookouts used for information gathering. Locations were places where raw materials were collected and/or processed — for example, chert collecting/workshop sites. Caches were places used for field storage of subsistence or technological goods, for example, meat or chipped stone tool preform stashes. The remains of the deceased were ceremonially interred at mortuary sites.

Most late prehistoric residential settlements in the Northern Plains have been found in proximity to rivers or lakes. Epp suggests that these "anomalous wooded environments" were selected not only because of the timber, water, and biotic diversity that they offered, but because bison were attracted to them throughout the year (1988:316). Oakwood Lakes (39BK7) may be either a residential base or field camp occupied by peoples with Besant-Sonota material culture (Nowak, Hannus, and Lueck 1982:25.17). Besant-Sonota tipi encampments were also established in the vicinity of prairie lakes and seasonal drainages (cf. Deaver 1985; Schneider 1982b). Some of these tipi ring sites in prairie-lakes settings contain earthen mound features (R. Fox 1982:102). Slow-moving streams with stands of wild rice, such as some of the eastern and western tributaries of the Red River (Jenks 1900), were also favored by Woodland groups for residential settlements.

Northeastern Plains peoples in terminal Middle Woodland times sometimes hunted big game and gathered wild plant foods including tuberous roots at sites in upland settings (cf. Deaver 1985:262). There are indications from excavations in the southern parts of the study area that people were also gardening (Benn 1986:28). *Cucurbita pepo* seeds were ubiquitous through all the Mid-America Woodland levels at the Rainbow site (Benn 1990:199). This is not surprising since contemporary folk in the riverine Midwest were growing squash and marsh elder (Kelley et al. 1984:125). Bison were the principal focus of attention in most subsistence economies, and they were also a focal point in religious and spiritual practices as evidenced by the interment of bison remains along with human remains in Sonota mortuaries (cf. Neuman 1975:89; Schlesier 1987:141). But other animal foods were also important. Based on excavation results from Archaic and Woodland components in the upper James River valley (cf. Haury 1987:384), it appears that domestic dogs were the most dependable, "storable" food resource that people had prior to the advent of full-blown horticulture. Similarly, Thurman (1988:167) has suggested that dogs were an "essential" food source for late prehistoric peoples to the southwest in the High Plains.

There are numerous extensive complexes of conical and linear mortuary mounds in the central and northcentral portions of the study area. People with Besant-Sonota material culture appear to have been the earliest builders of these mounds, specifically the dome-shaped tumuli. Evidence indicates that linear mounds were constructed later, from A.D. 500 to 1550 or so (Chomko and Wood 1973:15). Some earthworks raised during Besant-Sonota times continued in use as mortuary sites from Middle Plains Woodland times into the Plains Village period. The Jamestown Mounds, for example, were used and expanded over a period of more than a thousand years (Snortland-Coles 1985). The Blasky or Fordville mound group (32WA1) along the Forest River on the western Lake Agassiz beaches in eastern North Dakota was another outstanding mound complex that originally contained at least thirty-five conical mounds and four linear mounds with lengths ranging from 242 feet (74 m) to 2,688 feet (820 m) (Larson et al. 1986; Wilford 1970). They probably had an extended history of use similar to the Jamestown Mounds. It is likely that other large groups of mounds scattered throughout the Northeastern Plains and first investigated in the late nineteenth century (cf. Lewis 1886; Montgomery 1889, 1906) had intricate histories of use. Repeated use of such sacred sites indicates cultural or ethnic continuity within a region. Schlesier (1987:134–50) has suggested that some people with Besant-Sonota material culture were proto-Cheyenne, and it is widely accepted that the Cheyenne were one of several groups who lived in this subarea at the dawn of historic times. But in the 1800s when Middle Dakota people were asked about the Jamestown Mounds, they said they had no idea who might have built them (Fox 1985:2.13, citing Cyrus Thomas 1873).

A.D. 800 TO 900

The effects of the more mesic Neo-Atlantic climatic conditions began about A.D. 800. Population density then built toward the initial Plains Village demographic climax of several centuries later. Residential sites from this era are not prominent and have not received much attention in most parts of the study area, but mortuary sites are relatively common, and a number of them have been investigated (cf. Johnson 1973; Snortland-Coles 1985:4.25). Map 4.2 illustrates the approximate geographic locations of named archaeological complexes that were part of the cultural scene at that time.

Woodland sites dating around A.D. 1000 appear to be fairly numerous along the Red River (Foss et al. 1985; Michlovic 1978:12–13, 1981, 1983:24, 1987a). Several of these Woodland period occupations have

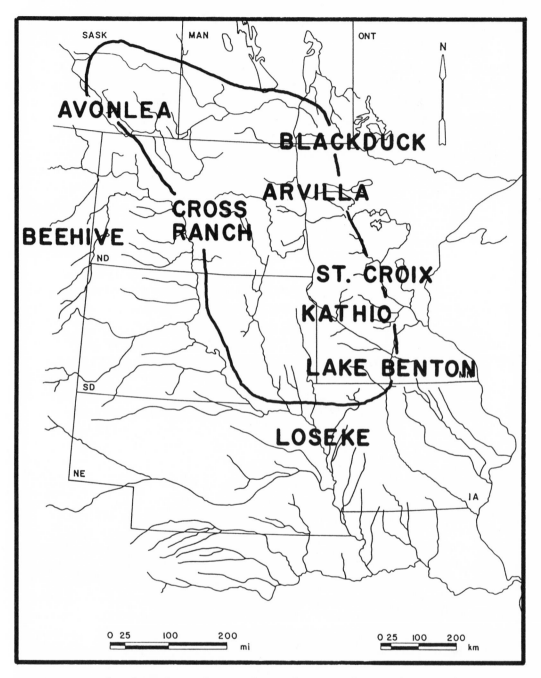

Map 4.2. Archaeological complexes in the Northeastern Plains and surrounding areas on an A.D. 800 to 900 Late Plains Woodland time level.

been excavated (Michlovic 1983, 1984, 1986, 1987a). The St. Croix complex is estimated to date from A.D. 500 to 800 in the prairie-lakes country of southwestern Minnesota and along most of the prairie-woodland ecotone (Anfinson 1979:169–74; Gibbon and Caine 1980:61–62).

Sites of the Blackduck complex are situated along the prairie-woodland ecotone from southern Manitoba to west-central Minnesota and northeastward into the woodlands (Joyes 1970; MacNeish 1954, 1958; Steinbring 1980; Tisdale 1978). Minor occurrences of Blackduck pottery have been recorded along the James River in southeastern North Dakota (Schneider 1982a). Similar late Plains Woodland pottery has also been found at sites beyond the Northeastern Plains to the west (e.g., Ahler, Lee, and Falk 1981:97–108). The earliest Blackduck sites date to about A.D. 800 (Evans 1961; Syms 1977:101). Sites with these ceramics came to dominate the prairie-woodland ecotone in subsequent centuries. European trade goods have been found in Blackduck sites in Ontario.

The Arvilla "complex" is represented at a number of late Plains Woodland burial sites in the eastern portion of the study area. The burials were capped with conical and sometimes perhaps linear earthen mounds (Jenks 1932). Both St. Croix and Blackduck ceramic vessels have been found as grave offerings in Arvilla sites (Johnson 1973:62; Syms 1979:300, 1982:158). The diversity of ceramics and other mortuary items indicates that a number of different ethnic groups used "Arvilla" cemetery sites.

Ceramic technological improvements in Plains Woodland times after A.D. 500 led to the production of not just more vessels, but thinner, better made, and generally larger vessels. Figure 4.3 illustrates a generic late Plains Woodland ceramic container exhibiting characteristics that were typical around A.D. 800 to 900.

Benn (1983:83) suggests that in northwestern Iowa around this time "more permanently situated residential groups" aggregated "to protect an ever-growing investment in horticulture." Some Woodland groups further north in the study area may also have been getting caught up in the process of horticultural development (cf. Johnson 1962:165). A packet of squash seeds (Cucurbita pepo, variety ovifera) was found within a leather pouch associated with a female burial dating from about A.D. 800, salvaged from the wall of a gravel pit near the Sheyenne River in southeastern North Dakota (Good 1975). But people in the prairie-lakes region of southwestern Minnesota, and probably extending northwestward into southeastern Saskatchewan, seem to have continued to subsist principally by hunting and gathering a broad array of wild resources (cf. Anfinson 1982).

Semipermanent settlement — living most of the year in one residential site with a heavy investment of labor in permanent settlement features — appeared at the southern end of the study area in western Iowa about A.D. 700. Larger and more numerous storage pits are good indica-

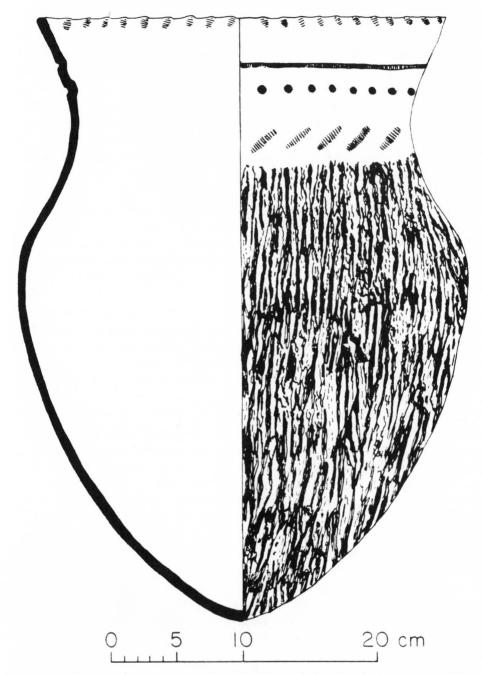

O   5   10   20 cm

Fig. 4.3. Illustration of a generic Plains Woodland ceramic vessel of the A.D. 800 to 900 period. The vessel shape is basically conoidal, but there is a distinct shoulder zone differentiating the vessel body from the neck and rim. Rims are straight to outcurved. Exterior surfaces are typically cordmarked, but the rim exteriors are often smoothed. Like earlier Plains Woodland pots, rim exteriors are sometimes decorated with punctates and nodes. Rim exteriors were also commonly decorated with cord-wrapped object impressions of various widths applied vertically, obliquely, and in horizontal bands.

tors of village settlements (Benn 1982b:42). Semipermanent settlement was essential for groups that were gardening. Although hunter-gatherers were also inclined to aggregate into large groups and stay together as long as resources were sufficient to support them (cf. Hanson 1983), fixed residential settlement was characteristic only of certain later Plains Villagers. Storage pits, houses, and high artifact densities — archaeological indicators of sedentism in the Northeastern Plains — are a coherent suite of traits found only at Plains Village residential sites.

A.D. 1100 TO 1200

On an A.D. 1000 to 1100 time level, Plains Village lifeways were developing among Woodland populations in southwestern Minnesota (Tiffany 1983:92), western Iowa (Anderson 1987), and the lower and central portions of the James River valley (Alex 1981b; Haberman 1983), as well as in the Middle Missouri subarea (Lehmer 1971:97; Toom 1988:69, 1992). Plains Woodland cultures were probably also thriving in the prairie-woodland transition zone and in the Red River valley as evidenced by the numerous Late Woodland sites recorded in surveys (e.g., Michlovic 1983:26). Map 4.3 illustrates general geographic locations where there are concentrations of sites of named archaeological complexes dating to this period.

The florescence of lifeways based on mixed horticultural-hunter-gatherer subsistence practises seems to have coincided with Neo-Atlantic climatic conditions that were more mesic than the present (cf. Haberman 1983:100; Syms 1977:137; Wendland 1978a:281; 1978b). Mesic conditions enabled the spread of corn gardening and promoted increase in the overall biomass which enhanced the productivity of hunting and gathering. Times were good for horticulturists as well as hunter-gatherers. For example, Alex suggested that the "deep middens . . . filled with elaborately decorated artifacts" at early Plains Village sites along the lower James "give the impression of village prosperity" (1981b:39). Some Woodland sites of this age have also been described in this way. The Blackduck component at the Lockport site (EaLf-1) "is unquestionably the richest" of that site's four components (Buchner 1988:30). Yet, environmental conditions were not consistently mesic throughout the Neo-Atlantic. At floodplain locations along the James River in North Dakota, some sites indicate two episodes of mesic conditions with an intervening droughty period during the Neo-Atlantic (Gregg et al. 1986, 1987).

The Cambria complex appeared in southwestern Minnesota along the Minnesota River (Johnson 1961; Knudson 1967; Ready 1979a). Obsidian and Knife River flint from western source areas at the Cambria site indicate east-west lines of interaction across the study area between A.D. 1100 and 1300 (Wattrall 1974). Cambria ceramics

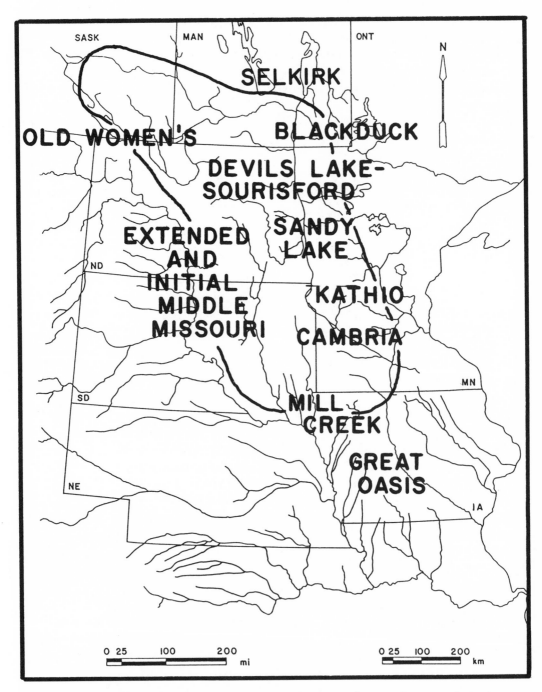

Map 4.3. Archaeological complexes in the Northeastern Plains and surrounding areas on an A.D. 1100 to 1200 early Plains Village time level.

provide evidence for technological and stylistic influences from surrounding Middle Missouri, Middle Mississippian, and Woodland populations (Knudson 1967). The extensive distribution of KRF in early
Plains Village sites throughout the central and northern portions of the
study area, coupled with the broad distributions and mixes of ceramic
stylistic traits, demonstrate widespread interactions between different
cultural groups at this time level.

Like Cambria, Great Oasis is viewed either as a terminal Late
Woodland or incipient Plains Village cultural complex of southwestern
Minnesota, northern Iowa, and eastern South Dakota dating around
A.D. 1100 (Alex 1980; Anfinson 1979; Henning and Henning 1978;
Johnson 1969; Keller and Keller 1983; Zimmerman 1985:75–82). The
Hartford Beach Village (39RO5) is one component on the west shore of
Big Stone Lake. It is a village site that was fortified by a defensive ditch
and palisade wall with bastions (Haug 1983). Across its range, a variety
of adaptations are associated with Great Oasis ranging from principally hunting and gathering in the prairie lakes regions to possibly
horticultural in northeastern Iowa–southeastern South Dakota riverine environments (Henning and Henning 1982:10–12). In its horticultural aspect, it is akin to other Initial Middle Missouri cultures.

Named ceramic types from the region include Sandy Lake, Blackduck, Brainard horizontal corded ware, Kathio, Buchanan Flared Rim
ware, Linden Everted Rim ware, Northeastern Plains ware, Red River
ware, Cambria, Great Oasis, and a variety of Initial Middle Missouri
wares and types at the southern end of the study area (e.g., Michlovic
1978:11–13; 1981:12–14; 1983:25–26; Wheeler 1963). It was in the southerly portions of the study area that Middle Mississippian ceramic
influences emanating from Cahokia had their greatest impact. At Mill
Creek sites, there are unique vessel forms such as bean pots and bowls
with effigy figures on the rims exactly like those made at Cahokia (cf.
Anderson 1987). Middle Mississippian influences are also seen in the
central portions of the study area in ceramic wares such as Cambria,
Great Oasis, Buchanan Flared Rim ware, and Linden Everted Rim ware
(figure 4.4). Such influences are to be expected if Elden Johnson is
correct that people with Cambria material culture produced bison
products for the Cahokia trade system (Johnson 1991).

Sites of the Sandy Lake complex are situated primarily in central and
western Minnesota, southern Manitoba, and eastern North Dakota,
straddling the prairie-woodland ecotone. Dates range from A.D. 1000 to
1700 (Anfinson 1979; Cooper and Johnson 1964; Michlovic 1985). This
and other Late Woodland complexes are defined principally on the
basis of ceramic wares, Sandy Lake ware in this case.

The key element in the Plains Village adaptive strategy has long been
thought by many to have been the production of a dependable, storable
surplus food supply primarily in the form of dried corn (e.g., Lovick and

Ahler 1982:55). In late prehistoric times, people who relied upon gardening for a large measure of their food production were limited to the southern half of the study area by the climatic restriction of the length of the frost-free growing season. Early Plains Village food production in the central portions of the study area involved hunting, gathering, and gardening. But unlike contemporary Plains Village cultures to the south in the Northeastern Plains and in the Middle Missouri subarea, there is no evidence for very heavy reliance on horticultural surpluses for subsistence (Schneider 1988). Typical garden crops were maize, sunflowers, and tobacco (e.g., Haberman 1983: 51). Bison remained the mainstay of the diet, supplemented with elk, deer, dogs, and smaller mammals (cf. Haury 1987:382). Gathering of wild plant foods (greens, fruits, seeds, and tuberous roots) also continued to be important as it had been for thousands of years (cf. Benz 1987).

Plains Village groups in the Northeastern Plains had highly advanced stone, bone, and shell technologies to match their ceramic technologies. Stone tool aggregates include finely flaked bifaces and unifaces, and carefully prepared ground stone axes, tablets, and pipes. Most of the earlier arrow points are classified as Prairie side-notched; the more uniformly made and straight-sided Plains side-notched forms are prevalent at later sites (cf. Kehoe 1966). Asymmetrical, bifacially chipped flint cutting tools, made for hafting in bone or wooden handles, are also characteristic (Gregg et al. 1987: fig. 12.6r). A great variety of bone tools and ornaments was made. Bone spatulates were often used as pressure flakers in making and refurbishing stone tools. Of course, bison scapula hoes are a hallmark implement of most native Plains horticulturists. Freshwater mussels were a source of shell stock material from which various utilitarian and ornamental objects were fabricated (cf. Picha 1987).

Early Plains Village settlement systems included villages, field camps, garden locations, mortuary sites, and the whole range of temporarily occupied sites associated with the procurement and processing of subsistence resources. Few of the villages appear to have been fortified with palisade walls or dry moats, which are typically also lacking in early villages along the Missouri River. Most of the residential sites were in the large river valleys. Actual garden plots have not been identified archaeologically as they have been in the Midwest and Southwest, but they must have been near the villages based on the finds of new and used scapula hoes in the village sites. Burial practices were variable, perhaps even within individual communities. At the Dirt Lodge Village site (39SP11) along the central James River, initial burial may have been on scaffolds with subsequent differential treatment of the cranial and postcranial remains (Haberman 1983:99). Mortuary practises of many villagers and nonvillagers alike throughout the study area involved the construction of cemetery mounds atop promi-

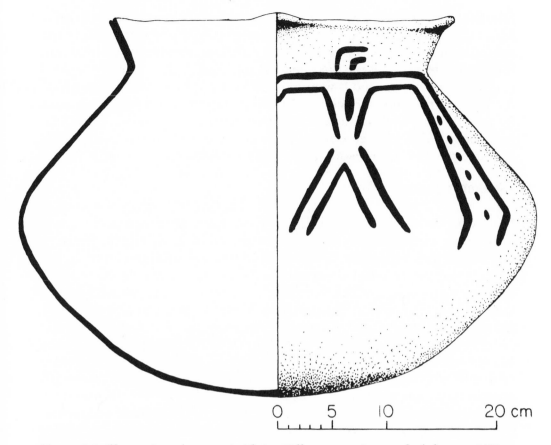

Figure 4.4. Illustration of a generic Plains Village ceramic vessel of the A.D. 1100 to 1200 period in the central portions of the Northeastern Plains. The vessel form is distinctly globular rather than conoidal; this vessel form characterized most Woodland pots of the same era in the prairie-woodland border area. Vessel profiles usually display pronounced deflections in the shoulder and neck zones. Exterior surfaces are characteristically smoothed or burnished, although many are cordmarked. Rim forms are usually straight to outcurved. Exterior rims are typically decorated with trailed lines and tool impressions. Lips are frequently embellished with channeling, tool-impressed decorations, and/or tab handles.

nences such as the edges of upland plains overlooking residential areas in river valley bottomlands (e.g., Alex 1981b; Swenson and Gregg 1988). Some burials with exotic goods in association have been termed Devils Lake–Sourisford mortuaries (Syms 1979). These exotic goods evince a resurgence of long-distance exchange relations, the likes of which had not been seen on the Northeastern Plains since Middle Woodland times.

Numerous Late Woodland sites with mixed Woodland and Plains Village ceramic traits have been recorded along the prairie-woodland border. These occurrences have fostered the study of prehistoric land use and other cultural phenomena from an ecotonal perspective (e.g.,

Nicholson 1988a). Wattrall (1985:71) suggested that "ethnically diverse
co-resident winter villages" documented in historic times along the
ecotone and generally thought to have developed under the influence of
the fur trade may also have been established prehistorically. Direct
exchange of material goods would likely have gone hand in hand with in-
terethnic coresidency. Exchange in this context could partly account
for the mixing of styles and materials that often characterize archaeological deposits along the ecotone such as at the Lake Bronson site (21KT1)
in northwestern Minnesota (Anfinson, Michlovic, and Stein 1978).

A.D. 1400 TO 1500

Low water levels and high salinity have been documented in cored
sediments dating between A.D. 1350 and 1650 from prairie lakes in
northeastern South Dakota. These findings are solid evidence of the
negative environmental effects of Pacific climatic episode droughts in
the southern portion of the Northeastern Plains (Radle 1981). There are
similar indications that the northern portions of the study area were
also adversely affected by drought. For example, most of the Devils
Lake basin in northeastern North Dakota dried up one or more times
between A.D. 1300 and 1535 (cf. Callendar 1968). Conditions were
probably not continuously adverse for centuries, just as they were not
continuously favorable during the Neo-Atlantic. However, during times
when the prairie lakes were dry or excessively saline, few residential
bases and field camps would have been situated away from the major
rivers and permanent springs.

Coincident with the beginnings of the Pacific climatic episode
around 1250 or 1300, there were dramatic changes in human adaptations at a number of places in the study area as there were elsewhere in
the Plains. Plains Village settlements in northwestern Iowa and southeastern South Dakota were abandoned (Alex 1981b:20; Benn 1986:30–
31). Social upheavals are indicated by the fact that nearly all of the
village sites known from this time period and later were fortified.
Droughts of the Pacific climatic episode led to excessive population
pressures on limited amounts of arable land which in turn resulted in
food shortages, malnutrition, and internecine warfare (cf. Gregg and
Zimmerman 1986).

Woodland cultures continued to dominate the prairie-woodland
ecotone, but they adopted a number of Plains Village traits. For example, there was no indication until recently that the Sandy Lake complex
was ever anything but Woodland. However, excavations at the Shea site
(32CS101) in southeastern North Dakota have documented a fortified
village supported by a mixed horticultural–hunter-gatherer subsistence base and a ceramic assemblage dominated by Sandy Lake ware
(Michlovic 1988:62; Michlovic and Schneider 1988). Radiocarbon dates

indicate occupation around A.D. 1450. The defensive ditch and defensive wall with bastions that surrounded the residential area are reminiscent of coeval Plains Village settlements. It now appears that late prehistoric people with Sandy Lake material culture had territories that extended from the woodlands of Minnesota across the prairie-woodland ecotone and into the Northeastern Plains. Some of these people may have depended upon gardening to such an extent that they were living what we would identify as a Plains Village lifeway. It has also been suggested that Plains Village lifeways were extended into parts of southern Manitoba during this period by an actual in-migration of people (Nicholson and Malainey 1991:88).

While Woodland cultures predominated along the ecotone, and Middle Missouri and Coalescent Plains Village cultures flourished in the central and western portions of the study area, Oneota cultures came to dominate the southern one-third of the study area by A.D. 1300 or so (map 4.4). Some of the Oneota complexes have been termed Blood Run, Olivet, and Correctionville–Blue Earth–Orr (cf. Alex 1981b; Stanley 1989:23). Oneota ceramic technological and stylistic influences in the form of shell tempering and broad trailed-line decorations have been identified as far north as the upper James River and Red River headwaters areas of North Dakota and Minnesota (Gregg et al. 1987:271; Michlovic 1983:25). People with Oneota material culture made extensive use of catlinite pipestone quarried in southwestern Minnesota (Sigstad 1973, 1983). They may have been the principal point-of-contact distributors in late prehistoric times when long-distance exchange of catlinite was most extensive (cf. Brown 1989).

A trade network known as the Middle Missouri system was linked with other exchange nodes across the entire continent in early historic times (Wood 1972a). The annual Dakota rendezvous on the James River in South Dakota was one well-known part of the Middle Missouri system. Wood suggests that this historic manifestation represents part of a pattern of intertribal trade that developed prehistorically. Exchange of this sort was certainly ongoing by A.D. 1400 to 1500 when Northern Plains peoples were receiving Northwest Coast *Dentalium* sp. ornamental shells, Rocky Mountain obsidian (cf. Anderson, Tiffany, and Nelson 1986; Baugh and Nelson 1988), Southeastern Ceremonial Cult design motifs and objects (Howard 1953), and Southern Plains trade vessels (Anderson and Tiffany 1987). Many aspects of native technologies reached their highest levels of development just before the influx of European goods and the devastating plagues that decimated the skilled native artisans during the fur trade period. In terms of durable material culture that is commonly recovered archaeologically, ceramics of this period are most extraordinary as regards technological advancements and stylistic embellishments. Forms characteristic of this period include elaborately decorated S-rims (fig. 4.5).

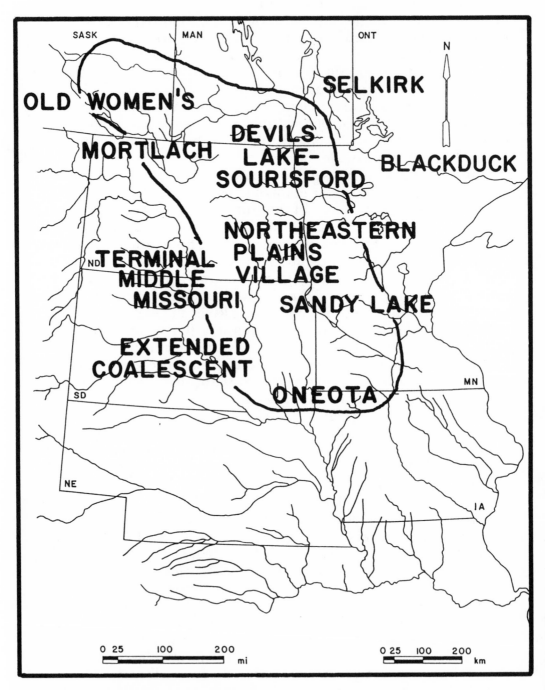

Map 4.4. Archaeological complexes in the Northeastern Plains and surrounding areas on an A.D. 1400 to 1500 late Plains Village time level.

Large residential bases with earthlodges were occupied semipermanently and permanently. Fortification walls and defensive ditches were constructed around villages such as at the Hendrickson III site (32SN403) along the upper James River (Good et al. 1977), the Shea site (32CS101) along the Maple River (Michlovic 1988:82; Michlovic and Schneider 1988), and Linden Village (39RO43) on the shore of Big Stone Lake (Haug 1983). Little is known about the residential and other settlements of Plains Village and Woodland groups in the northern portions of the Northeastern Plains at this time. Most villages were apparently not like the large fortified settlements of the Plains Village peoples along the Missouri River (Ahler, Theissen, and Trimble 1991). Cultural continuity with earlier Northeastern Plains peoples is indicated by perpetuation of Devils Lake–Sourisford mortuary practices and mound construction. Preservation of perishables in some of these mortuary mounds in the vicinity of Sourisford, Manitoba, points to mound interments very late in prehistory (cf. Thomas 1894:36–37). Other late Plains Village site types that have been documented include eagle trapping pits, stone-rimmed depressions with human burials (Wheeler 1963:221–22), boulder effigies often in the form of turtles (Thomas 1894:38), and stone procurement workshops (Gregg et al. 1986).

Maize horticulture continued to be practiced in the central portion of the study area, but perhaps not to the extent as in early Plains Village times (Schneider 1988). However, the only direct evidence for prehistoric corn horticulture in the Canadian portion of the study area comes from components of this age at the Lockport site just north of Winnipeg (Buchner 1988:30) and the Lovstrom site near the Assiniboine River in Manitoba (Nicholson 1988b; Nicholson and Malainey 1991:88). Lockport has yielded scapula hoes, milling stones, and bark-lined storage pits in addition to carbonized corn kernels as indicators of corn gardening (Buchner 1988:30). To the south, Oneota settlements appear to have been larger than the more northerly villages, and they may have been dependent upon stored surpluses of maize for their perpetuation. The continued importance of bison to peoples' livelihoods cannot be overstated.

ETHNIC GROUPS AND POPULATION DENSITY AT ABOUT A.D. 1500

Archaeological research, oral histories, and/or historic documentation have indicated the presence of the Dakota, Ojibwa, Cheyenne, Plains Cree, Assiniboine, Ioway, Mandan, Arapaho, Atsina, Oto, Missouri, and Hidatsa in the Northeastern Plains during protohistoric and historic times (Bowers 1965:482; Bray and Bray 1976:169–211; Michlovic 1983:26–27; Syms 1985; Wood 1971b). Ancestors of all of these peoples may have utilized parts of the Northeastern Plains around A.D. 1500, and they all had territories that overlapped with those of other groups (cf. Syms 1985:75).

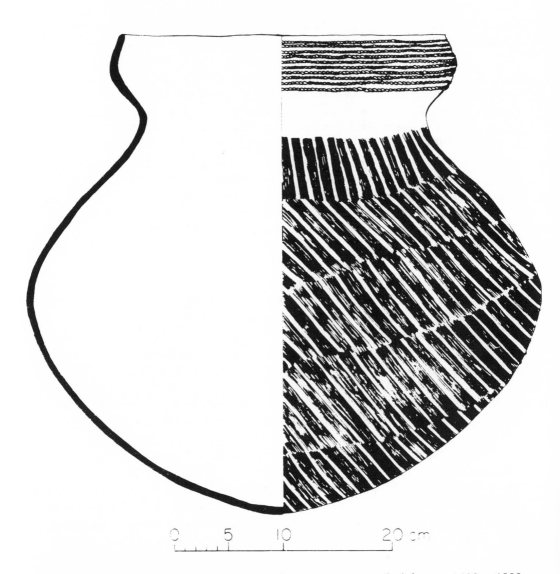

Fig. 4.5. Illustration of a generic Plains Village ceramic vessel of the A.D. 1400 to 1500 period. Vessel shapes continued to be globular as they were during earlier Plains Village times. Exterior surface treatments were often simple stamped, a result of malleating the vessel with a grooved or thong-wrapped paddle in the process of forming it prior to drying and firing. Check stamping and linear check stamping are other kinds of exterior surface treatments that appear on very late prehistoric ceramics. Cordmarked, smoothed, and brushed surfaces also occur. More complex rim forms such as S-rims and recurved S-rims became popular, while simpler straight and outcurved rim forms persisted as well. Upper rim zones were often decorated with complex patterns of cord impressions.

Ethnic Groups and Archeological Complexes

Some Blackduck sites in Ontario may have been occupied proto-historically, yet there is lack of agreement regarding the ethnicity of the makers of Blackduck ceramics. MacNeish (1958) and Wilford (1955) argued that it was the Assiniboine. Wright (1981) proposed it was the Ojibwa. Syms (1985:96) suggested a less specific association of Black-duck, along with other Woodland material including Laurel and Sel-kirk, with Algonquian groups in general.

Sandy Lake ceramics are thought to have been brought into historic times by the Middle Dakota or western Dakota (Yankton, Yanktonai, and Teton – Michlovic 1985) or the closely related Assiniboine (Partici-pants of the Lake Superior Basin Workshop 1988). This pottery has been recovered from firmly dated prehistoric contexts at both residential and mortuary sites in the center of the Northeastern Plains (e.g., Good et al. 1977; Michlovic and Schneider 1988; Snortland-Coles 1985). Whether proto–Middle Dakota, proto–Western Dakota, or proto-Assiniboine peoples made Sandy Lake pottery, the finds of this pottery in the central portions of the study area suggest that Siouan groups with strong Woodland ties were traditional prehistoric occupants of the Northeastern Plains. This interpretation of archaeological data is supported by ethnohistoric documentation of Yanktonai Dakota estab-lishing winter villages on the James River in South Dakota at least as early as 1725 (Howard 1976:20).

The Biesterfeldt site (32RM1) along the Sheyenne River in south-eastern North Dakota has been interpreted as a residential settlement of Cheyenne peoples living a Plains Village lifeway in an earthlodge village around 1750 (Wood 1971). Strong (1941) suggested that the Cheyennes may have dwelled in the Sheyenne valley by 1600 or earlier. The oral histories of the Dakota say that Cheyennes also lived at one time in the Devils Lake region (Grinnell 1972,1:8). So archaeological and ethnographic evidence indicates that the Algonquian-speaking Cheyenne, equestrian nomadic peoples of historic times, lived a Plains Village lifeway in the central part of the study area around A.D. 1500. Cheyenne culture may be traceable back in time to a connection with Besant-Sonota (cf. Schlesier 1987:134–50). This hypothesis would be strongly supported if physical anthropologists could confirm that proto-Cheyenne peoples are represented in Woodland burial popula-tions such as Arvilla dating between the time of the Besant-Sonota complex and the protohistoric period (cf. Ossenberg 1974:38; Syms 1985:88–93).

Hidatsa oral traditions hold that their Awaxawi subgroup occupied a territory that included the Sheyenne River valley and the headwaters of the Red River in late prehistoric times (Bowers 1965:22). If so, they probably shared this territory with the Cheyenne and some of the

Teton or Middle Dakota. The Hintz site (32SN3) along the James River
in North Dakota was an earthlodge village interpreted by Wheeler
(1963:229) and Wood (1986) as a protohistoric Hidatsa settlement. The
Schultz site on the Sheyenne River (Bowers 1948), the Sharbono site
(32BE419) on Graham's Island at Devils Lake (Schneider 1983), and the
Irvin Nelson site (32BE208) on the Devils Lake shoreline (S. Fox 1982)
are other late prehistoric sites posited to have been used by Hidatsas.
Sites of the Mortlach complex in the northwestern portions of the
Northeastern Plains may also be linked to Hidatsas (Finnigan 1988:44).
There is little doubt that at least one subgroup of the Hidatsa held
territory within the study area around A.D. 1500.

By that time, the southern one-third of the Northeastern Plains
appears to have been dominated by people with Oneota material
culture. Protohistoric and historic occupants of the Oneota settlements in the Blood Run locality straddling the border of Iowa and
South Dakota may have included the Ioway, Oto, and Omaha (cf. Alex
1981b:20; Stanley 1989:23).

Some historic tribal groups seem totally lost in prehistory. While
most of the historic tribes have been linked at least hypothetically
with archaeological complexes or specific sites, no one has yet identified prehistoric traces of the Arapaho and Atsina (Wood 1985:4).

Population Density

The study area covers about 140,000 square miles or 360,000 square
kilometers. Today's population density is about ten people per square
mile. Densities of hunter-gatherers around the world have been recorded ranging from 0.01 to 2.0 people per square mile (Hassan 1975:
38). Groups at the high end of the range occupied areas with rich and
reliable resource bases such as the Pacific Northwest Coast. As an
example of the low end of the range, Steward (1968:103) estimated
densities for the Great Basin Shoshone as 0.01 to 0.2 per square mile.
When biotic and social conditions were favorable on the Northern
Plains, as they were for the Villagers before the incursions of plagues
and hostile equestrian nomads, and when drought conditions did not
prevail, population densities may have been around 0.2 people per
square mile. If the Mandans and Hidatsas combined had a territory of
fifty thousand square miles and biotic and social conditions were
favorable, then they may have numbered ten thousand or so.

Around A.D. 1500, peoples of the Northeastern Plains are posited to
have been recovering from the damaging effects of Pacific climatic
episode droughts. These droughts must have had severe negative effects on horticultural pursuits as well as availability of wild plant and
animal resources. The central and northern portions of the study area
in 1500 were occupied primarily by groups living Plains Woodland

lifeways. Some lived in small fortified villages, but they appear not to have depended on horticultural produce for subsistence. Village-oriented peoples with Oneota material culture apparently dominated the southern part of the study area. Under generally poor biotic conditions, the overall population density may have been something on the order of 0.1 people per square mile, yielding a total of fourteen thousand people for the entire Northeastern Plains. Population density ought to have been higher than that several centuries earlier under the favorable conditions of the Neo-Atlantic and again several centuries later during the mesic Neo-Boreal. The vast bison herds and the denser human populations of protohistoric times developed under the generally lush biotic conditions of the Neo-Boreal (cf. Reher and Frison 1980:59).

CONCLUSIONS

Cultures of the Northeastern Plains cannot be viewed as peripheral to the late prehistory of either the Northern Plains or the prairie-woodland ecotone. A Plains Village lifeway based on a mix of horticulture, hunting, and gathering for food production evolved in this sub-area and spread throughout the Northern Plains. This occurred during the Neo-Atlantic climatic episode with the conjunction of warm temperatures, regular precipitation, and successful selection of garden crops that matured during short growing seasons. Perhaps even more important than the expansion of gardening practices was the overall buildup of regional biomass. Grasslands and bison flourished. Availability of bison seems to have been a persistent limiting factor for human population growth and stability throughout prehistory in the area.

The two-hundred-year period of A.D. 1000 to 1200 represents the highest peak in the cycle of human population growth and decline in the prehistory in the Northeastern Plains. The cycle turned down in the droughty environmental conditions of the 1300s and 1400s. An upsurge was under way during the mesic Neo-Boreal episode of the late 1500s, 1600s, and 1700s. But there never was a post-1500 peak because native peoples were decimated by the effects of the European invasions.

CHAPTER 5

NEIGHBORS TO THE NORTH: PEOPLES OF THE BOREAL FOREST

David Meyer and Scott Hamilton

THE study area (map 5.1) forms a broad band extending from the upper drainage basin of the Churchill River in western Saskatchewan, east across central Manitoba, and then southeast through northwestern Ontario[1] into the Rainy River drainage area of northern Minnesota. In Saskatchewan and Manitoba the southern edge of the study area coincides with the limits of the boreal forest; in Minnesota the southern limit of the study area falls along the Glacial Lake Agassiz bog lands, which separate the Rainy River drainage basin from that of the headwaters of the Mississippi River. The northern edge of the study area falls along the northern limits of the boreal forest.

Following the theme of this volume, the following chapter focuses on the period A.D. 500–1500 and provides an overview of the culture history of the study region. Also included are brief discussions of evidence for plains/forest cultural interaction. In terms of prehistory, this chapter will concentrate on the Woodland cultures of the study area. In part, we have elected this focus because the Woodland cultural assemblages contain ceramics of readily recognizable styles. Also, the material remains of those peoples who did not make pottery are poorly known.

ENVIRONMENTAL OVERVIEW

In broad terms the surficial geology is similar throughout the study area. The northern and eastern portions of the area are characterized by the Precambrian Shield (map 5.1), which is bordered on the south by Pleistocene and Holocene deposits. The latter consist mainly of glacial till, large areas of which were covered by glacial lakes—Glacial Lake Agassiz in particular. Lacustrine deposits characterize the beds of these glacial lakes. As a result of glacial scouring, soils on the Precambrian Shield are thin and bedrock outcrops are frequent. What sediment mantle there is on the bedrock is glacio-lacustrine, relating to the

We extend special thanks to Grace Rajnovich, who read and commented on this chapter. She and Paddy Reid also made available an unpublished paper outlining their current thinking with regard to Laurel. We must also thank Terrance Gibson for providing illustrative material and Phyllis Lodoen for preparing the drawing of an Avonlea pottery vessel. Also, Gary Wowchuk has very kindly allowed us to examine his surface-collected material from the Swan River, Manitoba, area.

[1]In the Canadian context, the term "northwestern Ontario" refers to that part of the province of Ontario which lies west and northwest of Lake Superior.

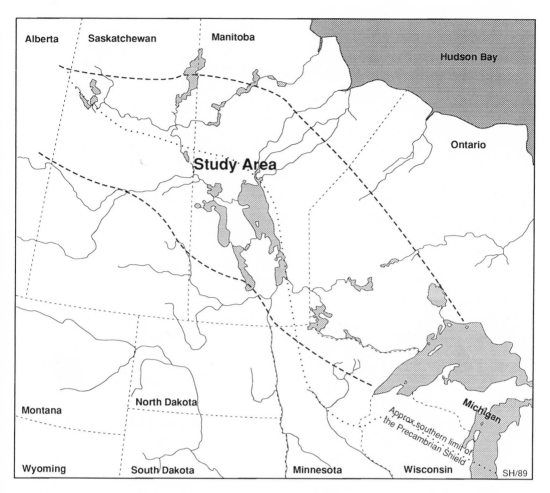

Map 5.1. Location of the study area.

glacial retreat. The terrain is generally rough, with ridges and hills between which are depressions which usually contain lakes or bogs.

Two major forest regions are present in the study area – the boreal forest and the Great Lakes–St. Lawrence forest (map 5.2). The Great Lakes–St. Lawrence forest occupies a large portion of northeastern North America, reaching its western extremity in southeastern Manitoba. It covers much of the northern half of Minnesota, exclusive of that state's northwestern corner (map 5.2). In northwestern Ontario, this forest zone is present in a relatively narrow east-west strip extending some eighty-five kilometers north of the international border. Particularly characteristic of this forest region is the presence of "eastern white and red pines, eastern hemlock and yellow birch" (Rowe 1972:11). Hardwood species characteristic of the deciduous forest region on the south are also common: red oak, sugar and red maples, basswood, and white elm. As well, most species common to the boreal forest region (discussed below) occur in appropriate environments in the Great Lakes–St. Lawrence forest region (Shay 1967:237).

This diversity of plants resulted in an environment very productive in those floral and faunal resources useful to past human occupants (Lugenbeal 1976:27–28). The pine-hardwood forest yielded a number of potential plant foods, including nuts, berries, and sap. Of major importance—at least to peoples of the Late Prehistoric period—was the presence of wild rice in that portion of the study area within the Great Lakes–St. Lawrence forest region. Wild rice was only one of the resources that made the aquatic environments vitally important to Late Prehistoric subsistence economies. Here too were substantial fish populations (including the highly esteemed sturgeon) as well as beavers and muskrats, and moose frequented the edges of the water bodies. The fauna of the Great Lakes–St. Lawrence forest region also included

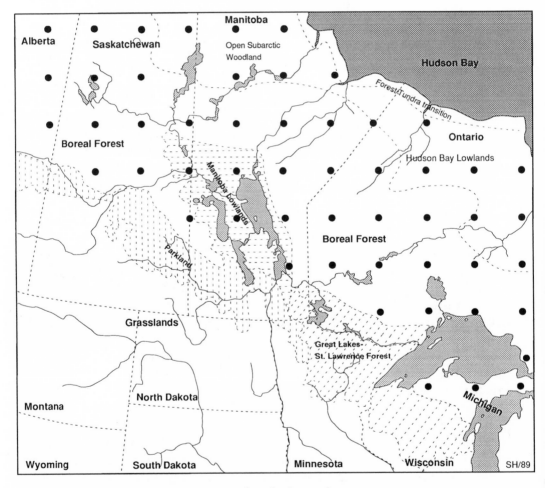

Map 5.2. Vegetation zones associated with the study area.

white-tailed deer, woodland caribou, and (occasional) wapiti. Waterfowl were common, particularly in the wild rice stands.

The climate of the Great Lakes–St. Lawrence forest region, with up
to 120 frost-free days, is somewhat less rigorous than that of the boreal
forest to the north. The latter region is characterized by conifers such
as white and black spruce, tamarack, balsam fir, and jackpine. Deciduous species include trembling aspen, white birch, and balsam
poplar. Compared to the Great Lakes–St. Lawrence forest, the boreal
forest is generally impoverished in terms of its floral and faunal
resources—especially on the Precambrian Shield. Perhaps a more appropriate representation of boreal forest ecology is one of "resource
patchiness" (Winterhalder 1983:32). This patchiness assures considerable diversity of plants and animals in localized communities. It
reflects the dynamics of ecological succession in response to climate,
wind, hydrology, altitude, sedimentation, and, particularly, cycles of
forest fires. As a result the ecology of the boreal forest is considerably
more diverse and dynamic than previously thought.

With the perspective of resource patchiness, the boreal forest can be
viewed as comprising a complex patchwork of localized communities
with highly variable levels of usable biomass. Some of these localized ecological communities yield limited or unreliable food resources (i.e.,
closed coniferous forest); others can be extremely productive and predictable. Examples of rich zones include lake and river situations associated
with wild rice, spawning fish or migratory wildfowl, and recently burned-
over areas colonized by pioneer plants and animals that browse on them.

The Manitoba lowlands stretch across much of central and west-
central Manitoba (map 5.2) and are characterized by an environment
not unlike that of the Great Lakes–St. Lawrence forest region. In this
area of large lakes (Winnipeg, Winnipegosis, Manitoba), with the Saskatchewan River delta on the northwest, are a number of tree species
not usual in the boreal forest: American elm, green ash, and Manitoba
maple (Rowe 1972:31). This is a relatively rich environment of lakes
and marshes which attains, perhaps, its peak in the Saskatchewan River
delta. From the north end of Lake Winnipeg this vast delta extends
some 170 kilometers west up the Saskatchewan River valley. The
productivity of this region in terms of large game (particularly moose
and black bears), aquatic mammals, fish, and waterfowl is very great.

PALEOCLIMATE, A.D. 500–1500

Pollen studies in Manitoba and Saskatchewan provide evidence for the
onset of essentially modern climatic conditions by 3,000–2,500 years ago
(Ritchie 1983:167–68). At this time the plant communities of the boreal
forest assumed their contemporary composition. As well, the southern
edge of the forest became established at about its present position.

In northern Europe and North America the centuries following A.D. 500 probably were characterized by climatic conditions very similar to those of the twentieth century, although it has been argued that this was a slightly milder period (Wendland 1978a:281). In any case, a "climatic optimum" was reached in the period about A.D. 1090–1230 (Porter 1986:42). This corresponds to a portion of the Neo-Atlantic episode (Bryson and Wendland 1967:294; Wendland 1978a:281), a period of significantly warmer climate in the northern hemisphere. In northern Canada, evidence for this warmer period is provided by forest remains in the barrengrounds west of Hudson Bay as much as 280 kilometers north of the present tree line (Bryson, Irving, and Larsen 1965). This forest has been dated to the period around A.D. 800–1100. Following this, the climate cooled quite quickly through to the late 1400s, following which it ameliorated for almost three-quarters of a century (Porter 1986:43; Lamb 1977:461). The following period, about 1550–1850, has been termed the "Little Ice Age" (Grove 1988), a period of significantly colder climatic conditions. For Europe this climatic deterioration has been described in considerable detail on the basis of historical documents (Lamb 1977:449–73), and similar conditions prevailed across the North Atlantic (Gribbin and Lamb 1978:70–74) and throughout northern North America (Porter 1986:43).

PREHISTORIC RECORD, A.D. 500

Northern Saskatchewan and Manitoba

Although the Churchill River system in northern Saskatchewan and Manitoba (map 5.3) almost certainly supported a human population at A.D. 500, archaeological evidence of its presence is very uncertain. This relates to the paucity of archaeological activity in this region. There is, however, a small amount of information. In 1981 and 1982, James V. Millar and students conducted archaeological surveys and excavations in the Buffalo Narrows region (map 5.3), at the headwaters of the Churchill River. On the basis of components at two sites, Millar (1983:94, 101) proposed the Chartier complex (ca. A.D. 600–700), which is characterized by bi-pointed lanceolate and medium-sized stemmed projectile points. Some side- and corner-notched points are also associated. Similarly, a few stemmed and lanceolate points are known from the Reindeer River (Meyer and Smailes 1975:58–61), which flows into the Churchill River toward the east side of the province. Millar (1983: 112–13) and Meyer (1983b:148–53) have considered these materials related to the Taltheilei tradition, which is best known from the barrengrounds of the Northwest Territories (e.g., Noble 1971, Gordon 1976).

In Manitoba, where work on the Churchill River has been concentrated on Southern Indian Lake, Taltheilei tradition materials have

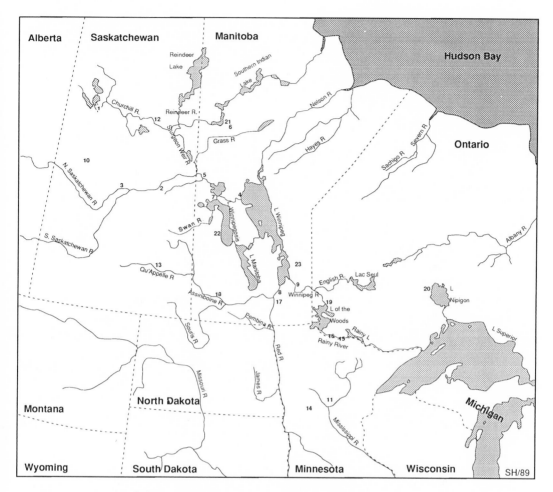

Map 5.3. Rivers, lakes, and archaeological sites referred to in the text.

been found at a number of sites (Dickson 1980:149–50). The peoples who produced the Taltheilei materials depended on the migratory herds of barrenground caribou for their subsistence. These herds sometimes penetrated as far south as the Churchill River system, and it appears that they were closely followed by the humans who depended upon them. In short, around A.D. 500 there was at least occasional occupation of the Churchill River system by peoples with northern cultural connections.

The nature of the occupation of the southern portion of the Saskatchewan forest at this time is very uncertain. It is possible that the Besant phase was present. For example a Besant component has been excavated at the Intake site, on the North Saskatchewan River (Meyer 1981a; see map 5.3). This site has yielded a number of Besant projectile points as well as shards of a single pottery vessel (Wilson 1982:835–39, 906, 975). This vessel, decorated with a row of punctates just below the lip, has an exterior textile impression and seems to have been conoidal in shape. A bone collagen sample from this occupation has been radiocarbon dated at 1205 ± 580 B.P. (S-2185).

Manitoba, Northwestern Ontario, Northern Minnesota

At A.D. 500 a large portion of the study area was occupied by peoples whose cultural remains we know as Laurel (map 5.4). Indeed, A.D. 500 marks about the middle of the Laurel time period, about 100 B.C.–A.D. 900. Syms (1977:80, 81) summarized the characteristics of Laurel assemblages this way:

[A]ll these archaeological units share a common core of traits: toggle head harpoons, overlapping projectile point typologies, and conical ceramic vessels with varying frequencies of pseudoscallop shell stamping, linear stamping

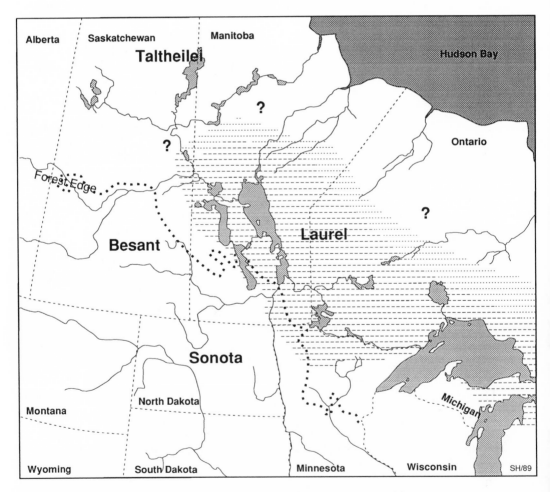

Map 5.4. Approximate extent of Laurel distribution, ca. A.D. 500.

and stab-and-drag stamping decorative techniques applied to the upper third of the vessel [fig. 5.1].

Other traits which are not ubiquitous . . . are small burial mounds, often containing bundle burials, a variety of stemmed and notched projectile points, the cold hammering of native copper into simple tools such as awls, barbs, chisels and beads, and hafted beaver incisor tools. . . . Burial mounds are in the southern portions of the Boreal Forest along the boundary between Manitoba [Ontario] and Minnesota, copper is more common in the eastern sites around the Great Lakes.

(For a more recent, detailed overview, see Mason 1981:284–92.) Since its initial recognition, Laurel has been subject to a good deal of research, and a number of temporal/regional phases have been proposed (Stoltman 1974, Lugenbeal 1976:570–88). As well, a number of Laurel pottery types have been identified: Dentate, Pseudo-Scallop Shell, Bossed, Incised, Plain, Punctate, Cord-wrapped Stick, Dragged Oblique, and Undragged Oblique (Stoltman 1973, Lugenbeal 1976).

Lugenbeal, following Stoltman (1973:115–17), has assigned the middle Laurel materials of northern Minnesota, adjacent Ontario, and southeastern Manitoba to the McKinstry phase, about A.D. 300–900. McKinstry phase ceramics are characterized by substantial percentages of Laurel Pseudo-Scallop Shell and the boss and punctate subtype of Laurel Bossed (Lugenbeal 1976:576). Arthurs (1986:139) has noted that Laurel components dating to this period are present "in the southern Boreal Forest in both northwestern and northeastern Ontario, as far as the edge of the Hudson Bay Lowlands." Arthurs (1986: 139) also has observed that these "tend to be small components, which have almost invariably yielded pseudo scallop shell decorated pottery, the hallmark of middle period Laurel."

During this period, Laurel also makes its appearance much farther north in Manitoba; for example, Lugenbeal (1976:582) has identified a McKinstry phase occupation at the Tailrace Bay site near the mouth of the Saskatchewan River on the northwestern corner of Lake Winnipeg (map 5.3) (Mayer-Oakes 1970). Farther upstream, in the Saskatchewan River delta, Tamplin (1977) has excavated a middle Laurel component at the Pas Reserve site (map 5.3). This is a relatively early Laurel occupation, as indicated by radiocarbon dates of 1820 ± 150 B.P. (A-1424) and 1590 ± 50 B.P. (A-1368). There is also some evidence of middle period Laurel occupation even farther north in Manitoba: Laurel Pseudo-Scallop Shell and Laurel Dragged Oblique (common in early and middle Laurel components) types on the Grass River system (Hlady 1970:106, 1971:42–49). To the east, stronger evidence is available from excavations at Site UNR 26, on Wapisu Lake. Two of the five Laurel vessels recovered here were of the Pseudo-Scallop Shell type, associated with a radiocarbon date of 1645 ± 195 B.P. (S-959).

Fig. 5.1. Laurel vessel from Department of Anthropology collection, Lakehead University, Thunder Bay, Ontario.

Because the Saskatchewan River delta extends westward well into Saskatchewan, Laurel components dating around A.D. 500 likely are present in that province. However, archaeological investigations on the Saskatchewan side of the delta have been too limited even to provide evidence of the presence of Laurel.

Following Syms (1977:83), Hamilton (1981:21) has outlined three different subsistence economies that are considered to have been followed by Laurel peoples:

1) large summer aggregates supported by the exploitation of concentrated fish resources and small winter groups relying upon diffuse land mammal resources. This strategy seems to be employed in the Lake-Forest regions in the vicinity of the Great Lakes (Fitting 1970:99,129–142).

2) a strategy employing seasonally available resources that imply movements from Mixed Conifer-Hardwood and Parkland biomes in Minnesota (Syms 1977:83).

3) a strategy represented by the scattered distribution of sites reflecting a reliance on diffuse resources in eastern and northern Manitoba and Northwestern Ontario. (Syms 1977:83; Wiersum and Tisdale 1977:1; Meyer and Smailes 1974)

The subsistence-settlement pattern which involved seasonal movement between the Great Lakes–St. Lawrence forest and the adjacent aspen parkland appears to have been restricted to southeastern Manitoba and northeastern Minnesota. Here, Laurel components are present in the parkland (e.g., Anfinson, Michlovic, and Stein 1978). More characteristic of Laurel subsistence strategies is that described above for the Laurel occupants of the upper Great Lakes because it also appears to have been followed by Laurel peoples in the Boundary Waters region. This would have involved major aggregations during the spring and early summer, when there were massive spawning runs of sturgeon, pickerel, and suckers (Hamilton 1981:22). Although there very likely was dispersal into smaller family groups for much of the summer, the run of autumn spawning fish (such as whitefish) and the wild rice harvest would have allowed (probably smaller) fall gatherings.

It is likely that a subsistence strategy basically like that described above characterized Laurel populations throughout the Manitoba lowlands. For instance the Tailrace Bay site (map 5.3) has yielded evidence of substantial Laurel occupation (Mayer-Oakes 1970). However, aggregation sizes may have been smaller and, given the absence of wild rice, fall aggregations may not have occurred. In the boreal forest of the Precambrian Shield it is also likely that aggregations occurred during the spring spawning runs; however, available evidence suggests that the gatherings were relatively small, reflecting either a sparse human population or a relatively limited fish resource.[2]

[2]Laurel in northwestern Ontario and northern Minnesota has been undergoing considerable new research and reevaluation over the past decade. New syntheses are as yet unpublished (Reid and Rajnovich n.d.). The initial definition and study of Laurel was centered in northern Minnesota and the Boundary Waters region, specifically associated with the mound-building complex that flourished in the region. Much of the new work has shifted direction and now is focused upon large-scale excavation of habitation sites in order to collect settlement data, definition of individual households, and regional economic orientations (Rajnovich, Reid, and Shay 1982; Hamilton 1981).

Lugenbeal (1976) proposed that, for the northern Minnesota area at least, variation in Laurel ceramic variation is linked directly to temporal change. Thus, in a region where archaeological deposits amenable to chronometric dating are rare, Laurel assemblages may be provisionally dated in very general terms on the basis of changing proportions of stylistic types of pottery.

This model of temporal change being reflected in the change in relative proportions of ceramic decorative styles has been given added complexity by recent studies in northwestern Ontario. It appears that temporally based stylistic variation is crosscut by ceramic variation which seems to be linked in part to geographic locations. In this line, Reid and Rajnovich (n.d.) offer a model of regional expressions of Laurel ceramic variation which may imply geopolitical divisions within the larger entity of Laurel over its thousand-year duration. Such a model, if borne out, will have very profound implications for the view of Laurel which has been offered here.

Forest/Plains Interaction

Although they are from contexts of questionable or at least uncertain cultural associations, several obsidian artifacts recovered in northwestern Ontario have been tentatively assigned to the Laurel culture (Godfrey-Smith and Haywood 1984:29–35 citing Rajnovich, Reid, and Shay 1982:174). Godfrey-Smith and Haywood (1984) conducted an X-ray florescence spectroscopy (XRF) obsidian source study on some of these finds, and found that four of the five items investigated originated from the Obsidian Cliff locality in Yellowstone National Park, Wyoming. The fifth yielded an XRF spectrum the source of which is unknown but which is consistently associated with the Yellowstone obsidian in other collections from across western Canada (Godfrey-Smith and Haywood 1984:174). These data forcefully indicate that very wide-ranging contacts and exchange networks existed in the prehistoric period (perhaps during Laurel times), which resulted in sporadic appearances of exotic western North American lithics deep in the boreal forest. Equally sporadic recoveries of Knife River flint objects in northwestern Ontario also attest to the occasional availability of these exotic western raw materials.

We can only speculate whether such recoveries of exotic lithics are the product of the famed Hopewellian Interaction Sphere which was contemporaneous with Laurel occupation of the boreal forest (see Mason 1981), or whether the occasional recovery of exotic materials reflects periodic, less formal contacts and "down the line" trade between forest and plains people throughout prehistory.

PREHISTORIC RECORD, A.D. 750

At A.D. 750, Laurel remained the dominant cultural manifestation in the study region (map 5.5) but regionalism was developing in Laurel pottery styles—probably as a result of the difficulty of maintaining contacts across huge areas of the boreal forest. Perhaps the fact that Blackduck began to take form in the southern part of the study area is related to this increasing cultural differentiation.

Northern Minnesota and Northwestern Ontario

For northern Minnesota and adjacent Ontario, two late Laurel phases have been proposed: Smith and Hungry Hall (Lugenbeal 1976:570–81). The Smith phase, characterized by the appearance of Laurel Cordwrapped Stick, is succeeded by Hungry Hall, and both phases are characterized by elevated amounts of the Laurel Dentate and Laurel Punctate types (Lugenbeal 1976:574, 578–80). The nature of the Laurel occupation farther north in Ontario at this time remains uncertain

(Arthurs 1986:139). However, Pilon (1986) has shown that Laurel occupation of the Hudson Bay lowland was very sparse although he (1986: 307, 388) did recover Laurel sherds from a site on the Sachigo River.

Manitoba and Saskatchewan

On the basis of materials from the Lockport and Anderson sites in southeastern Manitoba, Lugenbeal (1976:580) tentatively defined the Anderson phase, characterized by "extremely high percentages of Laurel dentate coupled with substantial amounts of Laurel Cord-wrapped stick and Laurel Punctate" (see also MacNeish 1958:59–61). In west-central Manitoba a Laurel component that dates to this period has been excavated at the Oscar Point site (Kelly and Connell 1978), on the north shore of Lake Winnipegosis. It is noteworthy that this component, dated at 1135 ± 65 B.P. (S-1079 – Dickson 1976:36–37), has

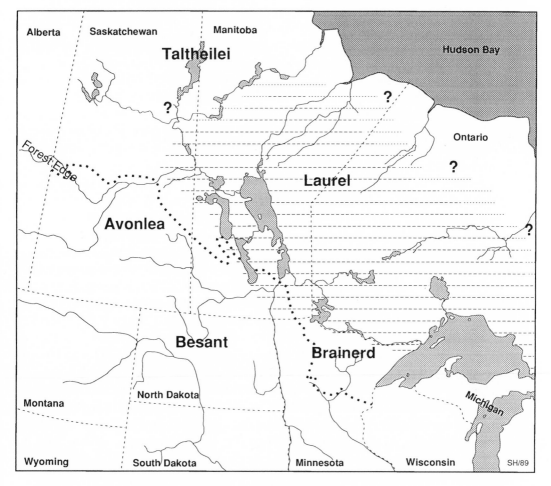

Map 5.5. *Approximate extent of Laurel distribution, ca. A.D. 750.*

yielded rimsherds of a Laurel Pseudo-Scallop Shell type vessel — unexpected in a Laurel assemblage of this period. Laurel components known to be of this age have not been investigated in the more northerly areas of Manitoba, although almost certainly a Laurel occupation was there at this time.

The presence of Laurel in Saskatchewan at this time is evidenced by data from one site in the Nipawin region. Here, at the Peterson Creek site (FhNb-72), is a stratigraphic sequence that includes two superimposed Laurel components. These components have yielded sherds of two vessels of the Laurel Bossed type (Boss and Punctate subtype and Punctate subtype). Two samples of fire-cracked rock from these components have produced thermoluminescence dates of A.D. 810 ± 230 (DUR88TL128–1AS) and A.D. 880 ± 220 (DUR88TL123–1AS). It is unlikely that Laurel was present in the more northerly parts of the Saskatchewan forest at this time. In all probability, peoples with a Taltheilei-related culture continued to occupy the Churchill River system.

At this time, the Avonlea phase was present in the parklands and adjoining grasslands of Saskatchewan. Avonlea assemblages (dating ca. A.D. 200–900) are conventionally known to include a distinctive type of delicate side-notched projectile point as well as consistent styles of pottery vessels (see Vickers this volume). This Avonlea pottery is generally net-impressed on the exterior although some fabric-impressed and smooth-surfaced vessels are also present. Conoidal or bag shapes are characteristic (Byrne 1973:355; see fig. 5.2). This pottery is present in many surface collections in the parklands and northern grasslands, and it is also known from a number of *in situ* components (in both Alberta and Saskatchewan). Indeed, Avonlea components in Saskatchewan regularly produce pottery, sometimes in substantial quantity (e.g., Morgan 1979; Klimko and Hanna 1988; Smith and Walker 1988).

The peoples whose remains we assign to the Avonlea phase were plains bison hunters, skilled at dispatching large numbers of bison in pounds and jumps (Kehoe 1973). However, they also were capable of exercising considerable flexibility in subsistence pursuits, as evidenced by an Avonlea fishing site on Katepwa Lake (map 5.3) in the Qu'Appelle valley (Smith and Walker 1988). This flexibility also is reflected in the degree to which some of these peoples penetrated the edge of the boreal forest — a number of Avonlea components are known in the forests of central Saskatchewan. These include the Yellowsky site (Wilson-Meyer and Carlson 1985) in the west central part of the province (map 5.3) and several sites on the Saskatchewan River toward the eastern side of Saskatchewan (Klimko 1985; Meyer, Klimko, and Finnigan 1988).

These Avonlea components in the edge of the forest contain assemblages much like those of the adjacent parklands and northern grass

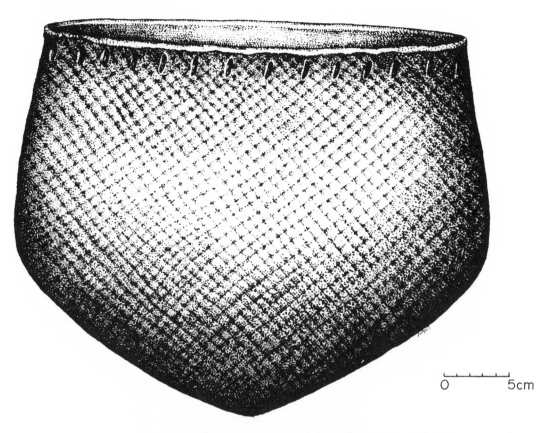

0   5cm

Fig. 5.2. Artist's conception of an Avonlea vessel, based on a partially reconstructed vessel from the Garratt site in south-central Saskatchewan (Morgan 1979). The base is conjectural. (Drawing by Phyllis Lodoen.)

lands, including the distinctive projectile points and net-impressed pottery. As yet the seasonality of this occupation remains uncertain, although the Wallington Flat site in the Nipawin area appears to have been occupied during the spring or early summer.

To the east, in Manitoba, Morgan Tamplin (1977) has identified an Avonlea component at the Pas Reserve site (map 5.3), on the Saskatchewan River. This component appears to contain some Avonlea projectile points; the associated pottery has not been described and illustrated. Farther south, in west-central Manitoba, surface collections from cultivated fields in the Swan River valley (map 5.3) indicate the presence of Avonlea projectile points — sometimes in association with net-impressed pottery (Gryba 1977, 1981; Gary Wowchuk pers. comm.).

Joyes (1988) has reviewed the status of Avonlea materials in Manitoba, noting that "Avonlea seems too poorly represented" and that "assemblages fully comparable to those on the western prairies have not been found" (1988:232). He has proposed a number of related reasons that may account for the paucity of Avonlea on the plains of Manitoba—in particular, the strong presence of a population responsible for the Besant-Sonota materials (see Gregg this volume): "It may simply have been that Avonlea was denied access to southern Manitoba until the Sonota subphase terminated in the Middle Missouri subarea" (Joyes 1988:228).

Forest/Plains Interaction

The aspen parkland zone borders the study area, extending northwestward from Minnesota across Manitoba and Saskatchewan (map 5.2). Given that this parkland zone is transitional between the grasslands and the boreal forest, it is conceivable that forest-adapted groups could have occupied it as an extension of the forest or, vice versa, that grasslands-adapted groups occupied it as an extension of the grasslands. Around A.D. 750 the latter situation characterized most of the study area. In Saskatchewan and western Manitoba, Laurel occupations have not been found in the parklands, but Avonlea and Besant components are common in the parklands and are sometimes present in the edge of the forest. The situation is not so clear in southeastern Manitoba or adjacent northwestern Minnesota; there Laurel components are in the parklands. Given the opportunity, Laurel peoples apparently were willing to leave the forest and exploit the rich seasonal resources (especially bison) of the parklands.

Although the distribution of certain archaeological materials with respect to environmental zones is revealing, the presence of occasional artifacts of one cultural group in components of another provides stronger evidence regarding contact and interaction. In this regard, the occasional recovery of net-impressed pottery in Laurel components is particularly significant. As was noted above, net-impressed vessels are characteristic of Avonlea assemblages in the Saskatchewan parklands and northern grasslands. However, net-impressed pottery also has been recovered in north and central Minnesota, where it is known as "Brainerd Ware" (Lugenbeal 1978, Anfinson 1979:45–50). The characteristics of the cultural phase that contains this ware are uncertain, although at the Gull Lake Dam site in central Minnesota (map 5.3), Johnson (1971:33, 61) believed it to be associated with side-notched projectile points. Vessels with horizontal exterior cord impressions may also be associated (Lugenbeal 1978). Apparently Brainerd ware in northernmost Minnesota was produced during and after the Laurel "withdrawal" from this region and, perhaps, before the development of Blackduck (Anfinson 1979:46).

The similarity between Avonlea and Brainerd net-impressed pottery is striking. This similarity has led Morgan (1979:205–15) to postulate a cultural relationship between Avonlea and certain archaeological remains in west-central Minnesota. Indeed she (1979:220) has argued that Avonlea had its origins in a westward expansion of peoples from the upper Mississippi Valley. This may be the case; if so, components with net-impressed pottery would be continuously distributed northwest from northern Minnesota through the Manitoba parklands and into Saskatchewan. However, as noted above, Avonlea-type projectile points and net-impressed pottery are only weakly represented in southern Manitoba. Despite this discontinuous distribution, it is noteworthy that there is considerable evidence of the interaction of Laurel peoples with peoples making net-impressed pottery in both the southeast and the northwest. In Minnesota, for example, Laurel and Brainerd net-impressed ware were found together at the Dead River site (Michlovic 1979:34), and Lugenbeal (1978:50) has noted them together at the McKinstry Mound 2 site (map 5.3) in northern Minnesota. Moving northwest, MacNeish (1958:171) recovered some net-impressed pottery in the Laurel components at the Lockport site. Lugenbeal (1976: 618–19) has identified this pottery as Brainerd ware.[3] This suggests a co-occupation of northern Minnesota and of southeastern and south-central Manitoba by makers of Laurel and Brainerd potteries. Looking farther to the northwest, along the forest edge, at least two sites in the Swan River valley (map 5.3), west of Lake Winnipegosis, have produced both Laurel and net-impressed (Avonlea) pottery (Gary Wowchuk pers. comm.). These are surface finds in cultivated fields, and the contextual data is lost, but these associations are suggestive. Farther northwest, on the Saskatchewan River in the Nipawin region, two examples of the co-occurrence of Laurel and Avonlea (net-impressed) ceramics have been encountered. Sherds of a Laurel vessel have been recovered from an Avonlea component at the Gravel Pit site (Klimko 1985:112–13), and a Laurel component at the Crown site has yielded sherds of net-impressed vessels (Quigg 1986:197–207).

It is apparent that both in Minnesota and in more northwesterly areas, peoples who made Laurel pottery were interacting (or sharing territory) with contemporaneous peoples who made net-impressed pottery. However, this interaction seems neither to have been intensive nor to have had an extensive cultural impact. Evidence of this interaction is present only on the borders of the Laurel "world"; Avonlea components are not found deep in the forest. Similarly, in Saskatchewan and southwestern Manitoba, Laurel vessels are rare or unknown beyond the forest edge. In contrast to the occasional co-occurrence of Avonlea and Laurel pottery, Besant pottery is not found in such contexts. In particular, Besant pottery might be expected in Laurel compo-

---

[3]In 1988 the senior author examined net-impressed potsherds from more recent excavations at the Lockport site and, unaware of Lugenbeal's identification, considered them to be Avonlea.

nents in the southern edge of the forest of west-central Manitoba where there is a strong Besant presence in the adjacent parklands.

This patterning of avoidance and co-occurrence provides suggestive evidence that the cultural materials recognized as Avonlea, Laurel, and Besant relate to three distinct cultural groups. These groups appear to have been characterized by ethnic boundaries. Across some of these there was little interaction (e.g., Avonlea/Besant, Laurel/Besant); in one case (Avonlea/Laurel), there was a certain amount. The fact that, in southeastern Manitoba and adjacent Minnesota, peoples making Laurel pottery did occupy the parkland and the grassland edge indicates that they were entirely capable of adapting to this new environment. Therefore, it seems that sociopolitical relations must have been a major factor restricting Laurel occupation of southwestern Manitoba and the Saskatchewan parklands. In short, it appears that the occupants of the Saskatchewan grasslands and parklands (Avonlea) and of southwestern Manitoba (Besant), did not allow movement of peoples of Laurel culture into their bison range.

THE PREHISTORIC RECORD, A.D. 1000

Between A.D. 750 and 1000 the Blackduck cultural unit took form in the southern portion of the study area, with Laurel remaining in the north (map 5.6). Indeed it appears that during this time, Laurel attained its most northerly distribution in Manitoba and its most northwesterly extent in Saskatchewan. As has been discussed previously, this was a period of considerably milder climate. Quite possibly subsistence economies were more productive, leading to population increase and, perhaps, territorial expansion. In any case, it is very likely that the appearance and spread of the Blackduck cultural unit, as well as the northern and northwestern expansion of Laurel, is related to this benign climatic episode. (For an overview of Blackduck, see Mason 1981:313–17.)

The Boundary Waters Region

The origin of Blackduck ware has been studied by a number of archaeologists. For example, Evans (1961c:52–53), Dawson (1974:88), Koezur and Wright (1976:22), and Buchner (1982:116; 1979:115–16, 120) have argued that Blackduck developed out of Laurel. In contrast, Wilford (1945:327–29), Hlady (1970), and Syms (1977:106) have argued against continuity between the two. Lugenbeal (1976:628), in a careful, studied review of the relevant data has concluded that the "total ceramic evidence . . . can reasonably, but not compellingly, be interpreted as indicating an *in situ* development of Blackduck ceramics out of Laurel ceramics in northern Minnesota."

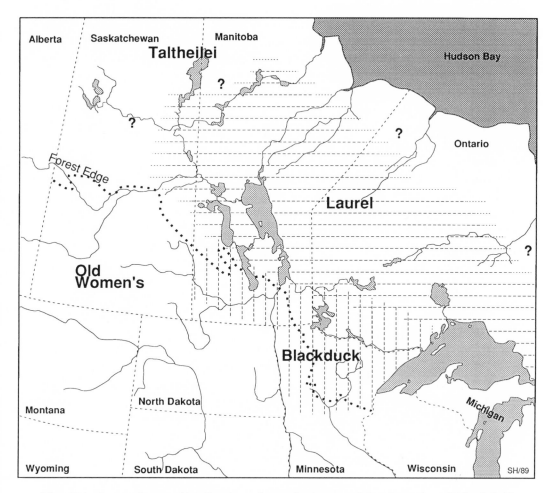

*Map 5.6. Approximate distribution of populations making Laurel and Blackduck
pottery, ca. A.D. 1000.*

The Blackduck cultural unit subsequently expanded north into
Ontario and also into southeastern Manitoba. This expansion either
was at the expense of a resident population that made Laurel pottery or
involved a radical, rapid change in ceramic styles by peoples who were
making Laurel pottery. Around A.D. 1100–1200, Blackduck contracted
northward, out of central Minnesota, and by the early 1200s it seems to
have been superseded in the Boundary Waters region (Arthurs 1986:
225).

Syms (1977:104) has presented this outline of the Blackduck cultural
unit: "The Blackduck Horizon has been identified primarily on the
basis of distinctive decorative traits on thin-walled, globular vessels
with flared rims; however, other traits are small triangular notched
and unnotched projectile points, end and side scrapers, awls, tubular
pipes, occasional unilateral harpoon and socketed bone projectile points,

bone spatulates, fleshers, copper beads and awls, beaver incisor gouges, and burial mounds generally containing seated burials." The rim and neck exteriors of Blackduck vessels are usually elaborately decorated with cord-wrapped tool impressions, often incorporating punctates or bosses (fig. 5.3). The exteriors of the vessels characteristically bear a vertically oriented textile impression. This is considered to have been produced either by a cord-wrapped paddle or by making vessels inside of a textile bag (Lugenbeal 1976:190).

On the basis of his work at the Smith Mound site (map 5.3), Lugenbeal identified an early Blackduck phase, for which he obtained one radiocarbon date: 1020 ± 565 B.P. (Wis. 616). Such early Blackduck components are found not only in the Boundary Waters area but also south into central Minnesota (map 5.6). This southern distribution of Blackduck is a significant departure from the situation of Laurel, which never extended southward into the Mississippi River drainage basin. Given this southerly position, it is perhaps not surprising that Lugenbeal (1976:611, 643), as a result of his comparisons of early

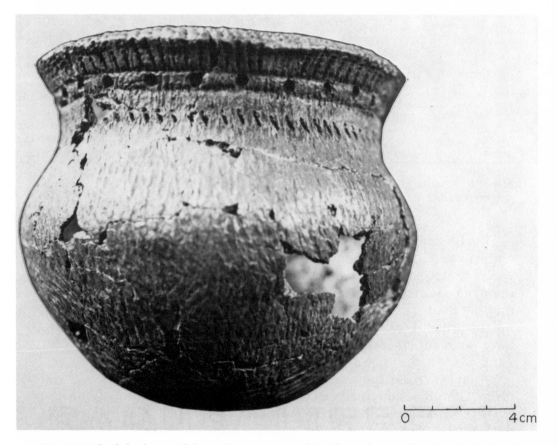

Fig. 5.3. Blackduck vessel from Department of Anthropology collection, Lakehead University, Thunder Bay, Ontario.

Blackduck ceramics with those of neighboring areas, concluded that the "regional affinities of the early Blackduck phase at the Smith site are southern, not eastern or northern" (Lugenbeal 1976:409). Also, employing a wider perspective, he noted that Blackduck is characterized by a number of traits shared with early Late Woodland wares throughout the upper Great Lakes: for example, cord-wrapped tool decoration, globular vessel shape, and manufacture by cord-wrapped paddle and anvil technique (1976:616–17).

The subsistence economies of the Blackduck peoples of the Great Lakes–St. Lawrence forest region and the boreal forest region appear to have been about the same as those described previously for Laurel times.

Southern Manitoba

There is good evidence that, in southeastern Manitoba at this time, the Laurel occupation had ended and that peoples making Blackduck pottery were in residence. This is best evidenced at the Lockport site on the Red River (map 5.3), where a long stratigraphic sequence and a battery of radiocarbon dates have led Buchner (1988:29) to conclude that the Laurel occupation ended about A.D. 800. The early presence of Blackduck in this part of Manitoba is also evidenced farther south on the Red River, at the Lord site (map 5.3) which has yielded a date of 1170 ± 90 B.P. (S-652) (Syms 1977:102).

In the period A.D. 750–1000, Blackduck culture expanded westward across the plains of southern Manitoba. Here, several Blackduck sites are present along the Assiniboine and Pembina rivers (Syms 1977:103), including a major Blackduck occupation at the Stott site (Tisdale 1978; Hamilton et al. 1981; Badertscher et al., 1987; see map 5.3). Significantly, the Blackduck occupation at this site seems to have occurred in two main periods, around A.D. 800–900 and around A.D. 1100–1200 (Tisdale 1978:100; Badertscher, Roberts, and Zoltai 1987:332).

Northern Ontario, Manitoba and Saskatchewan

It is increasingly apparent that, at least until A.D. 1100, a population making Laurel ware continued to occupy much of the boreal forest in the study area (map 5.6). For instance, Reid and Rajnovich (n.d.) have obtained Laurel dates of 710 ± 45 B.P. (DIC-2876), 710 ± 65 B.P. (DIC-2884), and 680 ± 55 B.P. (DIC-2885) from the Ballynacree site, at the north end of Lake of the Woods (map 5.3). Less firm is a date of 710 ± 175 B.P. (S-6811) from a site on the Wabinosh River near Lake Nipigon (Dawson 1981:39), but Dawson (1981:42) also argues for the presence of Laurel in northern Ontario until A.D. 900–1200. Similarly, there is evidence of late Laurel occupation in northern Manitoba. For instance, the Notigi Lake site (map 5.3), has produced sherds representing eleven Laurel vessels (Wiersum and Tisdale 1977:36–53). Two radiocarbon dates have been obtained relating to this component: 1200 ± 130 B.P. (S-746) and 920 ± 150 B.P. (S-744 — Wiersum and Tisdale 1977:18).

In Saskatchewan, Laurel vessels have been recovered from sites on the Saskatchewan, Sturgeon-Weir, Churchill, and Reindeer rivers (Meyer 1983a) — a total of thirty-three known occurrences. Given the pioneering nature of Laurel studies in this province, our understanding of this occupation remains limited. While Saskatchewan Laurel is sometimes difficult to relate to the Laurel typology of the Boundary Waters region, it is noteworthy that Pseudo–Scallop-Shell-impressed vessels have not been recovered from Saskatchewan. As well, dentate impressed vessels are very well represented, and the Laurel Punctate type is not uncommon. One or two cord-wrapped tool-impressed vessels have also been recovered, but Laurel Bossed is rare. On the whole, Laurel pottery in Saskatchewan exhibits a constellation of late decorative attributes (Meyer 1983a:20, 22). This observation is supported by two dates from the Nipawin study area. Here, a Laurel vessel has been recovered in an Avonlea component dated at 815 ± 135 B.P. (S-2355 — Klimko 1985:105), and a Laurel component at the Crown site has yielded two dates: 645 ± 70 B.P. (S-2527) and 785 ± 155 B.P. (S-2555 — Quigg 1986:32).

Forest/Plains Interaction

The Stott Site is the best known of several sites in southwestern Manitoba that contain associations of cultural debris that appear to reflect influences from both the plains and the forest. Stott remains the most important because it is one of the few subjected to considerable excavation and publication (MacNeish 1954; Tisdale 1978; Syms 1977; Hamilton et al. 1981; Badertscher, Roberts, and Zoltai 1987).

The Stott site is a large and complex site located on several valley terraces along the Assiniboine River in the aspen parkland zone. It is notable for its preponderance of Blackduck ceramics mixed with a range of projectile points classed as Late Plains and Prairie side-notched and triangular (Kehoe 1966). On this theme, Nicholson (1987: 50–53) also comments on the general mixing and melding of late side-notched point styles into the forest which he interprets as reflecting contact and social interchange between the forest and the plains.

The Stott site is also notable for its dense deposition of faunal debris, most of which is bison (Hamilton et al. 1981; Badertscher, Roberts, and Zoltai 1987) — consistent with a big-game hunting economy generally associated with the northern Plains. Lithic debitage recovered from some localities indicates heavy reliance on Knife River flint, which was obtained by quarrying expeditions to the western Dakotas or by trade and exchange with Plains groups to the south (Hamilton 1982).

The presence at the Stott site of a minority of ceramic vessels decorated with conventional motifs but using unconventional incising techniques is also noteworthy (Hamilton 1982). This incising technique, encountered frequently on Plains wares, is rather rare on Woodland ceramics. The co-occurrence of a higher-than-usual incidence of decorative incising on pottery, a plains-style economic orientation based upon bison hunting, and comparatively high recoveries of Knife River flint debitage suggests considerable contact and influence from the plains on this southwestern fringe Blackduck. This also attests to the considerable social and economic flexibility of prehistoric populations in responding to local ecological and social situations.

THE PREHISTORIC RECORD, A.D. 1250

Northwestern Ontario and Southern Manitoba

As noted above, it appears likely that Blackduck took form in the Boundary Waters area. From there, like the preceding Laurel distribution (Lugenbeal 1976:591–92), it eventually spread eastward along the northern shores of Lake Superior as far as northern Michigan (map 5.7). However, as has been discussed, Blackduck also expanded southward into central Minnesota and westward across the Manitoba plains, well beyond the limits of the Laurel distribution.

The northward expansion of Blackduck was relatively limited. In Manitoba, components dominated by Blackduck pottery are present only up to the northern end of Lake Winnipeg and into the adjacent Saskatchewan River delta. Farther north in Manitoba, and northwest into Saskatchewan, Blackduck occurrences are scattered and rare. In northwestern Ontario the northern expansion also seems to have been limited, although this interpretation may be a function of limited archaeological survey activity. Certainly, Pilon (1986) has shown that Blackduck is very rare in the Hudson Bay lowland. Indeed the Blackduck rim sherds that he has identified from the Severn River relate to a very unusual, even idiosyncratic, vessel (Pilon 1986:173, 388). In any case, at A.D. 1250, Blackduck appears to have been in place throughout the region extending from western Manitoba to eastern Lake Superior (map 5.7). According to Syms (1975:18), Blackduck in southern Manitoba dates through to the mid-1400s, and some archaeologists have posited an even later Blackduck occupation in northwestern Ontario (Dawson 1975:34, 1977:73, 1987:157–60; Arthurs 1986:226; Syms 1977:101).

Northern Manitoba

At A.D. 1250, the mild climatic conditions of the preceding century and a half were drawing to a close. Just as this milder period seems to have

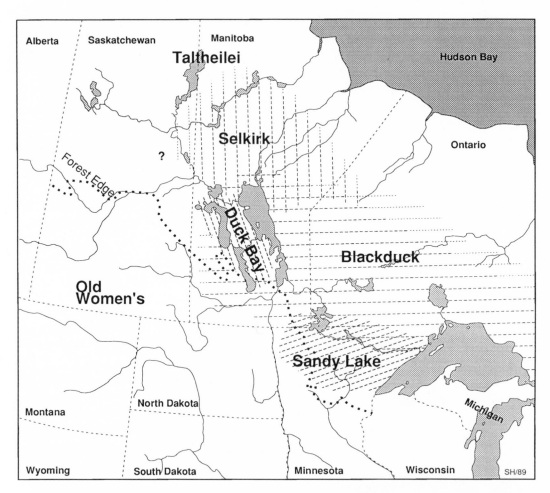

Map 5.7. *Approximate distribution of Selkirk, Blackduck, Duck Bay, and Sandy Lake cultural materials, ca. A.D. 1250.*

stimulated Blackduck developments, so too, we see the beginnings of Selkirk at this time. As has been noted, around A.D. 1000, a population in northern Manitoba, Saskatchewan, and Ontario continued to make Laurel pottery. Given this situation, it has been argued that Selkirk developed in the boreal forest of central or northern Manitoba around A.D. 1100, and that the population involved was the same one that had continued to make Laurel pottery there (Rajnovich 1983:52–59; Meyer and Russell 1987:24). By A.D. 1250, peoples making Selkirk pottery are thought to have occupied an area extending from the Churchill River in northern Manitoba southeastward into northwestern Ontario (map 5.7). The occupation of northern Saskatchewan at this time is uncertain—unless by a population that continued to make Laurel pottery.

Selkirk vessels generally are globular with constricted necks and excurvate rims (fig. 5.4). Very characteristic is the smoothed fabric impression present over the whole of the vessel exteriors. The nonceramic portion of the assemblages is very similar to that described above for Blackduck. Two major variations in Selkirk are recognized: (1) a northern tier found from the forests of western Saskatchewan east to northern Lake Superior, and (2) a southern expression which is present in southeastern Manitoba and adjacent Ontario and Minnesota (Meyer and Russell 1987:21).

Although there are not a large number of Selkirk dates, Selkirk does appear to be earliest in north-central Manitoba, where it dates from at least A.D. 1100 (Meyer and Russell 1987:13, 15). A number of researchers would accept beginning dates as early as A.D. 850 (e.g., Dickson 1980:150). Selkirk assemblages in neighboring regions have produced later dates. For instance, Selkirk sites in the Nipawin area of eastern Saskatchewan date no earlier than the late A.D. 1300s (Meyer and Russell 1987:17). Similar dates have been obtained for Selkirk in southeastern Manitoba and adjacent Ontario (Rajnovich 1983:54).

Fig. 5.4. Selkirk vessel from the Bushfield West site in east-central Saskatchewan. (Photograph courtesy of Terry Gibson.)

The subsistence-settlement patterns characteristic of Selkirk populations are not well understood. Most archaeological work has been concentrated on the largest, most prolific sites — those occupied in the spring and early summer. Such sites, whether on Southern Indian Lake or the Saskatchewan River, appear to have been chosen as locations at which fish spawning runs could be intercepted, providing food for large gatherings of the local population. Dispersal into smaller groups for the remainder of the year (particularly the winter) seems likely.

Central Manitoba

Centered on the Lake Winnipegosis region, an unusual set of archaeological remains makes its appearance about this time. These are characterized by Duck Bay ware. Duck Bay vessels have straight or S-shaped rims set on angular necks and angular shoulders. These shoulders, which Snortland-Coles (1979:28) describes as "sharply angled," are sometimes decorated. The vessel exteriors bear a smoothed fabric impression. Three types of Duck Bay ware have been recognized (Hanna 1982:4–5). The most common and distinctive is Duck Bay Punctate ware (fig. 5.5). According to Hanna (1978:3) it has "minimally three rows of punctates on the rim exterior. When additional rows are present these continue onto the shoulder and in some instances onto the body of the vessel" (quoted in Hanna 1982:4). The next most common type is Duck Bay Notched Lip, which is "characterized by shallow closely spaced punctates on the rim interior, extending onto the lip" (Hanna 1982:5). The least common type is Duck Bay Undecorated, which "maintains the overall vessel shape characteristic of the ware but lacks decoration" (Hanna 1982:5).

Duck Bay ware is best known from excavations at the Aschkibokan site which occupies an island in Duck Bay on the west side of Lake Winnipegosis. Here, portions of 410 vessels were recovered. Duck Bay ware occurs at a number of other sites on Lakes Winnipegosis and Manitoba, but none has an equally high percentage (47 percent) of the Duck Bay Punctate type. However, such a site has been examined on the west shore of Lake Winnipeg, some 145 kilometers west of the Aschkibokan site. As Snortland-Coles (1979:51) has noted: "Using Syms' (1976, 1977) Co-influence Sphere Model, the Manitoba Lowlands may have been the 'core' area of the makers of Duck Bay pottery while sites outside of this region represent seasonal (or other) movements into tertiary or secondary territories." Indeed, occasional Duck Bay Punctate vessels have been found as far afield as Drinking Falls (map 5.3) on the Churchill River (fig. 5.5) in northern Saskatchewan (Brace and Dyck 1978:11) and the Rainy River in northern Minnesota (Stoltman 1973:127).

The large amount of faunal remains recovered in the course of excavations at the Aschkibokan site indicate that a major fishery was

Fig. 5.5. Duck Bay vessel from the Drinking Falls site on the Churchill River, northern Saskatchewan. (Photograph courtesy Saskatchewan Museum of Natural History.)

operated here, primarily in the spring, but possibly in the fall as well. Numbers of moose and beaver also were taken, as were a few caribou. Waterfowl were well represented in the faunal recoveries (Snortland-Coles 1979:117–19). The time span of Duck Bay is not well established. Indeed, there are only two accepted radiocarbon dates, both from the Aschkibokan site: 695 ± 175 B.P. (GX-5516) and 770 ± 110 B.P. (GX-5517 — Hanna 1982:5).

The Aschkibokan site also yielded a number of Blackduck vessels, and it has been noted that most other Duck Bay sites also yield some Blackduck pottery (Snortland-Coles 1979:48). There has been some discussion among archaeologists about whether Duck Bay is more closely related to Blackduck or to Selkirk. Snortland-Coles (1979:51) suggests that "Duck Bay pottery developed out of Blackduck and was made by the same group, becoming more common later in the Late Woodland Period." Arthurs (1986:228), however, considers Duck Bay more closely related to Selkirk ware than to Blackduck. Indeed the angular and sometimes decorated shoulders of the Duck Bay vessels are traits shared with Selkirk ware (Pehonan complex) to the northwest (Meyer 1981b). Similarly, the emphasis on decoration of the rim and neck exterior with punctate rows is reminiscent of Selkirk ware to the north.

Northern Minnesota and the Boundary Waters

By A.D. 1250, peoples who made a kind of pottery known as Sandy Lake ware ranged as far north as the Boundary Waters region (map 5.7). Sandy

Lake ware is characteristic of the Wanikan culture (Birk 1977), first described by Cooper and Johnson (1964). In central Minnesota the Wanikan culture replaced Blackduck, beginning about A.D. 1100 (Arthurs 1986:225). Sandy Lake vessels have simple, globular shapes with slight neck constrictions and nonexistent shoulders (see Gibbon this volume). Rims are usually straight or slightly S-shaped. Decoration is sparse, generally consisting only of notches on the inner corner of the lip, although trailed lines also occur (Michlovic 1983:25). The exteriors are usually vertically cord impressed, although smooth exteriors are not uncommon. In the southern portion of its range, Sandy Lake ware is characteristically shell tempered although a minority of grit-tempered vessels are present. On the northern extremity of its distribution, Sandy Lake vessels are almost always grit tempered (Arthurs 1978:59).

Forest/Plains Interaction

On the Saskatchewan plains at this time were peoples who made projectile points of the Prairie side-notched type as well as a considerable amount of fairly low quality pottery. These assemblages generally have not been awarded a phase definition, although the senior author (1988) has suggested that they be assigned to the Old Women's phase (see Vickers this volume). On the basis of present information, the distribution of this archaeological material north into the forest edge of Saskatchewan and west-central Manitoba appears to be much more limited than was true of Avonlea. For instance, only one such component (Finnigan, Meyer, and Prentice 1983:141) has been found in the large Nipawin study area. Of course, as has been noted, it is not even certain what cultural unit was present in the central Saskatchewan forests during this time.

However, to the south is evidence of Blackduck interaction with Plains peoples. For instance, a Blackduck vessel is represented at the Lebret site (map 5.3), in the Qu'appelle valley of southern Saskatchewan (B. Smith 1986:149). Similarly, Blackduck pottery has been recorded from the James River in southeastern North Dakota (Schneider 1982a) and a vessel has been reported from western North Dakota (Ahler, Lee, and Falk 1981). Indeed, Blackduck has been considered to have had an important influence on cultural developments in southern Saskatchewan (Dyck 1983:126–29). The introduction of Prairie side-notched points to the latter region, as well as pottery with vertically oriented textile impressions on the exterior, may relate to Blackduck contacts.

THE SITUATION, A.D. 1500

Northern Manitoba and Saskatchewan

Between A.D. 1250 and A.D. 1500, Selkirk appears to have expanded to the west, east, and southeast out of northern Manitoba (map 5.8).

Remarkably, this expansion occurred during a period of very cool climatic conditions. By A.D. 1500, Selkirk had become well established on the Churchill River system in Saskatchewan. Although the pottery of the latter system is very similar to that of adjacent northern Manitoba, Selkirk in the Saskatchewan River valley exhibits a number of features that appear to reflect influence from cultural groups on the parklands and grasslands. These include angular rims and shoulders, decorated shoulders, and occasional S-shaped rims (Meyer 1981b). Millar (1983) has described similar Selkirk materials from the headwaters of the Churchill River.

Central Manitoba

The situation in central Manitoba at this time is not certain. However, it must be noted that Selkirk components are present to the east, north, and northwest of the Lake Winnipegosis region but are rare or absent in the latter area (Meyer and Russell 1987:25). In all likelihood, Selkirk occupation did not extend into the Lake Winnipegosis region because peoples making Duck Bay ware continued to reside there.

Southeastern Manitoba, Northwestern Ontario, and Northern Minnesota

Well before A.D. 1500, Selkirk also appeared in southeastern Manitoba, adjacent Ontario, and northernmost Minnesota—forming southern tier Selkirk. Southern tier Selkirk vessels are frequently undecorated, although some vessels bear cord-wrapped tool decorations which appear to be simplified versions of Blackduck motifs (MacNeish 1958:167, Rajnovich 1983:40). In northernmost Minnesota, Selkirk occurs mainly in the vicinity of wild rice stands (Arthurs 1986:263; Evans 1961c: 143–44). Arthurs (1986:263) has speculated that this may relate to "the limited penetration of northern Minnesota by Selkirk or related groups, on wild-rice harvesting expeditions."

Between A.D. 1250 and 1500, it appears that some peoples making Blackduck ware continued to occupy portions of northwestern Ontario. Contacts between the makers of Blackduck and Selkirk wares appear to have been extensive because many components contain mixtures of both wares and, as noted above, there was much borrowing of decorative features (Buchner 1979:120–21).

Although centered on the northern half of Minnesota (Anfinson 1979:177), it appears that by A.D. 1500, peoples making Sandy Lake ware had extended their range well into northwestern Ontario and southeastern Manitoba (Participants of the Lake Superior Basin Workshop 1988:49–56). Given this distribution (map 5.8), it would be expected that these peoples came into contact with northerners making Selkirk pottery. It is not surprising, therefore, that there are a number of

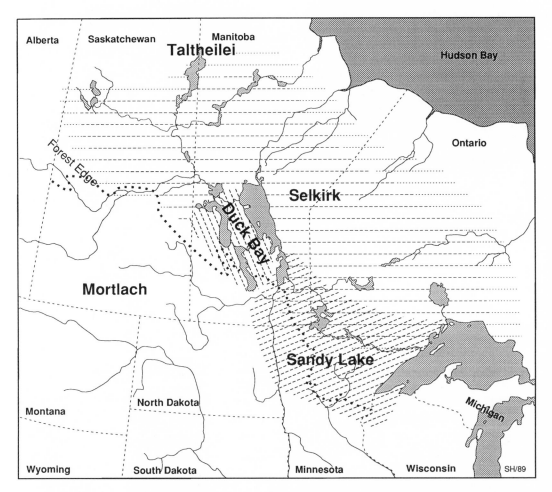

Map 5.8. Approximate distribution of Selkirk, Duck Bay, and Sandy Lake cultural materials, ca. A.D. 1500.

similarities between southern Selkirk ware and Sandy Lake ware. Arthurs (1986:264) noted: "A small number of Sandy Lake rims from the Boundary Waters and Lake of the Woods area (including one vessel from the Long Sault site), share certain attributes with Selkirk ceramics. Most notable are the few Sandy Lake vessels with fabric impressed surfaces." It is possible that these similarities are the result of contact and attribute borrowing, but the idea that there may be a cultural relationship between Sandy Lake and Selkirk must also be considered. Because of these similarities, some ceramics originally identified as Selkirk have now been identified as Sandy Lake. For instance, the "Selkirk" pottery from the Wanipigow Lake site (Saylor 1976, 1977) has been identified as Sandy Lake (Snortland-Coles pers. comm.; Participants of the Lake Superior Basin Workshop 1988:50).

Plains/Forest Interaction

In southern Saskatchewan at this time was a population whose archaeological remains have been assigned to the Mortlach "aggregate" (Joyes 1973, Syms 1977:125–26). In the parkland-grassland interface in Saskatchewan is considerable evidence of interaction of the latter peoples with northerners who made Selkirk pottery. For instance, the senior author has noted a number of Selkirk vessels in Mortlach phase components in this region (1984:44–45). Similarly, Mortlach phase vessels are sometimes recovered from Selkirk sites in the southern edge of the forest—as has been noted at sites in the Nipawin region (Meyer 1984).

In southwestern Manitoba at this time, Syms (1977:140) has also documented the presence of features in the regional pottery that are considered to reflect forest influences. These include fabric-impressed vessel exteriors. Selkirk is considered the likely origin of this influence, but Duck Bay, just to the north, is also a likely candidate. It is noteworthy that although Selkirk is very well represented in the boreal forest, right to edge of the parklands, expansion out of the forest was very limited (as was true of Duck Bay). The exception in this regard is the strong presence of Selkirk in the parklands and grasslands of the Red River valley of southwestern Manitoba. Given its general restriction to the forest, it is striking that Selkirk influence on northern Plains cultures was so extensive.

Ethnic Identifications

At A.D. 1500, therefore, the occupants of the study area made Selkirk, Duck Bay, and Sandy Lake ware. It cannot be assumed that each of these three archaeological manifestations equals a particular cultural group; however, it is likely that a large proportion of the individuals who produced a particular ware were members of the same cultural group (see also Dawson 1987:164–65).

Sandy Lake was produced in the northeastern Plains and adjacent forest regions in the Late Prehistoric/Protohistoric periods. As such, it generally has been identified with the Siouans who occupied this region protohistorically and were present at the time of European contact (Rackerby 1975; Michlovic 1983). It has been suggested that the more northerly Sandy Lake ceramics may have been produced by the ancestors of the most northerly branch of these Siouans—the Assiniboines (Arthurs 1986:263–64). On the other hand, Assiniboines are known to have occupied the parkland and southern boreal forest as far west as eastern Saskatchewan by the late 1690s (Doughty and Martin 1929, Russell 1982). Given this situation, a broader distribution of Sandy Lake ware to the west might be expected, and the fact that some

Sandy Lake ceramics in this region may have been misidentified as Selkirk or Duck Bay supports the possibility.

Selkirk ware appears to have been made across the boreal forest through to the time of European contact in the late 1600s and early 1700s. Because the occupants at this time were northern Algonquians (mainly the direct ancestors of the Crees), these peoples are identified, on the whole, with the Selkirk materials (Wright 1971:23–24, Meyer and Russell 1987:25–26). The identification of Duck Bay presents some problems, but it is thought to be the product of an Algonquian group (Meyer and Russell 1987:26). (For northwestern Ontario, Dawson [1987] has presented an alternate interpretation of protohistoric boreal forest ethnic groupings – including the major presence of Ojibwa.)

DISCUSSION AND SUMMARY

To demonstrate the broad sweep of cultural development and population interaction during the period A.D. 500–1500, this culture-history overview has concentrated on changing pottery styles. During the Laurel and Blackduck periods the Boundary Waters region was a cultural "heartland" in which new styles arose and then were passed along to the hinterlands. The cultural complexity of this heartland is also evidenced by the presence of burial mounds, the diversity of pottery styles, and the relatively high quality of most of the pottery. This apparent cultural intensification in the heartland probably was related to a relatively large and dense population characterized by greater social organizational complexity than more northerly populations of the times. The establishment and maintenance of this population was dependent upon a productive subsistence economy based in the bountiful environment of the northern edge of the Great Lakes–St. Lawrence forest. However, the expansion of middle period Laurel and, subsequently, of Blackduck peoples out of this heartland and northwest through Manitoba was very likely related to the presence of the Manitoba lowlands. This boreal forest region shares many biotic and physical characteristics with the Boundary Waters region.

It is noteworthy that the somewhat tentative occupation of the southeastern Manitoba parklands during Laurel times was followed by a major expansion westward across the Manitoba plains during the Blackduck period. If this Blackduck population was descended from the earlier Laurel population of the region, we may speculate that the Blackduck expansion was a logical result of a plains adaptation perfected by their ancestors.

In contrast to Laurel and Blackduck, Selkirk was not focused on the Boundary Waters and Manitoba lowlands regions, although it extended into these latter regions. Rather, it had a stronger presence in northern Manitoba and is found much farther to the west in northern Saskatchewan than either Laurel or Blackduck. Throughout Selkirk times, peoples making Duck Bay pottery continued to occupy Lakes Winnipegosis and Manitoba while peoples making Sandy Lake pottery clearly became major occupants of the parklands and environs of southeastern Manitoba and adjacent Minnesota and Ontario.

Interaction of the forest peoples with the occupants of the plains is evident throughout the period under consideration. There was Laurel occupation of the parklands in northwestern Minnesota and adjacent Manitoba, and here, as well as to the northwest along the forest edge, is considerable evidence of Laurel interaction with peoples who made net-impressed pottery. Subsequently, a population making Blackduck pottery occupied most of the plains of southern Manitoba. As might be expected, interaction with neighboring plains groups was extensive, and it has been argued that Blackduck influenced the cultural makeup of the Old Women's phase of southern Saskatchewan. Similarly, plains influences have been noted in Blackduck pottery, subsistence, and perhaps lithic technology. Selkirk (like Duck Bay) appears to have had extensive influence on Plains cultures, especially the Mortlach phase of southern Saskatchewan — although Selkirk pottery in the forests of central Saskatchewan also exhibits influence from Mortlach. In addition, Selkirk traits have been noted in southwestern Manitoba pottery.

The relationship of Selkirk and Sandy Lake, which overlapped in southeastern Manitoba and adjacent Ontario and Minnesota, is just beginning to be outlined. A good deal of exchange of ideas occurred between these groups. Considering the protohistoric distribution of Selkirk and Sandy Lake in relation to the distribution of Indian groups at the time of first contact, it seems very likely that Selkirk is the product of northern Algonquians, including those who became known as Crees in the historic period. Similarly, Sandy Lake is considered to relate to Siouans, with at least some of the more northerly materials being made by the ancestors of the historically known Assiniboines.

CHAPTER 6

CULTURES OF THE UPPER MISSISSIPPI RIVER VALLEY AND ADJACENT PRAIRIES IN IOWA AND MINNESOTA

Guy Gibbon

CULTURAL developments in the Eastern Woodlands are frequently cited as a stimulus for the appearance of new traits in the prairies and plains to the west. Perhaps the most frequently mentioned are Woodland pottery, burial mounds, and the horticulturally based village lifeway. In addition the Eastern Woodlands are widely regarded as a primary source of new peoples, such as the Sioux and Cheyenne, who each in their own way contributed substantially to Plains culture. In this chapter cultural developments in the upper Mississippi River Valley between A.D. 500 and 1500 are reviewed and an assessment is made of their impact on contemporary peoples living on the adjacent prairies to the west in Iowa and Minnesota.

The traditional definition of the upper Mississippi River Valley is that stretch of the valley between the junction of the Illinois and Mississippi rivers and the headwaters of the Mississippi in Lake Itasca, Minnesota. This stretch of some 1,280 kilometers (800 miles) is separated here into two cultural-environmental review areas, a southern, eventually occupied by horticulturists, and a northern occupied by wild rice harvesters. Although cultural developments in these two areas were not unrelated, a division based on differences in subsistence emphasis is a useful organizational device for our purposes. A convenient separation between these areas is a northwest-southeast line running from Lake Traverse at the headwaters of the Red River to Minneapolis–St. Paul (map 6.1).

SOUTHERN HORTICULTURISTS

At historic contact the southern section of the upper Mississippi Valley was a resource-rich gallery forest bordered by rolling upland prairies from the Illinois River juncture northward to the Driftless Area. To the north the river flows through stream-dissected terrain, including the heavily dissected Driftless Area, which was covered by southern deciduous hardwood forest interspersed with extensive prairie openings (Anfinson 1990; Conrad 1952; Curtis 1959; H. E. Wright 1968). For convenience, the culture history of this southern area of the upper

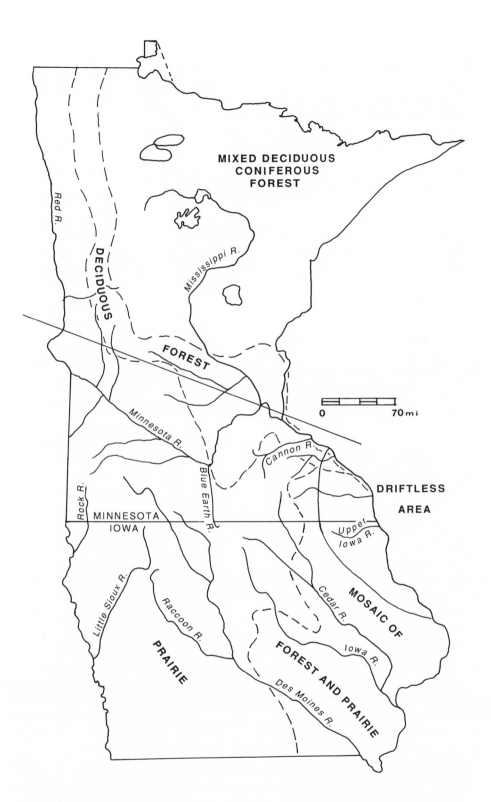

MIXED DECIDUOUS
CONIFEROUS
FOREST

Red R.

DECIDUOUS

Mississippi R.

FOREST

Minnesota R.

Cannon R.

DRIFTLESS
AREA

Rock R.

Blue Earth R.

MINNESOTA
IOWA

Upper
Iowa R.

0   70 mi

Little Sioux R.

Raccoon R.

Cedar R.

Iowa R.

MOSAIC OF

PRAIRIE

FOREST AND PRAIRIE

Des Moines R.

Map 6.1. Major vegetation regions in Iowa and Minnesota just before Euro-American settlement.

Valley is divided into three topical periods: Late Woodland and Emergent Mississippian (A.D. 500–900), Mississippian Expansion (A.D. 900–1200), and Mississippian Decline and Oneota Expansion (A.D. 1200–1500). The temporal divisions used here are only meant to be approximate, for different authors cite different dates for the same phenomena and some major events occurred at different times in different areas.

Late Woodland and Emergent Mississippian: A.D. 500–900

Until recently Late Woodland complexes in this area of the upper Valley have received little sustained interest (map 6.2). In fact they have often been regarded as rather drab, degenerate derivatives of earlier Havana-Hopewell complexes (Green 1986:22). These complexes are composed of components containing (earlier) Linn and (later) Madison ware in the north and (earlier) Weaver and (later) Maples Mills ceramics in the south.

The attitude toward these "good grey cultures" gradually changed with the shift in North American archaeology from a necessary concern with taxonomic problems to the more explicitly anthropological tasks of, for example, reconstructing social organizations, settlement-subsistence systems, and population sizes. Rather than "degenerate," the Late Woodland period in the deciduous forests and prairies of the upper Valley is now considered a dynamic period that witnessed a series of gradual but profound cultural changes. Among the most important of these were: an increase in numbers of camps, villages, and burial mounds; tighter packing of populations resulting in territory allocations; a spread of populations into more varied environments and greater exploitation of upland resources; the development of significant regional differences in local group size and complexity; an increase in sedentism in some areas; increasing dependence on cultivated starchy and oily seed plants, including maize; an intensification of aquatic resource (fish and mussel) harvesting in some areas; technological refinements in pottery vessels that increased their efficiency for boiling, storing, and processing food; and adoption of the bow and arrow. Although the causes of these changes remain speculative, they are thought to be interrelated responses to population growth, increased demand for food resources, the opportunistic appropriation of diffusing traits, and, perhaps, climatic amelioration (the moister Sub-Atlantic climatic episode). For reviews and studies of the Late Woodland period in this section of the upper Valley, see David W. Benn (1978, 1979, 1980), Melvin L. Fowler and Robert L. Hall (1978); William Green (1986), Harold Hassen (1985), W. D. Logan (1976), Stanley Riggle (1981), James B. Stoltman (1983), and James L. Theler (1987). Extensive cultural resource management (CRM) surveys throughout the Mississippi Valley are adding rapidly to our knowledge of this period as well (e.g.,

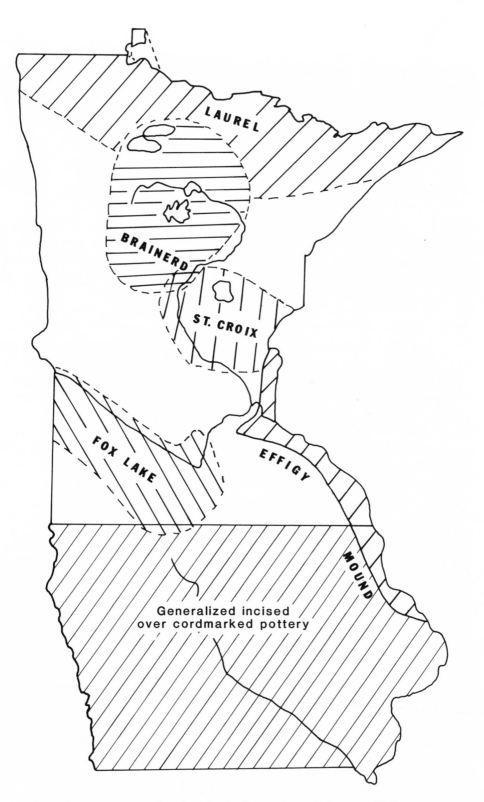

Map 6.2. Core areas of archaeological complexes in Iowa and Minnesota, ca. A.D. 650–800.

Barnhardt et al. 1983; Benn, Bettis, and Vogel 1988; Boszhardt and
Overstreet 1983; Hotopp 1977; Penman 1984).

A somewhat similar Late Woodland pattern of intensification of
natural and horticultural resources has been documented for portions
of the Illinois River valley (e.g., Ford 1977, 1979) and central Iowa (Benn
1981a, 1981b, 1982b, 1983), and for the heavily forested North Ma-
quoketa River valley in northeastern Jones County, Iowa (Benn 1980);
the discovery of maize in association with Late Woodland Madison
ware ceramics at the Nelson site near Mankato may indicate the
presence of this pattern in south-central Minnesota, too (Scullin 1981).
Not all resource-rich habitat zones in the upper Valley were "packed"
with Late Woodland populations, however, as the La Crosse area of
Wisconsin and the Red Wing area of Minnesota demonstrate, and not all
areas of the prairies—the prairie lake zone, for instance—participated
fully in these developments (Anfinson 1987). In addition settlement-
subsistence shifts in at least some upland headwaters areas in the
prairie peninsula show a different pattern of adjustment to changing
social and biophysical conditions than that suggested above for the
relatively densely settled large valleys of the Mississippi and Illinois
rivers (Green 1987).

Was the relationship between parallel developments in the upper
Valley and the western prairies a dependent one? It is clear that some
elements of, for example, ceramic technology did diffuse westward. For
instance, the distinguishing trait of ceramics in the late Late Woodland
period is single cord-impressed decoration in geometric patterns. This
pan-midwestern phenomenon, represented in western Illinois by Maples Mills Cord-Impressed and in Wisconsin and southeastern Minnesota by Madison ware, and earlier by Lane Farm Cord-Impressed in the
Driftless Area and south along the Mississippi River Valley, seems to
have rapidly penetrated Iowa (Madison, Minotts, and Maple Mills Cord
Impressed), southwestern Minnesota (Lake Benton ware), and the Plains
(Loseke ware; see Anfinson 1979b, 1987; Benn 1978, 1979, 1980, 1981b,
1982a, 1982b; Benn and Thompson 1977; Hudak 1983; Logan 1976;
Morgan 1985; Perry 1987; Tiffany 1986b). Nonetheless, Benn (1983:85)
argues, and I think correctly, that the developments that occurred
during the Late Woodland are more convincingly understood as inter-
nally generated responses to "the increased productive output that
followed the shift from gathering to collecting to harvesting; intermittent population growth; multiplying interpersonal relations; and historical events."

To the south of our review area in the American bottoms, trends
similar to those discussed above were occurring at about the same
time. These trends include the introduction of the bow and arrow,
changes in ceramic technology, population increases, the appearance of
nucleated villages (ca. A.D. 600), and economic dependence on maize

agriculture (ca. A.D. 800). In addition there is evidence of large-scale trade networks and an increasing emphasis on hierarchical social organization (Kelly 1987; Emerson 1991a). But different processes were occurring, too, that herald major changes in the upper Valley and western prairies during the subsequent A.D. 900–1200 period. These processes resulted in the emergence between A.D. 800 and 1000 of the new sociocultural system we recognize as Mississippian. Since "virtually nothing is known about the regional effects of this Emergent Mississippian stage" (Emerson 1991a), we will confine our discussion of the impact of American bottoms–based Mississippian cultures on the upper Valley and western prairies to the following two sections.

Mississippian Expansion and Decline: A.D. 900–1200

A major transformation occurred in our review area during the three centuries from A.D. 900 to 1200. This transformation involved in part the "mississippianization" of the upper Valley and western prairies, with Mississippian settlements or settlements most strongly influenced by Mississippian culture largely confined to the upper Valley, and Plains Village and Oneota villages distributed throughout the prairie province to the west (map 6.3). Although site descriptions and transformation/developmental models are relatively abundant, the specific mechanisms involved in this transformation and the nature of the relationships between communities in the American bottoms, in the upper Valley, and in the prairies to the west remain subjects of debate. In this section evidence of Mississippian expansion up the Mississippi Valley is reviewed first followed by a review of the emergence of complexes in the prairies to the west.

The origins of the Emergent Mississippian stage are rooted in the same processes that led to the development of complex societies throughout the Mississippi River Valley to the south of the American bottoms and in the Southeast by A.D. 800–1000 or earlier (for recent summaries, see Emerson and Lewis 1991, Milner 1990, and Smith 1986). Although discussion has focused on the expansion and impact of classic, fully developed Mississippian culture (the Lohmann and Stirling phases), there is increasing evidence of Emergent Mississippian interaction with our review area at least during the final half of the tenth century A.D. (the Lindeman and Edelhardt phases) (Emerson 1991a; also see Kelly et al. 1984; Emerson and Jackson 1984, 1987). Characteristic traits of this period include: single-post semisubterranean household structures; households clustered along ridge tops or around central courtyards; platform mound construction (apparently confined to Monks Mound); maize agriculture in combination with use of the starchy seed complex and wild plants (Johannessen 1984); exploitation of a wide variety of aquatic and terrestrial faunal re-

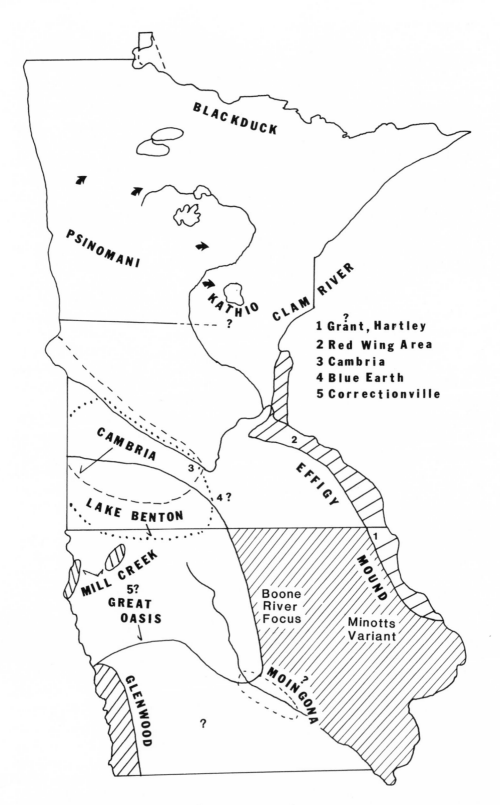

BLACKDUCK

PSINOMANI

KATHIO
?

CLAM RIVER

?
1 Grant, Hartley
2 Red Wing Area
3 Cambria
4 Blue Earth
5 Correctionville

CAMBRIA

2

3?
4?

EFFIGY

LAKE BENTON

MILL CREEK
5?
GREAT
OASIS

1

MOUND

Boone
River
Focus

Minotts
Variant

MOINGONA
?

GLENWOOD

?

Map 6.3. Archaeological complexes in Iowa and Minnesota, ca. A.D. 1100–1200.

sources (Kelly and Cross 1984); a transition in ceramics to forms that eventually typify those of early Mississippian assemblages (a shift from cordmarked to plain surfaces, an increase in the use of shell tempering and red slip, and vessel shape modification), and the introduction of new vessel forms (such as pans and hooded water bottles); the presence of tradeware vessels from the central and lower Mississippi Valley (Coles Greek Incised, Kersey Incised, Varney Red Filmed, and Larto Red Filmed), southern Indiana (Yankeetown), and northern and southern Illinois ("collared" forms).

A group of three rectangular platform mounds on a narrow jutting ridge crest in Trempealeau County, Wisconsin, apparently associated with this Emergent Mississippian period, may represent the earliest Mississippi site-unit intrusion into the upper Valley (Stevenson, Green, and Speth 1983). The ceramic assemblage appears chronologically early in that it is dominated by shell-tempered, red-slipped, and polished sherds, and contains early central Mississippi Valley types such as Varney Red Filmed, Kersey Incised, and Coles Creek Incised; it also lacks Woodland and Oneota ceramics. Although less well documented, pre–A.D. 1050 Mississippian groups and/or influences seem present in the central Illinois River valley (McConaughy, Jackson, and King 1985) and in the Red Wing area of southeastern Minnesota (George Holley pers. comm. 1989). At present, there is only scattered evidence of Emergent Mississippian peoples or influences in the remaining portions of the upper Valley or in the western prairies, though increasing familiarity with traits of this stage could substantially alter this conclusion. Emergent Mississippian ceramics, for example, have recently been identified in Mille Lacs Lake area sites in north-central Minnesota (George Holley pers. comm.).

Site-unit intrusion or at least substantial contact is much better documented for the classic American bottoms Stirling phase (ca. A.D. 1050–1150), perhaps because of its more easily recognizable "Old Village" assemblage of wall trench structures, platform mounds, and, in particular, distinctive ceramic types, Ramey Incised and Powell Plain. Actual (site-unit) intrusions of Mississippian populations northward have been apparently demonstrated for only two areas, the Illinois valley and the Apple River valley in northwestern Illinois (Emerson 1991a; also see Conrad 1991, Emerson 1991b). Other examples of contact of varying degrees of intensity occur in settings of the Late Woodland (Aztalan in south-central Wisconsin, the Hartley phase of northeastern Iowa); Oneota-related (the Silvernale phase in the Red Wing area of Minnesota); Middle Missouri tradition (the Great Oasis phase of northwestern Iowa and southeastern Minnesota, the Mill Creek culture of northwestern Iowa, the Cambria phase in southwestern Minnesota); and Central Plains tradition (the Nebraska culture in the Glenwood vicinity of southwestern Iowa).

A perennial focus of debate has been the ancestral role, if any, of Cahokia-based Mississippian cultures (through population intrusions and/or influence) in the emergence of the Oneota, Silvernale, Mill Creek, Cambria, and Glenwood complexes. Since J. B. Griffin's (1946, 1960; also see his 1967:189) original statement of Mississippian expansion and subsequent devolution in the harsher and perhaps deteriorating environment of the upper Valley and western prairies, radiocarbon dates and assemblage analyses have indicated that these transformations occurred before the Stirling expansion or were contemporary with it. The result has been a proliferation of alternative transformation models, none of which has gained universal support (R. A. Alex 1981; Anderson 1987; Benn 1984, 1989a; Gibbon 1974, 1982; Henning 1968, 1970, 1971; Tiffany 1983, 1991a, 1991b). In the majority of these models, the transformation was from a Late Woodland base, with contact with more complex Mississippian polities, climatic change, indigenous cultural developments, and other factors assuming varying degrees of importance in one model or another.

Since the 1960s, for example, archaeologists investigating Mill Creek culture have suggested that Mill Creek developed out of resident Late Woodland cultures, that it is part of the Middle Missouri rather than Mississippian tradition, and that the presence of Mississippian culture traits in Mill Creek sites is a result of contact with and acculturation to aspects of the Mississippian lifeway (Henning 1968, 1971; Anderson 1969, 1987; Tiffany 1982c). Evidence supporting these conclusions includes: absence of flat-topped pyramidal mounds; presence of indigenously derived traits in the earliest ceramic assemblages; an early date for the emergence of Mill Creek (ca. A.D. 900); and the absence of a Mississippian component in the earliest Mill Creek sites (Anderson 1981a; Tiffany 1982c). Instead groups represented by the Great Oasis phase are considered the probable ancestors of the Mill Creek culture (Henning 1971, 1983a:4.45; Henning and Henning 1982; Tiffany 1982c, 1983).

A confusing element in this scenario is the origin of many traits traditionally considered Mississippian. Though their histories cannot be traced in detail at present, it seems that shell tempering in ceramics, small side- and basally notched projectile points, globular jars with handles or lugs, more intensive agricultural practices, a tribal level of social organization, fortified villages, and, probably, elements of the Southern Cult are part of broader regional developments rather than specifically American bottoms' Mississippian traits (Tiffany 1991b; Hall 1967; Gibbon 1991). Shell tempering may be associated with the spread of corn agriculture through the upper Valley (Hall 1967:177–79; Gibbon 1974:133), for instance, and fortified villages with increased sedentism. Because of the diverse origins of these and other traits, it seems an error in procedure to conflate the processes of "mississippianization" and of agricultural intensification with its attendent social and material culture adjustments before close examination of their interrelationship in the Midwest, for the former is largely a phenomenon of the upper Mississippi Valley and adjacent regions, while the latter occurred almost simultaneously over a much broader area that stretched from the Plains to the Atlantic seaboard.

Not all Late Woodland peoples participated or participated as fully in this transformation. A Late Woodland enclave seems to have been present, for instance, in the Prairie du Chien area of Wisconsin (Theler 1987), and the Hartley (Tiffany 1982b) and Great Oasis (Henning and Henning 1978) phases, while on the same general level of development as Mill Creek, maintained a Woodland cast in their ceramic assemblages. Other areas, such as the expansive terraces and floodplain around La Crosse, Wisconsin, have produced little evidence of intensive occupation during either the Late Woodland period or period of Mississippian expansion. Perhaps because of their larger and more highly visible villages, most research on the A.D. 900–1200 period in our review area has concentrated on modeling developmental trajectories and/or intercultural interactions of Mill Creek, Oneota, Silvernale, and other newly emergent cultures rather than those of the surviving Woodland peoples. For general reviews of the complexes of this period, see L. M. Alex (1980), D. C. Anderson (1969, 1975, 1981b), S. F. Anfinson (1987), G. E. Gibbon (1991), D. R. Henning (1983a, 1983b), Elden Johnson (1991), J. B. Stoltman (1983, 1986), and J. A. Tiffany (1983, 1986c, 1991b).

Mississippian Decline and Oneota Expansion: A.D. 1200–1500

The major events in our review area between A.D. 1200 and 1500 are the disappearance of a Mississippian presence by A.D. 1250–1300, Oneota expansion after A.D. 1200, and the attendant readjustments that accompanied these events. Interpretations of the disappearance of Mississippian groups and influences from the region vary. T. E. Emerson (1991a), who believes that Mississippian communities colonized the upper Valley in the eleventh century, has argued that these communities began to diversify almost immediately in their new settlement locations because of cessation of contact with Cahokia, geographical isolation, independent political and cultural development, and the deterioration of their subsistence base that resulted from the absence of strains of maize adapted to the climatic conditions of the northern hinterlands. As devolution progressed, according to Emerson, the competitive advantage shifted to Late Woodland groups. The result was the eventual disappearance of Mississippian groups from the upper Valley region by about A.D. 1300–1350.

Alternatively, the collapse of a Cahokia-centered extractive network by A.D. 1250–1300 may have resulted in the disappearance of hinterland exchange nodes and relationships, along with the religious symbolism that tied the network together (Gibbon 1974). While it remains unclear whether Mississippian communities in the American bottoms maintained their status quo or began to experience a process of decentralization during the Moorehead phase (A.D. 1150–1250), nucleation had dissolved, with populations dispersing over the floodplains and into the surrounding uplands, by the Sand Prairie phase (A.D. 1250–1400) (Woods and Holley 1991; Farnsworth, Emerson, and Glenn 1991; Pauketat and Koldehoff 1983). It would be an extraordinary coincidence if these developments were unrelated in some manner to the disappearance of the Cambria, Silvernale, and Mill Creek complexes in the region by A.D. 1300, and, more broadly, to the major cultural transitions that were occurring from the Plains to the Atlantic seaboard in the northeastern United States during the A.D. 1200–1300 period.

A vigorous expansion of Oneota communities paralleled the demise of Mississippian culture in the upper Valley. The origin of the Oneota and the date of their expansion also remain subjects of dispute (Gibbon 1982). Oneota settlements seem concentrated during the A.D. 1000–1200 period in southern Wisconsin (Koshkonong and Grand River phases, Lake Winnebago area, Lake Pepin); in southeastern Minnesota (Red Wing area and probably the Blue Earth River valley); and in northeastern, northwestern, and possibly south-central Iowa—the Grant, Correctionville, and Clarkson sites, respectively (Dobbs 1982; Gibbon 1972, 1979; McKusick 1973; Osborn 1982; Penman 1988; Tiffany 1979). And it is these areas (except for the Lake Winnebago area, the Blue Earth River valley, and the central Des Moines River valley), perhaps not unsurprisingly, that are abandoned by about A.D. 1250–1300, if not earlier. The Oneota seem to have entered the La Crosse area of Wisconsin by about A.D. 1200 (Boszhardt 1982), the northern stretch of the central Illinois River valley between A.D. 1275 and 1350, southern and western Iowa (with the probable exception of the Correctionville sites) by about A.D. 1200 (Tiffany 1991a; Harvey 1979:222–23), and the Red River of the North by A.D. 1300 (Michlovic 1983). Their influence (in the form of Ogechie ceramics), if not actual populations, also spread into the mixed deciduous-coniferous forests of central Minnesota by A.D. 1300 (Ready 1979c). Their penetration into the southern stretch of the central Illinois valley, the lower Illinois valley, and the American bottoms was limited, however, to small temporary intrusions (Emerson 1991a). Emerson (1991a) suggests that their movement south was halted by the denser populations and stabler communities made possible by the greater agricultural productivity of this region.

The precise nature of Oneota interaction with other groups during their expansion has received little attention. It is, however, generally considered to have been aggressive. In the models of Mill Creek development and decline proposed by D. C. Anderson (1987) and D. R. Henning

(1982:281), for instance, competition with Oneota groups is considered a main reason for the consolidation of villages, construction of defensive fortifications, and reduced emphasis on long-distance bison procurement that is evident in Mill Creek settlements after A.D. 1200 or 1250; the Mill Creek homeland was eventually abandoned by about 1300. The suggested causes of Oneota expansion are many and varied (Benn 1989a; Emerson 1991a; Penman 1988).

Apparently, the Oneota emerge in history as the Winnebago in east-central Wisconsin, the Ioway in northern Iowa, southwestern Wisconsin, and southeastern Minnesota, the Oto in southern Minnesota and northern Iowa, and the Missouri along the Missouri River trench (map 6.5) (Gibbon 1972, 1986; Griffin 1960; Harvey 1979; Henning 1970, 1983b; Mason 1976; Mott 1938; M. M. Wedel 1981, 1986). What happened to the various peoples they supposedly displaced, such as Mill Creek, Cambria, and Lake Benton, remains a matter of speculation, but they are thought in general to have retreated westward (Watrall 1974).

For general reviews and studies of the Oneota culture in this review region, see Alex (1980), Anderson (1975, 1981b), C. A. Dobbs (1982, 1984), Dobbs and O. C. Shane (1982), J. P. Gallagher et al. (1985), Gallagher and Katherine Stevenson (1982), Gibbon (1979, 1983), A. E. Harvey (1979), Henning (1970, 1983b), N. M. Osborn (1982), Tiffany (1979, 1982a), and M. M. Wedel (1959).

NORTHERN WILD RICE HARVESTERS

The A.D. 500–1500 period in the northern forests and prairies of Minnesota exhibits many parallels with developments in the southern part of our review region. There was a transitional phase that lasted about five hundred years (A.D. 300–800); Native American population sizes dramatically increased; the size and number of habitation sites increased; a trend toward increasing sedentism and organizational complexity is apparent; burial mounds became more abundant and widespread; small unnotched triangular projectile points eventually replaced notched and stemmed forms; ceramic vessels became thinner and more globular; and dependency upon a single plant food, in this case wild rice, significantly increased.

North of St. Anthony Falls the Mississippi River flows from its source in southeastern Clearwater County in what has been called the headwaters lakes region (map 6.1) through a heavily forested area with numerous lakes. In general deciduous vegetation and prairie openings are common in the southern portion of the zone and a mixed coniferous-deciduous forest is present to the north. Most of this zone seems to have been unsuitable for growing prehistoric varieties of maize, though wild rice beds were extensive. To the west are the

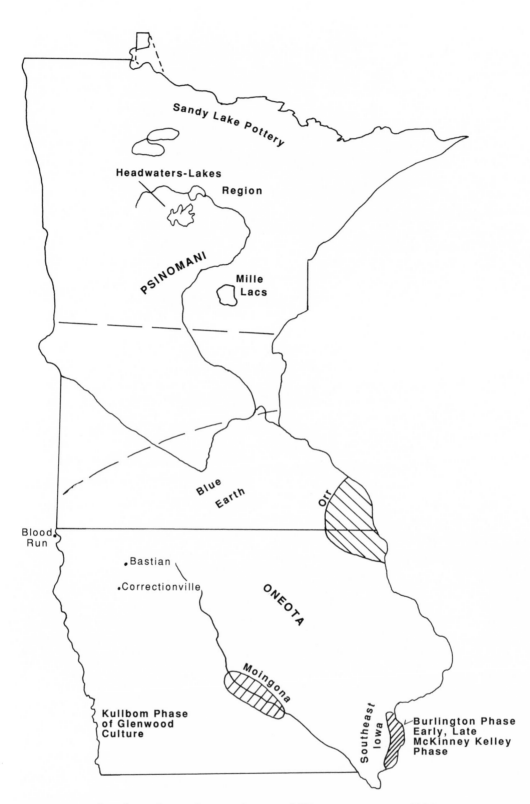

Map 6.4. Archaeological complexes in Iowa and Minnesota, ca. A.D. *1500.*

Map 6.5. General distribution of Native American linguistic/tribal groups in the upper Mississippi Valley, ca. A.D. 1650.

prairies of the flat plain of Glacial Lake Agassiz and the Red River valley (A. C. Ashworth and A. M. Cvancara 1983; S. F. Anfinson 1990).

The Transitional Phase: A.D. *300–800*

Two cultural phases may be defined for this period, although the archaeological cultures and cultural dynamics of the period remain poorly known. The St. Croix phase stretches from the northwestern corner of Wisconsin across eastern and central Minnesota into the Red River valley (map 6.2). Components associated with the phase, however, have their greatest density in the Mille Lacs Lake–Snake River region. The second phase, called the Brainerd phase here, stretches from the Mille Lacs–Nokasippi River region in the east into the aspen parkland in the west and northward, although its area of greatest concentration is the headwaters region. Dating of both phases remains uncertain. For instance, Brainerd ware appears very similar to ceramics associated with the Avonlea complex to the west and northwest that could date as late as A.D. 1200 (Morlan 1988).

Although St. Croix phase materials are known from some twenty-two excavated sites — fifteen habitation and seven burial sites — knowledge of the full range of artifacts associated with the phase is still limited, for no single-component St. Croix site has been excavated (Caine 1974; Caine-Holman 1983; George 1979; E. Johnson 1971, 1973). The material culture of the Brainerd phase is also poorly known, although Brainerd ware is present at many sites in the headwaters region (E. Johnson et al. 1977:33, 61; Lugenbeal 1978; George 1979).

St. Croix has been interpreted as having a hunting-gathering economy with perhaps some use of wild rice (George 1979). This static description, however, disguises a number of trends in adaptive strategy that may have been occurring at this time (Gibbon and Caine 1980:4; Caine-Holman 1983:255). These include increasing dependence on wild rice and a few large or abundant food animals as subsistence resources. The reasons for these trends may include: (1) the increasing availability of wild rice itself (McAndrews 1969; E. Johnson 1969); (2) possible readjustment to the colder and drier climatic conditions of the Scandic climatic episode (Baerreis and Bryson 1965, but see Anfinson and H. E. Wright 1990); and (3) an increase in population sizes with resulting pressure on traditional food resources. The shift in hunting strategy is thought to correlate with the shift from the atlatl to the bow and arrow as inferred from an increasing preponderance of small triangular projectile points at this time.

Whether Brainerd peoples experienced processes of change similar to these remains unknown at present. However, the size and number of Brainerd phase sites suggest significant population increases over earlier periods. Elden Johnson has suggested that population sizes were still relatively small and that the settlement pattern was probably not much different from the seasonal movements indicated by campsites reflecting the Archaic (Johnson et al. 1977:23). He suggests in addition, however, that an intensification of indigenous cultural practices was already present.

Elden Johnson (1973) has also identified a consistent and recurring pattern of burial traits that span the transitional period. The combination of traits diagnostic of this burial complex, which is called the Arvilla complex, includes linear and circular earthen mounds, deep subsoil burial pits, flexed and disarticulated primary and bundle secondary burials, frequent use of red and yellow ocher, associated utilitarian and ornamental grave goods dominated by bone and shell artifacts, Prairie side-notched and Broad side-notched projectile points, blade side scrapers of brown chalcedony, and small mortuary vessels of St. Croix Stamped or Blackduck ware (E. Johnson 1973:62). In the Arvilla burial complex, grave goods have been found associated with all modes of burial and with both male and female adult and adolescent burials. The burial complex has been found at sites from the St. Croix River valley across central Minnesota to the Red River valley and northward along the Red River through the Pembina plain to the Winnipeg area (Syms 1982).

The Arvilla burial program, which had a duration of four hundred years or so, appears over a wide, ecologically diverse area and was almost certainly associated with a series of different cultures (E. Johnson 1973:65). Although some Native Americans with a St. Croix phase material culture did participate in an adaptive system which included the Arvilla burial program (Caine-Holman 1983:248), not all St. Croix and Brainerd phase mound burials were part of the program (E. Johnson 1971; Caine-Holman 1983:215–16).

Clam River–Kathio–Blackduck Continuum: A.D. 800–1000/1100

By at least A.D. 800, the transition to a Late/Terminal Woodland adaptive pattern was probably complete. Cultural complexes after this date to about A.D. 1000 or 1100 are identifiable by a similar appearing material culture and by a subsistence base apparently even more dependent on the harvesting of wild rice (E. Johnson 1969, 1971). These complexes include: (1) the Clam River phase in the mixed deciduous-coniferous forests of northwestern Wisconsin and eastern Minnesota, (2) the closely related Kathio phase, located along the southern boundary of this forest zone in eastern and central Minnesota, and in the west-central "lakes district" that stretches across the deciduous forest zone into the prairies to the west, and (3) the (early) Blackduck phase, situated in the mixed deciduous-coniferous forests to the west and north of Kathio. Differences between these phases, although not pronounced, are primarily defined in terms of decorative motifs on pottery vessels (map 6.3) (Ready 1979b; Caine 1974; Caine-Holman 1983: 150; Lugenbeal 1976, 1978).

The material culture of this continuum is characterized by globular-shaped, grit-tempered, cordmarked pottery jars decorated with twisted cord or cord-wrapped stick impressions, and by small unnotched and side-notched triangular projectile points. Since most of the pottery associated with these phases has been recovered from multicomponent habitation sites, the association of other classes of artifacts with specific phases remains problematic (Evans 1961a, 1961b; Ready 1979b).

Sites with Kathio phase components apparently have their greatest density in the east central Mille Lacs Lake area, which has been considered the core settlement area of the Kathio culture (E. Johnson 1979:24). At least a dozen sites with Kathio components have been found around the Rum River outlet of the lake alone. It was material from a few of these sites that L. A. Wilford (1941, 1955) used in his original description of Kathio as an archaeological unit. Despite the number of excavated sites containing Kathio components, a Kathio settlement-subsistence pattern has never been fully documented in the literature, although several models have been proposed (E. Johnson 1985; Gibbon and Caine 1980). The pattern is generally thought to have revolved around the hunting of deer and other smaller mammals and the gathering of vegetal resources, especially wild rice, in the Mille Lacs region and the seasonal hunting of bison on the western prairies.

The heart of early phase Blackduck in Minnesota appears to be the Lake Winnibigoshish and Leech Lake basins in the headwaters region (E. Johnson et al. 1977:29), although its distribution extends from the prairies of the "lakes district" in the west-central region of the state (at the Dead River site, for example) to the Red River valley and across the far northern forests of the state. The location, size, and context of many sites suggest a hunting and gathering subsistence base with seasonal movement between resource zones. Examples of possible seasonal activities include spring fishing during the spawning season, spring and fall hunting of migratory waterfowl, bison hunting on the western prairies, and wild rice harvesting (E. Johnson et al. 1977:129; E. Johnson 1969, 1979:23). On the prairies the Dead River site in Ottertail County is thought to have been a generalized hunting camp at which fishing was important (Michlovic 1979), and the Lake Bronson site may have been used by Blackduck people for bison procurement (Anfinson, Michlovic, and Stein 1978). At least some of these sites in the northwestern prairies and in the aspen parkland may have served primarily as "exchange centers" where small numbers of people from two or more social groups met to exchange goods and information.

Johnson has been the main proponent of an association between early-phase Blackduck and the intensification of wild rice harvesting, and regards Terminal/Late Woodland cultures (Blackduck and Sandy Lake), at least in the headwaters region, as having intensive wild rice–bison economic systems (E. Johnson et al. 1977:24). The association between the Clam River–Kathio–Blackduck continuum and intensive wild rice harvesting is supported at present, however, only by circumstantial evidence and has not been conclusively demonstrated.

Mortuary sites of the Clam River–Kathio–Blackduck continuum are characterized by groups of conical mounds. There is an apparent difference between the Kathio and Blackduck phases, however, in the mode of burial within these mounds. Kathio people are thought to have been buried as secondary bundles without grave goods, with the bundles laid on the surface of the ground with very low conical mounds that are almost never cumulative erected over them (E. Johnson 1979: 24; Ready 1979b:103; Wilford 1964). Early phase Blackduck burials are usually partially flexed primary burials in what has been interpreted as a sitting or semisitting position (Evans 1961a, 1961b; E. Johnson 1979: 24; Lugenbeal 1979:24). Mounds are also circular and relatively small in size compared, for example, to earlier Laurel mounds.

The social organization of societies within the continuum was probably a segmentary lineage system that grew and fissioned throughout the period. The result was a similarity of material styles and way of life, and increasing population packing, throughout large areas of the mixed hardwood-coniferous forests. By about A.D. 1000 or 1100, the mixed forests of central Minnesota contained a widely distributed and large population, perhaps a population much larger than may have existed in the southern quarter of the state inhabited by maize horticulturists.

The Psinomani Culture: A.D. 1000/1100–1500

The Late Terminal/Late Woodland period in the forests and prairies of central Minnesota extends from about A.D. 1000 or 1100 to the beginning of the Historic period. Perhaps the single most important event in this period is the abrupt appearance and gradual spread throughout the mixed forests of central Minnesota of a new cultural complex called the Psinomani culture (maps 6.3 and 6.4). But other significant events occurred as well, such as the contraction northward of Blackduck culture, the spread throughout the region of Oneota and Plains Village ceramic traits, and, perhaps, the appearance for the first time of a fully developed wild rice parching and storage technology. As for other periods of prehistoric Minnesota, the volume of detailed published information is meager.

Psinomani is a Dakota word for a widespread archaeological complex that contains Sandy Lake ceramics and their associated artifacts and features in central Minnesota.[1] Estimates of the date of emergence of the cultural complex vary widely. D. A. Birk (1979:175), for example, suggests that the complex emerged by about A.D. 1000 and that Sandy Lake ceramics replaced Blackduck ware in the Mississippi headwaters region around A.D. 1100–1200, while Elden Johnson (1979:29) thinks this replacement occurred in both the headwaters region and in the east-central Kathio span of the continuum around A.D. 1300–1400. M. G. Michlovic (1987b) has stated that the component containing Sandy Lake ceramics at the Mooney site in the Red River valley is "fairly reliably dated to around A.D. 1000–1100." Establishing the time and place of origin of the complex is critical, for it is generally assumed that the Psinomani culture abruptly replaced the Clam River–Kathio–Blackduck continuum across central Minnesota and in the Wisconsin tributaries of the St. Croix River. While the Psinomani culture may have emerged as early as A.D. 1000, then, the timing of its spread across central Minnesota remains uncertain.

Except for ceramics, the Psinomani material culture has been considered very similar to that of Kathio and early Blackduck (E. Johnson 1979:26; Johnson et al. 1977:29). Sandy Lake ceramic vessels are globular with slight neck constrictions and generally straight but also incurved and out-flaring rims (Birk 1979; Peterson 1986). The laminated paste is usually tempered with crushed mussel shell or with shell and finely ground grit, and occasionally with grit only, across central Minnesota, and increasingly with grit alone as one traces its distribution northward. Exterior vessel surfaces are either cordmarked, smooth, or stamped with grooved paddles, and are rarely decorated. When present, decoration is usually confined to lip notching and notching and large punctate impressions on the interior rim surface. Nearly all Psinomani ceramic assemblages across central Minnesota contain small amounts of "northern" Oneota pottery (Anfinson 1979a:144; Ready 1979c) or Red River ware (or Northeastern Plains ware) in the Red River valley region (Michlovic 1987; Michlovic and Schneider 1988).

Surprisingly little information is available concerning Psinomani culture mortuary practices, but existing evidence documents the presence of at least three burial tracks: (1) primary flexed interment with an associated mortuary vessel in a shallow subsurface burial pit underneath a small circular conical mound; (2) intrusive mound interment; and (3) nonmound interment (Birk 1977; Lothson 1972).

[1]*Psinomani* (pronounced "see-no-mon-nee") is a Dakota word that can be translated "wild rice gatherer." D. A. Birk (1977) originally named this archaeological complex the Wanikan culture. *Wanikan*, an Ojibwa word, means "hole in the ground," and the name was intended to signify the importance of ricing jigs and wild ricing in this prehistoric culture. Since the complex is almost assuredly related to the historic Santee Dakota, there has been some dissatisfaction with the assignment of an Ojibwa term to a Dakota culture. Agreeing with Birk's insight that at least protohistoric cultures should be given Indian names, I have suggested a substitution of terms (Gibbon 1989).

In Minnesota Psinomani settlement-subsistence patterns remain poorly documented because of artifact mixing in shallow sites and a lack of detailed excavation reports. Elden Johnson (1985:163; Johnson et al. 1977:24, 29) considers these Late Terminal/Late Woodland societies as "forest fringe dwellers" with a forest-prairie edge area adaptation which included bison hunting, wild rice harvesting, fishing, the hunting of woodland mammals, and gathering and collecting activities in both biomes. They may, in fact, have been as actively engaged in prairie maintenance through the use of fire to maintain game levels (Johnson 1985:162) as they were in maintaining the quality and size of their wild rice beds. The Cooper and Wilford sites at the Rum River outlet of Mille Lacs Lake are examples of large year-round woodland villages, while the Shea and Mooney sites in the Red River valley region may be examples of seasonal prairie bison hunting camps (Michlovic 1985; Michlovic and Schneider 1988). The ceramic assemblages at Shea and Mooney indicate that considerable interaction between eastern woodland and prairie-plains dwellers persisted throughout the Terminal/Late Woodland period.

Although Elden Johnson (1979:26, 1985) regards the Psinomani settlement-subsistence patterns as similar to that of the preceding Clam River–Kathio–Blackduck continuum, I have argued that there is a considerable difference between the two patterns (Gibbon 1989). Unlike the extensive settlement pattern of the continuum, for example, the majority of large camps and villages of the Psinomani culture are clustered in a small number of widely separated localities; intervening areas are virtually abandoned except by seasonal extractive groups. Relatively large semipermanent palisaded villages, warfare, further population growth, the development of more formal sociopolitical alliances, and the intensification of wild rice harvesting in conjunction with a new roasting and storage technology appear at this time.

These societies emerge in the historic record as the rather amorphous groups of Dakota speakers that were labeled the Santee or eastern Dakota for convenience (map 6.5) (E. Johnson 1985; M. M. Wedel 1974).

The Tribalization Process in the Upper Valley

In broad overview cultural developments in the upper Valley during the A.D. 500–1500 period can be divided into three successive phases: the emergence and spread of early Late Terminal/Late Woodland lifeways; the dramatic and disjunctive appearance of a mosaic of large, defended villages and aggregated populations who depended in part on the intensive harvesting of maize or wild rice; and then domination of the region by the Oneota in the south and the Psinomani in the north.

Stimulating and possibly fruitful explanations have been suggested for developments within each of these phases. Coevolutionary and tribalization models, for instance, have been developed to explain the nature and elaboration of Late Woodland cultures in the general area in the first phase (e.g., Braun 1985, 1987, 1988; Braun and Plog 1982; O'Brien 1987), and various models have been used to trace the development of archaeological cultures in the second phase (e.g., Anderson 1987; Gibbon 1974). Until recently, few models have attempted to view all three phases as parts of a whole, as a continuum dominated by a common theme. An emerging set of models suggest that the unifying theme of this continuum is the tribalization process (Benn 1989a, 1989b; Gibbon 1989).

The concept "tribalization process," like the concept "tribe," is ill-defined (e.g., Sahlins 1968; Fried 1975; Lightfoot 1984; Braun and Plog 1982; Bender 1985; Niemczycki 1988; Dincauze and Hasenstab 1989). In broad perspective, however, the process refers to the appearance and elaboration of structurally decentralized and functionally generalized multicommunity alliances for nonaggression, mutual defense, and exchange among dispersed "egalitarian" populations. The causes of the process are as disputatious as its definition, with suggested causes ranging from neo-Darwinian risk mitigation models (e.g., Braun and Plog 1982) to social models that focus on the dynamics of social relations and social production within the context of alliance formation and exchange (e.g., Bender 1979, 1985; Nassaney 1987; Saitta 1983; Hindess and Hirst 1975). In the emerging set of models for the upper Mississippi Valley, the gradual elaboration of Woodland cultures and their rapid transformation to Oneota, Plains Village, and Psinomani cultural systems are regarded as historical processes "involving the reorganization of productive relations and the development of pan-ethnic symbols of dominance" (Benn 1989a:233); eventually, the expansive organization of the Oneota and Psinomani production systems resulted in their domination of the prairies and mixed deciduous-coniferous forests of the upper Valley; for detailed discussions of this process, see Benn (1989a, 1989b) and Gibbon (1989).

Although perhaps premature given our data base, this perspective raises interesting questions about cultural developments in the upper Valley between A.D. 500 and 1500. Posing these questions is an apt coda for this brief review: Would parallel developments have occurred throughout the upper Valley if maize and wild rice had not been available for intensive exploitation? What affect, if any, did contact with more complex polities to the south have on the form and tempo of this developmental pattern? What relationship, if any, was there between this developmental pattern and similar changes in social organization that were occurring at approximately the same time in the Southwest and in the northeastern woodlands? What role, if any, did population growth, diffusing innovations, warfare, social circumscription, new trade alliances, and climatic change have in this scenario? The active imagination can easily add to this short list.

CHAPTER 7

CULTURES OF THE MIDDLE MISSOURI
R. Peter Winham and Edward J. Lueck

THE Middle Missouri region as defined for this chapter is oriented strictly to the Missouri River trench (map 7.1), and extends from Fort Randall Dam at the south end of Lake Francis Case in South Dakota to the confluence of the Missouri River with the Little Missouri River in what is today Lake Sakakawea in North Dakota, a distance of approximately 605 river miles. In the 1950s and 1960s four major reservoirs, Lake Sakakawea, Lake Oahe, Lake Sharpe and Lake Francis Case, were constructed in this region. Only a small portion of the Missouri River between the Knife and Heart rivers in North Dakota retains its original setting. Intensive archaeological surveys and excavations took place in this region under the auspices of the Smithsonian Institution prior to the flooding of the reservoirs. Known as the Smithsonian Institution River Basin Surveys, this work focused on the larger, more prominent, earthlodge villages, particularly those along what today is Lake Oahe. The most comprehensive (although dated in several respects) summary of this work is provided in D. J. Lehmer's (1971) *Introduction to Middle Missouri Archeology.*

The next major archaeological undertaking to encompass this region was initiated because of federal historic preservation legislation requiring federal land-managing agencies, such as the U.S. Army Corps of Engineers, to manage their cultural resources. A first requirement, therefore, was to determine what cultural resources existed on the lands they managed around the major reservoirs. During the late 1970s and 1980s nearly all federal lands in the Middle Missouri region were intensively surveyed (Lake Sakakawea: Noisat, Campbell, and Moore 1986; Science Applications, Inc. and Overland Archeology, Inc. 1982; Van Hoy and Nathan 1983; Winham, Lippincott, and Lueck 1987; Winham, Lippincott, Hannus, and Lueck 1988. Lake Oahe: Falk, Peppert, and McCormick 1986; Lueck, Lippincott, and Winham 1989; Winham, Lippincott, and Lueck 1988; Winham and Lueck 1987; Larson et al. 1983, 1986; Sanders et al. 1987, 1988; Toom and Artz 1985. Lake Sharpe: Falk, Steinacher, and Toom 1984; Steinacher 1981; Toom and Picha 1984. Lake Francis Case: Lees, Brown, and Mandel 1985; Olson and Zimmerman 1979; Winham and Lueck 1984).

The information provided by these two regionwide evaluations, undertaken some thirty years apart and with very different resources and research goals, provides the data base for this chapter. We attempt

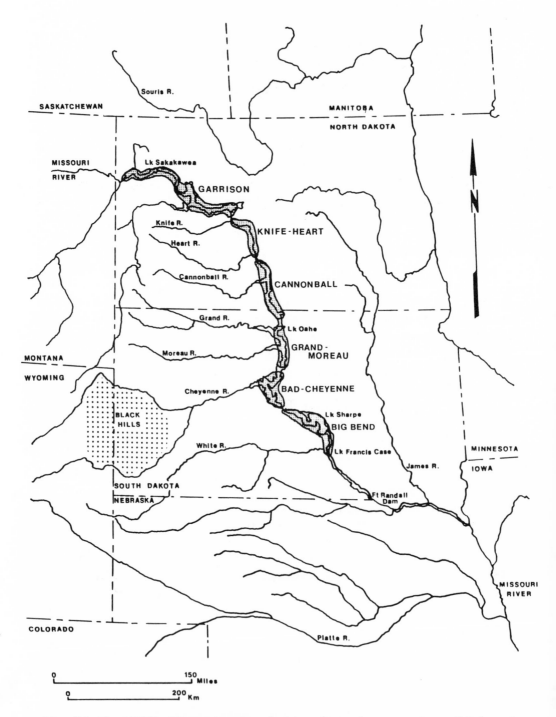

Map 7.1. *The Middle Missouri region showing the major reservoirs and Lehmer's regions (Garrison, Knife-Heart, Cannonball, Grand-Moreau, Bad-Cheyenne, and Big Bend).*

to summarize some of the major statements that have been made about the prehistory of the Middle Missouri region for the period A.D. 500–1500. Much of what has been written remains speculative, and will remain so until more problem-oriented research is undertaken. Unfortunately, in some areas important sites now lie under the reservoirs. This particularly applies to the Lake Francis Case area where sites critical to an understanding of Great Oasis and Initial Middle Missouri relationships likely lie submerged.

The Middle Missouri region occupies a prominent place in Great Plains prehistory through its role in the development, and later demise, of the Plains Village cultures. This appears to be an area where different peoples interacted and adapted to changes in the environment and external contacts by altering subsistence strategies and trade patterns which affected their social and political organization.

Groups recognized archaeologically as variants or phases may not relate on a one-to-one basis to past human groups. For instance there are Mandan and Hidatsa groups in the historic period that show little or no differentiation in the archaeological record. Archaeologically these two separate cultures might be classified as one.

A.D. 500: WOODLAND

At around 500 A.D. the Middle Missouri region was occupied by several groups of people sharing subsistence economies based on hunting and gathering, supplemented occasionally by limited horticulture. These peoples used corner-notched points and elongated pottery vessels with straight or slightly flaring rims, slight shoulders, and conoidal bottoms (Johnson in press).

Relatively little attention has been given to the composition, chronology, and taxonomy of Plains Woodland in the past, but recent investigations (Benn 1981) have emphasized the significance of such in addressing problems of the transition between Woodland and Plains Villagers, and insights into processes of culture change. Benn (1981c: chap. 9) discusses a number of changes that differentiate the Woodland organization of production from the preceding Archaic. These changes include the appearance of ceramics and storage pits. The latter indicates an increased storage capacity that might be interpreted as evidence for either an increasing supply of food or longer occupations at one location, or both. There is evidence of intensification of production and the bow and arrow appears during this period. "In general . . . the organization of Mid-America Woodland production is characterized by gradually increasing complexity stemming from evolutionary changes in the means of production and greater inputs of specialized labor" (Benn 1981c: chap. 9, p. 39).

Specific named Woodland manifestations in the Middle Missouri region (map 7.2) include Valley phase, Besant (Neuman 1975)-Sonota complex (following Reeves 1983), Truman Mound Builders, Loseke Creek phase (Hurt 1952), and Cross Ranch.[1] In addition to Woodland groups the region was also utilized by several nomadic hunter-gatherer groups, presumably including Avonlea and Old Women's complex (Reeves 1983a:47).

Besant is the most widespread of the Woodland groups. Besant groups practiced a sophisticated bison procurement strategy and are associated with mound burials. The mound burials are a feature of what has been named the Sonota complex, and perhaps reflect Besant groups who had a more settled lifeway afforded by efficient hunting and gathering subsistence strategies.

The current picture of the Woodland period in the Middle Missouri region is one of much variability, particularly in ceramic types. Settlements include both multiple dwellings, as probably represented at the Arp site (Gant 1967), and smaller camps, such as at the La Roche site (Hoffman 1968). A variety of burial practices is suggested, although primary and secondary inhumations in burial mounds appear most often. Temporal control over this variability is very limited, and a much tighter chronology is needed to distinguish changes through time from spatial variability in any one time.

The current distribution of Woodland period sites may be biased because of the limited studies undertaken to locate buried sites in this region. There was also a bias toward recording the larger Plains Village sites during the Smithsonian Institution River Basin Surveys. In general Woodland sites exist along the entire Middle Missouri region (map 7.2a). A major gap occurs between the Cheyenne and Moreau rivers in South Dakota but, as can be seen in all the site distribution maps presented in this chapter, no sites of the period A.D. 500–1500 are recorded in this area.

TRANSITION: WOODLAND TO PLAINS VILLAGE

In the Middle Missouri region Woodland groups are in a position to have played a role in the development or adoption of the Plains Village lifeway. It has been suggested that Loseke Creek pottery styles, Ellis Plain and Randall Incised, are very similar to the Great Oasis pottery types Great Oasis Plain and Great Oasis Incised (Johnston 1967:71). Also, similarities between Great Oasis and Initial Middle Missouri pottery types have been noted (Johnston 1967). Chronologically Valley

---

[1]Tables 7.1–7.6 list sites used to prepare the distribution maps. In several cases the assigned cultural/temporal affiliation of a site is speculative. Components at some sites are represented by only a few sherds and at other sites the affiliations are "suggested."

Table 7.1
Woodland Sites in the Middle Missouri Region

Valley phase ca. A.D. 1–600 (Total = 6)
39BR101   Arp Site
39GR2   Ellis Creek Village
39CH45   Hitchell Site
39LM238   Good Soldier Site
39GR1   Scalp Creek Site
39ST9   La Roche (component D)

Besant-Sonota ca. A.D. 1–600 (Total = 14)
39CA4   Rygh Site (Sonota-like ceramics)
39DW233   Swift Bird — burial
39DW240   Grover Hand Site — mounds
39DW242   Stelzer Site — occupation
39DW252   Arpan Mound Site
39ST9   La Roche (house 2)
39ST80   Woodland occupation
32DU2   Midipadi Butte
32ME103   High Butte Mound
32ML39   Nightwalkers Butte
32MO20   Schmidt Mound
132SI1   Boundary Mound
32SI6   Porcupine Creek (component)
32SI200   Alkire Mound

Loseke Creek ca. A.D. 600–800 (Total = 9)
39BF233   Side Hill Mounds
39BF234   Old Quarry Mound
39BR101   Arp Site
39BR102   Woodland village
39CH4   Wheeler Bridge Mound
39CH9   White Swan Mound
39CH45   Hitchell Site
39GR1   Scalp Creek Site
39GR2   Ellis Creek Village

Truman Mounds (39BF224)/Late Woodland ca. A.D. 600–800

Cross Ranch (various sites) ca. A.D. 900–1000

Unassigned Woodland Sites A.D. 1–900 (Total = 64)
39BF3   Talking Crow (Woodland ceramics)
39BF4   Occupation
39BF10   Walking Warrior Mounds
39BF44   Occupation
39BF49   Mound group
39BF101

Table 7.1 (Continued)

39BF201	Occupation
39BF208	Bill Voice Mound Group
39BF209	Mound group
39BF213	Wolf Creek Mounds
39BF216	Martin Ranch/Slow Mound
39BF219	McBride/Reddog Mound
39BF223	Olson Mounds
39BF225	Sitting Crow Mounds
39BF229	Artifact scatter
39BF235	Presbyterian Church Mound
39BF270	McBride II Mounds
39BR17	
39CA15	Artifact scatter
39CA101	Artifact scatter
39CA106	Artifact scatter
39CA113	Artifact scatter
39CA117	Artifact scatter
39CH20	Mound
39CH27	Occupation
39CH52	Williamson Mounds
39CH207	Burials
39CH210	Sunrise Hill Site (occupation)
39CH212	Occupation
39DW256	Mound
39HU48	Burials
39HU83	Woodland component at village
39HU89	Occupation
39HU102	Occupation
39HU173	Cairn
39HU205/241	Woodland component at village
39HU212	Huston Mounds
39HU221	Little Elk Site – occupation
39LM26	Oacoma Village – Woodland component
39LM27	Oacoma Village – Woodland component
39LM57	Fort Lookout – Woodland occupation
39LM81	Woodland village
39LM84	Component at village
39LM149	Mound
39LM201	Meander site
39LM221	Mound group
39LM235	Component
39LM261	Mound
39SL312	Hearth
39ST112	Cairn/artifact scatter
39ST122	Sitting Buzzard (component)
39WW22	Artifact scatter
39WW46	Artifact scatter

Table 7.1 (Continued)

39WW56	Artifact scatter
39WW58	Artifact scatter
32EM204	
32ME57	
32ME199/799	
32ME947	
32ML258	
32MO17	Sugarloaf Butte
32MO98	
32MO207	
32MO401	

precedes Loseke Creek, which precedes Great Oasis, and sites of these groups have almost identical spatial distributions in this region (see maps 7.2b and 7.3). Most of these sites, however, need additional studies and radiocarbon dating before detailed evaluations can be made.

While the focus of study into the transition from Woodland to Plains Village has been in the southern portion of the Middle Missouri region, and adjoining areas to the east, preliminary excavations at the Flaming Arrow site (32ML4) in the northern part of the Middle Missouri region may be "the oldest dated occupation by semisedentary village dwellers in the Knife-Heart region, ostensibly affiliated with the Awatixa [group of the Hidatsa tribe]" (Toom 1988). Available data are insufficient to assign this component to a defined archaeological taxonomic unit, although superficial similarities to the Plains Village tradition, Initial Middle Missouri variant, are noted. A Late Plains Woodland affiliation is also possible, which led to the conclusion that the component represents a cultural entity transitional from Plains Woodland to Plains Village lifeways (Toom 1988:51). Corrected radiocarbon dates from the site place the occupation between A.D. 920 and A.D. 1230. Since no report providing information on the context of the radiocarbon samples is available, an evaluation of this site must wait. Sites of the Clark's Creek phase (see below) are presently considered the earliest semisedentary village dwellers in the Knife-Heart region.

It is likely that the transition from one lifeway (Woodland) to another (Plains Village) is reflected to varying degrees in all Woodland groups present in the Middle Missouri region — that is, they were all adapting to changing circumstances. It has been suggested (below) for Great Oasis that some part of those peoples developed a more complete Plains Village lifeway, while others, contemporaneously, retained their Woodland lifeway. It would certainly be premature, therefore, to assign any groups existing around A.D. 500 in the Middle Missouri as proto-Mandan or proto-Hidatsa.

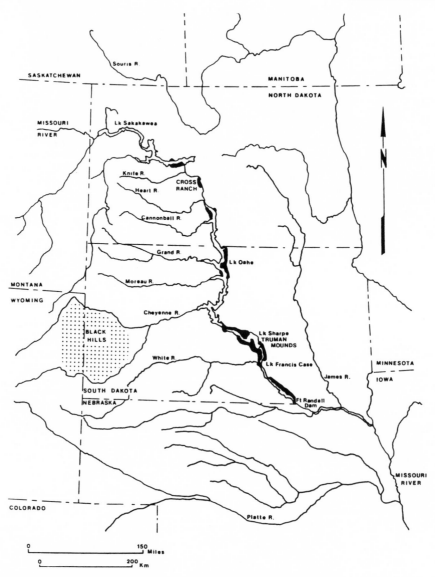

Map 7.2 (a). Truman Mounds, Cross Ranch, and unassigned Woodland sites.

GREAT OASIS ASPECT

One cultural manifestation that has long been recognized as central to the issue of the origin of Plains Village groups in the Middle Missouri region is the Great Oasis aspect or simply Great Oasis. Great Oasis peoples practiced different subsistence strategies in different regions. While primarily relying on hunting and gathering, they also practiced maize horticulture. These peoples represent a complex that has been viewed as bridging the Woodland and Plains Village traditions, or

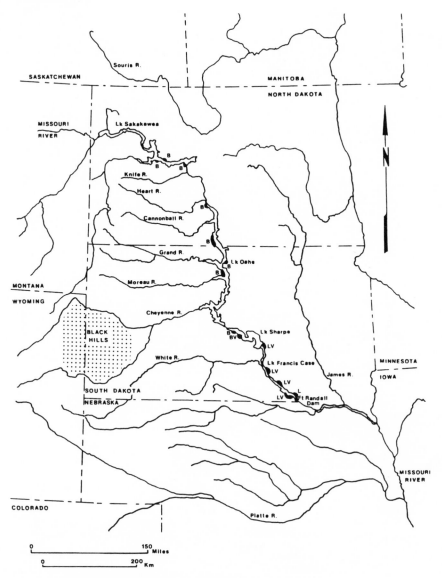

Map 7.2 (b). Valley phase (V), Loseke Creek (L), Besant-Sonota (B).

alternatively, as an eastern manifestation of the Initial Middle Missouri (IMM) tradition (Ludwickson, Blakeslee, and O'Shea 1981:139).

Tiffany (1983) has presented a detailed case for including Mill Creek and Cambria within the IMM tradition and that "the Initial variant of the Middle Missouri tradition is a part of, and an outgrowth of, indigenous Late Woodland cultures in the Middle Missouri subarea exemplified by groups utilizing Great Oasis pottery and related forms" (Tiffany 1983:96). Based on a suggested date range for Great Oasis of A.D. 850–1100 and on particular (Cahokia) pottery present in IMM but not Great Oasis sites, Great Oasis is seen to predate the Mill Creek

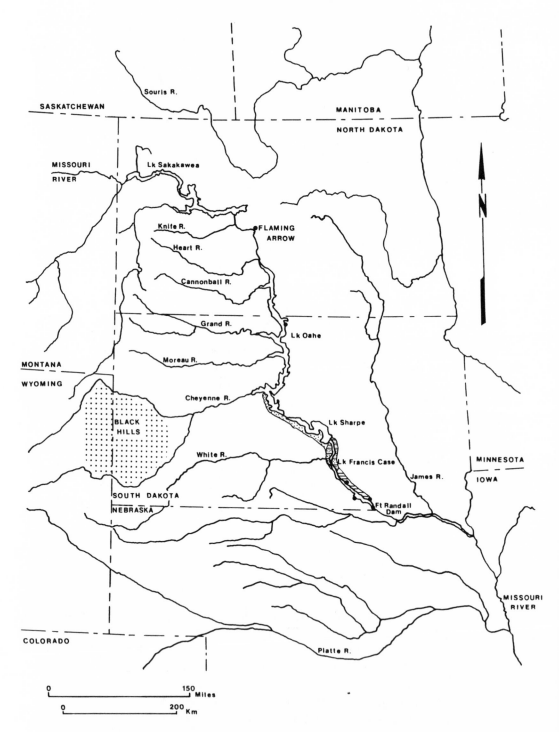

Map 7.3. *Great Oasis (hatched), Initial Middle Missouri (stipled/dots), and the Flaming Arrow site.*

Table 7.2
Great Oasis Sites in the Middle Missouri Region

Great Oasis ca. A.D. 800–1200 (Total = 11)	
39BF227	
39BR101	Arp Site
39BR202	
39CH5	Pease Creek Village
39CH7	Oldham Village
39CH29	Benge Creek Site
39CH45	Hitchell Site
39CH205	
39LM59	
39LM66	
39LM238	Good Soldier

culture and the Initial Middle Missouri variant and yet is contemporaneous with both.

Alex (1981a) has addressed the problem of the relationship between Great Oasis and the Initial Middle Missouri variant.

Great Oasis seems to precede, and yet be partly contemporary with, the Initial variant in much the same way as the Initial variant seems to be earlier and yet contemporary with the Extended variant. . . . What could cause a single archaeological culture to subdivide into two separate but related cultures? . . . We might speculate that about A.D. 900, those Great Oasis peoples who were situated in optimal areas for floodplain horticulture and with access to the northern Plains bison herds prospered more than those who lived in areas less desirable for horticulture . . . and developed a more complex social organization. . . . Their culture was transformed into what we refer to as the Initial Middle Missouri variant. . . . In the lakes region and beyond the northern Plains bison herds, however, the old Great Oasis lifeway continued for more than a century. (Alex 1981a:40)

MIDDLE MISSOURI TRADITION

By 1000 A.D. a semisedentary, horticultural way of life had been established in the Middle Missouri region. Floodplains were exploited for garden crops and uplands for game, especially bison, but to what degree the inhabitants relied on crops as opposed to game, and what subsistence variability existed, is not clearly established.

The Middle Missouri tradition provided the social and technological base for two of the historic village tribes in the Northern Plains: the Mandan, and their close cultural and linguistic neighbors, the Hidatsa.

A brief summary of Mandan culture history after W. R. Wood (1967) shows that the Mandan developed from Siouan-speaking horticultural

Table 7.3
Initial Middle Missouri Sites in the Middle Missouri Region

Initial Middle Missouri ca. A.D. 950–1350 (Total = 65)
39BF4
39BF11   Crow Creek component
39BF12   Pretty Bull component
39BF20
39BF44   Component
39BF215   Aiken Site – Occupation
39BF221   Akichita Site
39BF227   Village
39BF301
39BR13   Earthlodge Village
39BR16   Swanson Site
39BR29
39BR39
39BR101   Arp Site
39CA3   Jones Village
39CH5   Pease Creek Village
39CH205   Earthlodge Village
39GR53   Bozarth Site
39HU60   Chapelle Creek Village
39HU211   Huston Ranch Village
39HU213   St. Johns Village
39HU223   Fry Village
39LM1   Stricker Village
39LM2   Medicine Creek Village
39LM4   Hickey Brothers Village
39LM7   Springs Village
39LM33   Dinehart Village
39LM47   Clarkstown Village
39LM55   King Village
39LM57   Fort Lookout Village
39LM58   Artifact scatter
39LM59   Occupation
39LM84   Earthlodge Village
39LM146   Antelope Dreamer
39LM174   Artifact scatter
39LM208   Jiggs Thompson
39LM209   Langdeau Village
39LM212   Long Turkey Cabin
39LM225   Jandreau Village
39LM226   Gilman Village
39LM232   Pretty Head Village
39LM247
39LM248   Occupation
39ST9   La Roche Village
39ST11   Fay Tolton Village

Table 7.3 (Continued)

39ST12	H. P. Thomas Village
39ST16	Breeden's Village
39ST23	Gillette Village
39ST30	Dodd Village
39ST37	Hallam I Village
39ST38	Hallam II Village
39ST55	Antelope Creek Village
39ST56	Sommers Village
39ST88	Red Fire Village
39ST89	Artifact scatter
39ST91	
39ST214	Earthlodge Village
39ST223	Ketchen Village
39ST224	Cattle Oiler Village
39ST228	
39ST233	
39ST235	Stony Point Village
39ST238	Durkin Village

Flaming Arrow (32ML4) ca A.D. 920–1230

village groups that moved onto the Great Plains from the Eastern Woodlands. The nearest linguistic relatives to the Mandan were the Hidatsa and Crow.

Mandan migration traditions are separate and distinct from those of the Hidatsa, although each episode contains references to the other. There are two distinct and conflicting Mandan origin myths. In one version of creation (Bowers 1950:347–65), the Heart River is the heart of the universe and the Mandan are depicted as an indigenous group spontaneously originating in their historic habitat. In a second version (Bowers 1950:156–63), the creation of the Mandan originated on the right (west) bank of the Mississippi at its mouth near the ocean, where they emerged from beneath the earth, bringing corn with them. Moving northwards along the banks of the Mississippi River, they reached the mouth of the Missouri River. They crossed to the north bank of the Missouri and resided there for a time. They then moved on up the Mississippi, eventually leaving the river and traveling southwest, settling not far from the pipestone quarries in Minnesota. About this time one clan moved to a point north of the Turtle Mountains, where they remained until they later moved west to the Missouri River. The rest of the Mandan moved southward, rediscovered the Missouri River and moved west, building a village on the east bank opposite the White River. At this time the Awigaxa band vanished, and although some of them later returned, they talked differently. The rest of the tribe moved north along the Missouri until they reached the Heart River.

The Hidatsa tribe consists of three historically recognized groups, the Hidatsa proper, the Awatixa, and Awaxawi (Amahami) (Bowers 1965). The Amahami, like the Mandan, claim to have emerged from the earth far to the southeast, long ago. They then moved north, reaching Devils Lake before advancing to the Missouri River (arriving at the Painted Woods area near present day Square Buttes) where they found the Mandan, and a village of Awatixa nearby.

The Awatixa have a tradition of coming to the earth "from the sky under the leadership of the culture hero, Charred Body" (Wood and Hanson 1986:34). "The Awatixa had no traditions of living elsewhere than on the Missouri River between the Heart and Knife Rivers. . . . According to their tradition, they were the descendants of peoples who formerly lived near Painted Woods farther upstream where they were 'created'" (Bowers 1948:17–18).

The Hidatsa proper, including at that time the River Crow, separated from the Amahami in western Minnesota, moved north, then south to Devils Lake. They discovered the Mandan soon afterward and also moved to the Missouri River, taking up residence north of the Knife River and the Mandan villages. The River Crow separated from the Hidatsa proper here and moved west. The Hidatsa proper later moved to the mouth of the Knife River. Bowers (1965) suggests the existence of two major internal subgroups (northern and southern) during the prehistory of the Mandan prior to A.D. 1300. The northern subgroup eventually settled in the vicinity of the mouth of the Heart River in North Dakota. Bowers recognized three archaeological foci for this group, the Cannonball focus (Lehmer's Extended Middle Missouri), the Huff focus (Lehmer's Terminal Middle Missouri), and the Heart River focus (Lehmer's Post Contact Coalescent and Disorganized Coalescent).

Oral tradition indicates that simultaneously with the Mandan settlement in the Heart River area, the southern subgroup of the Mandan remained far to the south, eventually moving west toward the Black Hills, then moving back to the Missouri River, establishing villages at the mouths of the Cheyenne, Moreau, and Grand Rivers by about A.D. 1500 (Bowers 1948:96). By this time the southern Mandan had adopted the use of circular lodges and made pottery with predominantly tool-impressed decorations. It was after A.D. 1500 that oral tradition suggests the southern Mandan moved to the Knife-Heart region and the first of the Hidatsa groups moved onto the Missouri River from the east. However, some researchers have suggested that the Awatixa group of the Hidatsa tribe may already have been in the upper Knife-Heart region earlier (Wood and Hanson 1986:36).

Archaeologically the Initial Middle Missouri (IMM) and Extended Middle Missouri (EMM) variant groups are seen as in some way ancestral to the Mandan and Hidatsa. The Extended and Initial variants are distinct cultural, temporal, and geographic expressions of the Middle Missouri tradition, most likely stemming from a common ancestral group.

Recent research (see Ahler and Toom 1989: table 2.2) postulates only a fifty-year difference between the earliest dates for IMM (in South Dakota) and the earliest for EMM (in North Dakota). Given such a short time frame it would appear unlikely that the EMM in North Dakota was a development from the IMM in South Dakota. A more detailed review of the dating evidence is necessary before we have to conclude, however, following Wood (in press) that the IMM disappears from the archaeological record and there is no demonstrable association between them and any historic tribe in the Plains.

Within the Missouri River trench two phases have been defined for the IMM variant, the Anderson and Grand Detour phases. Ludwickson and coworkers (1981:143) have discussed the problems of phase-level taxon of the IMM stating that the "Grand Detour and Anderson phases seem to differ little in terms of any material culture parameter, and the differences perceived between the Missouri Trench sites and the James and Big Sioux sites [to the east] might change if a single, consistent ceramic typology was applied." For this chapter all IMM phase sites are considered as a whole.

Well over fifty sites are reported as having IMM materials from the region (map 7.3). These sites extend from north of Fort Randall Dam to the Cheyenne River with most sites concentrated in the area from around the White River to the Cheyenne River. IMM dates cluster between A.D. 950 and 1350. Many of the sites are fortified, and subsistence appears directed toward exploitation of bison, with lesser emphasis on floodplain fauna (Ludwickson, Blakeslee, and O'Shea 1981;151; Chomko 1976). Horticulture was also important (Benn 1974).

The Extended Middle Missouri (EMM) variant appears about A.D. 1000 and is distinguished from the IMM by ceramic differences and different features in the shape of the houses. EMM sites extend from the mouth of the Little Missouri River in North Dakota to south of the Big Bend region of South Dakota. More than eighty-five sites have materials assigned to this variant (map 7.4). Most of the northern sites are not fortified, while those in the south generally are. This has been seen as evidence of conflict between the IMM and EMM groups resulting from the intrusion of EMM groups downstream into IMM territory. Overlap between IMM and EMM groups is evidenced in the Bad-Cheyenne region by a number of sites which contain components of both variants.

Lehmer (1971) defined a "Modified Initial Middle Missouri variant" partly on the basis of the presence of IMM and EMM pottery together at the same site. He assigned seven sites to that taxon, but a reevaluation concluded that the sites "did not meet the content and temporal requirements for membership in the "Modified Initial Middle Missouri Variant" (A. M. Johnson 1979:157). Ann M. Johnson reassigned each site to either IMM or EMM:

[Reassignment] has important implications for the cultural dynamics and history of the Middle Missouri tradition. The presence of Extended Middle Missouri sites below the Cheyenne River, especially unfortified ones, would not be predicted by the model presented . . . (by) . . . Lehmer (1971). . . . We believe the presence of Initial pottery in Extended sites (and vice versa) is evidence of more friendly contact than previously believed. Because the Initial and Extended variants overlap and apparently coexisted for perhaps 200 years, it is reasonable that there would be contacts and exchanges of ideas and material objects. An important question may be why there is so little evidence of cultural mixing. . . . Although Lehmer (1971:101) did not recognize the presence of Initial and Extended components at the same site, the data from several sites may be interpreted as such; for example, Hickey Brothers in the Big Bend region (Caldwell et al. 1964), Cattle Oiler (Moerman and Jones n.d.), and King (Ehrenhard 1973). Breeden (Brown 1974) and Dinehart (39LM33 site file, Midwest Archeological Center) are cases in which Extended pottery represents a minor element in the Initial component." (A. M. Johnson 1979:161)

There are problems with all of the schemes that have been used to assign the Plains Village materials from the Middle Missouri region. These problems have been summarized by Lovick and Ahler (1982:54–65). Recent research in the upper Knife-Heart region (Lovick and Ahler 1982) has shown that none of the existing general culture-historic models for the prehistory of the Middle Missouri region (e.g., Lehmer 1971; Bowers 1948) can specifically be applied to the archaeological record.

[Bowers's] general concept of the prehistoric development and interaction among the Mandan, Hidatsa and Arikara may be generally accurate, but his organization of the archeological data base into foci can today be questioned due to his lack of control on absolute chronology and sampling problems related to mixed components and other factors. The models of Lehmer (1971) and earlier researchers (Will, Hecker, Wood) . . . appear to be even less useful . . . because they are structured according to overly simplistic ideas about diffusion and ethnic group interaction and migrations; above all, they make little attempt to mesh Mandan and Hidatsa oral traditions with complex archeological data directly from the upper Knife-Heart region." (Lovick and Ahler 1982:3–4)

For the upper Knife-Heart region, basic analytic units of component and phase are being formulated. For the Plains Village period six basic culture-historic units have been identified of which four overlap with the period A.D. 500–1500, namely Clark's Creek phase (A.D. 1000–1200 [Wood 1986]), the Nailati phase (A.D. 1200–1400 [Calabrese 1972; Lee

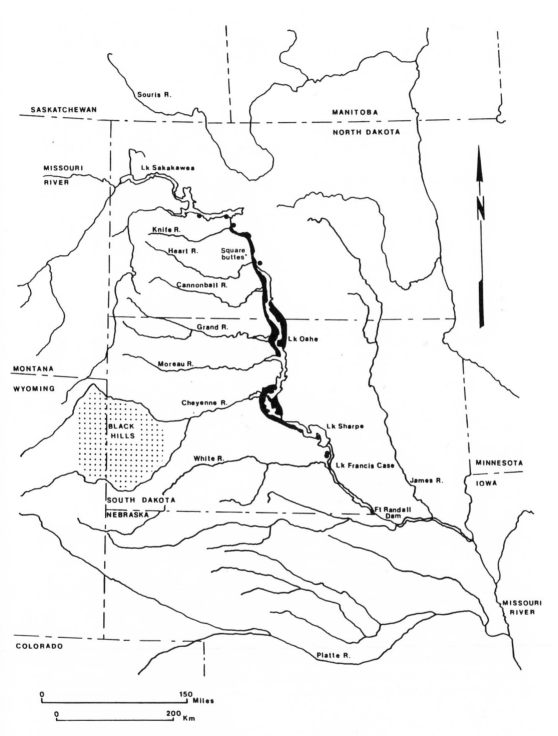

Map 7.4. Extended Middle Missouri.

Table 7.4
Extended Middle Missouri Sites in the Middle Missouri Region

Northern EMM — Fort Yates phase

Southern EMM — Thomas Riggs focus

Knife-Heart region

Clark's Creek phase (A.D. 1000–2000) [Earlier EMM Variant (Wood 1986:7)]

Nailati phase (A.D. 1200–1400) [Later EMM Variant (Wood 1986:7)]

Extended Middle Missouri ca. A.D. 1000–1500 (Total = 98)

39AR8	Alberts Creek Village
39AR201	McKensey Village
39AR210	Earthlodge Village
39CA1	Vanderbilt Village
39CA2	Keen's Village
39CA3	Jones Village
39CA4	Anton Rygh Site
39CA208	Helb Site
39CO1	Demery
39CO3	Kenel Village
39CO6	Jake White Bull
39CO201	Timber Creek Village
39CO212	Earthlodge Village
39CO213	Travis I Village
39DW101	
39DW213	
39DW223	
39DW224	Earthlodge
39DW225	Village
39DW231	Calamity Village
39DW232	
39DW233	Earthlodge Village (Swift Bird Mounds)
39HU1	Thomas Riggs Village
39HU16	Pitlick Village
39HU216	
39LM4	Hickey Brothers Village
39LM33	Dinehart Village
39LM53	
39LM55	King Village
39SL7	Sully School Village
39SL12	
39SL13	Earthlodge Village
39SL29	C.B. Smith Village
39SL41	Zimmerman Site
39SL42	Glasshoff Site

Table 7.4 (Continued)

39ST1	Cheyenne River Village
39ST3	Black Widow
39ST15	Indian Creek Village
39ST16	Breeden's Village
39ST38	Hallam II Village
39ST39	
39ST203	
39ST223	Ketchen Village
39ST224	Cattle Oiler Village
39ST238	Durkin Village
39WW89	Burial
32BL7	Apple Creek
32EM1	Havens
32EM7	Badger Ferry
32ME1	Clark's Creek (Clark's Creek phase)
32ME7	White Buffalo Robe (Nailati phase)
32ME8	Amahami (Nailati Phase)
32ME9	Buchfink (Nailati phase)
32ME12	Big Hidatsa
32ME59	Grandmother's Lodge
32ME101	Sagehorn (Clark's Creek phase)
32ME102	
32ME202	Steifel (Clark's Creek phase)
32ME407	Polly
32ME408	
32ME409	
32ME413	
32ME499	
32ME538	
32ML6	Stanton Ferry
32MO2	Bendish
32MO4	Upper Fort Rice
32MO5	Gwyther Farm
32MO8	Watson Homestead
32MO9	
32MO10	Smith Farm
32MO12	Jennie Graner
32MO13	
32MO19	Bernhard Schmidt
32MO21	Bad Water
32MO24/25	Barett
32MO28	Rippel
32MO31	Scattered Village
32MO35	Rock Haven
32OL3	Wetzstein Ranch
32OL6	Price
32OL8	Pretty Point

Table 7.4 (Continued)

32OL10	Wildwood (Clark's Creek phase)
32OL12	Upper Sanger
32OL14	Cross Ranch (Nailati phase)
32OL16	Bagnell (Nailati phase)
32OL21	Mandan Lake
32OL22	Mahhaha (Nailati phase)
32OL103	Shoreline (Clark's Creek phase)
32OL172	
32SI2	Fire Heart Creek
32SI3	Robert Zahn
32SI4	Paul Brave
32SI5	Slab Town
32SI7	Ben Standing Soldier
32SI8	Jerome Standing Soldier
32SI17	Redstone Site
32SI19	South Cannonball
32SI119	

Note: Some sites of the Heart River phase (A.D. 1400–1710) [Coalescent tradition (Wood 1986:13)] and Scattered Village complex (A.D. 1400–1700) [unaccounted for in the Lehmer (1971) scheme for the culture history of the subarea (Lovick and Ahler 1982:75)] appear prior to A.D. 1500.

1980]), the Heart River phase (A.D. 1400–1710 [Ahler and Weston 1981]), and the scattered village complex (A.D. 1400–1700 [Lovick and Ahler 1982]).

The Clark's Creek phase is broadly equivalent to the Fort Yates phase, represented by several sites in the Cannonball region. Villages are unfortified, consist of long rectangular houses, and yield "high frequencies of Riggs ware (straight rim) and Fort Yates ware (S-rim) pottery" (Lovick and Ahler 1982:70). "Among the differences between the pottery from Clark's Creek and that from downriver Fort Yates phase sites is the fact that 4.4% of the body sherds from Clark's Creek are check stamped; downriver, less than 1% of the sample from any given site is so treated" (W. R. Wood 1986b:9).

Sites of the Nailati phase are also characterized by unfortified villages of long rectangular houses. Ceramics are distinguished by relatively equal frequencies of Riggs ware and Fort Yates ware and significant amounts of check stamping on body sherds (Lovick and Ahler 1982:71–72).

The Heart River phase is characterized by circular earthlodges, as well as "relatively compact villages with large numbers of houses, deep middens . . . frequent use of fortification systems, and a high percentage of LeBeau S-rim pottery with cord impressed decorations" (Lovick and Ahler 1982:72). Both Mandan and Hidatsa are represented by Heart River phase components.

The scattered village complex is characterized by "scattered village plans, a lack of fortification, imprecise site boundaries, little surface expression of house location and house types" (Lovick and Ahler 1982:73).

In 1971 Lehmer observed:

It seems likely . . . that a unit corresponding to Hurt's Thomas Riggs focus, which will include the southern Extended Middle Missouri components [Southern Extended variant], will be distinguished. It may well prove to have early and late subphases. It seems probable that the Fort Yates phase will continue to be recognizable as a valid cultural entity which includes the northern villages [Northern Extended variant]. Again there is a strong likelihood that it will be possible to distinguish subphases. (Lehmer 1971:97)

W. R. Wood (1967) regarded sites of the Thomas Riggs focus to be the earliest village sites culturally cognate with the Mandan. By formally defining a Southern Extended variant (Mandan) and a Northern Extended variant (Hidatsa), Tiffany remarks that this "provides a means by which the Hidatsa can be included in the Middle Missouri tradition and Bowers ideas can be tested" (Tiffany 1983:104).

Lehmer saw every evidence of a direct cultural continuity from the Fort Yates phase into the Terminal Middle Missouri (TMM), with the small, unfortified sites of the Fort Yates phase being replaced by much larger, heavily fortified villages. TMM sites (map 7.5) are fewer in number than EMM sites. Dates from the Huff site (TMM) average A.D. 1490 ± 60 (Thiessen 1977: note 1). "Ceramics from TMM villages are indistinguishable from those of the EMM variant. They differ only in the proportion of various types" (Fawcett 1988:70–71).

ARIKARA AND CHEYENNE

Other protohistoric groups that inhabited the region in this period include ancestral Arikara and Cheyenne. The historic Arikara were a distinct sociopolitical entity with linguistic and cultural roots traceable to the Caddoan-speaking Pawnee of central Nebraska. At some time during the prehistoric period the ancestral Arikara groups split off from the Pawnee and migrated northward along the Missouri River in South Dakota. Considered to be represented archaeologically by the Initial and Extended Coalescent variants of the Plains Village pattern, these proto-Arikara groups penetrated into South Dakota as early as A.D. 1300.

Ludwickson, Blakeslee, and O'Shea (1981) provide a summary of Arikara origin traditions.

Some traditional accounts derive the Arikara, in a very general way, from the south or east (Dorsey 1904:12–40). . . . One version brings the Arikara and

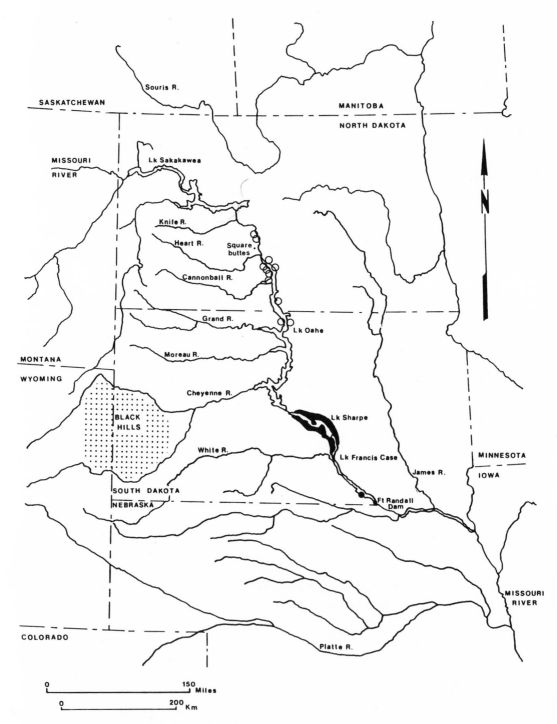

Map 7.5. Initial Coalescent (black), Terminal Middle Missouri (open circles).

Pawnee from big mountains in the south and into the Missouri River country via the Black Hills (Anonymous 1909). Gilmore's (1929:95) assertion that the Caddoans migrated from northern Mexico is undocumented speculation. Dorsey (1904:xiii, 1906:8–9) found some evidence in Pawnee traditions that the Arikara split from the Skidi (Awaho or "left-behind") in the Loup River area of Nebraska. Finally, Fletcher and La Flesche (1911) record that the Omaha remembered finding the Arikara in northeast Nebraska, and credit the Arikara with teaching them to build earthlodges and cultivate maize. . . . The Arikara of the earliest historic records appear to have been coalescing into a tribal unit from previously independent village units. . . . Excavations have provided a direct link of continuous development from before A.D. 1300 to the historic period. This line of development is known as the Coalescent tradition. The remains of the protohistoric Pawnee, the Lower Loup Focus, are very similar to the Initial and Extended Coalescent materials from South Dakota. Thus it is possible that the Pawnee, or some portion of the Pawnee, once were part of the Coalescent tradition of the Dakotas (Smith 1977:156)." (Ludwickson, Blakeslee, and O'Shea 1981:33–34)

The Cheyenne have traditions of having once lived in Minnesota (Wood 1971b), and may have left remains identified as belonging to the Coalescent Tradition (Ludwickson, Blakeslee, and O'Shea 1981:34). According to Cheyenne, Sioux, and Arikara traditions, the Cheyenne later occupied a number of villages along the Missouri River (Grinnell 1962, 1:8–9, 22–30). Schlesier (1988) has suggested that the Cheyenne may have been responsible for the Crow Creek massacre.

Around A.D. 1250 climatic deterioration was a one factor that may have influenced the movement of cultural groups out of the Central Plains into the Missouri River trench of South Dakota. The contact between the Middle Missouri and Central Plains traditions formed Lehmer's Coalescent Tradition. The earliest manifestation of this coalescence he called the Initial Coalescent variant (IC). Sites of this variant are found primarily in the Big Bend region, and consist of large, compact villages containing transitional Central Plains–like "circular earthlodges" randomly scattered within a bastioned fortification ditch. More than twenty IC sites are reported from South Dakota, and include Arzberger, Black Partisan, Talking Crow and the Crow Creek site (map 7.5). By about A.D. 1500 these groups had replaced IMM and EMM groups in the southern Middle Missouri subarea.

Around 1500 the Extended Coalescent (EC) variant appears as a direct outgrowth of Initial Coalescent. The number of EC sites shows a marked increase over the IC but this may be partly due to a shift from nucleated settlements to smaller sites (individual farms or hamlets) with relatively short occupations.

Ludwickson and coworkers (1981:161) note that the term "coalescent" has several different meanings. It has been used to refer to the fusion of cultural characteristics derived from the Middle Missouri and Central Plains traditions. It can also refer to the apparent concen-

Table 7.5
Initial Coalescent Sites in the Middle Missouri Region

Initial Coalescent c.a. A.D. 1300–1500 (Total = 31)

39BF3	Talking Crow
39BF4	
39BF11	Crow Creek
39BF44	Component
39BF63	Occupation
39BF220	Farm School Site
39BF228	Village
39BF301A	Voice Site
39BR13	
39DE233	
39GR1	Scalp Creek Village
39HU6	Arzberger Village
39HU61	Granny Two Hearts
39HU83	West Bend Site
39HU205/241	De Grey Village
39HU207	
39216	
39HU224	Denny Site
39HU225	Artifact scatter
39HU229	Arch Village
39HU242	Whistling Elk Village
39LM2	Medicine Creek Village
39LM6	Useful Heart/Over's Camel Creek V
39LM23	Earthlodge Village
39LM26	Sharpe/Oacoma Village II
39LM82	Earthlodge Village
39LM98	
39LM218	Black Partizan Village
39ST16	
39ST121	Artifact scatter
39ST235	

tration into a small region of peoples who had inhabited a considerably wider area. For example, as the Coalescent tradition formed, a whole host of earlier cultural lines terminated, including the Upper Republican, Smoky Hill, and Nebraska phases, the Steed-Kisker complex, and the Initial variant of the Middle Missouri tradition. A third type of coalescence is embodied in the formation of large, compact villages from the scattered farmsteads and loose hamlets of the earlier Central Plains tradition.

With regard to Lehmer's Coalescent tradition, Lovick and Ahler (1982:64) discuss three examples of the process of coalescence:

Table 7.6
Terminal Middle Missouri Sites in the Middle Missouri Region

Terminal Middle Missouri ca. A.D. 1500–1675 (Total = 15)

39CA208	Helb Site
39CO1	
39CO6	Jake White Bull
39CO212	
39DW231	
32BL5	Holbrook
32EM3	Tony Glas
32EM10	Shermer
32MO1	North Cannonball
32MO3	Lower Fort Rice
32MO7	Cadell Homestead
32MO11	Huff
32MO24/25	Barett
32OL4	Husfloen Farm
32OL5	Eidelbrock

. . . when Caddoan speaking villagers moved out of the Central Plains and established themselves as the ancestors of the Arikara in South Dakota . . . when the southern Mandan group borrowed architectural and ceramic traits from elsewhere while living in the vicinity of the Black Hills, and . . . when the two groups of Mandan and three groups of Hidatsa interacted in the Knife-Heart region. These three episodes of the process of coalescence [which] were not necessarily chronologically sequential and did not necessarily involve any single group of people in all three episodes . . . do not necessarily constitute a cultural "tradition" in the sense that Willey and Phillips (1958:37) defined it. (Lovick and Ahler 1982:64)

SUMMARY

Over the last two decades there have been extensive archaeological surveys along the Missouri River in both North and South Dakota (see references cited). Hundreds of new sites have been recorded and hundreds of square miles have been intensively evaluated (nearly 60 square miles alongside Lake Francis Case, 26 square miles by Lake Sharpe; 252 square miles bordering Lake Oahe, and more than 70 square miles within the defined Middle Missouri region alongside Lake Sakakawea). Unfortunately, the majority of the sites located by these surveys are of unknown temporal or cultural affiliation and major excavations, problem-oriented research investigations, and syntheses have been limited. There is also the problem of ambiguity and inaccessibility of information concerning many of the sites previously excavated in this region.

Ongoing research continues to define and refine archaeological variants and phases to comprehend better the complexity of the archaeological record. Given the homogeneity between village cultures in general, and the variability among individual occupational units that comprise each village site, current interpretations of the archaeological record may be limited by oversimplistic assumptions and extrapolations from limited excavation data.

A reworking of Middle Missouri culture history needs the establishment of a more refined chronology; a problem-oriented research program that addresses the complexities of the archaeological record and attempts to mesh these with Mandan, Hidatsa, and Arikara oral traditions; a clearer identification of Hidatsa and related groups in precontact sites; and an appraisal or reappraisal of information derived from River Basin Survey excavations, particularly sites that have not been adequately published.

The period A.D. 500–1500 in the Middle Missouri region was clearly a dynamic period, even if all the processes of adaptation and change are not clearly defined. Around A.D. 500 several Late Woodland groups were adapting to and experimenting with changing conditions brought about through processes of trade, population shifts, climatic changes, and the associated impacts on food resources. The practice of horticulture was undoubtedly begun by Woodland groups without "seriously modifying the usual hunting and gathering cycle" (Benn 1981c: chap. 9, p. 38). Nevertheless, a major change was brought about by the establishment of semisedentary horticultural village groups in the Middle Missouri region by 1000 A.D. "The development of the Middle Missouri tradition was multilinear in nature and, that through time, it came to serve as a cultural melting pot in the Northern Plains" (Tiffany 1983:107).

Oral traditions present a very complex picture, particularly for Mandan and Hidatsa groups in the Knife-Heart region. For the Mandan, Bowers (1948) describes a northern subgroup that eventually settled in the vicinity of the mouth of the Heart River. Simultaneously, the southern subgroup of Mandan remained far to the south, then moved to the west, then back to the Missouri River, establishing villages at the mouths of the Cheyenne, Moreau, and Grand rivers by A.D. 1500. By this time the southern Mandan had adopted the use of circular lodges and made tool-impressed pottery, both considered "Coalescent-like" traits. Later the southern Mandan moved up the Missouri valley north of the Heart River Mandan group and south of the Knife River. Eventually these two subgroups merged into the single generalized Mandan cultural pattern known from the historic era.

For the Hidatsa three subgroups are identified. The Awatixa claim always to have lived on the Missouri River, the Awaxawi arriving on the Missouri River from the east sometime later, and the Hidatsa proper later still.

The upper Knife-Heart region, north of Square Buttes, is traditional Hidatsa territory and the lower Knife-Heart region, south of Square

Buttes, traditional Mandan territory. Following Wood (1986:66) the archaeological sequence leading to historic Hidatsa begins with Clark's Creek phase followed by the Nailati phase, both predating A.D. 1500. Then comes the Heart River subphase II, then the Knife River subphase II. The archaeological sequence leading to historic Mandan begins with Fort Yates phase prior to A.D. 1500, followed by the Huff phase, the Heart River subphase I, and the Knife River subphase I. Within the time frame of this chapter the archaeology of the Arikara appears comparatively straightforward with the arrival of a population from the Central Plains referred to as the Initial Coalescent variant of the Coalescent tradition. The Coalescent tradition provides a continuous line of development to the historic Arikara villages. However, among sites assigned to the Coalescent tradition may be sites occupied by other tribes, including Pawnee, Cheyenne, and Mandan. Village cultures did not originate in the Middle Missouri region, but had their genesis to the east or south. Nevertheless, it was in the Middle Missouri region that these village groups developed their distinct identities as the Mandan, Hidatsa, and Arikara cultures we know from the historic period.

CHAPTER 8

CULTURES OF THE HEARTLAND: BEYOND THE BLACK HILLS

L. Adrien Hannus

PRIOR to an examination of past human living systems in the geographic area detailed by this chapter (map 8.1), one should consider the varied landforms that constitute the natural environment and that were exploited by prehistoric peoples. The diversity of the Northwestern Plains environment is evident in Frison's description. "Mountain ranges, minor uplifts, intermontane basins, major rivers, high altitude plateaus, and many other landforms are intruded into the Northwestern Plains. . . . Even the Plains areas within the Northwestern Plains are varied over short distances" (Frison 1978:4).

Much of the study area falls within the Missouri Plateau division of the Great Plains physiographic province. Badlands topography is common on the Missouri Plateau. This highly eroded, dissected terrain is characterized by numerous remnant buttes and drainage channels. In western North Dakota, the Little Missouri Badlands formed as a result of the diversion of the Little Missouri River in response to glacial advances. The largest area of badlands topography is the Big or White River Badlands, located at the western edge of the Tertiary tablelands in southwestern South Dakota.

To the west of the White River Badlands stand the Black Hills of South Dakota and Wyoming, an unglaciated, mountainous, domal uplift rising above the surrounding plains (Froiland 1978). The Black Hills are the easternmost extension of the Rocky Mountains and are an isolated feature, surrounded by rolling foothills and broad valleys which merge with the prairies. The Belle Fourche River and the Cheyenne River nearly encircle the Black Hills uplift. The two rivers join northeast of the Black Hills, flowing eastward to meet the Missouri River north of Pierre.

The mountain ranges closest to the Black Hills are the Laramie Mountains to the southwest and the Bighorn Mountains to the west. Further west, the deeply trenched North Platte River and its tributaries have produced a very rugged terrain with sparser grass cover. As one moves east from the Bighorn Mountains increased moisture has allowed a lusher grass cover. To the west beyond the Bighorn basin and extending to the upper Snake River drainage in Idaho are numerous mountainous features such as the Absaroka, Wind River, Gros Ventre and Teton ranges. Frison notes that "the Snake River Plain in south-

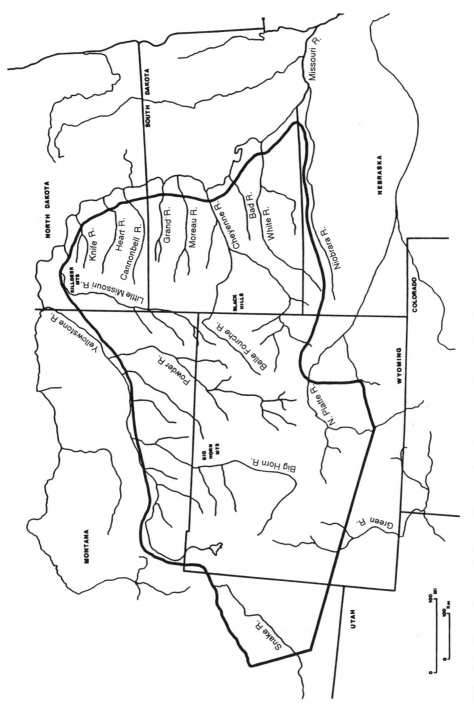

Map 8.1. General map of the study area: Northwestern Plains, detailing prominent drainages.

eastern Idaho presents an ecological and archaeological situation that may bear close relationships to the Northwestern Plains" (1978:6).

The Yellowstone River flows northeast across Montana and joins the Missouri River at the border with North Dakota. In the Yellowstone River valley, where the climate is somewhat milder and grass thrives, an excellent environment for buffalo existed in the past.

In North Dakota, both the glaciated and unglaciated subsections of the Missouri Plateau section are represented. An isolated feature present within the unglaciated Missouri Plateau, in west-central Dunn County, North Dakota are the Killdeer Mountains "suspended above the surrounding plain" (Wyckoff and Kuehn 1983:154).

ARCHAEOLOGY: ORDERING TIME AND SPACE

While a number of taxonomic approaches involving point typologies and cultural chronologies have been proposed for segments of the Northern and Northwestern Plains, considerably divergent opinions and uneven data sets persist. This statement is not meant as a negative reflection on previous investigations, but rather as a recognition that problematical gaps do exist in the archaeological schema. Important to this discussion are the units by which archaeologists systematize temporal/spatial contexts.

W. T. Mulloy (1958) constructed one of the earliest chronologies for the Northwestern Plains. He chose the concept of "periods" to order time across the physical landscape. Mulloy himself recognized and stated: "That these periods are justified in the sense of an earlier one having been replaced by a later different one in a short time is open to serious doubt. Changes were probably gradual and new items probably entered at many different times. The establishment of periods then is simply a convenient means of ordering the material" (Mulloy 1958:140). Mulloy's was a four-period system which included the Early Middle Prehistoric, Late Middle Prehistoric, Late Prehistoric, and Historic periods. Against these periods Mulloy categorized his projectile points stylistically with each marking a horizon/period. This system also accommodated recording the frequency of occurrence of other point styles present in each site during each period (Mulloy 1958:143–54). In addition, Mulloy produced a set of characterizations concerning the dominant settlement and subsistence systems associated with the changing habitat for each period.

In 1970, Brian O. K. Reeves refined and expanded the work of Mulloy both by reordering the time/space dimension and by broadening the physiographic areal coverage. Utilizing the Gordon R. Willey and P. Phillips (1958) concepts of phase and tradition and redefining both to be more applicable to the vast open environs of the Plains, Reeves proposed three named traditions and at least two unnamed traditions to order the time interval from 1000 B.C. to A.D. 1000 (1970:21–24). Reeves's proposed *Tunaxa* tradition is comprised of the Pelican Lake and Avonlea phases, with the insertion of local phases specific to restricted regions. The earlier McKean and Hanna phases are also encompassed by the *Tunaxa* tradition, but predate the temporal scope of Reeves's 1970 work. Reeves's second tradition is identified as *Napi-kwan* and contains the Sandy Creek, Besant, and Old Women's phases. Reeves's final tradition is the Plains Horticultural Tradition which contains such local phases as Valley, Loseke Creek, and Keith in Kansas, Nebraska, and the Dakotas.

In 1978, Frison published a cultural chronology specific to Wyoming and the Northwestern Plains, spanning twelve thousand years from the end of the Pleistocene. George C. Frison (1978) created six overlapping time periods: Paleoindian, Early Plains Archaic, Middle Plains Archaic, Late Plains Archaic, Late Prehistoric, and Protohistoric. Cultural complexes and projectile point typologies dominate the temporal/spatial divisions (1978:83). The units of temporal index established by Frison rely heavily on diagnostic projectile points due primarily to the fact that this region of the Northwestern Plains frequently lacks other diagnostic items in the toolkit to serve as cultural indices.

Other works more restricted in scope which contribute to the ordering of our temporal/spatial conundrum include those of Ken Deaver and Sherri Deaver (1988), I. G. Dyck (1983), Michael L. Gregg (1985), and Sally T. Greiser (1984). Deaver and Deaver's (1988) synthesis provides a review of the previous schema which have variously arranged the archaeological data in the Northwestern Plains region; they also propose useful refinements in their review of the growing body of cultural material items within this broad physiographic region.

While the time frame on which we are focused is A.D. 500–1500, an expansion of the temporal/spatial parameters is necessary to "set the stage" prior to presenting the perceived players in the last act.

A SEARCH FOR PROGENITORS

As the search for progenitors begins, it seems prudent to recognize the environmental constraints which affected past human groups living in the Northern and Northwestern Plains. Reeves recently wrote:

Life in the Northwestern Plains was tethered to the seasonal movements and behavior of the bison, on which natives relied for most of their material needs (cf. Reeves n.d.b). The yearly life cycle in these northern climes can be divided into two periods: overwintering and summering. The overwintering period extended from October to May when bison ranged through their fall, winter, and spring habitats. The ranges of the herds during these seasons were principally along the western and northern edges of the Plains. Some herds also wintered in such prairie mountain ranges as the Cypress Hills in southeastern Alberta and the Black Hills in South Dakota. . . .

A critical requisite for native settlement, from fall to spring, was fuel. All else being equal, depletion of local firewood supplies was the major reason camps had to be moved. . . .

In summer, water was the limiting resource for natives, their dogs, and bison. The bison had, after calving in May, moved out into their ranges on the shortgrass Plains area. As summer wore on and waterholes and streams dried up, the movements of herds and man became increasingly circumscribed and focused on major rivers. . . .

Wild plants were collected: tubers and root crops in the late spring and early summer in the foothills and mountains, and berries in mid- to late summer in the Plains area and foothills. . . .

Another important activity during the snow-free months was the acquisition of flakable stone for small tool manufacture. (Reeves 1990:171–72)

The description by Reeves of the complex and divergent cyclical activities required of human groups in the Northern Plains underscores a rather intractable circumstance for those desirous of utilizing the archaeological data base. Namely, the paucity of excavated site localities severely restricts attempts to recognize how these diverse and complex human activities manifest themselves archaeologically. A further limitation in the Northern and Northwestern Plains rests with the determination of cultural identities relying heavily, if not solely, on projectile point typology. Clearly, the more limited the data set, the more difficult it is to determine whether the same or separate cultural groups are represented in the changing toolkits as one moves from activity area to activity area.

Oxbow: 3500–2500 B.C.

The antecedent technocomplexes of Oxbow through Yonkee are presented due to their important ancestral connections to our specific data base. The Oxbow nomenclature was introduced by R. W. Nero and B. A. McCorquodale in 1958 from work at the Oxbow Dam site in southern Saskatchewan. Oxbow is distributed from its presumed heartland in southern Saskatchewan across southern Alberta and Manitoba into Montana, Wyoming, and western portions of North and South Dakota.

Deaver and Deaver (1988:99) report that, based on the earlier work of Greiser et al. (1983) and Dyck (1983), the Oxbow phase represents a lifeway adapted to upland hunting with bison being the predominant fauna represented in the archaeological context. Greiser et al. (1983) report the range of Oxbow phase dates as 3500–2500 B.C. Based on work at the Harder and Carruthers sites in Saskatchewan, Reeves (1983a:14) has noted the possibility that technologically Besant derives from Oxbow. These sites produced dates for Oxbow ranging from about 1300 to 1000 B.C., thus indicating that Oxbow persisted in this area after being replaced in the Plains by the McKean-Hanna/Pelican Lake sequence of *Tunaxa*.

McKean: 2500–1400 B.C.

Oxbow overlaps with the later McKean phase material, with McKean dating from 2500–1400 B.C. The area of geographic distribution for McKean is in general in accordance with that postulated for Oxbow. A number of authors have viewed McKean as a period of significant cultural expansion in the Northwestern Plains due to its correspondence with the Sub-Boreal climatic episode, which is felt to have generated expanded resource availability (Beckes and Keyser 1983; Frison 1978; Gregg 1985). The apparent proliferation of site assemblages in this temporal/spatial spectrum has produced evidence of a wider array of species hunted, including pronghorn and bison, with some evidence of forest forms such as mountain sheep and mule deer. Frison (1978) notes a tendency during the McKean phase for increased plant food preparation based on the recovery of grinding slabs and manos from areas within Wyoming's basins and foothills. L. Adrien Hannus et al. (1983) note a concordant phenomenon within the Cheyenne River region of South Dakota with the appearance of grinding slabs and manos. However, they place the appearance of these implements at the interface between Oxbow and McKean.

Duncan-Hanna: 1700–800 B.C.

For purposes of the present study, the Duncan-Hanna phase, named by R. P. Wheeler (1954), is subsumed under the McKean complex. Dates for the Duncan-Hanna phase span at least 1700–1100 B.C. Reeves (1983a: 255) suggests the possibility of an even younger 800 B.C. date for Hanna, which creates a temporal overlap with Pelican Lake point styles. While Duncan-Hanna is poorly documented archaeologically, this phase would appear to be a continuation of open upland living systems with a prairie hunting focus.

Yonkee: 1100–500 B.C.

The ensuing phase of Yonkee takes its name from the work of R. Bentzen (1961, 1962) at the Powers-Yonkee site in southeastern Montana. Frison (1978) would restrict the Yonkee phase largely to the Powder River basin of Montana and Wyoming. Gregg (1985:112) extends this point typology into central Montana and western North Dakota. Hannus et al. (1989) extend the range further east into west and west-central South Dakota. The basic adaptation of Yonkee phase peoples was communal bison hunting, including the utilization of traps, jumps, or pounds, with natural physiographic features such as arroyos being employed as entrapments. Dates for the Yonkee phase are 1100–500 B.C. (Deaver and Deaver 1988:106). Deaver and Deaver recognize Yonkee and Pelican Lake as coeval, indicating that "until a similar

range of site types can be documented for the Yonkee phase, we cannot
determine the relationship between the two co-occurring units *and
shouldn't ignore the possibility that the Yonkee phase is largely a
localized functional site type of a larger unit"* (1988:106; italics added).

Pelican Lake: 1500 B.C.–A.D. 300

The Pelican Lake phase was originally identified by B. Wettlaufer
(1955) within the lower level of the Mortlach site in southern Saskatchewan. Dates have generally been placed at 1000 B.C. to the
beginning of the Christian era (Frison 1978; Reeves 1970); however,
Gregg (1985) suggests a slightly expanded temporal span of 1500 B.C.–
A.D. 300. The Pelican Lake phase has a wide distribution, stretching
across major portions of southern Alberta, Saskatchewan, and Manitoba, and extending southward to Montana and Wyoming, and at least
as far east as the Missouri River in North and South Dakota.

In their review of Pelican Lake, Deaver and Deaver (1988:107–11)
note that a number of authors – including D. C. Fraley, M. Griffith, and
C. A. Novak (1982), Gregg (1985), Reeves (1983), and G. Ruebelmann
(1983a) – argue that human population increases occurred in the study
region as a response to moister conditions during the Sub-Atlantic climatic episode, suggesting increased carrying capacity in the bison range.
The Pelican Lake phase shows utilization of the multiple habitat zones
in the Northern and Northwestern Plains, with a concomitant and ex-
pectable set of expanded resource utilization schemes. Deaver and Deaver (1988), Frison (1978), Gregg (1985), and Reeves (1970, 1983a) all note
the broader spectrum of faunal utilization. Dyck, in considering the Pelican Lake phase, indicates that "although they were certainly not inventors of bison jumps and pounds, Pelican Lake peoples were the first to use
some mass kill locations that were used repeatedly, in some cases, more
intensively in later times" (1983:107). A. Simon, C. Sheldon, and K. Kiem
(1982) note that in the rugged terrain of the Little Missouri Badlands,
many of the sites occur along the divides and ridges which offered the
best transportation. Field observations by Hannus and others (Hannus
1985; Hannus et al. 1983, 1989; Ed J. Lueck et al. 1990; R. Peter Winham,
Lippincott, and Lueck 1988) suggest that the subtle refinement of techniques for utilizing diverse topographic features is a hallmark of Pelican
Lake hunting adaptations. In regard to hunting technology, Frison
(1978) views Pelican Lake projectile points as sharply contrasting with
earlier McKean-type projectile points and identifies them as the earliest of the corner-notched varieties of the Late Plains Archaic. In an
oft-quoted and succinct statement on morphology Frison notes, "Pelican Lake points are a true corner-notched type with wide, open notches
that form sharp points as they intersect blade edges and bases. Both
blade edges and bases may be straight or very slightly concave" (1978:56).

Reeves (1983a:136–37) categorizes Pelican Lake as a serial phase within a cultural tradition exhibiting a continuity which spans two and one-half millennia. This cultural tradition has been identified by Reeves as *Tunaxa*, with three temporal phases: McKean, Hanna, and Pelican Lake. While a strong basis for a northern origin accrues, Reeves does not rule out several other sources, including the Eastern Woodlands; areas to the west in British Columbia; and areas further south in central Idaho, ultimately suggesting even the possibility of a Southern Plains origin. Reeves (1983a:137) states that "thus it seems impossible to isolate at present any one area from which the barbed corner notched point may have been introduced into the plains" (see map 8.2, Pelican Lake distribution).

Sandy Creek: 800–300 B.C.

The Sandy Creek complex is characterized by small, shallow side-notched points and is coeval with Pelican Lake in the Saskatchewan basin. Reeves (1983a:14) sees Sandy Creek as being technologically transitional between Late Oxbow and some Besant side-notched forms.

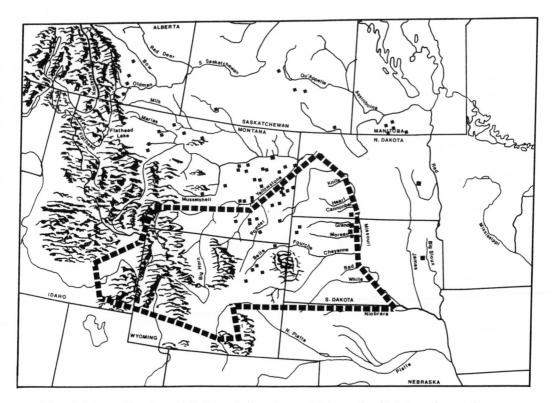

Map 8.2. Distribution of Pelican Lake sites within and adjoining the study area. (Adapted from Reeves 1970, 1983a; Winham, Lippincott, and Lueck 1988.)

Thus, Reeves perceives that Sandy Creek persists in the Canadian parklands during Pelican Lake times and emerges at approximately A.D. 0 as the Besant phase. Richard E. Morlan (1988:306, fig. 6), on the basis of cumulative histograms of radiocarbon dates for southern Canada, sees strength in the argument for the Sandy Creek transition into Besant.

Besant: 500 B.C.–A.D. 800

The Besant point complex appears on the Northern Plains around 500 B.C. and is initially identified by the characteristic atlatl dart point configuration having shallow notches and round shoulders, and known as Besant side-notched. A technological transition from atlatl to bow and arrow occurs between A.D. 420 and 750, with the Samantha side-notched point, the smaller corresponding arrow point of the Besant technocomplex, replacing Besant side-notched through time (Reeves 1970:89, 92). Evidence of Avonlea in Besant components and Besant types in Avonlea components indicates that Besant and Avonlea are coeval.

The *Tunaxa* tradition is seen by Reeves (1970, 1983a) to span at least two and one-half millennia, with the Pelican Lake phase represented by a number of locally adapted sociocultures which in time are replaced in certain areas by a transition to Avonlea. Reeves postulated a series of subcultures which evolved to replace the Pelican Lake phase across its wide area of distribution. Those subcultures to the east (Missouri River region — South and North Dakota) are represented by Valley/Loseke and Keith phases which are ceramic-producing, semi-permanent village dwellers with the concomitant habitation structures and storage facilities. Reeves sees the Plains horticultural subsistence traditions emerging in the Northern Plains as the result of a diffusion of traits (ideas) from the Middle Woodland period of eastern North America. Reeves (1983a:184) notes: "In other areas ecologically unsuited for stable corn horticulture at this time level, the Tunaxa cultural tradition continues as a basic hunting gathering adaptation into the Avonlea phase in the bison-rich Northwestern Plains, and into the Keyhole and Patten Creek phases in the Missouri and North Platte Basins in Wyoming."

The *Napikwan* cultural tradition as postulated by Reeves (1970) makes its appearance on the Plains relatively coeval with the *Tunaxa* cultural tradition as *Tunaxa* is viewed to be undergoing change and divergence. The *Napikwan* tradition is represented by the Besant phase, described by Reeves (1970, 1983a) as a nomadic hunting-gathering culture with a distinctive lithic artifact assemblage and regional manifestations to the east (Dakotas) which include ceramics, burial mounds and habitation structures. Reeves notes for Besant that "although origins are obscure, evidence suggests that it has been a resident Plains tradition on the Northeastern Periphery since possibly 500 B.C." (1983a:185). Salient to the overall consideration of Besant would be the underlying mechanisms responsible for this cultural tradition's spread into the Northern and Northwestern Plains since it appears to have lifeways strongly parallel to the indigenous and continuing *Tunaxa* tradition.

In viewing the arguable hegemony represented by Avonlea peoples, the premier producers and distributors of the bow-and-arrow technology, it appears difficult to characterize Besant as an intrusive cultural tradition. Reeves (1970, 1983a) presents an elaborate scenario of Besant as an egalitarian band society which underwent significant reworking of its cultural system due to participation in the interaction sphere of the Mississippi Valley Hopewellian cultural complex. By coming to participate in a complex system of trade in both utilitarian and non-utilitarian ritual items, Besant in some subtle ways could be characterized as an elaborated bison procurement system of middlemanship, expanding into the Northern and Northwestern Plains ecotones. In reviewing Besant, Deaver and Deaver (1988:112–14) suggest that the temporal span for this phase may be in the range of 500 B.C.–A.D. 800, thus overlapping with Avonlea and Pelican Lake. Considering temporal/spatial influences regarding Besant, they state:

The earliest dates are most common on the eastern edge of the Northern Plains, and the point types and adaptation developed somewhat later to the west. Interestingly, the dominance of Besant diagnostics persists in the Dakotas long after other point styles have appeared in the west. Transitional levels from Besant to Plains Village/Old Women's/Late Woodland components tend to fall in the 650–1000 BP range in the Dakotas (Kropp and Sisseton mounds, Dancing Grouse). Across the prairies of Montana and Alberta, Old Women's arrow points replace Besant styles by 1000–1300 BP (Deaver and Deaver 1987:100). The most appropriate range for the Besant phase in southeast Montana are 1300–2000 BP. (Deaver and Deaver 1988:112–14)

Robert W. Neuman (1975) described the Sonota complex, interpreted as a Besant manifestation characterized by bison hunting and exploitation of the Plains riverine environments of north-central North America. Neuman reckoned the western range of this culture to be in portions of southern Alberta and Saskatchewan, in Montana, and in the western part of the Dakotas. The predominant site types of the west are characterized as campsites and buffalo impounding or jump localities. The Sonota complex was originally defined by Neuman (1975) on the basis of materials from excavations at the Stelzer site (39DW242), as well as materials from the Swift Bird (39DW233), Grover Hand (39DW240), Arpan (39DW252), and Boundary Mound (32SI1) sites. The complex is recognized as having an emphasis on bison procurement, a predomination of tools made from Knife River flint, a distinctive variation of corner-notched projectile points very similar to Besant and Samantha side-notched forms, upright bones in village and kill sites, and small burial mounds containing multiple bundle burials as well as numerous bison remains. Sonota ceramics are shoulderless, conoidal vessels with straight walls and rounded bases. Most have a vertically cord-roughened surface similar to Valley ceramics. Both E. Leigh Syms (1977:90) and David W. Benn (1981a), however, see the Sonota and Valley complexes as two quite distinct groups despite the overlap.

The distribution of the Sonota complex is now recognized as being much larger than the regional aspect suggested by Neuman, extending throughout the narrow central plains of North and South Dakota and southern Manitoba, with some sites also found in Saskatchewan and Alberta (Syms 1977:89). Thomas W. Haberman (1979) has reported a small, temporary aceramic occupation site in Stanley County (39ST80) assignable to the Sonota complex which yielded two Besant-like points. The site is situated on the uplands at the edge of the Missouri Breaks.

In the Coteau des Prairie region of eastern South Dakota, the Sonota complex has been identified at the Oakwood Lakes site (39BK7). Timothy R. Nowak (1981:124) has noted that, based on the analysis of the stone tool assemblage and its cultural affinities, it appears that the Oakwood Lakes site represents a Sonota complex bison hunting and processing camp on the eastern prairie periphery of South Dakota dating about A.D. 200 to 700. "The similarities with aspects of the Valley complex to the south and west and with western periphery Laurel to the north suggests [sic] an interface of mobile hunting and gathering groups participating in multiple biome utilization and exploiting the bison herds of the tall grass prairies all along the eastern periphery of the Northeastern Plains" (Nowak 1981:125). This hypothesis is compatible with Syms's (1977) co-Influence sphere model and it is not unlikely that the Sonota complex is a composite of a number of regionally varied complexes similar in nature to Besant and Valley. It may, in fact, be the manifestation of the interface between the Besant complex of the Plains Archaic tradition and the ceramic and small-notched and un-notched point complexes of the Eastern Woodland tradition.

Reeves (1990:182–85) suggests that Besant origins lie in the earlier Oxbow complex, while Pelican Lake origins derive from the earlier McKean complex. He (1990:184–85) also postulates the exploitation of different lithic source areas by the Besant and Pelican Lake peoples. Reeves suggests that Besant peoples favored the Knife River flint quarries in North Dakota, while Pelican Lake period peoples preferred quarries in central and southern Montana, including the obsidian outcrops near Yellowstone National Park in northwestern Wyoming. While the notion that the quarrying of brown chalcedony has its focal locality in the Knife River quarries of North Dakota may prove to be

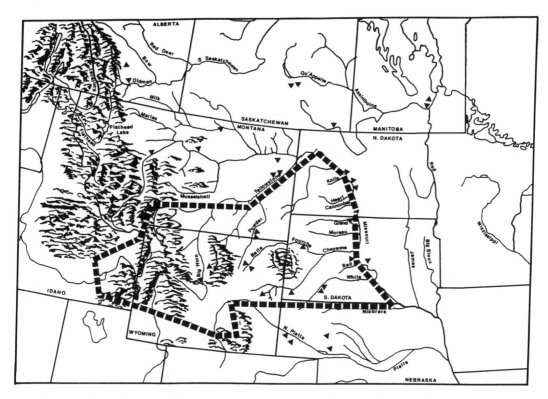

Map 8.3. Distribution of Besant sites within and adjoining the study area. (Adapted from Reeves 1979, 1983a; Fraley 1988.)

more perceived than real (Nowak and Hannus 1981), clearly the Pelican Lake and Besant flintworkers were selecting consistently finer-grained, higher quality materials than some of their predecessors and were involved in a much farther-flung geographic range for lithic procurement than earlier populations.

Besant projectile point types are found frequently in surface collections from the Black Hills (Tratebas 1978:141) and from the Pass Creek basin in the White River Badlands (Lueck and Butterbrodt 1984). Only one excavated Black Hills site has produced Besant points. A shallowly buried hearth containing red ocher, a large dart point, ovate knives, and antler flakers was excavated at 48CK209 (Wheeler n.d.).

The distribution of Besant is particularly difficult to determine due to the tremendous variability in point forms which have never been systematically quantified (map 8.3). While Besant likely evolves from Sandy Creek, it is the least well defined point technology and exhibits the broadest apparent variance, thus complicating questions of origins and distribution. A parallel issue not yet resolved is whether the Sonota complex actually represents a specialized subset of Besant or is a totally separate cultural manifestation.

AVONLEA: A.D. 100–1200

The Avonlea phase is named by Wettlaufer from his description of an "Avonlea culture" in southern Saskatchewan (Wettlaufer and Mayer-Oakes 1960). In 1970, Reeves recognized three subphases of Avonlea occurring largely in the Northwestern Plains. Thomas Kehoe (1973: 74–75) notes: "In comparison of Avonlea Point sequences from sites located in Manitoba, Saskatchewan, Alberta and Montana there seems to be a time-geographical difference among these points. Visual examination of the comparable sequences suggests that the earliest point varieties occur in the Prairie/Parkland edge-area environment of the Canadian Prairie Provinces and the later varieties are represented further to the south in Montana's Plains environments."

Kehoe (1973) saw the producers of the Avonlea point subsisting on woodland bison prior to A.D. 200, with the impounding of large game animals occurring by means of cultural diffusion along the parkland belt from the northwest, reaching into the prairie and plains to the south by approximately A.D. 700–900 (map 8.4). A number of authors, including L. B. Davis and John W. Fisher, Jr. (1988), Dennis C. Joyes (1988), Olga Klimko and Margaret G. Hanna (1988), Reeves (1988), and Tom E. Roll (1988) recognize that a wide variety of adaptive strategies, exhibiting a considerable range of choices and preferences, existed in the subsistence base of the Avonlea peoples. Coincident with varying subsistence foci, Hannus and Nowak see specialized hunting adaptations in South Dakota landforms.

It is our supposition that the physiographic similarities, i.e., the deeply incised ravine/gully terrain, of the Sandstone Buttes region where Ludlow Cave is situated and that of the White River Badlands provide a landform specifically selected for use by Avonlea hunters. The authors feel that specialized impoundment tactics were utilized within the framework provided by available landforms which facilitated the entrapment and killing of the fauna selected. (Hannus and Nowak 1988:188)

Roll, in considering Avonlea, indicates:

Sometime near the beginning of the first millennium A.D., it appears that a technology new to the Northwestern Plains and the Northern Rocky Mountains appeared and was added to the existing tool kit. From appearances, the bow and arrow rapidly replaced the atlatl and dart. By A.D. 800–1000, large projectile points appear infrequently, if at all, and accouterments such as the atlatl spur and atlatl weight go unmentioned in archaeological inventories for that interval.

For most of the Northwestern Plains and in selected localities, if not everywhere, in the Northern Rocky Mountains, small side- to corner-notched projectile points consistent with the Avonlea type herald the introduction of the bow and arrow. We now find sites that contain Avonlea points unevenly distributed over the southern one-half of Alberta and Saskatchewan, south-

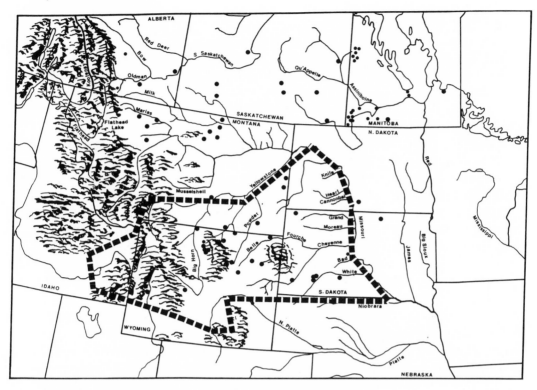

Map 8.4. Distribution of Avonlea sites within and adjoining the study area. (Adapted from Reeves 1970, 1983a; Fraley 1988; Hannus and Nowak 1988.)

western Manitoba, all of Montana, western North and South Dakota and northern Wyoming. They probably also occur in southeasternmost British Columbia and northern Idaho. From all appearances, the earliest dates fall into the northeastern two-thirds of this vast area and the most recent dates come from the western and southern margins. Throughout the area of distribution, substantial overlap in dates exists for the interval ranging from A.D. 600 to A.D. 1000. (Roll 1988:247)

Reeves (1990) has restated a position he assumed earlier (1970, 1983a), namely, that Avonlea derives from the earlier Pelican Lake phase, whereas the technological transfer occurs more slowly between Besant and Old Women's. To Reeves, "Avonlea flintworking is the finest since Paleoindian times. Many points are aesthetically beautifully made and finely finished, a pattern that also characterizes other small tools in their assemblage. Old Women's, by contrast, shows more variability in form and finishing, some of which appears perfunctorily performed" (1990:187).

Some researchers have chosen designations such as "Avonlea-like" to denote cultural entities separate from Avonlea, thus raising questions concerning the taxonomic constructs. One example is Lynn B. Fredlund's (1988:171–82) identification of the Benson's Butte–Beehive complex as a separate cultural entity distinct from Avonlea. Reeves (1988: 312–13) rejects Fredlund's framework. Clearly, there is a need to utilize systematic criteria in recognizing the presence of new technocomplexes.

The persistent issue of sequent cultural phases within a single tradition versus the intrusion of new (replacement) traditions bears heavily on any consideration of the Protohistoric period. Cogent to this consideration is Morlan's organization and interpretation of the radiocarbon dates assigned to Avonlea, as well as those that bear on earlier and later phases and coeval traditions. He (1988:306, fig. 6) constructed a cumulative histogram of radiocarbon determinations for the Pelican Lake and Avonlea phases of the *Tunaxa* tradition and the Sandy Creek, Besant, and Old Women's phases of the *Napikwan* tradition. Of particular value is Morlan's graphic representation of the progressive and rethought interpretation of these phases, expressed by Reeves in updating his 1970 work, as well as by Morlan's 1988 insights based on more current data.

To paraphrase Morlan, Reeves's position in 1970 viewed Besant as displacing Avonlea by approximately A.D. 700, ultimately giving rise to Old Women's phase. This early view has been invalidated by the expanded radiocarbon record available from additional archaeological localities; the Avonlea phase is now understood to persist well past the disappearance of the Besant phase. Reeves in 1983 revised his earlier scheme to show the Sandy Creek phase as predating Besant and incorporated it as an antecedent phase to Besant within the *Napikwan* tradition. Morlan's present conceptualization suggests either that Besant and Avonlea waxed and waned, trading places on the Northern Plains, or that Besant, Avonlea and Old Women's are in fact sequent phases of a single tradition. Morlan proceeds to reject the second proposition due to overriding evidence provided by Reeves (1983a) and others who uphold Avonlea and Besant as separate cultural traditions.

Additionally, it is important to recognize the variations between the other components within Old Women's phase, that is, Prairie vs. Plains side-notched points. As noted by Philip G. Duke (1988), Dyck (1983), Kehoe (1966), and Reeves (1969, 1983a) and reviewed by Morlan (1988), the Prairie side-notched points appear most similar to Besant, while Plains side-notched types are most reminiscent of Avonlea. Morlan, in commenting on the work of Duke (1988) and Reeves (1969, 1983a), hypothesizes that the distinguishing characteristics of the Prairie/Plains pieces either reflect the waning of the *Napikwan* tradition and waxing of the *Tunaxa* tradition, or are evidence of acculturation between Avonlea and Besant, with both contributing to the rise of Old Women's phase.

Duke (1988:268–69), in working with climatic and cultural data for southern Alberta, suggests that Avonlea peoples were the indigenous occupants of the area during the latter half of the Sub-Atlantic period.

Duke argues that as the climate ameliorated there were incursions into the area by Besant phase peoples. He expands this to hypothesize that ultimately Avonlea and Besant amalgamated to form a new phase, Old Women's, each one contributing elements to the new phase. To make our discussion even more interesting, Morlan's results (1988:306, fig. 6) see Besant as already established in the area of southern Alberta much earlier in the Sub-Atlantic episode, noting that the Avonlea phase emerged near the end of this episode. Morlan states that "it appears to me that the Avonlea phase may represent a highly successful adjustment to the Scandic episode [which follows the Sub-Atlantic] *at the eventual expense of the Besant phase*" (1988:307; italics added). In support of this argument, Fraley's (1988:132) graphic representation of Besant and Avonlea localities in eastern Montana indicates an overwhelming preponderance of Besant.

OLD WOMEN'S: A.D. 800–1700

Old Women's phase is defined from R. G. Forbis's (1962) excavation of the Old Women's Buffalo Jump in southern Alberta and is sometimes referred to as Late Plains or Prairie side-notched. Deaver and Deaver (1988:118) note:

Old Women's phase points occur across the entire northern Plains and, indeed, it is hard to distinguish among points of this age from most of western North America. However, the settlement and subsistence adaptation in central North and South Dakota is not the same as that in Montana, northern Wyoming and southern Alberta and Saskatchewan. Since a phase is based on consistency in both artifact style and adaptation, the geographic range for Old Women's phase includes only the Northwestern Plains and not the horticultural adaptation of the central Dakotas or the generalized foraging of the Rocky Mountains. Within the Northwestern Plains, Old Women's artifacts and sites are widespread and more common than any other phase.

Temporal parameters place Old Women's phase in Canada from A.D. 800 to 1700 (Reeves 1983a). Dates in Montana are somewhat more recent, ranging from A.D. 950 to 1700. In Morlan's (1988:305) evaluation of the radiocarbon data base, Old Women's phase terminates at A.D. 1600 due to the arbitrary assignment of A.D. 1950 for radiocarbon calibration. Deaver and Deaver (1988) characterize Old Women's phase as an extremely specialized cultural adaptation principally focused on upland game animals, specifically bison. Lowland localities were utilized as resource communities, but the vast majority of sites demonstrate open, upland locations with some 57 percent of excavated tipi rings in Montana producing diagnostics of Old Women's phase.

While forested areas were used during Old Women's phase, Michael R. Beckes and James D. Keyser (1983:285) note that the introduction of ceramics and the bow and arrow "resulted in a gradual, but noticeable, shift of settlement and exploitation away from the timbered uplands toward the larger, more open stream valleys and plains where optimal bison habitat was present."

Point styles of Old Women's phase are frequently distinguished as either Prairie side-notched or Plains side-notched (Dyck 1983; Kehoe 1966). As was noted earlier by Morlan (1988), Prairie types have been seen as more similar to Besant while the Plains types exhibit well-executed flaking and symmetry reminiscent of Avonlea. Many styles of ceramics have been found in association with Old Women's occupations. Deaver and Deaver (1988) note that some of the ceramic-bearing sites in Montana suggest Middle Missouri origins and are felt to represent "Village visitor" occupations. Keyser and C. M. Davis (1981) postulate a local ceramic style which they have called the Powder River Ceramic Tradition. This is seen to have links with the Middle Missouri villages vis-à-vis ceramic traditions but is believed to have developed in place between A.D. 1000 and 1600.

The Plains horticultural tradition impinges on our study area by means of contributing cultural influences from the east. During the early centuries of the Late Prehistoric period, while Avonlea and Besant nomadic hunting groups were spreading over the Northern and Northwestern Plains, manifestations of the Middle Woodland complex made their incursion into southeastern and eastern South Dakota.

The earliest Middle Woodland manifestation clearly recognized but poorly understood in South Dakota is the Valley phase, first described by A. T. Hill and M. F. Kivett (1941:91 Valley focus) on the basis of early ceramic sites in Nebraska. The proposed ceramic type is Valley Cord-roughened (Kivett 1949). The data on Valley phase subsistence are limited but evidence suggests emphasis on diffuse, riverine resources with bison being relatively unimportant (Kivett 1952, 1953, 1970). Shellfish are abundantly represented and small to medium-sized game such as antelope or deer, water birds, turtles, and rabbits were significant.

Burial mounds for disposal of the dead are associated with the Valley phase (O'Brien 1971), but the absence of diagnostic ceramics from excavated mounds in eastern South Dakota has hampered identification of the mound complex with Valley.

Sites containing Valley Cord-roughened pottery are distributed "on the Plains at least from the border of Kansas, north through Nebraska, and then gradually following the immediate valley of the Missouri River from southeastern South Dakota, northwest North Dakota, and as far west as Havre, Montana" (Neuman 1975:84). Syms (1977:88) has reported Valley phase pottery near the Moore Group mounds in southwestern Manitoba and notes that nothing similar to Valley Cord-roughened pottery has been found in Minnesota.

The Valley phase, based on comparison with material from the Taylor Mound in northeastern Kansas, is probably contemporaneous with Kansas City Hopewell and Illinois Hopewell sites (O'Brien 1971). Dates for Kansas City Hopewell range approximately from A.D. 8 to A.D. 680 (Syms 1977:88). The spatial configuration of Valley phase suggests that it is derived from the Central Plains tradition.

During the succeeding Late Woodland period, horticulture, a sedentary life-style, and increased complexity of social organization represent important changes developing on the eastern periphery of the plains and spreading up major rivers and creeks. In South Dakota this period is recognized by a configuration referred to as the Loseke Creek phase and is identified at sites found exclusively in the Missouri River drainage and along its tributaries, including the James and Big Sioux rivers in southeastern South Dakota and the Niobrara and Platte rivers in eastern Nebraska. Loseke Creek phase sites extend southward from the Chamberlain vicinity (Ludwickson, Blakeslee, and O'Shea 1981: 130) along the Missouri River in western Iowa until contact is made with the Sterns Creek phase configuration in southwestern Iowa and southeastern Nebraska.

The Loseke Creek phase is characterized by cord-roughened pottery having single-line cord-impressed decorations on the rim, generally in horizontal rows but occasionally in alternate triangles or oblique lines over the horizontal rows. Vessels change from the conoidal form of the Middle Woodland to rounded vessels with pronounced flaring rims and distinct shoulders. Vessel walls tend to be thinner with smoothing over cord roughening or simple stamping (Syms 1977:91; Ludwickson et al. 1981: 132).

The Loseke Creek Late Woodland configuration first recognized by Kivett (1952) at the Feye and Lawson sites in Nebraska has been identified in South Dakota at the Arp site (Gant 1967), the Hitchell site (Johnston 1967), the Tabor site (Hurt 1961), the Gavins Point site (Brown 1968), the Scalp Creek and Ellis Creek sites (Hurt 1952), Spawn Mound (Howard 1968) and the Split Rock Creek Mounds (Over and Meleen 1941). Excavations by Benn (1981a) at the Rainbow and MAD sites in western Iowa have provided significant information on the transition from Middle Woodland Valley phase configurations to Late Woodland Loseke Creek. The age of Loseke Creek phase Late Woodland sites is based primarily on four radiocarbon dates from the Arp site (Gant 1967) ranging from A.D. 420 to A.D. 810.

Recognition of Woodland period sites in southwestern South Dakota is not common. Wheeler (n.d.) found Woodland pottery at Mule Creek Rockshelter, associated with corner-notched points. Reeves (1970:80–81 finds these ceramics most closely comparable to Besant and Valley ceramics, and assigns the component to the Upper Miles subphase of Pelican Lake. Tratebas (1979:42–43) reports that stemmed points, similar to those found in Lens D at Ash Hollow Cave (Champe 1946) which are associated with corner-notched points and Woodland pottery, are found in the southern Black Hills (cf. Sigstad and Jolley 1975: figs. 1–3; Haug 1978: figs. 6, 7).

THE CRUCIBLE: MELTING POT FOR ALL

An abbreviated overview is presented below to summarize positions that selected investigators have taken in attempting to utilize ethnographic, linguistic, and archaeological data sets to correlate ethnic identities with tribal movements and distributions in and across the Northern and Northwestern Plains. Early investigators such as Julian H. Steward (1937), Betty H. Huscher and Harold A. Huscher (1942, 1943), E. T. Hall (1944a), Dolores A. Gunnerson (1956), Kehoe and McCorquodale (1961), Melvin C. Aikens (1966), and Kehoe (1973) considered movements and distributions relative to Southern Athapaskan origins.

More recently, J. Loring Haskell (1987) has written a synthesis of Southern Athapaskan migration for the period A.D. 200–1750. Haskell utilizes linguistic, ethnohistoric, and archaeological data in conjunction with a consideration of physiographic zones and subsistence systems. He identifies Avonlea as the archaeological manifestation of Athapaskan peoples and asserts that the peoples carrying this new point type (Avonlea) emerged from the taiga areas in Canada and are inextricably linked with the Chipewyan, Beaver, and Sarcee peoples who practiced communal caribou hunting (Haskell 1987:25). Haskell partially relies on the work of Kehoe (1973) in crediting the Avonleans with the introduction of a number of firsts in the Northwestern Plains, including communal hunting with a bow-and-arrow technology as well as impounding bison prior to their slaughter.

Haskell also suggests that some bands of Avonlea (Athapaskan) people filtered into the Missouri River trench zone of the Dakotas and likely intermarried with Siouan-speaking proto–Mandan-Hidatsa peoples. These events are seen to have occurred by the seventh century A.D.; only slightly later, perhaps by the eighth century A.D., further intermarriage took place with Lenapid peoples drifting into the area who had introduced the Prairie side-notched projectile point (Haskell sees Prairie side-notched points as direct lineal descendants of the Besant point).

Haskell's main research focus surrounds the evidence for a branch of Athapaskan-speaking peoples moving south and west through the Wyoming basins, continuing southward ultimately to become the western Apaches and the Navajos. In the course of delineating this hypothesis, he details the complex interactions in the Northwestern Plains among the Fremont, Athapaskan, indigenous Uto-Aztecan, and Kiowa-Tanoan participants. Haskell's efforts provide a base for framing new hypotheses for future investigations of the archaeological data in terms of Athapaskan migrations.

Utilizing a similar approach, Hannus (1972) reviewed the ethnographic, linguistic, and archaeological data base for the Northwestern Plains in an attempt to identify the presence and movements of Uto-Aztecan speakers from A.D. 400 to 1700. In a series of hypotheses specific to the archaeological data, it was suggested that items other than projectile points, including hearths filled with fire-cracked rock, and petroglyphs and pictographs depicting shield-bearing warrior motifs might represent diagnostic traits for establishing the early presence of Uto-Aztecan speakers from areas west of the Rocky Mountain cordillera, who spread their cultural influence over a wide area of the Northwestern Plains and intermontane area (Hannus 1972:138). Although no confirmation of Hannus's thesis has been forthcoming, the basic arguments have yet to be refuted.

Kehoe (1973:192) in his Gull Lake site monograph postulates the assignment of ethnic identities by suggesting:

The Avonlea people were perhaps Athabascans. If this attribution is correct, we can assume with confidence that they were familiar with communal hunting techniques, probably bison hunting or perhaps caribou hunting. The Prairie Side-Notched Type, which first appears at Gull Lake at about A.D. 700, may be associated with Algonkian peoples and be derived from the earlier Besant point of Saskatchewan's Middle Woodland period. The Plains Side-Notched Type replaces the Prairie Type at about A.D. 1300 and seems associated with the Mississippian sphere of influence. Apparently because of that influence, a point type based on the Mississippi triangular point became the model.

T. A. Foor (1988) reviewed prior hypotheses for assigning Avonlea ethnicities and notes that W. M. Husted (1969:95) chose to refute the Athapaskan connection of Kehoe's and rather suggested that the Avonlea points which make their appearance along the Missouri River of South Dakota by A.D. 1000 as part of the Initial Middle Missouri horizon would be much more aptly placed in affiliation with Siouan peoples (early Mandan/Hidatsa?).

Karl H. Schlesier's (1987) inquiry into the prehistoric origins of the Cheyenne is perhaps the most exhaustive of recent works seeking to establish linguistic/ethnic/tribal identities in the Northern and Northwestern Plains. While the subtleties and complexities of Schlesier's arguments far transcend the present investigation, a portion of his basic argument is important to this chapter. Schlesier's focus for Cheyenne origins rests with the hunters of the Shield Archaic, specifically from that zone west of Hudson Bay. The western groups of Shield Archaic hunters whom he sees as Algonquian speakers derive from ancestral proto-Algonquians, based on the linguistic work of Ives Goddard (1978a). Schlesier suggests that the movement of these Algonquian Shield Archaic peoples toward the Plains was triggered by the intrusion into their area of Pre-Dorset Eskimos, coupled with climatic deteriorations causing a retreat of the boreal forest west and east of Hudson Bay, an event he places at 1500 B.C. In commenting on the complex set of movements and adaptations of Algonquian groups Schlesier (1987:165) states:

It appears that the northernmost Algonquian groups left first. I believe that they passed other groups and, going south, eventually arrived in the northern plains, where they adapted to a different environment, which is known archaeologically as the Besant Phase. My identification of western Besant with groups ancestral to the various historic Blackfoot divisions and of eastern Besant with the Tsistsistas is in agreement with the linguistic data that gives both Blackfoot and Cheyenne, speakers of Plains or Western Algonquian, the greatest linguistic distance from the parental Proto-Algonquian core (Pentland 1978, figs. 1, 2).

Other Algonquian groups from west of Hudson Bay removed eastward through the boreal forest below Hudson Bay, where their presence may be reflected archaeologically in the Laurel and succeeding traditions.

Reeves (1970, 1983a) has dealt extensively with the geographic area and period currently under consideration in this chapter. While recognizing the arguments raised by a number of previously mentioned investigators concerning ethnicity/tribal affiliations posited for Avonlea, Besant, and Old Women's phase manifestations, Reeves (1983a:193) states:

I feel these are tenuous suppositions at best, and are based on reasoning which presupposes that point types associate with language families (Projectile Linguistics) and that one glottochronological construct is better than another. They fail to recognize that different linguistic groups may share the same material culture and vice versa. They assume that old languages never die, nor even fade away.

These linguistic speculative ideas and suggestions are antiquarian in nature and add nothing to Plains anthropological archaeology by an a priori assignment of point types.

While leaving little doubt as to his position regarding the assignment of ethnic identities to projectile point complexes, Reeves in no way fails to recognize the dynamics of linguistic/tribal distributions in the Northern and Northwestern Plains. In a recent article, Reeves (1990: 185) indicates that during Late Prehistoric times (A.D. 200–1750):

. . . dramatic changes occurred on the Northern Plains and its peripheries. Along the Missouri River, village horticultural societies developed, some of which budded off to become semi-nomadic bison hunters such as the prehistoric Crow. Other ethnic groups, the Shoshone and related peoples, appeared on the southwestern periphery, and the prehistoric forerunners of the Cree, Assiniboine, and others appear on the north and east. In the core area of the Northwestern Plains, the Upper Saskatchewan and Missouri River basins, cultures ancestral to the Blackfoot continued to dominate.

In considering the application of the direct historical approach in American archaeology, the works of Waldo R. Wedel (1936, 1938, 1940a) and William Duncan Strong (1940) represent important beginnings. Willey and Sabloff note that Strong's and Wedel's research "laid the firm groundwork for Plains archaeology, with its prehistoric Upper Republican, protohistoric, and Historic Pawnee cultural sequence in Nebraska" (1980:108). However, Strong himself recognized and stated: "Once beyond the historic period specific tribal organization merges into the complex stream of culture history. The known tribal terminations of these streams are essential to link history and prehistory. They convert archaeological sequence into historic reality and anchor archaeology to social science. *Yet, from the protohistoric to earlier periods, all tribal and linguistic appellations become increasingly fallacious*" (Strong 1940:377; italics added).

European contact with the indigenous peoples in the Northern and Northwestern Plains did not occur substantially until the mid-eighteenth century. However, it is becoming acutely clear that the demographic circumstance of New World peoples was catastrophically and irreversibly disrupted early in the sixteenth century through the introduction of European diseases. Ann F. Ramenofsky (1987:173–74) notes: "Because local or regional catastrophic population loss was early and occurred in less than 100 years, survivors were adapting to that loss at the time of initial descriptions. . . . The applicability of the direct historical approach or any other sort of analogical framework to even the late prehistoric record cannot be presumed. Although traits may have survived across the contact border, *survival of traits cannot and should not imply survival of systems*" (italics added). The widespread deaths from disease of the elderly keepers of tribal origin myths is clearly a factor of paramount importance. Faced with such devastating circumstances, one must question how cultural systems could retain the rich detail of their oral traditions. This situation is also discussed by Schlesier (this volume).

THROUGH A GLASS DARKLY: SUMMATION

Some of the potential pitfalls pervading endeavors to link ethnographically documented tribal identities and affiliated language groups with prehistoric manifestations have been noted above in comments by Strong (1940:377), Reeves (1983a:193) and Ramenofsky (1987:173–74). The discussions of the archaeological data base presented in this chapter bring to light other issues to be considered.

The distributional evidence of the diagnostic artifact(s) becomes a crucial issue in the case of the Northern and Northwestern Plains where many migration arguments are tied directly to projectile point complexes. As demonstrated in earlier portions of this chapter, as the areal distributions of archaeologically named traditions and phases have expanded (maps 8.2–8.4), boundaries which may previously have appeared distinct have become considerably more fluid and overlapping. Additionally, while the spatial (geographic) distributions of diagnostic points have been documented, the crucially needed temporal parameters for the same materials have not been obtained, due to the lack of stratigraphically secure site excavations. Thus, a curious irony exists whereby although the data base appears to be enhanced, our understanding of the movements of peoples and diffusion of technology has actually become more confounded.

The spatial and temporal divisions of the archaeological data set do not equate with the calendrical events of an extant cultural system, nor are they designed to do so. This is especially true for the Northern and Northwestern Plains where human cultural groups were adapting to particularly extreme climatic and physiographic pressures. In turn, these pressures served to focus and restrict the lifeways, and appear to have produced similar and overlapping strategies for survival. These strategies seem to have precluded cultural elaborations which can be easily read in the archaeological (artifactual) assemblage. The principal cultural diagnostic for the Northern and Northwestern Plains, the projectile point, is at present likely too subjective a category to produce the subtle definition required to mark peoples and language units.

In the search for new data sets, perhaps our most useful avenue for ascertaining ethnicity is contained in new directions and methodologies becoming available to physical anthropologists. Unfortunately, the very data set (human osteologic remains) that might provide unequivocal evidence for migrations in prehistory is in danger of being removed from the purview of physical anthropologists, archaeologists, and paleopathologists. While there are many seemingly inescapable dilemmas and inconsistencies affecting the topic discussed in this chapter, these various difficulties also serve to underscore the vitality of the discipline of anthropology.

CHAPTER 9

THE CENTRAL LOWLAND PLAINS: AN OVERVIEW A.D. 500–1500

Patricia J. O'Brien

THIS chapter will focus on the nature of the human occupation on the Central Lowland Plains between A.D. 500 and 1500. It will also attempt to link these prehistoric populations to historic Indian peoples living in the region in the eighteenth and nineteenth centuries where possible.

The Central Plains of the Great Plains of North America are traditionally bounded by the Rocky Mountains to the west, the Missouri River to the east, the Niobrara River to the north and the Arkansas River drainage to the south. The area is marked today by the modern states of Kansas and Nebraska and the flat eastern plains of Colorado and the southeastern fringes of Wyoming (Wedel 1961:79).

Fundamentally, the Central Plains have two major zones: the High Plains in the west and the Lowland Plains in the east. The boundary between the two is generally marked by the average twenty-inch rainfall line, around the hundredth meridian, which is also the area of change between predominantly short and tall grasses.

The Central Lowland Plains cover the eastern two-thirds of Kansas and Nebraska and the region is bisected by, or bounded by, several major drainages flowing west to east: the Platte in Nebraska and the Kansas in Kansas, with the central and western reaches of the Arkansas River forming part of its southern boundary, and the Niobrara, draining east to the Missouri, its northern boundary (W. R. Wedel 1961:79–84, W. R. Wedel 1986:7–16).

Because the basic description and characteristics of the environment of the Central Plains has been presented in an earlier chapter, mention will be made of only a few salient features which particularly affected human occupation.

As map 9.1 illustrates, in Kansas the Central Lowland Plains are divided into five main regions: the Osage plains, the dissected till plains, the Flint Hills, the dissected high plains, and the Arkansas River lowlands (Self 1978:35–50, W. R. Wedel 1959:6). The dissected till plains and the Flint Hills upland touch into Nebraska at the western edge of what Strong (1935:32) called the glacial area. Nebraska, as map 9.1 shows, has four main regions: the High Plains, the sand hills, the loess plains, and the glacial area (Strong 1935:32). The loess plains and the glacial area are totally in the Central Lowland Plains; the

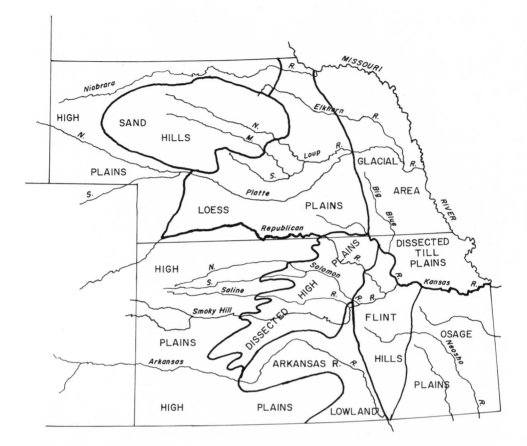

Map 9.1. The major physiographic regions of the Central Plains. The heavy black lines define their borders.

sand hills area is shared between the High Plains and Lowland Plains.

Each of these physiographic regions is bisected by major tributaries of the Kansas and Platte rivers, most of which trend west to east (map 9.1). Within some regions important resources are present or sacred places are found. For example, the Arkansas lowland is poorly drained and has salt marshes and ponds; the Flint Hills, with their east-facing limestone escarpments, have Permian limestones with layers of flint beds and nodules (W. R. Wedel 1959:13); and the dissected high plains on the Solomon River include a mineral spring called Waconda or Great Spirit Spring.

The major mineral used by the Indians of the Central Lowland Plains was chert or flint. The abundant blue-gray cherts of the Flint Hills were very important and consist of Florence, Three-Mile, and Schluyer deposits (Self 1978). Also present in the northern Flint Hills is Kansas pipestone, a red, fine-grained rock used to manufacture pipes and ornaments (James N. Gundersen pers. comm.). Additionally, the Flint Hills and the dissected till plains have large Sioux quartzite glacial boulders that were used to make metates, pounders, hammerstones, and axes. Foracker flint is available in the Osage plains while exposures of Spring Hill, Argentine, Westerville, and Winterset chert are found in the dissected till plains (Greene and Howe 1952). The southern glacial area of Nebraska has a major quarry area, located in Cass County and called Nehawka, which is a northern extension of the Flint Hills (Strong 1935:203). In the dissected and the loess plains, Cretaceous deposits of chalk contain nodules of a brown to yellow chert which is called Graham jasper (W. R. Wedel 1986:28) or sometimes Republican, Alma, or Smoky Hill jasper. It is even called Niobrara jasper. In Norton County, Kansas, a soft pinkish, whitish, or yellowish pipestone is found near a Graham jasper quarry (W. R. Wedel 1986:28). In the same broad region Dakota sandstone is found. It was used to manufacture abrading tools.

It is not without interest to note that there is little naturally occurring hematite (used for red paint pigment) in the Central Lowland Plains (O'Brien 1988:33–34). It is reported in pebble counts in glacial till, 1–2 pebbles per 1000, but is not economically exploitable. The nearest hematite deposits are in central Missouri. Also traded into the region from the Amarillo, Texas, area after A.D. 1000 is Alibates flint and Southwest obsidian (W. R. Wedel 1959:506–7).

W. R. Wedel (1986:43) has summarized chronologically the Late Pleistocene and Holocene climates of the Great Plains. For the period between A.D. 500 to 1500 four major changes occurred. From A.D. 300–400 to 700–750, in a period called the Scandic climatic episode, Atlantic conditions prevailed with strong westerly winds, and conditions were drier and/or warmer than today, especially on the northern Plains. This regime was followed by a Neo-Atlantic one, from about A.D. 700–750 to A.D. 1150–1200, with continued warmth and an influx of tropical air. There was an increase in summer rains and the prairies extended westward. Our period under study climatically ends at A.D. 1550 with a Pacific climate between A.D. 1150–1200 to 1550, during which the westerlies were strengthened, bringing seasonally dry air and lower temperatures and precipitation. There is some retreat of the prairie, and native horticultural populations withdrew from the western edge of the Central Lowland Plains.

THE A.D. 500 BASELINE: MIDDLE WOODLAND

The archaeological presence in the Central Lowland Plains at A.D. 500 is associated with what is called Woodland throughout the eastern United States. Within Illinois and other Midwest states the Woodland tradition is believed to have three major expressions: Early, Middle

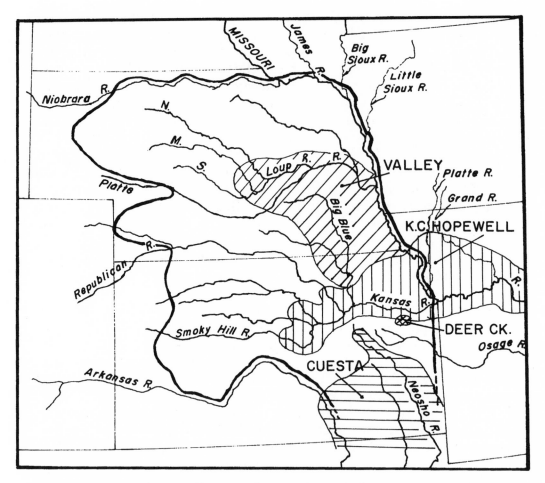

Map 9.2. Location of Hopewellian complexes or phases on the Central Lowland Plains, ca. A.D. 1–500.

(including Hopewellian), and Late. They are generally dated at 1000 to 500 B.C., 500 B.C. to 500 A.D., and A.D. 500 to 900, respectively (O'Brien 1984:45). Two major Middle Woodland components are present at the A.D. 500 dateline in the Central Lowland Plains: Kansas City Hopewell and the Cuesta phase. Also present is the less well defined Deer Creek phase, while a phase called Valley may just precede the dateline (map 9.2).

Kansas City Hopewell

Kansas City Hopewell materials are well defined on the eastern edge of the region at the confluence of the Kansas and Missouri rivers. Kansas City Hopewell was identified by J. Mett Shippee in the 1930s, and Waldo R. Wedel conducted the first full scale excavations at the Renner site in Missouri in the late 1930s (Wedel 1943). While a number of important Kansas City Hopewell sites are found on the Kansas side of the Missouri River, the most important excavations were at the Trowbridge site (Bell 1976).

Diagnostic artifacts associated with the complex include Stueben, Synder, Gibson, and Ensor projectile points, and blocky or circular end scrapers. Pottery consists of well-made sand-tempered globular jars often having S-shaped rims. Early pottery is decorated with cordmarking and at the top of the rim cord-wrapped stick impressions are found; below the impressions a horizontal line of embossing is present. Classic Kansas City Hopewellian vessels have smoothed surfaces, but near the rim incised cross-hatching and vertical or horizontal rocker-stamping occurs. Below the hatching, in the incurve of the S-rim, a row of punctates is typically found. The bodies of the vessels can be either plain or covered with rows of rocker stamping set in zones defined by incised lines. Late Kansas City Hopewellian pottery is usually plain, and the rims tend to flare out slightly. Their lips are plain, notched, or slightly crenelated (Johnson and Johnson 1975).

More exotic artifacts associated with the complex are platform pipes, copper celts, and obsidian flakes. The latter two items show that Kansas City Hopewellian peoples participated in the larger Hopewellian Interaction Sphere of the eastern United States for these latter materials come from Lake Superior and Yellowstone National Park respectively.

Also associated with Kansas City Hopewell are stone-vaulted burial mounds in which cremated human bone has been found. Osteological analysis of the fragmented bone reveals that adult men and women, adolescents, and children were interred in the mounds. The settlement system is defined by large, permanent villages with numerous straight-walled storage pits, situated at the mouths of major creeks with attendant ancillary, specialized limited-activity sites—for example, plant-processing camps, fishing camps, and quarry sites—found scattered up the creek (Johnson 1976:7–15).

The economy of these people is heavily focused on hunting deer as well as the utilization of beaver, rabbit, raccoon, turkey, migratory waterfowl, turtle, and some bison. A variety of wild tubers, seeds, nuts, and fruits were used, as was domesticated *Iva annua* (O'Brien 1982). Adair (1988:83–100) has summarized the evidence for the use of cultivated plants in Kansas City Hopewell times, and believes corn, squash and *Iva* were grown, but used with wild plants for greater seasonal security.

Kansas City Hopewellian materials have been recovered in sites within the Flint Hills region around Manhattan at the Ashland Bottoms site, 14RY603 (O'Brien et al. 1979), the Eggers site, 14RY609, and the Don Wells site, 14RY404 (O'Brien 1972). The Ashland Bottoms and Don Wells sites all seem to be specialized limited-activity camps. The

Eggers site may represent a more permanent settlement. Schultz and Spaulding (1948) reported a Kansas City Hopewellian burial mound in the Junction City area while Witty (1963:59) identified Hopewellian expressions at the Streeter site on the Republican River south of Clay Center, Kansas. In general Hopewellian materials are found south of the Nebraska border in the Republican River drainage (W. R. Wedel 1986:82–86). Scattered Hopewellian materials have been reported on the Smoky Hill and the Saline river drainages of Kansas too.

Kansas City Hopewellian materials are quite rare in the glacial area of southeastern Nebraska according to Strong (1935:285), although Kivett reported finding a burial of two possible Hopewellians in the Central High Plains in Red Willow County, Nebraska in the 1960s (Wedel 1986:91). It is possible that these individuals were associated with trade in obsidian. The Kelley site in Doniphan County, Kansas just south of the Nebraska border may represent the northern outpost of this complex (Katz 1969, 1976).

Kansas City Hopewellian materials have strong stylistic similarities to Illinois Hopewell, indeed Wedel in 1943 suggested the complex represented an intrusion of Hopewellians from the lower Illinois River up the Missouri River.

Cuesta Phase

In the Osage plains area of southeastern Kansas the Cuesta phase has been defined by Marshall (1972), Brogan (1981), and Thies (1985). This Hopewellian complex is related to the Cooper focus or phase found across the border in Oklahoma. Cooper was first identified by Baerreis (1939a, 1939b) from the type site on the Grand (Neosho) River drainage.

The Cuesta phase is defined by pottery which is grog tempered and globular in shape. It too has many classic Hopewellian traits including dentate stamping, embossing, crosshatching, rocker stamping, and punctation, often set in incised line zones, and Marshall (1972:230–31) called the pottery Cuesta Ware. Projectile points include Gary, Langtry, Synder, and Ensor types. Blocky and circular end scrapers are present while more exotic materials include cut and polished deer jaws and a polished hematite celt (Marshall 1972:229,81).

Cuesta phase houses have been recovered. In general they are round to oval enclosing about one thousand to two thousand square feet (Marshall 1972:227). Five houses discovered at one site, Infinity (14MY305), imply hamlets or very small villages while ancillary camps with only one or two structures have been excavated in Big Hill Lake (Brogan 1981:77). To date no adult burial materials for the complex have been recovered, and no mounds are reported near the villages. Two infants, buried in a flexed position, were recovered in a habitation site, and dog burials were also found at those sites (Marshall 1972:227–30).

The economy of these peoples is based on the hunting of deer, beaver, rabbit, raccoon, turkey, turtle, and canids, and collecting freshwater mollusca. They also exploited wild plants like sunflower and wild plum, and nuts like acorn and hickory. One corn kernel, suggesting some horticulture, was recovered (Brogan 1981:70).

Although Cuesta phase materials are stylistically similar to Hopewellian materials throughout the United States, the radiocarbon dates associated with the complex are late: A.D. 780, 970, and 960, almost three hundred years after Hopewell has disappeared. Very likely the radiocarbon dates are in error.

Cuesta's association with the more northerly Kansas City Hopewell is unclear, it is possible the complex is related to the more southerly Marksville materials from the lower Mississippi and Arkansas rivers to the southeast. One site — Arrowhead Island in John Redmond Lake in the Osage plains — has a mixture of Kansas City Hopewell (25 percent) and Cuesta Hopewell (75 percent) ceramics (Thies 1985:51). It also has a figurine similar to a type found at Trowbridge, a Kansas City Hopewell site (Thies 1985:48). It should be noted, however, that the Cooper focus/phase has figurines too. The site is approximately equidistant between the "centers" of the two cultural systems. Sites having Cuesta ceramics have been reported from the Council Grove Lake area in the Flint Hills (O'Brien 1983) and from El Dorado Lake on the eastern fringe of the Arkansas River lowland (Grosser 1973). In general the complex is found in the southeast Kansas and northeast Oklahoma.

Valley Phase

While the glacial area and loess plains of Nebraska do not have much of a Hopewellian penetration, there is one possible Middle Woodland complex found in the region: the Valley focus or phase. The Valley site, in Valley County within the Loup River drainage near the eastern edge of the sand hills, was excavated in the 1939 by Hill and Kivett (1940).

The most diagnostic artifact was pottery (Kivett 1949) which was grit tempered and overall cord roughened. The pots were globular jars with either a row of embossing or punctates encircling the rim below the squarish lip, or were marked with cord-wrapped stick impressions and embossing. Illustrated projectile points (Hill and Kivett 1940:169) are related to Gibson, Ensor, and Stueben types, and circular and blocky scrapers were found. Aside from the type site, the complex is best known from burial mounds excavated in Nebraska (Hill and Kivett 1940) and one, Taylor Mound, in Doniphan County, Kansas just across the Nebraska border (O'Brien 1972). It has even been suggested (Cummings 1958:54) that the Sweat Bee Mound near Manhattan, Kansas, overlooking the Big Blue River, might have a Valley affiliation based on its Woodland projectile points.

Burials are typically bundles of bones interred in low limestone cists and/or covered with limestone slabs, which are then covered with a mound of earth (O'Brien 1971). Evidence of a fire in the mounds suggests that mortuary practices included a ritual fire. Since these mounds do not hold all the members of the society these practices imply some type of social differentiation.

Unfortunately the complex is not well known. Taylor Mound has three radiocarbon dates of A.D. 10, A.D. 10, and A.D. 290 for an average of A.D. 100, suggesting it is partly contemporaneous with Kansas City Hopewell (O'Brien 1971). Additionally, Spaulding observed (1949) that this pottery might be Middle Woodland. Tiffany (1978:173) agrees with him, and believes it is related to wares found in southwest Iowa called Keg Creek and Rowe. Tiffany also proposes a correlation with the Havana Wares of Illinois. He argues that the complex is non-Hopewellian, and suggests it dates between 200 B.C. and A.D. 350 (Tiffany 1978:180).

Deer Creek Phase

Johnson (1968) working on the Wakarusa River in Clinton Lake discovered several very small sites with plain surface, grit-tempered pottery. Also present were large stemmed and corner-notched projectile points, and Scallorn-like points, and he discovered one rocker-stamped Kansas City Hopewell bodysherd. Johnson believed the complex dated between A.D. 1 and A.D. 790.

Since the scant materials, both lithic and ceramic, recovered by Johnson seem to be similar to materials found in the Manhattan area, I suspect that the Deer Creek phase is an expression of Kansas City Hopewell peoples moving west up the Kansas River and its tributaries.

Comments

Of these complexes, Kansas City Hopewell and Cuesta appear to be intrusive into the region from the east. Kansas City Hopewell is probably coming from the lower Illinois River area around the juncture of the Missouri and Mississippi rivers. Cuesta may come up the Arkansas River from the lower Mississippi River. The Deer Creek phase appears to be an expression of Kansas City Hopewell moving up the Kansas River. The Valley phase, however, may be a local development responding to the general Late Archaic–Early Woodland admixture in Iowa and Illinois (Tiffany 1978, 1986a:159–70). These Hopewellian complexes generally did not develop indigenously in the region: it is assumed that they moved in upon the Archaic peoples and transformed their lives. This is thought to be the case because the preceding Archaic life style does not appear to be present in the eastern Central Lowland Plains after the time of Christ.

Also found in the Flint Hills area is a burial complex called the Schultz focus which was defined by Eyman (1966) using data excavated by Floyd Schultz of Clay Center, Kansas. Part of the burial data seems to be related to either the Upper Republican or Smoky Hill phase of the Central Plains tradition which dates after A.D. 1000, but some of it is Woodland, and is related to what is called the Schultz phase (O'Brien 1981a). Several sites (14GE41, 14GE303 – the Elliott site, and 14GE607 – the C. C. Witt Mound) belong to this complex.

Pottery is either grit or limestone tempered, surface treatment is generally smooth, though some lips may be notched with a cord, and vessel forms are globular jars. Projectile points are typically Scallorn-type arrowheads. Present evidence suggests small temporary camps with a subsistence base focused upon hunting bison, deer, elk, small furbearers, and migratory waterfowl, and the gathering of wild plants (O'Brien et al. 1973, Parks 1978). Funerary practices point to burial in mounds, but the deceased were cremated first with the burnt bone being carried to the nearby bluffs and broadcast through the dirt fill as the mound was constructed.

Radiocarbon dates of A.D. 15, A.D. 415, and A.D. 700 (O'Brien 1984:54) are associated with the Schultz phase. One interpretation of this range of dates is that the complex was associated in some manner with Kansas City Hopewell in the area and succeeds it. Another is that the early date is incorrect and the complex is really a Plains or Late Woodland type dating after A.D. 500.

A.D. 500–900: LATE OR PLAINS WOODLAND

After approximately A.D. 500 a number different cultural complexes make their appearance in the Central Lowland Plains. They are traditionally called Plains Woodland although they are contemporaneous with complexes that are called Late Woodland in the Midwest and southeastern United States. Seven phases have been identified in Kansas: Keith, Butler, Greenwood, Schultz (previously mentioned), Grasshopper Falls, Hertha, Wakarusa, and an unnamed complex in the Kansas City area. In Nebraska we find Sterns Creek and Loseke Creek materials. Of these phases the best known in Kansas are Keith, Greenwood, Schultz, and Grasshopper Falls (map 9.3).

Keith Phase

Keith is associated with the west-central part of the Central Lowland Plains, being found in the upper reaches of the Republican River drainage, and the Solomon and Saline rivers. It is defined by the

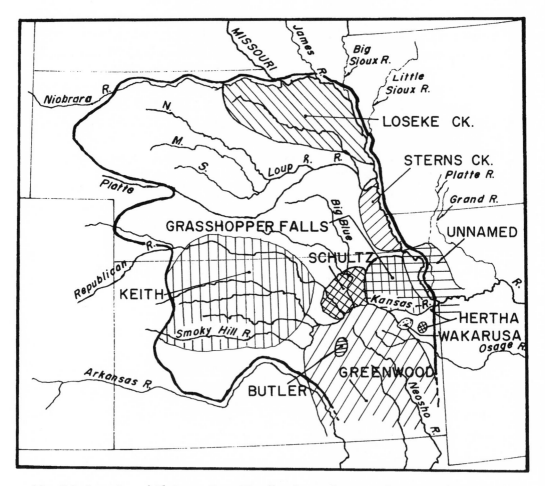

Map 9.3. Location of Plains or Late Woodland complexes or phases on the Central Lowland Plains, ca. A.D. 500–900/1000.

presence of Scallorn projectile points and Hardin Cord-roughened pottery. Vessels are globular with flat, straight rims, and are tempered with calcite. The best known site is the Woodruff Ossuary in Phillips County which was excavated by Kivett (1953), but there is also an excavated ossuary in Webster County, Nebraska (W. R. Wedel 1986:86). Associated with these ossuaries were hundreds of flat shell disc beads including a few trade beads made from *Olivella* and *Marginella* shell, and columella conch beads. The Marshall site ossuary also in Harlan County, excavated by Strong (1935:118–19), may belong to this complex for it too had hundreds of flat shell beads.

Although habitation site data for the complex are poorly known, sites basically being small and inconspicuous camps (W. R. Wedel 1986:85) with shallow basin shelters built of light poles and small pits for food storage, the ossuary mode of burial suggests a settlement of isolated homesteads or homebases, occupants of which were linked through social and ceremonial ties. No tools specifically associated with agricultural practices have been recovered (W. R. Wedel 1986), but deer, bison, and elk were hunted as were small furbearers and birds. Fish and freshwater mollusca were used too, so one aspect of the economy of these people is focused upon hunting.

Butler and Greenwood Phases

The Butler phase is known from the Synder site in Butler County within south-central Kansas. The pottery is tempered with limestone, the surface is overall cordmarked and the rims on the globular jars are rounded or flattened. Small corner-notched, Scallorn projectile points (arrowheads) are present (Grosser 1973).

To the east of Butler County in Greenwood County in the Osage plains are a series of sites which were used to define the Greenwood phase (Reynolds 1984). They were excavated by Calabrese (1967) who defined the Verdigris Wares, which are limestone tempered and cord roughened. Two vessel forms are present, both jars: one with a wide mouth, straight walls, and conical base; the other tapers from a slight shoulder at the rim to a nipplelike base. Scallorn projectile points are common, but some Ensor points occur. Burials are found in the village in a cemetery area. Villages covering up to twenty acres are reported, and long oval houses have been excavated (Reynolds 1984).

The Butler phase and Greenwood phase appear to be the same complex, and fundamentally they are found distributed over the Osage plains and the Arkansas lowlands in the vicinity of the Great Bend in the Arkansas River.

Grasshopper Falls Phase

Another recently defined complex is the Grasshopper Falls phase associated with the Delaware River drainage in the southern half of the dissected till plains of northeastern Kansas. Reynolds (1979, 1981) reports a settlement system of small communities — camps or villages — on the local drainages. He has excavated small sites, covering several acres, and found small trashed-filled pits and small oval houses with floor-space sizes ranging from 115 to 850 square feet. They lack internal hearths and were shallow basins covered with a light pole frame. The pottery is grit tempered with cordmarked or smoothed-over cordmarking. The vessels are globular jars with flared rims and rounded lips, and decoration is rare — occasionally tool impressions or wrapped-stick impressions below the lip. Projectile points are corner-notched; some are large, but most are Scallorn-like. Although an infant was found buried in a house floor, burial practices are not well known.

Wakarusa and Hertha Phases

Johnson (1968) defined the Wakarusa phase has having small wattle-and-daub houses, large stemmed and corner-notched projectile points, and grit- and sand-tempered pottery with overall cordmarking on elongated bodies. The vessels have slightly excurvate rims. Sites are confined to Douglas County and the Wakarusa drainage south of the Kansas River.

Recently the Hertha phase found in the Hillsdale Lake area in Johnson and Miami counties in the Osage plains, about fifty miles south-southeast of Kansas City, was proposed (Blakeslee and Rohn 1986). This phase is located south of the Kansas River and just east of the Wakarusa phase sites. According to Blakeslee and Rohn (1986:122–23) the pottery reportedly consists of subglobular jars with direct rims which are tempered with grog, crushed granite, sand, and crushed and burnt bone. Some sherds are even untempered. Decoration is rare and focused on the lip area. Projectile points are large and small corner-notched types, lanceolate points are occasionally found, and blocky end scrapers occur.

These two phases are linked because it is suspected that they are related. They are probably also related to the Unnamed Kansas City complex to be discussed, and may be part of the Grasshopper Falls phase just north of the Kansas River. Nathan (1980:172) implies as much for the Wakarusa phase in her comment that all the Woodland pottery she discovered in Clinton Lake was related to Grasshopper Falls ceramics.

The Unnamed Kansas City Complex

In the Kansas City area, especially on the Missouri side of the Missouri River, an undefined Late or Plains Woodland complex is present. It has been dated by two radiocarbon dates at A.D. 805 and A.D. 695. It is represented by Scallorn projectile points and a grit-tempered pottery with cordmarked, globular jar forms (McHugh 1980). Associated with the complex was one salvaged burial of a thirty-five-year-old female whose body was probably placed first on a scaffold. Later her bundled bones were interred in a pit, but only after some of the bones were deliberately broken (Frayer and Bradley 1979).

Sterns Creek and Loseke Creek Phases

Plains or Late Woodland complexes in the loess plains and glacial area of Nebraska include the Keith phase materials previously discussed on the Republican River drainage, but also the Sterns Creek and Loseke Creek foci. Both Sterns Creek and Loseke Creek are associated with the glacial area, which is part of the dissected till plains of north-eastern Kansas.

The type site of Sterns Creek, Walker Gilmore, excavated by Sterns, is situated in Cass County along the Missouri River (Strong 1935:175–85). The site was stratified with the Woodland materials below Nebraska culture materials. Remains of a reed-roof thatch house were found as well as pottery which defines the complex (Strong 1935:188–89). It is crumbly, gritty with a chalklike feel, and tempered with grit. The surface is smoothed but not polished, and rims have a "thumb-nail scallop" applied by a "pie-crust" technique or are simply incised or notched. Vessels are elongated globular jars with flaring rims. Projectile points were rare at the type site; only two were recovered (Strong 1935:190–91). One was a triangular type with a basal notch and single side notches—like points associated with the Nebraska culture. The other was triangular with a convex base and no notching. Of greatest interest was the recovery of squash and bottle gourd seeds as well as walnut and hickory shells (Strong 1935:193–94).

Loseke Creek focus or phase sites, in Platte County of northeastern Nebraska, have Feye pottery, globular jars with vertical to flaring rims and rounded or flat lips. Two ceramic types, Feye Cord Impressed and Feye Cord Roughened, exist (Kivett 1952:54–55). The latter's rim lips are occasionally notched, but are usually undecorated. The former's rims are impressed with single cords to create multiple lines or lineal designs of triangles, diagonals, and diamonds (Kivett 1952:54–55). The lithic and bone tool assemblages are poorly known, but corn has been recovered from a trash pit (Kivett 1952:57–58).

Comments

Plains or Late Woodland sites in the Central Lowland Plains share a number of fundamental features. Sites are typically small although larger ones, possibly representing villages, have been reported. Small camps and temporary activity sites abound. Pottery is generally globular jars and most vessels are cord roughened or smoothed-over cord roughened. Projectile points are commonly Scallorn and probably are arrowheads, suggesting the bow and arrow were in use. Burials when they occur are rarely in mounds, except for the Schultz phase, and are either individual interments or ossuaries. Bodies are either placed on scaffolds first or direct primary interment occurs. All these peoples exploit the bison, deer, elk and antelope of the prairie. Interestingly, as W. R. Wedel (1986:92) observes, there is no evidence of mass bison kills. All use the small game and furbearers, and all hunt birds, fish, and collect mollusca. Some evidence of the use of cultivated plants—corn, squash, and *Iva*—is present, but suggests that these complemented a fundamental hunting and gathering mode of living. The inadequate osteological data do not allow us to determine whether the populations were the ancient indigenous peoples developed from the Archaic period or peoples who were mixed through contacts with other populations. The Hopewellian presence at A.D. 500 is surely a cultural intrusion from the east, and may be a physical intrusion too, but the degrees of mixing can not be ascertained presently.

A.D. 1000–1500: THE CENTRAL PLAINS TRADITION

Around A.D. 900 to 1000 major changes occur throughout the Central Lowland Plains with the appearance of cultural remains which are called the Central Plains tradition, the appearance of Middle Mississippian influences with the Steed-Kisker phase in the Kansas City area,

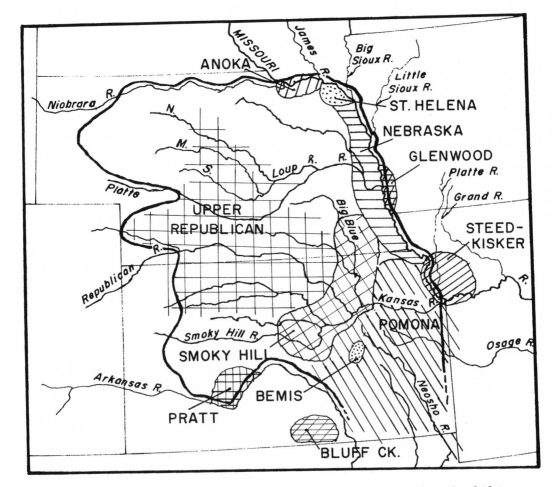

Map 9.4. *Location of Central Plains Tradition phases on the Central Lowland Plains, ca. A.D. 900/1000–1500.*

and in the Osage plains the presence of a complex called Pomona. Finally, in the southern part of the Flint Hills is the Bemis Creek phase (map 9.4).

The Central Plains tradition is characterized by at least three major complexes: the Nebraska phase (Blakeslee and Caldwell 1979, Cooper 1936, Gradwohl 1969, Sterns 1915, Strong 1935) focused in the dissected till plains (glacial area) along the Missouri River; the Upper Republican aspect or phase focused on the Republican River drainage of Kansas and Nebraska in the eastern High Plains and in the loess plains of Nebraska (Carlson 1971; Lippincott 1976, 1978; Strong 1935; W. R. Wedel 1934a, 1934b, 1986; Wood 1969); and the Smoky Hill aspect or phase (Brown 1981; A. E. Johnson 1973; O'Brien 1986; Sperry 1965; W. R. Wedel 1934c, 1959) focused in north-central Kansas in the Flint Hills and southern dissected high plains of central Kansas.

These complexes are all characterized by the presence of semisubterranean earthlodges with central fireplaces and four main interior support posts, rounded ceramic vessel forms — often collared; small, triangular projectile points — arrowheads; diamond-shaped bevel-edged knives; plano-convex end scrapers; bison scapula hoes; and evidence of corn, bean, squash, and sunflower agriculture. Extensive hunting of bison occurred. Scattered isolated earthlodges are distributed up and down the river and creek drainages and they are probably linked to larger hamlets and small villages. The settlement system is highly dispersed.

Upper Republican Phase

Strong (1935) and W. R. Wedel (1959) are our best sources for the Upper Republican Aspect, as it was originally called, while scholars like Lippincott (1976) and Wood (1969) have greatly increased our data base. Wedel recently (1986) has enlarged and summarized our present knowledge.

Upper Republican sites have been excavated in Glen Elder Lake on the Solomon River of the dissected high plains in Kansas (Krause 1969; Lippincott 1976, 1978), on Davies Creek in the North Loup River drainage of the loess plains of Nebraska (Strong 1935), in the Sweetwater area of the loess plains (Champe 1936), and in other isolated areas of the region (Wedel 1986:99). Aside from the presence of squarish or slightly rectangular semisubterranean earthlodges, sand-tempered pottery is the most diagnostic artifact. Two wares, Frontier and Cambridge, have been defined (Wood 1969:18–19) with the former having collared, often decorated, rims and the latter having straight or outsloping, mainly undecorated, rims. W. R. Wedel (1986:130–31) has reported the radiocarbon dates for the complex as about A.D. 1100 to 1400, and suggests that the population left the westerly Medicine Creek area by the end of the thirteenth century. He does not decide (Wedel 1986:132–33) whether they went south to join Texas–Oklahoma panhandle groups or east to become the historic Pawnee and Coalescent (Arikara) peoples. The period generally coincides with the close of the Neo-Atlantic climatic regime and the start of Pacific I. The Pacific I climatic period is thought to represent a cooling and drying of the region with lower temperatures and less rainfall (Wedel 1986:133). Probably the most interesting aspect of Upper Republican sites is that they represent a penetration of agricultural peoples beyond the hundredth meridian onto the Central High Plains. Burial is generally within an ossuary which potentially suggests some continuity from the previous Keith phase in western Kansas, but more importantly this funerary practice serves to integrate socially people who are scattered over the landscape.

Nebraska Phase

The Nebraska phase (or culture, as it is sometimes called) has received considerable attention beginning with the work of Sterns (1915), continuing with that of Strong (1935), Bell and Gilmore (1936), Gunnerson (1952), Gradwohl (1969), and Wood (1969), and culminating in a major reassessment by Blakeslee and Caldwell (1979). The complex is defined by its ceramics: McVey, Beckman, and Swoboda wares (Gunnerson 1952:34–44), all of which are tempered with sand or crushed rock or some mixture of the two, and have cord-roughened surfaces. McVey types have simple, straight to flaring rims, some of which are decorated; Beckman types have braced rims resulting in a collared effect, and some are also decorated; Swoboda types have S-rims which are commonly plain or cord-roughened. Its lithic and bone tool assemblages are similar if not identical to the Upper Republican and Smoky Hill phases.

Blakeslee and Caldwell (1979:112) date the complex between A.D. 1050 and 1450. They reject attempts by Krause (1969) and Brown (1967) to subdivide the phase into two units. They also point out the similarities and differences between the Nebraska phase and the Glenwood phase across the Missouri River in southwestern Iowa (Blakeslee and Caldwell 1979:116), but defer judgment as to whether the two should be linked. Most recently Blakeslee (1988:6–7) discusses the relationship between the Nebraska and St. Helena phases, and the latter's possible transitional position into the Coalescent tradition of the Middle Missouri trench north of the Central Lowland Plains. My own suspicion is that the Nebraska phase, via the St. Helena and the Anoka phases (see Witty 1962), turns into late prehistoric ancestral Arikara Indian.

Smoky Hill Phase

The Smoky Hill aspect or phase was first defined by W. R. Wedel (1959) as he summarized his earlier work (1934b, 1934c) at the Minneapolis site, and his later excavations in the Manhattan area (1959). The Smoky Hill phase includes the Budenbender site on the Blue River (Johnson 1973), the C. C. Witt site and mound beside the juncture of the Kansas, Smoky Hill, and Republican rivers (O'Brien 1986), the Whitford village and cemetery on the Saline River (Wedel 1959), and two lodges excavated in Milford Lake on the lower Republican River (Sperry 1965). It would also include sites excavated by the amateur, Floyd Schultz, in the 1920s and 1930s on the Republican River near Clay Center. The diagnostic pottery for the complex is called Riley Cordroughened and is generally sand-tempered with low, flaring rims or some low collaring of the rim. Many sites, though, have shell-tempered pottery with low, round rims and wide shoulders which are decorated with incised hatchered alternating triangles. Lithics and bone tools are like those of the other Central Plains tradition phases, and a detailed study of faunal use and bone tool manufacture has been presented by Brown (1981). Her data point to extensive utilization of all animals, waterfowl, fish, and mollusca found in the region.

Information on the religious ideology of Smoky Hill peoples, based on data from the C. C. Witt site, strongly documents the relationship of this complex to the historic Pawnee (O'Brien 1986), including evidence for a possible sacrifice to Morning Star at A.D. 1300. Based on radiocarbon dates, ignoring some late A.D. 1550 to 1700 samples, the Smoky Hill phase dates between A.D. 1000 and 1300; dates that are slightly earlier than those for Upper Republican or Nebraska. Indeed, Wedel (1959:564–65) has suggested that Smoky Hill could be the source of "classic" Upper Republican and Nebraska.

If Wedel's notion that Smoky Hill is the source of Upper Republican and Nebraska is correct, one could see the Smoky Hill phase representing a generalized northern Caddoan linguistic tradition which results in the Pawnee via an Upper Republican–Itskari–Lower Loup linkage, and the Arikara via a Nebraska–St. Helena–La Roche (with Anoka) linkage.

Another scenario could see the Smoky Hill phase as representing the South Bands of the Pawnee, with Upper Republican representing the Skidi Pawnee and Nebraska the Arikara. This interpretation makes some sense if the argument that the Smoky Hill phase C. C. Witt site is the home of a prehistoric cleric who probably was an ancestor of the South Band Pawnee. This is especially probable if the bobwhite quail is the symbol for the South Band Pawnee (O'Brien and Post 1988). If that is the case, then the three basic divisions of the northern Caddoan speakers – Skidi and South Band Pawnee, and Arikara – were established in prehistory, but not earlier than A.D. 1000.

At early historic times, especially in the eighteenth and nineteenth centuries, the Pawnee Indians are found in the heart of the Nebraska loess plains area on the Loup River, a tributary of the Platte River, associated with Lower Loup phase sites (Grange 1968, 1979). Ludwickson (1975) links Lower Loup to the Itskari (Loup River) phase which he then ties to Upper Republican. Two historic Pawnee villages, Monument, 14RP1 (Roberts 1978), and Bogan, 14GE1 (Marshall and Witty 1966), have been excavated on the lower Republican River in the northern Flint Hills of Kansas. Thus, historically the northern Caddoan-speaking Pawnee are present in the late prehistoric and early protohistoric periods in the northern range of Central Plains tradition sites. This without doubt must represent some aspect of their historically recorded traditions that they came from the south. At the same time the movement up the Missouri River by the historic Arikara has parallels in prehistory with the Nebraska, St. Helena, Anoka, and La Roche phases that chronologically progress up the Missouri River trench, replacing each other in turn and culminating in the Bad River phases of early historic times.

Pomona/Clinton Phase

The Pomona phase is a complex situated in the Osage plains of southeastern Kansas. Witty (1967, 1978) has defined the complex and notes that it lacks semisubterranean earthlodges, having oval, light pole frame structures and some interior posts, but not the four-post, central fireplace pattern. The ceramics are globular to rounded with simple, straight or flaring rims, and are tempered with indurated clay, shale, and crushed burnt bone. The subsistence system is based on the hunting of local fauna and the gathering of wild plants although agriculture is suggested by bison scapula hoes. The lithic assemblage has projectile points, knives, and plano-convex end scrapers commonly associated not only with the Central Plains tradition sites, but also with sites of the Southern Plains. The Pomona phase is the widely recognized name for this phase, but in 1968 Johnson defined the Clinton phase in Clinton Lake south of the Kansas River. Chambers et al. (1977:170) note though that Witty identified some of these sites as Pomona. Therefore I suspect the two phases are one and the same.

Witty (1978:61–62) has argued that Pomona is derived from existing Plains or Late Woodland groups and that it developed *in situ* from the preceding Plains or Late Woodland complex in the region, the Greenwood phase, whose pottery pastes match Pomona (Witty 1978:61). Certainly dates of A.D. 720 and 775 could be interpreted in that manner, although the complex also has some very late dates: A.D. 1490, 1495,

1560, and 1600 (O'Brien 1984:65). Witty notes that the range of A.D. 1000–1600 places the complex solidly in the time frame of the Central Plains tradition (Witty 1978:62). Witty (1978:62–63) has also noted some similarities between, on the one hand, Pomona, the Bluff Creek complex in south-central Kansas, and the Pratt Complex in west-central Kansas and, on the other, Southern Plains complexes like Washita in house form, particularly in the construction of light grass-pole structures, but he believes the Pomona phase is distinct from either the Central Plains tradition or Southern Plains tradition sites.

Because Pomona is contemporaneous with the Central Plains tradition, but lacks earthlodges and has pottery whose pastes go into Late or Plains Woodland, Witty argues that Pomona is separate and distinct. At the same time its lithics, scapula hoes, and the presence of Pomona pottery in eastern Smoky Hill phase sites and sites in the Soldier Creek area with Nebraska and Steed-Kisker phase ceramics suggest interaction of some type. This can be explained in three possible ways:

(1) Pomona is separate and evolves out of the Greenwood phase. Such a theory would require it to borrow most or all of its Central Plains tradition lithic assemblage.
(2) Pomona is really related to Smoky Hill and Nebraska which border it, that is, it is part of the Central Plains tradition, and its distinctive ceramic pastes are a product of locally available clays and not cultural choice. As such it reflects a thin, scattered, less permanent population in a region whose southern boundary is adjacent to the aggressive Caddo peoples associated with the Spiro complex in eastern Oklahoma.
(3) The few early dates are incorrect and the complex with its grass-pole structures and other Southern Plains features represents the initial northerly movement of peoples who would ultimately become the historic Wichita.

In interpretations two and three, Pomona would be associated with the central or northern Caddoan-speaking Indian groups. If theory number one holds, they are separate and their ancestors are more obscure — that is, they are Plains or Late Woodland.

Finally, most recently it has been argued that Pomona represents a prehistoric expression, in Kansas, of the Kansa Indians (A. E. Johnson 1991). That theory is highly controversial.

Bemis Creek Phase

In the late 1970s extensive excavations were conducted in El Dorado Lake in the southern Flint Hills. Some of this work focused on the Two Deer site (14BU55) which is dated, based on six averaged radiocarbon dates, to A.D. 1000 ± 25 years or between A.D. 975 and 1025 (Adair 1981:276). The site has been interpreted by Adair (1981:237–356) as documenting the transition between Plains Woodland and the Plains Village periods.

The Two Deer site has small corner-notched projectile points of the Scallorn variety and small blocky end scrapers of the type associated with Woodland. The pottery however is unique in that it is mainly bone tempered with some grog, limestone, and grit, although the exteriors are generally cord-roughened. Most vessels are conical in shape with an occasional globular jar. Rims are straight with flat or rounded lips. As Adair notes (1981:277–78), some bone tempering is associated with the Bluff Creek complex and generally occurs after A.D. 1000 with Middle Ceramic sites. The general shape and paste of the vessels are more like Plains Woodland. Finally, two wattle-and-daub houses, round and rectangular in shape, were defined (Adair 1981:254–55, 257). In some respects these structures are as poorly defined as Pomona houses.

Steed-Kisker Phase

The Steed-Kisker phase was first defined by Wedel (1943) and he said it included the earthlodge with four interior posts and a central fireplace; triangular arrowheads which are unnotched, single side-notched, multiside-notched, and/or basally notched; crescent-shaped knives, planoconvex end scrapers, bison scapula hoes, and Middle Mississippian shell-tempered pottery. The pottery is called Platte Plain and Platte Incised (Calabrese 1969, 1974). Burials were generally extended or flexed in cemeteries, sometimes covered with a mound of earth, on the bluffs overlooking habitation sites (O'Brien 1977, Wedel 1943). The complex dates between A.D. 1000 and 1250 (O'Brien 1984).

Because of the shell-tempered, incised pottery and its designs, Wedel (1943) believed the complex represented an intrusion of Middle Mississippian peoples from the Cahokia region near St. Louis. Additional data presently support this hypothesis (see O'Brien 1975, 1976, 1978a, 1978b, 1981b; McHugh 1980) including a partly wall-trenched house at the Coons site, and a solstice shrine in Smithville Lake (O'Brien and McHugh 1987).

This complex has been proposed as the source for the Doniphan phase of the Nebraska complex of the Central Plains tradition (Calabrese 1969, Krause 1969), but the data presently would seem to represent evidence of a population who intruded into the area, probably to control trade associated with the juncture of the Missouri and Kansas rivers (O'Brien 1988). These people disappear from the region after A.D. 1250. The disappearance may indicate a withdrawal back to Cahokia, or a movement north to join the Middle Mississippian–derived Mill Creek phase or Over focus populations of the Sioux City area, or more radically, to a retrenching in central Missouri via the Oneota tradition associated with the Utz site. The Utz site and the

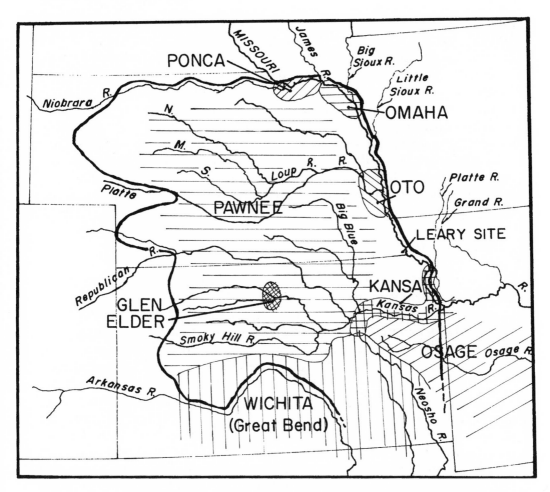

Map 9.5. Location of historic Indian tribes on the Central Lowland Plains, ca. A.D. 1500–1700.

Oneota tradition are ultimately associated with the appearance of the historic Missouri Indians in the late eighteenth century.

If the suggestion that Cahokia is associated with Siouan-speaking Indians is correct, this complex could be evidence for this people's appearance on the eastern border of the Central Lowland Plains (see Tiffany 1991a for a discussion of Mill Creek–Mandan relationships further north near the Missouri and Sioux rivers).

A.D. 1500: THE PROTO-HISTORIC PERIOD

This period of time is characterized by the presence in the Central Lowland Plains of historically known Indian peoples (map 9.5). Aside from the presence of the Pawnee Indians in the Loup River drainage of central Nebraska with the Itskari and Lower Loup phases, and the Wichita Indians with the Great Bend phase in the Arkansas River drainage around A.D. 1500, this region is marked by the appearance of the historic Kansa Indians at the Fanning site in northeastern Kansas (W. R. Wedel 1959) and the King Hill site in St. Joseph, Missouri (Henning 1988). Later they move further west to the Manhattan area and south to Council Grove (O'Brien 1984). Whether this intrusion is associated with an earlier presence of Oneota peoples at the Leary site in southeastern Nebraska (Hill and Wedel 1936, W. R. Wedel 1959), or more radically, with the Glen Elder phase, cannot be answered presently. Also, as mentioned, A. E. Johnson (1991) argues that the Kansa may be associated with the Pomona phase. Finally, at this time, or just a little later, the Osage Indians begin their penetration of the eastern edge of Kansas.

Itskari (Loup River) and Lower Loup Phases

Grange (1968, 1979) has defined the Lower Loup focus or phase and links it to the Historic Pawnee focus (Wedel 1936) in the northern half of the Central Lowland Plains; that is, *it is Pawnee.* Diagnostic artifacts include Lower Loup ceramics of eighteen different types, along with other historic artifacts of European manufacture. Ludwickson (1975) argued that the Upper Republican phase of the Central Plains tradition was linked to the Lower Loup phase via the Itskari or Loup River phase.

The Itskari phase has architecture, community patterning, and settlement distribution similar to those of the Upper Republican (Ludwickson 1975:99). Lithics and bone tools as well as the economy based on maize gardening are also Central Plains tradition practices (Ludwickson 1975:93). One difference is that house floors are larger and communities tend to be nucleated (Ludwickson 1975:99–100). Fundamentally this linkage allows us to document the antiquity of the Pawnee in the Central Lowland Plains back to A.D. 1000.

Glen Elder Phase

Also present in the eastern edge of the dissected high plains is the White Rock aspect (Rusco 1960) which includes the Glen Elder focus (Rusco 1960, Marshall 1967) on the Solomon River and the Blue Stone focus (Rusco 1960) on Prairie Dog Creek in Harlan County, Nebraska. The pottery is called Walnut Decorated and it has Oneota-like designs and vessel shapes, but is tempered with sand (Rusco 1960:30). Tempering materials may be of no great significance in this western region because Murray and Leonard (1962:83, 92) report only two species of mollusca in the waterways this far west, and neither may actually occupy the drainages where these sites are situated.

Marshall (1967:92) ultimately proposed to combine the two foci into one: the Glen Elder focus (phase), and attribute it to Siouan speakers in the region around the seventeenth century. Given the strong "Oneota" similarities of all these complexes it seems reasonable to suggest that Chiwere-speaking Siouan groups like the Oto, Missouri, and Iowa were associated with this complex. This is especially the case if Henning's (1988) powerfully argued theory that the Dhegiha-speaking Siouan Indians: Quapaw, Osage, Kansa, Omaha, and Ponca, are not associated with the Oneota tradition, is correct.

Whitman notes (1937:xi–xii) that the Oto Indians were very wide ranging and got on peacefully with their neighbors. He also mentions that they were reported by Marquette in 1673 as being west of the Missouri River around the fortieth or forty-first degree latitude. Although their distance west of the Missouri River is not stated, their latitude location is in an area adjoining and just north of the Glen Elder focus sites. Thus, it is quite possible the Glen Elder focus (phase) is protohistoric Oto.

Great Bend Phase

In the Great Bend area of the Arkansas River lowlands we discover the presence of the historic Wichita Indians at the time of Coronado's *entrada* in 1541 (W. R. Wedel 1959). These central Caddoan-speaking Indians have been linked by Wedel (1959) to the Great Bend aspect or phase in the immediate protohistoric period at the southern edge of the Central Lowland Plains. Sites with some Great Bend pottery have been reported as far east as Fall River Lake (O'Brien and Elcock 1980) and as far north as Council Grove Lake near the crest separating the Kansas and Arkansas river drainages (O'Brien 1983).

Great Bend phase sites date around A.D. 1500, and trade sherds dating about A.D. 1500–1700 from the American Southwest have been found in Great Bend phase sites. Such sherds are also found at the Pratt site, which is one of the reasons (the other being the nature of the local pottery) that the Pratt complex is a suggested ancestor of Great Bend. Great Bend pottery types, originally associated with two foci of the aspect, are called Cowley, a shell-tempered ware, and Geneseo, a grit-tempered ware. The rims of both are simple and straight or recurved and flaring. Both have generally flat bottoms with Geneseo jars being almost amphoralike (Wedel 1959:575–76). Many of the lithics are like those of the Central Plains or Southern Plains, but arrowheads are typically very small, finely knapped, unnotched triangles.

Pratt and Bluff Creek Complexes

Within the Arkansas River lowlands two complexes, Pratt and Bluff Creek, have been found. Pratt has five incompletely defined pottery types with Southwest trade sherds dating A.D. 1425–1550, as well as a squarish house with braced corners, four interior posts, and central fireplace (O'Brien 1984:63). Bluff Creek has pottery with strong similarities to Geneseo Plain including flat bases (O'Brien 1984:63). For these reasons it may be the immediate ancestor, from the Southern Plains via the Washita phase, to the Great Bend phase.

Finally, at this very late time, post–A.D. 1500, in the center of the western edges of the Central Lowland Plains there appear the Plains Apache with the Dismal River phase, and a small Pueblo ruin called El Quartelejo in western Kansas. Since these Indians are associated with the Central High Plains they will not be discussed here, except to note that they are Athapascan-speaking and must be associated in some manner with the entrance of the Navajo and Apache into the American Southwest.

SUMMARY AND CONCLUSIONS

When the Euro-Americans first appeared in the Central Lowland Plains, in 1541, the Quivira (Wichita) Indians were reported in the Arkansas River lowlands and the Harahey (Pawnee) were north of them. Our present evidence suggests the Wichita were tied to the Great Bend phase sites in the region, but originally the Wichita came into the region probably around A.D. 1400 from the Southern Plains. However, if the Wichita are related to the Pomona phase they would have begun to enter southeastern Kansas by A.D. 1300. They may have been there even earlier if they are linked to the Bemis Creek phase on the Walnut River drainage. The Pawnee were tied to Lower Loup sites found throughout the loess plains, and they can be traced back to an ancestral Central Plains tradition phase called Upper Republican. Upper Republican is probably especially linked to the Skidi, while the Smoky Hill phase of the Central Plains tradition is linked with the Pawnee South Bands. The historic Arikara Indians, relatives of the Pawnee, were historically encountered far to the north on the Missouri River, but their antecedents too can be traced back, via the Nebraska phase, to a generalized northern Caddoan source, called the Central Plains tradition.

At the time of Coronado there was also an intrusion of Siouan-speaking Indians, possibility Ponca or Omaha, and surely Kansa by A.D. 1724, onto the east edge of the region at the confluence of the Kansas River with the Missouri. These people, represented by the historic Kansa, moved up the Kansas River from the central Missouri area, presumably up the Missouri River. They probably followed their linguistic relatives the Ponca and Omaha who moved into the area north and south of the juncture of the Platte and Missouri rivers in Nebraska via a route up the Grand River, through north-central Missouri, and then north to the Des Moines before turning west to the Missouri River (Fletcher and La Flesche [1911] 1972:38–42, Jablow 1974:8).

Shortly before Coronado and other Europeans entered the region, and probably just ahead of the Kansa, the Glen Elder focus (phase) of the Oto, a Chiwere-speaking Siouan group, briefly entered north-central Kansas before moving to the juncture of the Platte and the Missouri River in Nebraska as historically reported. The Leary site, of the Oneota tradition, on the Missouri River just north of the Kansas border probably represents an early appearance of the Missouri Indians in their traditional move up the river to join the Oto by the early nineteenth century.

Thus, the northern Caddoan-speaking Indians are ancestral in the Central Lowland Plains to at least A.D. 1000. Whether those Indians are related to the Plains or Late Woodland peoples is presently not known. Because all the northern Caddoan-speaking Indians have traditions that they came from the south and west, maybe southwest Texas, they could have intruded into the region around A.D. 1000. This is distinctly possible because there is a profound break in material culture between the Central Plains tradition and the Late Woodland tradition.

Witty argues that Pomona arises from the preceding Plains or Late Woodland, and Adair takes the same position for the Bemis Creek phase. If they are correct, it is possible that Caddoan speakers have been in the region since A.D. 500, and are associated with all the different varieties of Plains or Late Woodland. That Plains or Late Woodland seems to have developed out of, or more likely devolved from, the Hopewellian intrusions would suggest that Hopewell itself has a Caddoan-speaking affiliation. The major change from the Archaic, predating the birth of Christ, to the Early Ceramic Hopewellian–derived complexes minimally implies the movement of ideas from the eastern Woodlands onto the Central Lowland Plains, or maximally the intrusion of new populations who either replaced the indigenous peoples or absorbed them.

If, however, the Caddoan speakers enter the region after A.D. 1000, appearing with developed agriculture, then it is possible that the Plains or Late Woodland populations represent a different linguistic group, possibly the Algonquians, who may represent widespread and ancient hunting and gathering populations. Finally, we should remember that the Athapaskans intrude on the western edge of this region by no later than A.D. 1500, while Siouan speakers are entering it from the east not much earlier than A.D. 1500. There may even be an earlier intrusion, at about A.D. 1000, if the Steed-Kisker population's arrival into the Kansas City area represents Siouan speakers from the Cahokia area.

CHAPTER 10

THE CENTRAL HIGH PLAINS: A CULTURAL HISTORICAL SUMMARY

Jeffrey L. Eighmy

PHYSIOGRAPHICALLY, the central portion of the High Plains province is composed of two main features. One of them is a Tertiary age mantle of sediments which once covered nearly the entire area. The other consists of wide basins where the major drainages (North and South Platte rivers and the Arkansas) have cut through the Tertiary mantle. The Colorado Piedmont along the South Platte river and the Goshen Hole lowlands along the North Platte river are the largest of these denuded basins. Escarpments between these two features (such as the Chalk Bluffs, Pine Bluffs, and Wildcat Ridge), produced by the downcutting of the major drainages, result in physiographic features of archaeological importance because the resulting relief and contrast can provide a variety of attractive resource opportunities over a short distance. Many other features such as the Palmer Divide in Colorado produce a topographic and environmental richness often overlooked by casual observation.

Within the High Plains province two major communities can be found—uplands and bottomlands. Despite the semiarid environment, both zones are characterized by rich plant life with a fairly even distribution of species. The upland community is dominated by buffalo and blue grama grasses with shallow roots which utilize water quickly (Costello 1969:23). Trees are by and large restricted to the river valley bottomlands community. Here the dominant species are cottonwood and willow along with elm, ash, hackberry, and box elder. A third community should be mentioned, the tree slope community found along the Colorado foothills of the extreme eastern edge of the Rockies and on many north-facing slopes of the upland breaks zones throughout the study area. Here ponderosa pine and juniper stands can be found alternating with mountain mahogany communities. This community provides numerous resource opportunities in close juxtaposition and in the case of the foothills, the area is an ecotone between the Rocky Mountains and the central High Plains proper.

Taken together, the three ecosystems provide rich and varied resources. In historic times, for example, the Cheyenne are reported to have used and/or eaten thirty-seven different plant species while living as plains nomads (Grinnell 1972, vol. 2), and at least fifty mammals have home ranges in the central High Plains (Lechleitner 1969).

THE CENTRAL HIGH PLAINS IN A.D. 500

In A.D. 500[1] the central High Plains were occupied by hunter-gatherers using atlatls, the bow and arrow, and pottery. The remains of these people are mostly found in numerous campsites. Although cultivation of maize and beans is well documented by contemporary people farther east and south, evidence for cultivation at sites dated to this period in the central High Plains does not exist, except for a single maize phytolith at the Greyrocks site (Tibesar 1980). For example, of the many pollen samples analyzed from sites in the South Platte basin by J. Wood, no pollen from cultivated species was noted in prehistoric context (report from Schoenwetter in Wood 1967:537–66).

Ceramic use in hunting-gathering economies is dated prior to A.D. 500 along the North Platte (Tibesar 1980), along the South Platte (J. Wood 1967), and in the Colorado foothills (Kainer 1976; Wynn, Huber, and McDonald 1985). The pottery and projectile points from sites dated at or prior to A.D. 500 indicate a Plains affiliation. A more specific affiliation for the peoples of this period from the central High Plains is difficult without larger samples from more sites dated prior to A.D. 500. The pottery is thick (5 to 20 mm) with cord-impressed or smoothed-over cord-impressed exteriors and made by the paddle and anvil technique. Rims and partially reconstructed vessels indicate a conical vessel shape with essentially direct rims and no decorations. The projectile points consist of small ovate arrow points (neck widths range between 5 and 7.5 mm) with corner notches, and side- or corner-notched dart points (neck widths range between 12 and 20 mm). Components dating around A.D. 500 in northeastern Colorado are grouped with later components from the area into a South Platte phase of the Colorado Plains Woodland Regional Variant (W. B. Butler 1986: 85–88); however, no consensus has been reached on the relationship of these early South Platte phase components to components in other parts of, or adjacent to, the central High Plains. Similar assemblages can be found in surrounding areas of the Plains at this time. An example is the Butler-Rissler site near Casper, Wyoming (Miller and Waitkus 1989). The pre–A.D. 500 Massacre Canyon site (Kivetts 1952), located just east of the study area in the Republican River drainage, has a point and ceramic assemblage very similar to those on the central High Plains. Mention of the Massacre Canyon site brings up one final observation about the archaeological record on the central High Plains by A.D. 500—burial sites. At Massacre Canyon, seven burials were

[1]Dates referred to in this chapter are based on radiocarbon assays with the exception of tree-ring determinations from Ash Hollow Cave. The radiocarbon assays are corrected for fluctuations in atmospheric carbon by Minze Stuiver and Gordon Pearson's high precision calibration (1986). For the period under consideration, the correction produces either little change or dates fifty to one hundred years younger than uncorrected conversions.

excavated clustered to the southeast of a number of pits and fire hearths. The burials were flexed and largely primary interments. Three dated burial sites are noted prior to A.D. 500 from Colorado (Scott 1979; Wade 1966, 1971). Unlike at Massacre Canyon, however, these burials are not associated with habitation sites and the six burials at Kerb-Klein (Scott 1979) were secondary bundle burials. The bodies were buried with simple grave goods – hammerstones, ground stone, bone beads, bone awls, and flakes.

A.D. 500 TO 1050: THE LATE WOODLAND

The 550-year period between A.D. 500 and 1050 saw a continuation of the pattern established during the previous 500-year period. The central High Plains seem to have been primarily the home of generalized hunter-gatherers who used cordmarked, conical-shaped pottery and placed their dead in primary, flexed burials. The cultural developments characteristic of the area in A.D. 500 continue over much of the area for the next five hundred years in what is known as the Woodland tradition or pattern (dating roughly A.D. 1 to 1050).

The density of sites dated to the second half of the Woodland period is high compared to both the preceding and succeeding five hundred years. At least twenty cord-impressed ceramic components in Colorado, western Nebraska, and southeastern Wyoming have been dated between A.D. 500 and 1050. Features (W. B. Butler 1981:16) at the undescribed Bayou Gulch site dated A.D. 1160 and 1220 and associated with material attributed to the Colorado Plains Woodland Regional Variant of the Plains Woodland Pattern add another dated component and 150 years to the Woodland Pattern in the central High Plains (W. B. Butler 1986:228).

At least fifty other components have been recognized in the literature as part of the Woodland Pattern (Reher 1989, 1971; Butler 1986; Travis 1988; Eighmy 1982; Carlson and Jensen 1973; J. Wood 1967). Surely, many if not most of the these components also date to the late Woodland period. Without absolute dates, however, cross-dating these components to the later half of the Woodland period will be difficult. Woodland ceramics give little help in distinguishing between early and late Woodland. The idea (C. Irwin and H. Irwin 1957; J. Wood 1967:615–17) that lip thickening is a later development within the Woodland period has never been substantiated (W. B. Butler 1986:220). The proportions of projectile points in various types do change through time and provide some help in identifying late Woodland components. William Butler (1986:245) gives vent to the commonly held view that small to medium "corner-notched dart and arrow points appear to predominate in the early part of the Woodland, and triangular, side-notched points seem to be more prevalent towards the end of the period." Based on this trend in projectile point types, it is possible to suggest that ceramic components at Franktown Cave and Cliff Swallow Cave, both located along the South Platte near Denver, are Late Woodland components. Here, wide-mouthed, cordmarked jars with conoidal bases and incurving rims were found with side-notched arrow points.

As a result of the difficulty in distinguishing between pre– and post– A.D. 500 Woodland components, some of what follows will apply to the entire Woodland period. Where possible, observations are restricted to the Late Woodland. In general, the late Woodland refers to components with cordmarked pottery and small side- and corner-notched arrow points.

Most central High Plains components dating between A.D. 500 and 1050 fall into this definition of late Woodland. A notable exception to the characterization of the A.D. 500 to 1050 period as the Woodland pattern is in the form of an aceramic component, 48PL24, in southeast Wyoming (Mulloy 1965a, Mulloy and Steege 1967). Although the site contained the only aceramic component dated to the Late Woodland period, the pattern exhibited by 48PL24 may be much more common; it is not hard to envision late Woodland hunter-gatherers during this time producing aceramic components. Site 48PL24 was excavated as part of the Glendo Reservoir salvage. It is a stone ring site where diagnostic projectile points appear to indicate superimposed Cody (a single Scottsbluff point base) and Besant occupations. No arrow points or pottery were recovered (Mulloy 1965a: 42, 32). However, radiocarbon dates from the lower component, A.D. 540, and from the upper component, A.D. 670, suggest that the site was, in fact, the site of aceramic hunter-gatherers living in tipis during the later half of the Woodland period. The only faunal or floral evidence reported was bison bone with the Scottsbluff point from the lower component. Even if we ignore the incongruity of the point and date association in the lower component, the better represented upper component still is an exception to the general characterization of the period.

The upper component at 48PL24 can be interpreted in two ways. It may reflect a conservative aceramic hunter-gatherer population living at the same time as ceramic, Woodland populations, or it may reflect a special-function camp of otherwise ceramic-using peoples. Mark Miller and Brian Waitkus (1989:1–3) argue that differences within High Plains Woodland material culture may reflect seasonal differences in subsistence activity. The nearby Greyrocks site, for example, dates earlier than the upper component at 48PL24 and also has a dart point and Woodland ceramics. Although it is not hard to imagine Woodland hunter-gatherers in special purpose camps without pottery, it is a little difficult to imagine why the assemblage would contain no arrow point styles. As an alternative, the component may represent the remains of peoples who were part of another cultural tradition without the bow and arrow and living contemporaneously with the Woodland peoples of the central High Plains. Precedent exists in other parts of the High Plains for this alternative scenario. Michael Beckes and James Keyser (1983:107) describe an example of different cultural groups living simultaneously in the Northwest Plains during the Archaic and late prehistoric periods.

Most of the components dated between A.D. 500 and 1050 on the central High Plains, however, easily fall in the late Woodland pattern. The components can be characterized as camps; permanent villages have not been found. While many of these components exhibit features of base camp activities—a large variety of functional tool classes, extensive midden accumulations, hearths, and pits—evidence for permanent habitation structures at the sites is rare. Typically, the components consist of charcoal-stained soil, fire pits, rock-lined hearths, and ash concentrations. The artifact assemblages consist of hunting and gathering tools such as bifaces, corner- and side-notched arrow points, scrapers, drills, flake tools, hammerstones, manos, metates, and bone and antler tools, along with cordmarked pottery.

The sites are often located along ecotones. Many are on stream terraces with easy access to the upland and bottomland communities (Kvamme 1979); many others are located along the Colorado foothills which border the High Plains upland community and the Rocky Mountain front range.

Structures or potential structures have been located at three sites in the Colorado foothills ecotone, and, other than tipi rings such as at 48PL24, these are the only potential habitation structures documented for the period (Morris et al. 1983). At the George Lindsay Ranch site (two features) (Nelson 1971) and at Kinney Springs (E. A. Morris pers. comm.) subrectangular stone foundations measuring about 1.5 by three meters have been uncovered. All three structures had ash concentrations and fire pits while the Kinney Springs structure had an extensive midden accumulation in and around the structure. W. B. Butler (1986:230) reports a pattern of post molds in a Woodland component at Bayou Gulch which may indicate a structure. It has been noted that warming chinook winds can moderate the winter conditions within the foothills, and this climatic condition should result in relatively more attractive winter camp locations. Therefore, the structures may be part of wintertime camping activity.

The foothills ecotone may have attracted Woodland hunter-gatherers for specialized resource exploitation and activity. One hundred and seventy whole and fragmented edge-ground cobbles were picked up at fifteen sites (three-quarters of all sites) in a survey of a small section of the Colorado foothills (Travis 1988). Similar artifacts have been found at other foothills sites in Larimer County, Colorado (Morris et al. 1983;

Grant, Zier, and Rosenberg 1988:174) and north through Wyoming and Montana (Arthur 1966; Frison 1967:18). Edge-ground cobbles have polish on one to five narrow facets of varying widths, and Oscar Lewis (1944) implies that these stones may have been used in hide tanning. The concentration of these artifacts in the Lauri Travis survey of the Colorado foothills is brought up in the context of a Woodland discussion because in Travis's most productive site, 5LR155, edge-ground cobbles were found in association with late Woodland-style arrow points and Woodland ceramic sherds, suggesting that the site may have been an important Woodland period specialized activity camp.

In addition to the structures and edge-ground cobbles, the late Woodland components in the Colorado foothills are distinctive from the late Woodland components farther east in Colorado in having a high frequency of serrated, corner-notched arrow points. Approximately 20 to 25 percent of the corner-notched arrow points in late Woodland components in the Colorado Piedmont have serrated edges. The percentage rises to about 40 to 50 percent within the foothills area.[2]

We know that late Woodland components are found throughout the northern and western part of the central High Plains, along the North Platte, South Platte, Lodgepole Creek, and the Colorado foothills (map 10.1). However, to date, no Woodland component has been reported on the High Plains remnent of eastern Colorado drained by the Republican or Smoky Hill rivers. Further, no Woodland component has been reported east of the foothills in the Arkansas drainage north of the river (i.e., Big Sandy, Rush, Horse, or Black Squirrel creeks). This pattern is partly a reflection of the relative lack of cultural resources management surveys in the area, but may also be an indication of a sparse utilization of the area at this time.

In the Southern Plains, the later part of the Woodland period is recognized as a time when bison were scarce and bison hunting was a relatively unimportant part of the prehistoric subsistence (Dillehay 1974). In this regard, available evidence suggests (W. B. Butler 1986:53–57) that the central High Plains resemble the Central Plains (W. R. Wedel 1986:91–92) in that bison hunting continued to be an important part of the late, as well as the early, Woodland economy, at least in the northern half and western part of the region. At Spring Gulch (Kainer 1976:157) bison may, in fact, account for more than three-quarters of the amount of usable meat represented by the faunal debris.

The basic pattern in the faunal portion of the late Woodland diet was first revealed at Ash Hollow Cave (Champe 1946:43). In the Woodland component seventeen different kinds of animal remains were identified. Antelope, beaver, birds, bison, *Canis*, cat, cottontail, deer, fish,

[2]The author is grateful to David Schaeffer, Colorado State University student, for tabulating point percentages. These percentages are based on counts and types identified in site reports. No reanalysis was attempted.

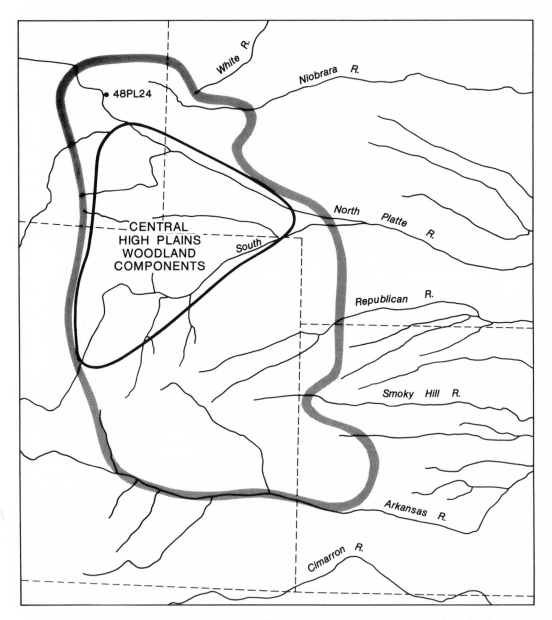

Map 10.1. Distribution of the late Woodland components in the central High Plains. *The aceramic component, 48PL24, discussed in the text, is also shown. Some of the components dated or cross-dated to the* A.D. *500–1050 period can be found in Burgess (1981), Carlson and Jensen (1973), Champe (1946), C. Irwin and H. Irwin (1957), H. Irwin and C. Irwin (1959), Kainer (1976), Kivett (1952), Lawrence and Muceus (1980), Metcalf (1974), Mulloy (1965a), Mulloy and Stege (1967), Nelson (1971), Reher (1989), Tibesar (1980), Travis (1988), J. Wood (1967), Wynn, Huber, and McDonald (1985), and Zier (1989).*

jackrabbit, mollusc, pocket gopher, prairie dog, skunk, turtle, elk, and woodrat were among the species found.

The broadly based hunting strategy is repeated over and over. At Uhl and Biggs (J. Wood 1967:168, 608–9), fifteen species of reptiles, amphibians, rodents, and other small mammals were found along with the remains of deer, pronghorn, and bison. At Site IV at Agate Bluff and LoDaisKa small mammals, pronghorn, bison, and elk were important to the diet (C. Irwin and H. Irwin 1957; H. Irwin and C. Irwin 1959). In addition to the bison at Spring Gulch, late Woodland hunters there were taking mule deer and other small mammals (Kainer 1976). At Owl Canyon Rockshelter (Burgess 1981:72–84) the late Woodland component contained the remains of deer, bison, small mammals, and rodents, most notably woodrat and rabbit.

The vegetable harvest is much less well known, but this fact is probably due to preservation and recovery problems. At Site IV of Agate Bluff (C. Irwin and H. Irwin 1957), the remains of sunflower, waxcurrant bush, wild grape, and yucca were found. At LoDaisKa microscopic evidence of *muhlenbergia* and *prunus* were identified along with evidence of popcorn and dent corn (H. Irwin and C. Irwin 1959: 132). At 5Wl453 near Johnstown, Colorado, flotation from a Woodland camp produced remains of goosefoot, sunflower, mustard, and sedge (Lawrence and Muceus 1980:11). Pollen analysis also revealed the presence of *chenopodium* and amaranth.

Burial practices established by A.D. 500 continue through the A.D. 500–1050 period. Burials dated to this period have been found at Aurora (Guthrie 1982), Hazeltine Heights (Buckles et al. 1963), and Red Creek (Butler, Chomko, and Hoffman 1986). In the most recent summary of central High Plains burial practices, Butler, Chomko, and Hoffman (1986:17) assign a total of thirty-eight burials to the Woodland period in the central High Plains. About three-quarters of these were primary flexed interments; the remainder were secondary bundle burials. Grave associations, particularly decorative or status items such as *unio* shell and exotic stone pendants, are rare. Most of the associations are hunting and gathering tools and bone beads.

This large burial sample may provide a good opportunity to study the racial affinities of the central High Plains Woodland population, depending on the condition of the skeletal collection. However, the necessary research has not been accomplished. Based on a very small sample George Gill and Rhoda Lewis (1977:72) hypothesize that the Late Middle Prehistoric (1500 B.C.–A.D. 500) population from Wyoming and western Nebraska contrasts with contemporary populations to the east in the Central Plains as described by Terrell Phenice (1969) in terms of overall "size, robusticity, and a few specific indices." The results from a subsequent study of a larger but still small sample of burials do not seem to support aligning Late Middle Prehistoric populations in the Northwest Plains with any specific populations farther east (Gill 1981:68).

Clearly, the biological relationships of the large number of Woodland burials on the central High Plains to populations in surrounding areas deserve further study because, culturally, the central High Plains peoples during late Woodland times seem clearly to affiliate with the Central Plains. All those who have worked in the area have agreed that the A.D. 500–1050 occupation is related to the Central Plains Woodland (e.g., J. Wood 1967; Reher 1971; Morris 1982). In the latest treatment of the Woodland cultural material from the Colorado portion of the central High Plains, William Butler (1986:227–34) defines a South Platte phase which he also affiliates with the Central Plains Woodland Pattern. It would be most interesting to compare the racial and cultural affiliations during the Woodland time period (Blakeslee 1981).

William Butler's (1986) South Platte phase provides the opportunity to consider internal variation within the central High Plains Woodland. The phase is defined (1986:227) on the basis of cordmarked, conical-shaped pottery with straight, incurving, or outcurving rims; small corner-notched or triangular, side-notched arrow points; and, possibly, expanding-base drills. The phase replaces an array of previously proposed but poorly defined taxonomic units applied to Woodland material within the South Platte drainage of Colorado. William Butler argues that, in fact, there is very little consistent variation documented throughout the South Platte area and throughout the entire period. The major exceptions to the image of geographic uniformity are, as mentioned earlier, the higher frequency of some artifact types (serrated points, edge-ground cobbles, and structures) along the Colorado foothills and the dart point–to–arrow point temporal shift. The variations in artifact types are not considered sufficient for the identification of separate phases. The variation in artifact assemblages between eastern Colorado and the foothills localities may reflect difference in exploitation during a hunting and gathering seasonal round rather than different social groups. The concentration of sites in the western and northern portions of the study area (see map 10.1) may reflect a subsistence adaptation at this time in which foothills/escarpment resources and locations were more important than those of the broad central High Plains to the east and south. Temporally, no economic, social, or cultural changes have been documented between A.D. 500 and 1050, although recent excavations at the Pine Bluffs site (Reher 1989:xxii) may change that situation.

Not only is it difficult to see significant deviation from the criteria of the South Platte phase within the South Platte drainage, but it is also difficult to see any significant difference between Woodland material on the South Platte River on the one hand and Ash Hollow Cave (Champe 1946), the other western Nebraska components (Bell and Cape 1936;

Carlson and Jensen 1973), and southeast Wyoming (Reher 1971; 1989) on the other hand. With the exception of the non–Woodland-like component at 48PL24, all central High Plains Woodland components for the entire thousand-year period exhibit the general traits listed by Butler for the South Platte phase.

The best possibility for identifying a more specific cultural affiliation for the central High Plains Woodland with a specific Woodland phase to the east (e.g., the Keith phase [Kivett 1952] or Valley phase [Hill and Kivett 1940]) lies in recognizing stylistic similarities in burial practices or in artifact classes such as pottery or projectile points, but none of these classes shows traits which would allow aligning it with specific phases farther east. The ceramic and projectile point traits and the burial practices are too indistinct to show a more specific taxonomic affinity (Butler 1982; 459–62). The most reasonable working hypothsis is that there is a general biological and cultural affinity between the central High Plains Woodland and Central Plains Woodland (Key 1983). In both aspects the model best describing this general affinity and the clinal east-west gradient in cultural traits is of a social network rather than a more centralized social structure (Blakeslee 1981:95). The major discordant note for this model is the discontinuous distribution of sites. Most central High Plains sites are not located to the east near central Plains Woodland sites; they are, rather, concentrated to the north and west.

A.D. 1050 TO 1500

The components dated or cross-dated to the A.D. 1050–1500 period noticeably decline in number and change in character from those of the late portion of the central High Plains Woodland. For example, from Colorado only five sites, Kasper, Biggs, Peavy Rockshelter (J. Wood 1967), Happy Hollow Rockshelter (Steege 1967), and T-W Diamond (Flayharty and Morris 1974) date to this period. Typologically, several other components can be assigned to this period throughout the central High Plains (e.g., Reher 1971), but a quantitative decline over the previous five hundred years is noted.

Peavy and Happy Hollow are rockshelters and Kasper and Biggs are open sites below caprock exposures in the South Platte drainage. They establish the existence of a generalized hunting and gathering subsistence strategy by groups culturally related to people of the Central Plains Village tradition. T-W Diamond is a tipi ring site in the Colorado foothills affiliated with the Intermountain tradition.

Focusing first on the numerically more important Plains Village tradition sites, the dated rockshelter components do not seem to differ functionally among themselves. Occupation zones consist of diffuse middens containing hearth and ash concentrations. Artifact assemblages include triangular, notched and unnotched points, knives, drills, flake tools, manos and metates, abraders, ceramics, and bone awls.

The ceramic assemblages at Peavy and Happy Hollow are large (for the central High Plains) and well preserved. In both cases the ceramic assemblages resemble the ceramics from the Upper Republican phase of the Plains Village tradition in the Republican River valley of Nebraska and Kansas (Sigstad 1969). Louis Steege (1967:20) and John Wood (1967:270–73) are quite definite about the similarities between their ceramic assemblages and those from the Upper Republican phase. Upper Republican ceramics have been used to cross-date a number of other components from the central High Plains to the A.D. 1050–1500 period and to show cultural affinity between the central High Plains components and the Upper Republican phase.

Upper Republican ceramics have been well described elsewhere (Strong 1935; W. R. Wedel 1959; Sigstad 1969). For our purposes it is enough to note that they are distinctive and come in two main varieties (Sigstad 1969): globular jars with collared rims (Frontier Ware) and globular jars with uncollared, flared rims (Cambridge Ware). Incised decoration is usually found on the exterior of the collared rims.

Components cross-dated by Upper Republican ceramics have been found along the North Platte (Strong 1935; Bell and Cape 1936), along Lodgepole Creek (Carlson and Jensen 1973), in southeast Wyoming (Reher 1971; Mulloy 1958:185–86), in eastern Colorado (W. Wood 1971), and in western Kansas (Bowman 1960). For convenience, these components will be called central High Plains Upper Republican components, but they are, in fact, very different from components of the Upper Republican phase proper. A number of these sites (Seven Mile Point, Gurney Peak Bench, Gurney Peak Butte, Red Butte, Coal-Oil Canyon and Buick Campsite) are large, open caprock campsites with commanding views of the surrounding area.

Concerning the cultural affiliation of the sites, three observations can be made. First, their distribution differs noticeably from the previous central High Plains Woodland. Utilization of the High Plains portions of the Upper Republican River (W. Wood 1971) and Smoky Hill River (Bowman 1960) is now documented, but no Upper Republican component has been recorded in the northern Arkansas River locality and only a few sherds have been recorded in the Colorado foothills. A few possible Upper Republican sherds were uncovered at 5PE56, the Avery Ranch site, located just outside the southwest edge of the study area (Zier, Kalasz, Peebles, Van Ness, and Anderson 1988:195). The site and several other nearby sites have pithouse structures and seem more similar to the southeast Colorado area (Eighmy 1982).

Secondly, in a classic example of site unit intrusion, the central High Plains Upper Republican components seem to be seasonal camps of Upper Republican hunters (W. R. Wood 1969:104, 1971a). No burials, structures, or agricultural tools have been found at these sites. Peter Bowman (1960:66) and Charles Reher (1971:155) point out that the seasonal hunting hypothesis needs to explain why Upper Republican hunters were coming hundreds of miles through "some of the best buffalo country on the Plains" just so they could hunt in places like Goshen Hole and Cedar Point. Detailed analysis of tools from these sites may help answer the question of site function. Bowman (1960:66), for example, notes unusually large proportions of arrow points (n = 614), knives, and scrapers at Coal-Oil Canyon. Preparation of large quantities of meat, skins, or bison scapulae for hoes should produce different types of camp debris.

Thirdly, ceramics assemblages from these camps are not all similar. Reher (1971:106, 122–23) recognized that Gurney Peak Butte and Seven Mile Point ceramics comprised only Cambridge Ware, and Gurney Peak Bench ceramics comprised only Frontier Ware. Peavy Rockshelter (J. Wood 1967:272–73) apparently only contained Cambridge Ware, and Happy Hollow Rockshelter (Steege 1967:20) apparently only contained Frontier Ware. Twenty-three of twenty-four vessels represented at 5EL1, Buick Campsite, were from Frontier Ware vessels (W. Wood 1971:67). Other large assemblages, Coal-Oil Canyon (Bowman 1960), Signal Butte (Strong 1935), and Smiley Rockshelter (W. Wood 1971a), were mixed in various proportions.

A number of things could account for the variation in the proportion of rim treatments. The sherd descriptions and identifications could be misleading; in which case a thorough, firsthand reanalysis is in order. In some cases the sherd frequencies are low, possibly representing the remains of the chance breakage of pots of only one type. However, the variation could reflect real differences in prehistoric usage of the central High Plains because sites in the Upper Republican River valley are also known to contain assemblages of only one type or the other (Grange 1980:96). In this event, the variation could reflect temporal differences as Roger Grange suggests (1980:159), or the variation could reflect use of the central High Plains by peoples from within different parts of the Upper Republican phase area. Waldo Wedel's early summary of Kansas archaeology reveals that some of the western Upper Republican sites (e.g., Pottorff site, W. R. Wedel 1959:398–399) have high frequencies of collared rims. Central High Plains Upper Republican sites with high frequencies of collared rims may be the remains of visitations by people from the more westerly portion of the Upper Republican heartland.

Also dated to this period is the T-W Diamond site. It contained about forty-seven stone rings, notched and unnotched triangular points, and 139 sherds from a single, flat-bottomed vessel. The vessel was regularly indented, possibly by fingernail impressions, and then smoothed over. The limited material culture assemblage is consistent with a hunter-gatherer toolkit — scrapers, ground stone, and bone and flake debris.

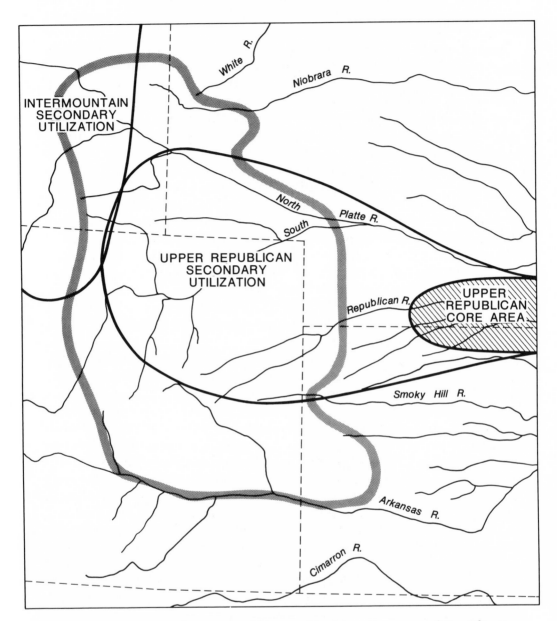

Map 10.2. Distribution of Upper Republican and Intermountain secondary utilization of the central High Plains. Some of the components dated or cross-dated to the A.D. 1050–1500 period can be found in Bell and Cape (1936), Bowman (1960), Carlson and Jensen (1973), Flayharty and Morris (1974), Ireland (1968), Reher (1971), Steege (1967), Strong (1935), Watts (1971), Witkin (1971), J. Wood (1967), W. Wood (1971a), and Zier, Kalasz, Peebles, Van Ness, and Anderson (1988).

Flat-bottomed pottery has also been found at Roberts Buffalo Jump (Witkin 1971), a bison kill and processing site. Little could be learned from the badly eroded and potted site, but at least eighteen bison had been part of the kill.

The ceramics from T-W Diamond and Roberts Buffalo Jump are more similar to Intermountain Ware than to Central Plains tradition pottery (Mulloy 1958). Intermountain Ware has been associated with hunting and gathering components in the Northwest Plains. Several years ago W. Raymond Wood (1972b:13) felt that no firm evidence had been found of Upper Republican occupation of either the Colorado foothills or the montane-alpine areas. The "intrusion" by the eastern Plains populations seems to have been restricted largely to the High Plains. In the succeeding fifteen years little has been reported to alter Wood's conclusion. The one exception is that Upper Republican components have been reported along the front range where the South Platte leaves the mountains (Windmiller and Eddy 1975). Penetration by peoples from the Northwest Plains, as represented by the distribution of Intermountain Ware, is restricted largely to the northwest portion of the area. Besides the Colorado foothills, Intermountain Ware has been found at single component and multicomponent sites in southeast Wyoming (Reher 1971) and, possibly, in northeastern Colorado (J. Wood 1967:647).

Modeling Upper Republican and Intermountain use of the central High Plains can be accomplished by utilizing elements of E. Leigh Syms's co-influence sphere model. The traditional phase concept, while appropriate for sedentary peoples further east and possibly for the resident but nomadic late Woodland populations of the previous five hundred years, is not easily fitted to the data for the central High Plains between A.D. 1050 and 1500. Syms argues that when people use different areas at different intensities and in different ways, the idea of core, secondary, and tertiary use areas may better model the data and the prehistoric utilization of the territory. With this model, core areas for Upper Republican and Intermountain peoples are postulated outside the central High Plains. The central High Plains were used by both Upper Republican and Intermountain peoples less frequently (and at least for the Upper Republican peoples for different purposes) than were their core areas (map 10.2). For a later period, John Bozell and John Ludwickson (1988) have identified a similar pattern of secondary utilization in northwestern Nebraska by Extended Coalescent or Redbird phase peoples from core areas further east.

SUMMARY

The A.D. 500 to 1500 period on the central High Plains saw two major eras. Early, until A.D. 1050, the area was occupied by a hunting and gathering population culturally most closely related to the Woodland

Pattern of the Central Plains. The biological affinity of these peoples has yet to be studied thoroughly. After A.D. 1050 these people have left the area and it, in fact, seems to be void of a resident population. For the next five hundred years the area appears to be a seasonal hunting territory of groups in surrounding areas, from the Northwest Plains and the Central Plains Village tradition. No burials attributed to this period have been documented.

CHAPTER 11

CULTURAL CONTINUITY AND DISCONTINUITY IN THE SOUTHERN PRAIRIES AND CROSS TIMBERS

Susan C. Vehik

THIS chapter will discuss the prehistory and early history of the southern prairies and Cross Timbers (map 11.1). The discussion emphasizes continuity and discontinuity among cultures in time and intercultural relationships over space. An attempt has been made to present all perspectives and therefore discussion is primarily limited to summarizing. Extensive references have been provided for anyone wishing to pursue details.

ENVIRONMENT

The northern boundary of the southern prairies and Cross Timbers was defined by the Smoky Hill and Kansas rivers. The eastern boundary essentially follows the contact between the tallgrass prairie with the Ozarks and Ouachita Mountains and then follows the western edge of the Blackland Prairie of eastern Texas. The southern boundary is marked by the Comanche and Edwards plateaus. The western boundary follows the caprock escarpment of the Llano Estacado and then trends northeastward crossing the Arkansas River west of the Great Bend.

Four basic environmental zones can be defined: floodplain forest, Cross Timbers, tallgrass prairie, and mixed grass prairie (Shelford 1963). The floodplain forest is a continuation of eastern deciduous floodplain forests and diminishes in size to the west and as stream size decreases. Fish, mussels, birds, deer, nuts, and farmable land would have been major resources. The Cross Timbers are composed of post oak, blackjack oak, and black hickory. Major resources were deer, turkey, and nuts. The remaining area consists of tall- and mixed grass prairies. Bison were common, especially where shorter grasses occurred, and pronghorn existed in drier areas. Rabbits, burrowing animals, prairie chickens, grouse, quail, and tubers were other grassland resources.

The area is notorious for its environmental instability. Wendland (1978a) summarizes possible climatic episodes and Hall (1982) suggests a period of drier climate beginning around A.D. 1000. The boundary between tall- and mixed grass prairies appears most unstable while that between grassland and forest is somewhat more stable. Periodic

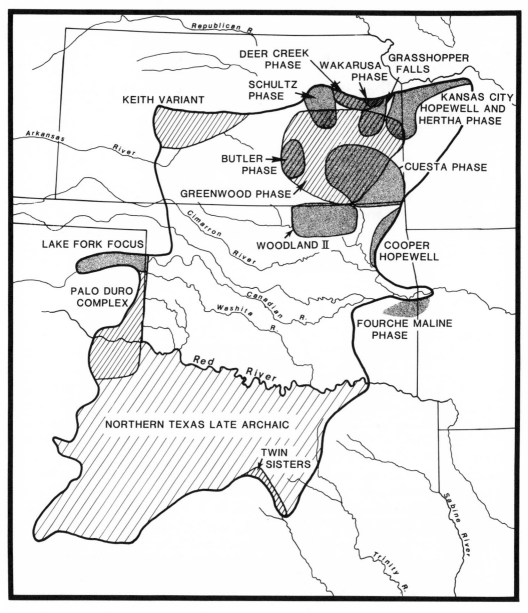

Map 11.1. Southern prairies and Cross Timbers, A.D. 500.

changes in the distribution or frequency of bison have also been suggested (Dillehay 1974; S. Baugh 1986).

SOUTHERN PRAIRIES AND CROSS TIMBERS: A.D. 500

Three cultures (table 11.1, map 11.1) have relatively close relationships to Hopewell: Kansas City Hopewell (A. E. Johnson 1976, 1979; Brown

Table 11.1.
Southern Prairies and Cross Timbers, A.D. 500

Culture	Date (A.D.)
Kansas City Hopewell	1–700
Wakarusa Phase	1–1000
Deer Creek Phase	1–750
Schultz Focus/Phase	1–700
Hertha Phase	365–760
Cuesta Phase	700–1000
Grasshopper Falls Phase	500–1000
Greenwood Phase	400–900
Butler Phase	500–800
Keith Variant	400–800
Cooper Hopewell	Uncertain
Woodland II	300–500
Fourche Maline Phase/Early Ceramic	300 B.C.–A.D. 500
Palo Duro Complex	120–870
Lake Creek Focus	1–1000
Northern Texas Late Archaic	1000 B.C.–A.D. 500
Twin Sisters	200–550

and Simmons 1987), Cuesta phase (Marshall 1972; Brown and Simmons 1987), and Cooper focus (Bell and Baerreis 1951; Vehik 1984, 1987). Migration from the Illinois River valley is seen as the origin of Kansas City Hopewell. Although migrations cannot be ruled out, Cuesta and Cooper seem more likely to have developed indigenously from Hopewellian contacts (Wyckoff 1980; Sabo and Early 1988; Vehik 1984), possibly from groups such as Kansas City Hopewell. The degree of interaction with Hopewellian populations further east may be limited as the mortuary patterns differ and evidence for involvement in the Hopewellian Interaction Sphere is not strong (S. Vehik 1982; Sabo and Early 1988). It is not known what became of these groups. All may have been ancestral to later Woodland complexes. Cooper may have been displaced by an Arkansas River Valley Caddoan expansion up the Neosho River (Wyckoff 1980) or assimilated into the following Delaware B focus (Purrington 1971).

There are several complexes that seem to have been less closely involved with Hopewell: Wakarusa, Deer Creek, and Schultz in Kansas (Brown and Simmons 1987; O'Brien et al. 1973) and Woodland I in Oklahoma (Vehik 1984, 1985). Origins are seen in indigenous local Archaic groups, often with Hopewellian influences. All are seen as ancestral to either later Plains Woodland or Plains Village tradition cultures. Schultz in particular exhibits ceramic and lithic technology similarities to Upper Republican and Smoky Hill variant cultures of the Plains Village tradition. In north-central Oklahoma a gradual change from a settlement pattern emphasizing an upstream exploitation of Arkansas River tributaries to one stressing cross-stream exploitation indicates continuity with later Woodland and Plains Village tradition occupations.

Several other cultures date somewhat later in time: Hertha phase, Grasshopper Falls phase, Greenwood phase, Butler phase, and Keith variant in Kansas (Brown and Simmons 1987; Reynolds 1979; Witty 1982; Grosser 1973; Kivett 1953), and Woodland II–III and Delaware B focus in Oklahoma (Vehik 1984, 1985; Purrington 1971). These are late Plains Woodland groups and are all assumed to have developed indigenously, generally from previous Woodland groups but sometimes from a Late Archaic culture. All may be ancestral to Plains Village tradition groups. Hertha and Greenwood are considered specifically to be ancestral to Pomona variant. Keith may be connected to developments in north-central Kansas and south-central Nebraska. In north-central Oklahoma Woodland II and III exhibit gradual changes from Woodland I occupations. Delaware B may have been displaced by or incorporated into, or continued to coexist with, Arkansas River Valley Caddoan occupations.

Although only occupying a small part of the area under consideration, the Fourche Maline phase (Galm 1984) and other complexes along the southeast margin of the southern prairie are extremely important for some later Plains developments. Fourche Maline phase represents a continuation from the Late Archaic Wister phase (1500–300 B.C.) with influences from the Mississippi River Valley, possibly Tchefuncte. Fourche Maline phase is ancestral to Arkansas River Valley Caddoan occupations of the area (Bell 1984). Similar occupations can be found in southeast Oklahoma (R. Vehik 1982; Wyckoff and Fisher 1985), southwest Arkansas and northwest Louisiana (Schambach 1982; Davis 1970), and northeast Texas (Davis 1970; Thurmond 1985; Bruseth and Perttula 1981; Shafer 1978; Story 1981a, 1981b; Story and Creel 1982). These also developed out of local Late Archaic complexes with influences from the Mississippi Valley. They are ancestral to various Caddoan occupations of the area.

The southern portion of the area in central, north-central, northwestern, and west-central Texas was occupied by Archaic cultures (Prewitt 1964, 1981, 1985; Etchieson, Speer, and Hughes 1979; Lynott 1981; Raab and Moir 1982; Shafer 1969; Hughes and Willey 1978). All share a series of artifact similarities that seem to relate more closely to the Southwest with the Edwards Plateau area than to anything further east. Much of southwestern Oklahoma is similar to northwestern Texas (Vehik 1984, 1987). The few Woodland occupations suggest continuity with later Plains Village tradition Custer phase.

In the Texas panhandle were the Palo Duro complex and the Lake Creek focus (Gunnerson 1987; Lintz 1986; D. Hughes 1987; J. Hughes

1962). There are connections to the west with Mogollon groups and connections to the east with Plains Woodland exhibited in the pottery. Similarities are also seen with local Late Archaic groups. Lake Creek is considered a likely ancestor of the Plains Village tradition Antelope Creek phase.

SOUTHERN PRAIRIES AND CROSS TIMBERS TO A.D. 1450/1500

The Pomona variant (table 11.2, map 11.2) dominates eastern Kansas (Witty 1967; Brown and Simmons 1987). Pomona is seen as probably being an indigenous development out of the Woodland tradition Greenwood phase. A northeastward movement may have occurred through time. In the north ceramics grade into those of the Smoky Hill variant. It is uncertain what happened to Pomona but its descendants are expected to have been located in northeast Kansas or southeast Nebraska. A. E. Johnson (1991) suggests they may have become the Kansa.

Bemis Creek phase and Bluff Creek complexes (Brown and Simmons 1987; O'Brien 1984; Witty 1978) are early occupations that are likely indigenous developments or, in the case of Bluff Creek, representative of a migration from the Washita River area of Oklahoma. Both are assumed to have evolved into later Plains Village tradition cultures.

Other complexes in Kansas and north-central Oklahoma include Smoky Hill variant, Pratt complex, and the Uncas site (W. R. Wedel 1959; Brown and Simmons 1987; Galm 1979; Vehik and Flynn 1982; Vehik and Ashworth 1983; Vehik and Swenson 1984). Origins have been

Table 11.2.
Southern Prairies and Cross Timbers to A.D. 1450/1500

Culture	Date (A.D.)
Pomona Variant	960–1430
Smoky Hill Variant	900–1500
Pratt Complex	1400–1500
Bemis Creek Phase	1000
Bluff Creek Complex	1050
Wilmore Complex	1370–1450
Uncas Complex	1300–1400
Arkansas River Valley Caddoans	900–1450
Red River Valley Caddoans	800–1400
Custer and Washita River Phases	800–1450
Zimms Complex	1370–1450
Antelope Creek Phase	1200–1450
Driftwood Phase	550–700
Austin Phase	700–1300
Toyah Phase	1300–1750

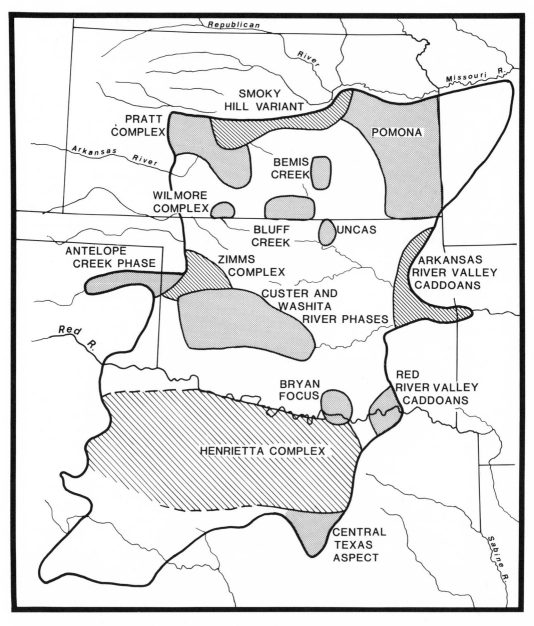

Map 11.2. Southern prairies and Cross Timbers to A.D. 1450/1500.

attributed to migrations and to indigenous development. Smoky Hill variant shares some ceramic similarities with Steed-Kisker and also had some trade connections with Caddoan populations to the southeast. Bell (1983, 1984) implies a migration of Arkansas River Valley Caddoans may be involved in the ancestry of both Steed-Kisker and Smoky Hill. Pratt complex had trade connections with Antelope Creek phase in the Texas panhandle and the Southwest. Uncas also had some lithic material from the Texas panhandle. Uncas has ceramic similarities to Smoky Hill.

Although sometimes suggested to be ancestral to Upper Republican and/or Nebraska variants, Smoky Hill appears to be contemporaneous (compare dates in Brown and Simmons 1987). O'Brien (1986) notes similarities between Smoky Hill ritual practices and Pawnee religious ideology. Pratt may be ancestral to the Great Bend aspect (Vehik 1976). Uncas has ceramic similarities to the Lower Walnut focus of the Great Bend aspect. Bluff Creek may be ancestral to later groups included within the Plains Village tradition.

The Wilmore complex is very poorly documented (Rowlison 1985; Brown and Simmons 1987; Lees 1991). Wilmore may have developed from Bluff Creek. The Buried City complex (Hughes and Hughes-Jones 1987) may be related to Wilmore, although it also resembles Antelope Creek phase in some aspects.

In south-central Kansas there are some village sites seldom discussed in the literature (Keller 1961). Trade connections exist with the Texas panhandle and the Southwest.

The Arkansas River Valley Caddoans occupied the Arkansas River drainage from the Neosho River eastward into southwest Missouri and northwest Arkansas (Bell 1984; Brown 1984; Sabo and Early 1988; Chapman 1980). Caddoan occupations occurred throughout the mountainous area of southwestern Arkansas and southeastern Oklahoma, continued into the Red River valley, and went on yet further south into Louisiana and Texas (Wyckoff and Fisher 1985; Davis 1970; Bruseth and Perttula 1981; Story 1981a). Caddoan society developed from the earlier Fourche Maline phase and similar occupations, possibly with some influence from Mississippi Valley Coles Creek. Trade occurred among Caddoan societies, with Plains societies, and with Mississippi Valley societies. The Caddoan occupations from this period can be traced into later periods.

Custer and Washita River phases are part of the same evolutionary trend (Hofman 1984; Bell 1984; Brooks 1987). Custer is earliest and likely developed locally from Woodland period residents. Trade becomes more important through time with earliest emphasis on trade to the east with Caddoan societies (Swenson 1986). Within Washita River there may have existed eastern and western subphases (Drass and Swenson 1986). Two other complexes, Bryan focus (Bell and Baerreis 1951) and Henrietta focus (Krieger 1947), are very similar, if not identical, to each other (Prewitt and Lawson 1972) and also very similar to Washita River (Krieger 1947; Lorrain 1967, 1969), but they are guess-dated to after A.D. 1450. Another related complex to the west is Zimms (Flynn 1986). The suggestion has been made that Washita River phase moved into the central Kansas area where it became Great Bend aspect (Bell 1973; Wedel 1961). Swenson (1986) and Baugh (1982) provide evidence to support an *in situ* transition to Wheeler phase (Edwards and Wheeler complexes). Krieger (1947) believed that Henrietta was not related to the historic Wichita Indians.

Antelope Creek phase likely is a local development out of the Lake Creek focus and not the Upper Republican variant of Kansas and Nebraska (Hughes and Hughes-Jones 1987; Gunnerson 1987; Lintz 1984, 1986). Trade connections exist both to the Southwest and the Plains. Antelope Creek phase distribution centered on the Alibates agatized dolomite quarries in the latter part of its temporal span. The destiny of Antelope Creek phase populations is uncertain. They may have become incorporated in Wheeler phase or Garza complex occupations or perhaps connections lie to the northeast in central Kansas where the trade of Alibates appears to have been more intense.

Societies in much of northern Texas may have essentially continued on an Archaic level (Lynott 1981; Prewitt 1985).

The Central Texas aspect covered central, south-central, and possibly west-central, north-central, and south Texas (Black 1986; Prewitt 1985; Skinner 1981). It has been suggested to represent a movement out of the southern Plains although no exact location is specified. Newcomb (1961) suggests an origin in the Edwards Plateau aspect. Trade with Caddoan populations to the east is indicated and some artifact styles are identical to those of the Plains Village tradition. The Toyah phase has been linked to the Jumano and, more commonly, the Tonkawa.

SOUTHERN PRAIRIES AND CROSS TIMBERS TO A.D. 1750

Covering much of central and south-central Kansas (table 11.3, map 11.3) were members of the Great Bend aspect (W. R. Wedel 1959; Rohn and Emerson 1984; Lees 1988; Brown and Simmons 1987). The origin of

Table 11.3.
Southern Prairies and Cross Timbers to A.D. 1750

Culture	Date (A.D.)
Great Bend Aspect	1450–1700
Dismal River Aspect	1675–1725
Fort Coffee Phase	1450–1600
Neosho Focus	1350–1600
Wheeler Phase	1450–1750
Garza Complex	1450–1750
Tierra Blanca Complex	1450–1650
Red River Valley Caddoans	1400–1750
Bryan Focus	Uncertain
Henrietta Focus	Uncertain
Norteño Focus	1600–1800

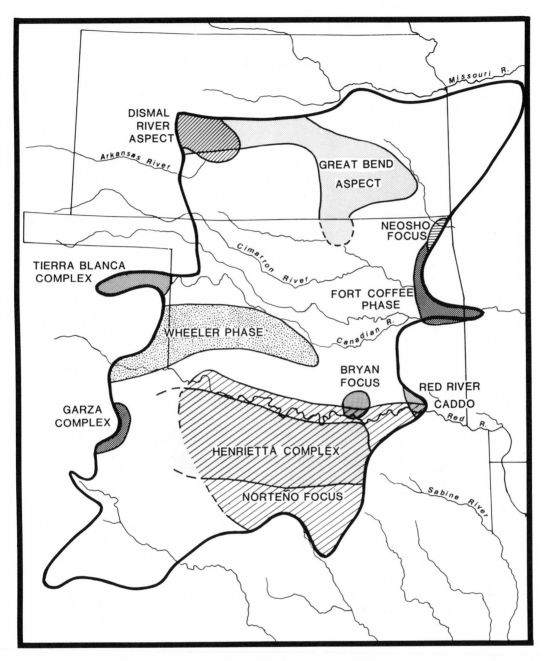

Map 11.3. Southern prairies and Cross Timbers to A.D. *1750.*

Great Bend may lie in either a migration of Washita River phase (Bell 1973; Wedel 1961) or an *in situ* development (Vehik 1976) from elements such as the Pratt, Zyba, Bluff Creek, and other similar sites and complexes. It is not at all obvious that the Smoky Hill and Pomona variants are uninvolved. There is evidence of widespread trade connections both to the southwest and to the north, although the intensity of southwestern connections may have decreased (Keller 1961). Great Bend aspect is ancestral Wichita (general sense) (W. R. Wedel 1959; Vehik 1992).

The Dismal River aspect reflects an Athapaskan migration southward and has been associated with the appearance of the Apache on the southern Plains (Gunnerson 1978; W. R. Wedel 1959; Brown and Simmons 1987). Trade with the Southwest is evident.

In the northeastern corner of Oklahoma was the Neosho focus (Rohrbaugh 1984). Neosho appears to be similar to the Top-Layer culture of northwest Arkansas and southwest Missouri. Chapman (1959) following Baerreis (1939b) sees this as reflecting an Osage intrusion into the area. Other researchers have suggested that it is a member of the Plains Village tradition (W. R. Wedel 1979b). An *in situ* development out of earlier Archaic and Woodland occupations has also been suggested (Freeman 1959, 1962; Sabo and Early 1988). Ceramic, lithic, and ceremonial similarities exist with the Arkansas River Valley Caddo (Rohrbaugh 1984; Purrington 1971; Dickson 1991; Muto et al. n.d.; Sabo 1986). Given that the area occupied by Neosho focus was earlier occupied by populations affiliated with the Arkansas River Valley Caddo, it would seem equally logical that Neosho focus represents the effects of the collapse of Spiro and loss of regional integration. The fate of Neosho focus is not known. However, there is evidence for a Pani/Pawnee (Plains Caddoan) occupation of the area in the eighteenth century (Vehik 1992).

Immediately adjoining Neosho focus to the south is the Fort Coffee phase (Rohrbaugh 1984). Fort Coffee phase represents the Arkansas River Valley Caddoans after the collapse of Spiro. The material culture assemblage suggests strong Plains influence. Trade is documented with the Plains, with Red River Caddoan groups, and to a limited extent with the Southwest (Wyckoff 1980). It has been suggested (Rohrbaugh 1982) that Fort Coffee is ancestral to the Norteño focus and the Kichai. Bell (1983) and Wyckoff (1980) suggest it is ancestral to the Lower Walnut focus of the Great Bend aspect.

Caddoan cultures occupied much of the eastern part of the Red River basin and into eastern Texas and western Louisiana. These represent continuations from the earlier occupations (Davis 1970; Wyckoff 1970) and their descendants were various Caddo groups.

Norteño focus occurs in the same general area as Henrietta (Woodall 1967; Bell and Bastian 1967; Jelks 1967; Harris et al. 1965; Duffield and Jelks 1961). The origin of Norteño has been suggested as being from Henrietta and as not at all involving Henrietta. An origin out of Fort Coffee phase has also been suggested (Rohrbaugh 1982). Major Norteño pottery types are considered to be in the Caddo tradition. The role of shell-tempered plain ware such as found in Henrietta and some of the

Washita River and other complexes is variable, reflecting time and/or space differences. Southwestern materials are present at some sites, but strongest connections are to the east. Rohrbaugh (1982) believes Norteño represents the Kichai and other authors have suggested either Kichai (Harris et al. 1965; Jelks 1967; Mallouf 1976) or Caddo (Davis 1961; Bruseth and Perttula 1981) connections for some Norteño sites. Other researchers consider Norteño to be Wichita (general sense) (Davis 1970; Duffield and Jelks 1961).

To the northwest was the Wheeler phase (T. Baugh 1982, 1986; Swenson 1986; Gunnerson 1987; Hofman 1984). Wheeler has been suggested to be an indigenous development from Washita River phase and possibly Antelope Creek phase. An alternative view sees it as intrusive from the north (Gunnerson 1987). Trade with the Southwest and to a more limited extent with the Southeast, is indicated, although local copying of some southeastern vessel types is indicated (Ferring and Perttula 1986 cited in Brooks 1987).

Further out on the Plains and extending only very slightly into the area under consideration was the Garza complex (T. Baugh 1986; Habicht-Mauche 1987, 1992; Runkles 1964; Johnson et al. 1977). Garza may represent a western extension of the Wheeler phase. Origins have been suggested to be local or from a northern intrusion. Trade with the Southwest is apparently greater than was indicated for Wheeler phase.

Researchers considering Wheeler phase and Garza complex as related to earlier Plains Village tradition sites also consider Wheeler-Garza to represent the Teya (Habicht-Mauche 1992), the Jumano (Baugh 1982), and/or the Escanjaque (Vehik 1986) and to consider these to be Plains Caddoans. Those researchers who see Wheeler-Garza as intrusive from the north consider them to represent the Apaches (Gunnerson 1987; Hofman 1984; Johnson et al. 1977).

To the north of Wheeler phase and Garza complex, and extending only slightly into the area under consideration here, was the Tierra Blanca complex. Very poorly defined in print, Tierra Blanca appears in the northern panhandle of Texas about the time Antelope Creek phase ends (Habicht-Mauche 1992). It is considered to represent the appearance of the Apache on the southern Plains (Habicht-Mauche 1992) at a date earlier than some (Wilcox 1981) assume.

SOUTHERN PRAIRIES AND CROSS TIMBERS: EARLY HISTORIC

The Coronado and DeSoto expeditions of 1540 were the first to provide eyewitness accounts of the area (map 11.4) under consideration (Winship 1896; U.S. De Soto Commission 1939). Quivira was visited by Coronado and it has long been accepted as having been in central Kansas where Wedel (1959) has tied it to the Little River focus of the Great Bend aspect and to the Wichita (general sense) and especially the

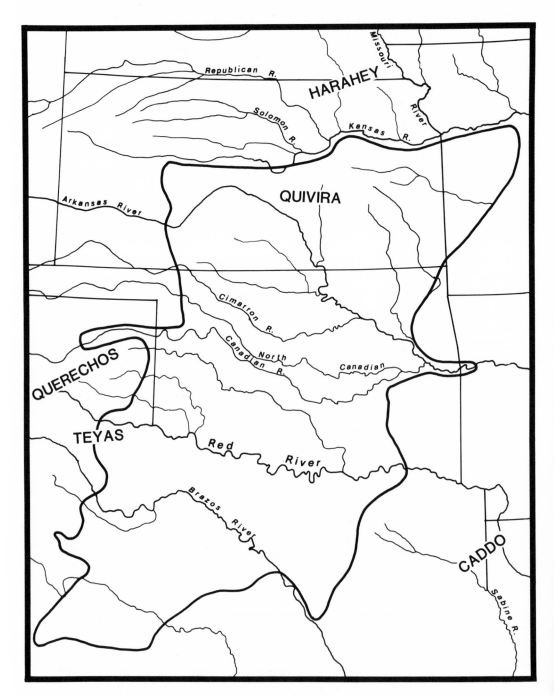

Map 11.4. Southern Prairies and Cross Timbers, Early Historic A.D. 1541.

Tawakoni subdivision (M. M. Wedel 1981; Vehik 1992). Coronado's Querechos have consistently been located in the Texas panhandle and adjacent New Mexico and considered Apache (Wilcox 1981; Habicht-Mauche 1992; Schroeder 1974; John 1975; Newcomb 1961). The area occupied by the Querechos coincides with that assigned to the Tierra Blanca complex. The Teya have also been located in the Texas panhandle and considered Apache or possibly Apache (Newcomb 1961; John 1975; W. R. Wedel 1959) or Jumano, Wichita, Caddoan, or Kichai (Habicht-Mauche 1987, 1992; Vehik 1992; Wilcox 1981; Schroeder 1974; John 1975; Swanton 1942; Bolton 1949). The location of the Teya appears to coincide with the area occupied by the Garza complex and possibly the Wheeler phase (Habicht-Mauche 1987, 1992).

The DeSoto expedition visited a variety of Caddo groups, especially those placed in the Hasinai confederacy of east Texas (Swanton 1946). The historic Hasinai have been placed in the Allen phase which is descended from the prehistoric Frankston focus/phase (Williams 1964; Story and Creel 1982; Davis 1970).

In 1601 Oñate made an *entrada* onto the Plains (Hammond and Rey 1953). A captured native later drew a sketch map of places with which he was familiar (Newcomb and Campbell 1982). This map and its possible ethnohistorical and archaeological correlations have been discussed in detail previously (Vehik 1986, 1992). The Indian was a member of a group called Escanjaques/Aguacanes (map 11.5). The Escanjaques/Aguacanes have been considered to be Apache (Newcomb 1961; W. R. Wedel 1959), Kansa (Hodge 1907), or the Iscani/Waco subdivision of the Wichita (Newcomb and Campbell 1982; Hughes 1968; Schroeder 1962; Vehik 1992). The Escanjaque were out on a hunting expedition when Oñate met them but they also had more permanent settlements to the southwest in the area occupied by the Wheeler phase (Edwards complex). Other places drawn by the captured Indian included Etzanoa, Tancoa, and Uayam. Etzanoa was likely located in the area occupied by the Lower Walnut focus of the Great Bend aspect and represents the Wichita (specific sense), Tancoa was in the area occupied by the Little River focus of the Great Bend aspect (but Newcomb and Campbell [1982] argue Tancoa represents the Tonkawa), and Uayam may have been either the Kansa, Osage, or Taovaya (Vehik 1986, 1992).

The last map (map 11.6) is a composite of several maps and reflects the general state of affairs around 1720. Not all of the cultural entities that appear on these maps were put on the composite. The composite only includes those entities that appear consistently on the maps and are discussed in documents.

On the southeast periphery were the Caddoan Hasinai (east Texas) and Kadohadacho (Great Bend of the Red River) confederacies. The Kadohadacho are represented in the historic Little River phase (Trubowitz 1984)

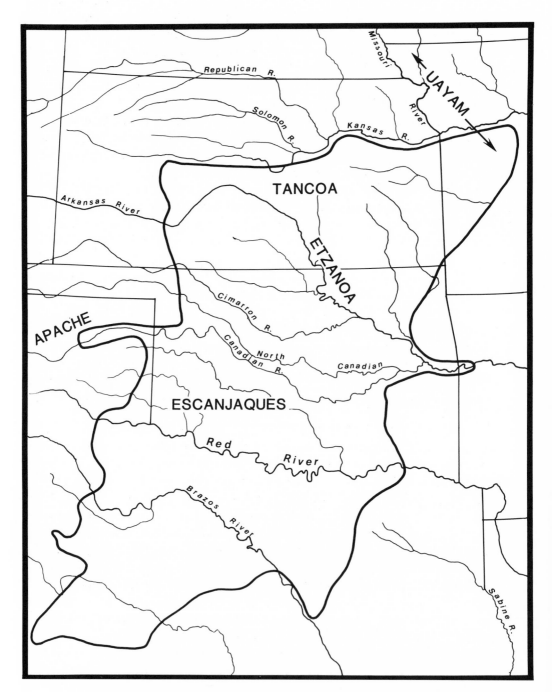

Map 11.5. Southern Prairies and Cross Timbers, Early Historic A.D. *1601.*

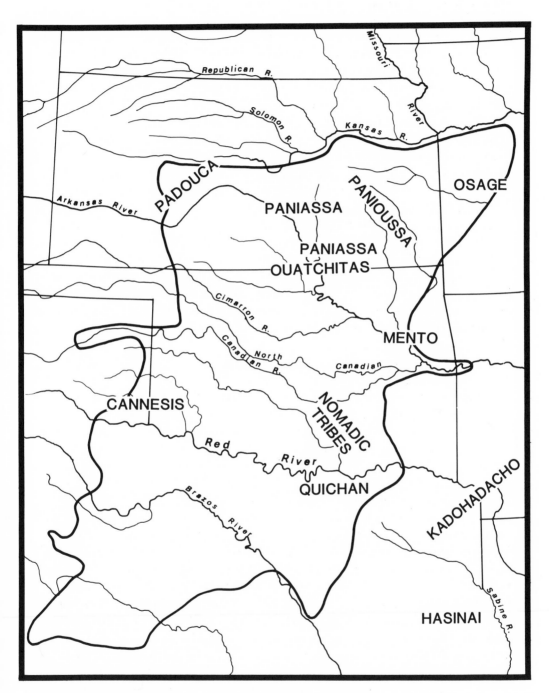

Map 11.6. Southern Prairies and Cross Timbers, Early Historic A.D. *1720.*

and then through the Texarkana and Belcher foci/phases to the prehistoric Bossier focus (Davis 1970; Hoffman 1970).

In 1719 LaHarpe established a post in the Kadohadacho area (M. M. Wedel 1978). From this post DuRivage traveled west and a quarter northwest, about seventy leagues, where part of the nomadic tribes were encountered (Smith 1959). Distance traveled (a French league = 2.76 miles — M. M. Wedel 1978) and mapped route (Temple 1975: pl. LXVI) suggest the area visited was north of the Washita River and not the Womack site of the Norteño focus (Harris et al. 1965; Mallouf 1976). The nomadic tribes consisted of the Quidehais, Naouydiches, Joyvan, Huanchane, Huane, and Tancaoye (Smith 1959). The identity of the Quidehais as Kichai, the Joyvan as the Tonkawan Youjaune, and the Toncaoye as Tonkawa proper is not in dispute (Newcomb and Field 1967). The Naouydiche are likely the Nabedache — a Caddo group (Newcomb and Field 1967). The identity of the Huanchane and Huane as Waco (Smith 1959 following Hodge 1907; Vehik 1992) is less certain, with Tonkawa being preferred by others (Newcomb and Field 1967). To the south, on the other side of the Red River were the Quichuan (Quichan, Quaineo), who have been suggested to be Kiowa (Hodge 1907) but are more likely Kichai (Newcomb and Field 1967). Further up the Red River, about sixty leagues from the place DuRivage visited, in the vicinity of the Red River forks were the Cannesis or Cancy. The Cancy were Apache, likely Lipan (Smith 1959; M. M. Wedel 1971; Newcomb and Field 1967).

LaHarpe undertook an expedition northward from the Kadohadacho post (Smith 1959). The place LaHarpe visited has been placed variously on the Arkansas and Canadian rivers as well as elsewhere (Smith 1959; M. M. Wedel 1971). One map (Temple 1975: pl. LXVI) equates the location visited with a group known as the Mento (for association of Mento with Wichita see Vehik 1992; Faye 1943; Wedel 1981, but some caution may be necessary — see Pease and Werner 1934; Cox 1905). Most maps place the Mento in association with a northern tributary of the Arkansas River that likely reflects the Three Forks area where the Neosho and Verdigris rivers join the Arkansas River (Vehik 1992). LaHarpe noted the settlement to be composed of the Touacaras, Toayas, Caumuche, Aderos, Ousitas, Ascanis, Quataquois, Quicasquiris, and Honechas (Smith 1959). The identity of the Touacaras as Tawakoni, Toayas as Taovaya or Tawehash, the Ousitas as Wichita (specific sense), and the Ascanis as Yscanis or Iscani is accepted (Newcomb and Field 1967; M. M. Wedel 1981). The Caumuche have been suggested to be Comanche (Smith 1959) but that is not agreed upon by Newcomb and Field (1967) who suggest it is a Wichita (general sense) term. The Aderos may be a Wichita (general sense) or Caddoan band (M. M. Wedel 1981; Smith 1959). The Quataquois have been suggested to be the Kiowa-Apache (Smith 1959), but Newcomb and Field (1967) think this was probably a Wichita (general sense) term. *Quicasquiris* is probably the Wichita term for themselves (Newcomb and Field 1967). Honechos have been identified as Waco (Smith 1959) or a Wichita (general sense) group (M. M. Wedel 1981; Newcomb and Field 1967).

Two Ascanis and Ousita villages were said to be sixty leagues distance to the north-northwest (Smith 1959). From the Three Forks area the villages would have been in the area of Wichita, Kansas (Vehik 1992). Maps from this period generally place two villages along the Arkansas River north of the Mento and near a north tributary. Sometimes identified as Ouatchitas and Paniassa, the villages may have been nearer the Walnut River juncture, possibly coinciding with the Deer Creek and Bryson-Paddock sites which were occupied at this time and have some elements suggestive of the Lower Walnut focus (M. M. Wedel 1981; Vehik 1992; Hartley and Miller 1977). Another set of Paniassa villages are located further upstream, possibly near Wichita, Kansas.

In the same year as DuRivage and LaHarpe, Dutisné also visited a group of Wichita (M. M. Wedel 1972). At forty leagues to the southwest of the Osage, the location visited would be just to the west of the Verdigris. Maps of the period place a Paniouassa village on a western tributary of the stream whose juncture with the Arkansas River was associated with the Mento. M. M. Wedel (1972) suggests correlation with an archaeological site near Neodesha, Kansas. Support is received from early nineteenth-century maps which place a Pani or Pawnee village on the Verdigris River. Other Panis (Wichita – general sense) or possibly Pawnee were to the west and northwest.

To the northwest and west of the Great Bend of the Arkansas were the Padouca. The Padouca have been identified as both Apache (Gunnerson 1974) and Comanche (Newcomb and Field 1967). LaHarpe described the people he visited as being unwilling to go far west because they might encounter the Cancy on their way to make war with the Padouca (Smith 1959). This would seem to suggest the Padouca were not Apache, at least in this context.

AN ESTIMATION OF POPULATION

Constructing an estimate of population sizes is extremely difficult. Wedel (1979a) has provided data for calculating population from house floor areas, but rarely is it known how many houses of what size existed in either prehistoric or historic situations. Oñate suggested eight to ten people occupied the larger houses at Etzanoa (Hammond and Rey 1953) and DeMézières also used ten people per house (Bolton 1914) to estimate the population of Wichita on the Red River. Later when enumeration of American Indian populations was undertaken the warriors were counted or estimated and then multiplied by three or five (Lowrie and Clarke 1832; Morse 1822).

It is commonly assumed that early observers suggesting large populations for American Indians were lying to please various crowns and popes. Thus a report in 1687 that the Osage had seventeen villages is considered to be in error (Chapman 1959). DeSoto's expedition, with certain exceptions, noted that the various Caddo groups were rather numerous (Swanton 1942). Similarly the Hasinai area was described as large and populous in 1686 (Cox 1905) and again in 1691 although many were said to have died (Hatcher 1927). Descriptions of Quivira suggest rather populous settlements as well, with some exceptions (Winship 1896). Comments in Oñate expedition accounts (Hammond and Rey 1953) may be used to construct some population estimates. In 1680 the Paneassa (Wichita, general sense) are described as not being inferior to the Pani-Maha (Skidi), who had twenty-two villages, the least of which had two hundred cabins (Cox 1905). However, in 1686 the manner of settlement in Quivira was said to leave an impression of more people than was really the case (Tyler and Taylor 1958).

Table 11.4 lists population data for the five historic cultures most discussed in this study. All are probably inaccurate in one or more ways — overestimation, underestimation, and incomplete enumeration. Compounding the problems of population estimation is the role of disease (Dobyns 1983). Definite indication of disease does not occur in the southern prairies and Cross Timbers until 1687–91 (table 11.5 — from Vehik 1989b). Because of inconsistency in population data and the complexity of disease ecology it is not presently possible to work out adequately a precontact population estimate, but previous estimates by Mooney (1928) and Kroeber (1963) are likely far too low.

CONCLUSIONS AND COMMENTS

The preceding pages serve to document that much of the sequence on the southern prairies and Cross Timbers is basically one of cultural continuity, albeit some sequences are better documented than others. Nonetheless, although cultural continuity seems to be indicated, important changes are also indicated over time. That these are more likely to reflect *in situ* adaptational processes than migrations is discussed in the pages to follow.

The survey began at a date well into the Woodland period (roughly A.D. 1–900). However, many cultures existing at A.D. 500 were apparently established much earlier. With the possible exception of Kansas City Hopewell it appears that most of the earlier Woodland period cultures were not introduced by migrations. Rather they seem more likely to be continuations of Late Archaic adaptations to which certain technological and social practices were added. Ceramics were added with ultimate sources varying depending upon geographic and probably cultural relationships. In most cases ceramics are a part of other

Table 11.4.
Available Historic Population Data and Estimates, A.D. 1540–1850

	Osage	Caddo	Kichai	Wichita	Apache
1542				14,000	
1601				46,000	
1680				44,000	
1698				44,000	
1699		3,000			
1700		2,450			
1709		2,500			
1716		4,030			
1718		1,900			
1719	1,000	750		6,000	
1720		400			
1721		1,778			
1722					5,000
1726			1,000	4,000	
1745					1,330
1748				1,500	
1750				2,500	
1754	4,750				
1758	4,750				
1760				1,250	1,500
1769	4,000				
1772	5,000		400	10,720	7,500
1773		765		5,000	
1777	5,750	675	125	2,000	25,000
1778		1,700	450	3,750	
1779		400		1,250	
1783		2,100			
1784	7,500				
1785	3,250				
1787				900	
1791				3,500	
1793	6,250			2,000	
1795	6,000				
1796	9,000	750		3,500	
1798	6,000				
1800	9,000				
1801	7,500				
1802	10,000				
1803	6,000				
1804	7,500	1,500	300	3,400	
1805	6,000	1,696	300	3,000	300
1806	6,300	1,600		2,000	
1807					2,500
1808				2,000	

Table 11.4 (Continued)

	Osage	Caddo	Kichai	Wichita	Apache
1809		1,500			
1812	6,000				
1813				3,500	2,500
1814	5,500	1,180	280	2,500	
1816	5,200	1,725	300	2,750	
1817	10,000				
1818		60		5,200	
1819	8,000	2,500	800		3,500
1820	10,000	4,000	1,000	3,200	3,800
1821	10,000				
1822	10,500				375
1824		538			
1825	5,200	538			
1826		26			
1827	20,000				
1828				1,500	
1829		450			
1830	6,000	850	300	1,500	3,000
1834		900			
1835		1,900		1,000	
1836	5,120	2,000		1,700	900
1837	7,000	225			20,280
1839	5,200				
1840		164			
1841	5,200	2,000			20,280
1842	4,102	2,000			20,280
1843	5,510	2,043	28	126	20,280
1844	4,102	2,000			20,280
1845	4,102	2,000			21,080
1846					4,000
1847	5,188	450		750	6,000
1848	3,500				
1849		1,400	300	1,000	4,000
1850	5,000	1,200	300		300

traded knowledge and things: raw materials, projectile point forms, and mortuary practices. Mortuary practices and often raw materials are modified to conform to local conditions. The projectile points reflect preferences in style and not new hunting technology. Ceramics suggest changes in cooking style and subsistence resources, possibly the increasing use of starchy seeds (Braun 1983). Available data indicate that the importance of ceramics was initially not great, suggesting a gradual change in cooking technology and subsistence practices.

Table 11.5.
Possible Plains Epidemic Events

Years	Disease	Probability for Southern Plains
1535	Unspecified	Possible
1592–93	Smallpox	Possible
1617–19	Smallpox	Possible
1619	Plague	Possible
1635–38	Smallpox and other rash-producing diseases	Possible
1647–48	Smallpox	Possible
1671	Unspecified (smallpox?)	Probable
1687–91	Smallpox likely	Definite
1708–10	Scarlet fever	Possible
1727–29	Measles, smallpox	Possible
1737–39	Smallpox	Definite
1750	Smallpox, possibly measles	Definite
1753	Malaria, dysentery	Possible
1755–60	Smallpox, possibly measles	Probable
1762–66	Smallpox	Definite
1769	Skin eruption diseases (measles, scarlet fever)	Possible
1777–78	Plague, typhoid, typhus	Definite
1780–81	Smallpox	Definite
1800–2	Smallpox	Definite
1815–16	Smallpox	Definite
1830–34	Cholera	Probable
1831–32	Smallpox	Definite
1837–40	Smallpox	Definite
1848–50	Cholera, smallpox	Definite

With the exception of Hopewellian-affiliated cultures, settlement emphasizes small, dispersed hamlets, and mobility. Johnson (1987) suggests that this pattern optimizes dispersed natural resources and that this same pattern is adaptive for slash-and-burn horticulture. In north-central Oklahoma the changes noted earlier in settlement pattern are accompanied by changes in artifact composition indicating that the major change is in the loss of a plant gathering-processing activity in the tributary stream occupations (Vehik 1985). It can only be presumed that this reflects increasing reliance on horticulture. Over much of the area the bow and arrow becomes the predominant hunting technology by late Woodland.

Along the southeastern periphery, Woodland period Fourche Maline phase continues the Late Archaic emphasis on nut processing and deer hunting (Galm 1984; Vehik 1989a). While ceramics increase in frequency throughout the period, there is little change in vessel form. There does appear to be a decrease in mobility (Vehik 1989a).

Out of Fourche Maline phase and related complexes along the south-eastern periphery developed the Arkansas and Red River Valley Caddo. The Arkansas River Valley Caddo expanded northward through north-eastern Oklahoma, northwestern Arkansas, and into southwestern Missouri (Bell 1984; Sabo and Early 1988; Chapman 1980). The Red River Caddo seem to have expanded similarly westward along the Red River and southwestward (Story 1981b; Story and Creel 1982). The possibly hostile interaction between Fourche Maline phase and Cooper Hopewell suggests this expansion may not have been without conflict (Galm 1978, 1984). Nonetheless it is entirely uncertain whether expansion involved actual movements of people, political/ideological incorporation of existing populations, or both.

The cause of expansion is equally uncertain. Story (1981a) suggests that the stimulus was an inability to compete with horticultural and expansionist Coles Creek, which led to the adoption of horticulture with a resulting expansion of territory. Data from the Fourche Maline Creek valley in eastern Oklahoma from the Late Archaic through Late Prehistoric periods indicates a trend of decreasing mobility, increasing intensity in occupation of the area, and, with the Late Prehistoric, centralization of political authority and a substantial decline in nut harvesting (Vehik 1989a). Possibly increasing sedentism was accompanied by population growth, displacement of excess population, and development of centralized systems of political organization to manage sociopolitical relations and resource distribution. Nonetheless, the role of horticulture may be minimal (Burnett 1988) or variable (Bruseth et al. 1987).

Most of the area under consideration was occupied by members of the Plains Village tradition after A.D. 1000. Early Plains Village tradition occupations are characterized by small hamlets organized in a dispersed settlement pattern similar to Woodland period occupations. Later Plains Village tradition occupations appear to involve fewer but larger villages. Increasing frequencies of ceramics, grinding implements, digging stick tips, and hoes, and increasing numbers and size of storage facilities suggest growing reliance on horticulture.

Beginning around A.D. 1450 major changes are indicated for the area. The centralized political system of the Arkansas River Valley Caddo collapses and although its descendants continue to live in the area until about 1600, their society is much different. Much speculation has been given as to the descendants of the Arkansas River Valley Caddo. Bell (1983) and Wyckoff (1980) suggest the Lower Walnut focus of the Great Bend aspect. However that entity was already in existence by A.D. 1600 (Brown and Simmons 1987; W. R. Wedel 1959; Thies 1991). Rohrbaugh (1982) suggests it became the Norteño focus and ultimately the Kichai. That suggestion ties several things together. First, the Kichai language is closest to Pawnee (Parks 1979a; Hughes 1969a, citing Lesser and Weltfish 1932 and Mooney 1896) and Caddo (Berlandier 1969) or both (Dorsey 1904b). A location in northeastern Oklahoma and adjacent areas would put the Kichai in a geographic position for those relationships to make sense. Second, Arkansas River Valley Caddoan populations traded extensively with Plains Village tradition and Red River Caddo societies (Vehik 1988; Brown 1984). Those interactions would explain the later history of the Kichai of often living with the Caddo and the Wichita (Swanton 1942; Rowland and Sanders 1932; Winfrey 1959, 1960; U.S. Department of the Interior 1858; Bolton 1913). Those relationships additionally explain the mixed nature of Norteño focus cultural assemblages, more Caddo in some contexts and more Wichita in others. It also explains the presence of certain Norteño pottery types in Caddoan contexts (Davis 1961; Thurmond 1985).

On the western side of the area an intrusion of Plains Apache is suggested and attached to several cultural entities. The present state of information (T. Baugh 1982, 1986; Swenson 1986; Habicht-Mauche 1987; Vehik 1986) suggests Wheeler phase and also possibly Garza developing out of Washita River phase, possibly with Antelope Creek admixture. The Teya and Escanjaque are the ethnohistoric representatives of these archaeological complexes and in turn they are likely to have been some subdivision of the Plains Caddoan Wichita, probably the Iscani/Waco (Vehik 1992). Ethnohistoric documentation suggests that these groups placed much less emphasis on horticulture than had their Washita River phase ancestors. The limited archaeological data available are supportive. Limited descriptions of social organization suggest an egalitarian arrangement (Vehik 1986, 1992).

The Apache are likely reflected in the Dismal River aspect and Tierra Blanca phase. Tierra Blanca appears in the Texas panhandle at about the same time Antelope Creek phase abandons it. It is possible the Apache movement into the area drove Antelope Creek phase occupations out. The trade in Alibates agatized dolomite to the northeast and east all but disappears with the demise of Antelope Creek phase. Present data suggest Antelope Creek phase occupations may have transformed their economy to emphasize bison hunting, joining the descendants of the Washita River phase and/or moving northeastward to join members of the Great Bend aspect.

The Little River focus of the Great Bend aspect has been tied to the Tawakoni subdivision of the Wichita (M. M. Wedel 1981; Vehik 1992). Little River focus had an extensive horticultural economy (W. R. Wedel 1959). Bison hunting was done at least partially by small hunting parties (Winship 1896). Although Coronado makes no note of it, it is possible they also obtained bison products through trade with the Teyas and Querechos who traded with Quivira as well as with Pecos and other Pueblos (Winship 1896). Ethnohistoric information from the Oñate and LaHarpe expeditions suggests the Tawakoni had a more complex social system (Vehik 1986, 1992) than has been indicated in most discussions (Dorsey 1904; Newcomb 1961) of the Wichita.

The Lower Walnut focus of the Great Bend aspect has been tied to the Wichita (specific sense; Vehik 1992). The location of the Etzanoa of the Oñate accounts appears to coincide with the location of the Lower Walnut focus. Oñate expedition accounts describe a society with a substantial horticultural economy and a somewhat centralized socio-political system (Vehik 1986, 1992). LaHarpe expedition accounts and maps from the early eighteenth century locate the Panioussa, Pani-piques, or sometimes the Ousita (Wichita) and Iscani in this area (Wedel 1981).

It is possible that there was an eastern division of Washita River phase that may not have participated in the transition to Wheeler phase. Henrietta/Bryan foci may be contemporaneous with Washita River phase or a later, more southerly manifestation. Hughes (1969a) suggests Henrietta became the Kichai. This view of the Kichai does not account easily for their linguistic relationships, however. The possi-bility that other groups of Wichita are represented in eastern Washita River/Henrietta/Bryan needs to be considered.

Having presented the above scenario of Late Prehistoric period cultural events, it is another matter to explain why. The decentraliza-tion of the Arkansas River Valley Caddo and their ultimate abandon-ment of the area has been associated with an increasing emphasis on bison hunting and interaction with Plains Village tradition societies (Wyckoff 1980). These changes have been attributed to a change in climate less favorable to horticulture and more favorable for bison population growth (Wyckoff 1980). However, it is possible that hor-ticulture only came to be intensively used after A.D. 1450 (Burnett 1988). A declining involvement in horticulture has also been consid-ered responsible for the transition of Washita River phase to Wheeler phase (Vehik 1986). Nonetheless, at the time of Coronado, DeSoto, and Oñate, horticulture was actively practiced by east Texas Caddo, the Pueblo, Quivira, and Etzanoa. Horticulture appears to have been in good shape on the peripheries of the western Plains. Trade and econom-ic data suggest the development of an economic specialization of sorts that may reflect the results of population growth, availability/depend-ability of certain areas to grow sufficient crops or other plant resources, overexploitation of local large game resources, distribution of special resources such as chert and salt, increasing numbers of the southern Plains bison herds, intrusion of Athapaskan speakers, and climatic change.

Later changes in cultural distributions reflect European diseases, declining populations — declines probably being greatest among seden-tary horticulturists — horses, guns, coalescence of populations, and increasing dependence upon and transformation of populations to a bison-hunting economy. The emphasis on bison hunting on the southern Plains probably reflects continued population growth in this resource. However, bison hunting provided an adaptive advantage of mobility in the face of disease and of mobility and food in the face of increasing Euro-American intrusions and expropriations of land.

Unlike Renfrew's (1987) explanation for the distribution of Indo-European languages, the Plains Caddoan language distributions in the southern Plains cannot be attributed to adoption and development of horticulture. Plains Caddoans, Arkansas River Valley Caddoans, and Red River Valley Caddoans all seem to have had representatives in place by the Late Archaic — an idea earlier proposed by Hughes (1969a). Continuity within the Archaic and Neoamerican occupations of northern, west-central, and central Texas is uncertain, especially with the Neoamerican period, but Skinner (1981) suggests continuity back to 9000 B.C. The Apache on the west and possibly the Osage on the east represent recent intrusions. As the historic period progressed those societies intruding into the southern Prairies and Cross Timbers came to outnumber those residing there prior to contact.

CHAPTER 12

HOLOCENE ADAPTATIONS IN THE SOUTHERN HIGH PLAINS

Timothy G. Baugh

EXTENDING from the Arkansas River to the Edwards Plateau, the southern High Plains consists of portions of five states. These include west Texas, New Mexico east of the Pecos River, the panhandle of Oklahoma, southeast Colorado, and southwest Kansas. The most prominent physiographic feature in this region is the Llano Estacado. This large, flat plain extends from the Edwards Plateau in the south to the Canadian River in the north. The eastern boundary is defined by the Caprock Escarpment while the western margin occurs at the Mescalero Escarpment.

Other prominent features include the Pecos trench, the Las Vegas Plateau, the Canadian River Breaks and Antelope Hills, the sand hills region, and the Park Plateau, which is dissected by deeply cut canyons creating an area of mesas and smaller tablelands such as the Chaquaqua Plateau. In addition to the Pecos and Canadian rivers, other important streams include the Arkansas, which marks the northern boundary of this region, the Purgatory (known locally as the Picketwire), Apishapa, Cucharas, Vermejo, Cimarron, and Red rivers. The Brazos River, which once flowed westward to the Pecos but now flows southeastward to the Gulf of Mexico due to stream piracy, is also an important drainage system. The old channel of the Brazos includes Blackwater and Yellowhouse draws, both of which are important drainages for Paleo-Indian hunters and gatherers. Today, the old channel of Blackwater Draw forms the sand hills region or Quaternary dune belts between Portales and Clovis, New Mexico. Many of these streams provide important resources for the native peoples of this area.

Lithic resources are commonly found along stream channels and various rock types are abundant in this region. One of the finer sources of lithic material, Alibates agatized dolomite, occurs along the Canadian River Breaks near modern day Fritch, Texas (Banks 1990; Green and Kelley 1960; Shaeffer 1958). Numerous cobbles flow downstream creating large float quarry areas which are still visible in the high terraces overlooking the Canadian River (Baugh 1984b:8; Wyckoff 1993). Along the eastern Caprock Escarpment other high quality lithic materials such as Tecovas jasper may be found (Green and Kelley 1960:413; Hughes and Willey 1978:47). Further south along the Callahan divide near Sweetwater, Texas, Edwards chert occurs in the

Georgetown formation (Banks 1990; Baugh 1982). To the north, several varieties of quartzite are also available. These include: (1) Ogallala quartzite, a fine to granular textured silicified sandstone (Lopez and Saunders 1973); (2) Dakota quartzite (known as Potter chert in Texas) which occurs in the Quaternary gravels of the major river systems throughout the area (Baugh 1984:291–92; Eddy 1982:402); and (3) Tesesquite quartzite which is also located throughout much of this region between the Canadian and Arkansas rivers (Lopez and Saunders 1973). In addition to these major sources of stone, locally available materials, such as petrified wood, were commonly used by prehistoric peoples throughout the region.

Elevational differences throughout the southern High Plains are correlated with climatic variation. In the Park Plateau, for example, an average elevation of around 1,677 meters (5,500 feet) is punctuated with peaks rising to as much as 4,152 meters (13,623 feet). The Llano Estacado, on the other hand, is comparatively flat and has an average elevation of about 1,219 to 1,372 meters (4,000 to 4,500 feet). River valleys, of course, tend to be lower in elevation with the Pecos occurring slightly below 1,036 meters (3,400 feet).

In addition to the north-south variation in precipitation, there is also an east-west difference. Precipitation throughout the region is relatively consistent with the western portions of the area being slightly drier. For example, Los Animas County, Colorado receives approximately 310 millimeters (12.2 inches) average annual rainfall (Eddy 1982:19) and Roswell, Chaves County, New Mexico about 295 mm (11.6 inches; Parry and Speth 1984:9). In contrast, Lubbock, Texas has an average annual precipitation nearing 457 mm (18 inches; Larkin and Bomar 1983:18). Generally, winter is the driest season with the spring and summer months having the greatest amounts of precipitation.

Temperature also varies in accordance with elevation. In the Park Plateau area temperatures range between − 29 and 32 degrees Celsius (− 20 to 90 degrees Fahrenheit) (Gleichman 1983:5–6). Lubbock County, Texas, has an average monthly low during the month of January of − 4 degrees C (24 degrees F) to an average monthly high of 33 degrees C (92 degrees F) in July. River valleys in the north portion of the region have 130 to 150 frost-free days, and in the south more than 200 frost-free days are common.

Botanically this region is divided into four biotic associations: the uplands (including mesas, plateaus, and the Llano); bottomlands; steep slopes; and sand hills. The upland association includes many of the shortgrasses characteristic of the region, for example, blue grama (*Bouteloua gracilis*) and buffalo grass (*Buchloe dactyloides*). The bottomlands provide a valuable source of wood and fruits, with species including cottonwoods (*Populus deltiodes* and *P. sargentii*), elm (*Ulmus alata*), and hackberry (*Celtis reticulata*). In addition to these woody plants, the bottomlands frequently contain Chickasaw plum (*Prunus angustifolia*) and chokecherry (*P. virginiana*). Other important grasses such as sideoats grama (*Bouteloua curtipendula*) and little bluestem (*Andropogon scoparius*) as well as sand dropseed (*Sporobolus cryptandrus*) occur in the steep slope and sand hill associations.

The shortgrasses are of special importance because of their high nutritive and protein content which once supported large herds of bison. Even though the tall bluestem grasses further east might provide more nutrients during their prime summer growth stages, during the winter they are almost totally deficient in calories. Shortgrasses, though, tend to retain more nutrients and calories during their dormant winter period (W. R. Wedel 1986:16). As a result, bison appear to have been available year-round to many of the people living in the southern High Plains, with summer perhaps being the most difficult time to locate these animals (Allen 1877:465; cf. Wallace and Hoebel 1952:54–55). In addition to seasonal variation, there were fluctuating climatic conditions that may have brought about short intervals of time when bison were absent due to a decrease in available plant species (Dillehay 1974; Creel, Scott, and Collins 1990).

Bison and other game species were not the only beneficiaries of these vegetal products, however. Lintz (1986a: table nine), for example, lists more than fifty potentially edible plants for the southern High Plains region, and these were used extensively by Plains people.

PALEOENVIRONMENTAL CONDITIONS

Paleoecologists have tended to focus much of their climatic research on the southern High Plains toward the Pleistocene and early Holocene fluctuations (Bryant and Shafer 1977; Oldfield and Schoenwetter 1964; Reeves 1976; Wendorf 1970; Wendorf and Hester 1975). The general conclusion of these studies is that post-Altithermal climatic change has been minor and relatively insignificant. Duffield (1970) began to challenge this traditional view when he recorded a shift from a high dependence on bison to pronghorn in eleven Antelope Creek phase sites. Hughes (1979:43) found a similar sequence based on the study of prairie voles. Support for Duffield's (1970) position, and a refinement of his chronology, has been accumulating during the 1980s (Ferring 1982; Hall 1982, 1984; Lintz and Hall 1983; Schuldenrein 1985; Speth 1983). Much of this work, however, has occurred outside of the southern High Plains. The major exceptions to this statement are the work of Schuldenrein (1985), who conducted an intensive geomorphological study of the Pinon Canyon Maneuver site in Los Animas County, Colorado, and Speth's (1983) and Hall's (1984) study of the Garnsey Springs site located on the eastern margins of the Pecos trench in Chaves County, New Mexico.

Schuldenrein's (1985:219–28) study concludes that after A.D. 1000 the paleoclimate of southeast Colorado was warm and dry with only minor mesic fluctuations. This mesic (Cycle 3) period was preceded by a warming and drying trend which was initiated about 350 B.C.

Other authors, such as Speth (1983) and Hall (1984), support these findings, and point to a post–A.D. 1350 date as initiating a severe drought on the southern High Plains. "All of the research tends to indicate that moist conditions were present during the first millennium, but after A.D. 1100–1300, the climate deteriorated towards drought (cf. Hall 1982)" (cited in Lintz 1986:65). There can be little doubt that human societies made at least some adjustments to these new conditions, and an examination of these cultural adaptations is now in order.

THE SOUTHERN HIGH PLAINS: A.D. 500 TO 1000

By A.D. 500, the Woodland or Early Ceramic period is represented at several localities throughout the southern High Plains (map 12.1). Despite this new adaptive strategy (based, at least in part, on the utilization of corn and the bow and arrow), hunting-and-gathering communities very similar to those of the Late Archaic seem to have persisted in places. Several foraging components dating into the sixth century have been recorded along Ute Creek (a tributary to the Canadian River) in northeast New Mexico (Hammock 1965), from several sites on the Chaquaqua Plateau in southeast Colorado (Campbell 1976:49), and perhaps Trinchera Cave also in southeast Colorado (Wood 1974; Wood-Simpson 1976), as well as the Kenton Caves (34CI39, 34CI48, 34CI49, 34CI50, 34CI68, 34CI69, and 34CI70) in the Oklahoma panhandle (Lintz and Zabawa 1984).

Early Ceramic sites in the southern High Plains tend to be small and scattered with relatively short occupations and little architecture. Much of our knowledge for this period, then, is derived from sites further east; hence the term Plains Woodland. In general, as this period continues Woodland people probably become somewhat more sedentary although a dependence on hunting and gathering continues. Several sites in the Colorado plains have yielded small quantities of maize (Campbell 1969; Eddy 1982; Galinat and Campbell 1967), but Zier and his colleagues (1988:21) speculate that only a few sites along the Arkansas River may have been horticultural centers which supplied the outlying areas. Not surprisingly then, some scholars have maintained that southeast Colorado may have been a major route for the movement of new varieties of maize from the Southwest to the Central Plains (Galinat 1985). Although cordmarked pottery indicates an adaptation based on an Eastern Woodland pattern, there is evidence in the southern High Plains of yet another type of Early Ceramic occupation based at least in part on Southwestern interrelationships. Before dis-

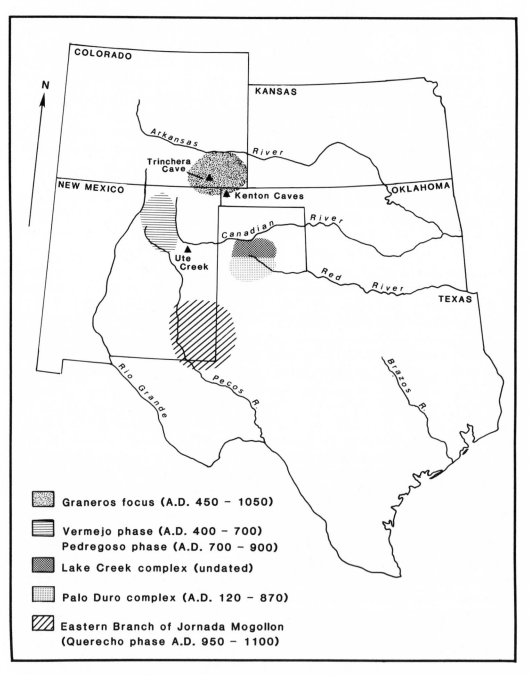

COLORADO

KANSAS

Arkansas River

Trinchera
Cave

NEW MEXICO

OKLAHOMA

▲ Kenton Caves

Canadian River

▲ Ute
Creek

Red River

TEXAS

Rio Grande

Pecos R.

Brazos R.

Graneros focus (A.D. 450 – 1050)

Vermejo phase (A.D. 400 – 700)
Pedregoso phase (A.D. 700 – 900)

Lake Creek complex (undated)

Palo Duro complex (A.D. 120 – 870)

Eastern Branch of Jornada Mogollon
(Querecho phase A.D. 950 – 1100)

Map 12.1. Plains Woodland and related archaeological manifestations on the southern High Plains.

cussing these Southwestern interconnections, however, a presentation of more traditional Plains Woodland cultures is in order.

Some of the earlier Woodland components in the southern High Plains are located at Easterwood (34TX37), Recon John Shelter (5PE648), and a series of other sites at John Martin Reservoir in southeast Colorado (Eddy 1982; Wyckoff and Brooks 1983; Zier and Kalasz 1985). These sites and similar ones throughout the area may represent the most westerly and southerly extensions of the traditional Plains Woodland complex as exemplified by the Valley and Keith foci of the Central Plains.

Not included in the more traditional Plains Woodland complex is a series of sites defined as the Graneros focus (Withers 1954; Campbell 1969, 1976). Characterized by cordmarked ceramics and circular structures or stone enclosures with dry lain masonry walls, this complex may have been the forerunner of the later Apishapa phase. Campbell (1976:52–58) places some fifty-three sites into the Graneros focus and divides this complex into three periods: Early (A.D. 450–750), Middle (A.D. 750–1000), and Late (A.D. 900–1050). On the basis of Campbell's divisions two other dated sites (5LA1053 and Belwood, 5PE278) have been placed in the Early period and one (5LA1110) in either the Middle or Late period (W. B. Butler 1981; Hunt 1975; Kingsbury and Nowak 1980). Two Oklahoma sites may also be associated with the Graneros focus (Saunders 1983). The earliest of these, 34CI115, falls within the Middle period, and the latest site, Carrizozo Creek Bridge (34CI199), may be associated with the Late period (Haury 1982; Saunders 1983).

Several pithouse sites in the Park Plateau, formerly associated with the Initial Sopris phase (A.D. 1000–1100), have been reevaluated (Eighmy and Wood 1984; C. E. Wood 1986) and are now considered to be Woodland. These sites (including 5LA1211 and 5LA1414B) may actually date between A.D. 630 and 875. The cultural assemblage for these proposed Woodland sites has not been carefully defined, however.

Moving south into northeast New Mexico, Glassow (1972, 1980:68–72, 1984) has assigned several sites to the Vermejo phase (A.D. 400–1000), which appears to be more Puebloan than Plains-like. Several authors have referred to the Vermejo phase as a Basketmaker II manifestation in the Cimarron valley (Glassow 1972, 1980; Cordell 1978). Only one site (VE-54) has yielded pottery in the form of unspecified Puebloan wares. The vast majority of these sites, however, have no associated ceramics indicating that basketry may have been of great importance to these people (Glassow 1980:78, 1984:99). One of these nonceramic sites (MP-4) has an uncalibrated radiocarbon date of A.D. 510 ± 50 which correlates with the Basketmaker periods (Cordell 1989:304; Glassow 1980:122, 136). Charred cobs of maize have been recovered from several sites, indicating that horticulture was being practiced. Manos and metates are rare, however, with grinding slabs being more common. Projectile points are of the small corner-notched variety. Circular structures (varying from three to six meters in diameter) have dry lain, horizontally placed sandstone slabs or blocks, or dacite cobbles, forming the foundation walls with mud or wood superstructures arising from these foundations. Despite the presence of maize, these people were more reliant on wild resources than domesticated plants, and as a result their sites appear to represent seasonal occupations (Cordell 1978; Glassow 1972; Kirkpatrick and Ford 1977).

The Vermejo phase is followed by the Pedregoso phase (A.D. 700–900), which is known from only one site – North Ponil 1 or NP-1 (Cordell 1978; Glassow 1980:72–73, 1984:99–100). There are two uncalibrated radiocarbon dates (A.D. 750 ± 80 and A.D. 755 ± 80) for NP-1, but Glassow (1980, 1984) maintains that this site may well be more recent. Overall, the Pedregoso phase is a Basketmaker III manifestation and appears to be quite similar to the Sambrito phase located in the Navajo Reservoir area of northwest New Mexico and southwest Colorado. In addition to maize and beans, the Pedregoso phase also has a rather thick, crude pottery associated with it. Open-end trough metates and grinding slabs and corner-notched projectile points are characteristic of this phase. Architectural features are not adequately known at this time, but contiguous rock circles (ranging from three to ten meters in diameter) are built of sandstone blocks or dacite cobbles and may be associated with the Pedregoso phase (Glassow 1984). Bottle-shaped roasting pits or cists are also common during this period. Maize, beans, nuts, and berries have been found in association with these sites, but the high degree of internal diversity associated with these cultigens argues for either horticultural experimentation with genetically variable plants or poor conditions due to climatic degradation or improper field maintenance (Cordell 1978; Kirkpatrick and Ford 1977). On the basis of information provided by Lorry Nordby, Cordell (1989:304) associates the Pedregoso phase sites with two pithouses excavated at Pecos National Monument.

Smooth-surface sherds are found in conjunction with cordmarked pottery in the Texas panhandle at Lake Creek focus sites (Hofman and Brooks 1989; J. Gunnerson 1987; J. Hughes 1962, 1991). Although tentatively dated between A.D. 200 and 800 or 900, only one chronometric date has been recorded for this focus (Hughes 1991). The single date of A.D. 520 is based on thermoluminescence dating of a Woodland sherd from the Tascosa Creek site in Oldham County, Texas (Couzzourt 1985, 1988). Most of the Lake Creek focus sites, such as Tascosa Creek and Lake Creek, occur along the northern boundary of the Llano Estacado where they are found on terraces of tributaries that flow into the Canadian River. These people had an economy based on wide-spectrum foraging with little dependence on bison.

The smoothed-surface sherds associated with the Lake Creek focus have been identified as a Jornada Mogollon brown ware known as Alma Plain. The presence of such sherds attests to Plains-Pueblo interaction at a relatively early date. This interaction, while sporadic, continues into the succeeding Plains Village period in this region. Sites belonging to the Lake Creek focus have corner-notched projectile points (Scallorn-like) which are made from locally derived lithic materials. The presence of local stone types, in conjunction with the cordmarked ceramics, leads archaeologists to the conclusion that the Lake Creek focus is an indigenous development and ancestral to the later Antelope Creek phase of the Plains Village or Middle Ceramic period.

Similar to the Lake Creek focus, but based primarily around the headwaters of the Red River drainage, is the Palo Duro complex, which tentatively dates between A.D. 300 and 900 (Hofman and Brooks 1989; Hughes 1991; Hughes and Willey 1978). Even though sites of the Palo Duro complex occur mainly in the Red River drainage, they have been reported as far north as the Canadian River. This complex represents a broad-based foraging people who relied on bison only minimally.

In general, the artifact assemblages of the northern Lake Creek focus and the more southern Palo Duro complex are quite similar. Like the Lake Creek focus, this Early Ceramic complex also contains cordmarked ceramics, but this pottery is found in association with greater quantities of the Southwestern-derived Alma Plain.

The Palo Duro complex is distinguished from the Lake Creek focus by more than geography and sherd counts. For example, possibly two Palo Duro complex sites — the Kent Creek site and a locality near Buffalo Lake (Cruse 1989; Hays 1986; Hughes 1991) — have or may have pit structures similar to those of the Mogollon. Like Lake Creek focus sites, hearths may be either earthen or rock-lined pits. The most distinctive artifact of the Palo Duro complex is the long-stemmed projectile point type known as the Deadman point. Typical sites associated with this complex include Blue Spring shelter, Deadman's shelter (Hughes and Willey 1978), Canyon City Club Cave (J. Hughes 1969b), and Chalk Hollow (Wedel 1975). The South Sage Creek site may be a late transitional site associated with this complex even though no Deadman points have been associated with this locality in Kent County, Texas (Boyd, Tomka, and Bousman 1992).

Along the southwestern edge of the Llano Estacado (or the Mescalero Escarpment) Mogollon interaction with Plains groups is even more apparent. Based on test excavations at several localities in west Texas and southeast New Mexico, Corley (1965) proposed an Eastern Extension of the Jornada branch of the Mogollon. The earliest cultural period of this manifestation is known as the Querecho phase (A.D. 950 to 1100) and represents an indigenous development from the preceramic Late Archaic phase that occurs throughout the Jornada area (Beckett 1979;

Collins 1969, 1971; Corley 1965; Lehmer 1948; Leslie 1979; Reed 1987; Whalen 1986). No structures have been identified with these open campsites which are not readily visible on the surface, but Leslie (1979) notes that "clay floor pads" are present at two sites belonging to the Querecho phase. The significance and function of these features is yet to be determined, however.

The cultural assemblage consists of lithic items, such as small corner-notched points and small dart points (occurring up to A.D. 1000). This transition in projectile point types is equated with the adoption of the bow and arrow, with these weapons being used to hunt small to medium-sized mammals (including rabbits, antelope, and deer). Oval basin metates with convex-faced manos may have been used to grind acorns and mesquite beans (Leslie 1979). By the end of the Querecho phase, such resources were brought back to small, rectangular pit-houses at some of the larger sites. Also included in this assemblage is a locally made brownware and a few trade wares (including Jornada brown, Jornada red-on-brown, Cebolleta black-on-white, and Mimbres black-on-white; Leslie 1979). Despite these interregional ties, Collins (1971) argues that these Eastern Jornada people became increasingly independent through time from the major Mogollon developments in south-central New Mexico.

EARLY PLAINS VILLAGE PERIOD: A.D. 1000 TO 1450

The transition from Early Ceramic or Plains Woodland cultures to the Plains Village period is marked by several changes. First and foremost is a greater reliance on horticulture with associated tools and implements such as bison scapula hoes and bison tibia digging stick tips. These changes may reflect the addition of new maize varieties that are better suited to the Plains environment, and hence to the subsistence economy of Plains people. In addition, this economic strategy finds more substantial structures being employed by the various farming groups. Even though such structures indicate a more sedentary pattern for Plains Village groups, there is a greater reliance on bison hunting than in the previous Plains Woodland period (Drass and Flynn 1990).

Speth and Scott (1989:78) argue that socioeconomic responses to farming in nonwestern societies may include a number of strategies. One of these is a greater reliance on communal hunts of large game species rather than utilizing small to medium-sized animals that were stalked individually. By concentrating on communal hunting patterns, horticulturalists are able to provide themselves with a greater return of protein in relation to the time and energy expended. Such a socio-economic perspective as provided by Speth and Scott (1989) carries a number of cultural implications that should be more closely examined in the context of Plains adaptations.

Previously, anthropologists attempted to correlate communal hunt- ing practices with the introduction of the bow and arrow or to changing environmental conditions which were favorable to herd animals. The archaeological record, in this case, shows that the introduction of the bow and arrow corresponded to the Plains Woodland period, but com- munal hunting patterns did not occur until the Plains Village period. In this same vein, Dillehay (1974) has argued that the occurrence of communal bison hunting corresponds with an amelioration in envi- ronmental conditions. Dillehay's position is somewhat tautological, however, in that the presence of bison is only examined within the archaeological record and does not include paleontological evidence. This perspective tends to bias the evidence in such a manner as to obscure socioeconomic processes that may be co-occurring.

Early Plains Village period sites yield more triangular forms of projectile points — which may be side-notched (Washita variety), side- and basally notched (Harrell variety), and/or unnotched (Fresno vari- ety) — than the earlier Plains Woodland sites. Other important tool types include diamond beveled knives and end scrapers, both of which would be useful for processing animal products. Pottery continues to be cordmarked in the Plains Village period, but vessel form is more spherical or globular in contrast to the conically shaped jars and pointed bottoms associated with the Plains Woodland period. Such changes are undoubtedly related to changing socioeconomic adapta- tions in the southern High Plains, indicating that similarities exist even though these changes are not identical throughout the region.

Beginning in the northwest portion of our study area (map 12.2), the Park Plateau, the Plains Village period is represented by the Sopris phase, which is the only archaeological manifestation associated with the Upper Purgatoire complex (Baker 1964; J. Gunnerson 1987; Wood and Bair 1980). As originally defined, the Upper Purgatoire complex contained an earlier phase known as the St. Thomas phase (Baker 1964), but later analysis of proposed St. Thomas sites has shown that they are more closely affiliated with the Sopris phase (Ireland 1970, 1971). The Sopris phase has been divided into three subphases: Initial (A.D. 1000– 1100), Early (A.D. 1100–1150), and Late (A.D. 1150 to about 1225) (Gleich- man 1983; Wood and Bair 1980:227).

The Initial subphase consists of wattle-and-daub or jacal surface structures which change to adobe and jacal units during the Early subphase. By the Late subphase, these buildings undergo changes once again as the Sopris people were living in dry lain sandstone slab roomblocks. The walls of these domiciles tend to have rounded corners with an occasional roof support occurring as well. Coinciding with these changing architectural features are differences in the ceramic and lithic assemblages. Sopris Plain and the closely related Taos Gray are the primary pottery types found in the Initial subphase (Wood

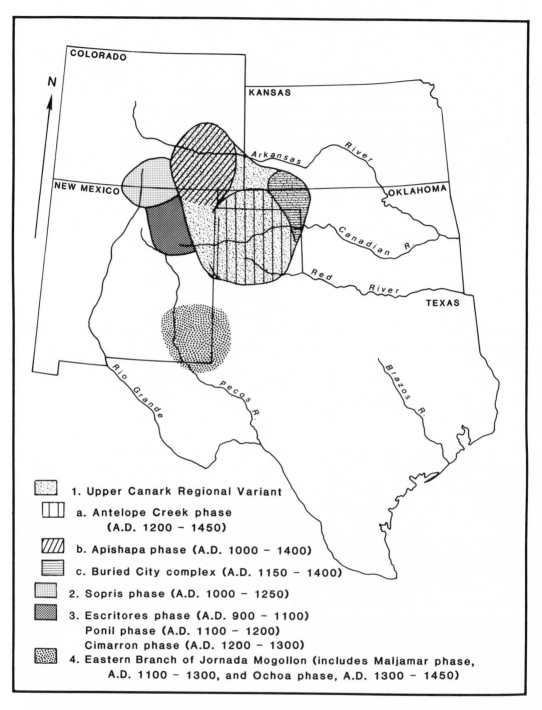

COLORADO

KANSAS

NEW MEXICO

Arkansas   River

OKLAHOMA

Canadian R.

Red   River

TEXAS

Rio Grande

Pecos R.

Brazos R.

N

1. **Upper Canark Regional Variant**
   a. **Antelope Creek phase
   (A.D. 1200 – 1450)**
   b. **Apishapa phase (A.D. 1000 – 1400)**
   c. **Buried City complex (A.D. 1150 – 1400)**
2. **Sopris phase (A.D. 1000 – 1250)**
3. **Escritores phase (A.D. 900 – 1100)
   Ponil phase (A.D. 1100 – 1200)
   Cimarron phase (A.D. 1200 – 1300)**
4. **Eastern Branch of Jornada Mogollon (includes Maljamar phase,
   A.D. 1100 – 1300, and Ochoa phase, A.D. 1300 – 1450)**

Map 12.2. *Early Plains Village and related archaeological manifestations on the southern High Plains.*

1986). Ground stone items include basin-shaped metates and elbow pipes, and chipped stone artifacts consist of corner-notched and side-notched projectile points.

During the Early subphase (represented by such sites as Leone Bluff [5LA1211] and Sopris [5LA1416A/B]), Sopris Plain/Taos Gray, Taos Gray Incised, cordmarked ceramics, corrugated sherds, and polished wares occur in conjunction with two black-on-white types, Taos and Red Mesa black-on-white. The presence of these black-on-white wares indicates interaction with local Puebloan groups and potential interconnections with the Chaco area. Lithic artifacts remain basically the same as those of the Initial subphase — one exception being the replacement of basin-shaped metates with the trough variety. One other addition includes the presence of stone and shell disc beads. Maize also appears for the first time during the Early subphase, but hunting and gathering continue to be important components of the economy.

During the Late subphase (as represented by components at Leone Bluff [5LA1211]; 5LA1413; Sopris [5LA1416]; 5LA1418; and 5LA1419), cordmarked pottery, polished vessels, and Red Mesa black-on-white decrease while Taos Gray Incised with herringbone motifs and Taos black-on-white increase. Sopris Plain/Taos Gray continues in common use as well. Slab metates replace the trough variety during this period, and grooved mauls appear for the first time. Not as abundant as in the Early subphase, but still present are shell disc beads. In general, the economy of these people seems to have been evenly divided between horticulture and hunting and gathering.

Sopris phase is the earliest archaeological manifestation in the southern High Plains to be correlated with an ethnographic group. Turner (1980) identified a high presence of triple-rooted molars in his study population (23 percent), indicating to him the possibility that Sopris phase people may be Athapaskan. Even though this correlation is relatively high, other physical and biological traits should be more closely examined before a specific association can be made with any ethnographic group. Interestingly enough, Gunnerson (1989:57) seems to reject this Athapaskan affiliation for the Sopris phase and instead places it within the Pueblo sphere.

Although the correlation between Sopris phase people and Athapaskans is tentative at best, it is interesting to note that archaeologists working in northwest New Mexico are equating a gray ware (dating between A.D. 1400 and 1700) with Southern Athapaskans as well (Hancock et al. 1988:774–859). Tentatively identified as the La Plata variety of Dinetah Gray, this type also corresponds with poorly made sherds of Chapin Gray (C. Dean Wilson pers. comm. 1990). Wilson argues that the association of the La Plata sherds with Jeddito yellow wares and the absence of Chapin black-on-white, plus the consistently poor quality of the La Plata sherds, differentiate this material from Chapin Gray.

Several problems exist with this cultural correlation, however. First, the context of these ceramics has not been well established and, second, the total assemblage with which these gray ware sherds are associated has not been adequately described. If such a correlation can be demonstrated, Plains and Southwest scholars alike will have to reevaluate the entry date of the Athapaskans into the Southwest. Most anthropologists currently accept this entry date at either the late fifteenth or early sixteenth century (D. Gunnerson 1956; Wilcox 1981).

South of the Sopris phase in northeast New Mexico is the Escritores phase that Glassow (1980:73; cf. Glassow 1972) suggests as dating between A.D. 900 and 1100. This temporal placement is based on the cross-dating of "a poorly defined and variable type of mineral painted black-on-white ware" (Kiatuthlanna and/or Red Mesa black-on-white) which needs to be more closely examined by petrographic studies and other means (Cordell 1978:35). Like the exotic Sopris ceramics, this material indicates interconnections with people living in the Chaco region. In addition to these poorly defined "trade sherds," a locally made, neck-banded gray ware with coarse sand tempering is also present. Tubular beads cut from the long bones of rodents appear during this period and continue through the two succeeding phases (Glassow 1980:77).

There are two tested sites (NP-1/Area 1 and NP-1/Area 3) associated with the Escritores phase (Glassow 1980; Lutes 1959). The only exca-vated structure, located at NP-1/Area 1, is a circular pithouse with four roof-support posts, a central collared fireplace, and a ventilator shaft. These features led Glassow (1980:73) to state that this pithouse is quite similar to the Basketmaker III/Pueblo I architectural style. Bottle-shaped roasting pits or cists occur in association with this house and are relatively common in Escritores phase sites — just as they are in the earlier Pedregoso phase occupations.

Succeeding the Escritores phase is the Ponil phase (A.D. 1100–1250) which is also dependent on the cross-dating of Southwestern trade wares. This phase was first defined by Baker (1964) and later refined by Glassow (1980) who places several tested sites in this cultural mani-festation. These include such sites as the three-room structure at NP-1/Area 2 (Lutes 1959), and rockshelters such as Lizard Cave (NP-2; Skinner 1964), Salt Lake Cave (NP-8), and Box Canyon Cave (MP-4). Box Canyon Cave is of interest because it has yielded a variety of perishable objects including yucca fiber sandals, basketry, and a rodent-skin bag as well as maize and cucurbits. Ceramics include Taos or Kwahe'e black-on-white, Taos incised, and Taos punctated, along with a plain culinary ware that is either incised or punctated with a chevron design (Glassow 1980, 1984).

According to Lutes (1959), the Ponil phase is more closely associated with Anasazi developments in the Rio Grande area than with the

Plains due to the presence of masonry houses, exotic ceramic types, yucca fiber sandals, basketry, and straight or "cloudblower" pipes. Cordell (1978) notes, however, that the absence of kivas, cranial deformation, and stone axes, as well as the extended reliance on hunting (as indicated by a variety of projectile points and faunal remains), argue against such an assumption. Indeed, Lintz (1986a:229; cf. Kershner 1984:122) accepts Cordell's position to the degree that he would combine Sopris phase in Colorado with the Ponil phase in the Cimarron district of New Mexico, because "the division along state lines seems artificial and unwarranted."

Be that as it may, the latest Puebloan occupation in northeast New Mexico, according to Glassow (1980), is represented by the Cimarron phase (A.D. 1200–1300). Occurring along the mouths of the Cimarron, Ponil, and perhaps Vermejo canyons, sites associated with this phase (including LP-19, MP-3, and MP-16) have relatively large, rectangular surface structures with contiguous rooms, separated by rock masonry or coursed adobe walls. Cimarron Gray Ware or Plain, with a sand quartz temper, and Santa Fe black-on-white appear for the first time during this period. Cimarron Plain may be neckbanded, incised, or punctated, and is generally more finely made than the ceramics associated with earlier phases. A variety of lithic items occur at these sites, but snub-nosed end scrapers indicate at least some interaction with Plains groups (Cordell 1978; J. Gunnerson 1959). Numerous grinding stones are found in conjunction with burned maize cobs and carbonized beans. The presence of these materials indicates a greater reliance on farming than in the earlier phases.

Further east, Lintz (1986a) has proposed the Upper Canark regional variant (A.D. 1100–1500) to include Plains Village cultures located in the Canadian and Arkansas river basins. The Upper Canark regional variant, then, includes the Apishapa phase (A.D. 1100–1350) of southeast Colorado and the Antelope Creek phase (A.D. 1200–1500) in the Oklahoma and Texas panhandles. Such a concept recognizes cultural similarities and implies related origins for the Apishapa and Antelope Creek phases. Concurrently, Lintz (1986a) notes that certain discontinuities (including less emphasis on farming and a corresponding assemblage difference — such as the absence of bison scapula hoes — for the Apishapa phase) also exist. Gunnerson (1989:126) disagrees with this assessment and maintains that the Apishapa phase represents the culmination of a local development labeled the Los Animas tradition. This tradition includes the earlier Graneros focus and Apishapa phase.

Apishapa phase sites (originally defined by Withers 1954) tend to be located atop steep sided canyons or isolated mesa tops where defensibility seems to have been a major concern. Representative sites include Snake Blakeslee I (5LA1247), Cramer (5PE484), Avery Ranch (5PE56), and Triple J (5LA5833) (Baugh et al. 1986; Chase 1951; J. Gunnerson 1989; Ireland 1968; Renaud 1942; Watts 1971, 1975; Zier et al. 1988). Several rockshelters, such as Medina (5LA22), Pyeatt (5LA550), Umbart (5LA125), and Trinchera Cave also contain Apishapa materials and make up about one-third of the total number of Apishapa phase sites (Campbell 1976; Lintz 1986a, 1986b; Wood 1974; Wood-Simpson 1976). Campbell (1969, 1976) has postulated that Apishapa phase people are ancestral to Antelope Creek, but Lintz (1978) has refuted this point of view. More recently, Gunnerson (1989:120–24) argues that, on the basis of projectile point styles, the Apishapa phase is more closely related to the Upper Republican than Antelope Creek phase people. From this perspective, both Lintz (1986a, 1986b) and Gunnerson (1989) would argue for a Plains Caddoan affiliation for the Apishapa phase people. The difference is that Lintz (1986a, 1986b) aligns both the Apishapa and Antelope Creek phases with a Wichita related group while Gunnerson (1989) would argue that the former are related to the Pawnee and the latter to the Wichita.

Architectural units at Apishapa phase sites are stone enclosures. These structures are most commonly individual rooms, which may be circular, oval, semicircular, or occasionally rectangular in outline. At the Cramer (5PE484) site, Gunnerson (1989:25–28, 130) compares the large circular structure (Room A) with a Pawnee earthlodge consisting of four central support posts (even though evidence was lacking for at least one of these) and upright rock-slab walls. A few sites may have contiguous room structures. Frequently associated with the stone enclosure sites are barrier walls. Structures and walls tend to be constructed of vertical sandstone or, in some cases, basalt slabs (Campbell 1969, 1976; Eighmy and Wood 1984; Kalasz 1985; Nowak and Kingsbury 1981; Zier et al. 1988).

With the absence of sizable middens, year-round habitation at any one site seems unlikely. Indeed, Kalasz (Zier et al. 1988) believes these sites may be associated with more efficient plant collection and storage techniques rather than horticultural practices. The economy of these people is based on hunting (including deer and antelope with occasional bison), plant collecting, and limited farming with at least five varieties of maize having been recovered (Campbell 1969, 1976; Eighmy 1982; Gunnerson 1987). Cordmarked pottery is present but not plentiful. Stone implements consist of side-notched projectile points (Washita and Harrell varieties), flake and core scrapers, flange drills, ovate knives, and choppers. Bone artifacts include awls, shaft wrenches, and tubular bone beads. The few trade items present at these sites indicate that interaction with other Plains groups as well as with the Pueblo occurred. Recovered Southwestern sherds from the Snake Blakeslee (5LA1247) site include Talpa black-on-white and Rowe black-on-white (J. Gunnerson 1989:57). The presence of Alibates agatized dolomite from the Texas panhandle and Medicine Creek jasper from southern

Nebraska attest to intra-Plains trade while small quantities of obsidian provide evidence for interregional exchange with Puebloan groups.

Antelope Creek phase sites are located to the south of the Apishapa region along the Canadian and North Canadian rivers in the Texas and Oklahoma panhandles. The geographical boundary between the Apishapa phase and Antelope Creek phase is the sand dune belt associated with the Cimarron River (Lintz 1986; Saunders and Saunders 1982), and the lower boundary extends southward to the headwaters of the Red River. Antelope Creek–like sites extend into western Oklahoma, and may occur as far west as the plains of eastern New Mexico. The type sites for the Antelope Creek phase include Alibates Ruin 28, Antelope Creek 22, and Conner (Duffield 1964; Lintz 1986a, 1986b). Other representative sites are Black Dog Village, Footprint, Arrowhead Peak, Saddleback Mesa, Stamper, Roy Smith, and Two Sisters (Green 1967; Holden 1933; Keller 1975; Lintz 1979, 1984; Schneider 1969; Watson 1950).

In general, site types associated with the Antelope Creek phase include villages, open campsites, and lithic scatters. Rockshelters are relatively rare in this region, but Plains Village materials recovered from the Kenton Caves may be associated with Antelope Creek occupants (Lintz and Zabawa 1984). Included in the village category are sites with architecture which may vary from single-room structures to room blocks containing up to twenty contiguous rooms. These structures may be either circular or rectangular.

The economy of these people was based on farming, hunting, and gathering. Two types of maize have been recovered from these sites along with cucurbits and beans. Animal remains include bison, deer, and antelope as well as a host of smaller species. Borger cordmarked is a relatively common ceramic type associated with these sites. Stone tools include a variety of triangular points (Washita, Harrell, and Fresno varieties). In addition to the lithic implements associated with the Apishapa phase, Antelope Creek phase sites yield diamond beveled knives, "guitar-pick" scrapers/preforms, and T-shaped drills. Bone artifacts include bison scapula hoes, bison tibia digging stick tips, squash knives, various types of awls, beads, wedges, bone rasps, antler-tine billets, and a variety of other tools. Trade items include materials representative of intra-Plains as well as Southwestern exchange. Plains items include catlinite pipes, implements made of Niobrara jasper, and cordmarked ceramic vessels with collared rims.

Lintz (1986a, 1986b; cf. Lintz 1984) divides Antelope Creek into Early (A.D. 1200–1350) and Late (A.D. 1350–1500) subphases. The Early subphase is characterized by multiple-household, contiguous-room structures while the Late subphase sites contain single-room structures. Correlated with this change in architectural type, however, is an increase in mean room size and total indoor living space (Lintz 1986a: table 52), which is interpreted as reflecting a population increase.

Concurrently, paleoenvironmental evidence indicates that climatic conditions were becoming more xeric. This, according to Lintz (1986a: 240–45) would have brought about population stress. Thus, the population would have dispersed over the landscape accounting for different settlement patterns and structural types.

Early subphase (A.D. 1250 to 1350) sites tend to be located closer to the Canadian River and its important floodplain and terraces, which may have been used for growing crops. Late subphase sites, on the other hand, are found along the lateral tributaries of the Canadian where springs fed by the Ogallala aquifer are a reliable source of potable water. A more dispersed population and new settlement locations are only two of the buffering mechanisms used by the Antelope Creek phase people, however. Lintz (1986a:253, 1991:101–4; cf. Baugh 1982) also points to an increase in the quantity of trade commodities from the eastern frontier Pueblo villages, indicating an expansion of exchange relationships. In addition, there may have been an increase in inter-ethnic raiding which would have denied outside groups access to the spring-fed tributaries and the Alibates chert quarries.

As one moves away from the Antelope Creek phase core area, related but slightly different variations occur. In the mixed grass prairie region of western Oklahoma and the eastern portion of the Texas panhandle, single-room structures with rounded corners, centrally depressed floor channels, and at least two interior support posts occur in association with ceramics more similar to the Washita River phase than Antelope Creek phase (Flynn 1984, 1986). The associated settlements (including Zimms [34RM72], Lamb-Miller [34RM25], New Smith [34RM400], Pyeatts #4 [34RM179], Chalfant [34RM35], Wickham #3 [34RM29], and Heading [34WD2]) tend to be small hamlets or isolated houses located along major terraces or ridge tops overlooking primary tributaries of major rivers (Brooks, Moore, and Owlsey 1992; Flynn 1984, 1986; Moore 1984). Ceramics (labeled Quartermaster Plain) have smooth surfaces with either shell or limestone tempering. Other artifacts include small triangular side-notched (Washita variety), tri-notched (Harrell variety), and unnotched (Fresno variety) points, diamond beveled knives, flake base drills, end and side scrapers, spokeshaves, gravers, celts, and other implements. Bone implements consist of an antler projectile point, bison tibia digging stick tips, bison scapula hoes, bone awls, and split deer metatarsals. Lithic material types indicate trade with both Southwestern (obsidian) and intraregional Plains groups (Alibates chert with quarry cortex and Florence-A chert; Baugh and Nelson 1986, 1987, 1988). The cultural placement of these farming people is uncertain, but the combination of Washita River phase artifact types in conjunction with Antelope Creek phase house styles represents a Plains Village variant labeled the Zimms complex, dated about A.D. 1265 to 1425 (Brooks 1989).

Another variation is found in the more northern tributaries (such as Wolf Creek) of the Canadian River in the northeast portion of the Texas panhandle. Known as the Buried City complex (D. Hughes 1986, 1991; D. Hughes and Hughes-Jones 1987), this archaeological manifestation extends from south of Perryton in Ochiltree County, Texas to western Oklahoma (cf. Drass and Turner 1989) and possibly through the Oklahoma panhandle into southern Kansas near Coldwater in Comanche County. D. Hughes and A. Hughes-Jones (1987:105) suggest a temporal span ranging from A.D. 1150 to 1350 or 1400 for the Buried City complex. Representative sites for this complex are the Handley ruins group (including Handley and Franklin ruins as well as Kent #1), the Courson ruins group (consisting of Courson A-D or 41OC26, 41OC27, 41OC28, and 41OC29), Gould ruins, and the Kit Courson ruins group. According to D. Hughes and Hughes-Jones (1987), another potential locality belonging to this complex is the Lonker site (34BV4) in Beaver County, Oklahoma.

Architectural patterns for the Buried City complex are poorly known, but appear to be similar to Antelope Creek phase types I and II (Lintz 1986a). They differ in that the former have wall-support posts located on either side of vertical caliche slabs placed ten to twenty centimeters apart forming the structure's foundation. A smaller room, used for processing and storage, may be attached to the southeast corner of such structures. Variation in wall construction and the presence or absence of this attached room may exist as well. Most of the known sites belonging to this complex are located above the floodplain of Wolf Creek in the northeast corner of the Texas panhandle.

Material culture is also quite similar to Antelope Creek phase sites, especially in terms of lithic and bone artifacts. Small triangular side-notched (Washita variety) and tri-notched (Harrell variety) points are present. In addition, there are diamond beveled knives, oval and flake knives, and suboval end scrapers. Large end scrapers are not present, however. Many of these tools are made of Alibates chert which appears to be acquired locally due to the presence of river cobble cortex. In contrast to Antelope Creek phase sites, trade items are relatively rare. The few trade commodities present occur in the form of Niobrara jasper from Nebraska and Florence-A chert from north-central Oklahoma and south-central Kansas (Vehik 1985; Vehik, Buehler, and Wormser 1979).

Bone implements are also common in Buried City complex sites. These include bison tibia digging stick tips, horn core scoops, scapula shovels, notched ribs, and rib-shaft wrenches. Additionally, deer mandible sickles and split deer metapodial awls and spatulates have been recovered. One site yielded bone pins, possibly for decorative purposes. Freshwater mussel shells occur in both unmodified and modified forms (the latter being used as scoops or scrapers and as pendants or other ornaments).

Pottery is perhaps the most distinctive artifact type in comparison to the Antelope Creek phase. Smooth-surface, obliterated cordmarked, and cordmarked vessels which are tempered with fine to very fine quartz sand are most common. Rims are commonly decorated. These may be pinched, incised, impressed, crenelated, filleted, gouged, punctated, or fluted. D. Hughes and A. Hughes-Jones (1987:78–80) have defined Courson Pinched as a tentative new type for this complex. According to Hughes and Hughes-Jones (1987:78, 106), this type is more similar to the Geneseo pottery types of western Kansas than to Antelope Creek wares.

As can be seen from this discussion, the Upper Canark regional variant includes the Apishapa phase, Antelope Creek phase, Zimms complex, and Buried City complex. Furthermore, this cultural manifestation covers a large portion of the southern Plains and is represented by cultural variation throughout the area.

Returning to the southwestern edge of the Llano Estacado and the Eastern Extension of the Jornada Mogollon, the previously discussed Querecho phase (A.D. 950–1100) is followed by the Maljamar (A.D. 1100–1300) and Ochoa (A.D. 1300–1450) phases. Maljamar phase sites, such as Boot Hill and Burro Lake, consist of twenty to thirty small, rectangular pithouses with hearths placed near the center of the back wall (Leslie 1979). Two types of locally made ceramics, a plain brownware and a corrugated brownware, are found in association with these pithouses. In addition, a wide variety of trade wares (including El Paso polychrome, Mimbres black-on-white, Playas red-incised, Three Rivers red-on-terracotta boldline, Three Rivers red-on-terracotta fine line, and Chupadero black-on-white) have been recovered from Maljamar phase sites (Collins 1971; Leslie 1979). Projectile point types change from small corner-notched to small triangular side-notched points during this period. Corresponding with this change in point styles in A.D. 1200 is a greater reliance on bison hunting. Oval basin metates and single hand manos were still in common use, but mortars and pestles had been added as well. These implements attest to the importance of plant foods in the subsistence pattern of these people.

Toward the end of the Maljamar phase much of the northern area was abandoned, with the major concentration of sites (such as Monument Spring) occurring in extreme southeast New Mexico (Leslie 1979). Several new trade wares make their appearance at this time, including the northern Rio Grande Glaze wares, Ramos polychrome, and Lincoln black-on-red. Leslie (1979) views this abandonment from A.D. 1300 to 1350 as a transitional period for the Eastern Extension of the Jornada Mogollon.

The latest complex in this sequence, the Ochoa phase (A.D. 1300–1450), consists of sites (such as Merchant and Salt Cedar), that are characterized by jacal or wattle-and-daub surface structures with rock or adobe foundations. These features occur as multiple, contiguous-room structures and as single-room structures. At least one site associated with the Ochoa phase also has pithouses occurring in association with the surface rooms. Bison hunting continues to be a primary subsistence practice, and small triangular side-notched points persist as the predominant type. Also included are shaft abraders, diamond beveled knives, and small end scrapers. Ceramics consist of the locally made Ochoa plain brown, Ochoa corrugated, and Ochoa indented brownware. A slightly modified but varied series of trade wares are also found. These include El Paso polychrome, Three Rivers red-on-terracotta fine line, Gila polychrome, Ramos polychrome, Aqua Fria glaze-on-red, Cienegilla glaze-on-yellow, Corona corrugated, Chupadero black-on-white, and Lincoln black-on-red (Leslie 1979).

Much of the temporal placement for all of these phases associated with the Eastern Branch of the Jornada Mogollon is dependent on cross-dating of these exotic ceramic types with very few radiocarbon or archaeomagnetic dates available. Still, the Eastern Branch of the Jornada Mogollon appears to have moved across much of the southern Llano Estacado at a relatively early date as established by work at the Salt Cedar and other sites in the Andrews Lake locality of west Texas (Collins 1968). In addition to Ochoa indented brownware, the Salt Cedar site yielded San Clemente Glaze A polychrome, Aqua Fria glaze-on-red, Chupadero black-on-white, and El Paso polychrome (Collins 1968, 1969).

To the west and north in New Mexico, Mogollon brownwares have been recovered from sites as far north as the Canadian River. These sites include the upper level of San Jon (Roberts 1942), the Hodges and other sites near Tucumcari (Dick 1953; Way 1984), as well as LA5573 and LA5575 in the Ute Reservoir area (Hammock 1965).

MIDDLE PLAINS VILLAGE PERIOD: A.D. 1450–1750

In the area previously occupied by Antelope Creek phase people, a new group of nomadic bison hunting groups took up residence in the Middle Plains Village period. Known as the Tierra Blanca complex (A.D. 1450–1650), this protohistoric culture extended southward from the Canadian River to the headwaters of the Red River in the Texas panhandle (map 12.3). Representative sites include Fatheree (A1286), Canyon Country Club Cave (A251), Fifth Green (A1363), Tierra Blanca (A264), Cita Mouth (A288), A148, and South Mouth (A1299) (Habicht-Mauche 1987, 1988, 1991; Holden 1931; J. Hughes 1991, n.d.; J. Hughes, Hood, and Newman 1978; Katz and Katz 1976; Spielmann 1982). The cultural material associated with the Tierra Blanca complex reflects a hunting-and-gathering–based economy. Small triangular notched (both Washita and Harrell varieties) as well as unnotched (Fresno variety) points

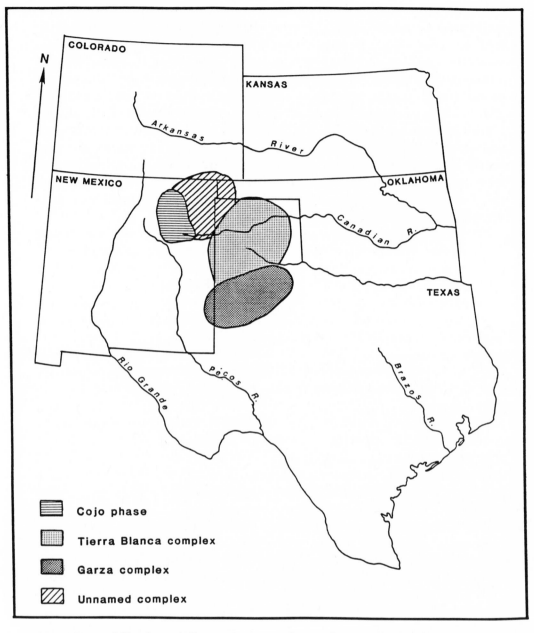

Map 12.3. Middle Plains Village cultures on the southern High Plains.

occur in association with end scrapers, side scrapers, drills, and diamond beveled knives. Most of these artifacts are made of Alibates chert
or the locally available Tecovas jasper. Obsidian occurs in only small
quantities. Bison scapula hoes and digging stick tips are absent, however. Ceramics include a series of Southwestern trade wares (i.e.,
intermediate and late glaze wares as well as a smeared, indented utility

ware). A thin, dark, faintly striated ware (Tierra Blanca Plain) is a locally made utility type using the Southwestern method of coiling and scraping rather than the Plains-derived paddle-and-anvil technique (Habicht-Mauche 1987, 1988, 1991). On the basis of the attributes of Tierra Blanca Plain, scholars in the area have placed this type within the realm of Eastern Apache ceramics (Baugh and Eddy 1987). Structural types associated with this complex are poorly known, but may be represented by stone circles (tipi rings) exclusively. J. Hughes (1991:36; n.d.) equates the Tierra Blanca complex with recently arrived Southern Athapaskans, but Habicht-Mauche (1988) notes that the initial dates of around 1450 for the complex indicate that Athapaskan speakers entered the Southern Plains much earlier than has generally been proposed (D. Gunnerson 1956; Wilcox 1981).

South of the headwaters of the Red River, along the Red River itself and the tributaries of the Brazos River and extending westward to the Pecos River is the Garza complex dated to A.D. 1450–1750 (T. Baugh 1986, 1992a; Habicht-Mauche 1988; J. Hughes 1991, n.d.). These people too relied upon bison hunting as the foundation of their economy with campsites, processing stations, and semisedentary base camps or villages being found throughout the area. Campsites and processing stations are represented by such sites as Garza (41GR1), Lubbock Lake (41LU1), Lott (41GR76), Blue Mountain rockshelter, Red Bluff shelter (41CX8), Johnson Creek, and the Garnsey Spring campsite (LA18400) near Roswell, New Mexico (Holden 1938; Johnson et al. 1977; Lorrain 1968; Parry and Speth 1984; Runkles 1964; Runkles and Dorchester 1986). Villages tend to be concentrated along the White River in Blanco Canyon near Lubbock, Texas. These sites include Montgomery (41FL17), Bridwell (41CB27), Pete Creek (41CB1), and Floydada Country Club (41FL1) (Baugh 1992a; Northern 1979; Parker 1982; Parsons 1967; Word 1963, 1965, 1991). Although no structures have been excavated at any Garza complex locality, the Bridwell site has a circular, raised earthen ridge measuring from forty-six to fifty meters in diameter (Baugh 1992b; Parker 1982). This circular feature may represent an intact fortification. Similar features have been recorded and tested for sites (e.g., Edwards I, 34BK2) affiliated with the Wheeler phase in southwest Oklahoma (T. Baugh 1986; cf. Vehik this volume).

Material culture includes small triangular, notched (Garza, Harrell, Washita, and Lott varieties) and unnotched points (Fresno). These occur along with snub-nosed scrapers, bifacial knives, and flake base drills. Edwards chert represents the predominant lithic material, but Alibates agatized dolomite, Tecovas jasper, and obsidian artifacts occur as well (T. Baugh 1986, 1992a; Baugh and Nelson 1987). Bone tools, such as awls and serrated metapodial fleshers, are also present. Decorative items are relatively common. Some of the shell objects (such as conus shell tinklers) are derived from the Southwest. Ceramics include

Plains wares associated with the Wheeler phase (A.D. 1450–1750) in southwest Oklahoma as well as early, intermediate, and late glaze wares from the Galisteo basin (T. Baugh 1986, 1992a). Because of the close relationships with the Wheeler phase, the Garza complex is affiliated with the Plains Caddoans, that is the Wichita (T. Baugh 1986; Habicht-Mauche 1988). Not all archaeologists agree on this point, however. Hofman (1989), J. Hughes (1991:36, n.d.), and J. Gunnerson (1987), for example, argue for a Plains Apache identity.

Northeast New Mexico during the transition from the Early to Middle Plains Village period appears to have been unoccupied except for occasional hunting or collecting forays by Puebloan people. During the late or perhaps mid-sixteenth century evidence for a new group of people, the Apacheans, becomes apparent. Glassow (1980:76–77, 1984:103) refers to this period as the Cojo phase (A.D. 1550/1600–1750) and places within it several sites along the Ponil, Cimarron, and Vermejo drainages. These include NP-12, NP-32A, VE-21, VE-21A, VE-124, VE-132A, and VE-169. Although J. Gunnerson (1969, 1979, 1987) is more reserved about the use of taxonomic names, he attributes several sites (including Glasscock [29MO20] and Sammis [29CX68]) in the headwaters of the Canadian River to this period. Dwellings associated with these sites range from stone circles (tipi rings), through an oval pit encircled with a low wall of rocks and covered by an unidentified superstructure, to a seven-room pueblo. The most distinguishing artifact associated with these sites is Ocate Micaceous, which is a thin, dark gray to black utility type that is affiliated with the Sangre de Cristo Micaceous wares (Baugh and Eddy 1987). This pottery type may occur in association with intrusive Puebloan sherds and historic European ceramics in the later sites. Lithic artifacts include side-notched and unnotched triangular projectile points, end scrapers, and "double bitted drills" (Gunnerson 1969, 1979, 1987). Ground stone implements consist of a distinctive convex-sided metate, basin metates, and sandstone abraders. Bone artifacts are not numerous, but occur as tubular bone beads, awls, beamers, and eagle bone whistles.

In southeast Colorado, a few tipi ring sites (e.g., 5LA1411) are associated with Ocate Micaceous ceramics exclusively (Ireland 1974:221–22; C. E. Wood 1986). C. E. Wood (1986:133–34) refers to these sites as the Carlana phase which ranges between A.D. 1525 and 1750. During this same period an unnamed complex occurs in eastern New Mexico. The type site for this complex is Ojo Perdido (29SM32), which exhibits over two hundred tipi rings (J. Gunnerson 1979, 1987; Gunnerson and Gunnerson 1971). The distinctive mica- and crushed-rock–tempered ceramic type for this site is known as Perdido Plain, which differs from Tierra Blanca Plain of the Texas panhandle (Baugh and Eddy 1987; Habicht-Mauche 1987, 1988). These sherds are found in association with Pecos and Picuris glaze wares that have been used to date the Ojo

Perdido site to the mid-seventeenth century. Between the Ojo Perdido site and Cojo phase localities are a number of sites containing both Ocate Micaceous and Perdido Plain. The significance of these intermediate sites has yet to be determined.

By A.D. 1750, the small farming sites occupied by the Apache had been besieged by the Comanche, more recent migrants to the southern Plains, and in many cases the Jicarilla and other Plains Apache groups had been displaced from the Plains altogether (Secoy 1953). Maintaining small farming communities, consisting of around eight dwellings, made the Apache easy targets for the well-mounted Comanche, and the Athapaskans suffered severe losses. As this situation demonstrates, the protohistoric period was a dynamic one involving not only Native American societies but the Spaniards as well (Baugh 1991). The dynamics of this and the later historic period are represented by the movement of other well-known southern Plains tribes, such as the Kiowa and Kiowa-Apache, who did not appear in the region until the early nineteenth century.

PREHISTORIC CULTURES OF THE SOUTHERN HIGH PLAINS: CONCLUSION

Technically this section should begin with post-Archaic cultures, but in order to understand the late prehistoric adaptations of the southern High Plains a brief preface concerning earlier societies is necessary. The Archaic peoples established an overall land-use strategy, which was certainly modified with the addition of horticulture, but the core principles of how people interacted with their landscape remained the same until the acquisition of the horse.

During the Paleo-Indian period (9000 to 6000 B.C.) prehistoric hunters and gatherers appear to have wandered freely across the Llano Estacado (Stanford and Day 1992). Because water was relatively dependable, occurring in the various playas, the location of herds was somewhat predictable. This made hunting of large game a rather low-risk proposition, and even though different bands certainly interacted there is little evidence for trade or exchange between them. These nomadic peoples may have obtained needed resources, such as lithic materials, through direct acquisition (Meltzer 1987). This pattern may have continued well into the Early Archaic period. Toward the end of the Early Archaic and with the advent of the Altithermal, however, much of this free-roaming movement from oasis to oasis (Shelley 1988) in pursuit of megafauna and later bison forms seems to have changed.

During the Altithermal, water sources tended to become fewer in number. As a result, these late Early to Middle Archaic foragers tend to rely on more dependable sources of water, which in many cases were hand-excavated wells at such localities as Mustang Springs in Texas, as

well as Blackwater Draw Locality No. 1 and Rattlesnake Draw, both in
New Mexico (Evans 1951; Green 1962; Hester 1972; Meltzer and
Collins 1987; Shelley 1988:20; Smith, Runyon, and Agogino 1966:306;
Warnica 1966). These people tended to cluster their sites along the
fringes of the Llano Estacado, and even though climatic conditions
improved in succeeding centuries, this pattern was followed by later
farming peoples.

The lack of water on the southern High Plains during the Middle
Archaic period may have been drastic enough to reduce the number of
bison. These animals may have moved northward and eastward to
escape the severe drought conditions (Meltzer and Collins 1987). This
led Dillehay (1974) to postulate his first bison absence period. As
Lubbock Lake indicates, however, not all sites on the southern Plains
lacked bison during this period (Johnson and Holliday 1986), but the
general trend was away from bison hunting. By the Late Archaic, bison
once again appeared in relatively large numbers in the southern Plains
and were being relied upon by Plains people. During this period sites
tend to be located near water sources such as "the rims and terraces of
playas, valleys, and canyons, especially the latter, and . . . some of the
deepest and richest sites occur at water sources near canyon heads.
Many more sites have been recorded in the canyons and breaks of the
Red River drainage, and in the Canadian breaks, than along the valleys
and around the playas on the High Plains" (Hughes 1976 cited in
Gunnerson 1987:37). Such a distinctive pattern of placing habitation
sites along the margins of the Llano where water was readily available
and using the uplands to exploit animal resources may be termed a
"tethered" economy. This tethered economy was well established by
A.D. 500, which represents the initial Woodland or Early Ceramic
period for the southern High Plains.

One of the more striking aspects of the Woodland or Early Ceramic
period for this region in general is that it began relatively late in
comparison to the Southwest, where cultigens have been found in use
by no later than 500 B.C. (Berry 1985; Lipe 1983:438), or eastern North
America where the Eastern Agricultural Complex played an important
role in the economy of Late Archaic peoples by about 2000 B.C. and
maize by no later than 200 B.C. (Berry 1985). Plains people were
certainly aware of the new cultigens being utilized in the Southwest for
early varieties of flint corns, or Maiz de Ocho, were moving through the
area to the Midwest (Galinat 1985; Upham et al. 1987). It was not until
the eighth century that southern Plains people began to adopt horticulture. This occurred with the "diffusion" of Maiz de Ocho from the
Southwest through northeast New Mexico and southeast Colorado to
eastern North America (Galinat 1985:267). The question is: Why did it
take southern Plains societies so long to take up this new subsistence
strategy and associated technology?

In attempting to account for the overall development of food production, Flannery (1986:515–16) suggests that the domestication of plants may have resulted from an attempt to reduce the search area for vegetable products. This process of minimizing the quest for plant foods may well have brought on an intensification in hunting as well. By concentrating on large game animals, such as bison, these hunters were able to maximize the acquisition of fats and proteins. Following this line of reasoning, if Plains foragers intensified their hunting strategies, they may have delayed or even offset the process of adopting domesticated plants since this would require a totally new adaptive strategy. This proposition certainly needs to be examined in more detail but it may help to explain partially why food production occurred at a relatively late date in the southern Plains region.

Once adopted, cultigens played an important role in southern Plains economies. Even then food production was not the ultimate stablizing force for the development of sedentism or even for providing all the necessary nutrient requirements for Plains societies. Hunting continued to play an important role, and trade with peoples to the west also had a significant impact on Plains people. The earliest exchange system seems to have developed through the Jornada branch of the Mogollon, but with the collapse of Casas Grandes and other Mogollon centers, this southern system was soon dominated by a more northern system (Baugh 1982, 1984a, 1991; Wilcox 1991). This northern system was first based in the pueblos of the Galisteo basin, but was later replaced by Pecos pueblo. The southern system did not completely disappear, however. The accounts dealing with Jumano traders (John 1975) who visited the Wichita and Caddo are evidence of the continued viability of this southern system that was operating parallel to the northern one. The northern system too underwent many changes as the Spaniards brought the southern Plains macroeconomy into the world economy of the seventeenth century. The southern Plains Village groups, then, present an excellent opportunity more thoroughly to examine mixed economies based on farming, hunting, gathering, and trading strategies. Such investigations will contribute substantially to anthropological research concerning cultural adaptation and change not only in the Plains but in comparable regions throughout the world.

CHAPTER 13

DEVELOPMENT IN THE SOUTHWEST AND RELATIONS WITH THE PLAINS

Albert H. Schroeder

THE plains of New Mexico and Colorado to the east of the Sangre de Cristo Mountains and to the east of the Pecos River flowing into west Texas are a region of temperature and precipitation extremes, at elevations ranging from 8,500 feet in the north to 2,500 feet in west Texas. Vulcanism accounts for a number of landmarks in northeastern New Mexico and southern Colorado, in contrast to the open plains to the south built up with Pleistocene and Holocene sands.

Grasslands are interspersed with streams lined with cottonwood and mesquite trees and shrubs, with shinnery oak on the sands of southeastern New Mexico and juniper on the outer slopes of the mountains on the west. Short drainages flow into the Pecos from the east, all others draining east from the mountains into the Southern Plains.

This is a region known for its early man—Clovis, Folsom, and other—sites, but little is known about its Archaic period development. By A.D. 500, the Eastern Anasazi along the Rio Grande, practicing horticulture supplemented with hunting and gathering, lived in scattered sites containing a few pithouses, perhaps seasonally occupied. Occasionally a larger settlement had one structure at least double the size of the associated houses, suggesting use as a community house for ritual, storage, or other possible extended family purpose.

THE EASTERN FRONTIER: PRE–A.D. 1200

Prior to A.D. 1000, major developments and cultural influences of the Southwest originated in and flowed from west of the continental divide to the Eastern Anasazi, particularly in regard to ceramics and architecture, including little kivas. The Jornada Mogollon to the south of the Eastern Anasazi, between the Rio Grande and Llano Estacado, never had big kivas and only had minor contacts with their northern neighbors, most being with the Mogollon on the west (Mera 1943; Jelinek 1967) prior to A.D. 1100. A few pre–A.D. 500 Jornada Brown sherds tempered with Sierra Blanca region material have been noted in the Texas panhandle (Hughes and Willey 1978:187, Baugh 1984a:157). Perhaps the lack of any long drainage on the east side of the Pecos River functioned as a deterrent to travel or trade into the Jornada district from the east. However, some Alibates and Edwards Plateau cherts and other material of eastern origin have been reported in Jornada sites prior to Jornada abandonment of the region about A.D. 1400.

Prior to A.D. 1100, a few Plains-derived items occur in the Southwest. The elbow pipe is found over a large area, beginning in the northern Southwest in Pueblo I (A.D. 700–900) times (Tichy 1945), perhaps derived from the Woodland complex where it has been reported (Wedel 1961:91). Beamers, which are reported in Eastern Anasazi sites, occur in the Navajo Reservoir district of the upper San Juan drainage prior to A.D. 1050 (Eddy 1966:497) and are now known to be present before A.D. 1300 (Wendorf 1953:98). These probably were introduced through contacts with the Upper Republican phase, where they were in use after A.D. 1000 (Wedel 1961:96). Stockaded sites in the Gobernador area on the west slope of the continental divide, dating from A.D. 800 (Hall 1944b; Eddy 1966:164, 201) into the late 1000s to 1100s and probably derived from Woodland barrier walls, as well as the presence of conical-base jars and cordmarked pottery (Hibben 1938; Seaman 1976) are additional features of Plains derivation, probably Woodland, as discussed below.

Early surveys in the San Luis Valley–Alamosa, Colorado locale on the east side of the divide recorded cordmarked and conical-base vessels associated with Anasazi pottery of Pueblo II to historic times (Mera 1935:34; Renaud 1942, 1947:49ff). The chronological placement of the non-Pueblo Woodland sherds was not demonstrated until later. In the region between Trinidad, Colorado and Cimarron Creek, New Mexico on the east side of the Sangre de Cristo Range, slab foundation structures are common after A.D. 1000 (Holden 1931; Krieger 1946; Wendorf and Reed 1955:140–41; Lutes 1959; Baker 1964; Glasgow 1984; Kershner 1984:122). The earliest Woodland ceramic period sites in the region, associated with circular rock or slab foundation structures to the north, occur in the early Woodland sites of A.D. 450–750 in the Chaquaqua Plateau (Campbell 1969) and between Pueblo and Walsenburg, Colorado (Withers 1983). Sites to the south in the Ponil Creek area date from A.D. 700, are few in number, and are not Woodland (Glasgow 1984:202). The lack of stockaded sites in this region suggests that the earlier Plains traits in the Gobernador entered by way of the southern tributaries of the upper Arkansas.

Table 13.1.
Southwestern Neighbors, A.D. 500

Culture District	Phase	Dates (A.D.)
Rio Grande Jornada Mogollon	Mesilla	300–1150
Rio Grande Mogollon	San Marcial	500–800
Rio Grande Anasazi	Developmental Pueblo	500–1200
Cimarron	Pedregosa	700–900

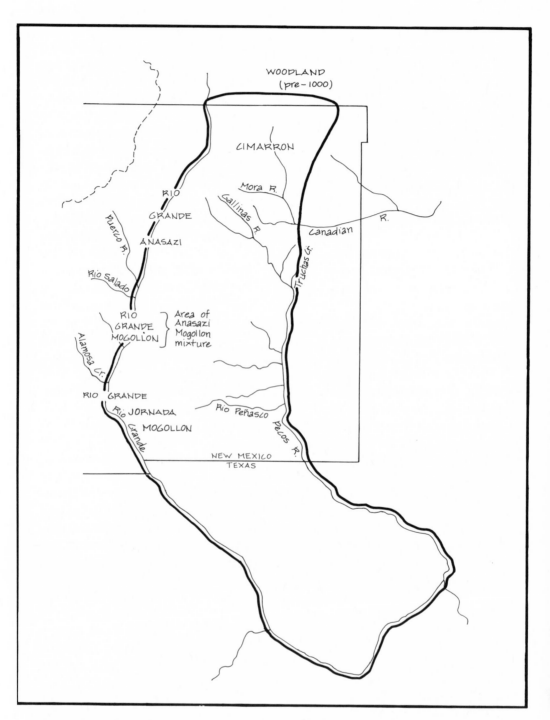

Map 13.1. Culture districts (otherwise Late Archaic), ca. A.D. *500 (see table 13.1).*

W. R. Wedel (1959) places the Woodland in eastern Colorado up to
A.D. 1000 and Alex Krieger (1946) has it in northern Texas up to 1050.
The work by Robert Campbell (1969) on the Chaquaqua Plateau places
this entire region in better perspective. His Plains Woodland period of
about A.D. 400–1000 contains the elements above noted in the Gobernador. He suggests that the change about A.D. 1000 from Woodland to
the Apishapa focus occurred *in situ* on the plateau and was not the
result of an influx since many of the Woodland elements continued
into the Apishapa focus. Hughes and Willey (1978) reached a similar
conclusion for the Antelope Creek phase. One change on the Chaquaqua Plateau was the shift from horizontal to vertical slab base foundations. Fred Wendorf and Erik Reed (1955:141) note that vertical slab
walls are present from A.D. 900 in the Rio Grande, perhaps an idea
picked up by the Plains Woodland.

Thus, it appears that the post–A.D. 1000 slab foundation structures
from Vermejo Creek north represent or are a variant of the Apishapa
focus. After this date, to the south in Ponil Creek area, Pueblo aspects,
including pottery and pithouses, are more evident, and later Pueblo
items continue to be present until the late 1200s. Joe Winter (1985:58)
further suggests that the Archaic foraging practice was maintained
when horticulture was added in Woodland times and that a semisedentary subsistence pattern continued during the Apishapa focus.

Michael Glassow (1980:13) suggests that sometime between A.D.
1000 and 1200 the population of the Taos area surpassed that of the
Cimarron on the east side of the mountains. This may well have
resulted from Albert Schroeder's proposed ancestral Tewa influx at
about A.D. 1050 from the upper San Juan into the area south of the
Picuris (Ford, Schroeder, and Peckham 1972: map 3), which displaced
the indigenous ancestral Tiwas who then concentrated in the Picuris-
Taos area. These Northern Tiwas prior to A.D. 1050 had been in a Late
Archaic (nonceramic) period. The Tewa intrusion introduced the neighboring Northern Tiwas to an Anasazi way of life derived from the upper
San Juan that differed from the contemporary Southern Tiwa, Red
Mesa Valley–derived Anasazi. The now ceramic period (beginning ca.
A.D. 1050–1100) of the Northern Tiwas, possibly due to overcrowding,
expanded east across the mountains (Wendorf and Reed 1955:140–41),
introducing this new Anasazi pattern to the non-Pueblo occupants of
the Cimarron area in the Ponil phase (A.D. 1100–1250).

A similar expansion (Wendorf and Reed 1955) occurred around the
south end of the mountains into the Pecos, Tecolote, and Mora drainages where pueblos of adobe and stone were built. A site near Watrous
with Pueblo III pottery yielded some bison bones in one adobe room
that exhibited three floors (Lister 1948). Multifloors are reported in
other eastern frontier pueblos of adobe in the Sacramento Mountains
(Bradfield 1929:4) and in the La Luz and Alamagordo areas, where the

Table 13.2.
Southwestern Neighbors, A.D. 1000

Culture District	Phase	Dates (A.D.)
Rio Grande Jornada Mogollon (south)	Mesilla	300–1150
	Dona Ana	1100–1200
Rio Grande Jornada Mogollon (north)	Capitan	pre-900–1100
	Three Rivers	1100–1200
	San Andres	1200–1300
Rio Grande Mogollon	Tajo	800–1000
	Early Elmendorf	950–1100
Rio Grande Anasazi	Developmental Pueblo	500–1200
	Coalition Period	1200–1325
Gran Quivira Mogollon	Pithouse Period	800–1200
	Jacal Period (Claunch)	1175–1350
Middle Pecos Jornada Mogollon	18 Mile	pre-800–950
	Mesita Negra	950–1100
Rio Hondo Jornada Mogollon	Glencoe	900–1350
	Corona	1100–1250
Eastern Jornada Mogollon	Querecho	pre-900–1100
	Maljamar	1100–1300
Santa Fe Anasazi	Red Mesa	900–1000
	Tesuque	1000–1200
	Pindi	1200–1275
	Galisteo	1275–1325
Cimarron Anasazi	Escritores	900–1100
	Ponil	1100–1250
	Cimarron	1200–1300
Upper Canadian	Woodland	pre-1000
Taos Anasazi	Valdez	1000–1200
	Pot Creek	1200–1250
Santa Rosa Anasazi	Pueblo	1050–1300

lowermost floors exhibit burned areas and the upper ones well-formed fire pits (Stubbs 1930:8). This type of situation, if it proves consistent among frontier pueblos, may imply seasonal use, at least in the earlier stages. No Plains pottery is reported at these sites. It appears that these frontier pueblos had little contact with Plains groups prior to their abandonment in the late 1200s.

Along the Rio Grande and south of the Socorro area the Jornada horticultural development of the Mesilla phase (ca. A.D. 300–1100) spread downriver as a result of increased precipitation, permitting rainfall farming (Kelley 1952:382). By the Dona Ana phase (A.D. 1100–1200) it had expanded south to about 125 miles below El Paso to El

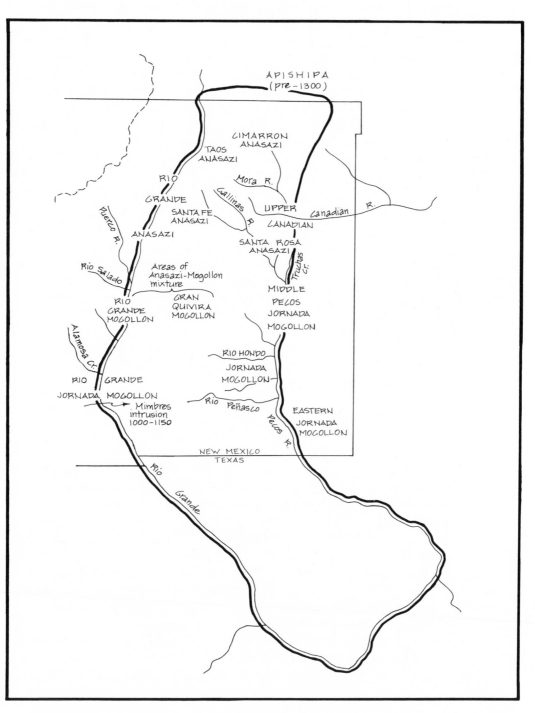

Map 13.2. Culture districts, ca. A.D. 1000 (see table 13.2).

Cajon. The Mogollon-like sites of the Chihuahua area to the west reflected the developments along the Rio Grande. During the El Paso phase (A.D. 1200–1400) in the north, contemporary horticultural sites appeared farther south in the locale of the Conchos River junction, from where they continue up this stream and Alamito Creek to the east some forty miles. In this region, the sites represent La Junta focus. All of these Rio Grande and Chihuahua villages — like those of the Jornada of southeastern New Mexico (Mera 1940:38) — were abandoned shortly after A.D. 1400 except for the latter focus which survived into the middle 1600s (Kelley 1952). These abandonments seemingly occur at the time of a drought between 1411 and 1424, or 1415 and 1425 (Mera 1940; Rose, Dean, and Robinson 1981:100).

By the early Spanish period, in the 1500s, the occupants of the La Junta area were referred to as Pataros or Rayas or Rayados in 1581; Pataraguates, Pataraguantes, or Patarabueyes, or Jumanos ("among themselves called Jamana") in 1582, and also called Otomoacos. Farther north were nonfarming Caguates or Jumanos, later called Sumas, and near El Paso more nonfarmers called Tampachoas, later called Mansos. South of the Conchos — Rio Grande confluence were the Cabri or Abriachis of 1582 and up the Conchos River the Conchos (Schroeder 1974:130–59; for confusion on the use of the name Jumanos, see pp. 160–72). Perhaps the nonfarmers represent descendants of the pre–A.D. 1400 horticulturists.

INSTABILITY IN THE WEST: A.D. 1100–1300

Beginning in the 1100s, a number of demographic shifts took place west of the continental divide (Schroeder 1955:22, 1961:87–88, 106–8, 1982: 16–17, 1985:107) that were to affect the Eastern Anasazi. The primacy of cultural influences from the west coast of Mexico seems to have begun to break down between 1150 and 1250 (Meighan 1971:767), perhaps causing similar disruption in contemporary Southwestern societies.

The potters of the Western Anasazi decorated their vessels with organic paint, a practice that replaced the use of mineral paint among their eastern Mesa Verde neighbors by the 1100s. Most of the Eastern Anasazi mineral paint decoration gave way to organic paint by the 1200s, the exceptions being the Taos, upper Canadian, Salinas, and Socorro areas where mineral paint continued in use (Schroeder 1982: 304). The above events appear to be a related episode.

As the west Mexican coast connection was breaking down, it was being replaced by that of the Casas Grandes (Schroeder 1982:16–17). During this period, the Eastern Anasazi districts developed their own distinctive ceramic decorations as a result of a variety of temporal contacts from different directions (Lang 1982:166–67). The instability west of the divide had little immediate effect on the Eastern Anasazi prior to the 1200s.

The dislocations of the 1100s west of the divide were followed by almost a century of successive droughts in the same region between A.D. 1215 and 1299. This contributed to the depopulation of certain areas and disappearance of some subcultures.

As for the Central Anasazi, some of the Mesa Verde people reoccupied several of the depopulated or abandoned Chacoan sites in the early 1200s. Many of the former occupants of Chaco Canyon had migrated east to the continental divide in the 1100s (Vivian and Matthews 1964) and probably by the 1200s were in the Rio Grande drainage. Also during this period, the occupants of the Gallina district dispersed, some into the Jemez area (Wendorf and Reed 1955:148) and others possibly to the Hopi country (Schroeder 1985).

By the end of the 1200s, most of the Four Corners region had been abandoned. Concentrations now survived in the Hopi region and along the middle and upper Little Colorado River as well as in the northern Mogollon region from Zuni south. The occupants of the last maintained contact with the Eastern Anasazi as their trade pottery in the Santa Fe–Albuquerque area indicates (Wendorf and Reed 1955).

Of little apparent connection in the late 1200s are the coincidental appearances of two cults far removed from one another. Krieger (1946: 216) notes the occurrence of the Southern Cult in his Sanders focus which he dates around A.D. 1300–1400 (now the Middle Caddo of A.D. 1200–1400). He placed this focus along the western edge of the Mississippi tradition. This cult also appears in the Spiro phase (A.D. 1250–1450) of eastern Oklahoma (Willey 1966:304–6) in the Arkansas River valley. James Ford and Gordon Willey (1941:358) in discussing possible origins for this cult considered Mexican influence or a religious revival based on stressful conditions similar to those that led to the Ghost Dance in the late nineteenth century.

Apparently at about the same time, the Kachina Cult appeared among the Western (and Eastern?) Anasazi which Randall McGuire (1986) places at the time of the major drought of the late 1200s west of the divide. He postulates that the long drought resulted in adoption of this new cult because of an ideological crisis that led to a reorganization of symbolical exchanges "derived ultimately from mesoamerican models," thus paralleling Ford and Willey's thoughts on cult origins. If either cult had any direct bearing on Southwest-Plains interaction, it presently is not apparent unless the weeping eye and awanyu symbols (rock art only in the Southwest) and presence of conch shell in both are of any significance.

Though the region east of the continental divide seems to have been free of severe droughts in the late 1200s, sites east of the Sangre de Cristos in the Cimarron area and south of Ocate were abandoned at this time, the occupants returning respectively to the Taos and Pecos districts (Wendorf and Reed 1955:148; Wendorf 1960). More recently, Campbell (1969) has proposed that the Apishapa focus of the Chaquaqua Plateau also was abandoned at this time and suggests that the inhabitants moved east and contributed to the development of the Antelope Creek phase in the Texas panhandle. If he is correct, perhaps those north of Cimarron in the Trinidad–Vermejo Creek area, also abandoned at this time and seemingly related to the Apishapa focus, joined in this move to the east.

The presence of black-on-white pottery types of the 1200s from the Bandelier, Galisteo basin, and Pecos areas on Texas panhandle sites (Baugh 1984a:157) at least demonstrates Pueblo contact in the late 1200s. The presence of Galisteo, Taos, and Chupadero black-on-whites, along with micaceous plain of the Taos-Picuris type, Jornada Brown, and Glazes E and F, as well as cordmarked sherds on a site thirty-five miles downstream from Conchas Reservoir on the Canadian River (Way 1984) strongly suggest Pueblo-Plains contact through this area continued to operate from the 1200s into historic times. Several sherds of Borger Cordmarked Ware recovered from Pueblo Alamo, ten miles south of Santa Fe and occupied in the late 1200s (Allen 1973:8), indicate Plains contact with the Eastern Anasazi.

EASTERN ANASAZI ADJUSTMENTS: A.D. 1300s

By the early 1300s, Central Anasazi-derived traits resulting from intrusions from the west included masonry pueblos which mostly replaced the Eastern Anasazi coursed adobe villages east of the mountains on the Pueblo frontier from Pecos south into the Galisteo basin as well as in the Jemez–Pajarito Plateau country on the west side. More or less contemporaneous was the introduction of Northern Mogollon items into the Albuquerque district, such as extended burials, rectangular little kivas, and perhaps the few masonry pueblos present there and in the area east of the mountains from Chilili south to Gran Quivira (the historic period Tompiro pueblos, Schroeder 1964). Between A.D. 1325 and 1350, locally made glaze paint decorated pottery, introduced from the Northern Mogollon, also appears in the Albuquerque area, from where neighboring potters adopted the practice (Wendorf and Reed 1955:149–52). However, black-on-white types continued to be preferred in the Taos-Picuris, Jemez, Pajarito, and Salinas districts. The influx from the west not only introduced new items but also led to an increase in numbers and sizes of pueblos. This situation no doubt placed a greater demand on local game, wild food products, and arable land. In addition, the Pueblo world was shrinking, even more so in the 1400s (compare Ford, Schroeder, and Peckham 1972, map 5, and Schroeder 1979:239 – Oñate map).

Whether this population build-up in the late 1200s–early 1300s led to Pueblo bison hunts in the Plains is debatable. Tom Dillehay (1974) suggests that prior to A.D. 1300 bison were not present (or did not occur in numbers sufficient to show up in contemporary sites?) in the Southern

Plains, but were present after that date, as bison bones in sites indicate. The increase could be accounted for by an expansion of herds south out of the Central Plains or perhaps an increase of a small shifting herd in the Southern Plains under more favorable ecological conditions, which might have been the same factor that drew the horticulturists from the Chaquaqua Plateau to the Southern Plains, as Campbell suggests.

That contact existed between New Mexico and the Plains during the 1300s and later is obvious. Small amounts of Glaze A (1315–1425) and B (1400–50) pottery occur in Texas panhandle horticultural villages and in Jornada sites of southeastern New Mexico (Spielmann 1983:263–64; Baugh 1984:157). Jornada occupation along the middle Pecos River, where intrusive cordmarked pottery has not been reported, was highest between A.D. 1000 and 1200, but it continued into the late 1300s (Jelinek 1967:58, 159, 164). During Agua Fria Glaze-on-red times (1300–1425) the Jornada district was abandoned except in the northwest corner where the cultural aspects became more typically Pueblo (Mera 1943:13–15) in the Gran Quivira area.

Plains items that appear among the Eastern Anasazi up to the 1300s are few in number and variety. Alibates dolomite tools are found primarily in post–A.D. 1350 associations (Wendorf 1953:36) in pueblos east of the Rio Grande with an occasional occurrence in the Chama valley (Spielmann 1983: table 1). Aside from Pecos Pueblo, such tools are scarce elsewhere. Bison bone, also in small quantity, has a similar distribution (Spielman 1983: table 2). As David Snow (1981:358) and Baugh (1984a:160) surmise, from the 1100s to 1300 or 1400, few items were traded and contacts appear to have been infrequent and of an open type requiring few if any cultural adaptations by the Plains or Pueblo groups involved. The presence of small quantities of nonindigenous material in both regions prior to A.D. 1300, a possible increase in the bison herd in the Southern Plains in the 1300s, but an increase in Plains items in the pueblos after 1400, lends little support to Pueblo bison hunts when the herd increased. Perhaps this increase in trade items in the 1400s was brought on by poor pasture conditions for bison in the Southern Plains which John Speth (1983:131, 170) suggests "may have been the norm throughout the year during the mid- to late fifteenth century . . ." Poor hunting locally also may have caused the nonhorticulturists of the mid-1400s to place greater dependence than before on trade with the Eastern Anasazi for corn and possibly other subsistence items, or the influx of Athapaskans on the plains in the mid-1400s may have contributed to this situation.

CHANGES IN EAST-WEST CONTACTS: A.D. 1400s

Snow (1981:361–62) indicates that after the decline of Casas Grandes (ca. 1400) there was a realignment of the northern Rio Grande pueblos, a situation that turned the Eastern Anasazi toward the Plains. An increase in bison tools and refuse as well as dolomite tools and debitage at Pecos Pueblo is evident (Kidder 1932:35, 170, 238, figs. 13, 14, 16a). A similar increase at Gran Quivira (McKusick 1981:65), but with few dolomite items, also includes Plains mussel shell ornaments which probably came from the upper waters of the Colorado and Concho rivers of Texas (McCusick 1981:40). Eastern Great Basin obsidian at pre-1400 Plains sites no longer is present on later sites (Baugh and Nelson 1987:326). Obsidian from New Mexico, some turquoise, and ceramics appear at Texas panhandle horticultural sites of the 1400s (Spielmann 1983:267–68).

Trade in the 1400s and later seems to have extended farther east on the Plains, Chupadero black-on-white being recorded in the Great Bend aspect (A.D. 1300–1800) on the Arkansas River as well as in sites of the Henrietta focus (1300–1600) of northeast Texas (W. R. Wedel 1959: 583). Krieger (1946:268) remarks on new "Caddo area" ceramic traits appearing at Pecos Pueblo in the 1400s, most specifically shouldered and carinated bowl forms adopted in Pecos Glaze III times and used in later types. He points to the similarity in shape of Late Caddo (A.D. 1400–1700, Krieger's Texarkana focus) vessels of the great bend of the Red River, and the use of a brushing technique on Pecos pottery surfaces like that of the Late Caddo (Krieger's Fulton aspect, Krieger 1946:216). This led him to suggest Pueblo contact with the Caddo area below Spanish Fort via the Red River (Krieger 1946:234–35).

Wendorf and Reed (1955:151) propose that the Fulton aspect, which exhibits engraved pottery (Krieger 1946:241), might have been the source for the development of Ptosuwi'i Incised (A.D. 1425–1500), a type found from Bandelier National Monument north into the Chama valley. I might add that the Southwestern type bears a strong resemblance to Maydelle Incised of northeast Texas (Suhm and Krieger 1954:324, pl. 46). The route of transmission to New Mexico also may have been along the Red River, or perhaps by way of the Washita and South Canadian rivers of western Oklahoma. This latter region, densely populated between A.D. 1000 and 1400, exhibits intrusive pottery, stone, and ornaments from the Mississippi Valley, Gulf Coast, eastern Oklahoma, and the Southwest (Wyckoff and Brooks 1983:64–65; Baugh 1984a:160). In any case, long distance contact of some type in the 1400s is obvious.

PROTOHISTORIC REGIONWIDE UPHEAVALS: MID-1400s INTO 1500s

Withdrawal northward of the northern Mogollon into the Zuni area in the early 1400s, abandonment of the middle Little Colorado district in favor of the Hopi country about 1450, the collapse of the middle Verde Valley pueblolike villages about 1425, plus similar events in the southern Southwest (which included the collapse of the Hohokam of southern Arizona in about 1400 and the abandonment of the Jornada region and south along the Rio Grande in the early 1400s) effectively cut off Southwestern relations with whatever might have remained in the 1400s of the Casas Grandes tradition of northern Mexico. Perhaps the drought of the early 1400s in the Southwest was more widespread and more intense than currently stated. In addition to all of this, as mentioned before, the Anasazi world was shrinking.

Wendorf (1960), on the basis of different pottery types than those used by Krieger, also places the end of the Antelope Creek phase at about A.D. 1450, his latest intrusive in Antelope Creek sites being Biscuit A (A.D. 1375–1450) and Glaze A. Glaze B from the Galisteo basin has since been reported on these horticultural village sites (Spielmann 1983:263–64). The disappearance of these sites at the time of droughts on the Plains, between 1439 and 1454 and a shorter one from 1459 to 1468, cannot be specifically interpreted as marking the

Table 13.3.
Southwestern Neighbors, A.D. 1500

Culture District	Phase	Dates (A.D.)
Rio Grande Jornada Mogollon (south)	La Junta	1200–1400
	Historic	1580s–
Rio Grande Jornada Mogollon (north)	El Paso	1200–1400
Rio Grande Mogollon	Ancestral Piro	1300–1540
	Colonial Piro	1540–1680
Rio Grande Anasazi	Classic Period	1325–1540
	Historic Period	1540–
Taos Anasazi	Talpa	1325–1375
	Vadito	1375–1540
	Historic Period	1540–
Galisteo Anasazi	Glaze A–D	1325–1550
	Glaze E–F	1550–1700
Pecos Anasazi	Glaze I–III	1350–1550
	Glaze IV–VI	1550–1700
Gran Quivira Anasazi	Gran Quivira	1300–1400
	Pueblo Colorado	1400–1500
	Salinas	1540–1670s
Middle Pecos Jornada Mogollon	McKenzie	1150–1350
	Post-McKenzie	1350–1450
Eastern Jornada Mogollon	Ochoa	1300–1450
Cimarron	Cojo (Apache)	1550–1750
Upper Canadian	Plains Village or Panhandle	1300–1450
	Plains Nomads	post–1450

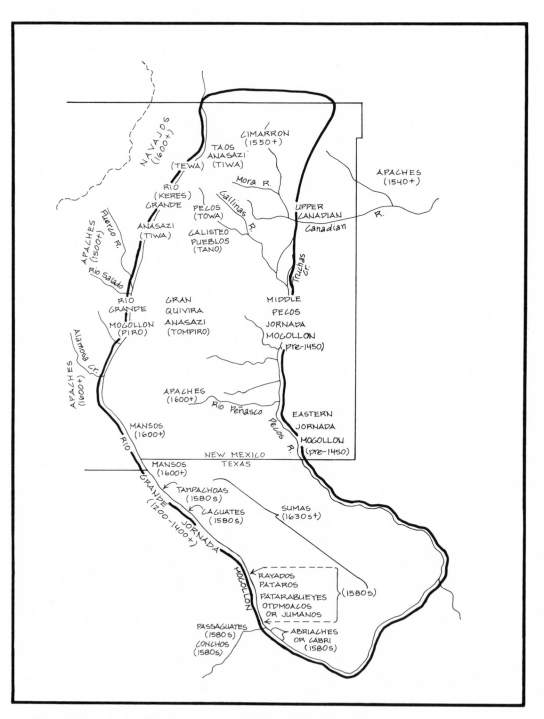

Map 13.3. Culture districts, ca. A.D. 1500, and locales of historic period tribes (see table 13.3).

demise of these people of the Panhandle aspect. The Upper Republican and Nebraska phase horticulturists of this period are thought to have moved north and east (W. R. Wedel 1959:571). Campbell (1969) suggests the survivors of the Apishapa focus of the Chaquaqua Plateau, who moved eastward to the Antelope Creek phase about A.D. 1300–1350, joined with the latter and moved down the Canadian River to become the Teyas reported by the Spaniards in 1540. When production of local pottery ceased in some areas on the High Plains, or horticulturists were replaced by nonpottery-making nomads, about 1450, Pueblo tradeware dominated hunter-gatherer sites in the Texas panhandle. At this time the nomads supplanted their lack or loss of horticulture by trading for food and other items from the eastern frontier Pueblos (Spielmann 1983:260, 263–62, 269), who by now had recovered from the early A.D. 1400 drought.

As for Pueblo contact, Baugh (1984a:158) reports that Glazes C (1425–1500) and D (1490–1515) from the Galisteo basin make up 14 to 50 percent of the pottery in the White River area of Texas, and obsidian up to 7 percent of the lithics. Katherine Spielmann (1983:264) points to Glazes C and D being dominant in sites of the 1450 and 1550 period on the interior drainage of the Llano Estacado and its eastern escarpment as well as C and D glazes from Tonque Pueblo and the Galisteo basin on sites near Hereford and Canyon, Texas where Pecos Glaze II (ca. A.D. 1400–1450) also had been reported (Holden 1931:51). She (Spielmann 1983:267) further remarks that 55 percent of Glaze C and 25 percent of Glaze D at Gran Quivira come from the same sources. This pueblo also may have transmitted these types to the above Texas sites since the local Chupadero black-on-white occurs in the upper Brazos drainage along with Pecos Glazes II through V (Holden 1931:51; Krieger 1946: 260–62).

In addition to the above, Picuris and Pecos pueblos began making glaze-decorated pottery in Glaze C times. Their products began to replace those of Tonque Pueblo and the Galisteo basin on late prehistoric Plains sites (Spielmann 1983:266). The western Oklahoma Wheeler phase of A.D. 1450 to 1750 exhibits horticultural sites and indigenous pottery, unlike the hunter-gatherer campsites lacking ceramics in the Texas panhandle region. The Edward site contains Caddo intrusive from northeastern Texas and southeastern Oklahoma as well as Glazes E and F and V and VI from Picuris and Pecos, and Jeddito Yellow Ware from the Hopi country, most of which date between 1500 and 1700 (Spielmann 1983; Baugh 1984a:16; 1986). Correlated with this shift in Pueblo pottery sources is an increased amount of Plains material in Glaze V times in Pecos Pueblo (Kidder 1958:313). The late glazes and obsidian that occur on the plains in small amounts, but at a greater distance east as far as the horticultural villages of central Kansas (W. R. Wedel 1959) and eastern Oklahoma (Spielmann 1983:268), Spielmann considers as having been down-the-line trade across the plains. This situation brings us into historic times when the Coronado expedition entered the Southwest and the Plains where he encountered the horticultural people of central Kansas in 1541.

Southwest-Plains relations between A.D. 500 and 1500 took place in a fringe area over which neither culture area established permanent control. It was a corridor over which Woodland influence crossed into the northeastern Southwest and where Pueblo settlement east of the Sangre de Cristos and north of Pecos Pueblo was short-lived. This also was the corridor over which Apaches and later Comanches and others ranged in historic times in their trade with and forays against Pueblos and Plains groups. Interaction between the two culture areas appears to have been seasonal and intermittent through time. While trade probably led to the establishment of several frontier pueblos by A.D. 1400, the interchange involved seems to have left little imprint on material, social, and religious aspects of late prehistoric eastern Pueblo culture. Plains traits among some eastern pueblos (Northern Tiwas) appear to have been derived from Pueblo refugee settlements in Kansas in the middle to late 1600s. Aside from more recent data herein, the general outline of Plains-Southwestern contacts presented by Wedel (1950) remains much the same today.

DISCUSSION

Snow (1981:357) remarks that eastern Pueblo exchange in early historic times was not a formal affair. The Pueblo household he considers as the basic production unit in subsistence, ritual, and economic affairs, and varying needs of the households or the craftsmen resulted in an irregular flow of goods (Snow 1981:355, 357). He also suggests an informal and unregulated system in Pueblo-Plains exchange involving small amounts of goods prior to the beginning of the protohistoric period, which he identifies as about A.D. 1250 (Snow 1981:368, 369). Following this, large pueblos developed on the frontier east of the mountains bordering the Rio Grande. Snow indicates that this latter situation, and the contemporary increased Plains interaction and exchange, required greater flexibility in economic pursuits at the household level, which continued to be the primary operational factor in the historic period.

Others have placed the shift in the quantity of goods exchanged to a later date. Spielmann (1983:268) designates the period of lesser trade prior to A.D. 1450 and suggests that the few items involved represent gifts by Pueblo hunters. The more common post–A.D. 1450 material on the plains she refers to as resulting from a process of exchange. Baugh (1984a:160) agrees, postulating that the pre–A.D. 1450 process was an open one requiring little or no social adjustment by either party, and that the later process was a closed system which necessitated certain social adjustments.

Spielmann's above reference to Pueblo hunters on the plains prior to A.D. 1450 as a means to explain exchange can be questioned. As a matter of fact, it is not known when and if Pueblo people might have hunted on the plains even after the entry of the Spaniards. Plains Apaches were bringing products derived from bison to Pecos Pueblo in the 1540s and later, and they were not driven off the plains by the Pawnees and Comanches until sometime between the 1720s and 1740s (Schroeder 1974:57–60; 1984:136). The last were enemies of Pecos Pueblo through most of the 1700s until the Comanches were subdued by the Spaniards in 1786 (Thomas 1932:294ff).

One of the earliest bison hunt references that I have been able to find is from 1811 and relates to punishment for members of the nonfrontier pueblo of Santa Ana who had hunted without having a license from the Spanish authorities (Spanish Archives of New Mexico, Roll 17, Jan. 16, 1811, Frame 350). An unsubstantiated report of a Pecos buffalo hunt in the 1740s, which supposedly resulted in the death of 150 men during a Comanche attack, was "a massacre that never happened" (Kessell 1979:379–80). Members of the nonfrontier pueblo of Santa Clara, along with individuals of other pueblos, made trips into the plains to trade, often spending several months on such ventures (Hill 1982:63, 65). These probably took place in the 1800s. It is somewhat doubtful that this practice was followed in prehistoric times since bison remains (and other Plains material) are scarce except on the eastern frontier (Snow 1981:363). Moreover, without laden animals to carry their goods for such long trips, before they obtained Spanish horses, the Pueblos would have had little chance to undertake trips of several months. David Wilcox (1984:142, 149) notes, however, that the Pueblos traded with one another in order for the frontier pueblos, which did not raise cotton, to have cotton blankets to trade to the Plains Apaches. He further observed that bison hides found to the south and west of the frontier pueblos must have been traded in return for the cotton goods.

Other circumstances suggesting that the Pueblos had little knowledge of the plains relate to two Spanish expeditions (Schroeder 1962). In 1541, two Plains Indians captive at Pecos Pueblo (Hammond and Rey 1940:219, 301)—not Pueblo Indians—led Vasquez de Coronado to Quivira (Little River focus of the Great Bend aspect) on the Arkansas River. Similarly, it was a Mexican Indian who had been captured on the plains, and later stayed among the Apaches and escaped to join the Spaniards in New Mexico, plus other guides captured east of the Apaches, who led Oñate's 1601 expedition (Hammond and Rey, 1953:754, 889) to Quivira (Lower Walnut focus of the Great Bend aspect).

The matter of the type of exchange involved at the time of the Spanish arrival is provided by the Valverde Investigation of 1601 (Hammond and Rey 1953). Various replies stated that the Pueblo Indians did not buy, sell, or barter among themselves, nor did they have public places for buying or exchanging (Hammond and Rey 1953:628, 647, 663). These erroneous observations were perhaps due to the Spaniards of 1601 having had little opportunity to observe household trade of the type Snow described, as noted above. But as was further recorded by the Spaniards (Hammond and Rey 1953:626–63), the Pueblo people hunted deer, hare, rabbits, and mountain sheep, although no mention is made of hunting bison. The Pueblos traded with the bison-hunting Vaquero Indians who brought them dried meat, fat, and dressed hides in exchange for maize and painted cotton blankets. They traded in special houses, not in the plazas (see Schroeder and Matson 1965:124 regarding such a house at Picuris in 1591). The Vaqueros (Apaches), sometimes in a party of up to four hundred, came from forty to fifty leagues away at harvest time and pitched tents three hundred to four hundred paces from the pueblo, where the Pueblos went to trade. The Vaquero dogs carried fifty-pound loads. Wilcox (1984:146–48) provides some interesting estimates on the amount of bison products such a party could provide. Unfortunately, this flourishing trade was disrupted by the Spaniards in the middle to late 1600s (Schroeder 1972:52).

One last item of interest relates to Campbell's above proposal that the "Panhandle aspect" survived into historic times as Teyas on the Canadian River. Of particular relevance in this regard are the Coronado and Oñate trips into the plains (Hammond and Rey 1940; 1953; see Schroeder 1974, part I, for maps covering their routes onto the plains, as well as for other Spanish expeditions, and see Schroeder 1962 for details and map of these two expeditions).

Coronado, ten to twelve days after crossing the Canadian River, probably halfway between the north boundary of the Texas panhandle and Lake Meredith, arrived at a Querecho (Apache) rancheria. The Querecho told the Spaniards that in the direction of the sunrise was a large river (Canadian) along which they could travel for ninety days from one settlement to another. The first was called Haxa according to these Athapaskans. While some Spaniards went east two days under Coronado's orders, on the basis of one of the guides' statement, Haxa was not reached, the Spaniards having turned northeast from the Canadian River before reaching the Oklahoma boundary.

Oñate followed the Canadian farther downstream to about the Oklahoma border before leaving the river to proceed in an east-northeast direction, but no settlements were encountered along the river. However, a map drawn by an Indian (Newcomb and Campbell, 1982) shows settlements along a river south of Oñate's route of travel while he was moving east-northeast. This river has to be the Canadian. The first settlement on the south side of the river is labeled Ahaccapan, according to this probable Caddoan-speaking Indian. This name bears a close resemblance to Haxa of Coronado's day. In any case, both of these expeditions missed the settlements that might represent the survivors of the Antelope Creek phase who moved out of the Texas panhandle about A.D. 1450 to join their kin of the Washita River phase.

Eastern Anasazi survivors into historic times and their antecedents as I see them, include, from south to north along the Rio Grande and on either side, the Piros out of a mixed Jornado-Mimbres-Mogollon base; the Tompiros east of the mountains from a Jornada-Anasazi mix; the Southern Tiwas on the river out of a local Albuquerque-area base; the Tanos in the Galisteo basin out of the local base with earlier Keres influence; the Keres from Acoma to the west edge of the Galisteo basin from Chaco–Mesa Verde (Central Anasazi) ancestors; the Tewas on the river north of the Keres out of the A.D. 1050 influx from the upper San Juan; the Northern Tiwas from a local base; and on either side of the Keresan and Tewa belt across the Rio Grande, the Towas of Pecos on the east side (forced off the Rio Grande at the time of the A.D. 1050 ancestral Tewa influx that also split the Towas?) from the late A.D. 1200s concentration into that area, and the Jemez from a local base plus a Gallina influx.

On the basis of early Spanish documents reporting the number of pueblos and population estimates, which run respectively into the low hundreds and from 30,000 to 60,000, a figure of 30,000 to 40,000 (or higher?) seems reasonable for the Pueblos alone.

CHAPTER 14

COMMENTARY: A HISTORY OF ETHNIC GROUPS IN THE GREAT PLAINS
A.D. 150–1550

Karl H. Schlesier

It is pusillanimous to avoid making our best efforts today just because they may appear inadequate tomorrow. . . . The data will never be complete and their useful, systematic acquisition is dependent upon the interpretation of the incomplete data already at hand. (Simpson 1944:xviii)

HENRY Kelsey, a young employee of the Hudson's Bay Company, spent the winters of 1690 and 1691 among Assiniboines in the aspen parklands and prairies of Saskatchewan, the first European to come so far. In his journal of 1691 (Doughty and Martin 1929), based on observations made among Assiniboines and Atsinas, he provides a first outline of some characteristics of a pattern of culture shared widely in the Northern Plains by groups of different origins and belonging to different language families. These, Kelsey's six "points," are the feather bonnet; use of a ceremonial pipe; the spirit lodge ritual; a curing ritual in which a specialist removed an illness from a patient by sucking it out; use of hunting charms; and belief in spirit helpers, or "familiars."

These characteristics were not invented in protohistoric time but must be very old. All, with the exception of the pipe, were also found among old ethnic groups in Siberia, the region from where the ancestors of American Indians originally came. If they were shared, in a general sense, by peoples of the Northern Plains and adjacent areas during prehistoric time, as is likely, they would not assist in identifying ethnic groups even if traces of them had survived in archaeological sites and features. But to visualize them as colorful images behind the cold, sparse objects of the archaeological collections fires the imagination necessary for an anthropologist to understand an essentially alien past.

This chapter attempts to identify all relevant archaeological entities discussed in this volume with their descendant historical ethnic groups. It is a formidable task, and the results will not be the last words on the subject. But it is a beginning; it provides a cultural frame within which the material in archaeological sites, features, and laboratories can be judged and compared. This process, it is hoped, should lead to clarification and a reliable historical and cultural fit. The initial steps are perhaps easier for an ethnographer to take than for an archaeologist, because the ethnographer is a second, more distant reader of the archaeological information. Also, because of experiences in living ethnic groups whose ancestors left the artifacts which are the stuff of archaeological collections, ethnographers may be more ready to slip into the shadow land where only the fools and tricksters of their host groups roam.

This chapter is organized according to language groups and follows their transformations over time. Given the fact that their movements bridged vast areas, a regional approach in an overview committed to all of the Great Plains would have made the task impossible. As important as the recognition of new groups entering the Great Plains around or shortly before A.D. 500 is the recognition of groups already present, some with an occupation history of thousands of years. All underwent transformations also. Some were edged to fringe areas, others remained; few groups, or segments of them, actually left the Great Plains altogether. Chapter sections appear with different starting dates due to cultural and population dynamics.

1. KUTENAI AND KIOWA-TANOAN TRANSFORMATIONS, 1300 B.C.–A.D. 1550

Kutenai is an isolated and independent language spoken by the Kutenais in southeastern British Columbia and northwestern Montana. No linguistic relationship of Kutenai with members of known language families has yet been firmly established although some linguists have pondered whether it might be included in a broader Algonquian phylum (Akira Yamamoto pers. comm.). Kiowa-Tanoan is a language family which includes, besides Kiowa, such Rio Grande Pueblo linguistic branches as Tiwa, Tewa, and Towa. Tiwa consists of a northern subgroup comprising two languages (Taos, Picuris), and a southern subgroup comprising two dialects (Sandia, Isleta). The Tewa branch is viewed by Hale and Harris (1979:171) as a single language which includes Arizona Tewa (Tano) and the Rio Grande dialects such as Santa Clara, San Juan, San Ildefonso, Nambe, Tesuque, and Pojoaque. The Towa branch of Tanoan is represented by Jemez; the now extinct Pecos has traditionally also been assigned to Towa. It is generally agreed that Rio Grande Anasazi was developed by Tanoans (excluding Kiowas); whether or not some San Juan Anasazi were Tanoans is still a matter of debate (Hale and Harris 1979:177).

Trager (1967) suspected a Plains derivation of the early Tanoans and judged that at most two millennia separate Kiowa from Tanoan. Hale and Harris's (1979) calculations arrived at a higher figure, from twenty-six hundred to three thousand years. The authors agree that the Kiowa divergence is the result of geographic and cultural separation. Hale and Harris (1979) have pointed out that the north-south extension of Kiowa-Tanoan speakers had taken place shortly before the beginning of the Christian era, thus excluding the northernmost representatives, the ancestors of the Kiowas, from participation in later developments in the Southwest, including the Anasazi tradition. This author (Schlesier 1990) has recently probed into Kiowa-Tewa relationships and found important concepts in religion and mythology shared on deep levels. This result supports Trager's and Hale and Harris's interpretation. It is also supported, this author believes, by a careful rethinking of the information extant in Northern Plains archaeology.

In his major work on the last three millennia of culture history in the Northern Plains, Reeves (1970) has defined two important traditions: Tunaxa and Napikwan. Tunaxa is a Kutenai term and refers to their Plains division of early times; Napikwan is a Blackfeet word meaning white people, specifically the white invaders of the nineteenth century. Reeves's Tunaxa includes the Pelican Lake and Avonlea phases, while he described the Napikwan tradition as represented by the Besant and the succeeding Old Women's phases. Recently he expanded the *Napikwan* tradition to include Oxbow and Sandy Creek as earlier phases (Reeves 1983:14). Questions arising from this reinterpretation are discussed later in this essay. Reeves thought that phase transition from Pelican Lake to Avonlea occurred around A.D. 150–250. In contrast, Kehoe (1973) has interpreted Avonlea as a third tradition independent of the other two, and has identified it with Athapaskan speakers.

Ancestral to Pelican Lake were the McKean and Hanna phases, the first of which appeared in the northwestern Plains around 3,600 B.C. (Gary Wright 1982). According to most researchers, the three are serial phases of the same tradition which entered the Plains from the Rocky Mountain west (Benedict and Olson 1983; Husted 1969; Greiser 1985). A gradual transition from Hanna to Pelican Lake was completed around 1300 B.C. (Foor 1982). Pelican Lake is the type name for a distinctive projectile point (Pelican Lake corner-notched) found in all components of this phase, although unnotched and stemmed points also occur. Reeves assigned some ninety archaeological components to this phase and divided it into eight regional subphases. These he conceptualized as representing a series of regionally adapted societies who participated to a greater or lesser degree in an overall unifying cultural tradition.

During its widest distribution, Pelican Lake extended from northern Colorado through nearly all of the Northern Plains (Reeves 1970: fig. 3; Foor 1982: fig 15; Hannus this volume). The largest concentrations of sites are in Wyoming and Montana. The available data indicate that the economy of the phase was based primarily on the communal hunting of bison where bison populations were dense. In other areas, a more

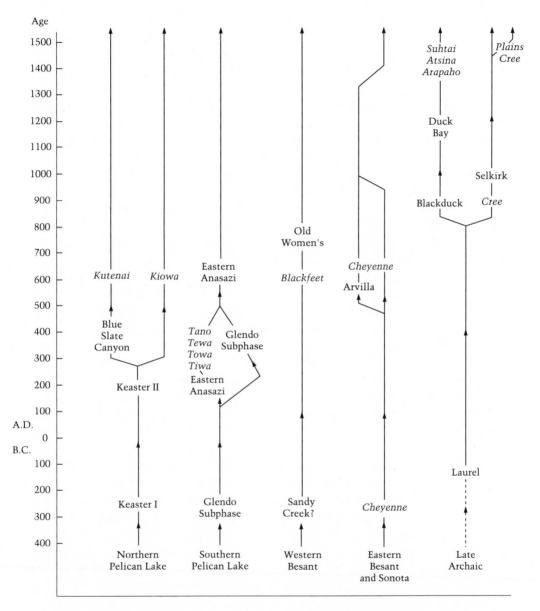

Fig. 14.1. Archaeological cultures to ethnic groups: Kutenais, Kiowa-Tanoans, Algon-quians, 400 B.C. to A.D. 1550. Historic groups are shown in italic.

generalized hunting pattern existed, with the grinding of wild plants for food. The Bighorns, the Black Hills, and the Montana and Alberta Rocky Mountains were used by Pelican Lake groups for hunting elk, deer, and sheep. Buffalo kill sites include jumps and pounds. The main hunting weapon for most of the period was the atlatl. If the Pecked Realistic rock art (Sundstrom 1984) in the southern Black Hills, often featuring game drives, was made by Pelican Lake groups, as is most likely, their locations in steep canyons may suggest that these canyons were used as game traps.

Temporal and spatial distributions of sites show a withdrawal of Tunaxa tradition groups westward from the eastern part of their range, beginning during the third century B.C. The retreat coincides with the arrival of Besant in the parklands of southwestern Manitoba and southeastern Saskatchewan, and its steady thrust to the west and southwest. By the third century A.D., Besant has essentially replaced Pelican Lake in the High Plains (Vickers, Greiser, Hannus, this volume). In the mountains of Alberta, Idaho, western Montana, and west-central Wyoming, however, Pelican Lake remains visible until A.D. 800–1000 (Foor 1982; Greiser this volume). Between the North and South Platte rivers, Pelican Lake lingers to A.D. 400 (see section 5).

The Pelican Lake transition from atlatl to bow technology took place around A.D. 250, two centuries earlier than for the Napikwan tradition. After A.D. 250 the arrow version of the corner-notched point, Keaster II, dominates assemblages from central Wyoming to Alberta. In some areas it is accompanied by the distinctive side-notched Avonlea arrow point or by Avonlea-like points. This association occurs, for instance, in the Blue Dome phase of the headwaters region of the Salmon River in southeastern Idaho, beginning around A.D. 300–500 (Butler 1981a), and in Roll's (1988) Warex phase on the Kootenai River, dated from A.D. 500 to 1200.

In this chapter, Avonlea is not regarded as a phase of Tunaxa but as a separate tradition. Avonlea entered the upper Saskatchewan and middle Saskatchewan basins during the first and second centuries A.D. (Morlan 1988; Vickers this volume), apparently from the mountains to the west and northwest. It is generally credited with having brought bow technology into the Northern Plains. Although the emphasis of researchers always has been on the classical, delicate side-notched point, corner-notched and unnotched points appear with it. Because the Keaster II arrow point is stylistically an expression of the traditional Pelican Lake corner-notched form, it would make sense if some Pelican Lake groups adopted the bow after initial contact with Avonlea groups in the mountains of Alberta and passed the knowledge south to related groups. By A.D. 250 it was clearly expressed in Wyoming.

Reeves was the first to stress Avonlea–Pelican Lake relationships which led him to perceive Avonlea as a succeeding phase of the same tradition. This is not possible, however, because in terms of established tool inventories Pelican Lake continued in the mountains and foothills until about A.D. 800–1000, while Avonlea remained visible in the northern Plains and parklands to A.D. 1200–1400 (Morlan 1988). Therefore they must be seen as contemporaries for a thousand years.

It is quite possible, however, that the traditional point types, the corner-notched and the Avonlea-like side-notched, crossed ethnic boundaries and became favored arrow points in the arsenals of some groups of traditions. If this were correct, the present interpretation of a clear separation between the two traditions may not be factual everywhere; it would be difficult to distinguish late Pelican Lake from Avonlea assemblages in or near the Rocky Mountains. When Reeves (1988) states that ceramics are not a significant element in Avonlea subphase assemblages in the Rocky Mountains, one might ask if he is not in reality dealing with the Pelican Lake tradition which shows strong Avonlea influences. The same question might be raised regarding Roll's Warex phase.

Napikwan aggression was apparently not — or rarely — leveled against Avonlea groups because the territory of the two traditions often overlapped. They actually existed side by side from the first century A.D. to historic time (see identification of Avonlea below). Avonlea might be viewed as playing a mediator or middlemen role between Pelican Lake and Napikwan, giving to both and receiving from both. Perhaps the development of the Prairie side-notched point by the Napikwan Old Women's phase was stimulated by Avonlea technology although stylistically it was based on the older tradition.

If we need models for long-lasting, close relationships between groups very different in regard to cultural tradition and language, the Kiowa and Kiowa Apaches, or Sarcees and Blackfeet, come to mind. We may go further. It is here proposed that Pelican Lake groups in Alberta and the northern half of Montana, as many prehistorians suspect, were indeed ancestral to the historic Kutenais, but that Pelican Lake groups in southwestern Montana and northwestern Wyoming were ancestral to the historic Kiowas. It is further proposed that Avonlea groups north of the Milk River became the historic Sarcees while Avonlea groups in northeastern Wyoming and western South Dakota (the Beehive phase, Fredlund 1988; Morlan 1988; Greiser, Hannus this volume) were ancestral to the Kiowa Apaches.

Concerning the ethnic composition of the Tunaxa tradition (Avonlea and Napikwan are treated in more detail later in this essay), this author believes that it consisted essentially of two language groups: Kutenai and Kiowa-Tanoan. Perhaps groups ancestral to the Sahaptin-speaking Nez Perces participated at times on the western edge of the Pelican Lake distribution, in southwestern Montana. The expansion of Napikwan forced Kutenai speakers into the foothills and mountains of northwestern Montana (Reeves's Blue Slate Canyon subphase) and Alberta, while Kiowa-Tanoan groups retreated to the region extending from southwestern Montana to northern Colorado. It seems that within two centuries some of the southern Tanoan groups abandoned the Plains altogether and moved south and southwest where their history took a different course. It led them to the upper San Juan and to the Cimarron Creek area on the east slope of the Sangre de Cristos before and at the beginning of Anasazi Basketmaker developments (see sections 5, 6; Schlesier 1990). This migration should be seen as a succession of moves made by independent but related bands, leaving and arriving at different times. This would account for the "splits" and linguistic variations among Rio Grande Tanoans which have puzzled prehistorians and linguists in the Southwest.

Northern Tanoan bands ancestral to the Kiowas remained in southwestern Montana and west-central Wyoming for another thousand years. Trager's suggestion of a Kiowa-Tanoan Plains derivation, and glottochronological calculations that range from two millennia to 2,600–3,000 years for the Tanoan separation from Kiowa, have already been mentioned. This early separation must have occurred in the region extending from the Black Hills to northern Colorado, not near the Southwest. Much of the Plains range abandoned by the southern Tanoan groups was invested by Avonlea groups.

The Proto-Kiowas comprised groups which had made the transition to bow technology with the Keaster II arrow point. Kiowa tradition concerning the early history of their culture is specific. It traces an early presence to the mountains of the "extreme north" (speaking from Oklahoma; Mooney 1898:247), to "their first remembered home, the 'Kiowa Mountains' near the Gallatin Valley in Montana" (Scott 1911: 368). Kiowa and Kiowa Apache traditions agree that their affiliation was of very long standing. Mooney learned from old Kiowa Apache informants that their ancestors had "come with the Kiowa from the extreme north," and that "their association with the Kiowa antedates the first removal of the latter from the mountains, as both tribes say that they have no memory of a time when they were not together." This association seems to date back to about A.D. 200–400, following a first contact between Avonlea and Pelican Lake groups in southwestern Montana and Wyoming. Most, if not all, of the Beehive complex (Greiser this volume) must represent the ancestors of the historic Kiowa Apaches.

Pelican Lake groups to the north of the Proto-Kiowas were ancestral to the Kutenais. The latter are linguistically isolated and unique, perhaps the remnant of an originally much larger population. The early Kutenais and Kiowas shared some specific religious concepts which survived to historic time (Schlesier 1990). In protohistoric time the Kutenais consisted of three tribes: Upper and Lower Kutenai, and the

Tunaxa (Teit 1930). While the range of the Upper Kutenais bridged areas to the east and west of the continental divide (they claimed the headwaters region of the Northern Saskatchewan River), the Tunaxa were a Plains tribe speaking a variant Kutenai dialect. The Tunaxa were destroyed by a smallpox epidemic (Turney-High 1941) (as were the Salish Tunaxe), perhaps that of 1780–82, which inflicted great losses on all Northern Plains groups and ended the Shoshone invasion. During the time of the Shoshone presence, about 1580–1785, the High Plains to the west of the Shoshones were occupied, north to south, by the Upper Kutenais (the country north of the Red Deer River), the Tunaxa (the country to the south as far as present Browning), and the Salish Tunaxe (to present Helena) (Teit 1930). During this period the Blackfeet tribes had been forced to retreat to the edge of the boreal forest.

The identification of Pelican Lake with Kutenai is relatively widely accepted among prehistorians. If we accept the identification of southern Pelican Lake groups with Kiowa-Tanoans, we must consider a cultural continuity for Kutenais and Kiowas that spans three millennia.

Salish groups such as the Flathead and Kalispel do not appear to have been part of the Pelican Lake phase although they came to occupy an area in western Montana between Kutenais and Kiowas. Perhaps their immigration from the Plateau was triggered by the Kiowa withdrawal eastward during the fourteenth or fifteenth century A.D. They were in place when the Shoshones came north from Wyoming, about A.D. 1500. Although the region between the Bitterroot Range and the continental divide remained their core area, Flathead tradition claims that their Salish Tunaxe (not to be confused with the Kutenai Tunaxa) division or tribe lived entirely east of the continental divide until consumed by a smallpox epidemic, perhaps the same one that had annihilated the Kutenai Tunaxa. According to Teit (1930), the Salish Tunaxe were called "Sun River People" by the Kutenais and at one time consisted of four main divisions. After the smallpox pandemic of 1780–82, and the Shoshone retreat to Wyoming, Flathead survivors strengthened their resistance to the Blackfeet through an alliance with the Nez Perces.

In historic time the Sahaptin-speaking Nez Perces were known for extended forays into the buffalo ranges of Montana and even northern Wyoming. Historic Nez Perce culture was a composite of Plateau and Plains elements (Spinden 1908). But there are some intriguing clues which suggest that groups ancestral to the Nez Perces may have bridged Plateau and Plains for a long time, and may represent a western outlier of the Pelican Lake phase.

The first deals with the earliest locations remembered. Nez Perce tradition places the earliest remembered occupation sites of the tribe in the Clearwater Mountains of eastern Idaho, in a position west of present Hamilton, Montana and on the headwaters of the Salmon River (McWhorter 1952). The second is contained in Nez Perce mythology.

Early Nez Perce stories collected by Phinney (1934), who was Nez Perce himself, describe the use of buffalo pounds in the "east country"; five mountain ranges had to be crossed to reach it. Game taken in the "east country" was forbidden to be mixed with game taken in the "west country." These stories belong to the cycle of Coyote tales and speak of a very distant past. In the story "Coyote the Interloper" (Phinney 1934:268–82) it was Coyote who brought death into the world on the last of the five mountain ranges when he crossed from the "west country" (identified with salmon) to the "east country" (identified with buffalo).

The archaeological record is fragmentary but promising. The Weis Rockshelter site near the Salmon River, in historic Nez Perce territory, is dominated during the Grave Creek phase (1490–105 B.C.) by Bitterroot side-notched points which are replaced in the following Rocky Canyon phase (105 B.C.–A.D. 400) by neck-stemmed, eared, and corner-notched points. The succeeding Camas Prairie phase (A.D. 400–1400) is dominated by corner-notched points (Butler 1962). Butler believes that at least the latter two phases represent the direct ancestors of the Nez Perces. He thinks that the Camas Prairie region was a refuge of early bison hunters who wandered into Idaho from the east.

2. ALGONQUIAN TRANSFORMATIONS, 500 B.C.–A.D. 1550

In linguistic classification, historic Algonquian languages in central and eastern North America are separated into Eastern, Central, and Plains languages. Eastern Algonquian languages were spoken along the Atlantic coast from New Brunswick to North Carolina. Goddard (1978a:70) believes that these descended from an ancestral Proto-Eastern Algonquian language (PEA). PEA is supposed to have undergone a period of independent development after it had branched off from the parent of the whole linguistic family, Proto-Algonquian (PA). Tuck (1978:44) has dated the beginning of a Proto-Eastern Algonquian movement across the St. Lawrence to the Atlantic coast around 1000 B.C.

Central Algonquian languages were spoken in the Great Lakes area and adjacent regions in Canada, extending from Newfoundland across James Bay to Saskatchewan. There were seven languages with local varieties of speech: Cree (including Naskapi and Montagnais), Ojibwa (including Salteaux, Ottawa, Mississauga, Nipissing, Algonquin), Potawatomi, Menomini, Fox (including Sauk and Kickapoo-Mascouten), Miami-Illinois, and Shawnee. Goddard (1978b:585–86) sees them as seven independent branches descending from Proto-Algonquian (PA).

The Plains Algonquian languages are generally listed as three: Blackfeet, Cheyenne, and Arapaho (including Atsina and three extinct dialects: Besawunena, Nawathinehena, and Hanahawunena). Suhtai, now extinct, is sometimes tentatively listed with Cheyenne (Pentland 1978); however, Goddard's (1978c) comparison of the few recorded Suhtai forms and phrases with Cheyenne reveals a considerable distance between the two. It is likely that Suhtai is closer to Arapaho dialects than to Cheyenne; this would make sense because the Cheyennes and Suhtais established relationships only as late as the 1730s (Schlesier 1990). Goddard (1978b, 1979) sees Plains Algonquian languages as having branched off from the original Proto-Algonquian nucleus to form three distinct speech communities. Although researchers emphasize that the linguistic classification is essentially a geographical one (Rhodes and Todd 1981), Pentland's (1978) studies have shown that Blackfeet and Cheyenne are linguistically distant from Central Algonquian groups and were, perhaps with the extinct Beothuck on the east, the first to split from the Proto-Algonquian core. In contrast, Arapaho-Atsina is related to Salteaux, Swampy Cree, and Eastern Montagnais of the Cree language group. Pentland's hypothesis is supported by the archaeological evidence (see below).

By reconstructing Proto-Algonquian words for certain birds, fish, mammals, and trees, and mapping the distribution of these species, Siebert (1967) concluded that the original homeland ("Urheimat") of the Proto-Algonquians lay in the narrow space between Georgian Bay and Lake Ontario, with outward migration beginning about 900 B.C. Goddard (1978b) essentially concurs; Snow (1976), however, postulated earlier dates and a much larger center of the Proto-Algonquian distribution which he thought included the Great Lakes lowlands (apart from those of Lake Superior), the St. Lawrence lowlands, New England, and the Maritime Provinces.

Siebert's model has exerted a considerable influence on Plains archaeology because it postulates westward migrations of Algonquian speakers from the eastern Great Lakes into the Great Plains, the parklands, and the boreal forests of Manitoba and Saskatchewan. The factual movement of some Cree and Ojibwa groups westward along the shores of Lake Superior during the seventeenth and eighteenth centuries, recorded by French eyewitnesses, is conjectured by many archaeologists to have been preceded by movements in prehistoric time. The Cree and Ojibwa migrations, however, are an anomaly and were triggered by the impact of epidemic diseases, the disorganization of aboriginal religious, economic and social systems, and the disruptive influence of European fur traders and missionaries (Schlesier 1990). Nevertheless, many Plains archaeologists conjure waves of Woodland immigrants although they are unable to identify groups ancestral to the Plains Algonquians with earlier homelands around the Great Lakes.

Siebert's model is flawed on all counts. The Proto-Algonquian original homeland was neither in Siebert's small nor in Snow's larger space although both regions to a degree shared in it. Instead, it was located on the Canadian Shield, extending northwest, west, south and east around Hudson Bay (map in J. V. Wright 1981: fig. 1). Half of the Shield was occupied from about 7000 B.C. onward (during the Paleo-Indian period); all of it was occupied during the Archaic period, beginning around 4000 B.C. Many of the Shield's ethnic groups survived to historic time and the present. This gives Proto-Algonquians and Algonquians the extraordinary continuity of about nine thousand years. The main direction of Proto-Algonquian movement was southward. The essential elements of Algonquian culture were developed, during thousands of years, *in situ* on the Canadian Shield.

Using archaeological, ethnohistorical, and linguistic evidence, J. V. Wright (1972a, 1972b, 1981) has concluded that the Shield Archaic evolved from a Paleo-Indian (Plano tradition) cultural base; that Shield Archaic people spoke Algonquian (Proto-Algonquian); and that Shield populations in the Northwest Territories abandoned the region between 1500 and 1000 B.C. due to a deteriorating climate and the advance of Pre-Dorset Eskimo groups who followed the expanding tundra south.

This author has proposed elsewhere (Schlesier 1987:152–66) that the refugee groups from the Mackenzie and Keewatin districts entered the Northern Plains where they became archaeologically the Besant phase of Reeves's Napikwan tradition. This author has further proposed that the Besant phase consisted essentially of two subphases, a western and an eastern one, of which the first represents the prehistoric Blackfeet divisions while the second represents the prehistoric Cheyennes (Schlesier 1987:134–50). These hypotheses have not been challenged with contradicting data but met with some disapproval, perhaps because most researchers are reluctant to accept the emergence of ethnic entities such as Blackfeet and Cheyenne as early as perhaps 800 B.C., and the continuation of the cultural systems of these groups over a period of more than two and a half millennia.

The evidence, it appears to this author, admits no other conclusion but that Besant represents the two Plains Algonquian language groups. The archaeological record shows no antecedents of Besant to the east, in the woodlands around the Great Lakes or the boreal forests of Ontario. On the contrary, Meyer and Hamilton (this volume) have stated that a

patterning of avoidance and co-occurrence provides suggestive evidence that the cultural materials recognized as Avonlea, Laurel, and Besant relate to three distinct cultural groups. These groups appear to have been characterized by ethnic boundaries. Across some of these there was little interaction (e.g., Avonlea/Besant, Laurel/Besant); in one case (Avonlea/Laurel), there was a certain amount. . . . In short, it appears that the occupants of the Saskatchewan grasslands and parklands (Avonlea) and of southwestern Manitoba (Besant), did not allow movement of peoples of Laurel culture into their bison range.

The linguistic distance between Blackfeet and Cheyenne and the Central Algonquian languages, including Arapaho-Atsina, points to a different origin and a history not shared with the other groups. The evidence favors the Mackenzie and Keewatin districts. Shield Archaic projectile points of this region include side-notched points (J. V. Wright 1972b, 1981). In his discussion of the origins of the Besant phase, Reeves (1970:173–76) mentioned the occurrence of Besant or Besant-like points in the Lockhart River area northeast of Great Slave Lake. MacNeish (1964:404–5, fig. 87) first recognized Besant points in the Lockhart River, Fisherman's Lake, and Taye Lake complexes, dated by him tentatively to 1500 to 1200 B.C. (MacNeish 1964: fig. 82). About Besant points he stated: "Further south in the Canadian Plains and Prairies they appear in late preceramic times" (MacNeish 1964:404). Noble (1981:104) redefined the Lockhart River complex and placed it in the Taltheilei Shale (Athapaskan) tradition; he omitted MacNeish's Besant points, however. J. V. Wright (1972b:53) discussed Lockhart River as part of the Shield Archaic.

Most recently the search for Besant origins has shifted to the Oxbow complex (Reeves 1983a:14). It is characterized by small side-notched atlatl points with convex shoulders and thinned concave bases. The complex seems to have developed out of a cultural complex which featured Bitterroot and Salmon River side-notched points; a Rocky Mountain and Plateau affiliation is implied. In 1973, Reeves summarized the existing information and dated Early Oxbow to about 3000–2500 B.C., Late Oxbow about 2500–2000 B.C. (Reeves 1973:1,236). Early Oxbow still included Bitterroot side-notched points. Subsequent cultural traditions such as Reeves's Mummy Cave complex (ca. 2500–1500 B.C.) exhibited Oxbow, McKean, and Bitterroot points, while Oxbow-McKean (ca. 2500–2000 B.C.) contained only the two point varieties. The following McKean complex featured McKean points only. Noble (1981:99) proposed dates of around 2500–1500 B.C. for the Oxbow complex in central Saskatchewan in order to accommodate the — undated — occurrence of Oxbow points at Fisherman's Lake near Fort Liard and in the Lockhart River area. He views their presence there as the result of a brief incursion of Northern Plains people. Hannus (this volume) mentions dates of about 1300–1000 B.C. for a late Oxbow pocket in Saskatchewan.

Oxbow points bear a certain resemblance to Besant points. Both may have been contemporaries in the Mackenzie district. Oxbow was intrusive; the Besant point appears to have been developed there and been carried south by refugee groups. If Besant was influenced by the Oxbow complex it is most likely that this would have happened in the Northwest Territories before removal. At the time of the Besant arrival in the Saskatchewan and Manitoba grasslands, the Oxbow complex had been superseded by the Pelican Lake phase of the Tunaxa tradition. In terms of language and ethnic identity, the Oxbow complex and the Tunaxa tradition archaeologically most likely represent the same or related people (see below).

The earliest date for Besant, so far, is about 250 B.C., for Boundary Mound 3, on the Missouri River in south-central North Dakota. This is a Sonota site; Sonota is here included in the eastern subphase of Besant. The author has proposed elsewhere (Schlesier 1987:134) that earlier dates must be expected farther north in the regions of the Besant entry, the parklands of Manitoba and Saskatchewan. Based on the evaluation of a Cheyenne sacred tradition, the author has proposed that the prehistoric Cheyennes, who are the people of the eastern Besant subphase, initiated their Massaum earth-giving ceremony in the grasslands between 500 and 300 B.C. (Schlesier 1987).

In the Saskatchewan basin, the still vaguely perceived Sandy Creek complex, tentatively dated to begin around 800 or 700 B.C. (Reeves 1983a:14; Morlan 1988:306–7; Hannus, Vickers, this volume), may actually be an early Besant variant in the fringe of the northwestern Plains. The complex is characterized by small, shallow side-notched points. This is contrary to the interpretation of Reeves, who now views Oxbow, Sandy Creek, Besant, and Old Women's as successive phases of a single tradition, Napikwan. Oxbow, however, cannot possibly be part of Napikwan because of its association with Rocky Mountain and Plateau points (Salmon River and Bitterroot) and its McKean association; it was clearly indigenous to the northwestern Plains and the mountains. Besant, in contrast, was clearly intrusive. Most researchers concur that Besant was intrusive although they may regard — without evidence — the eastern woodlands as the Besant area of origin (Greiser this volume).

At the time of the Besant arrival, the Pelican Lake phase occupied virtually all of the Northern Plains as far south as northern Colorado. The steady, apparently hostile thrust of Besant to the south and west replaced Pelican Lake groups in the High Plains within a few centuries (already discussed in the previous section). The situation in the Northern Plains changed again with the arrival and the expansion of Avonlea. In cooperation and, apparently, at times in competition with Besant, both traditions waxed and waned, effectively trading places in the Northern Plains during the following millennium. This is the conclusion offered by Morlan's (1988: fig. 6) cumulative histograms for Besant and Avonlea based on all carbon-14 dates currently available.

The archaeological transformations of the western subphase of Besant are quite clear. Around A.D. 750, Besant became the Old Women's phase which basically continued to historic time (Morlan 1988:305; Reeves 1983a). Besant and Besant-derived Samantha arrow points were replaced by Prairie side-notched arrow points about 750 and were superseded by Plains side-notched arrow points which lasted from A.D.

1200/1300 (Vickers, Greiser this volume) to the introduction of metal points in the early historic period. The gradual development from western Besant through the Old Women's phase is widely accepted as leaving no conclusion other than to view the carriers of this tradition as the divisions of the prehistoric and historic Blackfeet.

The archaeological transformations of the eastern subphase of Besant are more complex. Groups in the southwestern part of the range of the subphase (west and south of the Black Hills) abandoned the region about A.D. 400–500, slowly shifting back toward the east and northeast. They were replaced by the Avonlea tradition and the Avonlea-derived Beehive complex, with beginning dates around the Black Hills near A.D. 400 (Fredlund 1988; Hannus and Nowak 1988; Morlan 1988:300–1, 304–5). East of the Black Hills, and along the Missouri River in South and North Dakota, Besant groups eventually became embroiled in warfare with the newly arrived Proto-Mandans (Schlesier 1987:135–37) of the Initial Middle Missouri tradition (ca. A.D. 950–1350), and perhaps with the Proto-Awatixa (Hidatsa) in the Knife–Heart River region (A.D. 920–1230) (both sets of dates in Winham and Lueck this volume). These events led to a continuation of their withdrawal eastward. Later relationships with especially the Awatixa were amiable, however, as is reflected in the fact that Awatixa and Cheyennes shared the unique concept of sacred arrows which were featured prominently in ceremonies of both tribes (Schlesier 1990:16–17).

Terminal dates for Besant-Sonota in southern Manitoba may extend to about A.D. 1000 (Reeves 1970; Syms 1977:90); Gregg (this volume) places them somewhat earlier. Meyer and Hamilton (this volume) note that in the period A.D. 750–1000, Blackduck culture expanded its range from northern Minnesota across the Plains of southern Manitoba, with sites along the Assiniboine and Pembina rivers. This brought the Besant occupation of the region to an end. The withdrawal led southward along the Red River where the other bands of the subphase were already concentrated. Archaeologically eastern Besant became the Arvilla complex which occupied the tallgrass prairie along the lower Red and upper Minnesota rivers and the adjacent woodland edge. In essential elements of culture Arvilla did not change much from the preceding Besant. After the archaeological features of Arvilla disappeared, the protohistoric Cheyennes emerged. Directly to the west of the prehistoric and protohistoric Cheyennes were the early Hidatsas of the Devils Lake–Sourisford Burial complex, dated by Syms (1979:301–2) to A.D. 900–1400. The long-standing, beneficial relationship between Cheyennes and Hidatsas has already been discussed (Schlesier 1990); it was continued later when the Cheyennes moved to the Missouri River, and lasted well into the nineteenth century.

Syms (1982) agrees with proposed beginning dates of A.D. 500–600 for Arvilla but sees continuation to about A.D. 1350 because of trade items in Arvilla sites that reflect Mississippian trade generally dated from A.D. 800 to 1350. Gregg (this volume) notes the association of Besant-Sonota with dome-shaped burial mounds which lasted into Arvilla time. Some of these mounds were raised by Besant groups and were maintained and expanded over a period of more than a thousand years, such as the Jamestown Mounds. The Blasky or Fordville mound group on the Forest River in eastern North Dakota is another outstanding mound complex. Originally it contained at least thirty-five conical and four linear mounds which may have a history of use as long as that of the Jamestown group. Because ethnic groups generally do not bury their dead in the graveyards of an alien people, these mounds (and perhaps others) speak of the spiritual importance of places and the presence of the prehistoric Cheyennes in the area over a very long time.

Ossenberg (1974:38–39) has identified Arvilla skeletal remains as ancestral Cheyenne. Her interpretation has met with little general approval but has not been contradicted by fact. Syms (1982:37–38), after reviewing the evidence, at least agrees that "Arvilla includes a predominance of an Algonquian population." Gibbon (this volume) describes the emergence of the Psinomani culture in central Minnesota around A.D. 1000, but omits its neighbors to the west. *Psinomani* is a Dakota word for a widespread archaeological complex that contains Sandy Lake ceramics. It is clearly Dakota. Moore (1987:97–117, 145–54) has brought attention to the intimate and long-standing Cheyenne-Dakota relationship in this region which is supported by the oral traditions of both groups.

Considering historic Central Algonquian–speaking groups in the Northern Great Plains, the Plains Ojibwas, or Bungi, must be excluded here because they arrived in the upper Red River and Souris River locale later than the period covered in this volume. They began to infiltrate the edge of the tallgrass prairie in the 1760s and took it over after the northernmost of Cheyenne bands, the Omissis (Schlesier 1990), had abandoned it following a destructive Bungi raid in about 1770 (Thompson 1916:216–63; Howard 1965).

Most researchers agree that the origin of the various Cree groups, including the Plains Crees, lie within the Selkirk horizon which developed around A.D. 1100 in the boreal forest of central/northern Manitoba from an earlier Laurel population (Meyer and Hamilton this volume). Laurel had developed *in situ* from Shield Archaic antecedents. Selkirk sites in the Nipawin area of eastern Saskatchewan are dated no earlier than the late 1300s. After that date, Selkirk appears to have expanded west, and by A.D. 1500 had advanced to the forest edge along and south of the Saskatchewan River. This westernmost Selkirk expression should be identified with the Plains Crees; they occupied this locale in early historic time.

Concerning the whereabouts of the Central Algonquian-speaking Arapaho-Atsinas and their related dialects (Besawunena, Nawathinehena, Hanahawunena, extinct in historic time), and groups ancestral to the Suhtais, we must review negative evidence first. They cannot be included in the Mortlach and One Gun phases, dated from A.D. 1300 to 1730, which forced the protohistoric Blackfeet westward across the two branches of the Saskatchewan River. They dominated for a few centuries the grasslands of southern Saskatchewan and southeastern Alberta. This intrusion had come from the east and represents Siouan-speaking groups associated with Crow/Hidatsas (see Vickers, this volume).

They can be identified neither with the Selkirk Crees nor with Gibbon's Psinomani culture (A.D. 1000–1500), which was Dakota. The only archaeological entity that seems to qualify for the Arapaho group and the early Suhtais is Duck Bay. Duck Bay pottery makes its appearance around A.D. 1200. The Manitoba lowlands were the core area of the makers of this ware, and from it seasonal movements were made into the grasslands. Duck Bay pottery developed out of Blackduck pottery; vessels also share traits with Selkirk ware, which is to be expected (see Meyer and Hamilton this volume for discussion). Ultimately, the makers of Duck Bay descended from the people who carried the Blackduck expansion into the Plains edge of southern Manitoba, A.D. 750–1000. Only the waning of the Mortlach phase and the concentration of the protohistoric Hidatsa and Crow groups in the area extending from the Missouri River to the Yellowstone opened space for the early Arapaho-Atsinas and Suhtais. While the Atsinas invested territory in the parklands north of the headwaters of the Assiniboine River, the Arapahos left the area altogether and moved south to the Black Hills. The Suhtais may have been part of this action but took up a position in eastern South Dakota to the west of the Cheyennes. The sacred mountain of the Suhtais is located in the Timber Mountains of southwestern Minnesota, to the north of the pipestone quarries (Schlesier 1990). A reasonable estimate for these movements would be the period around A.D. 1550. If at that date the independent Besawunena, Nawathinehena, and Hanahawunena divisions had already ceased to exist, with elements having joined either the Arapahos or the Atsinas, the causal factor may have been the smallpox pandemic of 1520–24 hypothesized by Henry Dobyns (1983). This scenario seems to be supported by the fact that the Suhtais enter the protohistoric and early historic periods as but a single band of an originally larger body. The early warfare between Cheyennes and Suhtais, as mentioned in Cheyenne tradition, may have occurred at that time. It contributed eventually to the Suhtai removal westward to the Cheyenne River where they remained close to the Arapahos until finally, in the 1750s, they became a band of the Cheyenne tribe (Schlesier 1990).

3. ATHAPASKAN TRANSFORMATIONS, A.D. 50–1550

The historic Athapaskan language family (Krauss and Golla 1981) consists of three recognized geographical subdivisions: Northern Athapaskan, Pacific Coast Athapaskan, and Southern Athapaskan, or Apachean. Northern Athapaskan includes twenty-three languages; they once occupied a large, continuous area in the subarctic interior of Alaska and western Canada, extending from near the Alaskan west coast eastward to Hudson Bay, south as far as central British Columbia and the adjacent Plains of Alberta (Sarcee). Pacific Coast Athapaskan is a group of eight languages spoken by riverine tribes in California and Oregon. Southern Athapaskan, or Apachean, is a group of seven languages, spoken by tribes in and near the Southwest: Navajo, Western Apache, Chiricahua, Mescalero, Jicarilla, Lipan, and Kiowa Apache (Young 1983).

The parent of the language family is Proto-Athapaskan which became differentiated from another branch, Proto-Eyak, about 1500 B.C. Because of the degree of diversity within Athapaskan, Krauss and Golla (1981) believe that Proto-Athapaskan was still an undifferentiated linguistic unit until 500 B.C. or even later. They see the Proto-Athapaskan homeland in the eastern interior of Alaska, the upper drainages of the Yukon River, and northern British Columbia, or some part of this area. From there, largely before A.D. 500, intermontane and coastal migrations took Athapaskan speakers westward farther into Alaska and southward along the interior mountains into southern British Columbia. The Pacific Coast Athapaskan languages are viewed as an offshoot from British Columbia languages. Linguists believe that after A.D. 500 two other Athapaskan migrations occurred, one going eastward to Hudson Bay, the other leading south into the Southwest. Apachean languages have their closest linguistic ties in the north with Sarcee, the southernmost representative of the Northern Athapaskan language group (Krauss and Golla 1981:68). The authors emphasize that Proto-Athapaskan (and Proto-Eyak) were clearly languages of interior-oriented peoples.

Wilcox (1988) has traced the Southern Athapaskan or Apachean group through the prehistory of the language family to the Diuktai culture of the interior of Siberia. He has summarized the extant knowledge concerning the Apacheans as follows: (1) Apachean dialects are a single language network, with Kiowa Apache as a closely related but separate language; (2) Apachean dialects appear to have developed out of a protolanguage called "early Apachean"; (3) early Apachean populations must have become isolated from other Proto-Athapaskan speakers for a long enough time for linguistic shifts that differentiate early Apachean from Proto-Athapaskan to take place; and (4) the subsequent differentiation of Kiowa Apache and the other Apachean

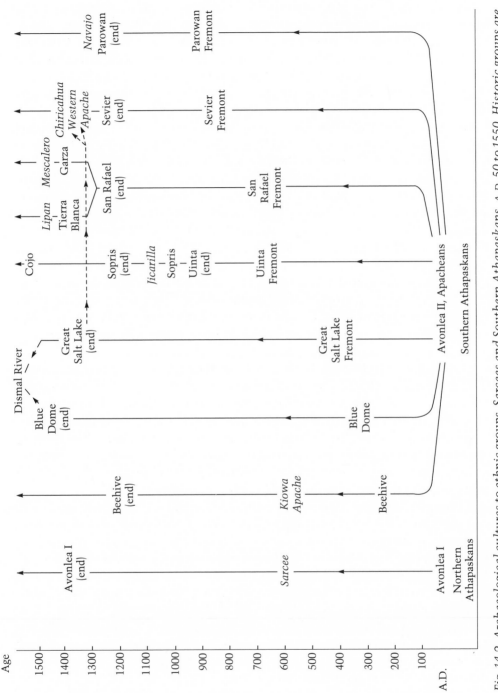

Fig. 14.2. Archaeological cultures to ethnic groups. Sarcees and Southern Athapaskans, A.D. 50 to 1550. Historic groups are shown in italic.

dialects occurred in the Plains, when the Kiowa Apaches became isolated from the others. Wilcox's interpretation of the Avonlea tradition as Athapaskan, first proposed by Kehoe (1973) and supported by the author (Schlesier 1987), is convincing and supported by the data. Wilcox (1981, 1988) has built a strong case for a Plains movement of Apacheans and a late (sixteenth-century) arrival in the Southwest. This is where this author partly disagrees and proposes a different scenario.

It is suggested here that there were at least four major movements of Athapaskan groups into the Great Plains. The first led into the northwest edge of the Northern Plains and proceeded into the upper Saskatchewan basin and eastward (beginning A.D. 50). The second came from the mountain regions including east-central Idaho and southwestern Montana, and the adjacent upper Snake River Plain, going into southeastern Montana and central and eastern Wyoming, quickly circling the Black Hills (beginning ca. A.D. 200). The third came across the Colorado Rocky Mountains and went to the Park Plateau in north-central New Mexico and southeastern Colorado (beginning A.D. 950). The fourth came from two directions: one by the intermontane route through southern Colorado (ca. A.D. 1350), the other passing through southern Wyoming and northern Colorado from the west (after A.D. 1600). Both led into the Colorado High Plains, and southward.

Of these, the last three movements were carried by early Apacheans. The first must clearly be considered a Proto-Athapaskan movement which remained associated with the Northern Athapaskan language division. Initially all these groups possessed the Avonlea tradition tool assemblage. Over time, separated and exposed to different environments and to the different cultural traditions of peoples already present in areas newly infiltrated or taken over, the culture and tool inventories were enriched through adoption of foreign elements.

The region of departure of the four Athapaskan movements lies in the interior of British Columbia, in the Proto-Athapaskan homeland as defined by linguists. From here, just before the beginning of the Christian era, some bands of Proto-Athapaskans moved south through the mountain ranges of Idaho and adjacent western Montana (south of the Bitterroot Range) when others went east into the upper and middle Saskatchewan basins. Apparently they did not simply enlarge their territories in British Columbia, but instead moved considerable distances. Perhaps the nearer space was closed by the forced concentration of prehistoric Kutenais of the Pelican Lake phase who were being driven off the Plains by Besant groups.

The first movement, here called Avonlea I, arrived in the upper and middle Saskatchewan basins around A.D. 50. Dates for Avonlea in this region extend to approximately A.D. 1200–1300; farther east, in the lower Saskatchewan basin, Avonlea begins around A.D. 900 and lasts to about 1400 (Morlan 1988; Meyer and Hamilton this volume). Avonlea sites include bison jumps (Head-Smashed-In, Gull Lake), pounds (Ramillies, Estuary), winter campsites (Larson, Morkin, Garrat), and tipi ring sites (Empress). The Lebret site was an Avonlea fishing station in the Qu'Appelle valley (Vickers this volume). The carbon-14 dates collected by Morlan (1988) suggest that Avonlea I essentially remained in the Saskatchewan basin from the time of its entrance to historic time. The region was also used by the western subphase of Besant. The two traditions did not merge but remained separate cultural entities, trading places in subareas over time. Avonlea I relationships with Pelican Lake and its descendant groups, and Besant groups, already discussed, appear to have been generally friendly. Numerically, Avonlea I groups were inferior to western Besant groups. Vickers (this volume) has stated that by 1986 in Alberta some 142 Besant components had been recorded as compared to fifty of Avonlea, and that a similar ratio existed in Saskatchewan. It is interesting that in historic time the Sarcees numbered about one third of the total of the three Blackfeet divisions.

While the distribution of groups of the western subphase of Besant (and its later Old Women's phase) included areas well to the south of the Saskatchewan basin, Avonlea I does not appear to have participated. There are virtually no Avonlea sites between the Milk River and the Missouri until about A.D. 750 (Greiser this volume). Morlan's (1988) tables also show this time gap. While some do not, some writers make a distinction between Avonlea point types in the north and those, with later dates, farther south. Davis (see Morlan, 1988, for discussion) calls the latter "not Avonlea, but contemporaneous"; Frison sees them as Avonlea-like; Fredlund regards them as a separate entity. Morlan's tables suggest a delayed Avonlea expansion southward. This is an incorrect impression, however.

South of the Missouri, even south of the Yellowstone River, Avonlea or Avonlea-like tradition groups (here termed Avonlea II) are present from approximately A.D. 200 on, distributed from the southeastern corner of Montana as far south as the Green River of Wyoming—the Wardell site—and the Yampa River in northern Colorado—the Serviceberry Shelter (Fredlund 1988: fig. 1). Perhaps the Wahmuza site, near Fort Hall on the upper Snake River (Holmer 1986), should be included; occupation level I, dated to the first century A.D., is said to contain Pelican Lake and Avonlea-like points mixed with Great Basin types such as Elko and others. These groups clearly did *not* come from the Saskatchewan basin because they did not pass through Greiser's area. The southern groups belong archaeologically to the Beehive complex and are interpreted here as early Apacheans (see below). Therefore, it is proposed here that Avonlea I chose to remain in its northern locale and thus became isolated from the other Athapaskans in the Great Plains. Because the Sarcees are linguistically Northern

Athapaskans, and their sites continue from A.D. 50 to about 1400, no other conclusion appears reasonable.

As others before him (for instance, Julian Steward, the Huschers, Grenville Goodwin, Oliver LaFarge, W. W. Hill, Cal Riley), Morris Opler (1971, 1975, 1983), the dean of Apachean ethnography, has steadfastly insisted on the intermontane advance of Apacheans toward the Southwest, contrary to the more widely supported Plains entry route. Recently Perry (1980) and Wilcox (1981, 1988) have summarized the different positions of this old controversy, the first opting for the intermontane, the second for the Plains route. That the Proto-Athapaskans were originally an interior, mountain-oriented people, is not questioned. Concerning the Apachean advance, it is here proposed that both the intermontane and the Plains region shared nearly equally in importance in Apachean prehistory and history.

The second movement (Avonlea II) arrived in east-central Idaho and southwestern Montana around A.D. 200, perhaps earlier. Because the entrance route did not follow the High Plains east of the continental divide, an intermontane approach on either side, or on both sides of the Bitterroot Range, must be considered. The earliest unquestioned date, so far, comes from southwestern Wyoming, the Wardell site, a buffalo corral on the upper Green River. The lower level at Wardell extends from A.D. 230 to 610; the upper level is dated from A.D. 875 to 1235 (Morlan 1988:300). Frison (1978) states that intermittent use of the site over a long period is indicated by thick beds of bison bone. The Serviceberry Shelter, a small rockshelter in Dinosaur National Monument in northwestern Colorado, is related but undated (Fredlund 1988:173). Both sites feature Avonlea points and are associated with the Beehive complex. The Spring Creek Cave site in north-central Wyoming, dated A.D. 225, may be a Pelican Lake site; Perry (1980:288), however, believes that the wooden foreshafts tipped with corner notched points (Frison 1978: fig 2.11) show a notable similarity to nineteenth-century Western Apache arrows. Butler (1981b:249) has stated that coiled basketry from this and a nearby cave has been identified as Fremont. To the northwest, in the headwaters region of the Salmon River in east-central Idaho, side-notched arrow points reminiscent of Avonlea points occur side by side with corner-notched points in the Blue Dome phase, dated to have begun about 300–500 (Butler 1981a:12). This phase is documented in a number of sites within a twenty-mile radius. Although it has not yet been included in the Beehive complex, this phase is clearly an expression of Apacheans. The same pertains to the Pilgrim stone circle site in southwestern Montana which produced an Avonlea component (Greiser this volume), and belongs to the same period.

It appears to this author that Avonlea II, after its arrival in the regions mentioned, split into essentially three divisions. One passed on south through the basins and mountains (discussed below), one continued east through western Wyoming (the Beehive complex), and one remained in place.

The latter includes the Blue Dome phase which was replaced by the Shoshonean Lemhi phase perhaps as late as the seventeenth century (Butler 1981a). It may also include, although generally perceived as Beehive, sites such as Wardell, with dates extending to A.D. 1235. From east-central Idaho and southwestern Montana, seasonal forays were made into the region lying between the upper Missouri and Milk rivers between A.D. 750 and 1000 (Greiser this volume), then ceased. Following the expansion of Shoshoneans into the region, beginning in the fifteenth century, this division finally removed south and became part of the Apachean withdrawal into the Colorado High Plains and beyond.

The second division became the Beehive complex in Wyoming, southeastern Montana, and western South Dakota. Fredlund's (1988: fig. 1) map shows its distribution. Morlan's (1988) table of carbon-14 dates lists twenty-one sites; they range in time from about A.D. 250 to 1200. His cumulative histograms of Beehive and Avonlea (I) dates (Morlan 1988: fig. 5) show that both cultures peaked at the same time, between A.D. 600 and 900. Fredlund (1988) discussed the differences in arrow point styles of the two cultures. While both types of Avonlea points are delicately made, the northern types have shallower notches than the Beehive points. The mingling of Beehive with Keaster II groups, who were already present in the area, speaks of amiable relationships between the two cultures and suggests the Kiowa–Kiowa Apache association (already discussed). In contrast, Beehive relationships with groups of the western subphase of Besant appear to have been hostile, and contributed to the Besant withdrawal from the region west of the Black Hills. The protohistoric Kiowas and Kiowa Apaches shifted their range east during the fourteenth century A.D., or later, encircling the Black Hills on all sides. Sacred places important to both groups, and still remembered today, are the Bear Tipi (Devil's Tower), Bear Butte, and Bear Butte Lake. Kiowa and Kiowa Apaches remained in the areas to the southeast, south, and west of the Black Hills until about A.D. 1800. Their southern High Plains experience as free nations spans only five decades (from the 1820s to the 1870s), the final episode in their very long history.

One of the markers of the Athapaskan, including Apachean, presence is the pre-horse shield-bearing warrior motif in rock art. The motif has been recorded in southern Alberta, in the Bitterroot valley of southwest Montana, in central Montana, central and northern Wyoming, in the Black Hills region (Loendorf 1990; Keyser 1984; Greiser this volume), and in the Fremont area (for instance, Gary Wright 1978; Aikens 1966, 1967; Schaafsma 1980, 1986). Often, but erroneously, this art motif has been associated with Shoshoneans. It does not, however, appear in the Great Basin outside of Fremont (which clearly was not Shoshonean), nor in the generally accepted western staging area of the Shoshonean expansion. Indeed, the motif is either restricted to areas occupied by Athapaskans in prehistoric and protohistoric time (including Fremont, discussed below), or was passed on by them to others, as in the Rio Grande area. Loendorf (1990) has recently resolved the controversy by establishing a radiocarbon date of A.D. 1104 for a shield-bearing warrior panel at the Valley of the Shields site, in south-central Montana. This date precedes the arrival of Shoshoneans in this area by nearly four centuries (see also Greiser this volume). Aikens (1967:11) has viewed shields and shield pictographs as characteristic Athapaskan culture elements. Late versions of the shield-bearing warrior motif are sometimes associated with horse armor (Keyser 1984), and horse armor has been specifically linked with Kiowa Apaches (Padouca) in their wars with the Poncas in the early eighteenth century (Fletcher and LaFlesche 1911:79).

It may be interesting to ponder whether some of the shield petroglyphs recorded by Keyser (1984: fig. 16) in the North Cave Hills in northwestern South Dakota, which possibly date to the early historic period, may be of Kiowa instead of Kiowa Apache origin; the close affiliation of the two groups must be considered here. The only Plains tribe that used shields as important features inside the ceremonial lodge of the protohistoric and historic so-called Sun Dance (Schlesier 1990), were the Kiowas, whose camp circle during the annual ceremonial included the Kiowa Apache camp on the north side (Scott 1911: 357). In the ceremony reported by Scott there were eight "Taime shields" fastened to the cedar screen behind the central figurine, the Taime. Their presence was required; during the year these shields were guarded by special keepers who were subjected to serious taboos (Spier 1921:443). The watercolor published by Scott (1911: pl. XXV) shows four red and four yellow and green shields, each with additional markings. Scott (1911:373–74) mentions that some of these shields were interpreted as bird shields (one specifically as a crane shield), and one as a buffalo shield, but did not pursue the question further or ask about their meaning. Loendorf (1990) has reported depictions of shields along with representations of shield-bearing warriors in northern Wyoming and in some locations in Montana; these are usually petroglyphs embellished with paint. Green is an important color there, but not common. Keyser's petroglyphs, already mentioned, show two buffalo shields and a bird shield. Whether there is a connection between some or all of these and the historic Taime shields remains a question. The latter could have come from the Kiowa Apaches directly, and could have been a protective contribution to the Taime and the associated ceremony, or they could be of Kiowa manufacture based on older Kiowa Apache concepts.

The third movement of Athapaskans (Apacheans here again) into the Great Plains arrived in the Park Plateau of north-central New Mexico and southeastern Colorado (the upper Purgatoire River valley) around A.D. 950. Its presence here is termed the Sopris phase; three successive subphases are dated from A.D. 1000 to 1225 (Baugh this volume). House features change over time from wattle-and-daub or jacal surface structures to adobe and jacal units, and eventually to dry lain sandstone roomblocks. Maize is already present during the early subphase, but hunting and gathering are important throughout (Baugh this volume). Ceramics and lithic assemblages also change over time. The earliest projectile points are side-notched and corner-notched arrow points. Sopris Plain and the ware termed Taos Gray are the primary pottery types throughout. The presence of black-on-white pottery may indicate interaction with local Puebloan groups and potential interconnections with the Chaco area (Baugh this volume). Baugh has noted that in northwest New Mexico a gray ware, dating between A.D. 1400 and 1700, is often equated with Athapaskans. Fremont pottery, it should be mentioned, is also a gray ware which appears in northern Utah by about A.D. 500, in the Uinta Basin by A.D. 600, and in central Utah by 900; a north-to-south time slope is clear and points to non-Pueblo origins (Madsen 1986:213, after Marwitt). Early Fremont pottery predates the earliest forms of Basketmaker III pottery (Madsen 1986:213).

A rare genetic anomaly occurs among Athapaskan populations in a relatively high frequency. This is the three-rooted mandibular first permanent molar (Wilcox 1988, after Turner). The link between this dental criterion and Athapaskan populations was firmly established by Turner (sources in Wilcox 1988). In his study of Sopris phase skeletal material he identified a high percentage (23 percent) of triple-rooted molars, and interprets this fact as suggestive evidence for an Athapaskan affiliation (Baugh this volume). The main reason for the general hesitance of anthropologists to accept his conclusion is an old bias that leads researchers to believe in a late arrival of Apacheans near and in the Southwest. One other important argument against Turner's position is that there are no traces of an Apachean passage southward along the Colorado foothills preceding Sopris (see Eighmy this volume). This author accepts Turner's verdict; if these Apacheans did not come through the Plains they must have come via the intermontane route. This author identifies the people of the Sopris phase with the prehistoric Jicarillas because the Sopris region matches exactly the territory of their occupation and the location of their sacred places in protohistoric time. In historic time (Tiller 1983: fig. 1) they had given up the northernmost part of their earlier range, around Jicarilla Lake (west of the Great Sand Dunes National Monument). This author further suggests that the Uinta Fremont variant of the Colorado Plateau and the Uinta Basin, dated A.D. 650–950 (Marwitt 1986:169) is the ancestral archaeological entity. The Uinta Fremont culture in turn seems to derive from the Avonlea II southern expression of the Beehive phase recognized in such sites as the Serviceberry Shelter in Dinosaur National Monument, in the very same area in which Uinta Fremont rose a few centuries later. Its disappearance in the tenth century A.D. is a fact. Regarding the time factor, the end of Uinta Fremont and the beginning of Sopris match closely. Now a reevaluation of the Fremont cultures becomes necessary.

Recent research agrees (Marwitt 1986) that most of the Fremont populations abandoned both the Great Basin and the Colorado Plateau provinces between A.D. 1225 and 1350; the Uinta basin was abandoned earlier, and an attenuated variety of Fremont seems to have persisted longer in the Snake River Plain of Idaho (see below). Post–fourteenth-century locations of the descendants of any of the Fremont cultures have not yet been identified. The archaeological data allow the conclusion that the Fremont were replaced culturally and ethnically by Numic-speaking peoples (Marwitt 1986:171–72). The origin of Fremont is essentially unknown although three theories have been explored: derivation from the Plains, from the Southwest, and an *in situ* development. Madsen (in Marwitt 1986) believes that all three theories have some degree of merit, especially because of the temporal unevenness of the Fremont emergence and the variability of Fremont material culture, indicating the presence of a number of separate groups. Within the area of Fremont occupation, the Great Salt Lake variant is dated A.D. 400–1350, Sevier to A.D. 880–1250, Parowan to A.D. 900–1250, Uinta to A.D. 650–950, and San Rafael to A.D. 700–1250. The first three variants are restricted to the Basin province, the latter two to the region east of the Wasatch Plateau. Boundaries between the variants appear to have overlapped. Despite the considerable variability an essential identity of the Fremont cultural tradition is not denied (Marwitt 1986:164).

Generally, the Fremont subsistence pattern featured a blending of horticulture with hunting and gathering, with emphasis on the latter in some areas. Fremont rock art (petroglyphs and pictographs) features shield bearers, anthropomorphs with horned and other types of head-dresses, and some geometric designs (see section 6), and has been interpreted as a shamanic art (Schaafsma 1980, 1986). San Rafael clay figurines, decorated with red, yellow, and green pigments, occur as male and female pairs (Tuohy 1986: fig. 9), and clearly belong in the realm of religion or magic. Within the Fremont area, anthropomorphic figurines, so far, are seen as restricted to the eastern Basin province and the Colorado Plateau (Tuohy 1986:236). This seems unlikely to this author because paired figurines are frequently important parts of Navajo ceremonial bundles. It might also be interesting to match the anthropomorphs of the rock art with the *ga'n*, *gahe*, or *hacti* (mountain spirit) concept of the Apaches.

Now to the question of origins and later transformations. The three Basin province variants, north to south, have these beginning dates: Great Salt Lake, A.D. 400; Sevier, A.D. 880; Parowan, A.D. 900. The two eastern variants, north to south, have these beginning dates: Uinta, A.D. 650; San Rafael, A.D. 700. This is a clear north-to-south time slope, suggesting that Fremont developed in the northern region, close to the Idaho border and in northwestern Colorado. This either includes or is very close to the southern edge of the Avonlea II distribution already discussed. The evidence indicates that Fremont was neither a peripheral Anasazi (although Parowan and San Rafael had contact with the northern outliers of Anasazi) nor a mysterious Uto-Aztecan branch (it was replaced *in toto* by Uto-Aztecans). The only reasonable option left is that the Fremont were Apacheans; because all variants shared in an essential Fremont identity, *all* were Apacheans. That Fremont exhibits some Archaic traits which had existed in the area in pre-Fremont times (Marwitt 1986:163) should be no surprise and should be taken as the result of cultural adaptation. It is proposed here that Fremont developed from Avonlea II antecedents, and that, after its removal, its variants became the bulk of the Apacheans in the Southwest. It should be noted that Aikens (1966, 1967) once proposed the Plains and Apachean links; this author sees no better fit for the evidence.

The transformations of the remaining four Fremont variants are linked with the fourth and last Apachean movement into the Plains. In the southern High Plains the Tierra Blanca (A.D. 1450–1650) and Garza (A.D. 1450–1750 complexes are identified as Apachean (Baugh this volume). Because there is no trace of an Apachean passage in the central High Plains, and Eighmy (this volume) sees this region as void of a resident population between A.D. 1050 and about 1650, these groups had come via the intermontane route. The best candidate for the ancestral entity is the San Rafael variant which had been the neighbor of Uinta in the south. It is proposed here that Tierra Blanca may represent the prehistoric Lipan Apaches, and that Garza is ancestral to the Mescaleros. Both were joined after 1750 by Apachean refugees from the Kansas plains who influenced the earlier culture (Schlesier 1972: 127–29).

It is proposed here that the Sopris phase became archaeologically the Cojo phase, dated A.D. 1550–1750 (Baugh this volume). There is presently a time lag between the last Sopris and the earliest Cojo dates. The Cojo sites, however, along the Ponil, Cimarron, and Vermejo drainages in northern New Mexico (Baugh this volume), are exactly where the Jicarillas were visited by Ulibarri in 1706, and by Valverde in 1719 (Schlesier 1972:105–16). Baugh also views Cojo as Apachean. Opler (1940:2–3) has noted that the Lipan kinship system resembles the Jicarilla and not the Chiricahua-Mescalero type. This is one reason for this author's tentative identification of Tierra Blanca with the Lipans.

The other is that the Lipans were stationed on the upper Canadian River, near the Jicarillas, until after 1725 (Schlesier 1972:115).

Two of the three remaining Fremont variants, Sevier and Parowan, do not appear to have played a role in the Southern Plains. It is proposed here that they became the protohistoric Western Apaches, Chiricahuas, and Navajos. Opler (1983:381) believes that the Western Apaches probably preceded the Navajos into the San Juan basin and later moved west and south to their historic territories, as the Navajos did subsequently. He observed that the Chiricahuas and Western Apaches show so few Plains traits that their entrance route was intermontane, as was that of the Navajos. David M. Brugge believes that the Apacheans must have been close to the northern periphery of the Anasazi region; whether they had any influence on the Puebloan abandonment of vast areas at that time is regarded as uncertain (but see section 6). Nevertheless, the Anasazi withdrawal and the disappearance of three variants at the same time must in some way be linked. Opler (1983:312), as this author, sees it as reasonable that the Apacheans may have entered the Southwest by 1400 or earlier; this is in sharp contrast to Wilcox's (1981) documentation. Against the Wilcox position of a late arrival, Brugge (1981:286) has argued that the Pueblos did not reoccupy lands abandoned during the thirteenth century, and that Navajos may not have used hogans until quite late in their history. This seems to be in agreement with Matthews' (1897:13–15) observations. He describes as the most common form of Navajo habitation "a conical frame, made by setting up a number of sticks at an angle of about 45 degrees. An opening is left on one side of the cone to answer as a doorway. The frame is covered with weeds, bark, or grass, and earth, except at the apex, where the smoke . . . is allowed to escape. . . . Some lodges are made of logs in a polygonal form." Even larger lodges he calls medicine-lodges were built on a "conical frame" (Matthews 1897: fig. 14), "somewhat on the same plan as the lodges formerly used by the Arickarees, Mandans, and other tribes on the Missouri."

Concerning the Navajo arrival, their origin legend may be of interest here. After they had arrived in the Fifth World, "then the people (Dine, Navahoes) began to travel" (Matthews 1897:80). Eventually they visited Chaco Canyon, where the great Pueblo of Kintyel (Broad House, Matthews' spelling) was under construction, but still far from completion (Matthews 1897:81; Zolbrod 1984:98–99). Matthews (1897:224) thought that this pueblo might have been Chetro Ketl. The Navajo origin story explains that people from the neighboring Pueblo of Ki'ndotliz (Blue House) were assisting in the construction (Matthews 1897:82; Zolbrod 1984:100–1). If the Navajo story reflects a factual, historic visit, this must have taken place around A.D. 1100, at the beginning of Pueblo III.

It is proposed here that the remaining Fremont variant, Great Salt Lake, or parts of it, represent the last flicker of the fourth Athapaskan movement into the Plains, at a time outside the scope of this volume. Great Salt Lake people, or some groups of them, appear to have survived in southern Idaho until the sixteenth and possibly the seventeenth century (B. R. Butler 1983, 1986). Their final removal, probably bringing along Apachean holdouts in southern Wyoming (not including Kiowa Apaches), led into the Central Plains where this amalgam became archaeologically the Dismal River aspect. This entity is dated from A.D. 1640 to 1750 (Gunnerson 1987:102–7; Schlesier 1972), and was clearly Apachean. To the north of the Jicarilla-Panhandle Lipan divisions, the Dismal River aspect consisted of a Colorado division (including the Carlana, Flechas de Palo, and Penxaye subtribes) and a Kansas division (including the Paloma, Cuartelejo, and Calchufine subtribes) (Schlesier 1972:109–10). Around 1750 these Apachean groups were driven by the Comanches either across the mountains (the Jicarillas) or into the Southern Plains, with the Lipans, where the survivors of the Colorado and Kansas groups eventually joined either with the Mescaleros or the Lipans (Schlesier 1972:131).

4. SIOUAN TRANSFORMATIONS, A.D. 100–1550

The historic Siouan language family consisted essentially of four subdivisions derived from Proto-Siouan: (1) a Southeastern group including Ofo and Biloxi in Mississippi (both extinct), and Tutelo, Catawba, and Woccon east of the Appalachians in Virginia and the Carolinas (all extinct); (2) a Mississippi Valley group including Chiwere, Dhegiha, and Dakota; (3) Mandan; and (4) the Missouri River group: Crow-Hidatsa (Chafe 1976; Rood 1979; Hollow and Parks 1980). Because of its location the southeastern group is not considered here. Neither is Dhegiha, one language comprising five dialects: Omaha, Ponca, Kansa, Osage, and Quapaw. Of these the first four represent historic tribes which immigrated into the eastern edge of the Central Plains during the seventeenth century (Schlesier 1975:187–88; 1990:14) from locations in Indiana. The time of their arrival lies outside the period covered here.

Of the Mississippi Valley groups, Chiwere consists of two languages: Winnebago, and one language which comprises three dialects, Missouri (extinct), Oto, and Iowa. Dakota separates into four major dialect groups: Yankton-Yanktonai, Assiniboine-Stoney, Santee, and Teton (Hollow and Parks 1980: fig. 1). It is relevant for the ethnic identification of archaeological entities in the Northeastern Plains, the upper Mississippi Valley, and the Iowa prairies that Crow-Hidatsa and Mandan constitute separate subfamilies despite the later proximity of their speakers on the Middle Missouri; the staging areas of their movements to the Missouri River should logically have been separate also. Hollow's (Hollow and Parks 1980:80) glottochronological investigations suggest that twenty-one centuries separate Hidatsa from Dakota, sixteen centuries separate Mandan from Dakota, and fifteen centuries separate Hidatsa from Mandan. These data may be perceived as a triangle in which the separation of Hidatsa from Mandan occurred later (fifteen centuries ago) than that of either from Dakota, Hidatsa breaking away as early as twenty-one centuries ago. Expressed in terms of space, the triangle, around A.D. 400–500, places the prehistoric Mandans to the west (or southwest) of the prehistoric Dakotas, and the prehistoric Hidatsas in the west (or northwest), already separated from the others but still rather close to the Mandans. This may appear as a circular argument because this is actually where these groups were at that time. The separation of Crow from Hidatsa took place about six centuries ago, according to Hollow – a date in agreement with the archaeological evidence (Mortlach phase as Crow, see section 2 and below).

The distribution of Siouan languages indicates that speakers of this family once occupied large sections of the American Midwest, the East, and the South. In the Great Plains, however, during the period here covered, Siouan speakers played a prominent role only in a limited area which included the tallgrass prairie of Iowa and the Middle Missouri region with the surrounding mixed grass prairie. The exception are the Crows who eventually took up residence on and south of the Yellowstone River. Other Siouan peoples remained in the woodlands of Minnesota and Wisconsin into historic time (the Winnebagos and all of the Dakotas). The Assiniboine-Stoney group advanced to the lower Red River country only around A.D. 1500 (against Cheyenne resistance), and the Teton and Yankton-Yanktonai movements westward across the Minnesota River began as late as the early eighteenth century.

Until the thirteenth century A.D., and the westward expansion of the – Siouan – Oneota cultures into the Prairie Peninsula, Siouan populations in the grasslands may not be called "Woodland" because they were Archaic populations with a long history of residence there, not immigrants from the eastern woods. The only exception is the so-called Kansas City Hopewell (A.D. 50–500): the people of this entity presumably were Siouan, came from the woodlands, stayed in eastern Kansas for a while, then vanished eastward. To call archaeological cultures in the Central and Southern High and lowland Plains "Plains Woodland" is a misnomer which precludes an understanding of the dynamics of (pre-) history. These were Northern Caddoan groups, most of whom had been Plains residents since the Archaic; their adoption of a few traits useful in the grasslands from their forest cousins testifies to their intelligence but did not make them over into "Woodland." They recognized a good thing when they saw it. Fitting (1978a:15) reminds us that the introduction of ceramics had little impact on life styles, and that the trait has little chronological significance.

To use the term Plains Woodland essentially means that Plains cultures are measured with the measuring rod from another region. It is a fallacy as severe as if Woodland cultures of the early historic period were measured against contemporary European cultures. It offends anthropological principles. Perhaps there is an underlying feeling in Plains archaeology that Plains cultures were inferior to the cultures of their cousins in the Southwest or the Woodlands. If this were so, it would be a matter of blindness because the ethnographic literature shows in countless examples that the world perception and the philosophical, religious, and ceremonial expressions of Plains cultures were as deep, complex, and powerful as those of any culture in Indian North America. It is necessary to study and discuss Plains prehistory on its own, not on borrowed terms.

In a recent synthesis of the "Woodland tradition" as it appears "manifested on the Plains-Prairies border," David Benn has defined three generalizations considered to be "the first major reorganization of these data in thirty years" (Ludwickson et al. 1981: 114–15):

(1) the intensification and elaboration of ritual behavior, symbolic artifacts, and cooperative construction efforts seemingly associated with birth (rebirth) and death;
(2) improved technologies (e.g., bow and arrow, ceramics, agriculture) and more cooperative production by larger and more complex human aggregates (i.e., an overall increase in production efficiency);
(3) a population increase that approaches limits perceived by Woodland people.

Because these generalizations are widely believed to be correct they deserve a critical analysis. There is nothing "Woodland tradition" in item (3) above. Population increase started with the first Siberian Upper Paleolithic band of hunters entering North America and continued in all regions until the smallpox pandemics ended it. In all areas productive for human subsistence, populations increased on steadily accelerating levels, including in the grasslands, although habitats in the latter, given the availability of large game and the continuing interest in hunting it, did not favor population densities as great as, for instance, portions of the Mississippi and Ohio valleys.

Part of item (2), "larger human aggregates," is included in item (3). That larger aggregates require a cooperative stance is self-evident, but where it may be assumed with good reason, as, for instance, in the Great Bend entity of Wichita confederacies, the issue is not investigated to conclusion; the Great Bend peoples are treated as a collection of simple artifacts. Regarding "improved technologies," there is nothing "Woodland tradition" about bow technology. The bow was introduced into Illinois by A.D. 700 (Fowler and Hall 1978:560) either from the Plains, where the weapon appeared first in A.D. 50, reaching Wyoming by A.D. 200, or from the north, where Pre-Dorset Eskimos carried bows to Hudson Bay and Labrador around 2000 B.C. There is nothing "Woodland tradition" about ceramics either. Ceramics were not invented in the northeast Woodlands but arrived via diffusion from the southeast, by about 1500 B.C. As a utensil a clay vessel is a rather insignificant object of material culture and an improvement over skin containers only for those who do not travel much. It is conceded that ceramics diffused from the Woodlands (and from the Southwest) into the Plains, but the trait is not regarded here as an improvement in technology.

The term "agriculture" in item (2) is incorrect; horticulture is more appropriate. Agriculture was brought to the Great Plains by European peasants who abhorred the wild community of animals and vegetation. Indian horticulture was part of an intricate mix in which domesticated and wild plants complemented the take of many animal species. This mix was embedded in religious practices and directed behavior regarding the world of the grasslands. In the Woodlands the first "efficient" agricultural systems developed from A.D. 800 to 1300 (Fitting 1978b:44; Gibbon, Gregg this volume). *Maiz de ocho* was present in New Mexico (via Mexico) by A.D. 750 and passed from there into the Plains. Although maize horticulture in the Great Plains arrived via diffusion, it is not necessarily a Woodland tradition trait. It is conceded that horticulture became a valuable asset in parts of the Great Plains.

Of the categories in item (1) only the oblique reference to burial mounds could be interpreted as a "Woodland tradition" trait complex that exerted some influence. But in time and space it had only a limited distribution in the Plains, and it came to an end during the protohistoric period. Evidence for the existence of a burial ritual goes back to the Paleo-Indian period (cremation), and Tuck (1978:42) has pointed out that mound burial in the northeast Woodlands is of northern origin, arriving via diffusion during the third millennium B.C. He has called attention to early burial mounds on the Labrador coast prior to 5000 B.C. Routes of diffusion are not sufficiently understood. Besant burial mounds in Manitoba and the Dakotas, prior to 300 B.C., may have been stimulated by Laurel neighbors; they also could have been brought in by Besant from the north. Because the trait complex diffused to the Woodlands, it makes sense that it also influenced adjacent areas in the Plains, embellishing what already existed. There is no reason to assume that an "intensification and elaboration of ritual behavior, symbolic artifacts," took place in the Plains under Woodland influence. Instead of searching for distant ancestors, complex rituals original to the Plains and its way of life should be considered first. The Cheyenne Massaum or the Kiowa K'ado ceremony (Schlesier 1987, 1990), for instance, do not have a grain of Woodland tradition but were as sophisticated and colorful as anything featured elsewhere. Some Woodland ideas and objects were adopted in the Plains; they were available because growing populations everywhere were connected with far-flung, efficient trade networks. This trade, however, was a two-way street.

In this chapter the obtuse term Plains Woodland is replaced with the proper ethnic confirmation. The Fox Lake phase in the tallgrass prairie of southwestern Minnesota represents a Late Archaic population that became visible as an archaeological entity after it adopted pottery. Evidence of the latter led to its characterization as Middle Woodland (Ludwickson, Blakeslee, and O'Shea 1981:116; Gregg this volume). The settlement pattern of the phase is not known. The subsistence orientation focused on buffalo hunting; there is no evidence for gardening or for burial mounds. Dates extend from about 100 B.C. to A.D. 850 (Ludwickson, Blakeslee, and O'Shea 1981:116–21); after 850 the phase vanished from the region. In Great Oasis and Lake Benton phase sites, which replace Fox Lake, Fox Lake material is absent.

It is proposed here that this culture moved northwestward and resettled in east-central North Dakota, between the Missouri and Sheyenne rivers, where it became the archaeological expression termed Devils Lake–Sourisford Burial complex ancestral to the historic Crow-Hidatsas. Its cultural transformation there occurred under the influence of the Besant-Arvilla complex (the prehistoric Cheyennes), located directly to the east, their territories overlapping. For a considerable period of time the essential elements of Fox Lake–Devils Lake–Sourisford culture changed little beyond the adoption of mound interment: buffalo hunting remained the main focus even later, after horticulture developed. In a comprehensive analysis of the complex, Leigh Syms (1979) has established a strong correlation of mounds and other finds with the annual cycles of bison movements in the Northeastern Plains. The greatest concentration of sites occurs in the Sourisford and Devils Lake regions, which were centers of spring and autumn herd migrations between the prairies and sheltered wintering grounds. Regarding cultural affiliations, Devils Lake–Sourisford is closest to Arvilla, with which it shares numerous traits; that there are also interesting differences should not be surprising. Both complexes shared in long-distance trade that brought in exotic Mississippian objects from the south. The optimum expansion of Mississippian materials into and near the Northeastern Plains occurred between A.D. 900 and 1300 (Syms 1979: 298–300). Although Arvilla traded also with Algonquian groups to the east and northeast, and with Siouan groups to the east and southeast — both Blackduck and St. Croix wares have been found as grave offerings in Arvilla burial sites (Gregg this volume) — Devils Lake–Sourisford does not appear to have participated in this. Instead, its interests lay in the west, in the Initial and Extended Middle Missouri variants.

The complexity of protohistoric Hidatsa (Devils Lake–Sourisford to this author) cultural history has been interpreted by Bowers (1965).

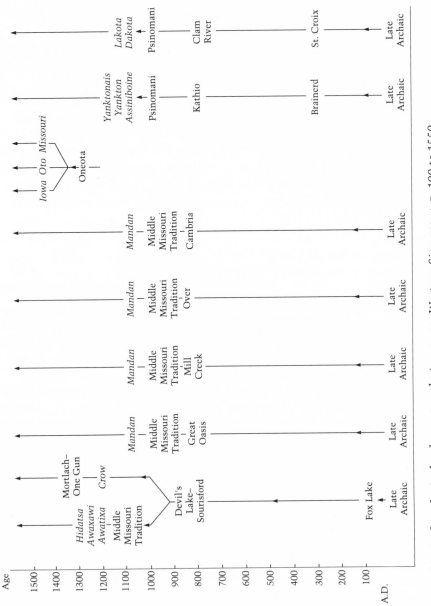

Fig. 14.3. *Archaeological cultures to ethnic groups: Western Siouans, A.D. 100 to 1550. Historic groups are shown in italic.*

This was not a unified culture but a loose confederation of divisions, each with an unknown number of subgroups. In protohistoric time at least five major divisions emerge: Awatixa, Awaxawi, and Hidatsa proper (or Mirokac), all of whom joined in the Extended Middle Missouri variant, and two divisions who remained nomadic buffalo hunters from the beginning to reservation time, Mountain and River Crow. The latter two expanded west into the Missouri basin, beginning during the thirteenth century; in the north they are visible in the archaeological entities Mortlach and One Gun phases, eventually pulling south to the Yellowstone (the River Crow division) (see also Vickers, Greiser, Gregg this volume). The southern division (Mountain Crows) eventually occupied the Bighorn Mountains and the Powder River country. Their first alliance west of the Black Hills was with the Kiowas (G. Wright 1978:131). Hidatsa tradition describes their three divisions moving to the Missouri River separately. First were the Awatixa, followed by the Awaxawi, who were followed later by the Mirokac (Hidatsa proper; Bowers 1965:21–22, 482). They settled on the river above the Knife, in a position to the north of the early Mandans. Because it is presently impossible to distinguish the early Hidatsa earthlodge settlements from those of the Mandans (W. R. Wood 1986a: 13), the exact time of the Awatixa arrival has not been fully established. It is possible that the first attempt was made around 920 A.D. (Tooms, in Winham and Lueck this volume). It took a few centuries for the three divisions to settle on the Missouri; they retained seasonal camps well to the east until historic time. They clearly participated in the Extended (A.D. 1000–1500) and Terminal Middle Missouri (A.D. 1500–1675; Winham and Lueck this volume) variants. Syms's (1979:301) closing dates for the Devils Lake–Sourisford complex, "at least late 1400 with a few elements persisting into the historic period," are in agreement with the dynamics of these transformations.

The Kansas City Hopewell complex was genuine Middle Woodland. It was concentrated at the confluence of the Kansas and Missouri rivers. It arrived from the Woodlands about A.D. 50 and retreated eastward about A.D. 500. During the last half of their occupation (ca. 300–500 – O'Brien 1984:48), some groups extended settlement about a hundred miles along the Kansas River. Associated with Kansas City Hopewell are stone-vaulted burial mounds which contain cremated human bone. The settlement system is defined by large permanent villages. The economy was focused on hunting deer, but smaller game and waterfowl were also taken; bison hunting was insignificant. Corn, squash and *iva* were grown in limited quantities, and were supplemented with collected wild foods. Along with ceramics some exotic artifacts occur, such as platform pipes, copper celts, and obsidian flakes. The materials of the latter two items come from Lake Superior and the Yellowstone National Park area, demonstrating participation in the greater Hopewellian Interaction Sphere (O'Brien this volume). According to O'Brien, Kansas City Hopewellian characteristics show strong similarities with Illinois Hopewell; she agrees with Wedel's original proposition that the complex represents an intrusion of Hopewellians from the lower Illinois River.

The Steed-Kisker phase (A.D. 1000–1250) may have been a follow-up of the first Woodland intrusion. O'Brien defines this phase as carried by a population which may have attempted to control trade associated with the confluence of the Kansas and Missouri rivers. It did not enter the grasslands and pulled east after a relatively short time. It is most likely that it was subsumed in central Missouri by the Oneota tradition, to emerge in protohistoric time as the Missouri tribe of the Chiwere group of Siouan speakers.

The Missouri River region north of the Kansas City Hopewell, to the mouth of the Big Sioux River, extending westward far into Nebraska, was occupied from about 50 B.C. to A.D. 500 by the Valley phase: Valley was Northern Caddoan and its transformations through Loseke–Sterns Creek to the Nebraska phase–Glenwood and the Coalescent tradition are discussed in the next section. The tallgrass prairie to the east of the Valley phase, and to the south of Fox Lake, was inhabited by Late Archaic hunting and gathering bands who had adopted pottery (for instance, Boyer and Arthur ware – Gregg this volume). Although the burial system of Valley included mound structures, and mounds were prominent features in the Mississippi Valley to the east, these bands did not adopt this burial concept. In the literature they are often called Woodland for no reason; their ancestors had been in the prairies for a long time and no intrusions from without have been demonstrated. They were clearly Siouan speakers. In a response to external influences and internal adjustments to a rise in population, these groups became the Great Oasis tradition which subdivided after its emergence (or continued already existing independent divisions) into at least four sociopolitical bodies: Great Oasis, Mill Creek, Over, and Cambria. All of these first explored then migrated to the Missouri River, where they became archaeologically the divisions of the prehistoric, Siouan-speaking Mandans of the Middle Missouri tradition.

Great Oasis is dated A.D. 800 to 1250, Mill Creek 950 to 1300, with the Over phase contemporary, and Cambria dating 900 to 1150 (Ludwickson, Blakeslee, and O'Shea 1981: 133–49); Winham and Lueck, Gibbon this volume). The tradition becomes first visible in northwest Iowa, from where it expanded slightly to the north and along the Missouri. In this process Great Oasis split into the four entities mentioned. In the archaeology of the Middle Missouri, the Great Oasis intrusion turns into the Initial Middle Missouri variant, dated A.D. 950 to 1350 (Winham and Lueck this volume). This is an issue important to regional archaeologists, but obviously the people of Great Oasis and its associated divisions remained the same people. One of the major inventions in their adaptation to the new setting was the development of the Okipa ceremony, which was in place during the Thomas Riggs focus (A.D. 1100–1400; W. R. Wood 1967:156–57). The Okipa required a permanent ceremonial lodge fronting a village plaza; this feature is an integral part of settlements of this so-called focus. From A.D. 1100 to the beginning of reservation time the Okipa lodge remained the center of every Mandan village, although plaza location and the structure of the lodge itself changed over time (Schlesier 1987:135–38). At the beginning of Thomas Riggs, Mandan settlements were distributed along the Missouri from the mouth of White River north to the mouth of the Little Missouri, over a stretch of 350 miles. In the latter area they were mixed with Hidatsa groups in the Clark's Creek (A.D. 1000–1200) and Nailati (A.D. 1200–1400) phases (dates in Winham and Lueck this volume).

Permanent settlement on the Missouri was preceded by exploration west toward the Black Hills. Mandan tradition names the Awigaxa division (or subtribe) in this advance and describes bitter warfare with the Cheyennes of the Besant phase (Schlesier 1987:136–37). Besant-Cheyenne sites and burial mounds extend along the Missouri from below the Cheyenne River north to the Little Missouri (Winham and Lueck this volume); during the wars with the Mandans in the south, and the Awatixa in the north (Schlesier 1987:137), Cheyenne burial mounds may in vain have served as markers of Cheyenne territorial claims. But this was a rearguard action fought by a few bands who soon followed the other Cheyenne divisions east to the Red and Minnesota rivers. The Awigaxa presence has been documented in the South Dakota Badlands, on the eastern slope of the Black Hills, and on the Belle Fourche River (Schlesier 1987:137). Dates for these sites cluster between A.D. 950 and 1300. It is believed that this Mandan division made extensive use of the Black Hills as a resource base; horticulture was attempted there but failed. "In the mountains they planted corn out there, but the seasons were too short, and the yields were small" (Bowers 1965:158–60). After A.D. 1100 Mandan sedentary villages were largely concentrated along the Missouri River.

Earlier, the Great Oasis people lived in open, unprotected villages composed of rectangular lodges. Excavated storage pits within house structures and the artifact inventory reveal that the economy mixed horticulture (sunflowers and corn) with collecting wild seeds and hunting (especially deer and elk, Anderson 1975:33–41). In some areas food collecting was more important than horticulture (Ludwickson, Blakeslee, and O'Shea 1981: 137), suggesting seasonal activities and/or differences among groups. The burial system did not include mounds but hilltop graves were favored. The Mill Creek, Over, and Cambria phases are generally considered eastern members of the Initial Middle

Missouri variant (Winham and Lueck this volume). Before removal to the Middle Missouri region, Mill Creek was restricted to northwestern Iowa, Cambria to southwestern Minnesota, and Over to locations on the lower James and middle Big Sioux rivers. The Mill Creek division practiced a more intensive horticulture than Great Oasis, growing corn, beans, and squash. Villages were of semisubterranean, earth-lodgelike houses; as in Great Oasis, the burial system used hilltop graves. Some Mill Creek villages featured ramps and bastions reminiscent of Initial Middle Missouri sites (Anderson 1975:53–61). Gibbon (this volume) connects Mill Creek fortifications after A.D. 1200, fifty years before complete removal, with the hostile advance of Oneota cultures from the east. After 1300 all four groups (Great Oasis, Over, Mill Creek, Cambria) were on the Middle Missouri as participants in the archaeological Initial Middle Missouri variant.

To these early Mandans the main event in South Dakota prior to the excruciating arrival of smallpox pandemics (after 1520) was the expansion of Caddoan groups north along the Missouri River. This began before A.D. 1300 and is expressed in the Initial Coalescent tradition (1300–1500; Winham and Lueck this volume) of the prehistoric Arikaras (see next section). Although the Caddoans had been peaceful neighbors to the west of Great Oasis throughout the existence of the latter, their advance northward led to the retreat of southern Mandan groups and a process of concentration of all Mandan tribes and divisions on the river between the mouth of Grand River and the Heart. They remained in this territory until the smallpox pandemics reduced all populations to shadows of an earlier existence.

The Oneota cultures are ancestral to the Chiwere group of Siouan speakers whose descendants were the historical Iowa, Oto, Winnebago, and Missouri tribes. These are the main subgroupings of survivors. During the early sixteenth century there may have been many more divisions and independent groups. They collapsed under the impact of European diseases and the seventeenth-century French advance into the western Great Lakes (Schlesier 1990) into the four known bodies. Of these only the Iowa and Oto groups are considered here. Gibbon (this volume) has traced the development of Oneota from its first expressions in southern Wisconsin and southeastern Minnesota (A.D. 1000–1200) through its expansion to northwestern Iowa (Correctionville sites) and southern Iowa (by A.D. 1250–1300). As others do (for instance, Anderson 1975), Gibbon also sees them as ancestral to the Chiwere group. He views the rise of Oneota as related to the decline of the Mississippian at A.D. 1250–1300. Red pipestone, catlinite, was one of the hallmarks of Oneota culture. From this material engraved tablets and pipe bowls were made and traded far; Oneota groups appear to have been the major distributors (Gregg this volume). It is suspected that besides corn and other crops, tobacco was also cultivated. In the northwest corner of the Oneota distribution, groups settled along the lower courses of the James and Big Sioux rivers in the wake of the Over and Mill Creek removal. The Oneota appear to have been originally Woodland people of whom two divisions (Oto, Iowa) became late residents of the prairie.

The Dakota language group with its four dialects — Yankton-Yanktonai, Assiniboine-Stoney, Teton, and Santee — were old dwellers in the Woodlands of whom only the first three groups, and well after A.D. 1500, became denizens of the grasslands. In Howard's (1966) classical categorization, in historic time they comprised these major divisions and sub-tribes: Santee or Eastern Dakota (Lower Council — Mdewakanton, Wahpekute; Upper Council — Wahpeton, Sisseton); Middle Dakota (Yankton, Upper Yanktonai, Lower Yanktonai); and Teton or Western Dakota, or Lakota (Hunkpapa, Minneconjou, Sihasapa, Two-Kettle, Brulé, Sansarc, Ogalala). The Assiniboine-Stoneys, who refer to themselves as Nakoda, originally derive from the Yanktonais (Howard 1966:19). This classification reflects the distribution of groups around A.D. 1800. In the heart of Santee country in western Wisconsin, excavations at Rice Lake revealed a late seventeenth-century burial mound group and ricing village (Brose 1978:578). Associated with historic artifacts in graves were Late Effigy Mound and Blackduck ceramics. The latter were certainly trade objects received from northern — Algonquian — neighbors. The presence of the former suggests that the Late Effigy Mound culture, which was subsumed farther south by Oneota during the thirteenth century, may have lingered in the northern woods to early historic time. The most likely creators of effigy mounds on the northern edge of the distribution of this fascinating feature, in north-eastern Iowa, southern Minnesota, and northern Wisconsin (Fitting 1978:52–56; Anderson 1981:43–51), dated generally from A.D. 650 to 1200, are Siouan groups, especially the Eastern Dakota. Or, perhaps, the Santees retained a semblance of the old tradition longer than the other divisions.

The heavily forested region of Minnesota north of St. Anthony Falls was occupied during A.D. 300 to 800 by two phases of Siouan speakers. These are defined only by two types of ceramics, Brainerd and St. Croix; associated with both are burial mounds. The St. Croix phase occupied east-central Minnesota when Brainerd was located in the north-central region of the state. Because the land of both phases was unsuitable for growing available varieties of corn, wild rice harvesting was important and was as intensive and productive as was corn horticulture elsewhere (Gibbon this volume). The careful maintenance of rice beds was a requirement. Eventually a fully developed wild rice parching and storage technology was in place. Brainerd and St. Croix burial mounds occur occasionally near Arvilla burial mounds, suggesting peaceful relations between Cheyenne and Siouan groups. St. Croix ware appears sometimes in Arvilla mounds. Brainerd ceramics are sometimes found together with Laurel pottery (Meyer and Hamilton this volume), reflecting trade contacts with northern neighbors. One trait of Brainerd ware (net impression) is regarded as similar to Avonlea pottery (Meyer and Hamilton this volume) and may be the result of long-distance trade, or even visits across friendly territories. Sizes and numbers of Brainerd and St. Croix sites show significant population increases over time. After A.D. 800 their ceramics are replaced by Kathio and Clam River styles, but the cultures remained the same. Gibbon (this volume) suspects that by A.D. 1000–1100 the mixed forests of central Minnesota held a population larger than that of corn horticulturists to the south.

With the rise of Psinomani culture (A.D. 1000–1500) the Dakotas enter the late prehistoric and protohistoric periods. Gibbon (this volume) introduced the term to replace the Ojibwa word Wanikan, used previously by Birk (see Gibbon this volume) for this complex. Because he sees it related to the historic Santees, he feels that a Dakota word (*psinomani* meaning "wild rice gatherer") is more appropriate. The dominant pottery style of this period is Sandy Lake ware. During Psinomani time wild rice harvesting intensifies with further population growth; large, semipermanent, palisaded villages appear. Mound burial continues but nonmound interment occurs also. Although in central Minnesota settlements were often occupied all year, western Psinomani groups made seasonal bison hunting forays into the tallgrass prairie near the Red River. Expansion, however, was not directed westward but northward.

In central Minnesota, the Psinomani culture replaced the Blackduck tradition beginning about 1100. By 1250 it was ranging to the Boundary Waters region, and by 1500 it had reached the lower Red River and the edge of Lake Winnipeg (Meyer and Hamilton this volume). This author concurs with Meyer and Hamilton that the northernmost Psinomani groups were Assiniboine-Stoneys; they would struggle for two more centuries for a place in the grasslands of southwestern Manitoba. The circuitous route was forced upon them by the Cheyennes who blocked the upper Red River and Sheyenne River country against them. Cheyenne tradition remembers the ancient enemies well and calls them by the Dakota word *Hohe*, meaning "rebels" or "outcasts," because in the developing conflicts between Crees and Dakotas the Assiniboine-Stoneys sided with the Crees against their Siouan relatives. By 1550 they were separated from the Yanktonais.

5. PLAINS (NORTHERN) CADDOAN TRANSFORMATIONS, 50 B.C.–A.D. 1550

The historic Caddoan language family consisted of two major subdivisions derived from Proto-Caddoan roots: Caddo and Northern or Plains

Caddoan. While some researchers thought that Caddo included at least four languages, each with additional dialects (Swanton, in J. Hughes 1969a:80), others (Newcomb 1961:282) believed that Caddo was a single language. It appeared as one during reservation time when tiny groups of Caddo-speaking survivors were settled around Anadarko in southwestern Oklahoma. In early historic time Caddo was spoken by more than two dozen tribes, most of whom were organized in large confederacies. These were spread throughout southeastern Oklahoma, southwestern Arkansas, western Louisiana, and eastern Texas. These Caddos were originally, and remained, Woodland peoples; because of their locations they are not included in this volume.

Northern or Plains Caddoan divides into three languages: Kitsai, Wichita, and Pawnee. The latter comprises the Skiri, South Band, and Arikara dialects (Hollow and Parks 1980:77). This, again, is a picture that emerges in late historic time. During the early sixteenth century, linguistic — and cultural — diversity must have been considerable but was lost with the great population decline resulting from epidemics of European diseases. The separation of Plains Caddoans from their Woodland cousins occurred early. Swadesh's (in J. Hughes 1969a:81–86) glottochronological studies suggest that 35 centuries separate Arikara from Caddo, 33 centuries separate Pawnee from Caddo, and 30 centuries separate Wichita from Caddo. Kitsai was not included in this investigation. Based on Swadesh's evaluation and his own interpretation of Caddoan archaeology, J. Hughes (1969a:86) believes that the separation between Woodland and Plains Caddoans took place about 1500 B.C. Because all Caddoans originated in the lower Mississippi Valley, the expansion of Plains Caddoan groups along river systems into the grasslands must have begun during Late Archaic time but continued into the late prehistoric period.

Concerning separation among the Northern Caddoans, Swadesh's earlier and Parks's (Parks 1979a:205–6; Hollow and Parks 1980:80) more recent glottochronological studies agree in one case: Wichita-Arikara, 20 centuries. They judge differently the Pawnee-Arikara separation, as 5 (Swadesh) or 3 centuries (Parks), and the Wichita-Pawnee separation, as 14 (Swadesh) or 19 centuries (Parks). Parks, who included Kitsai, finds that 12 centuries separate Kitsai from both Pawnee and Arikara, and that 19.5 centuries separate Kitsai from Wichita. It is odd that Kitsai is closer linguistically to Pawnee-Arikara than to Wichita because Kitsai speakers were, in historic time, geographically situated between the Hasinai Caddos and Wichita groups, and not at all near the Pawnees. J. Hughes (1969a:87) suggests that the break between groups eventually to become the Wichita and other Plains Caddoans may have occurred around 50 B.C. The conclusion that some Plains Caddoans were residents in the grasslands a century before the beginning of the Christian era has been confirmed by archaeology. How much earlier they may have been present is currently difficult to verify. A series of sites in eastern Kansas of a Late Archaic association (O'Brien 1984:40–43) may be ancestral to the Valley, Keith, or Greenwood phases. Two of these sites have dates of 550 ± 55 and 20 ± 110 B.C. (Snyder and Coffee sites of the Walnut phase; Johnson 1984:285–86). There was no evidence of ceramics.

Looking at the distribution of Northern Caddoans on the maps that accompany this chapter, it can generally be said that late prehistoric groups *north* of the (artificial) line separating the Central Lowland Plains from the southern prairies (the central and western reaches of the Arkansas River in Kansas; O'Brien, Vehik this volume) were Panian—that is, ancestral to the tribes and subdivisions of the Skiris, South Band Pawnees, and Arikaras. All groups ancestral to these historic entities were in the region to the north of the line by at least A.D. 250; some had been there centuries earlier.

The latter are the groups of the Valley phase (50 B.C.–A.D. 500). Distributed from northeastern Kansas along the Missouri to beyond the mouth of the Big Sioux, westward to the big bend of the Platte, it predates Kansas City Hopewell and was largely contemporary with this Woodland intrusion (O'Brien 1984:47–52, this volume). The most diagnostic artifact type is grit-tempered and cord-roughened pottery. Valley is best known from burial mounds excavated in Nebraska and Kansas. The burial system featured mounds raised over a subsurface limestone cist (for instance, Taylor Mound) or over surfaces upon which primary and secondary interments had been placed. Valley sites show no evidence of gardening; the economy was based on hunting and the collecting of wild foods. Buffalo hunting played a minor role; generally, deer and smaller game dominate faunal remains (Ludwickson, Blakeslee, and O'Shea 1981:123). Syms (1977:88–91) has discussed a secondary, temporal extension of Valley groups upriver on the Missouri as far as Havre, Montana. In South Dakota (Winham and Lueck this volume) their sites sometimes appear near Besant-Sonota burial mounds.

Phase transition of Valley began after A.D. 500. It split essentially into three archaeological entities: Loseke, beginning about A.D. 600, and Glenwood and Sterns Creek, both initiated around A.D. 900. The latter two emerged in the southern part of the earlier Valley range while Loseke occupied the north, extending along the Missouri as far as the mouth of the Cheyenne River. With the advance of Great Oasis into South Dakota around A.D. 850 (see preceding section), the northernmost Loseke phase groups evacuated the region and pulled south to below the Missouri bend, repeating the waning motion of their Valley ancestors five to six centuries earlier. The information recovered from Loseke and Sterns Creek sites tells that the range of subsistence activities included bottomland horticulture, gathering of wild plant

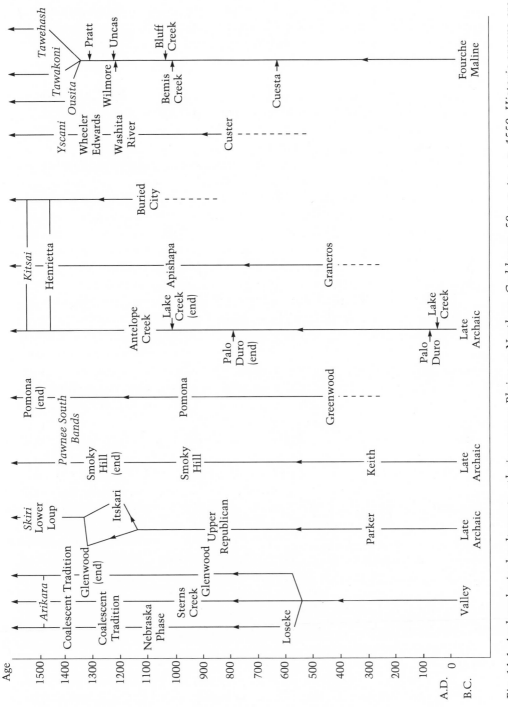

Fig. 14.4. Archaeological cultures to ethnic groups: Plains or Northern Caddoans, 50 B.C. to A.D. 1550. Historic groups are shown in italic.

foods, and hunting. Deer were still more important than bison. Loseke
burials featured low, conical mounds and subsurface pits. House structures of Loseke and Sterns Creek are not sufficiently understood. In
contrast, Glenwood phase settlements featured semisubterranean earthlodges, and the economy was based on corn, beans, and squash (Anderson 1975:44).

Phase transition of Loseke and Sterns Creek to the Nebraska phase
began around A.D. 1050 while Glenwood continued to about 1350.
Hamlets and small villages of semisubterranean earthlodges are a
hallmark of the Nebraska phase, following a system of subsistence and
settlement practiced by Glenwood groups earlier and probably adopted
from them. Bison hunting was still relatively insignificant (Ludwickson, Blakeslee, and O'Shea 1981:155). The feature of mound burials
seems to have become obsolete. By A.D. 1250 the Nebraska phase
becomes archaeologically the Basal Coalescent phase which led through
its St. Helena variant to the Initial Coalescent variant (A.D. 1300–1500),
following its migration northward on the Missouri River into South
Dakota and a position south of the early Mandans. It is proposed here
that the Glenwood bands followed their Caddoan relatives upriver. All
became the historic Arikaras. That a large number of originally independent groups participated in the Coalescent tradition is evidenced
by the fact that, even as late as on the eve of the smallpox epidemic of
1780–81, the Arikaras comprised no less than ten different tribes
(Tabeau 1939:123), with possibly as many as forty-five villages among
them. Each of these major subgroups spoke its own dialect and was
politically autonomous (Parks 1979b:215–29, 236).

The Loup River of Itskari phase, dated about A.D. 1250 to 1400, which
is sometimes included in the Basal Coalescent variant as ancestral
Arikara (for instance, Ludwickson, Blakeslee, and O'Shea 1981:161–
68), is here omitted from this tradition. Itskari was ancestral to Lower
Loup and the protohistoric Skiris, who had a different origin (see
below) and an independent history. The assumption that the Itskari
Skiris contributed directly to the Coalescent tradition Arikaras is
based on the misconception that Arikara speech is most closely related
to the Skiri dialect. This is false. Parks (in Murie 1981: notes, p. 177) has
provided evidence that linguistically Arikara is close to the South
Band Pawnee dialect, that Skiri is unintelligible to an Arikara speaker,
and that Arikara therefore cannot be a branch of Skiri.

The second major Panian grouping becomes visible archaeologically
about A.D. 300. This is the phase called Parker by Reeves (1970:121–25),
or South Platte by other researchers (Eighmy this volume). The Parker
advance into the South Platte basin put additional pressure on southern Tanoan groups who were already retreating before Besant south of
the Black Hills (see sections 1 and 2). Reeves (1970:68) calls these
southern Plains Tanoan groups the Glendo subphase of Pelican Lake,

after the Glendo Reservoir sites. Glendo subphase dates come to an end in the region lying between the South Platte and the headwaters of the Cheyenne River between A.D. 300 and 400 (Reeves 1970:331). After A.D. 400 the northern part of this range is controlled by Besant groups, the southern part by Parker groups. The fact that Parker dates in the southernmost part of its distribution start around A.D. 500, a full century later than to the north (Reeves 1970:122), suggests that the Parker intrusion occurred from a southeastern direction (via the upper Republican River), and that the last bands of southern Plains Tanoans may have lingered in the Denver basin a little longer before following related bands westward across the mountains or joining Tanoan relatives of the Vermejo phase (Basketmaker II, see below) on the east slope of the Sangre de Cristo Range, centered on the headwaters of the Canadian River and Cimarron Creek.

Parker occupations are located in caves or rockshelters or on stream terraces. Reeves (1970:125) defines Parker groups as generalized "nomadic hunter-gatherer-horticulturists." Parker ceramics most closely resemble those of the Keith phase (Reeves 1970:352). Eighmy (this volume), although not using the term Parker, describes a Plains affiliation of sites in this area during this period. Reeves's (1970:125–28) Ash Hollow phase, with beginning dates around A.D. 700, is here not viewed as a different phase but as a Parker variant or a Parker seasonal presence in the North Platte, Niobrara, and White River drainages. The archaeological record of Ash Hollow is virtually identical to that of Parker. Both, after A.D. 850, became archaeologically the Upper Republican phase. Most researchers (for instance, Ludwickson, Blakeslee, and O'Shea 1981; Blakeslee 1978) include Upper Republican in the Central Plains tradition, a term and concept first introduced by Lehmer in 1954 (see Roper 1989:29–33 for a brief discussion of its history). The concept is not used here because it is inadequate; there never was a single Central Plains tradition. From the beginning of the North Caddoan presence in the Central Plains region there were three different and distinct traditions: one leading to the Arikaras, one to the Skiris, and one to the South Band Pawnees. The first has already been traced. The second becomes visible with Parker–Ash Hollow and leads through Upper Republican and Itskari to Lower Loup and the Skiris. For the third, see below.

The Upper Republican temporal range is dated from about A.D. 850 to 1350 (Roper 1989:31). This phase occupied northwestern Kansas, northeastern Colorado, south-central and southwestern Nebraska. The westernmost sites do not contain earthlodges (Ludwickson, Blakeslee, and O'Shea 1981:157) and must be regarded as seasonal hunting camps. Corn, beans, squash, and sunflowers were cultivated. The subsistence pattern mixed hunting and horticulture. Remains of game species recovered from sites indicate emphasis on floodplain hunting, with bison of secondary importance. Eventually bison hunting became the primary focus of seasonal hunting activities. Phase transition to the Itskari (or Loup River) phase began after A.D. 1250; closing dates for Itskari are around A.D. 1450. That Upper Republican is ancestral to Itskari has not been seriously questioned by researchers. Centering on the Loup River valley, the Itskari phase was not simply the old Upper Republican in a new location. Some changes occurred in ceramics and other material traits, and it appears that the population was more tightly aggregated (Roper 1989:33).

It is proposed here that the major changes that led to the archaeological transition from Upper Republican to Itskari are in the realm of religion, which in turn brought about a certain degree of political control. Considering Wissler's (in Murie 1981:465–66) thoughts on this subject, it appears that the older concepts of animal power, animal lodges, doctors with animal power, and the like, were overlaid with influences coming from two directions: the Spiro center and the Anasazi Tanoans. The mother corn concept, the sacred ear of corn idea, the rain and cloud importance, and details of altar arrangements should be regarded as influences from the Rio Grande valley. Star ritualism, absent among the South Bands, and the human sacrifice ritual of the Skiris to the morning star came from Spiro and the Southern Cult. From the Skiris the human sacrifice ritual was passed to the Arikaras. A human arrow sacrifice is depicted in Spiro art (Brown 1984:258).

Phase transition of Itskari to the Lower Loup phase began after A.D. 1450; the phase persists to 1775 (Roper 1989:29). With this archaeological mode the Skiris enter the historic period. Permanent settlements were concentrated in a narrow space along the lower Loup River and the adjacent Platte, although seasonal bison-hunting camps ranged far to the west, in the north to the Niobrara River. According to native testimony in the early 1900s the Skiris formerly had eighteen villages, of which all but two were joined in a political and religious confederation. The smallpox epidemic of 1780–81 reduced the Skiris to a single village.

It is an important fact that only the Panian groups of Northern Caddoans had sacred bundles; these were often associated with specific villages or even tribes. The Skiris had a total of eighteen bundles; for the Arikaras ten sacred bundles are remembered (the same number as that of affiliated tribes), and the South Bands had at least fourteen bundles (Murie 1981:34–35, 183, 195–96, 199, 461). In contrast, the tribes of the Wichitas, Kitsais, and Woodland Caddos had not adopted the concept of sacred bundles. Because the number of bundles owned by the Pawnee South Bands lies between that listed for the Arikaras and Skiris, it is conceivable that the population of the South Bands may have been comparable in late prehistoric time to that of their relatives to the north, and significantly larger than the three to four villages known from the early historic period. The archaeological record seems to support this interpretation.

The early South Bands, the third major Panian grouping, became visible archaeologically about A.D. 300. They are represented by the phase called Keith; its temporal range is placed by Reeves (1970:350–51) between A.D. 300 and 900–1000. Keith ranged from the Smoky Hill River northward across the Saline and Solomon rivers to the upper reaches of the Republican River drainage (see O'Brien 1984:52–54, this volume). It does not appear to have made much use of the Central High Plains (Eighmy this volume). Keith is defined by the presence of specific projectile points (Scallorn) and a type of cord-roughened pottery (Hardin). The best known sites are ossuary pits with secondary burials. Habitation sites are inconspicuous, small camps (O'Brien this volume). Bison hunting was of marginal importance. Reeves (1970:120) thinks that corn horticulture was probably practiced; he defines Keith phase populations as semisedentary hunter-gatherer-horticulturists.

It was during the Keith phase, during the eighth century A.D., that Maiz de Ocho diffused from the Southwest to eastern North America through northeastern New Mexico and southeastern Colorado (Baugh this volume). Whether its passage had an influence on Keith and related Panian groups to the north is not yet fully understood. In the Caddo area of northeastern Texas the arrival of Maiz de Ocho led to the development of horticulture as the economic base of the emerging Caddo tradition (Story 1981:149).

After A.D. 900 the Keith phase becomes archaeologically the Smoky Hill phase. Phase transition was independent of the Parker–Upper Republican transition to the north, and occurred later. Contrary to a still widely held belief, Keith was not, as already shown, ancestral to Upper Republican but represents a different cultural tradition. Smoky Hill occupied essentially the same range as Keith earlier, perhaps with a slight eastward expansion to the Kansas River. The Solomon River phase (Ludwickson, Blakeslee, and O'Shea 1981:141–42) is here not considered as a phase but as a variant of the larger Smoky Hill, perhaps representing one of the major South Bands.

It is generally believed that Smoky Hill ended shortly after A.D. 1300. It is proposed here that Smoky Hill represents the protohistoric South Bands. If the above closing date is correct one might wonder about the whereabouts of the South Bands (Chawis, Kitkahahkis, and Pitahawiratas) between A.D. 1300 and 1550 (see below).

South Band culture differed from that of their Panian relatives. O'Brien and Post (1988) have recently reconstructed the meaning of an earthlodge and burial mound complex of the Smoky Hill phase, situated on a bluff spur overlooking the juncture of the Smoky Hill, Republican, and Kansas rivers, dated about A.D. 1300. Using South

Band ethnographic sources, they have demonstrated that the earth-lodge was the lodge of a Pawnee priest and that the South Band world perception and ritual was fully in flower at this place at this time.

It is proposed here that the sacred animal lodges of the South Bands already existed during Smoky Hill time, perhaps earlier. They held their importance into reservation time. Hyde (1974:108) mentions two sacred sites (animal lodges) of the South Bands: Pa:hu:ru, "Hill That Points the Way," now called Guide Rock, on the Republican River just above the Kansas-Nebraska line; and Kicawi:caku, "Spring on the Edge of a Bank," now called Waconda Spring, near the confluence of the South and North forks of the Solomon River in Kansas. The latter is now submerged under the waters of Glen Elder Reservoir. Parks and Wedel (1985:158–59) list two more sacred animal lodges associated with the South Bands: Pa:hu:a, Swimming Mound, an island in the Republican River in western Kansas; and Dark Island (also Lone Tree), an island in the Platte near present Central City, Nebraska. This author includes one more animal lodge in the sacred sites of the South Bands: Pawnee Rock (anonymous Pawnee informant, pers. comm.), located near the north bank of the Arkansas River, about fifteen miles south-west of Great Bend, Kansas. This remarkable landmark contains a spring, a feature important in the animal lodge concept. These five sites may not represent all the important animal lodges of the South Bands but may give a clue to the sacred geography developed by their shamans and priests. If O'Brien and Post's priest's lodge at the impor-tant juncture of the Kansas, Smoky Hill, and Republican rivers were considered as identifying the exact place of another animal lodge, we might see it as representing the ceremonial marker of the southeast. If this assumption were close to the truth, the ceremonial marker of the southwest direction would be Pawnee Rock, that of the northwest, Swimming Mound, and that of the northeast, Dark Island. Within these directional boundaries, Waconda Spring and Guide Rock would mark the center of the South Bands' territory — and this is the territory of the Keith to Smoky Hill phases.

This is a reasonable speculation but tells us nothing about the location of the South Bands after A.D. 1300. If they had indeed left their old lands — to which they returned after the possible episode of their absence — they might have gone north (to the Platte and Elkhorn rivers) or east and south? The latter is most likely. The Coronado expedition learned in Quivira in 1541 that downriver from the great bend of the Arkansas River were hunters who did not plant (Schroeder 1959:39–40), and also that groups to the east used grass and skin lodges. Blaine (1979) has looked into Skiri and South Band legends and found that all mention grass lodges, and that these groups claimed that "the grass house was the earliest type structure they knew and used" (Blaine 1979:243). It appears then, that Skiris and South Band Pawnees used three structures in prehistoric times: grass lodges, earthlodges, and skin tipis. If the South Bands had gone to eastern Kansas after A.D. 1300, they must have mingled with groups of the Pomona phase (dated ca. A.D. 980 to 1600 by O'Brien 1984:64–65, this volume). Pomona people used grass lodges but clearly did not become a Wichita division. They may have been a subdivision of the South Bands all along.

Looking again at the distribution of Plains Caddoans on the maps that accompany this chapter, it can generally be said that late prehistoric groups *south* of the — artificial — line separating the Central Lowland and High Plains from the Southern High Plains and prairies (O'Brien, Vehik this volume), as far south as the Red River, were ancestral to the tribes and subdivisions of the Wichita and Kitsai conglomerates. Some groups ancestral to these historic formations were in the region before the beginning of the Christian era, others emerged from the Woodland Caddo area later. Because of the confusing multitude of Plains Caddoan prehistoric complexes, phases, and foci recognized by archaeologists in the region, and the tendency to cut the pie into finer and finer slices, it seems advisable to divide the region into two major areas: the High Plains region and the prairies and Cross Timbers. The southern High Plains are taken up first.

Much of the southern half of this region, extending from the Red River to the southern edge of the High Plains and prairies, and including the Cross Timbers on the upper Brazos and Colorado rivers, was occupied throughout the period covered in this volume by groups ancestral to the historic Tonkawas. Linguistically they belong to the Coahuiltecan stock (Hoijer 1946:289). Skinner (1981) believes that they were present in this region for thousands of years, and that groups other than Tonkawas arrived during historic time. A Caddoan intrusion occurred in the eastern fringe of the area around A.D. 900 (Lynott 1981:105) but retreated eastward about A.D. 1200 (Lynott 1981:105; Skinner 1981:115).

The earliest dates for Caddoan groups with ceramics in the northern half of the region are those of the Palo Duro (A.D. 120–870) and Lake Creek (A.D. 1–1000) complexes (Vehik, Baugh this volume). These appear to be Late Archaic groups which adopted pottery. Both exhibit cordmarked pottery and Southwestern ware, indicating contacts to the west and east. Lake Creek sites occur along the northern boundary of the Llano Estacado, usually on terraces of tributaries of the Canadian River. Palo Duro sites are directly to the south, around the headwaters of the Red River drainage. It is generally believed that Lake Creek becomes archaeologically the Antelope Creek phase, dated A.D. 1200–1450 (Baugh, Vehik this volume). The fate of the Palo Duro complex is not known. Because the Antelope Creek distribution includes the area occupied earlier by Palo Duro, it is most likely that the latter merged via Lake Creek with the larger Antelope Creek formation if it had not been an affiliated band from the beginning.

Antelope Creek phase sites are concentrated along the Canadian and North Canadian rivers in the panhandles of Oklahoma and Texas, extending into northeastern New Mexico and western Oklahoma. In the south they reach the headwaters of the Red River. These sites include villages, open campsites, lithic scatters and, perhaps, rockshelters and caves (for instance, the Kenton Caves of extreme northwestern Oklahoma – Lintz and Zabawa 1984). Village sites vary from single-room structures to roomblocks containing up to twenty contiguous rooms (Lintz 1984:327–30; Baugh this volume). Possible burial mounds have been found at two sites, Alibates 28 and Spring Canyon, the first containing nine burials (Lintz 1986b:121). The economy of Antelope Creek groups was based on hunting, gathering, and horticulture. Two types of corn have been recovered along with beans and pumpkin seeds. Animal remains include buffalo, antelope, deer, and smaller game (Lintz 1984:331; Baugh this volume). Trade items in sites include objects from the Northern Plains (catlinite pipes, artifacts made of Niobrara jasper) and the Southwest. Lintz (1984:330) has discussed evidence of warfare but reports that sites are not fortified; some, however, are situated on nearly inaccessible mesa tops. Because groups of the Antelope Creek phase were forced by Apacheans to abandon all of their territory, episodes of warfare may relate mainly to the closing time of the phase (ca. A.D. 1400 to 1450).

Plains Caddoan neighbors to the north, and essentially contemporary with Antelope Creek, are groups of the Apishapa phase (A.D. 1100–1350 – Baugh this volume, after Lintz) and the Buried City complex (A.D. 1150–1500 – Hughes and Hughes-Jones 1987:105). The Apishapa phase derives from the earlier Graneros focus in the same area, the Arkansas River basin of southeastern Colorado. Graneros is dated through early, middle, and late periods from A.D. 450 to 1050 (Baugh this volume). It is characterized by cordmarked ceramics and circular structures or stone enclosures with dry lain masonry walls. The transition to Apishapa occurs after A.D. 1050. Architectural units of this phase are stone enclosures. Sites are generally located on high places with difficult access, suggesting that defense was a concern. This is not surprising because Athapaskans of the Sopris phase (beginning A.D. 1000, see section 3) were directly to the west. The boundary between Apishapa and Antelope Creek is fairly well established: the sand dune belt associated with the Cimarron River. Apishapa economy was based on hunting, collecting, and limited farming; at least five varieties of maize have been recovered. Trade items include Southwestern ware and material from Texas (Alibates agatized dolomite) and southern Nebraska (Medicine Creek jasper). Cordmarked pottery is rather rare. It has been argued on the basis of projectile point styles that Apishapa groups had closer relations to the Upper Republican (Skiris) phase than to Antelope Creek (Baugh this volume), which appears reasonable regarding their geographical distribution.

The Buried City complex (A.D. 1150–1400) was located to the southeast of Apishapa, extending from the northeastern part of the Texas panhandle through the Oklahoma panhandle into southwestern Kansas (Baugh this volume). Near the end of the occupation architectural structures progressed to large, rectangular, boulder-based houses with four or six center posts and well-defined internal activity areas (D. Hughes 1988). Ceramics are closer to Kansas Geneseo ware than to Panhandle varieties (Hughes and Hughes-Jones 1987:106), as may be expected. The origins of this complex are unknown. The differences between it and both Apishapa and Antelope Creek are significant enough to suggest that it may represent an independent group which may have come into the area from the southeast, that is, central Oklahoma.

The removal of these three Plains Caddoan groupings within one century, from 1350 to 1450, was matched by an Anasazi withdrawal westward from the east slope of the Sangre de Cristo Range, especially the headwaters region of the Canadian River, centering on Cimarron Creek. Tanoan Anasazi groups had used this region since A.D. 400. The first period of their presence is termed the Vermejo phase, dated A.D. 400–700; it is interpreted as a Basketmaker II manifestation in the Cimarron Creek valley (Baugh this volume; Cordell 1979). It is followed by the Pedregoso phase (700–900), interpreted as a Basketmaker III manifestation. Next come the Escritores phase with dates between 900 and 1100, the Ponil phase, 1100–1250, and the Cimarron phase, 1200–1300 (Baugh this volume). Sites and dates demonstrate an Anasazi occupation in this region near the High Plains over a period of nine hundred years. After A.D. 1300 the region was taken over by Apachean groups (see section 3) who had come across the Rocky Mountains of southern Colorado. Because there is no trace of a movement of groups into the Central High Plains between A.D. 1050 and the seventeenth century (Eighmy this volume), the Apachean groups who first replaced the Anasazi, then the Apishapa, Buried City, and Antelope Creek populations, did not come from the north. It is equally clear that none of the three Caddoan groups retreated north. This means that none of them contributed to Panian or to Quivira developments.

Now it becomes vital to consider the information provided by the Coronado expedition of the spring and summer of 1541. Albert Schroeder (1959) has made the most comprehensive assessment of the reports of the participants, and the following summary is based on his work.

The Coronado expedition reached the Canadian River after four days of travel east of Pecos Pueblo and crossed the river near the Conchas Reservoir area. Traveling in a northeasterly direction, four to five days after the crossing the Spaniards saw the first buffalos, and two to three days beyond these they came upon immense herds. On the eighth day after the crossing they met the first Apache ("Querecho") camp, and two days later a second camp; this took place in the northwest part of the Texas panhandle. The Apaches told of continuous settlements downriver on the Canadian; the first settlement was called Haxa. Five days of travel beyond the Apaches the Spaniards met with another group of buffalo hunters, the Teya, people who painted their bodies and faces and were enemies of the Apaches. For three days they passed through Teya camps. These were located around the northeastern edge of the Texas panhandle and below the North Canadian River in western Oklahoma. Castañeda, a member of the expedition, called this "a densely populated country" (Schroeder 1959:32).

The name Teya originated among Jemez-Pecos speakers and simply meant "People of the East" (Schroeder 1959:34). The term was given to them in 1525 when the Galisteo basin Pueblos were attacked by a Plains people from the east (Teya) who lived in houses of straw and raised corn but also hunted buffalo. The 1525 episode was their first hostile inroad into the Pueblo area (Schroeder 1959:35). It was also said that the Teyas were of the same type and dress as the people of Quivira. One day past the last Teya camp, on either the North Canadian or the Cimarron River, the army was ordered to return while Coronado pressed on with a small detachment. The Spaniards traveled for thirty days; no Indians were encountered. They reached the Arkansas River near Ford, Kansas, crossed to the north bank, and followed it downstream. Three days after the crossing they met Indians out hunting who had come from a Quivira settlement three to four days away. They found the first settlements on small streams that flowed into the large river, apparently the sites on Cow Creek and the Little Arkansas, thirty to forty miles east of Great Bend, Kansas. They traveled among the settlements for four or five days.

Coronado stated about Quivira (the Tawakoni division): "There are not more than twenty-five towns, with straw houses, in it, nor any more in all the rest of the country that I have seen and learned about." He also said: "All they have is the tanned skins of the cattle they kill, for the herds are near where they live, at quite a large river. They eat meat raw like the Querechos and Teyas. They are enemies of one another. . . . These people of Quivira have the advantage over the others in their houses and in the growing of maize" (Schroeder 1959:21). No Indians were encountered by the expedition on the return trip aside from an Apache camp in the northwest corner of the Texas panhandle, in the Stratford area.

The Querecho groups met by Coronado were Lipan Apaches (see section 3); the Teyas were Caddoan buffalo hunters whose permanent settlements were to the east and southeast. It is most likely that they represent groups of one or all of the archaeological cultures that had been driven out by the Lipans: Apishapa, Buried City, and Antelope Creek. Apparently they had been forced to encroach for some time upon settlements of the Edwards and Wheeler complexes of western Oklahoma. The Teya attack on the Tano Pueblos in 1525 is evidence for the turmoil deriving from their removal, their drifting away from lands occupied for a long time, and their difficulties in establishing new and safe territories. It is important that forty days of travel were required from the last Teya camp to reach Quivira, and that the country in between was devoid of people. It is almost as important that Quivira was described as being confined to the region well east of the great bend of the Arkansas. These facts lead to the conclusion that none of the three archaeological entities mentioned (Apishapa, Buried City, and Antelope Creek) took part in Quivira-Wichita developments, but instead may have been instrumental in the initiation of the Henrietta complex, with beginning dates between A.D. 1450 and 1500. Thus they appear to have become the subdivisions of the Kitsai grouping. This turn would explain why Kitsai is linguistically closer to Panian dialects than to Wichita. The Henrietta complex, located between the upper reaches of the Brazos River in the south and the area beyond the upper Red River in the north, takes the Kitsais into the historic period.

When in 1601 the Oñate expedition followed the first part of the Coronado trail through the Texas panhandle, the Teyas were gone. The Spaniards had met Lipan Apache camps (they called them Vaqueros) in the same general area where Coronado had seen them (as far east as Canadian, Texas), but neither saw nor heard of other Indians until they reached the "Escanxaques" (Schroeder 1959:46) below and on the Salt Fork of the Arkansas River in northern Oklahoma below Ponca City (see also Vehik 1986). The Teyas and the "continuous settlements" downriver on the Canadian had disappeared. It is proposed here that they had moved to the Red River, a distance about 120 miles south of where Coronado had placed them sixty years earlier.

Oñate's trail, leading northeast from the Antelope Hills on the Canadian toward the juncture of the Chikaskia River and the Salt Fork, passed through empty country until the Escanxaques were encountered. Two days beyond them were the Rayado villages (Schroeder 1959:47–50), located on Walnut River and Beaver Creek (Vehik 1986:23) east of the Arkansas; these were relatives of groups farther upstream. The vast empty space between the Antelope Hills and the Salt Fork suggests that European epidemics had visited. The Escanxaques were at war with their neighbors to the north (M. Wedel 1982:121, after B. Martinez). There is no choice but to identify the Escanxaques with the people of the archaeological Edwards and Wheeler complexes, who had moved away from their earlier territories farther west. When Oñate stated that the Escanxaques "did not plant or harvest, depending entirely for their food on the cattle" (Schroeder 1959:49), he was in error but may have caught them at a time when they were hunting.

Dates for Edwards lie between A.D. 1500 and 1650, beginning dates for Wheeler slightly later (Hofman 1984b:348–57). Perhaps the closing dates are too late and the Escanxaques represent the end of both complexes. Earlier, centering on the Canadian River in western Oklahoma, in the region found empty by Oñate, the economy of both complexes was based primarily on bison hunting and trading; differences in artifact inventories were insignificant between the two. Because of their geographical ranges, trade connections of Edwards were oriented westward (toward the Southwest), those of Wheeler eastward (toward Caddoan relatives). Researchers have reason to believe (Vehik 1986:30) that Edwards-Wheeler derive *in situ* from the Custer (A.D. 800–1100) and Washita River (A.D. 1250–1450) phases which were earlier in the same area but practiced extensive horticulture. The dates for the latter (Drass and Swenson 1986:46; Vehik this volume) allow for this transition. The Escanxaques represent the penultimate stage in the fate of a unique Plains Caddoan tradition that had lasted as an independent unit for nearly a thousand years until, decimated and displaced, its groups were subsumed, as were other originally independent groups, in that cauldron of survivors on the Red River during the eighteenth century called the Wichitas. If there ever was a Wichita confederacy, the term applies only to the Quivira visited by Coronado on the Little Arkansas and Cow Creek (the so-called Little River focus), "not more than twenty-five towns, with straw houses."

It is proposed here that the Escanxaques of 1601 are none other than the Yscanis of the eighteenth century. Oñate's Rayados may have been the Wichita proper, and in 1601 the settlements of the Tawakonis and Tawehash were still farther north. The relationship between these tribes, or groups of tribes, may have been similar to that between the Skiris and South Bands. In a reversal of the Panian arrangement one might see the Escanxaques-Yscanis as independent in a southern position, distantly related to three "North Bands," which cooperated with each other: Tawakonis, Tawehash, and Ousitas, or Wichita proper. The fact that the Escanxaques told Oñate that they were at war with the northern groups supports this interpretation.

It should be obvious now that, contrary to popular archaeological belief, none of the prehistoric groups of the High Plains and western Oklahoma participated in the Great Bend aspect (ca. 1450–1700), the archaeological manifestation of the historical divisions Tawakoni, Tawehash, and Wichita proper. Great Bend was a late expression of prehistoric groups which had come into the middle Arkansas River basin from a southeastern direction. Emerging from the Cross Timbers, ancestral groups went upriver on the Arkansas and its tributaries. During Great Bend time, beginning around A.D. 1450, the above-mentioned three divisions concentrated their settlements in essentially three areas. There were two northern locations, one on Cow Creek and the upper Little Arkansas River, one nearly straight east from there, on the Cottonwood River near Marion, Kansas, and one to the south, on the lower Walnut River. The first represents the Tawakonis, the second the Tawehash, the last the Wichita proper. About eighty miles separated the Tawakoni cluster of villages from that of the Tawehash, and about the same distance separated the latter from the Wichita proper. Although all these divisions hunted buffalo distances away from their sedentary villages, no effort was made to extend settlement farther west in the grasslands. The withdrawal of the two northern divisions southward on the Arkansas began after Oñate's visit to the Wichitas. The arrival of Dhegiha Siouan groups (Osage and Kansa) during the early seventeenth century, well to the east of the Tawehash and Wichita proper, played no role in this withdrawal. Another matter is the rise of the Apachean Dismal River aspect (ca. 1625–1750, Schlesier 1972) in western Kansas. These Apache groups clearly took over the hunting ranges of Tawakonis and Tawehash, and clashed with groups as far east as the Missouri River, between 1650 and 1725. If the Tawakoni-Tawehash pullout was partly due to Apachean pressures, epidemics of European diseases might have been a more powerful cause.

Directly ancestral to the "Wichita" divisions are archaeological entities such as the Wilmore complex (A.D. 1370–1450), the Pratt complex (A.D. 1400–1500), Uncas (A.D. 1300–1400), and Bluff Creek and Bemis Creek (A.D. 1050) (Vehik, O'Brien this volume). These in turn derive from the earlier Cuesta (Cooper) phase (A.D. 700–1000) of the Osage plains and the Neosho River. Back in time, all these Caddoan groups come from the Fourche Maline phase (300 B.C. to A.D. 500) of eastern Oklahoma, the hearth of Arkansas River Caddoan cultural developments. None of these archaeological cultures stems from Hopewellian roots although those near Kansas City Hopewell and Steed-Kisker (both Woodland intrusions from the St. Louis area) had trade relations with them, as is to be expected.

It is proposed here that the Pomona phase (A.D. 950–1600 — O'Brien this volume) of eastern Kansas, which developed *in situ* from the preceding Greenwood and Butler phases (A.D. 400–900), represents a tradition very different from that which led to the historic Tawakonis, Tawehash, and Wichitas. Pomona is related to Smoky Hill and appears to represent one of the South Bands, its distinctive ceramic pastes the product of locally available clays and not cultural choice, as O'Brien (this volume) has argued.

6. SOUTHWEST NEIGHBORS/RELATIVES: TRANSFORMATIONS, A.D. 400–1550

The small area of the Southwest included in this volume is confined to the country lying east of the Rio Grande, from the Taos area in the north to the great bend of the river in the south. The northern one-third of this region was part of the Eastern Anasazi (Tanoan, Keresan) territory. The lower two-thirds, originally occupied by Late Archaic hunting and gathering groups, experienced the rise and decline of the Eastern Mogollon, and the takeover of much of the country by Apaches.

Eastern Anasazi must be divided into two main components: Keresan speakers and Tanoans. The first, with a language for which as yet no external connections have been established (Hale and Harris 1979: 173), appear to have been the initial force in Eastern Anasazi developments, most likely under Mogollon influence. Viewed from the upper Rio Grande country, the Tanoans were clearly intruders from the north who adapted to the new country and the emerging Anasazi pattern through contact with the Keresans.

According to Cordell's (1979) summary, the earliest Basketmaker II sites of the Eastern Anasazi, dated from A.D. 1 to 500, are located in four clusters: the Durango, Colorado area, the Navajo Reservoir district, the Albuquerque area, and the Cimarron Creek area on the east slope of the Sangre de Cristos. The latter two are preceramic. With the exception of the Albuquerque-area sites, all the others are either to the northwest or to the northeast of the upper Rio Grande. In the Cimarron area, a continuous if small so-called Anasazi occupation extends from about A.D. 400 to 1200–1300 (see above; Baugh this volume); after the terminal dates the area was permanently abandoned for the Taos and Picuris locations. Earliest settlements in the Taos area date from A.D. 1000–1200 (Bodine 1979:257), and in the Picuris area to the last half of the twelfth century (Brown 1979:269). There is no question that the Cimarron groups are the ancestors of the Taos and Picuris people. They represent the Tiwa division of the Tanoan language group; today they are identified as Northern Tiwas.

Ford, Schroeder, and Peckham (1972:30) believed that the Tiwas developed *in situ* in the Rio Grande valley, a view contradicted by the new Cimarron evidence. The Tiwa discussion is complicated by the split of the original group into Northern and Southern Tiwas, the latter eventually occupying the Rio Grande valley from just north of Albuquerque south to Socorro. Wetherington (in Ford, Schroeder, and Peckham 1972:30) theorized that the Southern Tiwas moved out of the Taos area around A.D. 1300. It is likely, however, that groups ancestral to the Southern Tiwas passed from the Cimarron south along the eastern slopes of the Sangre de Cristos before settling on the Rio Grande. Two pithouses excavated at Pecos National Monument are associated with the Pedregoso phase of the Cimarron, dated from A.D. 700 to 900 (Baugh this volume). This time frame is close to Schroeder's tentative date for the Tiwa split, sometime before A.D. 1000. In any case, the Tiwa adjustment to the Anasazi tradition occurred *outside* the Rio Grande valley, after their bands arrived from the Northern Plains. Taos tradition states firmly that they had come from the north (Bodine 1979:258). It follows that Basketmaker II sites in the Albuquerque area were neither Tiwa nor belonged to a related Tanoan group; they should, therefore, be considered to have been of Keresan affiliation.

If this were correct, Keresan speakers would have been the only occupants of parts of the upper Rio Grande and two of its western tributaries (Rio Puerco, Rio San Jose) from Basketmaker to Pueblo III times. The latter period, dated to A.D. 1100–1300 (Cordell 1979:137), saw the abandonment of the northern Anasazi region — southern Colorado and northwestern New Mexico — and the removal of Keresan and Tanoan groups from there to the upper Rio Grande and adjacent areas west and east. These events constitute one of the major upheavals and population displacements to occur in the Southwest; they were concurrent with similar events that played on the Western Anasazi (Schroeder this volume). During a span of 150 years, from A.D. 1150 to 1300 (Ford, Schroeder, and Peckham 1972: maps 3–5), Keresan refugees from the north (Mesa Verde) and northwest (Chaco Canyon) moved to the upper Rio San Jose area (Western Keres), and the Rio Puerco and Rio de las Vacas (Eastern Keres), from where eventually some settled on the Rio Grande above Albuquerque. Of refugee Tanoan groups from the upper San Juan, the Tewas occupied the Rio Grande valley above Santa Fe, the related Tanos the upper Galisteo basin, and the Towas the upper Pecos River and the upper Rio de las Vacas are on the south slope of the Jemez Mountains. The Tiwas remained in place; the northern division held out at Taos and Picuris while the southern groups continued to occupy pueblos on the Rio Grande from Albuquerque (Sandia) southward (Isleta, etc.). All these groups were in these locations at the time of the Spanish *entrada* in 1540 led by Coronado (Schroeder 1979:238–39).

The Mogollon peoples of the southeastern part of the larger Southwest, as the Keresans of the Eastern Anasazi, were initially late Archaic populations who adopted horticulture and eventually a relatively sedentary way of life. The appropriate center of the Mogollon cultural distribution was the Rio Grande valley from Socorro in the north to below El Paso. The hearth of Mogollon cultural and economic developments was located in the western section of the Mogollon range, in the mountain country on both sides of the Arizona–New Mexico line. The roots of Mogollon are in the Archaic Cochise culture. Evidence from Tularosa Cave and Bat Cave indicates that the Cochise peoples were harvesting corn and squash by 2000 B.C. (Martin 1979:63; Jennings 1968:251), and pottery was introduced around 300 B.C. Domesticated plants and ceramics diffused into the western Mogollon area from Mexico, and were diffused north from there to the Anasazi (Willey 1966:189) and to groups incorporated in the Mogollon cultural pattern as far east as the Pecos River. By definition, the Mogollon begins when horticulture and ceramics appear side by side (Jennings

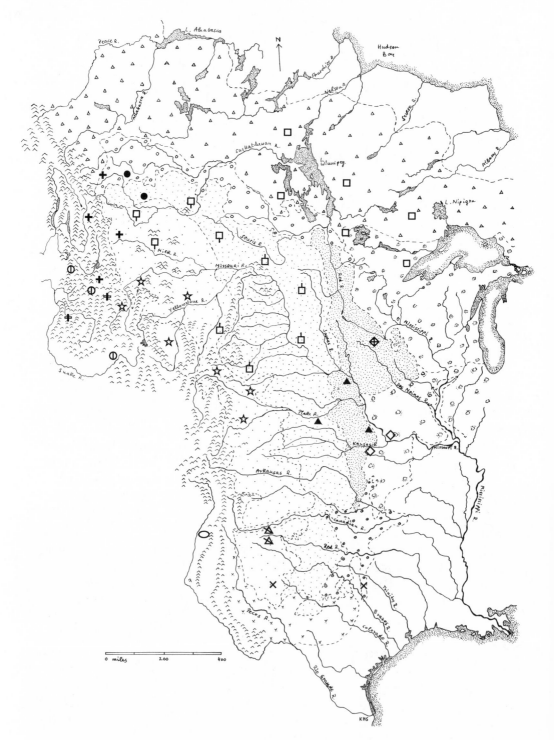

Map 14.1. Archaeological cultures to ethnic groups: the Great Plains and adjacent areas, A.D. 150.

✚ Pelican Lake groups ancestral to
   Kutenai

✚ Pelican Lake–associated Plateau
   groups ancestral to Nez Perce

☆ Pelican Lake groups ancestral to
   Kiowa and Anasazi Tanoans

● Avonlea I, Northern Athapaskans
   ancestral to Sarcee

◑ Avonlea II, Southern Athapaskans
   (Apacheans) ancestral to the
   Fremont cultures and Beehive
   (i.e., Kiowa Apache)

⌶ Western subphase of Besant groups
   ancestral to Blackfeet

⌶ Eastern subphase of Besant groups
   ancestral to Cheyenne

□ Laurel groups of the boreal forest
   and northern Minnesota ancestral
   to Central Algonquians

⊕ Fox Lake Siouan groups ancestral
   to Devil's Lake–Sourisford
   (i.e., the Hidatsa-Crow)

◇ Kansas City Hopewell intrusion,
   probably Siouan

▲ Valley groups ancestral to Loseke,
   Glenwood, and Sterns Creek
   (i.e., the Northern Caddoan Arikara)

◣ Lake Creek and Palo Duro groups
   ancestral to Antelope Creek
   (i.e., the Northern Caddoan Kitsai)

○ Keres

✕ Tonkawa

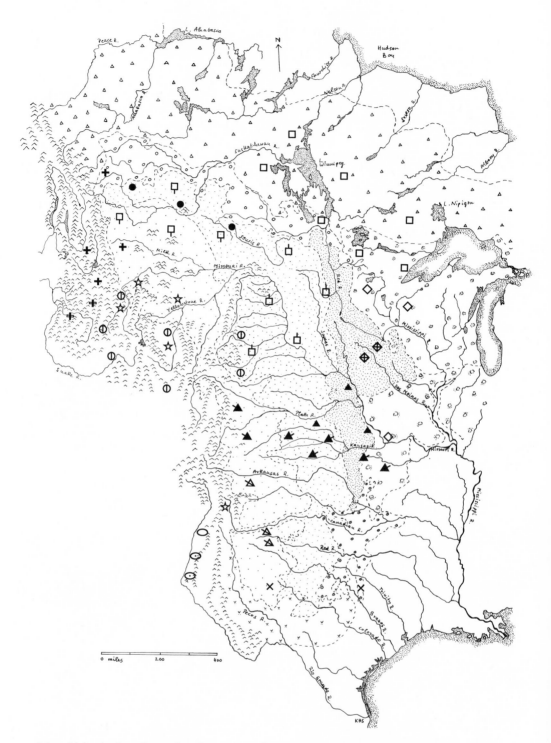

Map 14.2. Archaeological cultures to ethnic groups: the Great Plains and adjacent areas, A.D. 500.

✚ Pelican Lake groups ancestral to Kutenai

✛ Pelican Lake–associated Plateau groups ancestral to Nez Perce

☆ Pelican Lake groups in the Northern Plains ancestral to Kiowa; Tanoan groups on the headwaters of the Canadian River ancestral to the Tiwa divisions of the Anasazi Tanoans

● Avonlea I, Northern Athapaskans ancestral to Sarcee

◐ Avonlea II, Southern Athapaskans (Apacheans) ancestral to the Fremont cultures and Beehive (i.e., Kiowa Apache)

⊓ Western subphase of Besant groups ancestral to Blackfeet

⊔ Eastern subphase of Besant groups ancestral to Cheyenne

□ Laurel groups of the boreal forest and northern Minnesota ancestral to Central Algonquians

◇ Brainerd and St. Croix Siouan groups ancestral to Psinomani (i.e.,Dakota); Kansas City Hopewell intrusion ending

⊕ Fox Lake Siouan groups ancestral to Devil's Lake–Sourisford (i.e., the Hidatsa-Crow)

▲ Valley groups ancestral to Northern Caddoan Loseke, Glenwood and Sterns Creek (i.e., the Arikara)

◤ Parker groups ancestral to Upper Republican (i.e., Northern Caddoan Skiri)

◥ Keith and Greenwood groups ancestral to Northern Caddoan South Band Pawnee

◸ Lake Creek and Palo Duro groups ancestral to Antelope Creek (i.e., the Northern Caddoan Kitsai); Graneros groups, southeastern Colorado, ancestral to Apishapa (i.e., Northern Caddoan Kitsai)

○ Keres Anasazi

⊙ Mogollon

✕ Tonkawa

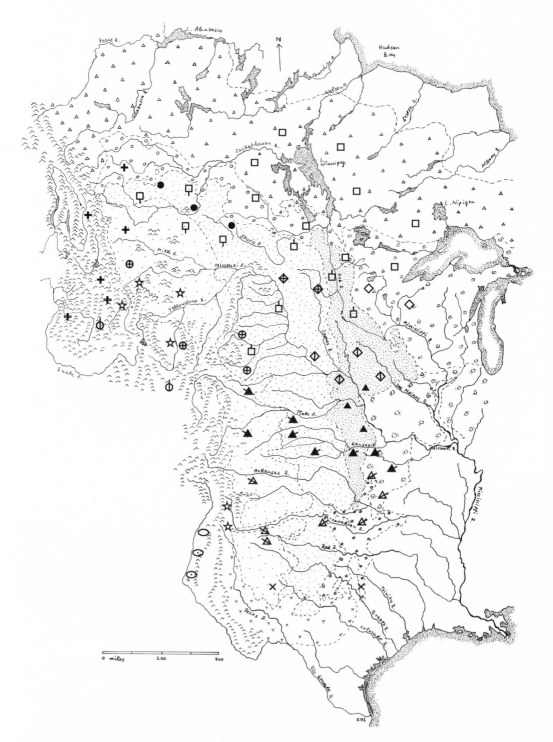

Map 14.3. *Archaeological cultures to ethnic groups: the Great Plains and adjacent areas,* A.D. 850.

✚ Pelican Lake groups ancestral to Kutenai

✛ Pelican Lake–associated Plateau groups ancestral to Nez Perce

☆ Pelican Lake groups in the Northern Plains ancestral to Kiowa; Tanoan groups on the headwaters of the Canadian and Pecos rivers ancestral to the Tiwa divisions of the Anasazi Tanoans

● Avonlea I, Northern Athapaskans ancestral to Sarcee

⊕ Avonlea II, Southern Athapaskans (Apacheans) ancestral to Kiowa Apache

⌽ Avonlea II, Southern Athapaskans (Apacheans) ancestral to the seventeenth–century Dismal River aspect (i.e., Central Plains Apaches)

⊟ Old Women's groups ancestral to Blackfeet

⊟ Eastern subphase of Besant and Arvilla groups (i.e., Cheyenne)

□ Laurel and Blackduck groups of the boreal forest and the parklands ancestral to Central Algonquians

◇ Kathio and Clam River Siouan groups ancestral to Psinomani (i.e., Dakota)

◈ Great Oasis groups ancestral to the Initial Middle Missouri variant (i.e., Mandan)

⊕ Devil's Lake–Sourisford Siouan groups ancestral to Hidatsa-Crow

▲ Loseke, Sterns Creek, and Glenwood groups ancestral to the Nebraska phase and the Coalescent tradition (i.e., the Arikara)

▲ Upper Republican groups ancestral to Itskari (i.e., the Skiri)

▲ Smoky Hill and Greenwood groups ancestral to South Band Pawnee

◺ Cuesta-Cooper groups ancestral to Great Bend (i.e., the Northern Caddoan Tawakoni, Tawehash, Wichita); Custer and Washita River groups, on the lower Canadian River, ancestral to the Edwards and Wheeler complexes (i.e., the Northern Caddoan Yscani)

◿ Graneros groups, southeastern Colorado, ancestral to Apishapa (i.e., the Northern Caddoan Kitsai); Lake Creek and Palo Duro groups ancestral to Antelope Creek (i.e., Kitsai)

◯ Keres Anasazi

◉ Mogollon

✕ Tonkawa

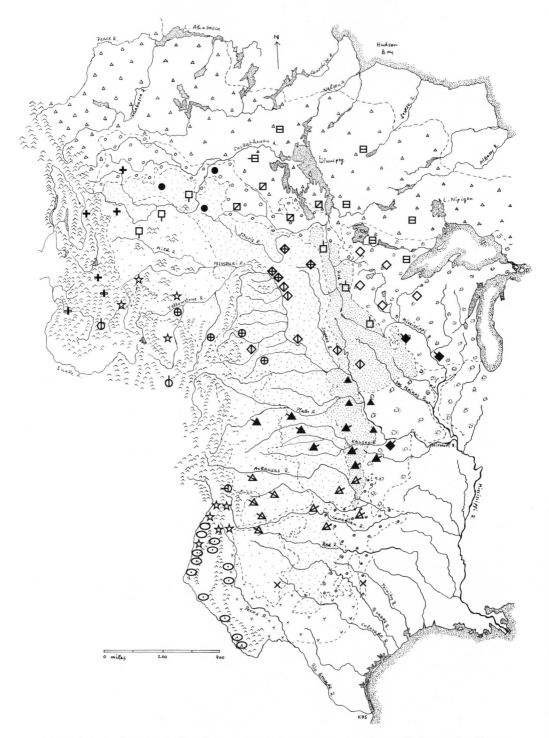

Map 14.4. Archaeological cultures to ethnic groups: the Great Plains and adjacent areas, A.D. *1200.*

✚ Kutenai

✚ Nez Perce

☆ Kiowa in the Northern Plains; Tanoan Anasazi Pueblos on and east of the Rio Grande

● Sarcee

⊕ Kiowa Apache

-⊕ Jicarilla

⬦ Apacheans ancestral to the seventeenth–century Dismal River aspect (i.e., Central Plains Apaches)

⊓ Blackfeet

⊔ Cheyenne

⊟ Cree

-⊟ Plains Cree

⬚ Duck Bay groups ancestral to Atsina, Arapaho, Suhtai

◇ Dakota

◈ Mandan

⬨ Hidatsa-Crow

◗ Oneota groups ancestral to Oto-Iowa

◆ Steed-Kisker groups ancestral to Missouri (?)

▲ Arikara

◤ Skiri

◢ Smoky Hill, Solomon River, and Pomona groups ancestral to South Band Pawnee

△ Bemis Creek and Bluff Creek groups, southern Kansas, ancestral to Tawakoni, Tawehash, Wichita; Custer and Washita River groups, on the lower Canadian River, ancestral to Yscani

◺ Apishapa, Buried City, and Antelope Creek groups (distributed north to south) ancestral to Kitsai

○ Keres Anasazi Pueblos

⊙ Mogollon Pueblos

✕ Tonkawa

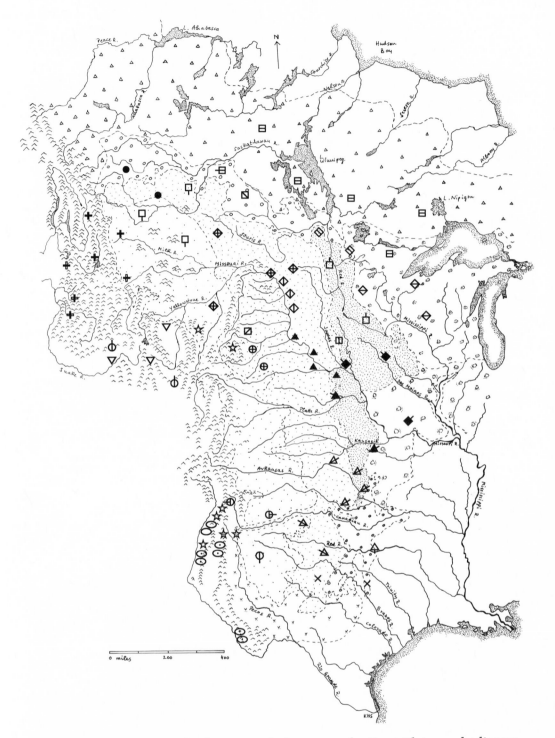

Map 14.5. *Archaeological cultures to ethnic groups: the Great Plains and adjacent areas*, A.D. 1550.

1968:251). For the center of Mogollon developments, in the mountain region astride the Arizona–New Mexico border, the Mogollon base line is dated to 300 B.C. In the center of the Mogollon distribution, on the Rio Grande, called the Jornada subarea, and on its eastern periphery, the adoption of horticulture and ceramics begins at A.D. 300 and later. On the Pecos River, Late Archaic populations made the transition to the Mogollon pattern about A.D. 950 (Baugh this volume). Some Late Archaic groups southeast of present El Paso, in the high country between the Rio Grande and the lower Pecos River, refused the adoption of Mogollon features and remained hunters and gatherers to the historic period; they disappeared as ethnic groups within the first century of Spanish control.

It is an interesting fact that the Mogollon world was expanding when the Anasazi world was shrinking. From A.D. 300 onward, the Jornada Mogollon spread downriver on the Rio Grande from near Socorro toward El Paso (Schroeder this volume), and by 1200 they had reached the La Junta area at the mouth of the Conchos River (Riley 1987:285). At the time of the Anasazi displacement in its northern realm, clusters of Jornada pueblos stood from the Tompiros (east of the Manzano Mountains, southeast of Albuquerque) and Piros (south of the Tiwa towns) in the north all along the Rio Grande to La Junta, a distance of about 450 miles. To the east, the Jornada had colonized the region as far as the middle stretches of the Pecos River. During the last phases of the Jornada on the Pecos (Maljamar, A.D. 1100–1300 and Ochoa, 1300–1450 – Baugh this volume), reliance on bison hunting in the Llano Estacado was significant. This branch of the Jornada came to an end (ca. 1450) with the arrival of the Mescalero Apaches of the Garza complex from the north.

The second major upheaval and population displacement to occur in the Southwest led to the eclipse of the Mogollon as a separate tradition. During merely a half-century, ending around A.D. 1400, most of the Mogollon area was abandoned. Northern Mogollon groups joined in the Zuni area when southern groups withdrew into Chihuahua. All of the Jornada towns between La Junta and the Piros were given up; clusters of Pueblos along a 350-mile stretch along the Rio Grande disappeared. After 1400 the closest Pueblo neighbors of the Jornada settlements of La Junta were the Piros upriver (Riley 1987:285). The Tompiro Pueblos remained in place also. At the same time the Hohokam culture west of the Mogollon collapsed (Schroeder this volume), and the heart of Casas Grandes in northern Chihuahua, the city of Paquimé, a major distribution center of Mexican influences, was violently destroyed in about 1340 (Di Peso 1979:98). It may be significant that the Jornada area on the middle Pecos, on the eastern periphery, was occupied longer than were the central and western Mogollon areas: the Apachean threat out of the southern High Plains developed only after 1450.

At the time of the *entrada* of the Spanish in 1540, the Jornada towns of the La Junta area may have numbered eleven (Riley 1987:295). Numbers of pueblos in the northern area on and near the Rio Grande, according to Schroeder (1979), were approximately the following: Piros (out of a mixed Jornada-Mimbres-Mogollon base) — twelve; Tompiros (out of a Jornada-Anasazi mix) — fifteen to sixteen; Southern Tiwas — sixteen; Northern Tiwas — two; Towas — twelve to fifteen; Tewas — twelve; Tanos — perhaps seven. The Keresan pueblos may have numbered perhaps fourteen.

Looking at the prehistory of the Southwest as an outsider, as a person not committed to any of the schools of thought that abound in Southwestern anthropology, this author believes that the two great upheavals and displacements mentioned are related. They are separated by approximately two hundred years. Some alarming events started at the northern edge of the Southwest and reached the southern part of the region during a second phase. Successively, from north to south, populations with long histories in specific, established areas scurried away, abandoning vast territories and seeking new places in habitats neglected before. It appears that a thrust was delivered at the very center of the Southwest from the north. The Puebloan world was forced to yield space at a time when its populations were increasing at a considerable rate.

There is no consensus among Southwestern prehistorians as to the cause of these displacements although a climatic explanation is generally favored. This author believes that they were caused mainly by the advance south from Utah of Apachean groups who were ancestral to the historic Western Apaches, Chiricahuas, and Navajos. This author (section 3) has identified Fremont as Apachean; it is important that the Sevier and Parowan variants disappeared from their homelands before A.D. 1250. It is proposed here that their move south may have begun about 1150, dispersing Anasazi to the west and southeast, and that the Western Apaches and Chiricahuas reached their historic territories in eastern Arizona and southwestern New Mexico not later than about 1300. The invasion of Mogollon space and the sacking of Casas Grandes do not seem to make any other explanation plausible.

It is a generally accepted theory among Southwestern specialists that the Kachina Cult appeared among the Western and Eastern Anasazi during the thirteenth century A.D. (Schroeder this volume). Usually the ubiquitous drought explanation is proposed, along with a projected "ideological crisis," during the late 1200s, to explain the rise of what is considered to have been a new cult (for instance, McGuire, in Schroeder this volume). It is further believed that the cult derived ultimately from Mesoamerican models (Anderson 1955). In addition, the appearance of the Kachina Cult is often related to architectural features, such as the development of the great kivas of the San Juan, including Chaco Canyon. Its introduction and maintenance may not have been without problems. In the origin myth of Acoma (Stirling 1942:70–75) some people were killed by kachina impersonators in a public spectacle during a specially arranged ceremonial gathering because they had mocked and criticized the kachinas. It is interesting that the symbolic house (*i'chini'*) which represented the Pueblo in this event was built from bison skins (Stirling 1942:71).

This author proposes a different scenario. It is suggested here that the Kachina Cult comprises a mix of four different complexes: one is Tanoan, one Apachean, one derives from a Late Archaic Southwestern base, and one is Mexican. The first three are ancient; the last represents the infusion of Mexican religious concepts during the thirteenth and fourteenth centuries. The first two ultimately originated in the Plains.

Regarding the term "kachina," Bandelier (in Anderson 1955:406) wrote this in 1893:

The origin of the word is found in the Tehua language, where "Ka-tzin-a" signifies the spirits of the fetishes of game. To dance a Katzina was therefore to perform some animal dance with the object of performing an incantation, either for the purposes of the hunt, or for war, or some other work of public utility. The deer dance ... the dance of the mountain sheep, the much discredited snake dance, in fact, all animal dances, are the original Cachinas. But the name was very soon extended to all idolatrous dances in general ... including even the scalp dance.

Rituals concerning game and the masters of game may have existed in the Southwest in Archaic times. Dances, in which masked performers dressed in animal costumes represented one species or a number of species together, appear to this author to have been brought into the Southwest by the Tanoans from whom the concept spread to neighboring groups. Among the Tanoans the Northern Tiwas (Taos, Picuris) have maintained the ancient custom in its purest form.

In the Northern Plains, earth-giving ceremonies, which also were game-calling and game propitiation ceremonies, are old; in these, masked animal impersonators were often important. In the Cheyenne Massaum, initiated between 500 and 300 B.C. (Schlesier 1987), animal lodges and masked performers representing many species were essential elements. The same holds true for the Okipa of the Mandans (Schlesier 1987). An important part of the Kiowa K'ado was the calling of a whole buffalo herd into the ceremonial lodge; impersonators were dressed in buffalo costumes. The Kiowa ceremony has been interpreted as ancient (Schlesier 1990). It is proposed here that the K'ado is an expression of very old Kiowa-Tanoan concepts from which the animal dances of the Northern Tiwas and other Rio Grande Tanoans (e.g., game animal dances, buffalo dance, elk dance, deer dance) derive also. In an interesting detail the Taos deer dance, besides the deer, also featured a whole bison herd. "The Buffalo, up to sixty-nine of them, mill about like a herd of the Great Plains. The Black Eyes hunt, shoot, and carry off animals" (Kurath 1958:447). These elements strike this author as reminiscent of both the Kiowa K'ado and the Cheyenne Massaum ceremonies (Schlesier 1990).

Panels of the Pecked Realistic art of the southern Black Hills, tentatively dated by Sundstrom (1984:68) to "2500 B.C. or later," depict drives of buffalo, elk, deer, and sheep, drive lanes and corrals, one-horned and two-horned drive leaders, or "herders," or game-calling shamans. This rock art is superseded by expressions of five later art styles, the earliest of which is dated to "A.D. 700 or earlier." The time frame and the location may allow the identification of the artists of the Pecked Realistic style as Tanoans of the Pelican Lake phase. It might be worthwhile to compare the Black Hills petroglyphs with the solidly pecked anthropomorphs of the Basketmaker II period near Bloomfield, east of Farmington, New Mexico. These are at the eastern end of Basketmaker anthropomorphs in rock art, in the region that must have been occupied by early Tanoan immigrants. They show the slightly tapered trapezoidal body shape and drooping hands and feet characteristic of Basketmaker figures elsewhere (Schaafsma 1980:117). The headgear is simpler, however, consisting only of horns and antlers (Schaafsma 1980: fig. 80). Nevertheless, the representation indicates that some of the figures wear animal costumes. Considering Bandelier's observation above it is quite possible that stone "fetishes of game" were brought into the Southwest by Tanoans, and were widely adopted by other Puebloan groups. Among the Kiowas, fetishes and figurines played key roles in ceremonies and were contained in sacred bundles kept by ordained keepers (Schlesier 1990).

It seems that principal elements of the iconography of the Black Hills petroglyphs are alive in Tanoan animal dances today. Reduced to its most basic forms, the Picuris deer dance (Brown 1980) consists of these: the deer (masked impersonators) are called from the mountains into the pueblo by two costumed women; they arrive with two "herders" and a bear and a bobcat; the deer dance in two lines led by the women; they are repeatedly struck by bear and bobcat but are healed by the women; after a series of dances accompanied by deer songs, the deer, "herders," bobcat and bear leave, returning to the mountains, the women remaining behind. No kiva is involved. Bear and bobcat obviously are animal helpers of the "herders," who in turn may represent the spirit protectors of the deer, or spirits of regions where the deer live (mountain spirits). Essentially, the deer dance either represents the symbolic impounding of deer in the pueblo, or a visit of the precious Deer People to their human counterparts, during which the appreciation of Picuris is reconfirmed. The invitation call of the women is crucial. These may be the "mothers" of Picuris who become the mothers of the animals who give themselves to human hunters.

Apachean groups are generally perceived by Southwestern specialists to have contributed little or nothing to Puebloan cultures but to
have been much influenced by them. This perception is based on the
assumption that Apacheans came into the Southwest late, after the
Puebloans had reached their classical period. If the Fremont cultures
were considered Apachean, and if a thirteenth- to fourteenth-century
entry of Western Apache and Chiricahua groups via southern Utah
were regarded as probable, the history of Southwestern ceremonialism
would have to be rewritten.

The hallmark of Fremont Apachean art everywhere is a broad-
shouldered human figure in ceremonial regalia (Schaafsma 1980:163–
81). It usually has a tapering torso, horns, or an elaborate headgear. The
bodies show costumes, ornaments, and necklaces. Some may represent
crown dancers (mountain spirits). Many hold shields; some wear masks.
Often the anthropomorphs are accompanied by animals, including
bison, bear, deer, elk, snakes, and lizards. Bear tracks and spirals appear
also. Often shield bearers and single shields are depicted. Hunting
scenes occur also; in these the animals surround antlered or horned
anthropomorphs. Sometimes the weeping eye motif appears. Actual
masks have been found in Uinta Fremont sites in Dinosaur National
Monument (Schaafsma 1980:175).

It is generally agreed that the Fremont cultural tradition is separate
from Anasazi tradition. To this author it already expresses the essential characteristics of the later Apache and Navajo ceremonial systems.
The figures of its art represent the holy people, mountain spirits, game
masters, shamans, and perhaps myths of origins and special events of
culture history. Some important religious ideas that originated with
the Apacheans were adopted by the Anasazi. One is the Fremont shield
and shield bearer, which is a hallmark of Fremont but appears in
Anasazi art late, in late Pueblo II and early Pueblo III times (Schaafsma
1980:171). One might wonder if the shield dances of the modern
Pueblos were thus initiated. The Jemez ceremony, however, is called
the Kiowa shield dance (Roberts 1980:113). The Kiowa shield complex
as probably derived from Apachean sources has already been discussed
(section 3). Another Apache concept is the flute player. Flute players,
both upright and reclining, appear in the rock art of the Fremont Uinta
variant (Schaafsma 1980:176) earlier than in Anasazi art; the terminal
date for Uinta is 950 A.D. (section 3). In sacred San Carlos and White
Mountain Apache stories (Goddard 1918:20, 1919:114), the flute serves
Naienezgani, the mysterious hero and son of the Sun, as magical flight
vehicle; when he plays it the flute wings him quickly any distance. In
Anasazi art he becomes Kokopelli, the hump-backed player; here his
first appearance is clearly dated later, to after A.D. 1000.

Another concept that originated with Apacheans is the clown who
achieved such an important position in Pueblo religion. The clown is

equally important in Apachean religion and seems to derive from the contrary idea and system of the Northern Plains. Contraries who were sacred clowns played central roles in Algonquian, Siouan, and Athapaskan ceremonies, and in religious and social life outside and beyond ceremonies (Schlesier 1987). Battey (1968:128–29) attended a Kiowa Apache "medicine dance" in 1873 in the Plains, and wrote:

All the performers, except two young women, wore hideous masks, some with distorted noses, grotesquely painted, and fantastically dressed, with feathers attached to their legs, arms, backs, and headdresses. The latter consisted of light wooden frames. Small bells were attached to their legs. . . . There were three sets who took part in the dance, one of which represented old, decrepit people apparently bent with age, and half starved, dressed in buckskins and rags, bearing masks of some white material over the face, with noses out of all proportion, and ears standing out several inches from the head; one of the women carrying an infant similarly masked.

This Kiowa Apache dance should be considered as ancient; it is clearly related to Navajo and Apache ceremonies, some of which are still held today.

Stone fetishes, figurines, and sacred bundle containers may have originated with both Tanoans and Apacheans in the Northern Plains, or perhaps Apacheans adopted the trait from Tanoans there. Matched male and female pairs of clay figurines such as those of the San Rafael Fremont variant (section 3) appear to have been models for later Anasazi forms but continue without a break in Navajo tradition.

In the nine-night Navajo Shootingway ceremony (McAllester 1980), Holy Young Man is attacked by the Thunder People and carried into the sky. The Sun befriends him, and gives him sky powers and four sacred arrows. All the Holy People come to the Sun's house where Holy Young Man receives their songs and power. Later, when traveling among the Buffalo People, he uses his sacred arrows on them but brings the dead back to life. He has a child with his buffalo wife. This sounds Northern Plains to this author. Said one of the Navajo singers to McAllester (1980:235) about the Shootingway: "There were two high points in the ceremony: the second sandpainting [the double sandpainting of Holy Young Man] and the White Buffalo sandpainting. These two are the most sacred to make, even though other sandpaintings like Monster Slayer, or Earth and Sky seem as though they ought to be more sacred. But these two are the ones—I don't know why that is."

It is interesting that the Navajos share with the Skiris one specific trait: the depiction of constellations important to their religion. While those of the latter were painted on hide (Chamberlain 1982: fig. 47), those of the Navajos are painted on the underside of overhangs and rockshelter ceilings. One Navajo informant knew about the existence of thirty-two (Schaafsma 1980:322). Most impressive, because of their virtually inaccessible locations high above the ground floors, are those in Canyon de Chelly. Schaafsma (1980:324) believes that in these planetaria are preserved the forms and the symbolic content that preceded the modern sandpaintings which may have replaced the rock art of the past.

Mexican influences on the Kachina Cult are documented by Schaafsma (1980:191–242) as they find expression in Mimbres and Jornada art. The Late Archaic–Basketmaker base of the Kachina Cult is partly represented by the San Juan Anthropomorphic Style (See Schaafsma 1980:108–20). Neither complex is discussed here because they are not affiliated with the Plains.

In the Kiowa origin stories of the Half-Boys, a Kiowa girl was taken to the sky and married the son of the Sun, with whom she had a son. Later, after she had fled back to earth, and died in the attempt, her son threw a gaming wheel against the sky. It was turned back and cut him in half. Thus he became twins, the Half-Boys, monster slayers who made the world safe for the Kiowas. After many adventures, one of the twins walked into a lake where he lives with the female Earth spirit; the other gave up his body to ten medicine bundles. This author believes that the now extinct Kiowa K'ado ceremony (Schlesier 1990) commemorated the return of the twin from the lake, and that he resided during the ceremony in the Taime doll. In the K'ado, for the time of the ceremony, both twins were reunited and became one person once more.

The Rio Grande Tanoans share the Kiowa story of the powerful boy. Here he is called Poseyemu; he is the son of the Sun, miraculously born to a poor girl. His name translates as "falling mist," or "dew falling" (Parmentier 1979:611). There is an etymological connection between his name and the ritual term for scalps, "little mists." In some Tewa stories he is associated with hunting and ritual knowledge. In other stories he was the first one outside at emergence, the place of emergence being at the center of the universe, where the house of the Sun and Earth spirit is, whence the dead return. Sometimes he is identified with World Man, who lives at the lake of emergence. Other stories tell that Poseyemu taught the people to hunt big animals, that the buffalo would satisfy their needs, and how to kill them. Before he departed, he taught the buffalo dance (Parmentier 1979:612). He is the mediator between heaven and earth. During the time of Spanish oppression, Tanoan myths explain how Poseyemu defended the Indian people against Jesus and claimed them as his charges (Parmentier 1979:614).

The Apacheans also share the story of the miraculous boy. Among Chiricahuas and Mescaleros he is called Child of the Water; his mother, White Painted Woman, was made pregnant through water by the Sun. Among some Western Apaches (San Carlos) he is Naienezgani, his father the Sun, and his mother, Changing Woman. Among other Western Apaches, Changing Woman gave birth to twins, one the son of the

Sun, the other the son of Black Water. The oldest twin, Slayer of Monsters, is the most important one. For the Jicarillas he is *ha'scin*, born in the underworld, and he made animals, birds, and First Man and First Woman. The first humans were descendants of these two before the emergence journey of the people to reach the earth's surface. In most Navajo stories the twins, Monster Slayer and Child of the Water, are the Sun's sons born to Changing Woman; in some stories the first is born to Changing Woman, the second to White Shell Woman. All of these Apachean heroes, as Poseyemu, are not the original creators but powerful inventors, lawmakers, and guardians who once purified the world and watch over it.

Among non-Tanoan Pueblo groups the central figure of the Sun Youth and culture hero is not as definite and comprehensive as among Tanoans and Apacheans. In Keres mythology the figure is split into two persons, the Christ-like Boshayanyi, and Sun Youth, both occurring in many myths. In Zuni, Poshayanki is the mediator between Sun-Father and humans, the leader at emergence. His double is Payatamu, who teaches corn rituals (Parmentier 1979:615). The tendency among non-Tanoan Pueblo groups to double, or to develop two aspects of one person into two persons, is further expressed in the concept of the Twin War Gods (Hopi, Zuni, Keres). These twins are either the sons of the Sun or the sons of the son of the Sun. They share characteristics of the single culture hero but are not prophets, as he was; they become ordinary humans after their exploits.

It is proposed here that Kiowa-Tanoans *and* Apacheans brought the original version of the story of the miraculous boy into the Southwest where it was adopted, embellished, and altered by Hopi, Zuni, and Keres ritualists. Because this figure is essentially absent among Northern Athapaskans, it may be concluded that it represents a fusion of Tanoan and Athapaskan — and, perhaps, Algonquian — philosophical concerns, and that its place of emergence was in the Plains where these linguistic groups had been in contact with each other (Schlesier 1990) for a considerable time.

THE CONTRIBUTORS

TIMOTHY G. BAUGH is an archaeologist with Western Cultural Resource Management. He received his doctorate in anthropology from the University of Oklahoma in 1978. In addition to serving as a research archaeologist for the Oklahoma Archeological Survey, Kansas State Historical Society, and Smithsonian Institution, he has taught at the University of Colorado and Eastern New Mexico University. He also has held a postdoctoral fellowship in remote sensing and archaeology at Boston University. His research has focused on late prehistoric to protohistoric economic structure and organization, and to this end he has conducted fieldwork in the Plains and Southwest.

PHILIP DUKE is an Associate Professor of Anthropology at Fort Lewis College, Durango, and a Fellow of the Society of Antiquaries. His research interests lie in postprocessual approaches to the past, especially their application to hunting-and-gathering societies of the western plains and mountains.

JEFFREY L. EIGHMY is currently professor of anthropology at Colorado State University where he has been teaching and conducting research since 1977. He received his B.A. from the University of Oklahoma and his M.A. and Ph.D. degrees from the University of Arizona. For the past fifteen years his research activity has been mostly in the area of archaeomagnetic dating. A sumary of his research on archaeomagnetic dating on the Great Plains has recently been published in the *Plains Anthropologist*.

GUY GIBBON received a B.S., M.S., and Ph.D. from the University of Wisconsin–Madison, and has taught at the universities of Illinois, Wisconsin–Milwaukee, and Minnesota, where he is currently a professor in the Department of Anthropology, director of an interdisciplinary graduate program in archaeology, and curator of the Wilford Laboratory of Archaeology. He continues to combine an interest in the social context and rhetorical justification of theoretical research programs in archaeology with an active program in midwestern prehistoric and historic archaeology.

SALLY T. GREISER is a senior archaeologist with Historical Research Associates in Missoula, Montana. She obtained her Ph.D. from the University of Colorado in 1980. Her main interests are the protohistoric and early historic periods in the Northwestern Plains and the Southwest, in addition to sacred geography of indigenous peoples.

MICHAEL L. GREGG received his Ph.D. in anthropology from the University of Wisconsin–Milwaukee in 1975. He has done contract archaeology since then, first with the Great Lakes Archaeological Research Center in Wisconsin, then with the Montana College of Mineral Science and Technology in Butte, Montana. For the past fourteen years, he has been at the University of North Dakota. He has worked on population estimates for the prehistoric Cahokia urban center, the appearance of Early Woodland cultures in the Northeastern Plains, and the evolution of Plains Village lifeways in the Northeastern Plains.

SCOTT HAMILTON is an Assistant Professor in the Department of Anthropology at Lakehead University in Thunder Bay, Ontario. He received his M.A. in 1985 from the University of Alberta and his Ph.D. in 1990 from Simon Fraser University. His research interests include the northwestern Canadian fur trade, and the archaeology of the Northern Plains and boreal forest. He also directs the Centre for Archaeological Resource Prediction, which is developing GIS-based heritage resource modeling and management techniques. Recent publications include "Western Canadian Fur Trade History and Archaeology: The Illumination of the Invisible in Fur Trade Society" and "Over-Hunting and Local Extinctions: Socio-Economic Implications of Fur Trade Subsistence."

L. ADRIEN HANNUS is Director of the Archeology Laboratory and Associate Professor of Anthropology at Augustana College. His Ph.D. in anthropology was granted by the University of Utah in 1985. Hannus served as president of the Plains Anthropological Society in 1992 and currently serves as editor of *South Dakota Archaeology* and president of the Council of South Dakota Archaeologists. His research interests include early man in the New World; communal land mammal hunting and butchering; and man and culture in the Pleistocene. His recent publications include "Flaked Mammoth Bone from the Lange/Ferguson Site, White River Badlands Area, South Dakota" in *Bone Modification* (1989) and "Mammoth Hunting in the New World" in *Hunters of the Recent Past* (1990).

EDWARD J. LUECK is Research Archaeologist for the Archaeology Laboratory, Augustana College. He received M.A. and B.A. degrees in anthropology with an emphasis on archaeology at the University of Nebraska–Lincoln in 1984 and 1976, respectively. He has participated in archaeological projects in Nebraska, Iowa, Minnesota, Wisconsin, Illinois, North Dakota, and South Dakota. His professional interests include Cultural Resource Management, mortuary practices, sociocultural collapse, and historic/economic trade patterns on the Plains.

DAVID MEYER is Associate Professor in the Department of Anthropology and Archaeology at the University of Saskatchewan. He received his M.A. in 1971 from the University of Manitoba and his Ph.D. in 1982 from McMaster University. His research interests include the archaeology and ethnography of the Canadian boreal forest and the archaeology of the Northern Plains. From 1976 to 1988 he was a consulting archaeologist on staff with the Saskatchewan Research Council. His recent publications include "North-South Interaction in the Late Prehistory of Central Saskatchewan" and "The Quest for Pasquatinow: An Aboriginal Gathering Centre in the Saskatchewan River Valley."

PATRICIA J. O'BRIEN is Distinguished Professor of Anthropology at Kansas State University and past editor of the *Plains Anthropologist* (1989–92). She received her Ph.D. in anthropology from the University of Illinois–Urbana in 1969. She is the author of many articles on the archaeology of Kansas, Missouri, and Illinois, including *Archaeology in Kansas* (1984). With James A. Brown she is the editor of *At the Edge of Prehistory: Huber Phase Archaeology in the Chicago Area* (1990).

KARL H. SCHLESIER, Professor Emeritus of Anthropology at Wichita State University, retired to Corrales, New Mexico, in 1992. He was educated at the universities of Bonn and Chicago. His research interests include the prehistory and ethnology of the Great Plains, Siberia, and the Magdalenian III–IV period of the east central Pyrenees.

He has published a number of books and many articles in professional journals. In 1980 he served on the Jury of the Fourth Russell Tribunal on the Rights of the Indians of the Americas. He is involved in a continuing action project, begun in 1969, with traditional Cheyenne leaders in Oklahoma.

ALBERT H. SCHROEDER retired from the National Park Service in 1976 after thirty years working primarily as an archaeologist. He served as a southwestern field and interpretive archaeologist with a special interest in linking late prehistoric and early historic period cultures. He has written a number of books and has contributed frequently to numerous scholarly journals on the subjects of archaeological, ethnological, and historical cultures relating primarily to the American Indians of the Southwest. He served on the boards of the Archaeological Society of New Mexico and the Historical Society of New Mexico until his death in late 1993.

SUSAN C. VEHIK is an Associate Professor of Anthropology at the University of Oklahoma. Her main research interests are Plains archaeology, resource procurement and distribution, and the prehistoric to historic transition. Her most recent publication is "Wichita Culture History" in *Plains Anthropologist* (1992).

J. RODERICK VICKERS is currently Plains Archaeologist with the Archaeological Survey, Provincial Museum of Alberta, Canada. He received a B.A. from McMaster University, and an M.A. from the University of Calgary. As part of the Archaeological Survey's "First Albertans Project," Vickers is involved with research at the Fletcher Site, a Cody Complex bison kill. Recent publications include "Seasonal Round Problems on the Alberta Plains" (1991) and, with A.B. Beaudoin, "A Limiting AMS Date for the Cody Complex Occupation at the Fletcher Site, Alberta, Canada" (1989).

MICHAEL CLAYTON WILSON is a consultant in archaeology, environmental sciences, and forensics. He is also Adjunct Associate Professor in the Department of Archaeology, University of Calgary, Alberta. In 1992 he completed a five-year appointment as a Canada Research Fellow in the Department of Geography, University of Lethbridge, Alberta. He then taught for a semester as Visiting Professor at Hokkaigakuen University in Sapporo, Japan. He is known to Plains archaeologists for studies of bison kill sites and postglacial bison evolution. Other research interests include Native-white Contact; arid-lands geoarchaeology; and ethnoarchaeology, particularly as regards the households of nomadic peoples. He has conducted field studies in the Plains and Plateau of North America, the Sahel of West Africa, the loess plateau of northwest China, and the northern Tibetan plateau.

R. PETER WINHAM is Assistant Director of the Archaeology Laboratory at Augustana College. He received M. Phil and B.A. (Hons) degrees in archaeology at the University of Southampton, England, in 1980 and 1975, respectively. Winham has worked on the Great Plains since 1980 and has participated in numerous projects across this region, with particular emphasis on the Missouri Trench in North and South Dakota.

BIBLIOGRAPHY

Adair, Mary J.
1981   "The Two Deer Site (14BU55): A Plains Woodland–Plains Village Transition." In *Prehistory and History of the El Dorado Lake Area, Kansas (Phase II)*, edited by M. J. Adair, pp. 237–356. Report submitted to the U.S. Army Corps of Engineers, Tulsa District.
1988   *Prehistoric Agriculture in the Central Plains.* Publications in Anthropology no. 16. University of Kansas, Lawrence.

Adams, Gary F.
1977   *The Estuary Bison Pound Site in Southwestern Saskatchewan.* Archaeological Survey of Canada Paper 68. National Museum of Man Mercury Series, Ottawa.

Ahler, Stanley A., C. H. Lee, and C. R. Falk
1981   *Cross Ranch Archaeology: Test Excavations at Eight Sites in the Breaks Zone, 1980–81 Program.* Department of Anthropology and Archaeology, University of North Dakota, Grand Forks.

Ahler, Stanley A., Thomas D. Theissen, and Michael K. Trimble
1991   *People of the Willows: The Prehistory and Early History of the Hidatsa Indians.* University of North Dakota Press, Grand Forks.

Ahler, Stanley A., and Dennis L. Toom (eds.)
1989   *Archaeology of the Medicine Crow Site Complex (39BF2), Buffalo County, South Dakota.* Illinois State Museum Society, Springfield. Submitted to Branch of Interagency Archaeological Services, U.S. National Park Service, Denver, Colo., Contract no. CX 1200-6-3547.

Ahler, Stanley A., and Julieann VanNest
1985   "Temporal Change in Knife River Flint Reduction Strategies." In *Lithic Resource Procurement: Proceedings from the Second Conference on Prehistoric Chert Exploitation*, edited by Susan C. Vehik, pp. 183–98. Center for Archaeological Investigations, Occasional Paper no. 4. Southern Illinois University, Carbondale.

Ahler, Stanley A., and T. Weston
1981   *Test Excavations at the Lower Hidatsa Village (32ME10), Knife River Indian Villages National Historic Site.* Report Submitted to the Midwest Archaeological Center, National Park Service, Lincoln.

Aikens, Melvin C.
1966   *Fremont-Promontory-Plains Relationship, including a Report of Excavations at the Injun Creek and Bear River Number 1 Sites, Northern Utah.* University of Utah Anthropological Papers 82, Salt Lake City.

1967   "Plains Relationship of the Fremont Culture: A Hypothesis." *American Antiquity* 32:198–209.

Alex, Lynn M.
1980   *Exploring Iowa's Past.* University of Iowa Press, Iowa City.

Alex, Robert
1981a "Villages off the Missouri River." In *The Future of South Dakota's Past*, edited by L. J. Zimmerman and L. C. Stewart, pp. 39–46. South Dakota Archaeological Society Special Publication 2.
1981b "The Village Cultures of the Lower James River Valley, South Dakota." Ph.D. dissertation, Department of Anthropology, University of Wisconsin, Madison.

Allen, J. A.
1877   *History of the American Bison,* bison americanus. United States Geological and Geographical Survey of the Territories, *Annual Report* 9, part 3, pp. 443–588. Washington, D.C.

Allen, J. W.
1973   *The Pueblo Alamo Project.* Museum of New Mexico Laboratory of Anthropology Notes no. 86, Santa Fe.

Anderson, Duane C.
1969   "Mill Creek Culture: A Review." *Plains Anthropologist* 14:137–43.
1975   *Western Iowa Prehistory.* Iowa State University Press, Ames.
1981a *Mill Creek Ceramics: The Complex from the Brewster Site.* Report 14. Office of the State Archaeologist, University of Iowa, Iowa City.
1981b *Eastern Iowa Prehistory.* Iowa State University Press, Ames.
1987   "Toward a Processual Understanding of the Initial Variant of the Middle Missouri Tradition: The Case of the Mill Creek Culture of Iowa." *American Antiquity* 52:522–37.

Anderson, Duane C., and Joseph A. Tiffany
1987   "A Caddoan Trade Vessel from Northwestern Iowa." *Plains Anthropologist* 32:93–96.

Anderson, Duane C., Joseph A. Tiffany, and Fred W. Nelson
1986   "Recent Research on Obsidian from Iowa Archaeological Sites." *American Antiquity* 51:837–52.

Anderson, Frank G.
1955   "The Pueblo Kachina Cult: A Historical Reconstruction." *Southwestern Journal of Anthropology* 11:404–19.

Anfinson, Scott F. (ed.)
1979a *A Handbook of Minnesota Prehistoric Ceramics.* Occasional Papers in Minnesota Anthropology no. 5. Minnesota Archaeological Society, Fort Snelling.
1979b "Effigy Mound Phase." In *Handbook of Minnesota Prehistoric Ceramics*, edited by S. F. Anfinson, pp. 73–78. Occasional Publications in Minnesota Anthropology no. 5. Minnesota Archaeological Society, Fort Snelling.

Anfinson, Scott F.
1982   "The Prehistoric Archaeology of the Prairie Lake Region: A Summary from a Minnesota Perspective." *Journal of the North Dakota Archaeological Association* 1:65–90.

1987   "The Prehistory of the Prairie Lake Region in the Northeastern Plains."
        Ph.D. dissertation, Department of Anthropology, University of Min-
        nesota, Minneapolis.
1990   "Archaeological Regions in Minnesota and the Woodland Period." In
        The Woodland Tradition in the Western Great Lakes, edited by Guy E.
        Gibbon, pp. 135–66. Publications in Anthropology 4. University of
        Minnesota, Minneapolis.
Anfinson, Scott F., M. G. Michlovic, and J. Stein
1978   *The Lake Bronson Site (32KT1): A Multi-component Prehistoric Site
        on the Prairie-woodland Border in Northwestern Minnesota.* Occa-
        sional Publications in Minnesota Anthropology no. 3. Minnesota
        Archaeological Society, St. Paul.
Anfinson, Scott F., and Herbert E. Wright, Jr.
1990   "Climatic Change and Culture in Prehistoric Minnesota." In *The
        Woodland Tradition in the Western Great Lakes*, edited by Guy E.
        Gibbon, pp. 213–32. Publications in Anthropology 4. University of
        Minnesota, Minneapolis.
Anonymous
1909   "Arikara Creation Myth." *Journal of American Folklore* 22(83): 90–92.
Arthur, George W.
1966   *An Archaeological Survey of the Upper Yellowstone River Drainage,
        Montana.* Agricultural Economics Research Report no. 26, Montana
        State University, Bozeman.
1975   *An Introduction to the Ecology of Early Historic Communal Bison
        Hunting Among the Northern Plains Indians.* Archaeological Survey of
        Canada Paper 37. National Museum of Man Mercury Series, Ottawa.
Arthurs, David
1978   "Sandy Lake Ware in Northwestern Ontario: A Distributional Study.
        Archae-Facts 5(2–3): 57–64.
1986   *Archaeological Investigations at the Long Sault Site (Manitou Mounds).*
        Northwestern Region Conservation Archaeology Report no. 7. On-
        tario Ministry of Citizenship and Culture, Toronto.
Ashworth, A. C., and A. M. Cvancara
1983   "Paleoecology of the Southern Part of the Lake Agassiz Basin." In
        Glacial Lake Agassiz, edited by J. T. Teller and L. Clayton, pp. 133–56.
        Geological Society of Canada, St. Johns.
Badertscher, P. M., L. J. Roberts, and S. L. Zoltai
1987   *Hill of the Buffalo Chase: 1982 Excavations at the Stott Site, D1Ma-1.*
        Papers in Manitoba Archaeology, Final Report no. 18. Department of
        Cultural Affairs and Historical Resources, Winnipeg.
Baerreis, David A.
1939a   "A Hopewell Site in Northeastern Oklahoma." *Society for American
        Archaeology Notebook*, vol. 1, pp. 72–78.
1939b   "Two New Cultures in Delaware County, Oklahoma." *The Oklahoma
        Prehistorian* 2(1): 2–5.
Baerreis, David A., and Reid A. Bryson
1965   "Climatic Episodes and the Dating of Mississippian Cultures." *The
        Wisconsin Archaeologist* 46:203–20.

Baker, Galen
1964   "The Archaeology of the Park Plateau in Southeastern Colorado."
       Southwestern Lore 30:1–18.

Bamforth, Douglas B.
1987   "The Numic Contraction: Great Basin Social Organization on the
       Great Plains." Paper presented at the Forty-fifth Annual Plains An-
       thropological Conference, Columbia, Mo.

Banks, Larry D.
1990   "From Mountain Peaks to Alligator Stomachs: A Review of Lithic
       Sources in the Trans-Mississippi South, the Southern Plains, and
       Adjacent Southwest." *Oklahoma Anthropological Society Memoir*
       no. 4.

Barnhardt, Michael L., David C. Dycus, Edward B. Jelks, Frederick W. Lange,
Floyd R. Mansberger, Joseph S. Phillippe, and Frederick S. Thomas
1983   "Preliminary Cultural Resource Survey and Geomorphological As-
       sessment of Selected Areas in Navigation Pool 16, Mississippi River."
       The Wisconsin Archaeologist 64:9–110.

Barry, P. S.
1991   *Mystical Themes in Milk River Rock Art.* University of Alberta Press,
       Edmonton.

Battey, Thomas C.
1968   *The Life and Adventures of a Quaker Among the Indians.* University
       of Oklahoma Press, Norman.

Baugh, S. T.
1986   "Late Prehistoric Bison Distributions in Oklahoma." In *Current Trends
       in Southern Plains Archaeology,* edited by T. G. Baugh, pp. 83–96.
       Plains Anthropologist Memoir 21.

Baugh, T. G.
1982   *Edwards I (34BK2): Southern Plains Adaptations in Protohistoric
       Period.* Studies in Oklahoma's Past, no. 8, Oklahoma Archaeological
       Survey, Norman.
1984a "Southern Plains Societies and Eastern Frontier Exchange During the
       Protohistoric Period." In *Collected Papers in Honor of Harry L. Had-
       lock,* edited by Nancy Fox, Papers of the Archaeological Society of
       New Mexico no. 9, pp. 157–67. Albuquerque Archaeological Society
       Press.
1984b *Archaeology of the Mixed Grass Prairie. Phase I: Quartermaster
       Creek.* Archaeological Resource Survey Report no. 20. Oklahoma
       Archaeological Survey, Norman.
1986   "Ecology and Exchange: The Dynamics of Plains/Pueblo Interaction."
       In *Farmers, Hunters, and Colonists: Interaction between the South-
       west and Southern Plains,* edited by Katherine A. Spielmann. Univer-
       sity of Arizona Press, Tucson.
1992a "Protohistoric Cultural Manifestations on the Southern Plains: A
       Reconsideration of the Wheeler Phase and Garza Complex." In *Cultur-
       al Encounters and Episodic Droughts: The Protohistoric Period in the
       Southern Plains,* edited by Eileen Johnson, pp. 21–39. Lubbock Lake
       Landmark Quaternary Research Center Series, no. 3. Lubbock.

1992b "The Bridwell site: A Protohistoric Community in the Texas South Plains." In *Cultural Encounters and Episodic Droughts: The Protohistoric Period in the Southern Plains*, edited by Eileen Johnson, pp. 41–42. Lubbock Lake Landmark Quaternary Research Center Series, no. 3. Lubbock.

Baugh, T. G., and F. W. Eddy
1987 "Rethinking Apachean Ceramics: The 1985 Southern Athapaskan Ceramics Conference." *American Antiquity* 52(4): 793–98.

Baugh, T. G., S. Karhu, S. Boerlin, and K. Googins
1986 "University of Colorado Fieldwork at the Triple J (5LA5833) Site, Las Animas County, Colorado." Paper presented at the Forty-fourth Annual Plains Anthropological Conference, Denver, Colo.

Baugh, Timothy G., and Fred W. Nelson, Jr.
1986 "Obsidian Studies at Landergrin Mesa (41QL2), Texas." Ms. on file, Texas State Archeologist's Office, Austin.
1987 "New Mexico Obsidian Sources and Exchange on the Southern Plains." *Journal of Field Archaeology* 14(3): 313–29.
1988 "Archaeological Obsidian Recovered from Selected North Dakota Sites and Its Relationship to Changing Exchange Systems in the Plains." *Journal of the North Dakota Archaeological Association* 3:74–94.
1991 "Ecology and Exchange: The Dynamics of Plains-Pueblo Interaction." In *Farmers, Hunters, and Colonists: Interaction Between the Southwest and the Southern Plains*, edited by Katherine A. Spielmann, pp. 107–27. University of Arizona Press, Tucson.

Beckes, Michael R., and James D. Keyser
1983 *The Prehistory of the Custer National Forest: An Overview.* U.S. Department of Agriculture, Forest Service, Billings, Mont.

Beckett, P. H.
1979 "Hueco phase: Fact or Fiction?" In *Jornada Mogollon Archaeology: Proceedings of the First Jornada Conference*, edited by P. H. Beckett and R. N. Wisemann, pp. 223–25. New Mexico State University, Las Cruces.

Bell, Earl H.
1936 *Chapters in Nebraska Archaeology.* University of Nebraska, Lincoln.

Bell, E. H., and R. E. Cape
1936 *The Rock Shelters of Western Nebraska in the Vicinity of Dalton, Nebraska.* Chapters in Nebraska Archaeology, vol. 1. University of Nebraska Press, Lincoln.

Bell, Earl H., and G. H. Gilmore
1936 "The Nehawka and Table Rock Foci of the Nebraska Aspect." In *Chapters in Nebraska Archaeology*, edited by E. H. Bell, pp. 301–56. University of Nebraska, Lincoln.

Bell, R. E.
1973 "The Washita River Focus of the Southern Plains." In *Variation in Anthropology, Essays in Honor of John C. McGregor*, edited by D. W. Lathrap and J. Douglas, pp. 171–87. Illinois Archaeological Survey, Urbana.

1983   "Reflections on Southern and Central Plains Pre-history." In *Prairie Archaeology: Papers in Honor of David A. Baerreis,* edited by G. E. Gibbon, pp. 1–13. Publications in Anthropology no. 3. University of Minnesota, Minneapolis.

1984   "Arkansas Valley Caddoan: The Harlan Phase." In *Prehistory of Oklahoma,* edited by R. E. Bell, pp. 221–40. Academic Press, Orlando.

Bell, R. E., and D. A. Baerreis
1951   *A Survey of Oklahoma Archaeology.* Bulletin of the Texas Archaeological and Paleontological Society 22:7–100.

Bell, R. E., and T. Bastian
1967   "Preliminary Report upon Excavations at the Longest Site, Oklahoma." In *A Pilot Study of Wichita Indian Archaeology and Ethnohistory,* assembled by R. E. Bell, E. B. Jelks, and W. W. Newcomb, pp. 54–118. Final Report to National Science Foundation.

Bell, Patricia
1976   "Spatial and Temporal Variability within the Trowbridge Site, A Kansas City Hopewell Village." In *Hopewellian Archaeology in the Lower Missouri River Valley,* edited by A. E. Johnson, pp. 16–58. Publications in Anthropology no. 8. University of Kansas, Lawrence.

Bender, Barbara
1979   "Gatherer-Hunter to Farmer: A Social Perspective." *World Archaeology* 10:204–22.

1985   "Emergent Tribal Formations in the American Midcontinent." *American Antiquity* 50:52–62.

Benedict, James B., and Byron L. Olson
1973   "Origin of the McKean Complex: Evidence from Timberline." *Plains Anthropologist* 18:323–27.

Benn, D. W.
1974   "Seed Analysis and its Implications for an Initial Middle Missouri Site in South Dakota." *Plains Anthropologist* 19(63): 55–72.

1978   "Woodland Ceramic Sequence in the Culture History of Northeastern Iowa." *Midcontinental Journal of Archaeology* 3:215–83.

1979   "Some Trends and Traditions in Woodland Cultures of the Quad-State Region in the Upper Mississippi River Basin." *The Wisconsin Archaeologist* 60:47–82.

1980   *Hadfields Cave: A Perspective on Late Woodland Culture in Northeastern Iowa.* Report 13. Office of the State Archaeologist, University of Iowa, Iowa City.

1981a   "Archaeological Investigations at the Rainbow Site. Plymouth County, Iowa." Contract Completion Report, Ms. on file, Luther College, Decorah.

1981b   "Ceramics from the MAD Sites and Other Prairie Peninsula and Plains Complexes." In *Archaeology of the MAD Sites at Denison, Iowa.* Iowa State Historical Department, Division of Historic Preservation, Iowa City.

1981c   "Archaeology of the MAD Sites (13CF101 and 13CF102) at Denison, Iowa." D. W. Benn, Principal Investigator. 3 parts. Draft Report on File, State Historical Society of Iowa, Des Moines.

1982a "The Ceramic Assemblage." In *A Preliminary Report on the Arthur Site, East Okoboji Lake, Iowa*, edited by J. A. Tiffany, pp. 38–86. Research Papers 7-1. Office of the State Archaeologist, Iowa City, Iowa.

1982b "Woodland cultures of the Western Prairie Peninsula: An Abstract." In *Interrelations of Cultural and Fluvial Deposits in Northwest Iowa*, edited by E. A. Bettis and D. M. Thompson, pp. 37–52. Association of Iowa Archaeologists, Iowa City.

1983 "Diffusion and Acculturation in Woodland Cultures on the Western Prairie Peninsula." In *Prairie Archaeology*, edited by Guy E. Gibbon, pp. 75–85. Publications in Anthropology 3. University of Minnesota, Minneapolis.

1984 "Excavations at the Christenson Oneota Site (13PK407). Central Des Moines River Valley, Iowa." A phase III data recovery for the U.S. Army Corps of Engineers, Rock Island District. Ms. on file, Center for Archaeological Research, Southwest Missouri State University, Springfield.

1986 *The Western Iowa Rivers Basin; An Archaeological Overview.* Iowa River Basin Report Series, vol. 3. Center for Archaeological Research, Southwest Missouri State University, Springfield, Mo.

1989a "Hawks, Serpents, and Bird-men: Emergence of the Oneota Mode of Production." *Plains Anthropologist* 34:233–60.

1989b "Social and Political Causes for the Emergence of Intensive Agriculture During the Late Prehistoric Period." Paper presented at the Forty-Seventh Annual Plains Anthropological Conference, Sioux Falls, S.D.

Benn, David W. (ed.)
1990 *Woodland Culture on the Western Prairies: The Rainbow Site Investigations.* University of Iowa, Office of the State Archeologist report 18. Iowa City.

Benn, David W., E. Arthur Bettis III, and Robert C. Vogel
1988 *Archaeology and Geomorphology in Pools 17–18. Upper Mississippi River.* Center for Archaeological Research, Southwest Missouri State University, Springfield, and the Iowa Department of Natural Resources, Geological Survey Bureau, Iowa City. Submitted to the U.S. Army Corps of Engineers, Rock Island District, Contract no. DACW25-87-C-0017.

Benn, David W., and Dean M. Thompson
1977 "The Young Site, Linn County, Iowa, and Comments on Woodland Ceramics." *Journal of the Iowa Archaeological Society* 24:1–61.

Bentzen, R.
1961 *The Powers-Yonkee Bison Trap.* Report of the Sheridan Chapter, Wyoming Archaeological Society.
1962 "The Powers-Yonkee Bison Trap." *Plains Anthropologist* 7:113–18.

Benz, Bruce F.
1987 "Seeds from the Naze Site." In *Archaeological Excavation at the Naze Site (32SN246)*, edited by Michael L. Gregg, pp. 304–28. Department of Anthropology, University of North Dakota, Grand Forks. Submitted to the U.S. Bureau of Reclamation, Billings, Mont.

Berlandier, J. L.
1969   *The Indians of Texas in 1830.* Smithsonian Institution Press, Washington, D.C.

Berry, M. S.
1985   "The Age of Maize in the Greater Southwest: A Critical Review." In *Prehistoric Food Production in North America,* edited by Richard I. Ford, pp. 279–307. Anthropological Papers no. 75. Museum of Anthropology, University of Michigan, Ann Arbor.

Binford, Lewis R.
1968   "Archaeological Perspectives." In *New Perspectives in Archaeology,* edited by L. R. Binford, pp. 1–3. Aldine Press, Chicago.
1980   "Willow Smoke and Dogs' Tails: Hunter-Gatherer Settlement Systems and Archaeological Site Formation." *American Antiquity* 45:4–20.

Birk, Douglas A.
1977   "The Norway Lake Site: A Multicomponent Woodland Complex in North Central Minnesota." *The Minnesota Archaeologist* 36:16–45.
1979   "Sandy Lake Ceramics." In *A Handbook of Minnesota Prehistoric Ceramics,* edited by S. F. Anfinson, pp. 175–82. Occasional Publications in Minnesota Anthropology no. 5. Minnesota Archaeological Society, Fort Snelling.

Black, S. L.
1986   *The Clemente and Herminia Hinojosa Site, 41JW8: A Toyah Horizon Campsite in Southern Texas.* Special Report no. 18. Center for Archaeological Research, University of Texas, San Antonio.

Blaine, Martha Royce
1979   "Mythology and Folklore: Their possible use in the Study of Plains Caddoan Origins." *Nebraska History* 60:240–48.

Blake, Michael
1981   "Archaeological Investigation at the Wild Horse River Site (DjPv 14)." Occasional Paper 6. Heritage Conservation Branch, Province of British Columbia.

Blakeslee, Donald J.
1975   "The Plains Interband Trade System: An Ethnohistoric and Archaeological Investigation." Ph.D. dissertation, University of Wisconsin, Milwaukee. University Microfilms International, Ann Arbor.
1981   "Toward a Cultural Understanding of Human Microevaluation on the Plains." In *Progress in Skeletal Biology of Plains Population,* edited by Richard L. Jantz and Douglas H. Ubelaker. Memoir 17, *Plains Anthropologist* 26 (94, pt. 2): 93–106.

Blakeslee, Donald J. (ed.)
1978   *The Central Plains Tradition: Internal Development and External Relationships,* Office of the State Archaeologist, Iowa City.

Blakeslee, Donald J., and Warren W. Caldwell
1979   *The Nebraska Phase: An Appraisal.* Reprints in Archaeology, vol. 18. J & L Reprint, Lincoln.
1988   "St. Helena Archaeology: New Data, Fresh Interpretations." Reprints in Archaeology, vol. 39. J & L Reprint, Lincoln.

Blakeslee, Donald J., and Arthur H. Rohn
1986   *Man and Environment in Northeastern Kansas: The Hillsdale Lake Project.* 6 vols. Report submitted to the U.S. Army Corps of Engineers, Kansas City District.
Boas, Franz
1918   *Kutenai Tales.* Bureau of American Ethnology Bulletin 59.
Bodine, John J.
1979   "Taos Pueblo." In *Southwest,* edited by Alfonso Ortiz, pp. 255–67. Vol. 9, *Handbook of North American Indians.* Smithsonian Institution, Washington, D.C.
Bolton, H. E.
1913   *Athanase de Mézières and the Louisiana-Texas Frontier 1768–1780,* vol. 1. Arthur C. Clark, Cleveland.
1914   *Athanase de Mézières and the Louisiana-Texas Frontier 1768–1780,* vol. 2. Arthur C. Clark, Cleveland.
1949   *Coronado, Knight of Pueblos and Plains.* University of New Mexico Press, Albuquerque.
Bonney, Rachel A.
1970   "Early Woodland in Minnesota." *Plains Anthropologist* 15:302–4.
Boszhardt, Robert F.
1982   "Archaeological Investigations in the Lowland Floodplain of Navigation Pool 10 near Prairie du Chien, Crawford County, Wisconsin." M.A. thesis, Department of Anthropology, University of Wisconsin, Madison.
Boszhardt, Robert F., and David F. Overstreet
1983   "Preliminary Investigations: Archaeology and Sedimentary Geomorphology, Navigation Pool 12, Upper Mississippi River." *The Wisconsin Archaeologist* 64:111–83.
Bowers, A. W.
1948   "A History of the Mandan and Hidatsa." Ph.D. dissertation, University of Chicago.
1950   *Mandan Social and Ceremonial Organization.* University of Chicago Press, Chicago.
1965   *Hidatsa Social and Ceremonial Organization.* Bureau of American Ethnology Bulletin 194. Washington, D.C.
Bowman, Peter W.
1960   *Coal-Oil Canyon: Report on Preliminary Investigations.* Kansas Anthropological Association, Wichita.
Boyd, Douglas K., Steve A. Tomka, and C. Britt Bousman
1992   "Data Recovery at the South Sage Creek site, 41KT33." In *Data Recovery at Justiceburg Reservoir (Lake Alan Henry), Garza and Kent Counties, Texas: Phase III, Season 1.* Prewitt and Associates, Inc., Reports of Investigations, no. 84, Austin.
Bozell, John R., and John Ludwickson
1988   *Highway Archaeological Investigations at the Slaughterhouse Creek Site and Other Cultural Resources in the Pine Ridge Area.* Nebraska State Historical Society, Lincoln.
Brace, Ian G., and I. G. Dyck
1978   "The M. A. Welsh Collection." *Saskatchewan Archaeology Newslet-*

ter 53(3): 6–11.

Bradfield, Wesley
1929   "Excavations in the Sacramentos." *El Palacio* 27:3–6.

Brasser, Ted J.
1982   "The Tipi as an Element in the Emergence of Historic Plains Indian Nomadism." *Plains Anthropologist* 27(98): 309–21.

Braun, D. P.
1983   "Pots as Tools." In *Archaeological Hammers and Theories*, edited by J. A. Moore and A. S. Keene, pp. 107–34. Academic Press, New York.

1985   "Ceramic Decorative Diversity and Illinois Woodland Regional Integration." In *Decoding Prehistoric Ceramics*, edited by Ben A. Nelson, pp. 128–53. Center for Archaeological Investigations, Southern Illinois University, Carbondale.

1987   "Coevolution of Sedentism, Pottery Technology, and Horticulture in the Central Midwest, 200 B.C.–A.D. 600." In *Emergent Horticultural Economies of the Eastern Woodlands*, edited by W. F. Keegan, pp. 153–82. Center for Archaeological Investigations, Southern Illinois University, Carbondale.

1988   "The Social and Technological Roots of 'Late Woodland.'" In *Interpretations of Culture Change in the Eastern Woodlands During the Late Woodland Period*, edited by R. W. Yerkes, pp. 17–38. Occasional Papers in Anthropology no. 3. Department of Anthropology, Ohio State University, Columbus.

Braun, David P., and Stephen Plog
1982   "Evolution of 'Tribal' Social Networks: Theory and Prehistoric North American Evidence." *American Antiquity* 47:504–25.

Bray, Edmund C., and Martha Coleman Bray (trans. and eds.)
1976   *Joseph Nicollet on the Plains and Prairies.* Minnesota Historical Society, St. Paul.

Brink, Jack
1986   *Dog Days in Southern Alberta.* Occasional Paper no. 28. Archaeological Survey of Alberta, Edmonton.

Brink, J., M. Wright, B. Dawe, and D. Glaum
1985   *Final Report of the 1983 Season at Head-Smashed-In Buffalo Jump, Alberta.* Manuscript Series no. 1. Archaeological Survey of Alberta, Edmonton.

1986   *Final Report of the 1984 Season at Head-Smashed-In Buffalo Jump, Alberta.* Manuscript Series no. 9. Archaeological Survey of Alberta, Edmonton.

Brogan, William T.
1981   *The Cuesta Phase: A Settlement Pattern Study.* Anthropological Series no. 9. Kansas State Historical Society, Topeka.

Brooks, Robert L.
1987   *The Arthur Site: Settlement and Subsistence Structure at a Washington River Phase Village.* Studies in Oklahoma's Past, no. 15. Oklahoma Archaeological Survey, Norman.

1989   "Village Farming Societies." In *From Clovis to Comanchero: Archeological Overview of the Southern Great Plains*, edited by Jack L. Hofman, Robert L. Brooks, Joe S. Hays, Douglas W. Owsley, Richard L.

Jantz, Murray K. Marks, and Mary H. Manhein, pp. 71–90. Arkansas Archeological Survey Research Series, no. 35.

Brooks, Robert L., Michael C. Moore, and Douglas Owsley
1992 "New Smith, 34RM400: A Plains Village Mortuary Site in Western Oklahoma." *Plains Anthropologist* 37(138): 59–78.

Brose, David S.
1978 "Late Prehistory of the Upper Great Lakes Area." In *Northeast,* edited by Bruce G. Trigger, pp. 569–82. Vol. 15, *Handbook of North American Indians.* Smithsonian Institution, Washington, D.C.

Brown, Donald N.
1979 "Picuris Pueblo." In *Southwest,* edited by Alfonso Ortiz, pp. 268–77. Vol. 9, *Handbook of North American Indians.* Smithsonian Institution, Washington, D.C.
1980 "Dance as Experience: The Deer Dance of Picuris Pueblo." In *Southwestern Indian Ritual Drama,* edited by Charlotte J. Frisbie, pp. 71–92. University of New Mexico Press, Albuquerque.

Brown, Ian W.
1989 "The Calumet Ceremony in the Southeast and Its Archaeological Manifestations." *American Antiquity* 54:311–31.

Brown, J. A.
1984 "Arkansas Valley Caddoan: The Spiro Phase." In *Prehistory of Oklahoma,* edited by R. E. Bell, pp. 241–63. Academic Press, Orlando.

Brown, K. L., and A. H. Simmons (eds.)
1987 *Kansas Prehistoric Archaeological Preservation Plan.* Office of Archaeological Research, University of Kansas, Lawrence.

Brown, Lionel A.
1967 *Pony Creek Archaeology.* Publications in Salvage Archaeology, Smithsonian Institution River Basin Surveys. Lincoln.
1968 "The Gavins Point Site (39YK203). An Analysis of Surface Artifacts." *Plains Anthropologist* 13(40): 118–31.
1974 *The Archaeology of the Breeden Site. Plains Anthropologist Memoir* 10.

Brown, Marie E.
1981 "Cultural Behavior as Reflected in the Vertebrate Faunal Assemblages of Three Smoky Hill Sites." M.A. thesis, Department of Anthropology, University of Kansas, Lawrence.

Brugge, David M.
1981 "Comments on Athabaskans and Sumas." In *The Protohistoric Period in the North American Southwest, A.D.1450–1700,* edited by David R. Wilcox and W. Bruce Masse, pp. 282–90. Arizona State University Anthropological Research Papers no. 24. Tempe.

Brumley, John H.
1976 *Ramillies: A Late Prehistoric Bison Kill and Campsite Located in Southeastern Alberta, Canada.* Archaeological Survey of Canada Paper 55. National Museum of Man Mercury Series, Ottawa.
1983 "An Interpretive Model for Stone Circles and Stone Circle Sites within Southeastern Alberta." In *From Microcosm to Macrocosm: Advances in Tipi Ring Investigation and Interpretation,* edited by L. B. Davis, pp. 171–91. Plains Anthropologist Memoir 19.

1985   "The Ellis Site (EcOp-4): A Late Prehistoric Burial Lodge/Medicine Wheel Site in Southeastern Alberta." In *Contributions To Plains Prehistory*, edited by D. Burley, pp. 180–232. Occasional Paper no. 26. Archaeological Survey of Alberta, Edmonton.

Brumley, John H., and Barry J. Dau

1988   *Historical Resource Investigations within the Forty Mile Coulee Reservoir.* Occasional Paper no. 13. Archaeological Survey of Alberta, Edmonton.

Brumley, John H., and Carol Rushworth

1983   "A Summary and Appraisal of Alberta Radiocarbon Dates." In *Archaeology in Alberta 1982*, edited by D. Burley, pp. 142–60. Occasional Paper no. 21. Archaeological Survey of Alberta, Edmonton.

Bruseth, J. E., and T. K. Perttula

1981   *Prehistoric Settlement Patterns at Lake Fork Reservoir.* Texas Antiquities Permit Series, Report no. 2. Southern Methodist University and Texas Antiquities Committee, Dallas.

Bruseth, J. E., D. E. McGregor, and W. A. Martin

1987   "Hunter-Gatherers of the Prairie Margin: Summary of the Prehistoric Archaeological Record." In *Hunter-Gatherer Adaptations along the Prairie Margin: Site Excavations and Synthesis of Pre-historic Archaeology*, edited by D. E. McGregor and J. E. Bruseth, pp. 229–56. Richland Creek Technical Series, vol. 3. Southern Methodist University, Dallas.

Bryant, V. M., Jr., and H. J. Shafer

1977   "The Late Quaternary Paleoenvironment of Texas: A Model for the Archaeologist." *Texas Archaeological Society Bulletin* 48:1–25.

Bryson, R. A., W. N. Irving, and J. A. Larsen

1965   "Radiocarbon and Soil Evidence of Former Forest in the Southern Canadian Tundra." *Science* 147:46–48.

Bryson, R. A., and W. M. Wendland

1967   "Tentative Climatic Patterns for some Late-glacial and Post-glacial Episodes in Central North America." In *Life, Land and Water*, edited by W. J. Mayer-Oakes, pp. 271–99. Occasional Paper no. 1. Department of Anthropology, University of Manitoba, Winnipeg.

Buchner, Anthony P.

1976   "Cultural Dynamics in the Grassland-boreal-deciduous Transitional Zone of Southeastern Manitoba: 1000 B.C.–A.D. 1000." M.A. thesis, Department of Anthropology, University of Winnipeg.

1979   *The 1978 Caribou Lake Project, Including a Summary of the Prehistory of East-Central Manitoba.* Papers in Manitoba Archaeology, Final Report no. 8. Department of Cultural Affairs and Historical Resources, Winnipeg.

1982   *Material Culture of the Bjorklund Site.* Papers in Manitoba Archaeology, Miscellaneous Paper no. 13. Department of Cultural Affairs and Historic Resources, Winnipeg.

1988   "The Geochronology of the Lockport Site." *Manitoba Archaeological Quarterly* 12(2): 27–31.

Buckles, W. G., G. H. Ewing, N. Buckles, G. J. Armelagos, J. J. Wood, J. D. Haug, and J. H. McCullough

1963   "The Excavation of the Hazeltine Heights Site." *Southwestern Lore* 29(1): 1–36.

Burgess, Robert J.
1981   "Cultural Ecological Investigations in the Owl Canyon Rockshelter
        (5LR104)." M.A. thesis, Department of Anthropology, Colorado State
        University, Fort Collins.
Burley, David, D. Meyer, and E. Walker
1981   "Recent Evidence for a Long Range Exchange Network in the Sas-
        katchewan Pehonan Complex." *Saskatchewan Archaeology* 2:73–76.
Burnett, B. A.
1988   "The Bioarchaeological Synthesis." In *Human Adaptation in the Ozark
        and Ouachita Mountains*, pp. 171–220. Final Report Study Unit 1,
        Ozark-Arkansas-Ouachita Archaeological Research, Synthesis, and
        Overview Report. U.S. Army Corps of Engineers, Southwestern Divi-
        sion, Dallas.
Butler, B. Robert
1962   *Contributions to the Prehistory of the Columbia Plateau.* Occasional
        Paper no. 9. Idaho State College Museum, Pocatello.
1968   *A Guide to Understanding Idaho Archaeology* (2d ed.) Special Pub-
        lication, Idaho State University Museum, Pocatello.
1971   "A Bison Jump in the upper Salmon River Country of Eastern Idaho."
        Tebiwa 14:4–32.
1978   "Bison Hunting in the Desert West before 1800: the Paleo-Ecological
        Potential and the Archaeological Reality." In *Bison Procurement and
        Utilization: A Symposium*, edited by L. B. Davis and M. C. Wilson, pp.
        106–12. *Plains Anthropologist Memoir* 14.
1981a   *When Did the Shoshoni Begin to Occupy Southern Idaho? Essays on
        Late Prehistoric Cultural Remarks from the Upper Snake and Salmon
        River Country.* Occasional Paper no. 32. Idaho Museum of Natural
        History, Pocatello.
1981b   "Late Period Cultural Sequences in the Northeastern Great Basin Sub-
        area and their Implications for the Upper Snake and Salmon River Coun-
        try." *Journal of California and Great Basin Anthropology* 3:245–56.
1983   *The Quest for the Historic Fremont and a Guide to the Prehistoric
        Pottery of Southern Idaho.* Occasional Paper no. 33. Idaho Museum of
        Natural History, Pocatello.
1986   "Prehistory of the Snake and Salmon River Area." In *Great Basin*,
        edited by Warren L. D'Ayevedo, pp. 127–34. Vol. 11, *Handbook of
        North American Indians.* Smithsonian Institution, Washington, D.C.
Butler, William B.
1981   "Eastern Colorado Radiocarbon Dates." *Southwestern Lore* 47(2): 12–31.
1986   "Taxonomy in Northeastern Colorado Prehistory." Ph.D. dissertation,
        University of Missouri. University Microfilms, Ann Arbor.
Butler, William B., Stephen A. Chomko, J. Michael Hoffman
1986   "The Red Creek Burial, El Paso County Colorado." *Southwestern Lore*
        52(2): 6–25.
Byrne, William J.
1973   *The Archaeology and Prehistory of Southern Alberta as Reflected by
        Ceramics.* Archaeological Survey of Canada Paper 14. National Muse-
        um of Man Mercury Series, Ottawa.

Caine, Christy A. H.
1974   "The Archaeology of the Snake River Region in Minnesota." In *Aspects of Upper Great Lakes Anthropology*, edited by E. Johnson, pp. 55–63. Minnesota Prehistoric Archaeology Series no. 11. Minnesota Historical Society, St. Paul.

Caine-Holman, Christy A.
1983   "Normative Typological and Systemic Stylistic Approaches to the Analysis of North Central Minnesota Ceramics." Ph.D. dissertation, Department of Anthropology, University of Minnesota, Minneapolis.

Calabrese, Francis A.
1967   *The Archaeology of the Upper Verdigris Watershed.* Anthropological Series no. 3. Kansas State Historical Society, Topeka.
1969   "Doniphan Phase Origins: An Hypothesis Resulting from Archaeological Investigations in the Smithville Reservoir Area, Missouri: 1968." Ms. submitted to the National Park Service, Omaha.
1972   "Cross Ranch: A Study of Variability in a Stable Cultural Tradition." *Plains Anthropologist* 18(62): 344–49.
1974   "Archaeological Investigations in the Smithville Reservoir Area, Missouri: 1969." Ms. submitted to the National Park Service, Omaha.

Caldwell, Warren W., Lee G. Madison, and Bernard Golden
1964   *Archaeological Investigations at the Hickey Brothers Site (39LM4), Big Bend Reservoir, Lyman County, South Dakota.* Bureau of American Ethnology Bulletin 189, River Basin Surveys Papers 36.

Callender, Edward
1968   "The Post Glacial Sedimentology of Devils Lake, North Dakota." Ph.D. dissertation, Department of Geology, University of North Dakota, Grand Forks.

Campbell, R. G.
1969   "Prehistoric Panhandle Culture on the Chaquaqua Plateau, Southeast Colorado." Ph.D. dissertation, University of Colorado, Boulder.
1976   *The Panhandle Aspect of the Chaquaqua Plateau.* Graduate Studies no. 11. Texas Tech University, Lubbock.

Carlson, G. F.
1971   "A Local Sequence for Upper Republican Sites in the Glen Elder Reservoir Locality, Kansas." M.A. thesis, Department of Anthropology, University of Nebraska.

Carlson, Gayle F., and Richard E. Jensen
1973   *Archaeological Salvage and Survey in Nebraska.* Publication in Anthropology no. 5. Nebraska State Historical Society, Lincoln.

Chafe, Wallace L.
1976   "Siouan, Iroquoian, and Caddoan." In *Native Languages of the Americas*, edited by Thomas A. Sebeok, pp. 527–672. Plenum Press, New York.

Chambers, M. E., S. K. Tompkins, R. L. Humphrey, and C. R. Brooks
1977   *The Cultural Resources of Clinton Lake, Kansas: An Inventory of Archaeology, History and Architecture.* Report by Iroquois Research Institute submitted to the U.S. Army Corps of Engineers, Kansas City District.

Chamberlain, Von del
1982 *When the Stars Came Down to Earth.* Ballena Press, Los Altos.
Champe, John L.
1936 "The Sweetwater Culture Complex." In *Chapters in Nebraska Archaeology*, edited by Earl H. Bell, pp. 249–97. University of Nebraska, Lincoln.
1946 *Ash Hollow Cave. A Study of Stratigraphic Sequence in the Central Great Plains.* University of Nebraska Studies no. 1, Lincoln.
Chapman, C. H.
1959 "The Origin of the Osage Indian Tribe: An Ethnographical, Historical and Archaeological Study." Ph.D. dissertation, University of Michigan. University Microfilms International, Ann Arbor.
1980 *The Archaeology of Missouri, II.* University of Missouri Press, Columbia.
Charles, Douglass K., and Jane E. Buikstra
1983 "Archaic Mortuary Sites in the Central Mississippi Drainage: Distribution, Structure, and Behavioral Implications." In *Archaic Hunters and Gatherers in the American Midwest*, edited by James L. Phillips and James A. Brown, pp. 117–45. Academic Press, N.Y.
Chase, H.
1951 "Field Report of the Excavation of Snake Blakeslee I by the Columbia University Summer Field Expedition." Ms. on file, Department of Anthropology, University of Denver.
Chomko, Steven A.
1976 "Faunal Exploitation in the Initial Middle Missouri Variant." In *Fay Tolton and the Initial Middle Missouri Variant*, edited by W. Raymond Wood, pp. 35–41. Missouri Archaeological Society Research Series no. 13. Columbia, Missouri.
Chomko, Steven A., and W. Raymond Wood
1973 "Linear Mounds in the Northeastern Plains." *Archaeology in Montana* 14(2): 1–19.
Choquette, Wayne
1984 "A Proposed Cultural Chronology for the Kootenai Region." In *Cultural Resource Investigations of the Bonneville Power Administration's Libby Integration Project Northern Idaho and Northwestern Montana*, edited by S. Gough. *Archaeological and Historical Services, Eastern Washington University Reports in Archaeology and History* 100:303–16.
Choquette, Wayne, and C. Holstine
1980 "A Cultural Resource Overview of the Bonneville Power Administration's Proposed Transmission Line from Libby Dam, Montana to Rathdrum, Idaho." Washington State University Project Report 100. Washington Archaeological Research Center, Pullman.
Clark, Frances
1982 "Knife River Flint and Interregional Exchange." M.Sc. thesis, Department of Anthropology, University of Wisconsin, Milwaukee.
1984 "Knife River Flint and Interregional Exchange." *Midcontinental Journal of Archaeology* 9:173–98.

Clark, Gerald, and Michael Wilson
1981   "The Ayers-Fraxier Bison Trap (24PE30): A Late Middle Period Bison Kill
        on the Lower Yellowstone River." *Archaeology in Montana* 22(1): 23–77.
Collins, M. B.
1968   "The Andrews Lake Locality: New Archaeological Data from the
        Southern Llano Estacado, Texas." M.A. thesis, University of Texas,
        Austin.
1969   "What Is the Significance of the Southwestern Ceramics Found on the
        Llano Estacado?" *Transactions of the Fifth Regional Archaeological
        Symposium for Southeastern New Mexico and Western Texas.* El
        Llano Archaeological Society, Portales, N.M.
1971   "A Review of Llano Estacado Archaeology and Ethnohistory." *Plains
        Anthropologist* 16(52): 85–104.
Conrad, H. S.
1952   "The Vegetation of Iowa." *Studies in Natural History* 14(4). State
        University of Iowa, Ames.
Conrad, Lawrence
1991   "The Middle Mississippian Cultures of the Central Illinois River Valley."
        In *Cahokia and the Hinterlands,* edited by Thomas E. Emerson and R.
        Barry Lewis, pp. 119–56. University of Illinois Press, Urbana.
Cooper, Paul
1936   "Archaeology of Certain Sites in Cedar County, Nebraska." In *Chap-
        ters in Nebraska Archaeology,* edited by E. H. Bell, pp. 11–146. Univer-
        sity of Nebraska, Lincoln.
Cooper, L. R., and E. Johnson
1964   "Sandy Lake Ware and Its Distribution." *American Antiquity* 29:474–
        79.
Cordell, L. S.
1978   *A Cultural Resources Overview of the Middle Rio Grande Valley, New
        Mexico.* For the Albuquerque District, Bureau of Land Management,
        Santa Fe, N.M.
1979   "Prehistory: Eastern Anasazi." In *Southwest,* edited by Alfonso Ortiz,
        pp. 131–51. Vol. 9, *Handbook of North American Indians.* Smithso-
        nian Institution, Washington, D.C.
1989   "Northern and Central Rio Grande." In *Dynamics of Southwest Pre-
        history,* edited by Linda S. Cordell and George J. Gumerman, pp. 293–
        335. Smithsonian Institution Press, Washington, D.C.
Corley, J. A.
1965   "Proposed Eastern Extension of the Jornada Branch of the Mogollon."
        Transactions of the First Regional Archaeological Symposium for
        Southeastern New Mexico and Western Texas. *Lea County Archae-
        ological Society Bulletin* 1:30–36. Hobbs, N.M.
Costello, David F.
1969   *The Prairie World.* Thomas Y. Crowell, New York.
Coues, Elliot (ed.)
1897   *New Light on the Early History of the Greater Northwest: The Manu-
        script Journals of Alexander Henry and David Thompson, 1799–1814.*
        Reprint. Ross and Haines, Minneapolis, 1965.

Couzzourt, Jim
1985 "Preliminary Report: Testing at the Tascosa Cree site, Oldham County, Texas." In *Transactions of the Twentieth Regional Archeological Symposium for Southeastern New Mexico and Western Texas*, pp. 65–142.
1988 "Tascosa Creek site." In *Transactions of the Twenty-third Regional Archeological Symposium for Southeastern New Mexico and Western Texas*, pp. 44–79.
Cox, I. J.
1905 *The Journeys of Rene Robert Cavelier Sieur de LaSalle.* Allerton Book Co., New York.
Creel, D., R. F. Scott, IV, and M. B. Collins
1990 "A Faunal Record from West Central Texas and Its Bearing on Late Holocene Bison Population Changes in the Southern Plains." *Plains Anthropologist* 35(127): 55–69.
Croes, Dale R.
1989 "Prehistoric Ethnicity on the Northwest Coast of North America: An Evaluation of Style in Basketry and Lithics." *Journal of Anthropological Archaeology* 8:101–30.
Cruse, J. Brett
1989 "Archeological Investigations at the Kent Creek site (41HL66): Evidence of Mogollon Influence on the Southern Plains." M.A. thesis, Department of Anthropology, Texas A&M University.
Cummings, Robert B., Jr.
1958 *Archaeological Investigations at the Tuttle Creek Dam.* Smithsonian Institution River Basin Surveys Paper no. 10. Bureau of American Ethnology Bulletin 169. Washington, D.C.
Curtis, John T.
1959 *The Vegetation of Wisconsin.* University of Wisconsin Press, Madison.
Davis, E. M.
1961 "Proceedings of the Fifth Conference on Caddoan Archaeology." *Bulletin of the Texas Archaeological Society* 31:77–143.
1970 "Archaeological and Historical Assessment of the Red River Basin in Texas." In *Archaeological and Historical Resources of the Red River Basin*, edited by H. E. Davis, pp. 25–65. Publications in Archaeology, Research Series no. 1. Arkansas Archaeological Survey, Fayetteville.
Davis, Leslie B. (ed.)
1988 *Avonlea Yesterday and Today: Archaeology and Prehistory.* Saskatchewan Archaeological Society, Saskatoon.
Davis, Leslie B.
1972 "Prehistoric Use of Obsidian: Northwestern Plains." Ph.D. dissertation, University of Calgary.
1976 "Comments on Radiocarbon Dates from the Wahkpa Chu'gn Site, by John Brumley." *Archaeology in Montana* 17(172): 83–95.
1982a "Archaeology and Geology of the Schmitt Chert Mine, Missouri Headwaters." In *Guidebook for Field Trip Held in Conjunction with the Thirty-fifth Annual Meeting of the Rocky Mountain Section of the Geological Society of America*, edited by Donald C. Smith. Montana State University, Bozeman.

1982b "Montana Archaeology and Radiocarbon Dates: 1962–1981." *Archaeology in Montana*, Special Issue 3.

Davis, Leslie B., Stephen A. Aaberg, Michael Wilson, and Robert Ottersberg
1982   *Stone Circles in the Montana Rockies, Systematic Recovery and Culture-Ecological Inferences.* Report by Montana State University submitted to the Montana Army National Guard.

Davis, Leslie B., and Jack W. Fisher, Jr.
1988   "Avonlea Predation on Wintering Plains Pronghorns." In *Avonlea Yesterday and Today: Archaeology and Prehistory,* edited by Leslie B. Davis. Saskatchewan Archaeological Society, Saskatoon.

Davis, Leslie B., and Troy Helmick
1982   "Inundated Prehistoric Occupation Sites Along Canyon Ferry Lake." *Archaeology in Montana* 23(3): 41–84.

Davis, Leslie B., and Charles D. Zeier.
1978   "Multi-Phase Late Period Bison Procurement at the Antonsen Site, Southwestern Montana." In *Bison Procurement and Utilization: A Symposium,* edited by L. B. Davis and M. Wilson, pp. 222–35. *Plains Anthropologist Memoir* 14.

Dawe, Robert J.
1987   "The Triangular Projectile Point in Plains Prehistory: A Preform Trade Hypothesis." In *Archaeology in Alberta 1986,* edited by M. Magne, pp. 150–62. Occasional Paper no. 31. Archaeological Survey of Alberta, Edmonton.

Dawson, Kenneth C. A.
1974   *The McCluskey Site.* Archaeological Survey of Canada Paper no. 25. National Museum of Man Mercury Series, Ottawa.
1975   "The Western Area Algonkians." In *Papers of the Sixth Algonquian Conference, 1974,* edited by W. Cowan, pp. 30–41. Ethnology Service Paper 23. National Museum of Man Mercury Series, Ottawa.
1977   "Northwestern Ontario Historic Populations." *Man in the Northeast* 18:14–31.
1981   "The Wabinosh River Site and the Laurel Tradition in Northwestern Ontario." *Ontario Archaeology* 36:3–46.
1987   "Northwestern Ontario and the Early Contact Period: The Northern Ojibwa, 1615–1715." *Canadian Journal of Archaeology* 11:143–87.

Deaver, Ken (ed.)
1985   *Mitigation of the Anderson Tipi Ring Site (32Ml111), McLean County, North Dakota.* Ethnoscience, Billings, Mont. Submitted to Falkirk Mining Co., Bismarck, N.D.

Deaver, Ken, and Sherri Deaver
1987   *Dancing Grouse, A Tipi Ring Site in Central North Dakota.* Ethnoscience, Billings, Mont. Submitted to Falkirk Mining Co., Bismarck, N.D.

Deaver, Sherri, and Ken Deaver
1988   *Prehistoric Cultural Resource Overview of Southeast Montana,* vol. 1. Ethnoscience, Billings, Mont. Submitted to Bureau of Land Management, Miles City, Mont., Contract no. YA-551-RFP6–340030.

De la Vega, Garcilaso
1962   *The Florida of the Inca. A History of the Adelantado, Hernando de*

Soto, Governor and Captain General of The Kingdom of Florida, and of other Heroic Spanish and Indian Cavaliers, written by the Inca, Garcilaso de la Vega, an Officer of his Majesty, and a Native of the Great City of Cuzco, Capital of the Realms and Provinces of Peru. Translated and edited by John G. Varner and Jeannette J. Varner. University of Texas Press, Austin.

Dempsey, Hugh A.

1956   "Stone 'Medicine Wheels': Memorials to Blackfoot War Chiefs." *Journal of the Washington Academy of Science*, 46(6): 177–82.

1973   *William Parker, Mounted Policeman.* Glenbow-Alberta Institute, Calgary, and Hurtig Publishers, Edmonton.

Dick, H. W.

1953   *The Hodges site, 1. Two Rock Shelters Near Tucumcari, New Mexico.* River Basin Survey Papers no. 5, pp. 271–84. Bureau of American Ethnology Bulletin 154. Washington, D.C.

Dickson, D. R.

1991   *The Albertson Site: A Deeply and Clearly Stratified Ozark Bluff Shelter.* Research Series no. 41, Arkansas Archaeological Survey, Fayetteville.

Dickson, Gary A.

1976   *Recent Radiocarbon dates from Northern Manitoba.* Papers in Manitoba Archaeology, Miscellaneous Paper no. 3. Department of Cultural Affairs and Historic Resources, Winnipeg.

1980   *The Kame Hills Site.* Papers in Manitoba Archaeology, Final Report no. 9. Department of Cultural Affairs and Historical Resources, Winnipeg.

Dillehay, Tom D.

1974   "Late Quaternary Bison Population Changes of the Southern Plains." *Plains Anthropologist* 19 (65): 180–96.

Di Peso, Charles C.

1979   "Prehistory: O'otam." In *Southwest*, edited by Alfonso Ortiz, pp. 91–99. Vol. 9, *Handbook of North American Indians.* Smithsonian Institution, Washington, D.C.

Dincauze, Dena, and Robert Hasenstab

1989   "Explaining the Iroquois: Tribalization on a Prehistoric Periphery." In *Centre and Periphery: Comparative Studies in Archaeology*, edited by T. Champion, pp. 67–87. Unwin Hyman, London.

Dobbs, Clark A.

1982   "Oneota Origins and Development: The Radiocarbon Evidence." In *Oneota Studies*, edited by G. Gibbon, pp. 91–106. Publications in Anthropology 1. University of Minnesota, Minneapolis.

1984   "Oneota Settlement Patterns in the Blue Earth River Valley, Minnesota." Ph.D. dissertation, Department of Anthropology, University of Minnesota, Minneapolis.

Dobbs, Clark A., and Orrin C. Shane, III

1982   "Oneota Settlement Patterns in the Blue Earth River Valley, Minnesota." In *Oneota Studies*, edited by G. Gibbon, pp. 55–68, Publications in Anthropology 1. University of Minnesota, Minneapolis.

Dobyns, Henry F.
1983   *Their Number Become Thinned.* University of Tennessee Press, Knoxville.

Dorsey, G. A.
1904a   *Traditions of the Arikara.* Publication 17. Carnegie Institution of Washington, Washington, D.C.
1904b   *The Mythology of the Wichita.* Publication 21. Carnegie Institution of Washington, Washington, D.C.

Doughty, Arthur G., and Chester Martin
1929   *The Kelsey Papers.* Published by the Public Archives of Canada and the Public Record Office of Northern Ireland. Ottawa.

Drass, R. R., and P. Flynn
1990   "Geographic and Temporal Variations in Southern Plains Village Subsistence Practices." *Plains Anthropologist* 35:175–90.

Drass, Richard R., and Fern E. Swenson
1986   "Variation in the Washita River Phase of Central and Western Oklahoma." *Plains Anthropologist* 31:35–49.

Drass, Richard R. and Christopher L. Turner
1989   *An Archeological Reconnaissance of the Wolf Creek Basin, Ellis County, Oklahoma.* Archeological Resource Survey Report no. 35. Oklahoma Archeological Survey, Norman.

Driver, Jonathan C.
1978   "Holocene Man and Environments in the Crowsnest Pass, Alberta." Ph.D. dissertation, University of Calgary.

Duffield, L. F.
1964   "Three Panhandle aspect sites at Sanford Reservoir, Hutchinson County, Texas." *Bulletin of the Texas Archaeological Society* 35:19–81.
1970   "Some Panhandle aspect Sites in Texas: Their Vertebrates and Paleoecology." Ph.D. dissertation, Department of Anthropology, University of Wisconsin.

Duffield, L. F., and E. B. Jelks
1961   *The Pearson Site: A Historic Indian Site in Iron Bridge Reservoir, Rains County, Texas.* Anthropology Series no. 4. University of Texas, Austin.

Duke, Philip G.
1981   "Systems Dynamics in Prehistoric southern Alberta: 2000 B.P. to the Historic Period." Ph.D. dissertation, Department of Archaeology, University of Calgary.
1988   "Models of Cultural Process During the Avonlea Phase." In *Avonlea Yesterday and Today: Archaeology and Prehistory,* edited by L. B. Davis, pp. 265–72. Saskatchewan Archaeological Society, Saskatoon.
1991   *Points in Time: Structure and Event in a Late Plains Hunting Society.* University Press of Colorado, Boulder.

Dumond, Don E.
1965   "On Eskaleutian Linguistics, Archaeology, and Prehistory." *American Anthropologist* 67:1,231–57.
1969   "Toward a Prehistory of the Na-Dene, with a General Comment on Population Movements Among Nomadic Hunters." *American Anthropologist,* 71:857–63.

Dyck, Ian
1983   "The Prehistory of Southern Saskatchewan." In *Tracking Ancient Hunters: Prehistoric Archaeology in Saskatchewan*, edited by H. T. Epp and I. Dyck, pp. 63–139. Saskatchewan Archaeological Society, Regina.

Eddy, Frank W.
1966   *Prehistory in the Navajo Reservoir District, North-Western New Mexico.* Museum of New Mexico Papers in Anthropology no. 15, Santa Fe.
1982   *A Cultural Resources Inventory of the John Martin Reservoir, Colorado.* Edited by Science Applications, Boulder.

Ehrenhard, John E.
1973   "The King Site." Ms on file, Midwest Archaeological Center, National Park Service, Lincoln.

Eighmy, Jeffrey L.
1982   *Colorado Plains Prehistoric Context.* Office of Archaeology and Historic Preservation, Colorado Historical Society, Denver.

Eighmy, J. L., and C. Wood
1984   "Dated Architecture on the Southern Colorado Plains." In *Papers of the Philmont Conference on the Archaeology of Northeastern New Mexico*, edited by C. J. Condie, pp. 273–90. *New Mexico Archaeological Council Proceedings* 6(1).

Elvas, Knight of
1904   *Narratives of the Career of Hernando de Soto in the Conquest of Florida, as told by a Knight of Elvas.* Translated by Buckingham Smith, edited with an introduction by Edward G. Bourne, vol. I. Allerton Book Co., New York.

Emerson, Thomas E., and Douglas K. Jackson
1984   *The BBB Motor Site (11-Ms-S95).* American Bottom Archaeology FA1–270 Site Reports, vol. 6. University of Illinois Press, Urbana.
1987   "The Edelhardt and Lindeman Phases: Setting the Stage for the Final Transition to Mississippian in the American Bottom." In *The Emergent Mississippian: Proceedings of the Sixth Mid-South Archaeological Conference, June 6–9, 1985*, edited by Richard A. Marshall, pp. 172–93. Occasional Papers no. 87–101. Cobb Institute of Archaeology, Mississippi State University, Mississippi State.

Emerson, Thomas E.
1991a "Some Perspectives on Cahokia and the Northern Mississippian Expansion." In *Cahokia and the Hinterlands*, edited by T. E. Emerson and R. Barry Lewis, pp. 221–36. University of Illinois Press, Urbana. In press.
1991b "The Apple River Mississippian Culture of Northwestern Illinois." In *Cahokia and the Hinterlands*, edited by Thomas E. Emerson and R. Barry Lewis, pp. 164–82. University of Illinois Press, Urbana. In press.

Emerson, Thomas E. and R. B. Lewis (eds.)
1991   *Cahokia and the Hinterlands: Middle Mississippian Cultures in the Midwest.* University of Illinois Press, Urbana.

Epp, Henry T.
1988   "Way of the Migrant Herds: Dual Disperson Strategy Among Bison." *Plains Anthropologist* 33:309–20.

Etchieson, G. M., R. D. Speer, and J. T. Hughes
1979   *Archaeological Investigations in the Crowell Reservoir Area, Cottle,
        Foard, King, and Knox Counties, Texas.* Archaeological Research
        Laboratory, Kilgore Research Center, West Texas State University,
        Canyon.
Evans, G. Edward
1951   "Prehistoric Wells in Eastern New Mexico." *American Antiquity*
        17:1–9.
1961a   "A Reappraisal of the Blackduck Focus or Headwaters Lakes Aspect."
        M.A. thesis, Department of Anthropology, University of Minnesota,
        Minneapolis.
1961b   "Ceramic Analysis of the Blackduck Ware and Its General Cultural
        Relationships." *Minnesota Academy of Science, Proceedings* 29:33–
        54. St. Paul.
1961c   "Prehistoric Blackduck–Historic Assiniboine: A Reassessment." *Plains
        Anthropologist* 6:271–75.
Ewers, John C.
1955   *The Horse in Blackfoot Culture.* Bureau of American Ethnology Bulle-
        tin 159. Smithsonian Institution, Washington, D.C.
1958   *The Blackfeet: Raiders of the Northwestern Plains.* University of
        Oklahoma Press, Norman.
Eyman, C. E.
1966   "The Schultz Focus: A Plains Middle Woodland Burial Complex in
        Eastern Kansas." M.A. thesis, University of Calgary. National Library
        of Canada, Ottawa.
Falk, Carl R., Robert E. Pepperl, and Mary E. McCormick
1986   *A Cultural Resource Survey of the East Shore of Lake Oahe, South
        Dakota.* 9 vols. Division Archaeological Research, Department of
        Anthropology, University of Nebraska, Lincoln. Submitted to U.S.
        Army Corps of Engineers, Omaha District, Contract no. DACW45-78-
        C-0159.
Falk, Carl R. (ed.), T. L. Steinacher, and D. L. Toom
1984   *Archaeological Investigations within Federal Lands Located on the
        East Bank of the Lake Sharpe Project Area, South Dakota 1978–1979
        Final Report.* 8 vols. Division of Archaeological Research, Department
        of Anthropology, University of Nebraska. Technical Report no. 83-04.
        Submitted to U.S. Army Corps of Engineers, Omaha District, Contract
        no. DACW45-78-C-1036.
Farnsworth, Kenneth B., Thomas E. Emerson, and Rebecca Miller Glenn
1991   "Patterns of Late Woodland/Mississippian Interactions in the Lower
        Illinois Valley Drainage: A View from Starr Village." In *Cahokia and
        the Hinterlands,* edited by Thomas E. Emerson and R. Barry Lewis, pp.
        83–118. University of Illinois Press, Urbana.
Fawcett, W. B., Jr.
1987   "Communal Hunts, Human Aggregations, Social Variation, and Cli-
        matic Change: Bison Utilization by Prehistoric Inhabitants of the
        Great Plains." Ph.D. dissertation, Department of Anthropology, Uni-
        versity of Massachusetts, Amherst.

1988 "Changing Prehistoric Settlement Along the Middle Missouri River: Timber Depletion and the Historic Context." *Plains Anthropologist* 33(119): 67–94.

Faye, S.
1943 "The Arkansas Post of Louisiana: French Domination." *Louisiana Historical Quarterly* 26:633–721.

Ferring, C. R. (ed.)
1982 *The Late Holocene Prehistory of Delaware Canyon, Oklahoma.* Institute of Applied Sciences, Contributions to Archaeology 1. North Texas State University, Denton.

Finnigan, James T.
1988 "The Green Site: A Late Prehistoric Campsite Located in Southeastern Saskatchewan." *Journal of the North Dakota Archaeological Association* 3:28–50.

Finnigan, J. T., D. Meyer, and J. Prentice
1983 *Resource Inventory, Assessment and Evaluation.* Nipawin Reservoir Heritage Study Volume 5, edited by David Meyer. Saskatchewan Research Council Publication no. E-903-9-E-83, Saskatoon.

Fitting, James E.
1970 *The Archaeology of Michigan.* Natural History Press, Garden City, N.Y.
1978a "Prehistory: Introduction." In *Northeast,* edited by Bruce Trigger, pp. 14–15. Vol. 15, *Handbook of North American Indians.* Smithsonian Institution, Washington, D.C.
1978b "Regional Cultural Development, 300 B.C. to A.D. 1000." In *Northeast,* edited by Bruce Trigger, pp. 44–57. Vol. 15, *Handbook of North American Indians.* Smithsonian Institution, Washington, D.C.

Flannery, K. V.
1986 *Guila Naquitz: Archaic Foraging and Early Agriculture in Oaxaca, Mexico.* Academic Press, Orlando.

Flayharty, Ross A., and Elizabeth A. Morris
1974 "T-W Diamond, A Stone Ring Site in Northern Colorado." *Plains Anthropologist* 19(65): 161–72.

Fletcher, A., and F. La Flesche
1911 *The Omaha Tribe.* Bureau of American Ethnology Annual Report 27:17–672. Smithsonian Institution, Washington, D.C. Reprint. University of Nebraska Press, Lincoln, 1972.

Flynn, P.
1984 "An Analysis of the 1973 Test Excavations at the Zimms site (34RM72)." In *Archaeology of the Mixed Grass Prairie,* Phase I: Quartermaster Creek, edited by T. G. Baugh, pp. 215–90. Archaeological Resource Survey Report no. 20. Oklahoma Archaeological Survey, Norman.
1986 "Analysis of Test Excavations at the Zimms site (34RM72), Western Oklahoma." In *Current Trends in Southern Plains Archaeology,* edited by T. G. Baugh, pp. 129–140. *Plains Anthropologist Memoir* no. 21.

Foor, Thomas Allyn
1982 "Cultural Continuity on the Northwestern Great Plains, 1300 B.C. to A.D. 200: The Pelican Lake Culture." Ph.D. dissertation, University of Michigan. University Microfilms International, Ann Arbor.

1985 "Archaeological Classification in the Northwestern Plains Region." *Plains Anthropologist* 30(108): 123–35.

1988 "Avonlea Systematics and Culture History." In *Avonlea Yesterday and Today: Archaeology and Prehistory*, edited by L. B. Davis, pp. 257–63. Saskatchewan Archaeological Society, Regina.

Forbis, Richard G.

1962 "The Old Women's Buffalo Jump, Alberta." *Contributions to Anthropology 1960*, part 1, pp. 57–123. Bulletin 180. National Museum of Canada, Ottawa.

1963 "The Direct Historical Approach in the Prairie Provinces of Canada." *Great Plains Journal* 3(1): 9–16.

1977 *Cluny, an Ancient Fortified Village in Alberta.* Occasional Paper no. 4. Department of Anthropology, University of Calgary.

Ford, James A., and Gordon R. Willey

1941 "An Interpretation of the Prehistory of the Eastern United States." *American Anthropologist* 43:325–63.

Ford, Richard I.

1977 "Evolutionary Ecology and the Evolution of Human Ecosystems: A Case Study from the Midwestern U.S.A." In *Explanation of Prehistoric Change*, edited by J. N. Hill, pp. 153–84. University of New Mexico Press, Albuquerque.

1979 "Gathering and Gardening: Trends and Consequences of Hopewell Subsistence Strategies." In *Hopewell Archaeology*, edited by D. S. Brose and N. Greber, pp. 234–38. Kent State University Press, Kent, Ohio.

Ford, Richard I., Albert A. Schroeder, and Stewart L. Peckham

1972 "Three Perspectives on Puebloan Prehistory." In *New Perspectives on the Pueblos*, edited by Alfonso Ortiz, pp. 19–39. University of New Mexico Press, Albuquerque.

Foss, J. E., Michael G. Michlovic, J. L. Richardson, J. L. Arndt, and Michael E. Timpson

1985 "Pedologic Study of Archaeological Sites along the Red River." *North Dakota Academy of Science* 39:51.

Fowler, Melvin L., and Robert L. Hall

1978 "Late Prehistory of the Illinois Area." In *Northeast*, edited by Bruce G. Trigger, pp. 560–68. Vol. 15, *Handbook of North American Indians.* Smithsonian Institution, Washington, D.C.

Fox, Gregory L.

1985 "Historical Research." In *The Jamestown Mounds Project*, edited by J. Signe Snortland-Coles, pp. 2.12–2.19. State Historical Society of North Dakota, Bismarck.

Fox, Richard A., Jr.

1982 "The Souris Basin in Northeastern Plains Prehistory." *Journal of the North Dakota Archaeological Association* 1:91–112.

Fox, Steven J.

1982 *Excavations at the Irvin Nelson Site, 32BE208.* North Dakota State University, Fargo. Submitted to the U.S. Fish and Wildlife Service, Denver Regional Office, Colo.

Fraley, David C.
1988 "Avonlea and Besant in Eastern Montana: Archaeological Distributions in the Lower Yellowstone Region." In *Avonlea Yesterday and Today: Archaeology and Prehistory,* edited by L. B. Davis, pp. 129–36. Saskatchewan Archaeological Society, Regina.

Fraley, David C., M. Griffith, and C. A. Novak
1982 "24DW87 and Ayers-Frazier: Soils and Archaeology at Two Sites in Eastern Montana." Paper presented at the Fortieth Annual Plains Anthropological Conference, Calgary, Alberta.

Frayer, D. W., and L. Bradley
1979 "A Late Woodland Burial from Platte County, Missouri." *Plains Anthropologist* 24(83): 21–27.

Fredlund, Lynn Berry
1981 "Southeastern Montana in the Late Prehistoric Period: Human Adaptation and Projectile Point Chronology." Ph.D. dissertation, Department of Archaeology, Simon Fraser University, Vancouver.
1988 "Distribution and Characteristics of Avonlea South of the Yellowstone River in Montana." In *Avonlea Yesterday and Today: Archaeology and Prehistory,* edited by Leslie B. Davis, pp. 171–82. Saskatchewan Archaeological Society, Saskatoon.

Freeman, J. E.
1959 "The Neosho Focus, A Late Prehistoric Culture in Northeastern Oklahoma." Ph.D. dissertation, University of Wisconsin, Madison. University Microfilms International, Ann Arbor.
1962 "The Neosho Focus: A Late Prehistoric Culture in Northeastern Oklahoma." *Oklahoma Anthropological Society Bulletin* 10:1–26.

Fried, Morton H.
1975 *The Notion of Tribe.* Cummings, Menlo Park, Calif.

Frison, George C.
1967 "The Piney Creek Sites, Wyoming." *University of Wyoming Publications,* 33(1): 1–92.
1970 "The Kobold Site, 24BH406: A Post-Altithermal Record of Buffalo-Jumping for the Northwestern Plains." *Plains Anthropologist* 15(47): 1–35.
1971 "Shoshonean Antelope Procurement in the Upper Green River Basin, Wyoming." *Plains Anthropologist* 16(54): 258–84.
1978 *Prehistoric Hunters of the High Plains.* Academic Press, New York.
1982 "Sources of Steatite and Methods of Prehistoric Procurement and Use in Wyoming." *Plains Anthropologist* 27(1): 273–86.
1988 "Avonlea Contemporaries in Wyoming." In *Avonlea Yesterday and Today: Archaeology and Prehistory,* edited by Leslie B. Davis, pp. 155–70. Saskatchewan Archaeological Society, Saskatoon.

Froiland, Sven G.
1978 *Natural History of the Black Hills.* Center for Western Studies, Augustana College, Sioux Falls, S.D.

Fryxell, Roald and R. A. Daugherty
1962 "Interim Report, Archaeological Salvage in the Lower Monumental Reservoir, Washington." Reports of Investigations 21. Washington State University Laboratory of Anthropology, Pullman.

Galinat, W. C.

1985   "Domestication and Diffusion of Maize." In *Prehistoric Food Production in North America*, edited by Richard I. Ford, pp. 245–78. Anthropological Papers no. 75. Museum of Anthropology, University of Michigan, Ann Arbor.

Galiant, W. C., and R. G. Campbell

1967   *The diffusion of Eight-rowed Maize from the Southwest to the Central Plains.* Monograph Series no. 1. Massachusetts Agricultural Experiment Station, Amherst.

Gallagher, James P., Robert F. Boszhardt, Robert F. Sasso, and Katherine Stevenson

1985   "Oneota Ridged Field Agriculture in Southwestern Wisconsin." *American Antiquity* 50:605–12.

Gallagher, James P., and Katherine Stevenson

1982   "Oneota Subsistence and Settlement in Southwestern Wisconsin." In *Oneota Studies*, edited by G. Gibbon, pp. 15–27. Publications in Anthropology 1. University of Minnesota, Minneapolis.

Galm, J. R.

1978   *Archaeological Investigations at Wister Lake, LeFlore County, Oklahoma.* Research Series no. 1. Archaeological Research and Management Center, University of Oklahoma, Norman.

1979   *The Uncas Site: A Late Prehistoric Manifestation in the Southern Plains.* Research Series no. 5. Archaeological and Research Management Center, University of Oklahoma, Norman.

1984   "Arkansas Valley Caddoan Formative: The Wister and Fourche Maline Phases." In *Prehistory of Oklahoma*, edited by R. E. Bell, pp. 199–219. Academic Press, Orlando.

Gant, Robert D.

1967   *Report of the Archaeological Investigations at the Arp Site, 39BR101, Brule County, South Dakota 1961.* Archaeological Studies Circular no. 12. W. H. Over Dakota Museum, Vermillion, South Dakota.

George, Douglas

1979   "St. Croix Stamped Series." In *A Handbook of Minnesota Prehistoric Ceramics*, edited by S. F. Anfinson, pp. 169–74. Occasional Papers in Minnesota Anthropology no. 5. Minnesota Archaeological Society, Fort Snelling.

Gibbon, Guy E.

1972   "Cultural Dynamics and the Development of the Oneota Life-Way in Wisconsin." *American Antiquity* 37:166–85.

1974   "A Model of Mississippian Development and Its Implications for the Red Wing Area." In *Aspects of Upper Great Lakes Anthropology*, edited by Elden Johnson, pp. 129–37. Minnesota Prehistoric Archaeology Series no. 11. Minnesota Historical Society, St. Paul.

1979   *The Mississippian Occupation of the Red Wing Area.* Minnesota Prehistoric Archaeology Series no. 13. Minnesota Historical Society, St. Paul.

1982   "Oneota Origins Revisited." In *Oneota Studies*, edited by Guy E. Gibbon, pp. 85–89. Publications in Anthropology 1. University of Minnesota, Minneapolis.

1983 "The Blue Earth Phase of Southern Minnesota." *Journal of the Iowa Archaeological Society* 30:1–84.

1986 "The Mississippian Tradition: Oneota Culture." In *Introduction to Wisconsin Archaeology,* edited by W. Green, J. B. Stoltman, and A. B. Kehoe, pp. 314–38. *The Wisconsin Archaeologist* 67(3–4).

1989 "Tribalization and Its Causes in Late Woodland Central Minnesota." Ms. on file, Wilford Laboratory of Archaeology, University of Minnesota, Minneapolis.

1991 "The Middle Mississippian Presence in Minnesota." In *Cahokia and the Hinterlands,* edited by Thomas E. Emerson and R. Barry Lewis, pp. 207–20. University of Illinois Press, Urbana and Chicago.

Gibbon, Guy E., and Christy A. H. Caine
1980 "The Middle to Late Woodland Transition in Eastern Minnesota." *Midcontinental Journal of Archaeology* 5:57–72.

Gibbon, Guy E., and Clark A. Dobbs
1991 "The Middle Mississippian Presence in the Red Wing Area, Minnesota." In *New Perspectives on Cahokia: Views from the Peripheries,* edited by James B. Stoltman, pp. 281–305. Monographs in World Archaeology no. 2. Prehistory Press, Madison.

Gill, George W.
1981 "Human Skeletal Populations of the Northwestern Plains: A Preliminary Analysis." In *Progress in Skeletal Biology of Plains Populations,* edited by Richard L. Jantz and Douglas H. Ubelaker. *Plains Anthropologist Memoir* 17, 26(94, pt. 2): 57–70.

Gill, George W., and Rhoda O. Lewis
1977 "A Plains Woodland Burial from the Badlands of Western Nebraska." *Plains Anthropologist* 22 (75): 67–74.

Gilmore, M. R.
1929 "The Arikara Book of Genesis." *Papers of the Michigan Academy of Science* 12:95–120.

Glassow, M. A.
1972 "Changes in the Adaptations of Southwestern Basketmakers: A Systems Perspective." In *Contemporary Archaeology,* edited by M. P. Leone, pp. 289–302. Southern Illinois University Press, Carbondale.

1980 *Prehistoric Agricultural Development in the Northern Southwest: A Study of Changing Patterns of Land Use.* Ballena Press Anthropological Papers no. 16. Menlo Park, Calif.: Ballena Press.

1984 "An Archaeological Survey of the Vermejo Canyon, Colfax County, New Mexico." In *Papers of the Philmont Conference on the Archaeology of Northeastern New Mexico,* edited by C. J. Condie, pp. 93–114. *New Mexico Archaeological Council Proceedings* 6(1).

Gleichman, P. J.
1983 *Segundo East and West: Archaeological Inventory of a Portion of the Upper Purgatoir River Valley.* Highway Salvage Report no. 40. Colorado Department of Highways.

Goddard, Ives
1978a "Eastern Algonquian Languages." In *Northeast,* edited by Bruce G.

Trigger, pp. 70–77. Vol. 15, *Handbook of North American Indians.* Smithsonian Institution, Washington, D.C.

1978b "Central Algonquian Languages." In *Northeast,* edited by Bruce G. Trigger, pp. 583–87. Vol. 15, *Handbook of North American Indians.* Smithsonian Institution, Washington, D.C.

1978c "The Sutaio Dialect of Cheyenne: A Discussion of the Evidence." In *Papers of the Ninth Algonquian Conference,* edited by William Cowan, pp. 68–80. Carleton University, Ottawa.

1979 "Comparative Algonquian." In *The Languages of Native America,* edited by Lyle Campbell and Marianne Mithun, pp. 70–132. University of Texas Press, Austin.

Goddard, Pliny Earle

1918 "Myths and Tales of the San Carlos Apache." *Anthropological Papers of the American Museum of Natural History* 24(1): 1–86. New York.

1919 "Myths and Tales of the White Mountain Apache." *Anthropological Papers of the American Museum of Natural History* 24(2): 86–139. New York.

Godfrey-Smith, D. I., and L. Haywood

1984 "Obsidian Sources in Ontario Prehistory. *Ontario Archaeology* 41:29–35.

Good, Kent N.

1975 "The Lisbon Burial: 32RM201." Ms. on file, Department of Anthropology, University of North Dakota, Grand Forks.

Good, Kent N., James C. Dahlberg, Thomas Larson, Bruce Benz, and Fred Schneider

1977 *Archaeological Investigations of the Hendrickson II Site, 32SN403, LaMoure-Oakes Project, Garrison Diversion, North Dakota.* Department of Anthropology and Archaeology, University of North Dakota, Grand Forks. Submitted to the U.S. Bureau of Reclamation, Billings, Mont.

Gordon, Bryan H. C.

1976 *Migod: 8000 Years of Barrenground Prehistory.* Archaeological Survey of Canada Paper no. 56. National Museum of Man Mercury Series, Ottawa.

Gradwohl, David M.

1969 *Prehistoric Villages in Eastern Nebraska.* Publications in Anthropology no. 4. Nebraska State Historical Society, Lincoln.

Grange, Roger T., Jr.

1968 *Pawnee and Lower Loup Pottery.* Publications in Anthropology no. 3. Nebraska State Historical Society, Lincoln.

1979 "An Archaeological View of Pawnee Origins." *Nebraska History* 60(2): 135–60.

1980 *Archaeological Investigations in the Red Willow Reservoir.* Publications in Anthropology 9. Nebraska State Historical Society, Lincoln.

Grant, Marcus P., Christian J. Zier, and Robert G. Rosenberg

1988 *Supplement Report: Cultural Resource Investigations in Stage One Areas of the Basin Study Extension, Cache La Poudre Water and Power Project, Larimer County, Colorado.*

Graspointer, Andreas
1980 "Southern Alberta: The Nomadic Culture." In *Alberta Archaeology: Prospect and Retrospect*, edited by T. A. Moore, pp. 83–95. Archaeological Society of Alberta, Lethbridge, Canada.

Green, F. E.
1962 "Additional Notes on Prehistoric Wells at the Clovis site." *American Antiquity* 28:230–34.
1967 *Archaeological Salvage in the Sanford Reservoir Area.* Report no. 14-10-0333-1126, submitted to the National Park Service, Washington, D.C.

Green, F. E., and J. H. Kelley
1960 "Comments on Alibates Flint." *American Antiquity* 25(3): 413–14.

Green, William
1986 "Prehistoric Woodland Peoples in the Upper Mississippi Valley." In *Prehistoric Mound Builders of the Mississippi Valley*, edited by James B. Stoltman, pp. 17–24. Putnam Museum, Davenport, Iowa.
1987 "Between Hopewell and Mississippian: Late Woodland in the Prairie Peninsula as Viewed from the Western Illinois Uplands." Ph.D. dissertation, Department of Anthropology, University of Wisconsin, Madison.

Greene, F. C., and W. B. Howe
1952 *Geologic Section of Pennsylvanian Rocks Exposed in the Kansas City Area.* Information Circular no. 8. Missouri Geological Survey and Water Resources, Rolla.

Gregg, John B., and Larry J. Zimmerman
1986 "Malnutrition in 14th Century South Dakota: Osteopathological Implications." *North American Archaeologist* 7:191–214.

Gregg, Michael L.
1985 "Archaeological Classification and Chronology for Western and Central North Dakota." In *An Overview of the Prehistory of Central and Western North Dakota*, edited by Michael L. Gregg and Dale Davidson, pp. 67–78. Bureau of Land Management, Billings, Mont.
1987a *Archaeological Excavation at the Naze Site (32SN246)*, edited by Department of Anthropology, University of North Dakota, Grand Forks. Submitted to the U.S. Bureau of Reclamation, Billings, Mont.
1987b "Knife River Flint in the Northeastern Plains." *Plains Anthropologist* 32:367–77.

Gregg, Michael L., and Paul R. Picha
1989 "Early Plains Woodland and Middle Plains Woodland Occupation of the James River Region in Southeastern North Dakota." *Midcontinental Journal of Archaeology* 14(1): 38–61.

Gregg, Michael L., Paul R. Picha, Cynthia Kordecki, Fern E. Swenson, and Cherie E. Haury
1986 *Test Excavations at Eight Archaeological Sites on the James River in Stutsman and LaMoure Counties, North Dakota.* Department of Anthropology, University of North Dakota, Grand Forks. Submitted to the U.S. Bureau of Reclamation, Billings, Mont.

Gregg, Michael L., Fern E. Swenson, Paul R. Picha, Cynthia Kordecki, Cherie E. Haury, and Christopher Quinn
1987   *Test Excavations at 15 Archaeological sites Along the James River in Stutsman and LaMoure Counties, North Dakota.* Department of Anthropology, University of North Dakota, Grand Forks. Submitted to the U.S. Bureau of Reclamation, Billings, Mont.
Greiser, Sally T.
1983   "Rethinking Late Prehistoric Culture History and Relationships in the Powder River Basin." Paper presented at the Forty-second Annual Plains Anthropological Conference, Lincoln.
1984   "Projectile Point Chronologies of Southwestern Montana." *Archaeology in Montana* 25(1): 35–52.
1985   "Predictive Models of Hunter-Gatherer Subsistence and Settlement Strategies on the Central High Plains." *Plains Anthropologist Memoir* 20, vol. 30.
1986   "Artifact Collections from Ten Sites at Canyon Ferry Reservoir." *Archaeology in Montana* 27(1–2): 1–190.
1988   "Lost Terrace Avonlea Material Culture." In *Avonlea Yesterday and Today: Archaeology and Prehistory,* edited by L. B. Davis, pp. 119–28. Saskatchewan Archaeological Society, Saskatoon.
Greiser, S. T., T. W. Greiser, S. M. Vetter, and A. L. Stanfill
1983   *Sun River (24CA74): A Stratified Pelican Lake and Oxbow Occupation Site Near Great Falls, Montana.* Historical Research Associates, Missoula, Mont. Submitted to U.S. Army Corps of Engineers, Omaha District, Contract no. DACW45-82-C-0152.
Gribbin, J. and H. H. Lamb
1978   "Climatic Change in Historical Times." In *Climatic Change,* edited by John Gribbin, pp. 68–82. Cambridge University Press.
Griffin, James B.
1946   "Culture Change and Continuity in Eastern United States Archaeology." In *Man in Northeastern North America,* edited by Frederick S. Johnson, pp. 37–95. Papers of the Robert S. Peabody Foundation for Archaeology no. 3. Phillips Academy, Andover, Mass.
1960   "A Hypothesis for the Prehistory of the Winnebago." In *Culture in History,* edited by Stanley Diamond, pp. 809–65. Columbia University Press, N.Y.
1967   "Eastern North American Archaeology: A Summary." *Science* 156: 175–91.
Grinnell, George B.
1962   *The Cheyenne Indians: Their History and Ways of Life.* 2 vols. Reprint. Cooper Square Publishers, New York.
1972   *The Cheyenne Indians: Their History and Ways of Life.* Reprint. University of Nebraska Press, Lincoln.
Griswold, Gillett
1970   "Aboriginal patterns of Trade between the Columbia Basin and the Northern Plains." *Archaeology in Montana* 11:1–96.
Grosser, R. D.
1973   "A Tentative Cultural Sequence for the Snyder Site, Kansas." *Plains Anthropologist* 18:228–38.

Grove, Jean M.
1988   *The Little Ice Age.* Methuen, London and New York.
Gruhn, Ruth
1961   "The Archaeology of Wilson Butte Cave, South Central Idaho." Occasional Paper no. 6. Idaho State Museum, Pocatello.
1971   "Preliminary Report on the Muhlbach Site: A Besant Bison Trap in Central Alberta." *National Museum of Canada Bulletin* 232:128–56. Ottawa.
Gryba, Eugene M.
1977   "The Prehistoric Occupation of the Lower Trout Creek–Hubble Creek Drainage Area in the Swan River Valley of Manitoba." *Napao* 7(1–2): 8–28.
1981   "An Introduction to the Prehistoric Human Occupation of the Southeastern Section of the Swan Valley, Manitoba." *Napao* 11 (1–2): 17–40.
Gunnerson, D. A.
1956   "The Southern Athabascans: Their Arrival in the Southwest." *El Palacio* 63(11–12): 346–65.
1974   *The Jicarilla Apaches.* Northern Illinois University Press, DeKalb.
Gunnerson, James H.
1952   "Some Nebraska Culture Pottery Types." *Plains Anthropological Conference Newsletter* 5(3): 39–49.
1959   "Archaeological Survey in Northeastern New Mexico." *El Palacio* 66(5): 145–54.
1969   "Apache Archaeology in Northeastern New Mexico." *American Antiquity* 34(1): 23–39.
1978   *An Introduction to Plains Apache Archaeology – The Dismal River Aspect.* Reprints in Anthropology, vol. 12. J&L Reprint, Lincoln.
1979   "Southern Athapaskan Archaeology." In *Southwest*, edited by Alfonso Ortiz, pp. 162–69. Vol. 9, *Handbook of North American Indians.* Smithsonian Institution, Washington, D.C.
1987   *Archaeology of the High Plains.* Cultural Resource Series, no. 19. Bureau of Land Management, Denver, Colo.
1989   *Apishapa Canyon Archaeology: Excavations at the Cramer, Snake Blakeslee and Nearby Sites.* Reprints in Anthropology, vol. 41. J & L Reprint, Lincoln.
Gunnerson, J. H., and D. A. Gunnerson
1971   "Apachean Culture: A Study in Unity and Diversity." In *Apachean Culture History and Ethnology*, edited by K. H. Basso and M. E. Opler, pp. 7–27. Anthropological Paper no. 21. University of Arizona, Tucson.
Guthrie, Mark R.
1982   *The Aurora Burial: Site 5AH244.* Report to the City of Aurora History Center, University of Denver.
Haberman, Thomas W.
1979   *Test Excavations and Evaluation of 39ST80: A Plains Woodland Site in Stanley County, South Dakota.* Contract Investigations Series 3. South Dakota State Archaeological Research Center, Fort Meade.
1983   "The Early Plains Village Component at the Dirt Lodge Village Site, Spink County, South Dakota." Ms. on file, South Dakota Archaeological Research Center, Rapid City.

Habicht-Mauche, J. A.

1987   "Southwestern-Style Culinary Ceramics on the Southern Plains: A Case Study of Technological Innovation and Cross-Cultural Interaction." *Plains Anthropologist* 32(16):175–89.

1988   "An Analysis of Southwestern Style Utility Ware Ceramics from the Southern Plains in the Context of Protohistoric Plains-Pueblo Interaction." Ph.D. dissertation, Harvard University, Cambridge. University Microfilms International, Ann Arbor.

1991   "Evidence for the Manufacture of Southwestern-Style Culinary Ceramics on the Southern Plains." In *Farmers, Hunters, and Colonists: Interaction Between the Southwest and the Southern Plains*, edited by Katherine A. Spielmann, pp. 51–70. University of Arizona Press, Tucson.

1992   "Coronado's Querechos and Teyas in the Archaeological Record of the Texas Panhandle." *Plains Anthropologist* 37:247–59.

Hale, Kenneth, and David Harris

1979   "Historical Linguistics and Archaeology." In *Southwest*, edited by Alfonso Ortiz, pp. 170–77. Vol. 9, *Handbook of North American Indians.* Smithsonian Institution, Washington, D.C.

Hall, E. T.

1944a   "Recent Clues to Athapascan Prehistory in the Southwest." *American Anthropologist* 46:98–105.

1944b   *Early Stockaded Settlements in Gobernador, New Mexico.* Columbia University Press, New York.

Hall, Robert L.

1967   "The Mississippian Heartland and Its Plains Relationship." *Plains Anthropologist* 12:175–83.

Hall, Steven A.

1982   "Pollen Analysis of the Garnsey Bison Kill Site, Southeastern New Mexico." In *The Garnsey Spring Campsite: Late Prehistoric Occupation in Southeastern New Mexico*, edited by William J. Parry and John D. Speth, pp. 85–111. Research Reports in Anthropology Contribution no. 10. Museum of Anthropology, University of Michigan, Ann Arbor.

1984   "Pollen Analysis of the Garnsey Bison Kill Site, Southeastern New Mexico." In *The Garnsey Spring Campsite: Late Prehistoric Occupation in Southeastern New Mexico*, edited by William J. Parry and John D. Speth, pp. 85–108. Technical Reports no. 15. Museum of Anthropology, University of Michigan, Ann Arbor.

Hamilton, Scott

1981   "The Archaeology of the Wenesaga Rapids." Archaeology Research Report 17. Archaeology and Heritage Planning Branch, Ontario Ministry of Culture and Recreation, Toronto.

1982   "The Blackduck Culture: Plains Periphery Influences." In *Approaches to Algonquian Archaeology*, edited by M. Hanna and B. Kooyman, pp. 97–118. Proceedings of the 13th Annual Conference, Archaeological Association of the University of Calgary.

Hamilton, S., W. Ferris, S. Hallgrimson, G. McNeely, K. Sammons, E. Simonds, and K. Topinka

1981   "1979 Excavations at the Stott Site (D1Ma-1): with Interpretations of

Cultural Stratigraphy." Papers in Manitoba Archaeology, Miscellaneous Paper no. 12. Department of Cultural Affairs and Historical Resources, Winnipeg.

Hammock, L. C.
1965 "Archaeology of the Ute Dam and Reservoir, Northeastern New Mexico." Papers in Anthropology no. 14. Museum of New Mexico, Santa Fe.

Hammond, George P., and Agapito Rey
1940 *Narratives of the Coronado Expedition, 1540–1542.* University of New Mexico Press, Albuquerque.
1953 *Don Juan de Oñate – Colonizer of New Mexico 1595–1628.* University of New Mexico Press, Albuquerque.

Hancock, P., T. M. Kerns, R. A. Moore, A. C. Reed, L. Wheelbarger, and P. Whitten
1988 *Excavations in the Middle La Plata Valley.* Studies in Archaeology no. 6. Division of Conservation Archaeology.

Hanna, Margaret G.
1978 "A Preliminary Description of Duck Bay Ware." Paper presented at the Eleventh Annual Meeting, Canadian Archaeological Association.
1982 "Pots and Populations: Alternate Analytical Techniques for using Ceramics as Indicators of Social Units." Ph.D. dissertation, Department of Archaeology, University of Calgary.

Hannus, L. Adrien
1972 "A Northwestern Plains Subculture, A.D. 400–1700." M.A. thesis, Department of Anthropology, Wichita State University, Wichita.
1985 *An Overview and Summary of the Archaeology of the Northern Border Pipeline Project in Montana, North Dakota, South Dakota, Minnesota and Iowa.* Archaeology Laboratory of the Center for Western Studies, Augustana College, Sioux Falls, S.D. Submitted to Northern Border Pipeline Company, Omaha, Nebr.

Hannus, L. Adrien, Philip Bjork, John Butterbrodt, David Miller, Timothy Nowak, and Everett White
1983 *A Cultural Resources Survey of a Portion of the South Fork of the Cheyenne River, Fall River county, South Dakota.* Publications in Anthropology no. 1. Archaeology Laboratory, South Dakota State University, Brookings. Submitted to State Historical Preservation Center, Vermillion, S.D.

Hannus, L. Adrien, J. M. Butterbrodt, E. J. Lueck, T. T. Nowak, and E. M. White
1989 *An Archaeological Survey of Selected Areas Within Fog Creek, Babby Butte Canyon and Lower Cain Creek in Shannon and Pennington Counties, South Dakota.* White River Badlands Regional Research Project Report, vol. 7. Archaeology Laboratory, Augustana College, Sioux Falls, S.D. Draft originally compiled in 1983 as Publications in Anthropology 4, Archaeology Laboratory, South Dakota State University, Brookings.

Hannus, L. Adrien, and Timothy R. Nowak
1988 "Avonlea: A Point Industry Surfaces in South Dakota or Archers on the March." In *Avonlea Yesterday and Today: Archaeology and Prehis-*

tory, edited by L. B. Davis, pp. 183–89. Saskatchewan Archaeological Society, Regina.

Hanson, Jeffrey R.

1983   "Bison Ecology and Nomadic Settlement/Subsistence Structure for the North Dakota Region." In *Archaeology of the Northern Border Pipeline, North Dakota: Test Excavations,* edited by Matthew J. Root and Michael L. Gregg, pp. 1,342–417. Department of Anthropology and Archaeology, University of North Dakota, Grand Forks. Submitted to the Northern Border Pipeline Co., Omaha, Nebr.

Harris, R. K., I. M. Harris, J. C. Blaine, and J. Blaine

1965   "A Preliminary Archaeological and Documentary Study of the Womack Site, Lamar County, Texas." *Bulletin of the Texas Archaeological Society* 36:287–363.

Hart, Jeff

1976   *Montana: Native Plants and Early Peoples.* Montana Historical Society, Helena.

Hartley, J. D., and A. F. Miller

1977   *Archaeological Investigations at the Bryson-Paddock Site, An Early Contact Period Site on the Southern Plains.* Archaeological Site Report no. 32. Oklahoma River Basin Survey, Norman.

Harvey, Amy E.

1979   *Oneota Culture in Northwestern Iowa.* Report 12. Office of the State Archaeologist, University of Iowa, Iowa City.

Haskell, J. Loring

1987   *Southern Athapaskan Migration, A.D. 200–1750.* Navajo Community College Press, Tsaile, Ariz.

Hassan, Fekri A.

1975   "Determination of the Size, Density, and Growth Rate of Hunting-Gathering Populations." In *Population, Ecology, and Social Evolution,* edited by S. Polgar, pp. 27–52. Aldine, Chicago.

Hassen, Harold

1985   "Late Woodland Diversity in the Fall Creek Locality, Adams County, Illinois." *The Wisconsin Archaeologist* 66:282–91.

Hatcher, M. A.

1927   "Descriptions of the Tejas or Asinai Indians, 1691–1722." *Southwestern Historical Quarterly* 30:283–304.

Haug, James K.

1978   *Cultural Resources Survey of Selected Silver King Mine Properties in Custer and Fall River Counties, South Dakota.* South Dakota State Archaeological Research Center, Fort Meade. Submitted to Tennessee Valley Authority, Contract no. TV-46932A.

1983   "Early Plains Village Sites in Northeastern South Dakota." Paper presented at the Forty-first Annual Plains Anthropology Conference, Rapid City, S.D.

Haury, C. E.

1982   *The Prehistory and Paleoenvironment of the Black Mesa Locality, Cimarron County Oklahoma.* Laboratory of Archaeology, Department of Anthropology, University of Tulsa.

Haury, Cherie E.
1987   "Vertebrate Faunal Remains from the Naze Site." In *Archaeological Excavation at the Naze site (32SN246)*, edited by Michael L. Gregg, pp. 343–85. Department of Anthropology, University of North Dakota, Grand Forks. Submitted to the U.S. Bureau of Reclamation, Billings, Mont.

Hayes, Alden C., Jon Nathan Young, and A. H. Warren
1981   *Excavations of Mound 7, Gran Quivira National Monument.* National Park Service Publications in Archaeology 16, Washington, D.C.

Hays, Joe S.
1986   "An Archeological Survey of Portions of the Buffalo Lake National Wildlife Refuge, Randall County, Texas." Report prepared for the U.S. Department of the Interior, Bureau of Reclamation, Southwest Region, Amarillo.

Henige, David
1986   "Primary Source by Primary Source? On the Role of Epidemics in New World Depopulation." *Ethnohistory* 33:293–312.

Henning, Dale R.
1968   "Climatic Change and the Mill Creek Culture of Iowa: Part 1." *Journal of the Iowa Archaeological Society* 15:1–191.
1970   "Development and Interrelationships of Oneota Culture in the Lower Missouri River Valley." *The Missouri Archaeologist* 32:1–180.
1971   "Origins of Mill Creek." *Journal of the Iowa Archaeological Society* 18:6–13.
1982   *Subsurface Testing Program: Proposed Perry Creek Dam and Reservoir Area, Plymouth County, Iowa.* Technical Report 82-05. Department of Anthropology, University of Nebraska, Lincoln.
1983a   "The Initial Variant of the Middle Missouri Tradition." In *Archaeological Reconnaissance Survey of the Northern Border Pipeline for the Northern Plains Natural Gas Company—Iowa Segment*, vol. 1, edited by G. Joseph Hudak, pp. 4.43–4.66. Archaeological Field Services, Stillwater, Minnesota.
1983b   "The Oneota Cultural Tradition." In *Archaeological Reconnaissance Survey of the Northern Border Pipeline for the Northern Plains Natural Gas Company—Iowa Segment*, vol. 1, edited by G. Joseph Hudak, pp. 4.67–4.81. Archaeological Field Services, Stillwater, Minnesota.
1988   "The Ethnohistory of the Dhegihan-Speaking Tribes." *Forty-sixth Annual Plains Conference Program and Abstracts*, p. 43.

Henning, Dale R., and Elizabeth Henning
1978   *Great Oasis Ceramics.* Occasional Publications in Minnesota Anthropology no. 2. Minnesota Archaeological Society, St. Paul.

Henning, Elizabeth, and Dale Henning
1982   "Great Oasis-Mill Creek Interrelationships." In *Interrelations of Cultural and Fluvial Deposits in Northwest Iowa*, edited by E. A. Bettis and D. M. Thompson, pp. 10–14. Association of Iowa Archaeologists, Iowa City.

Hester, J. J.
1972   *Blackwater Locality Number 1: A Stratified Early Man Site in Eastern*

New Mexico. Fort Burgwin Research Center Paper no. 8. Southern Methodist University, Dallas.

Hewes, Gordon
1948 "Early Tribal Migrations in the Northern Great Plains." *Plains Archaeological Conference Newsletter* 1(4):3–12. Lincoln, Nebr.

Hibben, Frank C.
1938 The Gallina Phase. *American Antiquity* 4:131–36.

Hill, A. T., and Marvin Kivett
1941 "Woodland-like Manifestations in Nebraska." *Nebraska History* 21(3): 145–243.

Hill, A. T., and Waldo R. Wedel
1936 "Excavations at the Leary Indian Village and Burial Site, Richardson County, Nebraska." *Nebraska History* 17(1): 3–73.

Hill, W. W.
1982 *An Ethnography of Santa Clara Pueblo, New Mexico.* University of New Mexico Press, Albuquerque.

Hindess, B., and P. Q. Hirst
1975 *Pre-Capitalist Modes of Production.* Routledge and Kegan Paul, London.

Hlady, Walter M.
1970 "Manitoba: The Northern Woodlands." In *Ten Thousand Years*, edited by W. M. Hlady, pp. 93–121. Manitoba Archaeological Society, Winnipeg.
1971 "An Introduction to the Archaeology of the Woodland Area of Northern Manitoba." *Manitoba Archaeological Newsletter* 8(2–3).

Hodder, Ian
1988 *Reading the Past.* Cambridge University Press, Cambridge.

Hodge, F. W., (ed.)
1907 *Handbook of American Indians North of Mexico.* Bureau of American Ethnology Bulletin 30. Smithsonian Institution, Washington, D.C.

Hoffman, J. J.
1968 *The La Roche Site.* Publications in Salvage Archaeology no. 11. Smithsonian Institution. River Basin Surveys. Lincoln.

Hoffman, M. P.
1970 Archaeological and Historical Assessment of the Red River Basin in Arkansas. In *Archaeological and Historical Resources of the Red River Basin*, edited by H. E. Davis, pp. 135–94. Publications in Archaeology, Research Series no. 1. Arkansas Archaeological Survey, Fayetteville.

Hofman, J. L.
1984a "The Plains Villagers: The Custer Phase." In *Prehistory of Oklahoma*, edited by R. E. Bell, pp. 287–305. Academic Press, Orlando.
1984b "The Western Protohistoric: A Summary of Edwards and Wheeler Complexes." In *Prehistory of Oklahoma*, edited by R. E. Bell, pp. 347–62. Academic Press, Orlando.
1989 "Protohistoric Culture History on the Southern Great Plains." In *From Clovis to Comanchero: Archaeological Overview of the Southern Great Plains*, edited by Jack L. Hofman, Robert L. Brooks, Jose S.

Hays, Douglas W. Owsley, Richard L. Jantz, Murray K. Marks, and
Mary H. Manhein. Publications in Archaeology, Research Series no.
35. Arkansas Archaeological Survey, Fayetteville.

Hofman, Jack L., and Robert L. Brooks
1989 "Prehistoric Culture History: Woodland Complexes in the Southern
Great Plains." In *From Clovis to Comanchero: Archeological Over-
view of the Southern Great Plains,* edited by Jack L. Hofman, Robert L.
Brooks, Joe S. Hays, Douglas W. Owsley, Richard L. Jantz, Murray K.
Marks, and Mary H. Manhein, pp. 61–70. Publications in Archaeology,
Research Series no. 35. Arkansas Archeological Survey, Fayetteville.

Hoijer, Harry
1946 "Tonkawa." In *Linguistic Structures of Native America,* pp. 289–311.
Viking Fund Publications in Anthropology no. 6. Viking Fund, New
York.
1956 "The Chronology of the Athapaskan Languages." *International Journal of American Linguistics* 22:219–32.
1971 "The Position of the Apachean Languages in the Athabaskan Stock."
In *Apachean Culture History and Ethnology,* edited by Keith H. Basso
and Morris E. Opler, pp. 3–6. Anthropological Paper no. 21. University
of Arizona, Tucson.

Holden, W. C.
1930 "The Canadian Valley Expedition of March 1930." *Texas Archaeological and Paleontological Society Bulletin* 2:21–32.
1931 "Texas Tech Archaeological Expedition Summer 1930." *Texas Archaeological and Paleontological Society Bulletin* 3:43–52.
1933 "Excavations at Saddleback ruin." *Texas Archaeological and Paleontological Society Bulletin* 5:39–52.
1938 "Blue Mountain Rock Shelter." *Texas Archaeological and Paleontological Society Bulletin* 10:208–21.

Hollow, Robert C., and Douglas R. Parks
1980 "Studies in Plains Linguistics." In *Anthropology on the Great Plains,*
edited by W. Raymond Wood and Margot Liberty, pp. 68–97. University
of Nebraska Press, Lincoln.

Holmer, Richard N., (ed.)
1986 *Shoshone-Bannock Culture History.* Reports of Investigations 85–16.
Swanson-Crabtree Anthropological Research Laboratory, Idaho State
University, Pocatello.

Hotopp, J.
1977 "Iowa's Great River Road Cultural and Natural Resources: A Preliminary Survey." Contract Completion Report 108. Office of the State
Archaeologist, Iowa City, Iowa.

Howard, James H.
1953 "The Southern Cult on the Northern Plains." *American Antiquity*
19:130–38.
1965 *The Plains-Ojibwa or Bungi.* Anthropological Papers no. 1. South
Dakota Museum, University of South Dakota, Vermillion.
1966 *The Dakota or Sioux Indians.* Anthropological Papers no. 2. South
Dakota Museum. University of South Dakota, Vermillion.

1968   "Archaeological Investigations at the Spawn Mound, 39LK201, Lake
        County, South Dakota." *Plains Anthropologist* 13(40): 132–45.
1976   *Yanktonai Ethnohistory and the John K. Bear Winter Count. Plains
        Anthropologist Memoir* 11.
Hudak, G. Joseph
1983   "The Prairie Lakes Subarea Woodland Period." In *Archaeological Re-
        connaissance Survey of the Northern Border Pipeline for the Northern
        Plains Natural Gas Company—Iowa Segment*, vol. 1, edited by G.
        Joseph Hudak, pp. 4.21–4.42. Archaeological Field Services, Stillwater,
        Minnesota.
Hudecek, Caroline R.
1988   "The Empress Site (EfOo 130): A Late Prehistoric Tipi Ring Site in
        Southeastern Alberta." Report on file, Archaeological Survey of Alber-
        ta, Edmonton.
Hughes, David T.
1986   "The Courson 1986 Archaeological Project." Paper presented at the
        Annual Meeting of the Texas Archaeological Society, Laredo.
1988   "Prehistoric Architecture Along Wolf Creek, Ochiltree County, Texas."
        Paper presented at the Forty-sixth Plains Anthropology Conference,
        Wichita.
1991   "Investigation of the Buried City, Ochiltree County, Texas: With an
        Emphasis on the Texas Archeological Society Field Schools of 1987
        and 1988." *Bulletin of the Texas Archeological Society* 60:107–148.
Hughes, David T., and A. Alicia Hughes-Jones
1987   *The Courson Archeological Projects: A Final Report of the 1985
        Investigations and Preliminary Report of the 1986 Work.* Courson
        Archaeological Projects, Perryton, Texas.
Hughes, Jack T.
1962   "Lake Creek: A Woodland Site in the Texas Panhandle." *Bulletin of the
        Texas Archaeological Society*, 32:65–84.
1969a   "Prehistory of the Caddoan-Speaking Tribes." Ph.D. dissertation, Co-
        lumbia University. University Microfilms International, Ann Arbor.
1969b   *The Canyon City Club Cave, Randall County, Texas.* Report submit-
        ted to the Texas Historical Commission by West Texas State Univer-
        sity, Canyon.
1976   "The Panhandle Archaic." In *The Texas Archaic: A Symposium*, edited
        by Thomas R. Hester, pp. 28–38. Special Report no. 2. Center for
        Archaeological Research, University of Texas, San Antonio.
1979   "Archaeology of Palo Duro Canyon." In *The Story of Palo Duro Can-
        yon*, edited by Duane Guy, pp. 35–58. Canyon, Texas.
1991   Prehistoric Cultural Developments on the Texas High Plains. *Bulletin
        of the Texas Archaeological Society* 60:1–55.
n.d.   "Cultural Developments During the Archaic and NeoIndian Stages on
        the Texas High Plains." Ms. on file, Archaeological Research Labora-
        tory, Killgore Research Center, West Texas State University, Canyon.
Hughes, J. T., H. C. Hood, and B. P. Newman
1978   "Archaeological Testing in the Red Deer Creek Watershed in Gray,
        Roberts, and Hemphill Counties, Texas." Report submitted to the

National Park Service. Ms. on file, Archaeological Research Laboratory, Kilgore Research Center, West Texas State University, Canyon.

Hughes, J. T., and P. S. Willey
1978 *Archaeology at Mackenzie Reservoir.* Archaeological Survey Report 24. Office of the State Archaeologist, Austin, Tex.

Hultkrantz, Ake
1957 "The Indians in Yellowstone Park." *Annals of Wyoming* 29:125–49.

Hunt, G. O.
1975 "The Archaeology of the Belwood Site." M.A. thesis, University of Denver.

Hurt, Wesley R.
1952 *Report on the Investigation of the Scalp Creek Site 39GR1 and the Ellis Creek Site 39GR2, Gregory County, South Dakota.* Archaeological Studies Circular 4. South Dakota Archaeological Commission, Pierre.
1961 Archaeological Work at the Tabor and Arp Sites. *Museum News* 22(8): 1–6. W. H. Over Museum, University of South Dakota, Vermillion.

Huscher, Betty H., and Harold A. Huscher
1942 "Athapascan Migration Via the Intermontaine Region." *American Antiquity* 8:80–88.
1943 "The Hogan Builders of Colorado." *Southwestern Lore* 9:1–92.

Husted, W. M.
1969 *Bighorn Canyon Archaeology.* Publications in Salvage Archaeology no. 12. Smithsonian Institution River Basin Surveys. Lincoln.

Hyde, George E.
1974 *The Pawnee Indians.* University of Oklahoma Press, Norman.

Ireland, S. K.
1968 "Five Apishapa Focus Sites in the Arkansas Valley, Colorado." M.A. thesis, University of Denver.
1970 *Purgatoire River Reservoir Salvage Archaeology, 1969: Sites TC:C9:4 and TC:C9:9.* Ms on file, National Park Service, Midwest Archaeological Center, Lincoln.
1971 "The Upper Purgatoire complex-A Re-Appraisal." *Southwestern Lore* 37(2): 37–51.
1974 "Trinidad Reservoir Salvage Archaeology, 1972." Ms. on file with the National Park Service, Midwest Archaeological Center, Lincoln, Nebr.

Irwin, Cynthia C., and Henry T. Irwin
1957 "The Archaeology of Agage Bluff Area, Colorado." *Plains Anthropologist* 8:15–38.

Irwin, Henry, and Cynthia C. Irwin
1959 *Excavations at LoDaisKa Site.* Proceedings no. 8. Denver Museum of Natural History.

Jablow, Joseph
1974 *Ponca Indians.* Garland Publishing, New York.

Jelinek, Arthur J.
1967 *A Prehistoric Sequence in the Middle Pecos Valley, New Mexico.* Anthropological Papers no. 31. Museum of Anthropology, University of Michigan, Ann Arbor.

Jelks, E. B. (ed.)
1967 "The Gilbert Site: A Norteño Focus Site in Northeastern Texas." *Bulletin of the Texas Archaeological Society* 37:1–248.
Jenks, Albert E.
1900 "The Wild Rice Gatherers of the Upper Great Lakes: A Study in American Primitive Economics." In Bureau of American Ethnology Annual Report (1897–98). 19:1,013–1,137.
1932 "The Culture from the Arvilla Gravel Pits." *American Anthropologist* 34:455–66.
Jennings, Jesse D.
1968 *Prehistory of North America.* McGraw-Hill, New York.
Jeter, Marvin D.
1977 *Archaeology in Copper Basin, Yavapai County, Arizona.* Anthropological Research Paper no. 11. Arizona State University, Tempe.
Johannessen, Sissel
1984 "Paleoethnobotany." In *American Bottom Archaeology,* edited by Charles J. Bareis and J. W. Porter, pp. 197–214. University of Illinois Press, Urbana.
John, Elizabeth A. H.
1975 *Storms Brewed in Other Men's Worlds: The Confrontations of Indians, Spanish, and French in the Southwest, 1540–1795.* Texas A&M University Press, College Station.
Johnson, Alfred E.
1968 *Archaeological Investigations in the Clinton Reservoir Area Eastern Kansas.* Report submitted to the U.S. Department of the Interior, National Park Service, Midwest Archaeological Center, Lincoln.
1973 "Archaeological Investigations at the Budenbender Site, Tuttle Creek Reservoir, North-Central Kansas." *Plains Anthropologist* 18(62): 271–99.
1976 "A Model of the Kansas City Hopewell Subsistence and Settlement System." In *Hopewellian Archaeology in the Lower Missouri Valley,* edited by A. E. Johnson, pp. 7–15. Publications in Anthropology 8. University of Kansas, Lawrence.
1979 "Kansas City Hopewell." In *Hopewellian Archaeology: The Chillecothe Conference,* edited by D. S. Brose and N. Greber, pp. 86–93. Kent State University Press, Kent, Ohio.
1983 "A Summary of Archaeological Investigations at El Dorado Lake, 1977–1980." In *Phase IV Archaeological Investigations at El Dorado Lake, Butler County, Kansas, Summer 1980,* edited by A. E. Johnson, pp. 185–228. Project Report Series no. 52. Museum of Anthropology, University of Kansas, Lawrence.
1984 "Temporal Relationship of Late (Plains) Woodland components in Eastern Kansas." *Plains Anthropologist* 29:277–88.
1987 "Late Woodland Adaptive Patterns in Eastern Kansas." *Plains Anthropologist* 32:390–402.
1991 "Kansa Origins: An Alternative." *Plains Anthropologist* 36(133): 57–65.
In press "Plains Woodland." Plains vol., *Handbook of North American Indians.* Smithsonian Institution, Washington, D.C.

Johnson, A. E., and Ann M. Johnson
1975 "K-Means and Temporal Variability in Kansas City Hopewell Ceramics." *American Antiquity* 40(3): 283–95.
Johnson, Ann M.
1970 "Montana Projectile Point Types: Avonlea." *Archaeology in Montana* 11(1): 45–57.
1977 "The Dune Buggy Site: 24RV1, and Northwestern Plains Ceramics." *Plains Anthropologist* 22(75): 35–49.
1977 "Woodland and Besant in the Northern Plains: A Perspective." *Archaeology in Montana* 18(1): 27–41.
1979 *Extended Middle Missouri Components in the Big Bend Region, South Dakota.* Special Publication no. 1. South Dakota Archaeological Society, Rapid City.
1988 "Parallel Grooved Ceramics: An Addition to Avonlea Material and Culture." In *Avonlea Yesterday and Today: Archaeology and Prehistory,* edited by L. B. Davis, pp. 137–43. Saskatchewan Archaeological Society, Saskatoon.
Johnson, Ann M., and Becky Kallevig
1988 "Nollmeyer." Paper presented at the Montana Archaeological Society Annual Meeting, Missoula.
Johnson, Elden
1961 "Cambria Burial Mounds in Big Stone County." *Minnesota Archaeologist* 23:53–81.
1962 "The Prehistory of the Red River Valley." *Minnesota History* 38(4): 157–65.
1969 *Prehistoric Peoples of Minnesota.* Minnesota Historical Society, St. Paul.
1969 "Preliminary Notes on the Prehistoric Use of Wild Rice." *The Minnesota Archaeologist* 30:31–43.
1971 "Excavations at the Gull Lake Dam (21CA27)." *The Minnesota Archaeologist* 31:44–69.
1973 *The Arvilla Complex.* Minnesota Prehistoric Archaeology Series no. 9. Minnesota Historical Society, St. Paul.
1979 "Cultural Resources Investigation of the Reservoir Shorelines: Gull Lake, Leech Lake, Pine River and Lake Pokegama." 3 vols. Ms. submitted to the U.S. Army Corps of Engineers, St. Paul District. Contract no.: DACW 37-77-C-0141.
1985 "The 17th Century Mdewakanton Dakota Subsistence Mode." In *Archaeology, Ecology, and Ethnohistory of the Prairie-Forest Border Zone of Minnesota and Manitoba,* edited by J. Spector and E. Johnson, pp. 154–66. Reprints in Anthropology, vol. 31. J & L Reprint, Lincoln, Nebr.
1991 "Cambria and Cahokia's Northwestern Periphery." In *New Perspectives on Cahokia: Views from the Peripheries,* edited by James B. Stoltman, pp. 307–17. Monographs in World Archaeology no. 2. Prehistory Press, Madison.
Johnson, Elden, Christina Harrison, and Jeanne Schaaf
1977 "Cultural Resources Inventory of Land Adjacent to Lake Winnibigoshish." Ms. submitted to the U.S. Army Corps of Engineers, St. Paul District. Contract no. DACW 37-76-C-0181.

Johnson, E., and V. T. Holliday
1986   "The Archaic Record at Lubbock Lake." In *Current Trends in Southern Plains Archaeology*, edited by Timothy G. Baugh, pp. 7–54. *Plains Anthropologist Memoir* no. 21.
Johnson, E., V. T. Holliday, M. J. Kaczor, and R. Stuckenrath
1977   "The Garza Occupation at the Lubbock Lake site." *Bulletin of the Texas Archaeological Society* 48:83–109.
Johnston, R. B.
1967   *The Hitchell Site.* Publications in Salvage Archaeology no. 3. Smithsonian Institution River Basin Surveys. Lincoln.
Joyes, Dennis C.
1973   "The Shippe Canyon Site." *Archaeology in Montana* 14(2): 49–85.
1988   "A Summary and Evaluation of Avonlea in Manitoba." In *Avonlea Yesterday and Today: Archaeology and Prehistory*, edited by L. B. Davis, pp. 227–36. Saskatchewan Archaeological Society, Saskatoon.
Kainer, Ronald E.
1976   "Archaeological Investigations at the Spring Gulch Site (5LR252)." M.A. thesis, Department of Anthropology, Colorado State University, Fort Collins.
Kalasz, S. M.
1985   "Prehistoric Architectural Remains." In *A Chronological Framework of the Fort Carson Pinon Canyon Maneuver Site, Las Animas County, Colorado*, vol. 2, edited by C. Lintz, pp. 104–34. Fort Carson Pinon Canyon Cultural Resource Project, Contribution no. 2. Center for Archaeological Research, Denver University.
Katz, Paul R.
1969   "An Analysis of the Archaeological Data from the Kelley Site, Northeastern Kansas." M.A. thesis, Department of Anthropology, University of Kansas, Lawrence.
1976   "A Technological Analysis of the Kansas City Hopewell Chipped Stone Industry." Ph.D. dissertation, Department of Anthropology, University of Kansas, Lawrence.
Katz, P. R., and S. R. Katz
1976   *Archaeological Investigations in Lower Tule Canyon, Briscoe County, Texas.* Archaeological Survey Report no. 16. Texas Historical Foundation, Texas Tech University. Texas Historical Commission, Office of the State Archaeologist.
Kehoe, Thomas F.
1960   "Stone Tipi Rings in North-Central Montana and the Adjacent Portion of Alberta, Canada: Their Historical, Ethnological and Archaeological Aspsects." Anthropological Paper 62. *Bureau of American Ethnology Bulletin* 173:417–74. *Smithsonian Institution, Washington, D.C.*
1966   "The Small Side-notched Point System of the Northern Plains." *American Antiquity* 31(6): 827–41.
1973   *The Gull Lake Site: A Prehistoric Bison Drive Site in Southwestern Saskatchewan.* Publications in Anthropology and History no. 1. Milwaukee Public Museum, Milwaukee.

1974 "The Large Corner-notched Point System of the Northern Plains and Adjacent Woodlands." In *Aspects of Upper Great Lakes Anthropology, Papers in Honor of Lloyd A. Wilford*, edited by E. Johnson, pp. 103–14. Minnesota Historical Society, St. Paul.

Kehoe, Thomas F., and Alice B. Kehoe
1968 "Saskatchewan." In *The Northwestern Plains: A Symposium*, edited by Warren Caldwell and S. W. Conner. Occasional Papers no. 1. Center for Indian Studies, Rocky Mountain College, Billings, Mont.

Kehoe, Thomas F., and Bruce A. McCorquodale
1961 "Avonlea Point-Horizon Marker for the Northwestern Plains." *Plains Anthropologist* 6:179–88.

Keller, G. N.
1961 "The Changing Position of the Southern Plains in the Late Prehistory of the Great Plains Area." Ph.D. dissertation, University of Chicago.

Keller, J. E.
1975 *The Black Dog Village Site: A Panhandle Aspect Manifestation in Hutchinson County, Texas*. Publications in Archaeology, Report no. 5. Texas Highway Department, Austin.

Keller, Stephen W., and Renee Keller
1983 *Volume IV, James River Survey, Brown County, South Dakota, 1983*. South Dakota Archaeological Research Center, Rapid City.

Kelley, J. Charles
1952 "Archaeological Notes on the Excavation of a Pithouse near Presidio, Texas." *American Anthropologist* 54:356–87.

Kelly, John E.
1987 "Emergent Mississippian and the Transition from Late Woodland to Mississippian: The American Bottom Case for a New Concept." In *The Emergent Mississippian: Proceedings of the Sixth Mid-South Archaeological Conference, June 6–9, 1985*, edited by Richard A. Marshall, pp. 212–26. Occasional Paper no. 87-01. Cobb Institute of Archaeology, Mississippi State University, Mississippi State.

Kelly, John E., Fred A. Finney, Dale L. McElrath, and Steven J. Ozuk
1984 "Late Woodland Period." In *American Bottom Archaeology*, edited by Charles J. Bareis and James W. Porter, pp. 109–27. University of Illinois Press, Urbana.

Kelly, Lucretia S., and Paula G. Cross
1984 "Zooarchaeology." In *American Bottom Archaeology*, edited by Charles J. Bareis and James W. Porter, pp. 215–32. University of Illinois Press, Urbana.

Kelly, M. E. and B. R. Connell
1978 *Survey and Excavations of the Pas Moraine: 1976 Field Season*. Papers in Manitoba Archaeology, Final Report no. 4. Department of Cultural Affairs and Historical Resources, Winnipeg.

Kershner, J. M.
1984 "Chronology of the Middle Vermejo River Drainage." In *Papers of the Philmont Conference on the Archaeology of Northeastern New Mexico*, edited by C. J. Condie, pp. 115–23. *New Mexico Archaeological Council Proceedings* 6(1).

Kessell, John L.
1979   *Kiva, Cross and Crown: The Pecos Indians and New Mexico, 1540–1840*, National Park Service, Washington, D.C.
Key, Patrick J.
1983   *Craniometric Relationships Among Plains Indians.* Report of Investigations no. 34. Department of Anthropology, University of Tennessee, Knoxville.
Keyser, J. D.
1975   "A Shoshonean Origin for the Plains Shield Bearing Warrior Motif." *Plains Anthropologist* 20:207–16.
1977   "Writing-On-Stone: Rock Art on the Northwestern Plains." *Canadian Journal of Archaeology* 1:15–80.
1984   *Rock Art of Western South Dakota.* Section 1. The North Cave Hills. Special Publication of the South Dakota Archaeological Society no. 9, pp. 1–51. Archaeology Laboratory, Augustana College, Sioux Falls.
Keyser, J. D., and C. M. Davis
1981   *Highwalker–One Bear: 1979 Archaeological Excavation on the Ashland Division, Custer National Forest.* Cultural Resources Report no. 3. U.S. Forest Service, Northern Region, Missoula, Mont.
Keyser, James D., and Linea Sundstrom
1984   *Rock Art of Western South Dakota.* Special Publication of the South Dakota Archaeological Society no. 9.
Kidder, Alfred V.
1932   *The Artifacts of Pecos.* Papers of the Southwestern Expedition no. 6, Robert S. Peabody Foundation in Archaeology. Yale University Press, New Haven.
1958   *Archaeological Notes.* Papers of the Robert S. Peabody Foundation for Archaeology, vol. 5, Andover, Mass.
Kingsbury, L. A. and M. Nowak
1980   *Archaeological Investigations on Carrizo Ranches, Inc.* Publications in Archaeology no. 2. Colorado College, Colorado Springs.
Kirkpatrick, D. T., and R. I. Ford
1977   "Basketmaker Food Plants from the Cimarron District, Northeastern New Mexico." *The Kiva* 42(3–4): 257–69.
Kivett, M. F.
1949   "A Woodland Pottery Type From Nebraska." *Proceedings of the Fifth Plains Conference for Archaeology*, pp. 67–89.
1952   *Woodland Sites in Nebraska.* Publications in Anthropology 1. Nebraska State Historical Society, Lincoln.
1953   *The Woodruff Ossuary, A Prehistoric Burial Site in Phillips County, Kansas.* River Basin Surveys Paper 3. Bureau of American Ethnology Bulletin 154. Smithsonian Institution, Washington, D.C.
1970   "Early Ceramic Environmental Adaptions." In *Pleistocene and Recent Environments of the Central Great Plains*, edited by W. Dort, Jr., and J. K. Jones, Jr., pp. 93–102. Department of Geology Special Publication 3. University of Kansas, Lawrence.
Klimko, Olga
1985   *The Gravel Pit and Eastcott Flat Sites: Final Excavation Reports.*

Nipawin Reservoir Heritage Study, vol. 7, edited by David Meyer. Saskatchewan Research Council Publication no. E-903-8-E-85, Saskatoon.

Klimko, Olga, and M.G. Hanna
1988 "The Avonlea Type Site Revisited: A Report on Excavations and Ceramic Analysis." In *Avonlea Yesterday and Today: Archaeology and Prehistory*, edited by L. B. Davis, pp. 25–31. Saskatchewan Archaeological Society, Saskatoon.

Knudson, Ruth Ann
1967 "Cambria Village Ceramics." *Plains Anthropologist* 12:247–99.

Koezur, Polly, and J. V. Wright
1976 *The Potato Island Site, District of Kenora, Ontario.* Archaeological Survey of Canada Paper no. 51. National Museum of Man Mercury Series, Ottawa.

Krause, Richard A.
1969 "Correlation of Phases in Central Plains Prehistory." In *Two House Sites on the Central Plains: An Experiment in Archaeology*, edited by W. R. Wood, pp. 82–96. *Plains Anthropologist Memoir* no. 6.

Krauss, Michael E., and Victor K. Golla
1981 "Northern Athapaskan Languages." In *Subarctic*, edited by June Helm, pp. 67–85. Vol. 6, *Handbook of North American Indians.* Smithsonian Institution, Washington, D.C.

Krieger, Alex D.
1946 *Culture Complexes and Chronology in Northern Texas.* University of Texas Publication no. 4640, Austin.
1947 *Culture Complexes and Chronology in Northern Texas with Extension of Puebloan Datings to the Mississippi Valley.* University of Texas Publication no. 4641, Austin.

Kroeber, A. L.
1963 *Cultural and Natural Areas of Native North America.* University of California Press, Berkeley.

Kuechler, A. W.
1964 "Potential Natural Vegetation of the Conterminous United States." Manual to accompany map. Special Publication no. 36. American Geographical Society, New York.

Kvamme, Kenneth L.
1979 "Settlement Variability in the High Plains of Northeastern Colorado: The South Platte River." *Southwestern Lore* 45(4): 18–28.

Lamb, H. H.
1977 *Climate: Present, Past and Future*, vol. 2. Methuen, London.

Lang, Richard W.
1982 "Transformations in White Ware Pottery of the Northern Rio Grande." In *Southwestern Ceramics: A Comparative Review*, edited by Albert H. Schroeder, pp. 153–200. *The Arizona Archaeologist* no. 15. Arizona Archaeological Society, Phoenix.

Larkin, T. J., and G. W. Bomar
1983 *Climatic Atlas of Texas.* Texas Department of Water Resources, Austin.

Laroque, Francois A.
1910   *Journal of F. A. Laroque from the Assiniboine to the Yellowstone,*
       1805, edited by L. J. Burpee. Canadian Archives Publication 3. Ottawa.
Larson, Thomas K., Dori M. Penny, John D. Benko, and Ross G. Hillman
1986   *The 1985 Forest River Survey: A Class II Cultural Resources Inven-*
       tory, Grand Forks and Walsh Counties, North Dakota. Larson-Tibesar
       Associates, Laramie, Wyoming. Submitted to the State Historical
       Society of North Dakota, Bismarck.
Larson, Thomas K., Kurt P. Schweigert, Steven A. Chomko and W. Raymond
Wood
1983   *A Cultural Resource Inventory of Proposed Recreation Areas, Lake*
       Oahe: Emmons, Morton, and Sioux Counties, North Dakota. 2 vols.
       Larson-Tibesar Associates, Laramie, Wyoming. Submitted to U.S.
       Army Corps of Engineers, Omaha District, Contract no. DACW45-82-
       M-1985.
Larson, Thomas K., Kurt P. Schweigert, Keith H. Dueholm and Dori M. Penny
1986   *A Cultural Resource Inventory of the Left Bank of Lake Oahe: Bur-*
       leigh and Emmons Counties, North Dakota. 4 vols. Larson-Tibesar
       Associates, Laramie, Wyoming. Submitted to U.S. Army Corps of
       Engineers, Omaha District, Contract no. DACW45-83-C-0243.
Lawrence, B., and C. Muceus
1980   "Preliminary Report of Test Excavations at 5WL453 Near Johnstown,
       Colorado." Ms. on file, Colorado Historical Society, Denver.
Lechleitner, R. R.
1969   *Wild Mammals of Colorado: Their Appearance, Habitat and Abun-*
       dance. Pruitt Publishing, Boulder.
Lee, C. H. (ed.)
1980   *The Archaeology of the White Buffalo Robe Site.* Report submitted to
       Stearns-Roger Engineering Corp., Denver.
Lees, W. B.
1988   "Emergency Salvage Excavations at Site 14MN328, A Great Bend
       Aspect Site at Marion, Kansas." *Journal of the Kansas Anthropological*
       Association 9:60–82.
Lees, W. B.
1991   "Chronological Placement of the Booth Site: Implications for the
       Wilmore Complex and Southern Plains Culture History." *Plains An-*
       thropologist 36:255–59.
Lees, William B., Marie E. Brown, and Rolfe D. Mandel
1985   *Cultural Resource Reconnaissance Along the Lower West Bank of*
       Lake Francis Case in Gregory and Lyman Counties, South Dakota.
       Office of Archaeological Research, Museum of Anthropology, Univer-
       sity of Kansas, Lawrence. Submitted to U.S. Army Corps of Engineers,
       Omaha District, Contract no. DACW45-83-C-0236.
Lehmer, D.J.
1948   *The Journada Branch of the Mogollon.* Social Sciences Bulletin no. 17.
       University of Arizona Bulletin.
1971   *Introduction to Middle Missouri Archaeology.* Anthropological Pa-
       pers 1. U.S. Department of the Interior, National Park Service.

Leslie, R. H.
1979 "The Eastern Journada Mogollon, Extreme Southeastern New Mexico." In *Journada-Mogollon Archaeology,* edited by P. Beckett and R. N. Wiseman, pp. 179–99. Santa Fe.

Lewis, Oscar
1942 *The Effects of White Contact upon Blackfoot Culture, with Special Reference to the Role of the Fur Trade.* Monograph no. 6. American Ethnological Society.
1944 "Edged (Tanning?) Stones from South Central Montana and North Central Wyoming: Their Possible Use and Distribution." *American Antiquity* 9:336–38.

Lewis, Theodore H.
1886 "Mounds of the Red River of the North." *The American Antiquarian* 8:369–71. On file, Department of Anthropology, University of North Dakota, Grand Forks.

Lightfoot, Kent
1984 *Prehistoric Political Dynamics: A Case Study from the American Southwest.* NIU Press, Dekalb.

Lintz, Christopher L.
1978 "Architecture and Radiocarbon Dating of the Antelope Creek focus: A Test of Campbell's Model." *Plains Anthropologist* 23(82): 319–28.
1979 "Radiocarbon and Archaeomagnetic Dates from the Two Sisters site, 34Tx-32, Texas County, Oklahoma." *Oklahoma Anthropological Society Newsletter* 27(6): 1–9.
1984 "The Plains Villagers: Antelope Creek." In *Prehistory in Oklahoma,* edited by R. E. Bell, pp. 18–39. Academic Press, Orlando.
1986a *Architecture and Community Variability within the Antelope Creek phase of the Texas panhandle.* Studies in Oklahoma's Past no. 14. Oklahoma Archaeological Survey, Norman.
1986b "The Historical Development of a Culture Complex: The Basis for Understanding Architectural Misconceptions of the Antelope Creek Focus." In *Current Trends in Southern Plains Archaeology,* edited by Timothy G. Baugh, pp. 111–28. *Plains Anthropologist Memoir* 21, vol. 31.
1991 "Texas Panhandle-Pueblo Interactions from the Thirteenth through the Sixteenth Century." In *Farmers, Hunters, and Colonists: Interaction Between the Southwest and the Southern Plains,* edited by Katherine A. Spielmann, pp. 89–106. University of Arizona Press, Tucson.

Lintz, C. L., and S. A. Hall
1983 *The Geomorphology and Archaeology of Carnegie Canyon, Fort Cobb Laterals Watershed, Caddo County, Oklahoma.* Archaeological Research Report no. 10. Oklahoma Conservation Commission, Tulsa.

Lintz, C., and L. G. Zabawa
1984 "The Kenton Caves of Western Oklahoma." In *Prehistory of Oklahoma,* edited by R. E. Bell, pp. 161–74. Academic Press, Orlando.

Lipe, W. D.
1983 "The Southwest." In *Ancient North Americans,* edited by Jesse D. Jennings, pp. 421–93. W. H. Freeman, San Francisco.

Lippincott, Kerry A.
1976   "Settlement Ecology of Solomon River Upper Republican Sites in North Central Kansas." Ph.D. dissertation, Department of Anthropology, University of Missouri.
1978   "Solomon River Upper Republican Ecology." In *The Central Plains Tradition: Internal Development and External Relationships*, edited by D. J. Blakeslee, pp. 81–93. Report 11. Office of the Iowa State Archaeologist, Iowa City.

Lister, Robert H.
1948   "Notes on the Archaeology of the Watrous Valley, New Mexico." *El Palacio* 55:35–41.

Loendorf, Larry
1973   "The Shield-Bearing Warriors Motif and its Implications on the Northwestern Plains." Paper presented at the Plains Anthropological Conference, Columbia, Mo.
1988   "Rock Art Chronology in Carbon County, Montana and The Valley of the Shield Site, 24CB1094." Paper presented at the Montana Archaeological Society, Missoula.
1990   "A Dated Rock Art Panel of Shield Bearing Warriors in South Central Montana." *Plains Anthropologist* 35:45–54.

Loendorf, Lawrence L., Stanley A. Ahler, and Dale Davidson
1984   "The Proposed National Register District in the Knife River Flint Quarries in Dunn County, North Dakota." *North Dakota History* 51:4–20.

Lofstrom, Ted
1987   "The Rise of Wild Rice Exploitation and Its Implications for Population Size and Social Organization in Minnesota Woodland Period Cultures." *The Minnesota Archaeologist* 46(2): 3–15.

Logan, W. D.
1976   *Woodland Complexes in Northeastern Iowa.* Publications in Archaeology no. 15. U.S. Department of the Interior, National Park Service, Washington, D.C.

Longley, Richard W.
1972   *The Climate of the Prairie Provinces.* Climatological Studies no. 13. Environment Canada, Toronto.

Lopez, D. R., and R. Saunders
1973   "Current Lithic Studies in Oklahoma." *Oklahoma Anthropological Society Newsletter* 21(9): 1–4.

Lorrain, D.
1967   "The Glass Site." In *A Pilot Study of Wichita Indian Archaeology and Ethnohistory*, assembled by R. E. Bell, E. B. Jelks, and W. W. Newcomb, pp. 24–44. Final Report to National Science Foundation.
1968   "Excavations at Red Bluff Shelter (Sotol site) 41CX8 Crockett County, Texas." *Transactions of the Fourth Regional Archaeological Symposium for Southeastern New Mexico and Western Texas*, pp. 18–39.
1969   *Archaeological Excavations in the Fish Creek Reservoir.* Contributions in Anthropology no. 4. Southern Methodist University, Dallas.

Lothson, Gordon A.
1972   "Burial Mounds of the Mille Lacs Lake Area." M.A. thesis, Department of Anthropology, University of Minnesota, Minneapolis.

Loveseth, Beatrice
1980   "The Crowsnest Lake Dancehall Site (DjPp-3): Interpretation based on Lithic Artifact and Type Analysis." M.A. thesis, University of Calgary.

Lovick, Steven K., and Stanley A. Ahler
1982   *Cultural Resource Reconnaissance in the Knife River Indian Villages National Historic Site.* Department of Anthropology and Archaeology, University of North Dakota, Grand Forks. Submitted to the Midwest Archaeological Center, National Park Service, Lincoln.

Lowrie, W., and M. St. Clarke
1832   *Documents, Legislative and Executive of the Congress of the United States 1789–1815.* Class 2, Vol. 4, *Indian Affairs.* Gales and Seaton, Washington, D.C.

Ludwickson, John
1975   "The Loup River Phase and the Origins of Pawnee Culture." M.A. thesis, Department of Anthropology, University of Nebraska.

Ludwickson, John, Don Blakeslee, and John O'Shea
1981   *Missouri National Recreational River: Native American Cultural Resources.* Nebraska State Historical Society, Lincoln.

Lueck, Edward J., and John M. Butterbrodt
1984   *Cultural Resource Surveys at Pass Creek, Nelson Butte, Babby Butte, Squaw-Humper Creek and Cuny Table in Jackson (Washabaugh) and Shannon Counties, South Dakota.* White River Badlands Regional Research Project Report, vol. 3. Archaeology Laboratory, Augustana College, Sioux Falls, S.D. Submitted to Historical Preservation Center, Vermillion, S.D.

Lueck, Edward J., Kerry Lippincott, and R. Peter Winham
1989   *Cultural Resource Reconnaissance in Dewey County, South Dakota, From Below the Moreau River to the Forest City Recreation Area.* 2 vols. Archaeological Contract Series no. 46. Archaeology Laboratory, Augustana College, Sioux Falls, S.D. U.S. Army Corps of Engineers, Omaha District, Contract no. DACW45-88-C-0261.

Lueck, Edward J., K. Lippincott, R. P. Winham, and L. A. Hannus
1990   *Cultural Resource Reconnaissance of U.S. Army Corps of Engineers Land Alongside Lake Sakakawea and Audubon Lake in McLean County, North Dakota.* Archaeological Contract Series no. 58. Archaeology Laboratory, Augustana College, Sioux Falls, S.D. For U.S. Army Corps of Engineers, Omaha District, Contract no. DACW45-88-C-0260.

Lugenbeal, Edward N.
1976   "The Archaeology of the Smith Site: A Study of the Ceramics and Culture History of Minnesota Laurel and Blackduck." Ph.D. dissertation, Department of Anthropology, University of Wisconsin, Madison.
1978   "Brainerd Ware Occurrence and Chronological Relationships." In *Some Studies of Minnesota Prehistoric Ceramics,* edited by Alan R. Woolworth and Mark A. Hall, pp. 47–55. Occasional Publications in Minne-

sota Anthropology no. 2. Minnesota Archaeological Society, Fort Snelling.

1979 "Blackduck Ware." In *A Handbook of Minnesota Prehistoric Ceramics*, edited by Scott F. Anfinson, pp. 23–37. Occasional Publications in Minnesota Anthropology no. 5. Minnesota Archaeological Society, Fort Snelling.

Lutes, E.
1959 "A Marginal Prehistoric Culture of Northeastern New Mexico." *El Palacio* 66(2): 59–68.

Lynott, Mark J.
1981 "A Model of Prehistoric Adaptation in Northern Texas." *Plains Anthropologist* 26:97–110.

MacGregor, J. G.
1966 *Peter Fidler: Canada's Forgotten Surveyor 1769–1822.* McClelland and Stewart, Toronto.

MacNeish, Richard S.
1954 "The Stott Mound and Village, Near Brandon, Manitoba." In *Annual Report of the National Museum of Canada, 1952–1953*, pp. 20–65. National Museum of Canada Bulletin no. 157. Queen's Printer, Ottawa.

1958 *An Introduction to the Archaeology of Southeastern Manitoba.* National Museums of Canada Bulletin 157. Ottawa.

1964 "Investigations in Southwest Yukon: Archaeological Excavations Comparisons and Speculations." In *Investigations in Southwest Yukon.* Papers of the Robert S. Peabody Foundation for Archaeology, vol. 6, no. 2. Phillips Academy, Andover, Mass.

Madsen, David B.
1986 "Prehistoric Ceramics." In *Great Basin*, edited by Warren L. D'Azevedo, pp. 206–14. Vol. 11, *Handbook of North American Indians.* Smithsonian Institution, Washington, D.C.

Magne, Martin (ed.)
1987 "Distribution of Native Groups in Western Canada, A.D. 1700 to A.D. 1850." In *Archaeology in Alberta 1986*, edited by M. Magne, pp. 220–32. Occasional Paper no. 31. Archaeological Survey of Alberta, Edmonton.

Magne, Martin P. R., and Michael A. Klassen
1991 "A Multivariate Study of Rock Art Anthropomorphs at Writing-On-Stone, Southern Alberta." *American Antiquity* 56(3): 389–418.

Malouf, Carling I.
1967 "Historic Tribes and Archaeology." *Archaeology in Montana* 8:1–16.
1968 "The Shoshonean Migrations Northward." *Archaeology in Montana*, 9(3): 1–19.
1982 "A Study of the Prehistoric and Historic Sites along the Lower Clark Fork River Valley, Western Montana." Contributions to Anthropology 7. Department of Anthropology, University of Montana, Missoula.

Mallouf, R. J.
1976 *Archaeological Investigations at Proposed Big Pine Lake, 1974–1975, Lamar and Red River Counties, Texas.* Archaeological Survey Report 18. Office of the State Archaeologist, Texas Historical Commission, Austin, Tex.

Marshall, James O.
1967 "The Glen Elder Focus." M.A. thesis, Department of Anthropology, University of Nebraska.
1972 *The Archaeology of the Elk City Reservoir.* Anthropological Series no. 6. Kansas State Historical Society, Topeka.

Marshall, J. O., and T. A. Witty, Jr.
1966 "The Bogan Site, 14GE1: An Historic Pawnee Village." Kansas State Historical Society, Topeka. Manuscript.

Martin, Paul S.
1979 "Prehistory: Mogollon." In *Southwest,* edited by Alfonso Ortiz, pp. 61–74. Vol. 9, *Handbook of North American Indians.* Smithsonian Institution, Washington, D.C.

Marwitt, John P.
1986 "Freemont Cultures." In *Great Basin,* edited by Warren L. D'Azevedo, pp. 161–72. Vol. 11, *Handbook of North American Indians.* Smithsonian Institution, Washington, D.C.

Mason, Carol I.
1976 "Historic Identification and Lake Winnebago Focus Oneota." In *Cultural Continuity and Change,* edited by C. E. Cleland, pp. 335–48. Academic Press, New York.

Mason, Ronald J.
1981 *Great Lakes Archaeology.* Academic Press, New York.

Matthews, Washington
1897 *Navajo Legends.* Memoirs of the American Folklore Society, vol. 5. New York.

Mayer-Oakes, William J.
1970 *Archaeological Investigations in the Grand Rapids, Manitoba, Reservoir, 1961–1962.* Occasional Paper no. 3. Department of Anthropology, University of Manitoba, Winnipeg.

McAllester, David P.
1980 "Shootingway: An Epic Drama of the Navajos." In *Southwestern Indian Ritual Drama,* edited by Charlotte J. Frisbie, pp. 199–238. University of New Mexico Press, Albuquerque.

McAllister, J. G.
1937 "Kiowa-Apache Social Organization." In *Social Anthropology of the North American Tribes,* edited by Fred Eggan, pp. 99–169. University of Chicago Press, Chicago.

McAndrews, J. H.
1969 "Paleobotany of Wild Rice Lake in Minnesota." *Canadian Journal of Botany* 47:1,671–79.

McConaughy, Mark A., C. Jackson, and Francis King
1985 "Two Early Mississippi Period Structures from the Rech Site (11P4), Peoria County, Illinois." *Midcontinental Journal of Archaeology* 10: 171–94.

McCracken, H., Waldo R. Wedel, Robert Edgar, John H. Moss, H. E. Wright, W. Husted, and W. Mulloy
1978 *The Mummy Cave Project in Northwestern Wyoming.* Buffalo Bill Historical Center, Cody, Wyoming.

McCullough, Edward J.
1982 *Prehistoric Cultural Dynamics of the Lac La Biche Region.* Occasional Paper no. 18. Archaeological Survey of Alberta, Edmonton.

McGuire, Randall H.
1986 "Economics and Modes of Production in the Prehistoric Southwestern Periphery." In *Ripples on the Chichimec Sea,* edited by Frances Joan Mathion and Randall H. McGuire, pp. 243–69, Southern Illinois University Press, Carbondale and Edwardsville.

McHugh, William P.
1980 *Before Smith's Mill: Archaeological and Geological Investigations in the Little Platte River Valley, Western Missouri.* Report submitted to the U.S. Army Corps of Engineers, Kansas City District.

McKusick, Charmion R.
1981 "The Faunal Remains of Las Humanas." In *Contributions to Gran Quivira Archaeology,* edited by Alden C. Hayes, pp. 39–65. Publications in Archaeology no. 17. National Park Service, Washington, D.C.

McKusick, Marshall B.
1973 *The Grant Oneota Village.* Report 4. Office of the State Archaeologist, University of Iowa, Iowa City.

McWhorter, L. V.
1952 *Hear Me, My Chiefs! Nez Perce Legend and History.* Caxton Printers, Caldwell, Idaho.

Meighan, Clement W.
1971 "Archaeology in Sinaloa." In *Archaeology of Northern Mesoamerica,* edited by Robert Wauchope. *Handbook of Middle American Indians,* vol. 11, no. 2, pt. 2. University of Texas Press, Austin.

Meltzer, D. J.
1987 "Were There Exchange Systems Among North American Paleo-Indians?" Paper presented at the Fifty-second Annual Meeting of the Society for American Archaeology, Toronto.

Meltzer, D. J., and M. B. Collins
1987 "Prehistoric Water Wells on the Southern High Plains: Clues to Altithermal Climate." *Journal of Field Archaeology* 14(1): 9–28.

Mera, Harry P.
1935 *Ceramic Clues to the Prehistory of Northcentral New Mexico.* Laboratory of Anthropology Technical Series Bulletin no. 8, Santa Fe.
1940 *Population Changes in the Rio Grande Glaze Paint Area.* Laboratory of Anthropology Technical Services Bulletin no. 9, Santa Fe.
1943 *An Outline of Ceramic Development in Southern and Southeastern New Mexico.* Laboratory of Anthropology Technical Series Bulletin no. 11, Santa Fe.
1944 "Jaritas Rock Shelter, Northeastern New Mexico." *American Antiquity* 9:295–301.

Metcalf, Michael D.
1974 "Archaeological Excavations at Dipper Gap: Stratified Butte Top Site in Northeastern Colorado." M.A. thesis, Department of Anthropology, Colorado State University, Fort Collins.

Meyer, David
1981a "Excavation at the Intake Site, 1981." *Saskatchewan Archaeology* 2(6): 114–16.
1981b "Late Prehistoric Assemblages from Nipawiwin: The Pehonan Complex." *Saskatchewan Archaeology* 2:4–38.
1983a "Saskatchewan Laurel: an Overview." *Saskatchewan Archaeology* 4: 3–24.
1983b "The Prehistory of Northern Saskatchewan." In *Tracking Ancient Hunters: Prehistoric Archaeology in Saskatchewan*, edited by H. T. Epp and I. G. Dyck, pp. 141–70. Saskatchewan Archaeological Society, Regina.
1984 "Anent the Pehonan Complex." *Saskatchewan Archaeology* 5:43–46.
1988 "The Old Women's Phase on the Saskatchewan Plains: Some Ideas." In *Archaeology in Alberta, 1987*, edited by M. Magne, pp. 55–63. Occasional Paper no. 32. Archaeological Survey of Alberta, Edmonton.
Meyer, D., O. Klimko, and J. Finnigan
1988 "Northernmost Avonlea in Saskatchewan." In *Avonlea Yesterday and Today: Archaeology and Prehistory*, edited by L. Davis, pp. 33–42. Saskatchewan Archaeological Society, Saskatoon.
Meyer, David, and Dale Russell
1987 "The Selkirk Composite of Central Canada: A Reconsideration." *Arctic Anthropology* 24(2): 1–31.
Meyer, David, and S. Smailes
1974 "Churchill Archaeology Study, Saskatchewan." *Canadian Archaeological Association Bulletin* 6:229–32.
Michlovic, Michael G.
1978 "Preliminary Report on the Archaeological Survey of Clay County, Minnesota, 1978." Department of Sociology and Anthropology, Moorhead State University, Moorhead, Minn. Submitted to the Minnesota Historical Society, St. Paul.
1979 *The Dead River Site (210T51).* Occasional Publications in Minnesota Anthropology no. 6. Minnesota Archaeological Society, Fort Snelling.
1981 "Preliminary Report on the Middle Red River Archaeological Survey, Norman County, Minnesota." Department of Sociology and Anthropology, Moorhead State University, Moorhead, Minn. Submitted to the Minnesota Historical Society, St. Paul.
1983 "The Red River Valley in the Prehistory of the Northern Plains." *Plains Anthropologist* 28:23–31.
1984 *The Archaeology of the Mooney Site (21NR29) on the Red River in Minnesota.* Department of Sociology and Anthropology, Moorehead State University, Moorhead, Minn. Submitted to the St. Paul District Corps of Engineers, Minn.
1985 "The Problem of the Teton Migration." In *Archaeology, Ecology and Ethnohistory of the Prairie-Forest Border Zone of Minnesota and Manitoba*, edited by Janet Spector and Elden Johnson, pp. 131–45. J & L Reprint, Lincoln, Nebr.
1986 "The Archaeology of the Canning Site." *The Minnesota Archaeologist* 45(1): 3–36.

1987a *Archaeological Survey and Test Excavations in Cass County, N.D.* Moorhead State University, Moorhead, Minn. Submitted to the State Historical Society of North Dakota, Bismarck.

1987b "The Archaeology of the Mooney Site." *The Minnesota Archaeologist* 46(2).

1988 "The Archaeology of the Red River Valley." *Minnesota History* 51:55–62.

Michlovic, Michael G., and Fred Schneider

1988 "The Archaeology of the Shea Site (32CS101)." Ms. on file, State Historical Society of North Dakota, Bismarck.

Millar, James V.

1983 "The Chartier Sites: Two Stratified Campsites on Kisis Channel near Buffalo Narrows." Ms. on file, Archaeological Resource Management Section, Saskatchewan Department of Culture and Recreation, Regina.

Miller, Mark E., and Brian R. Waitkus

1989 "The Butler-Rissler Site: Plains Woodland Along the North Platte River, Wyoming." *The Wyoming Archaeologist* 32(1–2): 1–38.

Milne, Laurie Ann

1988 "The Larson Site (DlOn-3) and the Avonlea Phase in Southeastern Alberta." In *Avonlea Yesterday and Today: Archaeology and Prehistory,* edited by L. B. Davis, pp. 43–66. Saskatchewan Archaeological Society, Saskatoon.

Milner, George R.

1990 "The Late Prehistoric Cahokia Cultural System of the Mississippi River Valley: Foundations, Florescence, and Fragmentation." *Journal of World Prehistory* 4:1–43.

Moerman, Daniel E., and David T. Jones

n.d. "Investigations at the Cattle Oiler Site, 39ST224, Big Bend Reservoir, South Dakota." Ms. on file, Midwest Archaeological Center, National Park Service, Lincoln.

Montgomery, Henry

1889 "Aboriginal Monuments of North Dakota." *Proceedings of the American Association for the Advancement of Science* 38:342–44.

1906 "Remains of Prehistoric Man in the Dakotas." *American Anthropologist* 8:640–51.

Mooney, James

1898 "Calendar History of the Kiowa Indians." In *Bureau of American Ethnology Annual Report,* 17:129–445. Smithsonian Institution, Washington, D.C.

1928 *The Aboriginal Population of America North of Mexico.* Smithsonian Miscellaneous Collections, vol. 80, no. 7. Washington, D.C.

Moore, John H.

1987 *The Cheyenne Nation.* University of Nebraska Press, Lincoln.

Moore, Michael C.

1984 "A Reconnaissance Survey of Quartermaster Creek." In *Archaeology of the Mixed Grass Prairie Phase I: Quartermaster Creek,* edited by Timothy G. Baugh, pp. 51–214. Archeological Resource Survey Report, no. 20. Oklahoma Archeological Survey, Norman.

Morgan, D. T.
1985 "Late Woodland Ceramics from the Fall Creek Locality, Adams County, Illinois." *The Wisconsin Archaeologist* 66:265–81.

Morgan, R. Grace
1979 *An Ecological Study of the Northern Plains As Seen Through the Garratt Site.* Occasional Papers in Anthropology no. 1. Department of Anthropology, University of Regina.
1980 "Bison Movement Patterns on the Canadian Plains: An Ecological Analysis." *Plains Anthropologist* 25(88): 143–60.

Morlan, Richard E.
1988 "Avonlea and Radiocarbon Dating." In *Avonlea Yesterday and Today: Archaeology and Prehistory,* edited by Leslie B. Davis, pp. 291–310. Saskatchewan Archaeological Society, Saskatoon.

Morris, Elizabeth A.
1982 "Archaeological Research Strategy in the South Platte River Valley of Northeastern Colorado." In *Directions in Archaeology: A Question of Goals,* edited by P. D. Francis and E. C. Poplin, pp. 219–36. Proceedings of the Fourteenth Annual Conference, Archaeological Association of the University of Calgary.

Morris, Elizabeth A., Daniel Mayo, Richard C. Blakeslee, and Patrick W. Bower
1983 "Current Perspectives on Stone Ring Structures in Northeastern Colorado." *Plains Anthropologist* 18(102, pt. 2): 45–58.

Morse, J.
1822 *A Report to the Secretary of War of the United States, of Indian Affairs.* Davis and Force, Washington, D.C.

Mott, Mildred
1938 "The Relation of Historic Indian Tribes to Archaeological Manifestations in Iowa." *Iowa Journal of History and Politics* 36:227–314.

Mulloy, William T.
1958 "A Preliminary Historical Outline for the Northwestern Plains." *University of Wyoming Publications* 22(1).
1965a "Archaeological Investigations Along the North Platte River in Eastern Wyoming." *University of Wyoming Publications* 31(2): 24–51.
1965b "The Indian Village at Thirty Mile Mesa, Montana." *University of Wyoming Publications* 31(1).

Mulloy, William T., and Louis C. Steege
1967 "Continued Archaeological Investigations Along the North Platte River in Eastern Wyoming." *University of Wyoming Publications* 33(3): 169–233.

Murie, James R.
1981 *Ceremonies of the Pawnee,* edited by Douglas R. Parks. University of Nebraska Press, Lincoln.

Murphy, Robert F., and Y. Murphy
1986 "Northern Shoshone and Bannock." In *Great Basin,* edited by Warren L. D'Azevendo, pp. 127–34. Vol. 11, *Handbook of North American Indians.* Smithsonian Institution, Washington, D.C.

Murray, E. M., T. Smith, and B. O. K. Reeves
1976   "Archaeological Salvage Investigations Alberta Highways and Trans-
        portation Projects Hwy. 1, Hartell Creek." Report on file, Archaeologi-
        cal Survey of Alberta, Edmonton.

Murray, H. D., and A. B. Leonard
1962   *Handbook of Unionoid Mussels of Kansas.* Miscellaneous Publications
        no. 28. University of Kansas Museum of Natural History, Lawrence.

Muto, G. R., M. S. Mayo, and K. Zahrai
n.d.   "From Hunting and Gathering to Business and Banditry: Holocene
        Adaptations in Lee's Creek Valley, an Anthropological Assessment."
        Ms. on file, Oklahoma Archeological Survey, Norman.

Nassaney, M. S.
1987   "On the Causes and Consequences of Subsistence Intensification in
        the Mississippi Alluvial Valley." In *Emergent Horticultural Econ-
        omies of the Eastern Woodlands,* edited by W. F. Keegan, pp. 129–52.
        Occasional Paper no. 7. Center for Archaeological Investigations,
        Southern Illinois University, Carbondale.

Nathan, Michele
1980   "Survey and Testing of Archaeological Resources at Clinton Lake,
        Kansas." Report submitted to the U.S. Army Corps of Engineers,
        Kansas City District.

Nelson, Charles E.
1971   "The George W. Lindsay Ranch Site, 5JF11." *Southwestern Lore* 37(1):
        1–14.

Nero, R. W., and B. A. McCorquodale
1958   "Report of an Excavation at the Oxbow Dam Site." *The Blue Jay* 16(2):
        82–90. Regina.

Neuman, Robert W.
1975   *The Sonota Complex and Associated Sites on the Northern Great
        Plains.* Publications in Anthropology 6. Nebraska State Historical
        Society, Lincoln.

Newcomb, W. W.
1961   *The Indians of Texas from Prehistoric to Modern Times.* University of
        Texas Press, Austin.

Newcomb, W. W., and T. N. Campbell
1982   "Southern Plains Ethnohistory: A Re-Examination of the Escanjaques,
        Ahijados, and Cuitoas." In *Pathways to Plains Prehistory: Anthro-
        pological Perspectives on Plains Natives and Their Pasts,* edited by
        D. G. Wyckoff and J. L. Hofman, pp. 29–43. Oklahoma Anthropologi-
        cal Society Memoir 3 and Cross Timbers Heritage Association Contri-
        butions 1.

Newcomb, W. W., and W. T. Field
1967   "An Ethnohistoric Investigation of the Wichita Indians in the Southern
        Plains." In *A Pilot Study of Wichita Indian Archaeology and Eth-
        nohistory,* assembled by R. E. Bell, E. B. Jelks, and W. W. Newcomb, pp.
        240–396. Final Report to National Science Foundation.

Nicholson, B. A.
1987   "Culture History of the Forest/Grassland Transition Zone of Western

Manitoba and Relationships to Cultures in Adjacent Regions." *Manitoba Archaeological Quarterly* 11(2,3).

1988a "Modeling Subsistence Strategies in the Forest/Grassland Transition Zone of Western Manitoba During the Late Prehistoric and Early Historic Periods." *Plains Anthropologist* 33:351–65.

1988b "Prehistoric Pottery of the Northern Aspen Parkland." Paper presented at the fall meeting of the North Dakota Archaeological Association, Bismarck.

Nicholson, B. A., and Mary Malainey
1991 "Report on the 1991 Field School Excavations at the Lovstrom Site (DjLx-1), Southwestern Manitoba." *Manitoba Archaeological Journal* 1(2): 51–93.

Niemczycki, M. A.
1988 "Seneca Tribalization: An Adaptive Strategy." *Man in the Northeast* 36:77–87.

Noble, William C.
1971 "Archaeological Surveys and Sequences in Central District of Mackenzie, Northwest Territories." *Arctic Anthropology* 8:102–35.
1981 "Prehistory of the Great Slave Lake and Great Bear Lake Region." In *Subarctic*, edited by June Helm, pp. 97–106. Vol. 6, *Handbook of North American Indians*. Smithsonian Institution, Washington, D.C.

Noisat, Brad, Jeff Campbell, and Gary Moore
1986 *A Reconnaissance Survey and Preliminary Assessment of the Cultural Resources of Lake Sakakawea in Williams and McKenzie Counties, North Dakota*. 2 vols. Overland Associates, Research Paper no. 1. Submitted to U.S. Army Corps of Engineers, Omaha District, Contract no. DACW45-83-C-0192.

Northern, M. J.
1979 "Archaeological Investigations of the Montgomery site, Floyd County Texas." M.A. thesis, Texas Tech University, Lubbock.

Nowak, M., and L. A. Kingsbury
1981 *Archaeological Investigation in Southern Colorado*. Publications in Archaeology no. 4. Colorado College, Colorado Springs.

Nowak, Timothy R.
1981 "Lithic Analysis of the Oakwood Lakes Site (39BK7), Brookings County, South Dakota: A Woodland Period Stone Tool Assemblage of the Northeastern Prairie Periphery." In *Archaeological Excavations at 39BK7, Brookings County, South Dakota*, edited by L. A. Hannus, pp. 51–152. Contract Investigations Series 33. South Dakota Archaeological Research Center, Rapid City.

Nowak, Timothy R., and L. A. Hannus
1981 "Knife River Flint: I Know It When I See It — Or Do I? An Alternative Primary Source from South Dakota." Paper presented at the Thirty-ninth Annual Plains Anthropology Conference, Bismarck, N.D.

Nowak, Timothy R., L. Adrien Hannus, and Edward J. Lueck
1982 "A Prehistoric and Historic Overview of Northeastern South Dakota." In *Cultural Resources Investigations of the South Dakota Segment of the Northern Border Pipeline Project*, vol. 4, edited by L.

Adrien Hannus, pp. 25.1–25.74. Northern Plains Natural Gas, Omaha, Nebr.

O'Brien, Michael
1987   "Sedentism, Population Growth, and Resource Selection in the Woodland Midwest: A Review of Coevolutionary Development." *Current Anthropology* 28(2): 177–97.

O'Brien, Patricia J.
1971   "Valley Focus Mortuary Practices." *Plains Anthropologist* 16(53): 165–82.
1972   "The Don Wells Site (14RY404), A Hopewellian Site Near Manhattan and Its Implications." *Kansas Anthropological Association, Newsletter* 17(5): 1–11.
1975   *Archaeological Excavation Smithville Lake Project.* Report submitted to the U.S. Army Corps of Engineers, Kansas City District.
1976   *Archaeological Survey Smithville Lake Project.* Report submitted to the U.S. Army Corps of Engineers, Kansas City District.
1977   *Cultural Resources Survey of Smithville Lake, Missouri, Volume 1: Archaeology.* Report submitted to U.S. Army Corps of Engineers, Kansas City District.
1978a   "Steed-Kisker: A Western Mississippian Settlement System." In *Mississippian Settlement Patterns,* edited by B. D. Smith, pp. 1–19, Academic Press, New York.
1978b   "Steed-Kisker and Mississippian Influences on the Central Plains." In *George Metcalf Festschrift on Central Plains Archaeology,* edited by Donald J. Blakeslee, pp. 67–80. Report no. 11. Office of the Iowa State Archaeologist, Iowa City.
1981a   "Schultz 'Phase': A Woodland Complex in the Central Plains." *Society for American Archaeology Abstracts,* p. 86.
1981b   "Steed-Kisker: A Cultural Interpretation." *Missouri Archaeologist* 42:97–108.
1982   "The Yeo Site (23CL199), a Kansas City Hopewell Limited Activity Site in Northwestern Missouri, and Some Theories." *Plains Anthropologist* 27(95): 37–54.
1983   *Cultural Resources Survey of Council Grove Lake, Kansas.* Report submitted to the U.S. Army Corps of Engineers, Tulsa District.
1984   *Archaeology in Kansas.* Public Education Series no. 9. Museums of Natural History and Anthropology, University of Kansas, Lawrence.
1986   "Prehistoric Evidence for Pawnee Cosmology." *American Anthropologist,* 88(4): 939–46.
1988   "Ancient Kansas City Area Borders and Trails." *Missouri Archaeologist,* 49:27–39.

O'Brien, P. J., M. Caldwell, J. Jilka, L. Toburen, and B. Yeo.
1979   "The Ashland Bottoms Site (14RY603): A Kansas City Hopewell Site in North-Central Kansas." *Plains Anthropologist* 24(83): 1–20.

O'Brien, P. J., and D. G. Elcock.
1980   *Cultural Resources Survey of Fall River Lake, Kansas.* Report submitted to the U.S. Army Corps of Engineers, Tulsa District.

O'Brien, P. J., C. S. Larsen, J. O'Grady, B. O'Neill and A. S. Stirland
1973 "The Elliott Site (14GE303), A Preliminary Report." *Plains Anthropologist* 18(59): 54–72.

O'Brien, P. J., and W. P. McHugh
1987 "Mississippian Solstice Shrines and a Cahokian Calendar: An Hypothesis Based on Ethnohistory and Archaeology." *North American Archaeologist* 8(3): 227–47.

O'Brien, Patricia J., and Duane M. Post.
1988 "Speculations about Bobwhite Quail and Pawnee Religion." *Plains Anthropologist* 33:489–504.

Oldfield, F., and J. Schoenwetter
1964 "Late Quaternary Environments and Early Man on the Southern High Plains." *American Antiquity* 38:226–29.

Olson, Gary D., and Larry J. Zimmerman
1979 *A Cultural Resources Reconnaissance of the Federal Lands on the East Bank of Lake Francis Case, South Dakota.* 2 vols. Augustana Research Institute, Sioux Falls, and Archaeology Laboratory, University of South Dakota, Vermillion. Submitted to U.S. Army Corps of Engineers, Omaha District, Contract no. DACW45-78-C-0018.

Opler, Morris E.
1940 "Myths and Legends of the Lipan Apache Indians." *Memoirs of the American Folklore Society,* vol. 36. New York.
1971 "Pots, Apaches, and the Dismal River Culture Aspect." In *Apachean Culture History and Ethnology,* edited by Keith H. Basso and Morris E. Opler, pp. 29–34. Anthropological Paper 21. University of Arizona, Tucson.
1975 Review of *The Jicarilla Apaches, A Study in Survival* by Delores H. Gunnerson. *Plains Anthropologist* 20:150–57.
1983 "The Apachean Culture Pattern and Its Origins." In *Southwest,* edited by Alfonso Ortiz, pp. 368–92. Vol. 10, *Handbook of North American Indians.* Smithsonian Institution, Washington, D.C.

Osborn, Nancy M.
1982 "The Clarkson Site (13WA2), An Oneota Manifestation in the Central Des Moines River Valley." *Journal of the Iowa Archaeological Society* 29:ii–108.

Ossenberg, Nancy S.
1974 "Origins and Relationships of Woodland Peoples: The Evidence of Cranial Morphology." In *Aspects of Upper Great Lakes Anthropology,* edited by Elden Johnson, pp. 15–39. Minnesota Historical Society, St. Paul.

Over, W. H., and Elmer E. Meleen
1941 *A Report on an Investigation of the Brandon Village and the Split Rock Creek Mounds.* Archaeological Studies Circular 3. University of South Dakota, Vermillion.

Parker, W.
1982 *Archaeology at the Bridwell Site.* Crosby County Pioneer Memorial Museum, Crosbyton, Texas.

Parks, Douglas R.
1979a "The Northern Caddoan Languages: Their Subgrouping and Time Depths." *Nebraska History* 60:197–213.

1979b "Bands and Villages of the Arikara and Pawnee." *Nebraska History* 60:214–39.

Parks, Douglas R., and Waldo R. Wedel
1985 "Pawnee Geography: Historical and Sacred." *Great Plains Quarterly* 5:143–76.

Parks, Sharon
1978 *Test Excavations at 14GE41: A Schultz Focus Habitation Site at Milford Lake, Kansas.* Report submitted to Military Planning Branch, U.S. Army Corps of Engineers, Kansas City District.

Parmentier, Richard J.
1979 "The Mythological Triangle: Poseyemu, Montezuma, and Jesus in the Pueblos." In *Southwest,* edited by Alfonso Ortiz, pp. 609–22. Vol. 9, *Handbook of North American Indians.* Smithsonian Institution, Washington, D.C.

Parry, W. J., and J. D. Speth
1984 *The Garnsey Spring Campsite: Late Prehistoric Occupation in Southeastern New Mexico.* Research Reports in Anthropology Contribution no. 10. Museum of Anthropology, University of Michigan, Ann Arbor.

Parsons, M. L.
1967 *Archaeological Investigations in Crosby and Dickens Counties, Texas During the Winter, 1966–1967.* Report no. 7, pp. 1–108. Texas State Building Commission Archaeological Program, Austin.
1988 "Desperately Seeking Siouans: The Distribution of Sandy Lake Ware." *The Minnesota Archaeologist* 47(1): 43–48.

Pauketat, Timothy R., and Brad Koldehoff
1983 "Emerald Mound and the Mississippian Occupation of the Central Silver Creek Valley." Paper presented at the Twenty-eighth Annual Midwest Archaeological Conference, Iowa City.

Pease, T. C., and R. C. Werner
1934 *The French Foundations 1680–1693.* French Series, vol. 1. Collections of the Illinois State Historical Library, vol. 23. Illinois State Historical Library, Springfield.

Penman, John T. (ed.)
1981 "Archaeology of the Bluff Siding Site (47-Bf-45), Buffalo County, Wisconsin." *The Wisconsin Archaeologist* 62:1–52.

Penman, John T.
1984 *Archaeology of the Great River Road: Summary Report.* Archaeological Report no. 10. Wisconsin Department of Transportation, Madison, Wisconsin.
1988 "Neo-Boreal Climatic Influences on the Late Prehistoric Agricultural Groups in the Upper Mississippi Valley." *Geoarchaeology* 3:139–45.

Pentland, David H.
1978 "A Historical Overview of Cree Dialects." In *Papers of the Ninth Algonquian Conference,* edited by William Cowan, pp. 104–26. Carleton University, Ottawa.

Perry, M. J.
1987 "Late Woodland Ceramics in Southeast Iowa: A Perspective from the

Lower Skunk Valley." *Journal of the Iowa Archaeological Society* 34:57–62.

Perry, Richard J.
1980 "The Apachean Transition from the Subarctic to the Southwest." *Plains Anthropologist* 25:279–96.

Peterson, L. A.
1986 "An Attribute Analysis of Sandy Lake Ware from Norman County and North Central Minnesota." M.A. thesis, Department of Anthropology, University of Nebraska, Lincoln.

Phenice, Terrell W.
1969 *An Analysis of the Human Skeletal Material from Burial Mounds in North Central Kansas.* Publications in Anthropology no. 1, University of Kansas, Lawrence.

Phinney, Archie
1934 *Nez Perce Texts.* Columbia University Press, New York.

Picha, Paul R.
1987 "Shell Remains from the Naze Site." In *Archaeological Excavation at the Naze Site (32SN246),* edited by Michael L. Gregg, pp. 386–412. Department of Anthropology, University of North Dakota, Grand Forks. Submitted to the U.S. Bureau of Reclamation, Billings, Mont.

Pilon, Jean-Luc
1986 *Ecological and Cultural Adaptation along the Severn River in the Hudson Bay Lowlands of Ontario.* Conservation Archaeology Report Northwestern Region, Report no. 10. Ontario Ministry of Citizenship and Culture, Toronto.

Potter, J. G.
1965 *Snow Cover.* Climatological Studies no. 3. Canada Department of Transport Meteorological Branch, Toronto.

Porter, Stephen C.
1986 "Pattern and Forcing of Northern Hemisphere Glacial Variations During the Last Millennium." *Quaternary Research* 26:27–48.

Prewitt, E. R.
1964 "Excavations at the Terri and Lightfoot Sites, Proctor Reservoir, Comanche County, Texas." *Bulletin of the Texas Archaeological Society* 35:143–92.
1981 "Cultural Chronology in Central Texas." *Bulletin of the Texas Archaeological Society* 52:65–89.
1985 "From Circleville to Toyah: Comments on Central Texas Chronology." *Bulletin of the Texas Archaeological Society* 54:201–38.

Prewitt, E. R., and D. A. Lawson
1972 *An Assessment of the Archaeological and Paleontological Resources of Lake Texoma, Texas-Oklahoma.* Texas Archaeological Salvage Project Survey Reports, no. 10. University of Texas, Austin.

Purrington, B.
1971 "The Prehistory of Delaware County, Oklahoma: Cultural Continuity and Change on the Western Ozark Periphery." Ph.D. dissertation, University of Wisconsin, Madison. University Microfilms International, Ann Arbor.

Quigg, J. Michael
1986 *Nipawin Reservoir Heritage Study Volume 8: the Crown Site (FhNa-86) Excavation Results,* edited by David Meyer. Saskatchewan Research Council Publication no. E-903-7-E-86, Saskatoon.
1986 *Ross Glen: A Besant Stone Circle Site in Southeastern Alberta.* Manuscript Series no. 10. Archaeological Survey of Alberta, Edmonton.

Raab, L. M., and R. W. Moir
1982 "Research Synthesis, with Special Consideration of Future Work." In *Settlement of the Prairie Margin: Archaeology of the Richland Creek Reservoir, Navarro and Freestone Counties, Texas 1980–1981,* pp. 203–13. Archaeological Research Program, Department of Anthropology, Southern Methodist University, Dallas.

Rackerby, F.
1975 "Current Research: the Northwest." *American Antiquity* 40(4): 479–85.

Radle, Nancy Jean
1981 "Vegetation History and Lake-Level Changes at a Saline Lake in Northeastern South Dakota." Master's thesis, University of Minnesota.

Rajnovich, Grace
1983 *The Spruce Point Site: a Comparative Study of Selkirk Components in the Boreal Forest.* Conservation Archaeology Report Northwestern Region, Report no. 1. Ontario Ministry of Citizenship and Culture, Toronto.

Rajnovich, G., C. S. Reid, and C. T. Shay
1982 "Rescue Excavations at the Fisk Site (D1Kp-1) in Northwestern Ontario." In *Two Conservation Archaeology Sites: The Lady Rapids and Fisk Sites,* edited by C. S. ("Paddy") Reid, pp. 65–177. Archaeology Research Report no. 18. Archaeology and Heritage Planning Branch, Ontario Ministry of Citizenship and Culture, Toronto.

Ramenofsky, Ann F.
1987 *Vectors of Death. The Archaeology of European Contact.* University of New Mexico Press, Albuquerque.

Ranere, Anthony, J. Ranere, and J. Lortz
1969 "The Monida Pass Tipi Ring Site." *Tebiwa* 12:39–46.

Ray, Verne F.
1939 *Cultural Relations in the Plateau of Northwestern America.* Publications of the Fredrick Webb Hodge Anniversary Publication Fund, Los Angeles.

Ready, Timothy
1979a "Cambria Phase." In *A Handbook of Minnesota Prehistoric Ceramics,* edited by Scott F. Anfinson, pp. 51–65. Occasional Publications in Minnesota Anthropology no. 5. Minnesota Archaeological Society, Fort Snelling.
1979b "Kathio Series." In *A Handbook of Minnesota Prehistoric Ceramics,* edited by Scott F. Anfinson, pp. 103–107. Occasional Publications in Minnesota Anthropology no. 5. Minnesota Archaeological Society, Fort Snelling.

1979c "Ogechie Series." In *A Handbook of Minnesota Prehistoric Ceramics,* edited by Scott F. Anfinson, pp. 143–48. Occasional Publications in Minnesota Anthropology no. 5. Minnesota Archaeological Society, Fort Snelling.

Reed, P. F.
1987 "Reinterpreting Jornada Mogollon Prehistory." *North American Archaeologist* 8(3): 193–208.

Reeves, Brian O. K.
1969 "The Southern Alberta Paleo-Cultural–Paleo-Environmental Sequence." In *Post-Pleistocene Man and His Environments on the Northern Plains,* edited by R. G. Forbis, L. B. Davis, O. A. Christensen, and G. Fedirchuk, pp. 6–46. University of Calgary Archaeological Association, The Student's Press, Calgary.
1970 "Culture Change in the Northern Plains: 1000 B.C.–A.D. 1000." Ph.D. dissertation, Department of Archaeology, University of Calgary. (Updated and published as Reeves 1983a.)
1972 "The Prehistory of Pass Creek Valley, Waterton Lakes National Park." Manuscript Report 69. National Historic Sites Service, Ottawa.
1973 "The Concept of an Altithermal Cultural Hiatus in Northern Plains Prehistory." *American Anthropologist* 75:1,221–53.
1974 "Prehistoric Archaeological Research on the Eastern Slopes of the Canadian Rocky Mountains 1967–1971." *Canadian Archaeological Association Bulletin* 6:1–31.
1976 "Quaternary Stratigraphy and Geological History of Southern High Plains, Texas and New Mexico." In *Quaternary Stratigraphy of North America,* edited by W. C. Mahaney, pp. 213–33. Dowden, Hutchinson and Ross, Stroudsburg, Pennsylvania.
1978 "Head-Smashed-In: 5500 Years of Bison Jumping in the Alberta Plains." *Plains Anthropologist Memoir* 14, 23(82) pt. 2:151–74.
1983a *Culture Change in the Northern Plains: 1000 B.C.–A.D. 1000.* Occasional Paper no. 20. Archaeological Survey of Alberta, Edmonton.
1983b "The Kenney Site: A Stratified Campsite in Southwestern Alberta." *Archaeology in Montana* 24(1): 1–135.
1985 "Northern Plains Culture Historical Systematics." In *Contributions to Plains Prehistory,* edited by D. Burley, pp. 3–21. Occasional Paper no. 26. Archaeological Survey of Alberta, Edmonton.
1988 "From Napi's World: Avonlea in Perspective." In *Avonlea Yesterday and Today: Archaeology and Prehistory,* edited by L. B. Davis, pp. 311–13. Saskatchewan Archaeological Society, Saskatoon.
1990 "Communal Bison Hunters of the Northern Plains." In *Hunters of the Recent Past,* edited by L. B. Davis and B. O. K. Reeves, pp. 168–94. Unwin Hyman, London.
n.d. "Late Pleistocene Seasonal Settlement Patterns in Southern Alberta." Manuscript.

Reher, Charles
1971 "A Survey of Ceramic Site in Southeastern Wyoming." M.A. thesis, Department of Anthropology, University of Wyoming.

1988   "Discussion of Papers and General Comments." In *Avonlea Yesterday and Today: Archaeology and Prehistory,* edited by L. B. Davis, pp. 283–84. Saskatchewan Archaeological Society, Saskatoon.

1989   "The High Plains Archaeological Project: Interim Report." *The Wyoming Archaeologist* 32(1–2): xvii–xxvi.

Reher, Charles A., and George C. Frison

1980   "The Vore Site, 48CK302, A Stratified Buffalo Jump in the Wyoming Black Hills." *Plains Anthropologist Memoir* 16.

Reid, C. S., and G. Rajnovich

n.d.   "Laurel: A Re-evaluation of the Spatial, Social and Temporal Paradigms." Manuscript.

Renaud, E. B.

1942   "Indian Stone Enclosures of Colorado and New Mexico." Archaeological Series no. 2. Department of Anthropology, University of Denver.

1947   *Archaeology of the High Western Plains: Seventeen Years of Archaeological Research.* Department of Anthropology, University of Denver.

Renfrew, C.

1987   *Archaeology and Language: The Puzzle of Indo-European Origins.* Cambridge University Press, New York.

Reynolds, John D.

1979   *The Grasshopper Falls Phase of the Plains Woodland.* Anthropological Series no. 7. Kansas State Historical Society, Topeka.

1981   "Grasshopper Falls Phase: A Newly Defined Plains Woodland Cultural-Historical Integration Phase in the Central Plains." *Missouri Archaeologist* 42:85–95.

1984   *The Cow-Killer Site, Melvern Lake, Kansas.* Anthropological Series no. 12. Kansas State Historical Society, Topeka.

Rhodes, Richard A., and Evelyn M. Todd

1981   "Subarctic Algonquian Languages." In *Subarctic,* edited by June Helm, pp. 52–66. Vol. 6, *Handbook of North American Indians.* Smithsonian Institution, Washington, D.C.

Richards, Thomas H., and M. K. Rosseau

1987   "Late Prehistoric Cultural Horizons on the Canadian Plateau." Publication 16. Department of Archaeology, Simon Fraser University, Vancouver.

Riggle, Stanley

1981   "The Late Woodland Transition in the Central Mississippi Valley: A.D. 700–1100." *South Dakota Archaeology* 5:5–18.

Riley, Carroll L.

1987   *The Frontier People. The Greater Southwest in the Protohistoric Period.* University of New Mexico Press, Albuquerque.

Ritchie, J. C.

1983   "The Paleoecology of the Central and Northern Parts of the Glacial Lake Agassiz Basin." In *Glacial Lake Agassiz,* edited by J. T. Teller and L. Clayton, pp. 157–70. Special Paper 26. Geological Association of Canada, St. John's.

Roberts, Don L.
1980 "A Calendar of Eastern Pueblo Indian Ritual Dramas." In *South-western Indian Ritual Drama*, edited by Charlotte J. Frisbie, pp. 103–24. University of New Mexico Press, Albuquerque.

Roberts, Frank H. H., Jr.
1942 *Archeological and Geological Investigations in the San Jon District, Eastern New Mexico*. Smithsonian Miscellaneous Collections 103(4). Washington, D.C.

Roberts, Ricky L.
1978 "The Archaeology of the Kansas Monument Site: A Study in Historical Archaeology on the Great Plains." M.A. thesis, Department of Anthropology, University of Kansas.

Rohn, A. H., and A. M. Emerson
1984 *Great Bend Sites at Marion, Kansas*. Publications in Anthropology no. 1. Wichita State University, Wichita.

Rohrbaugh, Charles Lawrence
1982 "An Hypothesis for the Origin of the Kichai." In *Pathways to Plains Prehistory: Anthropological Perspectives of Plains Natives and Their Pasts*, edited by D. G. Wyckoff and J. L. Hofman, pp. 51–64. Oklahoma Anthropological Society Memoir 3 and Cross Timbers Heritage Association Contribution 1. Norman.
1984 "Arkansas Valley Caddoan: Fort Coffee and Neosho Foci." In *Prehistory of Oklahoma*, edited by R. E. Bell, pp. 265–85. Academic Press, Orlando.

Roll, Tom E.
1988 "Focus on a Phase: Expanded Geographical Distribution and Resultant Taxonomic Implications for Avonlea." In *Avonlea Yesterday and Today: Archaeology and Prehistory*, edited by L. B. Davis, pp. 237–50. Saskatchewan Archaeological Society, Regina.

Rood, David S.
1979 "Siouan." In *The Languages of Native America: Historical and Comparative Assessment*, edited by Lyle Campbell and Marianne Mithun, pp. 236–97. University of Texas Press, Austin.

Roper, Donna C.
1989 *Proto-Historic Pawnee Hunting in the Nebraska Sand Hills: Archaeological Investigations at Two Sites in the Calamus Reservoir*. Report of the U.S. Department of the Interior, Bureau of Reclamation, Great Plains Region, Billings.

Rose, Martin R., Jeffery S. Dean, and William J. Robinson
1981 *The Past Climate of Arroyo Hondo, New Mexico Reconstructed From Tree Rings*. School of American Research Press, Santa Fe.

Rowe, J. S.
1972 *Forest Regions of Canada*. Bulletin 123, Canadian Department of Northern Affairs and National Resources, Ottawa.

Rowland, D., and A. G. Sanders
1932 *Mississippi Provincial Archives 1704–1743 French Dominion*, vol. 3. Mississippi Department of Archives and History, Jackson.

Rowlison, D. D.
1985 "A Preliminary Report of the Bell Site and the 1985 Kansas Archaeol-

ogy Training Program." *Journal of the Kansas Anthropological Association* 5:117–18.

Ruebelmann, G.
1983   "An Overview of the Archaeology and Prehistory of the Lewistown BLM District, Montana." *Archaeology in Montana* 24(3): 1–165.

Runkles, F. A.
1964   "The Garza site: A Neo-American Campsite near Post, Texas." *Bulletin of the Texas Archaeological Society* 35:101–25.

Runkles, F. A., and E. E. Dorchester
1986   "The Lott site (41GR56): A Late Prehistoric site in Garza County, Texas." *Bulletin of the Texas Archaeological Society* 57:83–115.

Rusco, Mary K.
1960   *The White Rock Aspect*. Note Book no. 4. Laboratory of Anthropology, University of Nebraska, Lincoln.

Russell, Dale
1982   "The Ethnohistoric and Demographic Context of Central Saskatchewan to 1800." In *Nipawin Reservoir Heritage Study Volume 3 Regional Overview and Research Considerations*, edited by D. Burley and D. Meyer, pp. 150–85. Saskatchewan Research Council, Saskatoon.

Sabo, G., III
1986   "Preliminary Excavations at the Huntsville Site." In *Contributions to Ozark Prehistory*, edited by G. Sabo III, pp. 55–76. Research Series no. 27. Arkansas Archaeological Survey, Fayetteville.

Sabo, G., III, and A. M. Early
1988   "Prehistoric Culture History." In *Human Adaptation in the Ozark and Ouachita Mountains*, pp. 34–120. Final Report Study Unit 1, Ozark-Arkansas-Ouachita Archaeological Research, Synthesis and Overview Report. U.S. Army Corps of Engineers, Southwestern Division, Dallas.

Sahlins, Marshall
1968   *Tribesmen*. Prentice-Hall, Englewood Cliffs, N.J.

Saitta, D. J.
1983   "On the Evolution of 'Tribal' Social Networks." *American Antiquity* 48:820–24.

Sanders, Paul H., Dori M. Penny, Thomas K. Larson, Michael L. McFaul, and Keith H. Dueholm
1988   *The 1986 Cultural Resource Inventory of Portions of Lake Oahe, Corson and Dewey Counties, South Dakota*. 2 vols. Larson-Tibesar Associates, Laramie, Wyo. Submitted to U.S. Army Corps of Engineers, Omaha District, Contract no. DACW45-86-C-0246.

Sanders, Paul H., Dori M. Penny, Michael L. McFaul, Keith H. Dueholm, Kurt P. Schweigert, and Thomas K. Larson
1987   *A Cultural Resource Inventory of Portions of Lake Oahe, Corson County, South Dakota*. 2 vols. Larson-Tibesar Associates, Laramie, Wyo. Submitted to U.S. Army Corps of Engineers, Omaha District, Contract no. DACW45-85-C-0223.

Sanger, David
1967   "Prehistory of the Pacific Northwest Plateau as seen from the Interior of British Columbia." *American Antiquity* 32:186–97.

1969 "Cultural Traditions in the Interior of British Columbia." *Syesis* 2:189–200.

Saunders, R. S.
1983 "The Carrizozo Creek Bridge site: A Plains Woodland site on the Oklahoma/New Mexico Border." Papers in Highway Archaeology no. 7. Oklahoma Department of Transportation.

Saunders, R., and K. Saunders
1982 "Distribution and Density Patterns of Lithic Materials: Clues to Prehistoric Land Use in Cimarron County, Oklahoma." In *Pathways to Plains Prehistory*, edited by D. G. Wyckoff and J. L. Hofman, pp. 99–110. Oklahoma Anthropological Society Memoir 3.

Saylor, Stanley
1976 *The 1975 Excavations at EgKx-1, Wanipigow Lake.* Papers in Manitoba Archaeology, Preliminary Report no. 3. Department of Cultural Affairs and Historical Resources, Winnipeg.
1977 *The 1976 Excavations at EgKx-1, Wanipigow Lake.* Papers in Manitoba Archaeology, Preliminary Report no. 4. Department of Cultural Affairs and Historical Resources, Winnipeg.

Schaafsma, Polly
1980 *Indian Rock Art in the Southwest.* University of New Mexico Press, Albuquerque.
1986 "Rock Art." In *Great Basin*, edited by Warren L. D'Azevedo, pp. 215–26. Vol. 11, *Handbook of North American Indians.* Smithsonian Institution, Washington, D.C.

Schaeffer, Claude
1940 "The Subsistence Quest of the Kutenai." Ph.D. dissertation, University of Pennsylvania.

Schambach, F. F.
1982 "An Outline of Fourche Maline Culture in Southwest Arkansas." In *Arkansas Archaeology in Review*, edited by N. L. Trubowitz and M. D. Jeter, pp. 132–97. Research Series no. 15. Arkansas Archaeological Survey, Fayetteville.

Schlesier, Karl H.
1972 "Rethinking the Dismal River Aspect and the Plains Athapaskans, A.D. 1692–1768." *Plains Anthropologist* 17:101–33.
1975 "Die Irokesenkriege und die Grosse Vertreibung, 1609–1656." *Zeitschrift fuer Ethnologie* 100:157–94.
1987 *The Wolves of Heaven; Cheyenne Shamanism, Ceremonies, and Prehistoric Origins.* University of Oklahoma Press, Norman.
1988 "An Ethnohistoric Overview for the Cheyenne River Arm Survey." In *Cultural Resources Reconnaissance along the Cheyenne River Arm of Lake Oahe in Dewey, Haakon, Stanley and Ziebach Counties, South Dakota*, edited by R. Peter Winham, Kerry Lippincott and Edward J. Lueck, pp. 77–106. Archaeology Laboratory, Augustana College, Sioux Falls, S.D. Archaeological Contract Series no. 30. Submitted to U.S. Army Corps of Engineers, Omaha District, Contract no. DACW45-86-C-0235.
1990 "Rethinking the Midewiwin and the Plains Ceremonial Called The Sun Dance." *Plains Anthropologist* 35:1–27.

Schneider, F.
1969   "The Roy-Smith site (Bv-14), Beaver County, Oklahoma." *Bulletin of the Oklahoma Anthropological Society* 18:119–79.

Schneider, Fred E.
1982a   "A Model of Prehistoric Cultural Developments in the James River Valley of North Dakota." *Journal of the North Dakota Archaeological Association* 1:113–33.
1982b   "Sprenger: A Tipi Ring site in Central North Dakota." In *Pathways to Plains Prehistory*, edited by D. G. Wyckoff and J. L. Hofman, pp. 175–98. Oklahoma Anthropological Society Memoir 3.
1983   "The Sharbono Site, Devils Lake." *Newsletter of the North Dakota Archaeological Association* 4(2): 7–20.
1988   "Prehistoric Plant Use in Eastern North Dakota: Evidence and Interpretation." Paper presented at the Forty-sixth Annual Plains Anthropological Conference, Wichita, Kans.

Schneider, Fred, and Jeff Kinney
1978   "Evans: A Multi-component Site in Northwestern North Dakota." *Archaeology in Montana* 19(1–2): 1–39.

Schroeder, Albert H.
1955   *Archaeology of Zion Park.* Anthropological Paper no. 22. University of Utah, Salt Lake City.
1959   "A Study of the Apache Indians. Part I. The Apaches and Their Neighbors, 1540–1700." Manuscript.
1961   *The Archaeological Excavations at Willow Beach, Arizona, 1950.* Anthropological Paper no. 50. University of Utah, Salt Lake City.
1962   "A Reanalysis of the Routes of Coronado and Onate into the Plains in 1541 and 1601." *Plains Anthropologist* 7:20–23.
1964   "The Language of the Saline Pueblos: Piro or Tiwa? *New Mexico Historical Review* 39:235–49.
1972   "Rio Grande Ethnohistory." In *New Perspectives on the Pueblos*, edited by Alfonso Ortiz, pp. 41–70. School of American Research Book, University of New Mexico Press, Albuquerque.
1974   *A Study of the Apache Indians.* Garland Press, New York.
1979   "Pueblos Abandoned in Historic Times." In *Southwest*, edited by Alfonso Ortiz, pp. 236–54. Vol. 9, *Handbook of North American Indians.* Smithsonian Institution, Washington, D.C.
1982   "Historical Overview of Southwestern Ceramics." In *Southwestern Ceramics: A Comparative Review*, edited by Albert H. Schroeder, *The Arizona Archaeologist* no. 15, pp. 1–26, Arizona Archaeological Society, Phoenix.
1984   "The Protohistoric and Pitfalls of Archaeological Interpretation." In *Collected Papers in Honor of Harry L. Hadlock*, edited by Nancy Fox, Papers of the Archaeological Society of New Mexico no. 9, pp. 133–39. Albuquerque Archaeological Society Press.
1985   "Hopi Traditions and Rio Grande Migrations." In *Prehistory and History of the Southwest, Collected Papers in Honor of Alden C. Hayes*, edited by Nancy Fox, Papers of the Archaeological Society of New Mexico Papers no. 11, pp. 105–12. Ancient City Press, Santa Fe.

Schroeder, Albert H., and Daniel Matson
1965   *A Colony on the Move: Gaspar de Castano de Sosa's Journal, 1590–1591.* School of American Research, Santa Fe.
Schuldenrein, J.
1985   *Geomorphological Investigations at the U.S. Army Fort Carson-Pinon Canyon Maneuver Site, Las Animas County, Colorado.* Report submitted to the National Park Service, Interagency Archaeological Services, Denver.
Schultz, F., and A. C. Spaulding
1948   "A Hopewellian burial Site in the Lower Republican Valley, Kansas." *American Antiquity* 13(4): 306–13.
Science Applications, Inc. and Overland Archaeology, Inc.
1982   *A Cultural Resources Inventory of Eastern Portions of Lake Sakakawea, North Dakota (Mercer and McLean Counties).* Science Applications, Inc., Golden, Colo. Submitted to U.S. Army Corps of Engineers, Omaha District, Contract no. DACW45-81-C-0220.
Scott, Douglas D.
1979   "A New Note on Colorado Plains Woodland Mortuary Practices." *Southwestern Lore* 45(3): 13–24.
Scott, H. L.
1911   "Notes on the Kado, or Sun Dance of the Kiowa." *American Anthropologist* 13:345–79.
Scullin, Michael
1981   "Minnesota's First Farmers? Late Woodland Ceramics and Maize on the Blue Earth River, the Nelson Site (21BE24)." Paper presented at the Council for Minnesota Archaeology Spring Symposium, Hamline University, St. Paul.
Seaman, Timothy J.
1976   *Excavation of LA 11843: An Early Stockaded Settlement of the Gallina Phase.* Museum of New Mexico Laboratory of Anthropology Notes 111G, Santa Fe.
Secoy, F. R.
1953   *Changing Military Patterns on the Great Plains.* American Ethnological Society Monographs 21. J. J. Augustin Publisher, Locust Valley, New York.
Self, Huber
1978   *Environment and Man in Kansas.* Regents Press of Kansas, Lawrence.
Schaeffer, J. B.
1958   "The Alibates Flint Quarry, Texas." *American Antiquity* 24(2): 189–191.
Shafer, H. J.
1969   *Archaeological Investigations in the Robert Lee Reservoir Basin, West Central Texas.* Papers of the Texas Archaeological Salvage Project no. 17. Austin.
1978   *Lithic Technology at the George C. Davis Site, Cherokee County, Texas.* Department of Anthropology, Texas A&M University, College Station.
Sharrock, Floyd W., and J. D. Keyser
1975   "Montana Highway Archaeological Salvage Testing Program, 1973 Report to Montana Highway Commission." In *Collected Papers in*

Highway Salvage Archaeology, 1972–74, edited by S. R. Sharrock, pp. 117–204. Contributions to Anthropology no. 5. University of Montana. Missoula.

Shay, C. Thomas
1967   "Vegetation History of the Lake Agassiz Basin During the Past 12,000 Years." In *Life, Land, and Water,* edited by W. J. Mayer-Oakes, pp. 230–52. University of Manitoba Press, Winnipeg.

Shelford, V. E.
1963   *The Ecology of North America.* University of Illinois Press, Urbana.

Shelley, P.
1988   "Review of the Archaic Archaeology of the Llano Estacado and Adjacent Areas of New Mexico." Manuscript.

Shimkin, Holmes
1941   "Shoshone-Comanche Origins." *Sixth Pacific Science Conference, Proceedings,* 4:17–25.

Shumate, Maynard
1950   "The Archaeology of the Vicinity of Great Falls, Montana." Anthropology and Sociology Papers, Montana State University, Missoula.

Siebert, Frank T., Jr.
1967   "The Original Home of the Proto-Algonquian People." In *Contributions to Anthropology: Linguistics 1 (Algonquian),* pp. 13–47. Anthropological Series no. 78, National Museum of Canada Bulletin 214. Ottawa.

Sigstad, John S.
1969   "Pottery." In *Two House Sites in the Central Plains: An Experiment in Archaeology,* edited by W. Raymond Wood. *Plains Anthropologist Memoir* 6, 14(44, pt. 2): 17–22.
1973   "The Age and Distribution of Catlinite and Red Pipestone." Ph.D. dissertation, University of Missouri, Columbia. University Microfilms International, Ann Arbor.
1983   "A Report of the Archaeological Investigations, Pipestone National Monument, 1965 and 1966." Reprinted in *The Minnesota Archaeologist* 42(1,2). (Originally published 1970, *Journal of the Iowa Archaeological Society* 17:1–51.)

Sigstad, J. S., and R. Jolley
1975   *An Archaeological Survey of Portions of Fall River and Custer Counties, South Dakota.* South Dakota Archaeological Research Center, Fort Meade. Submitted to Tennessee Valley Authority.

Simon, A., C. Sheldon, and K. Keim
1982   *Anderson Divide Archaeological Test Excavations, Billings County, North Dakota.* Contribution 183. Department of Anthropology and Archaeology, University of North Dakota, Grand Forks. Submitted to Supron Energy Corporation, McGregor, N.D.

Simpson, G. G.
1944   *Tempo and Mode in Evolution.* Columbia University Press, New York.

Skinner, S. A.
1964   Lizard Cave: A Rock Shelter in Northeastern New Mexico. *El Palacio* 71(3): 22–29.

1981 "Aboriginal Demographic Changes in Central Texas." *Plains Anthropologist* 29:111–18.

Smith, Brian
1986 "The Lebret Site." M.A. thesis, Department of Anthropology and Archaeology, University of Saskatchewan, Saskatoon.

Smith, Brian J., and Ernest G. Walker
1988 "Evidence for Diverse Subsistence Strategies in an Avonlea Component." In *Avonlea Yesterday and Today: Archaeology and Prehistory*, edited by L. B. Davis, pp. 81–88. Saskatchewan Archaeological Society, Saskatoon.

Smith, Bruce D.
1986 "The Archaeology of the Southeastern United States: From Dalton to de Soto, 10,500–500 B.P." *Advances in World Archaeology* 5:1–92.

Smith, C.
1977 *The Talking Crow Site.* Publications in Anthropology 9. University of Kansas, Lawrence.

Smith, C. B., J. Runyon, and G. Agogino
1966 "A Progress Report on a Pre-ceramic Site at Rattlesnake Draw, Eastern New Mexico." *Plains Anthropologist* 11:302–13.

Smith, R. A.
1959 "Account of the Journey of Benard de la Harpe and Discovery Made by Him of Several Nations Situated in the West." *Southwestern Historical Quarterly* 62:525–41.

Snortland-Coles, J. Signe
1979 *The Duck River or Aschkibokahn Site of West-Central Manitoba: The Role of the Northern Marsh in the Subsistence of Late Woodland Peoples.* Papers in Manitoba Archaeology, Final Report no. 7. Department of Cultural Affairs and Historical Resources, Winnipeg.
1985 *The Jamestown Mounds Project.* State Historical Society of North Dakota, Bismarck.

Snow, David A.
1981 "Protohistoric Rio Grande Pueblo Economics: A Review of Trends." In *Protohistoric Period in the North American Southwest, A.D. 1450–1700*, edited by David R. Wilcox and W. Bruce Masse, pp. 354–77. Anthropological Research Papers no. 24. Arizona State University, Tempe.

Snow, Dean R.
1976 "The Archaeological Implications of the Proto-Algonquian Urheimat." In *Papers of the Seventh Algonquian Conference*, edited by William Cowan, pp. 339–46. Carleton University, Ottawa.

Snow, Dean R., and Kim M. Lanphear
1988 "European Contact and Indian Depopulation in the Northeast: The Timing of the First Epidemics." *Ethnohistory* 35:15–33.

Spaulding, Albert C.
1949 "The Middle Woodland Period In the Central Plains." In *Proceedings of the Fifth Plains Conference for Archaeology*, pp. 105–111. Note Book no. 1. Laboratory of Anthropology, University of Nebraska, Lincoln.

Spencer, Robert F.
1965   "Western North America: Plateau, Basin, California." In *The Native Americans*, edited by R. F. Spencer, J. D. Jennings et al., pp. 213–82. Harper and Row, New York.

Sperry, James E.
1965   "Cultural Relationships of the Miller and Rush Creek Archaeological Sites on the Lower Republican River of Kansas." M.A. thesis, Department of Anthropology, University of Nebraska.

Speth, J. D.
1983   *Bison Kills and Bone Counts: Decision Making by Ancient Hunters.* University of Chicago Press, Chicago.

Speth, D. J., and S. L. Scott
1989   "Horticulture and Large-Mammal Hunting: The Role of Resource Depletion and the Constraints of Time and Labor." In *Farmers as Hunters: The Implications of Sedentism*, edited by Susan Kent, pp. 71–79. Cambridge University Press, Cambridge.

Spielmann, K. A.
1982   "Inter-societal Food Acquisition Among Egalitarian Societies: An Ecological Study of Plains/Pueblo Interaction in the American Southwest." Ph.D. dissertation, University of Michigan. University Microfilms International, Ann Arbor.
1983   "Late Prehistoric Exchange Between the Southwest and Southern Plains." *Plains Anthropologist* 28:257–72.

Spier, Leslie
1921   "Notes on the Kiowa Sun Dance." *Anthropological Papers of the American Museum of Natural History*, vol. 16, part 6, pp. 431–50. New York.

Spinden, Herbert Joseph
1908   "The Nez Perce Indians." *Memoirs of the American Anthropological Association*, vol. 2, pt. 3.

Stanford, Dennis J., and Jane S. Day
1992   *Ice Age Hunters of the Rockies.* Denver Museum of Natural History and University Press of Colorado, Niwit, Colorado.

Stanley, David G.
1989   *Phase 1 Reconnaissance Survey of Selected Tracts Within the Blood Run Locality, Lyon County, Iowa.* Bear Creek Archaeology, Decorah, Iowa. Submitted to the Iowa Bureau of Historic Preservation, Ames.

Steege, Louis C.
1967   "Happy Hollow Rockshelter." *Wyoming Archaeologist* 10(3): 11–23.

Steinacher, Terry L.
1981   *Archaeological Survey and Investigations of Selected Federal Lands on the West Bank of the Lake Sharpe/Big Bend Project Area, South Dakota: 1980.* 2 vols. Division of Archaeological Research, Department of Anthropology, University of Nebraska, Lincoln. Technical Report no. 81–07. Submitted to U.S. Army Corps of Engineers, Omaha District, Contract no. DACW45-80-M-2929.

Steinbring, Jack
1980   *An Introduction to Archaeology on the Winnipeg River.* Papers in

Manitoba Archaeology, Miscellaneous Paper no. 9. Department of Cultural Affairs and Historical Resources, Winnipeg.

Sterns, Fred H.
1915 "The Archaeology of Eastern Nebraska, With Special Reference of the Culture of the Rectangular Earth Lodges." Ph.D. dissertation, Harvard University.

Stevenson, Katherine, William Green, and Janet Speth
1983 "The Middle Mississippian Presence in the Upper Mississippi Valley: The Evidence from Trempealeau, Wisconsin." Paper presented at the Twenty-eighth Annual Midwest Archaeological conference, Iowa City, Iowa.

Steward, Julian H.
1937 *Ancient Caves of the Great Salt Lake.* Bureau of American Ethnology Bulletin 116:1–123. Smithsonian Institution, Washington, D.C.
1938 *Basin-Plateau Aboriginal Sociopolitical Groups.* Bureau of American Ethnology Bulletin 120. Smithsonian Institution, Washington, D.C.
1942 "The Direct Historical Approach to Archaeology." *American Antiquity* 7:337–43.
1968 "The Great Basin Shoshonean Indians: An Example of a Family Level of Sociocultural Integration." In *Man in Adaptation: The Cultural Present,* 2d ed., edited by Yehudi A. Cohen, pp. 101–15. Aldine, Chicago.

Stirling, Matthew W.
1942 "Origin Myth of Acoma." *Bureau of American Ethnology, Bulletin* 135.

Stoltman, James B.
1973 *The Laurel Culture in Minnesota.* Minnesota Prehistoric Archaeology Series no. 8. Minnesota Historical Society, St. Paul.
1974 "An Examination of Within-Laurel Variability in Northern Minnesota." In *Aspects of Upper Great Lakes Anthropology,* edited by Elden Johnson, pp. 74–89. Minnesota Historical Society, St. Paul.
1983 "Ancient Peoples of the Upper Mississippi River Valley." In *Historic Lifestyles in the Upper Mississippi River Valley,* edited by J. Wozniak, pp. 197–255. University Press of America, New York.
1986 "The Appearance of the Mississippian Cultural Tradition in the Upper Mississippi Valley." In *Prehistoric Mound Builders of the Mississippi Valley,* edited by James B. Stoltman, pp. 26–34. Putnam Museum, Davenport, Iowa.

Story, D. A.
1981a *Archaeological Investigations at the George C. Davis Site, Cherokee County, Texas: Summers of 1979 and 1980.* Occasional Paper no. 1. Texas Archaeological Research Laboratory, University of Texas, Austin.
1981b "An Overview of the Archaeology of East Texas." *Plains Anthropologist* 29:139–56.

Story, D. A., and D. G. Creel
1982 "The Cultural Setting." In *The Deshazo Site, Nacogdoches County, Texas,* edited by D. A. Story, pp. 20–34. Texas Antiquities Permit Series, no. 7. Texas Antiquities Committee, Austin.

Strong, William D.
1935   *An Introduction to Nebraska Archaeology.* Smithsonian Miscellaneous Collections 93(10). Washington, D.C.
1940   "From History to Prehistory in the Northern Great Plains." In *Essays in the Historical Anthropology of North America in Honor of John R. Swanton.* Smithsonian Miscellaneous Collections 100:353–94.
1941   "Arikara and Cheyenne Earth Lodge Sites in North and South Dakota." *North Dakota Historical Quarterly* 8(3): 157–66.

Strong, W. L., and K. R. Leggat
1981   *Ecoregions of Alberta.* Alberta Energy and Natural Resources Technical Report no. T/4. Edmonton.

Stubbs, Stanley
1930   "Preliminary Report of Excavations near La Luz and Alamagordo, New Mexico." *El Palacio* 29:3–14.

Stuiver, Minze, and Gordon W. Pearson
1986   "High-precision Calibration of the Radiocarbon Time Scale, A.D. 1950–500 B.C." *Radiocarbon* 28(2B): 805–38.

Suhm, Dee Ann, and Alex D. Krieger
1954   *An Introductory Handbook of Texas Archaeology.* Abilene.

Sundstrom, Linea
1984   *Rock Art in Western South Dakota. Section 2.* The Southern Black Hills. Special Publication no. 9, pp. 53–142. South Dakota Archaeological Society, Archaeology Laboratory, Augustana College, Sioux Falls.

Swanson, Earl H.
1972   *Birch Creek, Human Ecology in the Cool Desert of the Northern Rocky Mountains 9,000 B.C.–A.D. 1850.* Idaho State University Press, Pocatello.

Swanton, John R.
1942   "Source Material on the History and Ethnology of the Caddo Indians." *Bureau of American Ethnology Bulletin* 132. Smithsonian Institution, Washington, D.C.
1946   "The Indians of the Southeastern United States." *Bureau of American Ethnology Bulletin* 137. Smithsonian Institution, Washington, D.C.
1953   "The Indian Tribes of North America." *Bureau of American Ethnology Bulletin* 145.

Swenson, F. E.
1986   "A Study in Cultural Adaptations to Climatic Shifts on the Southern Plains: Washita River Phase and Edwards Complex Cultural Continuity." M.A. thesis, Department of Anthropology, University of Oklahoma, Norman.

Swenson, Fern E., and Michael L. Gregg
1988   "A Devils Lake-Sourisford Mortuary Vessel from Southeastern North Dakota." *Journal of the North Dakota Archaeological Association* 3:1–15.

Syms, E. Leigh
1975   "An Assessment of the Archaeological Resources of the Cherry Point Site in Southwestern Manitoba." *Archae-facts* 5(2,3): 49–56.

1977   "Cultural Ecology and Ecological Dynamics of the Ceramic Period in Southwestern Manitoba." *Plains Anthropologist Memoir* 12.

1979   "The Devils Lake–Sourisford Burial Complex on the Northern Plains." *Plains Anthropologist* 24:283–308.

1982   "The Arvilla Burial Complex: A Re-assessment." *Journal of the North Dakota Archaeological Association* 1:135–66.

1985   "Fitting People into the Late Prehistory of the Northeastern Plains: A Need to Return to a Holistic Anthropological Approach." In *Archaeology, Ecology and Ethnohistory of the Prairie-Forest Border Zone of Minnesota and Manitoba*, edited by Janet Spector and Elden Johnson, pp. 73–107. J & L Reprint, Lincoln.

Tabeau, Pierre Antonine
1939   *Tabeau's Narrative of Loisel's Expedition to the Upper Missouri*, edited by Annie H. Abel. University of Oklahoma Press, Norman.

Tamplin, Morgan
1977   "Prehistoric Occupation and Resource Exploitation on the Saskatchewan River at the Pas, Manitoba." Ph.D. dissertation, Department of Anthropology, University of Arizona, Tucson.

Taylor, Dee
1973   "Archaeological Investigations in the Libby Reservoir Area, Northwestern Montana." Contributions to Anthropology 3. University of Montana, Missoula.

Temple, W. C.
1975   *Indian Villages of the Illinois Country*, pt. I, Atlas Supplement. Scientific papers, vol. II. Illinois State Museum, Springfield.

Teit, J.
1930   "The Salishan Tribes of the Western Plateau." In *Bureau of American Ethnology Annual Report* (1927–1928)45:23–396.

Theler, James L.
1987   *Woodland Tradition Economic Strategies; Animal Resource Utilization in Southwestern Wisconsin and Northeastern Iowa*. Report 17. Office of the State Archaeologist, University of Iowa, Iowa City.

Thies, Randall M.
1985   *Arrowhead Island: A Middle Woodland Village in East Central Kansas*. Contract Archaeology Publication no. 3. Kansas State Historical Society, Topeka.

1991   "New Data on Lower Walnut Focus." Paper presented at the Forty-ninth Plains Anthropological Conference.

Thiessen, T. D.
1977   "A Tentative Radiocarbon Chronology for the Middle Missouri Tradition." In *Trends in Middle Missouri Prehistory: A Festschrift Honoring the Contributions of Donald J. Lehmer*, edited by W. Raymond Wood, *Plains Anthropologist Memoir* 13:59–82.

Thomas, Alfred Barnaby
1932   *Forgotten Frontiers*. University of Oklahoma Press, Norman.

Thomas, Cyrus
1873   "Ancient Mounds of Dakota." *U.S. Geological and Geographical Survey of the Territories, Annual Report* 6 (1982):655–58.

1894   *Report on the Mound Explorations of the Bureau of Ethnology. Bureau of American Ethnology Annual Report,* 12:1–742. Smithsonian Institution, Washington, D.C. Reprinted 1985.

Thompson, David
1916   *David Thompson's Narrative of His Explorations in Western America, 1784–1812,* edited by J. B. Tyrrell. Publication no. 12. Champlain Society, Toronto.

Thompson, Raymond H.
1956   "The Subjective Element in Archaeological Inference." *Southwestern Journal of Anthropology* 12(3): 327–32.

Thoms, Alston V.
1984   "History and Summary: Cultural Resources Investigations in the Libby Reservoir Area." In *Environment, Archaeology, and Land Use Patterns in the Middle Kootenai River Valley,* vol. 1. Project Report 2, edited by A. V. Thoms, pp. 7–15. Center for Northwestern Anthropology, Washington State University, Pullman.

Thoms, Alston V., and R. F. Schalk
1984   "Prehistoric Land Use in the Middle Kootenai River Valley." In *Environment, Archaeology, and Land Use Patterns in the Middle Kootenai Valley, Vol. 1,* edited by A. V. Thoms. Center for Northwestern Anthropology, Project Report 2:363–377. Washington State University, Pullman.

Thurman, Melburn D.
1988   "On the Identity of the Charaticas . . . : Dog Eating and Pre-Horse Adaptation on the High Plains." *Plains Anthropologist* 33:159–70.

Thurmond, J. P.
1985   "Late Caddoan Social Group Identifications and Sociopolitical Organization in the Upper Cypress Basin and Vicinity, Northeastern Texas." *Bulletin of the Texas Archaeological Society* 54:185–200.

Tibesar, William L.
1980   "An Intra-Site Discussion of the Greyrocks Archaeological Site, 48PL65." M.A. thesis, Department of Anthropology, University of Wyoming.

Tichy, Marjorie F.
1945   "The Distribution of Early Elbow Pipes." *El Palacio* 52:70–73.

Tiffany, Joseph A.
1978   "Middle Woodland Pottery Typology from Southwest Iowa." *Plains Anthropologist* 23(81): 169–82.
1979   "An Overview of Oneota Sites in Southeastern Iowa: A Perspective from the Ceramic Analysis of the Schmeiser Site (13DM101), Des Moines County, Iowa." *Proceedings of the Iowa Academy of Science* 86:89–101.
1982a   "Site Catchment Analysis of Southeast Iowa Oneota Sites." In *Oneota Studies,* edited by Guy E. Gibbon, pp. 1–13. Publications in Anthropology no. 1. University of Minnesota, Minneapolis.
1982b   "Hartley Fort Ceramics." *Proceedings of the Iowa Academy of Science* 89:133–50.
1982c   *Chan-Ya-T: A Mill Creek Village.* Report 15. Office of the State Archaeologist, University of Iowa, Iowa City.

1983   "An Overview of the Middle Missouri Tradition." In *Prairie Archaeology*, edited by Guy E. Gibbon, pp. 87–108. Publications in Anthropology no. 3. University of Minnesota, Minneapolis.

1986a   "The Early Woodland Period in Iowa." In *Early Woodland Archaeology*, edited by K. B. Farnsworth and T. E. Emerson, pp. 159–70. Kampsville Seminars in Archaeology no. 2. Center for American Archaeology Press, Kampsville.

1986b   "Ceramics from the F-518 Project." In *Archaeological Investigations Along the F-518 Corridor*, edited by S. C. Lensink, pp. 227–45. Iowa Quaternary Studies, Contribution 9. University of Iowa, Iowa City.

1986c   "The Mississippian Tradition and Iowa's Prehistoric Peoples." In *Prehistoric Mound Builders of the Mississippi Valley*, edited by James B. Stoltman, pp. 35–39. Putnam Museum, Davenport, Iowa.

1991a   "Modeling Mill Creek-Mississippian Interaction." In *New Perspectives on Cahokia: Views from the Periphery*, edited by J. B. Stoltman, pp. 319–47. Monographs in World Archaeology no. 2. Prehistory Press, Madison.

1991b   "Models of Mississippian Culture History in the Western Prairie Peninsula: A Perspective from Iowa." In *Cahokia and the Hinterlands*, edited by Thomas E. Emerson and R. Barry Lewis, pp. 183–92. University of Illinois Press, Urbana.

Tiller, Veronica E.
1983   "Jicarilla Apache." In *Southwest*, edited by Alfonso Ortiz, pp. 440–61. Vol. 10, *Handbook of North American Indians*. Smithsonian Institution, Washington, D.C.

Tisdale, M. A.
1978   "Investigations at the Stott Site: A Review of Research from 1947 to 1977." Papers in Manitoba Archaeology, Final Report no. 5. Department of Cultural Affairs and Historical Resources, Winnipeg.

Tisdale, M. A., and S. M. Jamieson
1982   *Investigations at Wapisu Lake, 1972–1976*. Papers in Manitoba Archaeology, Final Report no. 11. Department of Cultural Affairs and Historical Resources, Winnipeg.

Toom, Dennis L.
1988   "A Preliminary Statement on the Archaeology and Radiocarbon Dating of the Flaming Arrow Site (32ML4), McLean County, North Dakota." *Journal of the North Dakota Archaeological Association* 3:51–73.

1992   "Early Village Formation in the Middle Missouri: Subarea of the Plains." In *Research in Economic Anthropology, Supplement 6: Long-Term Subsistence Change in Prehistoric North America*, edited by D. R. Croes, R. A. Hawkins, and B. L. Isaac, pp. 131–91. JAI Press, Greenwich, Conn.

Toom, Dennis L., and Joe Alan Artz
1985   *An Archaeological Survey of Selected Federal Lands on the West Bank of Lake Oahe, Oahe Dam Vicinity, Stanley County, South Dakota, 1984*. 2 vols. Contribution no. 215. Department of Anthropology and Archaeology, University of North Dakota, Grand Forks. Submitted to U.S. Army Corps of Engineers, Omaha District, Contract no. DACW45-84-C-0191.

Toom, Dennis L., and Paul R. Picha
1984   *An Archaeological Survey of Selected Federal Lands on the West Bank of the Big Bend/Lake Sharpe Project Area, Lyman and Stanley Counties, South Dakota 1983.* 2 vols. Contribution no. 198. University of North Dakota, Department of Anthropology and Archaeology. Submitted to U.S. Army Corps of Engineers, Omaha District, Contract no. DACW45-83-C-0142.

Trager, George L.
1967   "The Tanoan Settlement of the Rio Grande Area: A Possible Chronology." In *Studies in Southwestern Ethno-linguistics: Meaning and History in the Languages of the American Southwest,* edited by Dell H. Hymes and William E. Bittle, pp. 335–50. Mouton, The Hague.

Tratebas, Alice M.
1978   *Archaeological Surveys in the Black Hills National Forest, South Dakota (1975–1977).* South Dakota Archaeological Research Center, Fort Meade. Submitted to U.S. Forest Service, Black Hills National Forest.
1979   *Archaeological Surveys in the Black Hills National Forest, South Dakota (1977–1978).* Contract Investigations Series 5. South Dakota Archaeological Research Center, Fort Meade. Submitted to U.S. Forest Service, Black Hills National Forest.

Travis, Lauri
1988   "An Archaeological Survey in the Plains Foothills Ecotone, Northern Colorado." *Plains Anthropologist* 33(120): 171–86.

Trubowitz, N. L.
1984   *Cedar Grove: An Interdisciplinary Investigation of a Late Caddo Farmstead in the Red River Valley.* Research Series no. 23. Arkansas Archaeological Survey, Fayetteville.

Tuck, James A.
1978   "Regional Cultural Development, 3000 to 300 B.C." In *Northeast,* edited by Bruce Trigger, pp. 28–43. Vol. 15, *Handbook of North American Indians.* Smithsonian Institution, Washington, D.C.

Tuohy, Donald R.
1986   "Portable Art Objects." In *Great Basin,* edited by Warren L. D'Azevedo, pp. 227–37. Vol. 11, *Handbook of North American Indians.* Smithsonian Institution, Washington, D.C.

Turnbull, Christopher J.
1977   "Archaeology and Ethnohistory in the Arrow Lakes, Southeastern British Columbia." Archaeological Survey of Canada Paper 65. National Museum of Man Mercury Series, Ottawa.

Turner, C. G., II
1980   "Appendix I: Suggestive Dental Evidence for Athabascan Affiliation in a Colorado Skeletal Series." In *Trinidad Lake Cultural Resource Study, Part II: The Prehistoric Occupation of the Upper Purgatoire River Valley,* edited by C. E. Wood and G. A. Bair. Laboratory of Contract Archaeology, Trinidad State Junior Colelge, Trinidad, Colo.

Turney-High, Harry H.
1933   "Cooking Camas and Bitter Root." *Scientific Monthly* 36:262–63.

1937   "The Flathead Indians of Montana." *American Anthropological Association Memoir* 48:1–160.

1941   "Ethnography of the Kutenai." *American Anthropological Association Memoir* 56.

Tyler, S. L., and H. D. Taylor

1958   "The Report of Fray Alonso de Posada in Relation to Quivira and Teguayo." *New Mexico Historical Review* 33:285–314.

Upham, S., R. S. MacNeish, W. C. Galinat, and C. M. Stevenson

1987   "Evidence Concerning the Origin of Maiz de Ocho." *American Anthropologist* 89(2): 410–19.

U.S. Department of Interior

1858   *Annual Report of the Commissioner of Indian Affairs to the Secretary of the Interior.* U.S. Government Printing Office, Washington, D.C.

U.S. De Soto Commission

1939   *Final Report of the United States De Soto Expedition Commission.* House Document no. 71, 76th Congress, 1st Session. U.S. Government Printing Office, Washington, D.C.

Van Hoy, Thomas, and Randy Nathan (portions edited by David D. Kuehn and Arleyn Simon)

1983   *Phase I Intensive Cultural Resource Inventory of Selected Recreation Areas in the West Portion of Lake Sakakawea, North Dakota – Dunn, McKenzie and Williams Counties.* Department of Anthropology and Archaeology, University of North Dakota, Grand Forks. Submitted to U.S. Army Corps of Engineers, Omaha District, Contract no. DACW45-81-C-0222.

Vehik, R.

1982   *The Archaeology of the Bug Hill Site (34Pu116): Pushmataha County, Oklahoma.* Archaeological Research and Management Center Series, no. 7. Norman, Okla.

Vehik, S. C.

1976   "The Great Bend Aspect: A Multivariate Investigation of its Origins and Southern Plains Relationships." *Plains Anthropologist* 21:199–206.

1982   "Burial Mounds, Mortuary Rituals, and Social Organization: The Impact of the Hopewell Interaction Sphere on the Plains." Paper delivered to University of Oklahoma, Department of Anthropology, Colloquia Series.

1984   "The Woodland Occupations." In *Prehistory of Oklahoma,* edited by R. E. Bell, pp. 175–97. Academic Press, Orlando.

1985a   "Late Prehistoric Settlement Strategy and Exploitation of Florence A. Chert." In *Lithic Resource Procurement: Proceedings from the Second Conference of Prehistoric Chert Exploitation,* edited by Susan C. Vehik, pp. 81–91. Occasional Paper no. 4. Center for Archaeological Investigations, Southern Illinois University, Carbondale.

1985b   "Conclusions." In *Cultural Resource Assessments in Osage and Kay Counties, North-Central Oklahoma,* edited by S. C. Vehik, pp. 302–30. Department of Anthropology, University of Oklahoma. Submitted to the Oklahoma Historical Society, Oklahoma City.

1986   "Oñate's Expedition to the Southern Plains: Routes, Destinations, and Implications for Late Prehistoric Cultural Adaptations." *Plains Anthropologist* 31:13–33.

1987   "Woodland Occupations." Paper presented at the annual meeting of the Oklahoma Anthropological Society.

1988   "Late Prehistoric Exchange on the Southern Plains and its Periphery." *Midcontinental Journal of Archaeology* 13:41–68.

1989a   *An Assessment of Wister Reservoir Archaeological Resources.* Report submitted to the U.S. Army Corps of Engineers, Tulsa District.

1989b   "Problems and Potential in Plains Indian Demography." In *Plains Indian Historical Demography and Health: Perspectives, Interpretations, and Critiques,* edited by G. R. Campbell, pp. 115–25. Plains Anthropologist Memoir 23.

1992   "Wichita Culture History." *Plains Anthropologist* 37:311–32.

Vehik, S. C., and K. Ashworth

1983   *Kaw Lake Hydropower: Further Archaeological Investigations at the Uncas Site (34Ka-172).* Report submitted to the U.S. Army Corps of Engineers, Tulsa District.

Vehik, S. C., and T. G. Baugh

In   "Prehistoric Plains Trade." In *Prehistoric Exchange Systems in North*
press   *America,* edited by J. E. Ericson and T. G. Baugh.

Vehik, S. C., K. J. Buehler, and A. J. Wormser

1979   *A Cultural Resource Survey of the Salt Creek Valley, Osage County, Oklahoma.* Oklahoma Archaeological Survey, Archaeological Resources Survey Report 8. University of Oklahoma, Norman.

Vehik, S. C., and P. Flynn

1982   "Archaeological Investigations at the Early Plains Village Uncas Site (34Ka-172)." *Oklahoma Anthropological Society Bulletin* 31:5–70.

Vehik, S. C., and F. E. Swenson

1984   *Excavations at the Late Prehistoric Uncas Site (34Ka-172) House IV: A Consideration of Internal Patterning and External Relationships on the Southern Plains.* Report submitted to the U.S. Army Corps of Engineers, Tulsa District.

Vickers, J. Roderick

1983   "An Introduction to Alberta Radiocarbon Dates." In *Archaeology in Alberta 1982,* edited by D. Burley, pp. 134–41. Occasional Paper no. 21. Archaeological Survey of Alberta, Edmonton.

1986   *Alberta Plains Prehistory: A Review.* Occasional Paper no. 27. Archaeological Survey of Alberta, Edmonton.

1986   *Alberta Plains Prehistory: A Review.* Occasional Paper no. 27. Archaeological Survey of Alberta, Edmonton.

Vivian, Gordon, and Tom W. Matthews

1964   *Kin Kletso: A Pueblo III Community in Chaco Canyon, New Mexico.* Southwestern Monuments Association Technical Series vol. 6, pts. 1, 2, Globe.

Voegelin, C. F.

1941   "North American Indian Languages Still Spoken and Their Genetic Relationships." In *Language, Culture and Personality: Essays in Mem-*

ory of Edward Sapir, edited by L. Spier, pp. 14–40. Sapir Memorial
Publication Fund, Menasha, Wisconsin.

Wade, William D.
1966   "The Hutcheson Burial Site." *Southwestern Lore* 21(4): 74–80.
1971   "Burial 1 from Michaud Site A." *Plains Anthropologist* 16(54): 321–23.

Walker, Deward E., Jr.
1967   "Mutual Cross-Utilization of Economic Resources in the Plateau: An
        Example from Aboriginal Nez Perce Fishing Practices." Report of
        Investigations 41. Laboratory of Anthropology, Washington State University, Pullman.

Wallace, E., and E. A. Hoebel
1952   *The Comanches: Lords of the South Plains.* University of Oklahoma
        Press, Norman.

Warnica, J. W.
1966   "New Discoveries at the Clovis Site." *American Antiquity* 31:345–57.

Watrall, Charles R.
1974   "Subsistence Pattern Change at the Cambria Site: A Review and
        Hypothesis." In *Aspects of Upper Great Lakes Anthropology; Papers
        in Honor of Lloyd A. Wilford*, edited by E. Johnson, pp. 138–42.
        Minnesota Historical Society, St. Paul.
1985   "A Structural Comparison of the Maplewood, Scott, and Lake Midden
        Sites." In *Archaeology, Ecology and Ethnohistory of the Prairie-Forest
        Border Zone of Minnesota and Manitoba*, edited by Janet Spector and
        Elden Johnson, pp. 65–72. J & L Reprint, Lincoln.

Watson, V.
1950   "The Optima Focus of the Panhandle Aspect: Description and Analysis." *Bulletin of the Texas Archaeological and Paleontological Society*
        21:7–68.

Watts, H. K.
1971   "The Archaeology of the Avery Ranch Site on Turkey Creek, Southeastern Colorado." M.A. thesis, Department of Anthropology, University of Denver.
1975   "The Avery Ranch Site." *Southwestern Lore* 14:15–27.

Way, J. E.
1984   "Preliminary Results of an Archaeological Survey along the Canadian
        River, Chappell-Spade Ranch, Tucumcari, San Miguel County, New
        Mexico." In *Papers of the Philmont Conference on the Archaeology of
        Northeastern New Mexico*, edited by C. J. Condie, pp. 201–26. *New
        Mexico Archaeological Council Proceedings* 6(1).

Wedel, Mildred M.
1959   "Oneota Sites on the Upper Iowa River." *Missouri Archaeologist* 21(2–
        4): 1–181.
1971   "J.-B. Bérnard, Sieur de la Harpe: Visitor to the Wichitas in 1719."
        Great Plains Journal 10:37–70.
1972   "Claude-Charles Dutisné: A Review of His 1719 Journeys." *Great
        Plains Journal* 12:4–25.
1974   "Le Sueur and the Dakota Sioux." In *Aspects of Upper Great Lakes
        Anthropology*, edited by Elden Johnson, pp. 157–71. Minnesota Prehis-

toric Archaeology Series no. 11. Minnesota Historical Society, St. Paul.

1978   *La Harpe's Post on Red River and Nearby Caddo Settlements.* Bulletin 30. Texas Memorial Museum, University of Texas, Austin.

1981   *The Deer Creek Site, Oklahoma: A Wichita Village Sometimes Called Ferdinandina, An Ethnohistorian's View.* Series in Anthropology no. 5. Oklahoma Historical Society, Oklahoma City.

1981   "The Ioway, Oto, and Omaha Indians in 1700." *Journal of the Iowa Archaeological Society* 28:1–13.

1982   "The Wichita Indians and the Arkansas River Basin." In *Plains Indian Studies: A Collection of Essays in Honor of John C. Ewers and Waldo R. Wedel,* edited by Douglas H. Ubelaker and Herman J. Viola, pp. 118–34. Smithsonian Contributions to Anthropology no. 30. Smithsonian Institution, Washington, D.C.

1986   "Peering at the Ioway Indians Through the Mist of Time: 1650–circa 1700." *Journal of the Iowa Archaeological Society* 33:1–74.

Wedel, Waldo R.

1934a   "Contributions to the Archaeology of the Upper Republican Valley, Nebraska." *Nebraska History* 15(3): 133–209.

1934b   "Minneapolis 1: A Prehistoric Village Site in Ottawa County, Kansas." *Nebraska History* 15(3): 210–38.

1934c   "Salina 1: A Protohistoric Village Site in McPherson County, Kansas." *Nebraska History* 15(3): 239–50.

1936   "An Introduction to Pawnee Archaeology." *Bureau of American Ethnology Bulletin* 112. Smithsonian Institution, Washington, D.C.

1938   *The Direct Historical Approach in Pawnee Archaeology.* Smithsonian Miscellaneous Collections 97(7). Washington, D.C.

1940   "Culture Sequence in the Central Great Plains." In *Essays in the Historical Anthropology of North America in Honor of John R. Swanton,* pp. 291–352. Smithsonian Miscellaneous Collections 100, Washington, D.C.

1943   *Archaeological Investigations in Platte and Clay Counties, Missouri.* Bulletin 183. U.S. National Museum, Washington, D.C.

1950   "Notes on Plains-Southwestern Contacts in Light of Archaeology." In *For the Dean,* edited by Erik K. Reed and Dale S. King, pp. 99–116, Hohokam Museums Association, Tucson, and Southwestern Monuments Association, Santa Fe.

1954   "Earthenware and Steatite Vessels from Northwestern Wyoming." *American Antiquity* 19(4): 403–9.

1959   "An Introduction to Kansas Archaeology." *Bureau of American Ethnology Bulletin* 174. Smithsonian Institution, Washington, D.C.

1961   *Prehistoric Man on the Great Plains.* University of Oklahoma Press, Norman.

1963   "The High Plains and Their Utilization by the Indians." *American Antiquity* 29(1): 1–16.

1975   "Chalk Hollow: Culture Sequence and Chronology in the Texas Panhandle." *Actas del XLI Congreso Internacional de Americanistas* 1:271–75. Mexico, D.F.

1979a "House Floors and Native Settlement Populations in the Central Plains." *Plains Anthropologist* 24:85–98.

1979b "Some Reflections on Plains Caddoan Origins." *Nebraska History* 60:272–93.

1986 *Central Plains Prehistory.* University of Nebraska Press, Lincoln.

Wendland, Wayne M.

1978a "Holocene Man in North America: The Ecological Setting and Climatic Background." *Plains Anthropologist* 23:273–87.

1978b "Holocene Man's Utilization of the Great Plains Environment." *American Antiquity* 28:159–71.

Wendorf, Fred

1953 *Salvage Archaeology in the Chama Valley, New Mexico.* Monograph no. 17. School of American Research, Santa Fe.

1960 "The Archaeology of Northeastern New Mexico." *El Palacio* 67:55–65.

1970 "The Lubbock Subpluvial." In *Pleistocene and Recent Environments of the Central Great Plains,* edited by Wakefield Dort and J. Knox Jones, Jr., pp. 23–37. *Special Publication* 3. Department of Geology, University of Kansas. University of Kansas Press, Lawrence.

Wendorf, F., and J. J. Hester

1975 *Late Pleistocene Environments of the Southern High Plains.* Fort Burgwin Research Center Publication 9, Dallas.

Wendorf, Fred, and Erik K. Reed

1955 "An Alternative Reconstruction of Northern Rio Grande Prehistory." *El Palacio* 62:131–73.

Wettlaufer, B. N.

1955 *The Mortlach Site in the Besant Valley of Central Saskatchewan.* Anthropological Series 1. Department of Natural Resources, Regina.

Wettlaufer, B., and William J. Mayer-Oakes.

1960 *The Long Creek Site.* Anthropological Series 2. Saskatchewan Museum of Natural History, Regina.

Whalen, M. E.

1986 "Small Site Analysis in the Hueco Bolson of Western Texas." *Journal of Field Archaeology* 13(1): 69–81.

Wheeler, R. P.

1954 "Two New Projectile Point Types: Duncan and Hanna Points." *Plains Anthropologist* 1:7–14.

1963 "The Stutsman Focus: An Aboriginal Culture Complex in the Jamestown Reservoir Area, North Dakota." *Bureau of American Ethnology Bulletin* 185:167–233, pls. 27–36. Smithsonian Institution, Washington, D.C.

n.d. "Archaeological Remains in the Angostura Reservoir Area, South Dakota, and in the Keyhole and Boysen Reservoir Areas, Wyoming." Ms. on file, National Park Service, Midwest Archaeological Center, Lincoln.

White, Thain

1959 "Tipi Rings in the Flathead Lake Area, Western Montana." Anthropology and Sociology Papers 19. Montana State University, Bozeman.

Whitman, William

1937 *The Oto.* Columbia University Press, New York.

Wiersum, Wayne E., and M. A. Tisdale
1977   *Excavations at UNR23, The Notiqi Lake Site.* Department of Cultural Affairs and Historical Resources/Manitoba Museum of Man and Nature, Winnipeg.

Wilcox, David E.
1984   "Multi-Ethnic Division of Labor in the Prehistoric Southwest." In *Collected Papers in Honor of Harry L. Hadlock,* edited by Nancy Fox, Papers of the Archaeological Society of New Mexico 9, pp. 141–55, Albuquerque Archaeological Society Press.

Wilcox, David R.
1981   "The Entry of Athapaskans into the North American Southwest: The Problem Today." In *The Protohistoric Period in the North American Southwest, A.D. 1450–1700,* edited by David R. Wilcox and W. Bruce Masse, pp. 213–56. Anthropological Research Paper no. 24. Arizona State University, Tempe.
1988   "Avonlea and Southern Athapaskan Migrations." In *Avonlea Yesterday and Today: Archaeology and Prehistory,* edited by Leslie B. Davis, pp. 273–80. Saskatchewan Archaeological Society, Saskatoon.
1991   "Changing Contexts of Pueblo Adaptations, A.D. 1250–1600." In *Farmers, Hunters, and Colonists: Interaction Between the Southwest and the Southern Plains,* edited by Katherine A. Spielmann, pp. 128–54. University of Arizona Press, Tucson.

Wilford, Lloyd A.
1941   "A Tentative Classification of the Prehistoric Cultures of Minnesota." *American Antiquity* 6:231–49.
1945   "The Prehistoric Indians of Minnesota: The Headwaters Lakes Aspect." *Minnesota History* 26:312–29.
1955   "A Revised Classification of the Prehistoric Cultures of Minnesota." *American Antiquity* 21:130–42.
1964   "The Eck Mound and Burial Area (21HE2)." *Minnesota Archaeological Newsletter* 6:1–6.
1970   *Burial Mounds of the Red River Headwaters, Minnesota.* Minnesota Prehistoric Archaeology Series 5. Minnesota Historical Society, St. Paul.

Wilford, Lloyd A., Eldon Johnson, and Joan Vicinus
1969   *Burial Mounds of Central Minnesota.* Excavation Reports. Minnesota Historical Society, St. Paul.

Willey, Gordon R.
1966   *An Introduction to American Archaeology,* vol. 1, North and Middle America. Prentice-Hall, Englewood Cliffs.

Willey, G. R., and P. Phillips
1958   *Method and Theory in American Archaeology.* University of Chicago Press, Chicago.

Willey, Gordon R., and Jeremy A. Sabloff
1980   *A History of American Archaeology,* 2d ed. W. H. Freeman, San Francisco.

Williams, S.
1964   "The Aboriginal Location of the Kadohadacho and Related Tribes." *In*

Explorations in Cultural Anthropology, Essays in Honor of George Peter Murdock, edited by W. H. Goodenough, pp. 545–70. McGraw-Hill, New York.

Wilmeth, Roscoe Hall
1972   *The Woodland Sequence in the Central Plains.* University Microfilms International, Ann Arbor.

Wilson, James S.
1982   "Archaeology and History." In *Environmental Baseline Study of the Saskatchewan River, Saskatchewan, in the Vicinity of Choiceland and the 'Forks,'* edited by A. E. Pipe, pp. 743–975. Saskatchewan Research Council Report no. C-805-25-E-80. Saskatoon.

Wilson, Michael Clayton
1988   "Bison Dentitions from the Henry Smith Site, Montana: Evidence for Seasonality and Paleoenvironments at an Avonlea Bison Kill." In *Avonlea Yesterday and Today: Archaeology and Prehistory,* edited by Leslie B. Davis, pp. 203–26. Saskatchewan Archaeological Society, Saskatoon.

Wilson, Robert L.
1980   "Archaeological Investigations near Kamloops." In *The Archaeology of Kamloops,* edited by R. L. Wilson and C. Carlson, pp. 1–86. Publication 7. Department of Archaeology, Simon Fraser University.

Wilson-Meyer, Dianne, and M. Carlson
1985   "The Yellowsky Site (FjOd-2): an Avonlea Component in West-central Saskatchewan." *Saskatchewan Archaeology* 6:19–32.

Windmiller, Ric, and Frank W. Eddy
1975   "An Archaeological Study of Aboriginal Settlements and Land Use in the Colorado Foothills." Ms. on file, State Historical Society of Colorado, Denver.

Winfrey, D. H.
1959   *Texas Indian Papers 1825–1843.* Texas State Library, Austin.
1960   *Texas Indian Papers 1844–1845.* Texas State Library, Austin.

Winham, R. Peter, and Edward J. Lueck
1984   *Report of a Cultural Resources Reconnaissance of Selected Areas Along the White River and Along the West Bank of Lake Francis Case.* 2 vols. Archaeological Contract Series no. 11. Archaeology Laboratory, Augustana College, Sioux Falls, S.D. Submitted to U.S. Army Corps of Engineers, Omaha District, Contract no. DACW45-83-C-0184.
1987   *Cultural Resource Reconnaissance Along Portions of Lake Oahe in Stanley and Dewey Counties, South Dakota.* 2 vols. Archaeological Contract Series no. 25. Archaeology Laboratory, Augustana College, Sioux Falls, S.D. Submitted to U.S. Army Corps of Engineers, Omaha District, Contract no. DACW45-85-C-0325.

Winham, R. Peter, K. Lippincott, L. A. Hannus, and E. J. Lueck
1988   *Cultural Resource Reconnaissance of U.S. Army Corps of Engineers Land Alongside Lake Sakakawea in Dunn County, North Dakota.* Archaeological Contract Series 23. Archaeology Laboratory, Augustana College, Sioux Falls, S.D. Submitted to U.S. Army Corps of Engineers, Omaha District, Contract no. DACW45-85-C-0304.

Winham, R. Peter, Kerry A. Lippincott, and Edward J. Lueck
1987 *Cultural Resource Reconnaissance of U.S. Army Corps of Engineers Land Alongside Lake Sakakawea in Mountrail County, North Dakota.* 2 vols. Archaeological Contract Series no. 22. Archaeology Laboratory, Augustana College, Sioux Falls, S.D. Submitted to U.S. Army Corps of engineers, Omaha District, Contract no. DACW45-85-C-0285.
1988 *Cultural Resources Reconnaissance Along the Cheyenne River Arm of Lake Oahe in Dewey, Haakon, Stanley and Ziebach Counties, South Dakota.* 2 vols. Archaeological Contract Series no. 30. Archaeology Laboratory, Augustana College, Sioux Falls, S.D. Submitted to U.S. Army Corps of Engineers, Omaha District, Contract no. DACW45-86-C-0235.
Winship, G. P.
1896 "The Coronado Expedition, 1540–1542." *Bureau of American Ethnology Annual Report* 14:329–637. Smithsonian Institution, Washington, D.C.
Winter, Joe
1985 *Stone Circles, Ancient Forts, and Other Antiquities of the Dry Cimarron Valley.* Office of Contract Archaeology, University of New Mexico, Albuquerque.
Winterhalder, B. P.
1983 "History and Ecology of the Boreal Zone in Ontario." In *Boreal Forest Adaptations: The Northern Algonkians,* edited by A. T. Steegman, Jr., pp. 9–54. Plenum Press, New York.
Withers, A. M.
1954 "Reports of Archaeological Fieldwork in Colorado, Wyoming, New Mexico, Arizona, and Utah in 1952 and 1953: University of Denver Archaeological Fieldwork." *Southwestern Lore* 19(4): 1–3.
1983 "O-way-wa-ha-an-ba-yoh in Northeastern New Mexico." In *Collected Papers in Honor of Charlie R. Steen, Jr.,* edited by Nancy Fox, Papers of the Archaeological Society of New Mexico 8, pp. 35–48. Albuquerque Archaeological Society Press.
Witkin, Max
1971 *An Archaeological Interpretation of the Roberts Buffalo Jump Site, Larimer County, Colorado.* M.A. thesis, Colorado State University, Ft. Collins.
Witty, Thomas A., Jr.
1962 "The Anoka Focus." M.A. thesis, Department of Anthropology, University of Nebraska.
1963 *The Woods, Avery and Streeter Archaeological Sites, Milford Reservoir, Kansas.* Anthropological Series no. 2. Kansas State Historical Society, Topeka.
1967 "The Pomona Focus." *Kansas Anthropological Association Newsletter* 12(9): 1–5.
1978 "Along the Southern Edge: The Central Plains Tradition in Kansas." In *The Central Plains Tradition: Internal Development and External Relationships,* edited by D. J. Blakeslee, pp. 56–66. Report 11. Office of the State Archaeologist, Iowa City.

1982 *The Slough Creek, Two Dog, and William Young Sites, Council Grove Lake, Kansas.* Anthropological Series no. 10. Kansas State Historical Society, Topeka.

Wood, C. E.

1974 "Excavations at Trinchera Cave, 1974." *Southwestern Lore* 40(3): 53–56.

1986 "Archaeology of the Upper Purgatoire River Valley, Las Animas County, Colorado: Chronology and Origins." *The Wyoming Archaeologist* 29(1–2): 125–43.

Wood, C. E., and G. A. Bair

1980 *Trinidad Lake Cultural Resource Study, Part II: The Prehistoric Occupation of the Upper Purgatoire River Valley.* Laboratory of Contract Archaeology, Trinidad State Junior College, Trinidad, Colo.

Wood, John T.

1967 "Taxonomy in Northeastern Colorado Prehistory." Ph.D. dissertation, University of Colorado. University Microfilms International, Ann Arbor.

Wood, W. Raymond

1967 "An Interpretation of Mandan Culture History." *Bureau of American Ethnology Bulletin* 198. Smithsonian Institution, Washington, D.C.

1971a "Pottery Sites Near Limon, Colorado." *Southwestern Lore* 37(3): 53–85.

1971b *Biesterfeldt: A Post-Contact Coalescent Site on the Northeastern Plains.* Smithsonian Contributions to Anthropology 15. Washington, D.C.

1972a "Contrastive Features of Native North American Trade Systems." In *For the Chief: Essays in Honor of Luther S. Cressman,* edited by F. Voget and R. Stephenson. University of Oregon, Anthropological Papers 4:153–69.

1972b "Archaeological Interpretive Report: Pueblo Reservoir, Eastern Colorado." Manuscript on file, Colorado Historical Society, Denver.

1985 "The Plains-Lakes Connection: Reflections from a Western Perspective." In *Archaeology, Ecology and Ethnohistory of the Prairie-Forest Border Zone of Minnesota and Manitoba,* edited by Janet Spector and Elden Johnson, pp. 1–8. J & L Reprint, Lincoln.

1986a "Cultural Chronology of the Upper Knife-Heart Region." In W. Raymond Wood, Ed., *Ice Glider,* 320L110, pp. 7–24. Sioux Falls: South Dakota Archaeological Society no. 10.

1986b "Introduction." In *Papers in Northern Plains Prehistory and Ethnohistory, Ice Glider 320L110,* edited by W. R. Wood, p. 124. Special Publication of the South Dakota Archaeological Society no. 10.

In "Prehistory: Plains Villagers: Middle Missouri Tradition." Plains vol.,
press *Handbook of North American Indians.* Smithsonian Institution, Washington, D.C.

Wood, W. Raymond (ed.)

1969 *Two House Sites in the Central Plains: An Experiment in Archaeology.* Plains Anthropologist Memoir 6.

Wood, W. Raymond, and J. R. Hanson

1986 *The Origins of the Hidatsa Indians: A Review of Ethnohistorical and Traditional Data.* Reprints in Anthropology 32. J & L Reprint, Lincoln.

Wood-Simpson, C. E.
1976   "Trinchera Cave: A Rock Shelter in Southeastern Colorado." M.A. thesis, University of Wyoming, Laramie.
Woods, William I., and George R. Holley
1991   "Upland Mississippian Settlement in the American Bottom Region." In *Cahokia and the Hinterlands,* edited by T. E. Emerson and R. Barry Lewis, pp. 46–60. University of Illinois Press, Urbana.
Woodall, J. N.
1967   "The Coyote Site." In *A Pilot Study of Wichita Indian Archaeology and Ethnohistory,* assembled by R. E. Bell, E. B. Jelks, and W. W. Newcomb, pp. 15–23. Final Report to National Science Foundation.
Word, James H.
1963   "Floydada Country Club site, 41-FL-1." *Bulletin of the South Plains Archaeological Society* 1:37–63.
1965   "The Montgomery Site in Floyd County, Texas." *Bulletin of the South Plains Archaeological Society* 2:55–102.
1991   The 1975 Field School of the Texas Archeological Society. *Bulletin of the Texas Archaeological Society* 60:57–106.
Wright, Gary A.
1978   "The Shoshonean Migration Problem." *Plains Anthropologist,* 23(80): 113–37.
1982   "Notes on Chronological Problems on the Northwestern Plains and Adjacent High Country." *Plains Anthropologist* 27:145–60.
Wright, Herbert E., Jr.
1968   "History of the Prairie Peninsula." In *The Quaternary of Illinois,* edited by R. E. Bergstrom, pp. 78–88. Report no. 14. College of Agriculture, University of Illinois, Urbana.
Wright, James V.
1968   "The Boreal Forest." In *Science, History, and Hudson Bay,* vol. 1, edited by C. S. Beals, pp. 55–68. Department of Energy, Mines and Resources. Queen's Printer, Ottawa.
1971   "Cree Culture History in the Southern Indian Lake Region." In *Contributions to Anthropology VII: Anthropology and Physical Anthropology,* pp. 1–31. Bulletin no. 232. National Museums of Canada, Ottawa.
1972a   *Ontario Prehistory.* National Museum of Man. National Museums of Canada, Ottawa.
1972b   *The Shield Archaic.* Publications in Archaeology no. 3. National Museum of Man, National Museums of Canada, Ottawa.
1981   "Prehistory of the Canadian Shield." In *Subarctic,* edited by June Helm, pp. 86–96. Vol. 6, *Handbook of North American Indians.* Smithsonian Institution, Washington, D.C.
Wyckoff, D. G.
1970   "Archaeological and Historical Assessment of the Red River Basin in Oklahoma." In *Archaeological and Historical Resources of the Red River Basin,* edited by H. A. Davis, pp. 67–134. Research Series no. 1. Arkansas Archaeological Survey, Fayetteville.
1980   "Caddoan Adaptive Strategies in the Arkansas Basin, Eastern Oklahoma." Ph.D. dissertation, Washington State University, University Mi-

crofilms International, Ann Arbor.
1993   "Gravel Sources of Knappable Alibates Silicified Dolomites." *Geo-archaeology* 8(1): 35–58.

Wyckoff, D. G., and R. L. Brooks
1983   *Oklahoma Archaeology: A 1981 Perspective of the State's Archae-ological Resources, Their Significance, Their Problems and Some Proposed Solutions.* Archaeological Resource Survey Report no. 16. Oklahoma Archaeological Survey, Norman.
1983   *Oklahoma Archaeology: A 1981 Perspective.* Archaeological Resources Survey Report no. 16. Oklahoma Archaeological Survey, Norman.

Wyckoff, D. G., and L. R. Fisher
1985   *Preliminary Testing and Evaluation of the Grobin Davis Archaeological Site 34Mc-253, McCurtain County, Oklahoma.* Archaeological Re-source Survey Report no. 22. Oklahoma Archaeological Survey, Norman.

Wyckoff, J., and David D. Kuehn
1983   "The Physiographic Background." In *Archaeology of the Northern Border Pipeline, North Dakota: Survey and Background Information,* vol. 2, part 1, edited by M. J. Root and M. L. Gregg, pp. 135–76. Contribution 194. Department of Anthropology and Archaeology, University of North Dakota, Grand Forks. Submitted to Northern Border Pipeline Company, Omaha, Nebr.

Wynn, Thomas, Thomas Huber, and Robert McDonald
1985   "Early Woodland Occupation at Jackson Creek." *Southwestern Lore* 51(1): 3–13.

Young, Robert W.
1983   "Apachean Languages." In *Southwest,* edited by Alfonso Ortiz, pp. 393–400. Vol. 10, *Handbook of North American Indians.* Smithsonian Institution, Washington, D.C.

Zier, Christian J.
1989   *Archaeological Excavation of Recon John Shelter (5PE648) on the Fort Carson Military Reservation, Pueblo County, Colorado.* Centennial Archaeology, Fort Collins.

Zier, C. J. and S. M. Kalasz
1985   *Archaeological Survey and Test Excavations in the Multi-Purpose Range Complex Area, Fort Carson Military Reservation, Colorado.* Centennial Archaeology, Fort Collins.

Zier, Christian J., Stephen M. Kalasz, Anne H. Peebles, Margaret A. Van Ness, and Elaine Anderson
1988   *Archaeological Excavations of the Arvery Ranch Site (5PE56) on the Fort Carson Military Reservation Pueblo County, Colorado.* Centen-nial Archaeology, Fort Collins.

Zimmerman, Larry J.
1985   *Peoples of Prehistoric South Dakota.* University of Nebraska Press, Lincoln.

Zolbrod, Paul G.
1984   *Diné bahane. The Navajo Creation Story.* University of New Mexico Press, Albuquerque.

INDEX

Algonquian (language stock), 18, 43, 46, 49, 93, 126, 195, 223, 309, 316–319, 322, 339, 345, 379, 381

Anasazi, 70, 276, 290, 293, 296–301, 307, 309, 310, 314, 333, 334, 352, 357, 362, 363, 374, 378, 379

Antelope Creek phase, 243–46, 249, 261, 266, 271, 277–83, 293, 298, 301, 303, 307, 355–57, 359

Apache, 17, 194, 249, 251, 254, 255, 263, 285, 287, 304, 305, 306, 332, 358, 378, 379; Plains, 222, 261, 286, 287, 305. *See also names*

Apachean, 51, 286, 324, 326–329, 331, 333, 334, 335, 357, 361, 374, 375, 376, 378, 380, 381

Apishapa phase, 269, 277, 278, 279, 282, 293, 297, 303, 356, 357, 359

Arapaho, xxi, 91, 94, 316, 317, 319, 323

Arikara, xxi, 164, 169, 171–175, 214, 215, 216, 222, 334, 347, 348, 350, 351, 352

Arvilla complex, 81, 93, 143, 321, 322, 339, 345, 346

Assiniboine, 3, 5, 18, 28, 30, 72, 91, 125, 127, 308, 323, 335, 336, 345, 346

Athapaskan (language stock), 17, 18, 39, 40, 41, 43, 46, 50, 51, 54, 67, 68, 70, 193, 194, 222, 223, 248, 262, 275, 276, 285, 287, 299, 306, 310, 324, 326, 328–31, 334, 356, 379

Atsina (Gros Ventre), xxi, 28, 30, 31, 32, 44, 48, 52, 54, 67, 91, 94, 308, 316, 317, 319, 322

Avonlea phase, 7, 13, 14–23, 31, 32, 36, 38, 39–43, 46, 49, 51, 54, 65–70, 74, 108–12, 122, 152, 178, 183, 184, 185, 187–90, 321, 326, 327, 328, 346; Avonlea I, 326–27, 329; Avonlea II, 327–29, 332, 333; origins, 324–30

Bannock, 61, 63

Basketmaker, 269, 270, 276, 331, 357, 362, 363, 377, 380

Beaver (tribe), 67, 194

Beehive complex, 40, 51, 54, 189, 313, 321, 327, 328, 329, 332

Besant phase, 7, 9–14, 16, 19–22, 32, 35, 36–38, 41, 42, 43, 46, 48, 49, 54, 64, 65, 74, 76, 101, 110, 111, 112, 178, 180, 182, 183–93, 195, 196, 227, 310, 312, 319, 320, 322, 326, 327, 329, 338, 343, 350, 351; eastern subphase, xxii, 195, 318; western subphase, 15, 195, 318, 320; origins, 11, 186–87, 195–96, 318–22

Blackduck complex, 81, 83, 85, 93, 106, 110, 112, 113–19, 121, 122, 123, 126, 127, 143–47, 321, 339, 345, 346

Blackfeet, xxi, 3, 5, 6, 18, 26, 28–31, 38, 44, 46–50, 52, 54, 62, 63, 66, 68, 69, 195, 310, 313, 315–19, 321, 322

Blood (Blackfeet division), 3, 5, 32, 44, 67

Brainerd phase, 110, 111, 142, 143, 345, 346

Buried City complex, 245, 281, 282, 356, 357, 359

Cabeza de Vaca, xx

Caddoan (language stock), 173, 223, 244, 278, 344, 346, 350; central, 217, 221; northern, 215, 217, 347, 348, 351, 352; Plains, 286, 346, 347, 355, 356, 357, 360

Cahokia, 85, 136, 137, 157, 218, 223

Cambria complex, 83, 85, 135, 136, 138, 139, 157, 342, 343, 344

Casas Grandes, 296, 299, 301, 374, 375

Chaco Canyon, 297, 307, 331, 334, 363, 375

Cheyenne, xxi, xxii, xxiii, xxiv, 72, 79, 91, 93, 128, 169, 171, 175, 195, 224, 316–23, 336, 338, 339, 343, 345, 346, 376, 377

Chipewyan, 194

Chiricahua, 324, 333, 334, 375, 378, 380

Cholera, xviii, 259

Cluny complex, 25, 26

Coalescent tradition, 169–73, 175, 213, 237, 342, 344, 350

Coeur d'Alene, 60, 62

Cojo phase, 286, 287

Comanche, 50, 287, 304, 305, 335

Coronado, Francisco Vasquez de, xvii, xx, 221, 222, 249, 251, 262, 304–307, 354, 357, 358, 359, 363

Cree, 18, 26, 28, 30, 126, 127, 316, 317, 322, 323, 346; Plains, 3, 5, 91, 322

Crow, xxi, 25, 28, 29, 50, 51, 54, 63, 161, 162, 323, 335, 336, 339, 341

Cuesta phase, 201, 204–205, 206, 241, 361

Custer phase, 245, 360

Dakota, xxi, 72, 91, 322, 323, 335, 336, 345

De la Vega, Garcilaso, xviii

De Soto, Hernando, xviii, 249, 251, 256, 262

De Vaca, Cabeza, xx

Devils Lake–Sourisford complex, 87, 91, 321, 339, 341

Diphtheria, xviii
Duck Bay complex, 120, 121, 123, 125, 126, 127, 323

Elvas, Knight of, xviii
Escritores phase, 276
Ethnicity, xxiii–xxiv, 34, 93, 125–26, 195

Flathead, 49, 54, 60, 315
Fourche Maline phase, 242, 245, 259, 260, 361
Fremont, 68, 69, 70, 194, 328, 329, 330, 332–33, 334, 375, 378, 379; origins, 331–34

Garcilaso de la Vega, xviii
Garza complex, 246, 249, 251, 261, 285, 286, 333, 374
Glen Elder phase, 220–221
Glenwood complex, 135, 136, 214, 342, 348, 350
Graneros focus, 269, 277, 356
Great Bend aspect, 220, 221, 222, 245, 246, 248, 249, 251, 260, 262, 300, 305, 337, 360–61
Great Oasis phase, 85, 135, 136, 137, 151, 152, 155, 156–59, 339, 342, 343, 344, 348
Greenwood phase, 207, 208–209, 217, 242, 348, 361
Gros Ventre. See Atsina

Henrietta focus, 245, 246, 248, 262, 300
Hidatsa, xxi, 25, 28, 29, 72, 91, 94, 151, 155, 161–64, 168, 173, 174, 175, 194, 195, 321, 323, 335, 336, 339, 341, 343
Hopewell, 14, 130, 192, 223, 241, 259, 260, 342
Hopewellian interaction sphere, 13, 41, 106, 184, 203, 241, 342

Influenza, xviii
Iowa (tribe), xxi, 72, 91, 139, 221, 335, 344, 345
Isleta (pueblo), 309
Itskari phase, 220, 350, 351, 352

Jicarilla, 287, 324, 331, 333, 334, 335, 381

Kachina cult, 297, 375, 376, 380
K'ado ceremony, 338, 376, 377, 380
Kalispel. See Pend d'Oreille
Kansa (tribe), xxii, 217, 220, 221, 222, 251, 361
Kansas City Hopewell, 192, 201–207, 211, 240, 241, 256, 336, 341, 342, 348, 361
Kathio culture, 85, 143–47, 346
Keaster II complex, 17, 38–39, 41, 43, 54, 312, 314, 329
Keith phase, 178, 184, 207–208, 214, 233, 242, 269, 348, 351, 353, 354
Kelsey, Henry, 48, 308
Keresan (language stock), 362, 363, 375, 380
Kiowa, xxi, xxiv, xxv, xxvi, 51, 54, 287, 309, 310, 313, 314, 315, 329, 330, 338, 341, 376, 377, 378, 380
Kiowa Apache, xxi, xxv, xxvi, 51, 287, 313, 314, 324, 326, 329, 330, 335, 379
Kiowa-Tanoan (language stock), 194, 309, 313, 314, 315, 350, 351, 352, 357, 362, 376, 380, 381

Kitsai confederation (also Kichai), xxi, 248, 249, 251, 254, 260, 261, 262, 347, 352, 355, 359
Kutenai, xxv, 28, 38, 40, 41, 46, 48, 49, 54, 60, 61, 65–68, 309, 310, 313–15, 326

LaHarpe, Bernard de, 254, 262
Lake Creek focus, 242, 243, 246, 270, 271, 355
Lakes (tribe), 61
Laurel tradition, 74, 76, 93, 102–108, 110–13, 115–18, 126, 127, 186, 322, 338, 346
Lipan Apache, 254, 324, 333, 334, 335, 359
Loseke Creek phase, 152, 155, 178, 184, 192, 193, 207, 210–11, 342, 348, 350
Lower Loup phase, 216, 220, 222, 350, 351, 352

McKean phase, 13, 17, 178, 180, 181, 182, 186, 310, 319, 320
Malaria, xviii, 259
Mandan, xxi, 50, 91, 94, 151, 155, 159, 161–64, 168, 173, 174, 175, 194, 195, 218, 321, 334, 335, 336, 341–44, 350, 376
Massaum ceremony, xxii, 320, 338, 376, 377
Measles, xviii, xx, 259
Mesa Verde, 297, 363
Mescalero, 324, 333, 335, 374, 380
Middle Missouri tradition, 151, 152, 157, 159–69, 174, 321, 339, 341, 342, 343–44
Mill Creek culture, 85, 135–39, 157, 218, 342–45
Mississippian culture, 85, 130–39, 195, 322, 339, 344
Missouri (tribe), 91, 139, 221, 335, 344
Mogollon, 243, 271, 272, 282, 283, 289, 290, 291, 294–96, 297, 298, 300, 307, 362, 374, 375
Mortlach phase, 7, 24–26, 29, 94, 125, 127, 323, 336, 341

Napikwan tradition, 11, 35, 38, 67, 178, 184, 189, 190, 310, 312, 313, 318, 320
Narvaez, Panfilo de, xvii
Navajo, 17, 194, 222, 324, 332, 334, 375, 378, 379, 381
Nebraska phase, 172, 212, 214–18, 222, 245, 303, 342, 350
Nez Perce, 61–64, 68, 313, 315–16
Numic speakers, 61, 332

Ojibwa, 91, 93, 126, 316, 317, 346; Plains, 72, 322
Old Women's phase, 7, 11, 13, 14, 18, 19, 20–24, 25, 26, 28–31, 44, 46, 65, 67, 122, 127, 152, 178, 185, 188, 189, 190–93, 196, 310, 313, 320, 321, 327
Omaha (tribe), xxi, xxii, 221, 222, 335
Oñate, Juan de, 251, 255, 256, 262, 305, 306, 359, 360, 361
One Gun phase, 7, 24–26, 29, 323, 341
Oneota culture, 89, 91, 94, 95, 130, 133, 135, 136, 137–39, 146, 147, 148, 218, 220, 223, 336, 342, 344–45
Osage, xxii, 220, 221, 248, 251, 255, 256, 263, 335, 361

Oto, 91, 139, 221, 222, 335, 344, 345
Oxbow phase, 11, 13, 180, 182, 186, 310, 319, 320

Paleo-Indian, 318, 338
Palo Duro complex, 242, 271, 355
Parker phase, 350–51, 353
Pawnee, xxi, 169, 171, 175, 213, 215, 219, 220, 222, 248, 259, 260, 278, 305, 347, 348, 354; South Bands, 215, 222, 347, 348, 350, 351, 353, 354, 355, 360, 361
Pecos (pueblo), 261, 270, 289, 297, 298, 300, 303, 304, 305, 307, 357, 362
Pedregoso phase, 270, 276, 362
Pelican Lake phase, 13, 17, 18, 32, 35, 36, 38, 39, 41, 67, 178, 180, 181–86, 188, 189, 193, 310–15, 319, 320, 326, 327, 328, 350, 377
Pend d'Oreille, 49, 54, 60, 62, 315
Picuris (pueblo), 293, 303, 309, 362, 363, 377
Piegan (Blackfeet division), 3, 5, 26, 28, 32, 44, 46, 48, 49, 67
Plague, xviii, xx, 259
Pomona phase, 212, 216–17, 218, 220, 222, 223, 242, 243, 247, 355, 361
Ponca, xxii, 220, 221, 222
Ponil phase, 276, 277, 293, 357
Pre-Dorset Eskimo, 195, 318, 338
Pueblo cultural tradition, 276, 278, 280, 286, 291, 293, 298, 299, 303–306, 331, 334, 358, 374, 375, 376, 378
Psinomani culture, 145–47, 148, 322, 323, 346

St. Croix phase, 74, 81, 142, 143, 339, 345, 346
St. Helena phase, 214, 216, 350
Salishan (language stock), 49, 55, 68
Sandia (pueblo), 309, 363
Sandy Creek complex, 11, 13, 178, 182–83, 186, 189, 190, 310, 320
Sandy Lake complex, 85, 88, 89, 93, 121, 123–127, 145, 146, 322, 346
Sanpoil, 61
Santee (eastern Dakota), 147, 335, 345, 346
Sarcee, 3, 5, 18, 28, 67, 194, 313, 324, 327
Scarlet fever, xviii, 259
Sekani, 67
Selkirk phase, 24, 28, 30, 93, 118–21, 123–127, 322, 323
Shield-bearing warrior motif, 30, 49, 50, 51, 194, 329, 330, 332, 378
Shoshone, 28, 30, 48–52, 55, 61, 63, 69, 70, 94, 315, 329, 330
Shuswap, 60, 61, 67, 68
Siouan (language stock), 18, 52, 54, 125, 127, 159, 218, 222, 335–36, 339, 342, 344, 345, 346, 379
Sioux, 128, 171
Skidi, 215, 222, 256
Skiri, xxi, 347, 348, 350, 351, 352, 354, 355, 356, 360, 379
Smallpox, xvii, xviii, 29, 259, 315, 323, 337,

344, 352
Smoky Hill phase, 172, 206, 212, 215–16, 217, 222, 241, 243, 244, 245, 247, 353, 354, 361
Snake (tribe), 26–30
Sonota subphase of Besant, 13, 14, 18, 74, 76, 78, 79, 93, 152, 185, 186, 320, 321, 322
Sopris phase, 269, 273, 275, 277, 331, 332, 333, 356
Spokan, 61
Steed-Kisker complex, 172, 212, 217, 218, 223, 244, 342, 361
Sterns Creek phase, 192, 207, 210–11, 342, 348, 350
Suhtai, xxv, 316–17

Taltheilei tradition, 100, 101, 108, 319
Tano (language), 309, 359, 363, 375
Taos (pueblo), 293, 296, 297, 309, 362, 363, 376
Teton (western Dakota), 93, 94, 335, 336, 345
Tewa (language), 293, 309, 310, 363, 375, 380
Thompson, David, 26
Tierra Blanca complex, 249, 251, 261, 283, 285, 286, 333
Tiwa (language), 293, 304, 307, 309, 362, 375
Tonkawa, 246, 251, 254, 355
Towa (language), 309, 363, 375
Tunaxa tradition, 17, 35, 36, 38, 66, 67, 178, 180, 182, 184, 189, 190, 310, 312, 313, 315, 319, 320
Typhus, xviii, 259

Upper Republican phase, 172, 206, 213–14, 215, 220, 222, 234, 237, 241, 245, 246, 278, 291, 303, 351, 352, 353, 356
Uto-Aztecan (language stock), 194, 333

Vaca, Cabeza de, xx
Valley phase, 152, 178, 184, 186, 192, 193, 205–206, 233, 269, 342, 348
Vega, Garcilaso de la, xviii
Vermejo phase, 269, 270, 293, 351, 357

Wallawalla (tribe), 61
Wanikan culture, 122, 146
Washita River phase, 217, 222, 245, 249, 261, 262, 280, 307, 360
Western Apache, 324, 328, 334, 375, 378, 380
Wheeler phase, 246, 249, 251, 261, 262, 285, 286, 359, 360
Wichita confederation, xxi, 217, 220, 221, 222, 248, 249, 251, 254, 255, 256, 261, 262, 278, 286, 289, 337, 347, 352, 355, 358–61
Winnebago, 139, 335, 336, 344

Yankton (middle Dakota), 93, 335, 336, 345
Yanktonai (middle Dakota), 93, 335, 336, 345, 346

Zuni (pueblo), 297, 300, 381